Texas Politics Today

2013 – 2014 EDITION

William Earl Maxwell	**San Antonio College**
Ernest Crain	**San Antonio College**
Adolfo Santos	**University of Houston–Downtown**

with

Elizabeth N. Flores	Del Mar College
Joseph Ignagni	The University of Texas at Arlington
Cynthia Opheim	Texas State University–San Marcos
Christopher Wlezien	Temple University

WADSWORTH
CENGAGE Learning·

Australia • Brazil • Japan • Korea • Mexico • Singapore • Spain • United Kingdom • United States

WADSWORTH
CENGAGE Learning·

Texas Politics Today: 2013–2014
William Earl Maxwell, Ernest Crain, Adolfo Santos

Senior Publisher: Suzanne Jeans

Executive Editor: Carolyn Merrill

Development Editor: Jennifer Jacobson, Ohlinger
    Publishing Services

Assistant Editor: Scott Greenan

Media Editor: Laura Hildebrand

Marketing Brand Manager: Lydia LeStar

Marketing Communications Manager: Linda Yip

Content Project Manager: Cathy Labresh Brooks

Art Director: Linda May

Manufacturing Planner: Fola Orekoya

Rights Acquisition Specialist: Jennifer Meyer Dare

Production Service and Compositor:
    Integra Software Services

Text and Cover Designer: Lou Ann Thesing

Cover Image: Glow Images/©Getty Images

For product information and technology assistance, contact us at
Cengage Learning Customer & Sales Support, 1-800-354-9706

For permission to use material from this text or product,
submit all requests online at **www.cengage.com/permissions.**
Further permissions questions can be emailed to
permissionrequest@cengage.com.

Library of Congress Control Number: 2012952069

ISBN-13: 978-1-133-60212-5

ISBN-10: 1-133-60212-6

Wadsworth
20 Channel Center Street
Boston, MA 02210
USA

Cengage Learning is a leading provider of customized learning solutions with office locations around the globe, including Singapore, the United Kingdom, Australia, Mexico, Brazil and Japan. Locate your local office at **international. cengage.com/region**

Cengage Learning products are represented in Canada by Nelson Education, Ltd.

For your course and learning solutions, visit **www.cengage.com.**

Purchase any of our products at your local college store or at our preferred online store **www.cengagebrain.com.**

Instructors: Please visit **login.cengage.com** and log in to access instructor-specific resources.

Printed in Canada
1 2 3 4 5 6 7 16 15 14 13 12

*We dedicate this book to all the students of Texas politics.
May they remain engaged in the Texas political process.*

Brief Contents

Contents

Chapter 1

TEXAS CULTURE AND DIVERSITY   1

Chapter 2

TEXAS IN THE FEDERAL SYSTEM   29

Chapter 6

Chapter 7

Chapter 8

Chapter 9

THE GOVERNOR   223

Chapter 10

THE BUREAUCRACY   244

Chapter 11

TEXAS JUDICIARY   271

Chapter 14

LOCAL GOVERNMENT   365

Although you and other intelligent, well-meaning Texans may strongly disagree about public policies, the policies of Texas state and local governments dramatically affect each of our lives—every day. If you refuse to participate, you relinquish your role in our democracy and your natural right to control your own future. The real losers in the political game are those who do not play.

Human beings are political by their very nature. Understanding government is necessary for intelligent development of a political ideology and for acceptance of conflicting ideologies as legitimate. We hope that this book's fact-based discussion of recent controversial issues will engage your interest and that its explanation of ongoing principles of Texas politics will help you understand opposing views in context. *Texas Politics Today* is your invitation to join the dynamic conversation about politics in the Lone Star State. You should be impressed neither by what the authors know nor by what your professors know, but by the opportunities available for you to become part of civil discourse and by what you can do for yourself and for others as you become a part of this political world of ours.

We use a comparative approach because you can understand Texas politics only in the context of the state's unique political culture, its institutions, its elites, and its legal structures compared to other states. You will find out who makes up the Texas political elite, how power politics works within state institutions, and how the state's public policy results from bargaining among unelected political insiders and elected officials in an environment conditioned by public opinion and ideology.

We designed the 2013–2014 edition of *Texas Politics Today* to meet your needs as students in introductory college and university-level courses. We wrote this reader-friendly text for you to use in courses specializing in Texas government and, because of its comparative approach, we believe the book works well with national government texts for courses that integrate both state and national politics.

We explain the background, rules of the game, political players, and framework of political institutions that give birth to the public policies that most affect you. You can explore major historical, demographic, political, and cultural trends and the role of political interest groups throughout the text. You can use vignettes, figures, tables, diagrams, and photos as active visual learning tools, and you can enjoy the humor of Ben Sargent's Pulitzer Prize–winning cartoons, which illustrate important issues that you will recognize in Texas politics.

You can exploit student-centered learning aids: Each chapter opens with **learning objectives** to help you track your progress. **Review questions** and **bulleted summaries** at the end of each chapter and key terms with definitions in the margins throughout each chapter facilitate study and review. **Chapter summaries** recap important points that you should understand and remember. **Get Active!** boxes at the beginning of each chapter offer ways to increase your own political involvement, and **Logging On** features include specific new ideas about projects to explore current issues, evaluate data, and draw conclusions about the Texas political scene. Carefully written photo, figure, and table captions direct you to the major takeaways from the visuals. Critical analysis questions help you get started in thinking about Texas politics.

The hallmark **comparative approach** of *Texas Politics Today* is highlighted in the **How Does Texas Compare?** sections, maps, and figures in every chapter, and the *How Texas Compares* element is summarized at the end of each chapter. These features help put Texas political institutions into context and direct students to debate the merits of alternative institutions and policies used in other states.

Review questions focus on main themes you should consider and analyze. Provocative **Join the Debate** features at the end of each essay pose broad questions that you should raise in class discussions and consider for debate and research on contemporary political issues.

NEW TO THIS EDITION

Instructors will recognize the most effective elements of previous editions, but this edition also analyzes the latest available data and discusses current issues, recent legal and structural changes, as well as contemporary demographic and political developments. Enticing new features and material in the 2013–2014 edition include the following:

★ **NEW! Texas Insiders** is our unique new feature in every chapter that puts a face on Texas's foremost campaign contributors, interest groups, and powerful behind-the-scenes operators while it provides students specific challenges about how to think about the role that Texas's political elites play in politics and policymaking in Texas. Examples include "The Suite 8F Crowd: The Power of Economic Ties and Personal Loyalties" (Chapter 1); "James Leininger and the Battle to Ban Same-Sex Marriage in the Texas Constitution" (Chapter 3); and "Texans for Lawsuit Reform: Interest-Group Style Justice" (Chapter 12).

★ **NEW!** The 2013–2014 edition covers the 2012 election results, the latest on legislative redistricting, and the recent changes in public policy, including health care and education. This edition also analyzes the latest data, issues, structural and legal changes, demographics, and more.

★ **NEW!** A **prologue**, "Texas's Political Roots," discusses Texas government and politics from the early years of statehood through the early twenty-first century. This means Chapter 1 of the new edition now focuses entirely on Texas culture and diversity.

★ **NEW!** Federalism is explained in an entirely new Chapter 2 that discusses not only the general theory of federalism but also how it now directly impacts the state in practical ways ranging from grants-in-aid to environmental quality to same-sex marriage.

★ **NEW!** Five new essays, including "The Texas Political Culture: Shaped by the Old South's Traditionalism and the Frontier Experience's Individualism" by Brian K. Dille, Odessa College (Chapter 1); "Texas Won't Forget These Federal Bureaucracies!" by Neal Coates, Abilene Christian University; and "Capital Punishment in Texas: Holding Steadfast in a Changing Era" by David Branham, Sr., University of Houston–Downtown (Chapter 12). These contemporary end-of-chapter essays—each contributed by one of Texas's leading political scientists—add perspective and support to chapter material. Essay topics include the governor's appointment power, tuition deregulation, the new media in politics, the politics of the blocking bill, the cultural divide in the politics of public education, and the experiences of a small-town mayor. Author introductions help students see the essay's significance within the framework of the chapter, and "Join the Debate" critical-thinking questions help students apply what they have learned.

★ **NEW!** *Did You Know?* facts in every chapter add interesting talking points that enhance the narrative.

★ **Texas's political culture and political ideology** are thoroughly examined throughout the book. Chapter 13 includes a new analysis of the politics of redistribution and the latest developments in the state's public policies on taxing, spending, education, and health care.

★ **Environmental issues** and the Texas view of sustainability are addressed in Chapters 2, 6, and 10.

★ **Citizen rights** is an important new focus. Chapter 1 discusses the historical development of ethnic and sexual minority rights and the struggle in Texas for equal rights; Chapter 2 explains how the Fourteenth Amendment affects the concepts of states' rights, minority rights, and individual liberty; Chapter 3 focuses on the Texas Bill of Rights guarantees; Chapter 4 traces the development of voting rights, and Chapter 12 examines rights under civil law and the rights of those accused of a crime.

★ **Redistricting** is discussed in Chapter 7, which features the new legislative district maps and an end-of-chapter essay examining the redistricting process.

★ **Results of the 2012 elections** are incorporated into the political Chapters 4, 5, and 7.

★ **Recent U.S. Supreme Court rulings** about health care reform, affirmative action, corporate political contributions, and conflicts of interest generated by campaign contributions are discussed in Chapters 2, 4, 6, 11, and 13.

★ **Get Active!** sections put tools into students' hands to examine the politics of polarization for themselves. These sections are rich in fresh online resources that invite students to link up with activist groups in Texas politics; to sample liberal, conservative, and libertarian opinions; and to decide where they stand on the ideological spectrum.

Each chapter contains important new contents:

Chapter 1 now begins with a new discussion of the relationship among political culture, public opinion, ideology, and public policy and has a special focus on Texas political culture; our discussion of diversity features a newly expanded section about Texans' struggle for equal rights.

Chapter 2 is a new chapter that defines the concept of federalism, the key elements in the U.S. Constitution that have helped shape our understanding of federalism, and how Texas has had an impact on and has been impacted by the changing understanding of the relationship between the national government and the state of Texas.

Chapter 3 substantially expands discussion of the Texas Bill of Rights, puts Texas's constitutions into historical perspective, and illustrates the interaction of elites and public opinion in the amending process.

Chapter 4 analyzes the election process with a special new focus on the role of campaign contributions and puts a face on megadonors in Texas politics.

Chapter 5 discusses the organization and characteristics of Texas political parties with a special emphasis on factionalism in the Republican party and differences in leadership styles among the majority party's elites. It makes clear the ideological and policy differences between the two parties, features county-by-county results in the 2012 presidential election, and details the rise of the Tea Party in Texas politics.

Chapter 6   concisely covers all aspects of interest group influence and illustrates such groups' power with a special Texas Insiders feature about how a Texas premiere lobbying outfit operates.

Chapter 7   analyzes the 2011 redistricting process and includes a new essay that puts the redistricting process into perspective. Discussion of legislative elections includes a new Texas Insiders feature about the role campaign contributions play in both the electoral process and legislative decision making.

Chapter 8   includes a reorganized and simplified discussion of the legislative process that focuses on bargaining between the legislature's leaders, its members, and interest groups. A new Texas Insiders feature examines the revolving door between the legislature and lobbyists.

Chapter 9   describes the governor's bargaining powers among bureaucrats, legislators, and interest groups. The new Texas Insiders feature shows Mike Toomey's masterful influence while lobbying the governor's office.

Chapter 10   includes a more streamlined coverage of the state's plural executive system and the part that appointed agencies play in negotiating public policy decisions. The new Texas Insiders feature explores the controversies surrounding the Texas Enterprise Fund and reveals the link between subsidies and campaign contributions. The stimulating essay about the State Board of Education looks at its curriculum decisions in the context of a polarized political environment.

Chapter 11   puts new perspective on judicial elections with a special focus on how campaign contributors such as trial lawyers and business groups compete to impose different perspectives on the courts.

Chapter 12   is restructured to focus on the judicial process, tort reform, and the rights of the accused. It includes a new Texas Insiders feature revealing the power of tort reformers on the judicial decision-making process and a new essay about the latest developments in the death penalty controversy.

Chapter 13   combines tax, spending, and state service policies into a new comprehensive public policy chapter. It features the latest U.S. Supreme Court ruling on health care reform and how it affects Texas. The impact of state budget cuts, tuition increases, the politics of income inequality, the latest policy developments, and the role of think tanks round out this chapter.

Chapter 14   includes an expanded analysis of local elections in a more plainly written narrative that includes a thorough discussion of the structures and functions of local government and how they operate in the state and federal system. The Insiders feature shows how local governments use their influence to lobby for their agendas at the state and national levels.

RESOURCES FOR BOTH STUDENT AND INSTRUCTOR

✱ A variety of student and instructional aids are available separately. Contact your Cengage sales representative for details about the following products and more print and online resources.

✱ On **CengageBrain.com**, students can save up to 60 percent on their course materials through our full spectrum of options. Students have the option to rent their textbooks or purchase print textbooks, e-textbooks, individual e-chapters, and audio books, all at substantial savings over average retail prices. CengageBrain.com also includes access to Cengage Learning's broad range of homework and study tools, including the student resources discussed here. Go to **www.cengagebrain.com** to access your *Texas Politics Today* resources.

✱  **Aplia**™ for *Texas Politics Today, 2013–2014 Edition*. Easy to use, affordable, and effective, Aplia helps students learn and saves instructors' time. It's like a virtual teaching assistant! Aplia helps instructors have more productive classes by providing assignments that get students thinking critically, reading assigned material, and reinforcing basic concepts—all before coming to class. The interactive questions also help students better understand the relevance of what they're learning and how to apply those concepts to the world around them. Visually engaging videos, graphs, and political cartoons help capture students' attention and imagination, and an automatically included eBook provides convenient access. Aplia is instantly accessible via CengageBrain.com or through the bookstore via printed access card. Please contact your local Cengage sales representative for more information, and go to www.aplia.com/politicalscience to view a demo.

IAC ISBN: 9781285071732 (Instant Access Code)

Bundle ISBN for the text with Aplia Printed Access Card: 9781285490045

✱  **CourseReader: Texas Politics (0-30 Selections)** allows you to create your reader, your way, in just minutes. This affordable, fully customizable online reader provides access to thousands of permissions-cleared readings, articles, primary sources, and audio and video selections from the regularly-updated Gale research library database. This easy-to-use solution allows you to search for content and to select the exact material you need for your courses. Each selection includes a descriptive introduction that provides important background context and is further supported by critical-thinking and multiple-choice questions designed to reinforce key points. The CourseReader is loaded with convenient pedagogical features like highlighting, printing, note taking, and the option to download MP3 audio files for each reading. CourseReader: Texas Politics is the perfect complement to any class and is updated throughout the year.

It can be bundled with your existing textbook, sold alone, and integrated into your learning management system. Please see your Cengage sales representative for details.

PAC ISBN: 9781133350286 (Printed Access Card)

IAC ISBN: 9781133350279 (Instant Access Code)

To demo CourseReader: Texas Politics, please visit us at: login.cengage.com. Click on "Create a New Faculty Account" and fill out the registration page. Once you are in your new SSO account, search for "CourseReader" from your dashboard and select "CourseReader: Texas Politics." Then click "CourseReader 0-30: Texas Politics Instant Access Code" and click "Add to my bookshelf." To access the live CourseReader, click on "CourseReader 0-30: Texas Politics" under "Additional resources" on the right side of your dashboard.

★  **Political Science CourseMate** *for Texas Politics Today, 2013–2014 Edition* brings course concepts to life with interactive learning, study tools, and exam preparation tools that support the printed textbook. Use Engagement Tracker to assess student preparation and engagement in the course, and watch student comprehension soar as your class works with the textbook-specific website. An interactive eBook allows students to take notes, highlight, search, and interact with embedded media. Other resources include video activities, animated learning modules, simulations, case studies, interactive quizzes, and timelines. Purchase instant access via CengageBrain or via printed access card in your bookstore. Visit **www.cengagebrain.com** for more information. CourseMate should be purchased only when assigned by your instructor as part of your course.

IAC ISBN: 9781285419459 (Instant Access Code)

Bundle ISBN for the text with CourseMate Printed Access Card: 9781285490052

For Students Only:

★ The Free **Companion Website** for *Texas Politics Today, 2013–2014 Edition,* accessible through **cengagebrain.com,** offers access to chapter-specific interactive learning tools, including flashcards, quizzes, learning objectives, and more.

For Instructors Only:

★ **PowerLecture DVD with ExamView for Texas Politics Today, 2013–2014 Edition (ISBN: 9781133960010)** is an all-in-one multimedia resource for class preparation, presentation and testing. This DVD includes Microsoft® PowerPoint® slides, a Test Bank in both Microsoft® Word and ExamView® formats, an Instructor Manual, and a Resource Integration Guide. The book-specific slides of lecture outlines, as well as photos, figures, and tables from the text, make it easy for you to assemble lectures for your course, while the media-enhanced slides help bring your lecture to life with audio and video clips, animated learning modules illustrating key concepts, tables, statistical charts, graphs, and photos from the book as well as outside sources. The test bank, offered in Microsoft Word® and ExamView® formats, includes 60+ multiple-choice questions with answers and page references along with 10 essay questions for each chapter. ExamView® features a user-friendly testing environment that allows you to not only publish traditional paper and computer based tests, but also Web-deliverable exams. The Instructor's Manual includes learning objectives, chapter outlines, summaries, discussion questions, class activities, lecture launchers, and suggested readings and Web resources. A Resource Integration Guide provides a chapter-by-chapter outline of all available resources to supplement and optimize learning. Contact your Cengage representative to receive a copy upon adoption.

★ **Latino American Politics Supplement (ISBN: 9781285184296)** by Fernando Piñon of San Antonio College is a revised and updated thirty-two-page supplement which uses real examples to detail politics related to Latino Americans.

ACKNOWLEDGMENTS FOR THE 2013–2014 EDITION

The authors thank the following reviewers for their useful suggestions toward this revision:

Jessika Stokley, Austin Community College

John David Rausch, Jr., West Texas A&M University

Eric Miller, Blinn College

Jack Goodyear, Dallas Baptist University

Woojin Kang, Angelo State University

David Smith, University of Texas at Dallas

ACKNOWLEDGMENTS FOR EARLIER EDITIONS

The following reviewers also contributed greatly through feedback on recent prior editions of *Texas Politics Today*:

Sarah Binion, Austin Community College

Larry E. Carter, The University of Texas–Tyler

Neil Coates, Abilene Christian College

Malcolm L. Cross, Tarleton State University

Laura De La Cruz, El Paso Community College

Kevin T. Davis, North Central Texas College

Brian R. Farmer, Amarillo College

Frank J. Garrahan, Austin Community College

Glen David Garrison, Collin County Community College–Spring Creek

Robert Paul Holder, McLennan Community College

Timothy Hoye, Texas Woman's University

Casey Hubble, McLennan Community College

Charles R. Knerr, The University of Texas–Arlington

Mel Laracey, The University of Texas–San Antonio

Dennis B. Martinez, The University of Texas–San Antonio

Jalal K. Nejad, Northwest Vista College

J. D. Phaup, Texas A&M University–Kingsville

John David Rausch, Jr., West Texas A&M University

Jo Marie Rios, Texas A&M University–Corpus Christi

Allan Saxe, The University of Texas–Arlington

Charles Vernon Wilder, Texarkana College

The English–Scots–Irish culture, as it evolved in its migration through the southern United States, played an essential part in the Texas Revolution. Sam Houston, Davy Crockett, Jim Bowie, and others were of Scotch–Irish descent, and these immigrants from the Scots–English border, by way of Northern Ireland, led the Anglo-American movement west and had a major impact on the development of modern mid-American culture.

The successful end to the Texas Revolution in 1836 attracted more immigrants from the southern United States. Subsequently, the Anglo-Texan population grew dramatically and became the largest Texas ethnic group. As a result, Anglo Texans controlled the politics and economy and Protestantism became the dominant religion.

The Anglo concept of Manifest Destiny was not kind to Latino and Native Texans. Native Americans were killed or driven into the Indian Territory, and many Latino families were forced from their property. Even Latino heroes of the Texas Revolution with names like Navarro, Seguin, de Zavala, and de Leon were not spared in the onslaught.[1]

As evidence of the dominance of the Anglo-Scotch culture, all the presidents of the republic and the governors of the state have been Protestant and had surnames linked to the British Isles.

POLITICS AND GOVERNMENT: THE EARLY YEARS

The Republic of Texas had no political parties. Political conflict revolved around pro-Houston and anti-Houston policies. Sam Houston, the hero of the battle of San Jacinto, advocated peaceful relations with the eastern Native Americans and U.S. statehood for Texas. The anti-Houston forces led by Mirabeau B. Lamar believed that Native-American and Anglo-American cultures could not coexist. Lamar envisioned Texas as a nation extending from the Sabine River to the Pacific.[2]

Joining the Union

Texas voters approved annexation to the United States in 1836, almost immediately after Texas achieved independence from Mexico. However, because owning human property was legal in the republic and would continue to be legal once it became a state, the annexation of Texas would upset the tenuous balance in the U.S. Senate between proslavery and abolitionist senators. This and other political issues, primarily relating to slavery, postponed Texas's annexation until December 29, 1845, when it officially became the 28th state.

Several Texas articles of annexation were unique. Texas retained ownership of its public lands because the U.S. Congress refused to accept their conveyance in exchange for payment of the republic's $10 million debt. Although millions of acres were ultimately given away or sold, those remaining continue to produce hundreds of millions of dollars in state revenue, largely in royalties from the production of oil and natural gas. These royalties and other public land revenue primarily benefit the Permanent University Fund and the Permanent

School Fund. The annexation articles also granted Texas the privilege of "creating . . . new states, of convenient size, not exceeding four in number, in addition to said State of Texas."[3]

Early Statehood and Secession: 1846–1864

The politics of early statehood soon replicated the conflict over slavery that dominated politics in the United States. Senator Sam Houston, a strong Unionist alarmed by the support for secession in Texas, resigned his seat in the U.S. Senate in 1857 to run for governor. He was defeated because secessionist forces controlled the dominant Democratic Party. He was, however, elected governor two years later.

The election of Abraham Lincoln as president of the United States in 1860 triggered a Texas backlash. A secessionist convention was called and it voted to secede from the Union. Governor Houston used his considerable political skills in a vain attempt to keep Texas in the Union. At first, Houston declared the convention illegal, but the Texas legislature later upheld it as legitimate. Although only about 5 percent of white Texans owned slaves, the electorate ratified the actions of the convention by an overwhelming 76 percent.[4]

Houston continued to fight what he considered Texans' determination to self-destruct. Although he reluctantly accepted the vote to secede, Houston tried to convince secessionist leaders to return to republic status rather than join the newly formed Confederate States of America—a plan that might have spared Texans the tragedy of the U.S. Civil War. Texas's secession convention rejected this political maneuver and petitioned for membership in the new Confederacy. Houston refused to accept the actions of the convention, which summarily declared the office of governor vacant and ordered the lieutenant governor to assume the position. Texas was then admitted to the Confederacy.

Post–Civil War Texas: 1865–1885

The defeat of the Confederacy resulted in relative anarchy in Texas until it was occupied by federal troops beginning on June 19, 1865, a date celebrated by African Texans as freedom day. Texas and other southern states resisted civil rights and equality for freed slaves, resulting in radical Republicans gaining control of the U.S. Congress. Congress enacted punitive legislation prohibiting former Confederate soldiers and officials from voting and holding public office.

Texas government was controlled by the U.S. Army from 1865 through 1869, but the army's rule ended after the new state constitution was adopted in 1869. African-Texan men were granted the right to vote, but it was denied to former Confederate officials and military. In the election to reestablish civilian government, Republican E. J. Davis was elected governor and Republicans dominated the new legislature. Texas was then readmitted to the United States, military occupation ended, and civilian authority assumed control of the state. Unlike either previous or subsequent constitutions, the 1869 Constitution centralized political power in the office of the governor. During the Davis administration, Texas began a statewide public school system and created a state police force.

Republican domination of Texas politics was a new and unwelcome world for most white Texans, and trouble intensified when the legislature increased taxes to pay for Governor Davis's reforms. Because Texas's tax base was dependent on property taxes, eliminating human property from the tax rolls and the decline in value of real property placed severe stress on the public coffers. Consequently, state debt increased dramatically. Former Confederates were enfranchised in 1873, precipitating a strong anti-Republican reaction from the electorate, and Democrat Richard Coke was elected governor in 1875.

Texas officials immediately began to remove the vestiges of radical Republicanism. The legislature authorized a convention to write a new constitution. The convention delegates were mostly Democrats, Anglo Texans, and agrarian interests. The new constitution decentralized the state government, limited the flexibility of elected officials, and placed public education under local control. It was ratified by the voters in 1876 and an often-amended version is still in use.

POLITICS AND GOVERNMENT: 1886–1945

Many reform measures were enacted and enforced in Texas in the 1880s, especially laws limiting corporate power. Attorney General James S. Hogg vigorously enforced new laws curtailing abuses by insurance companies, railroads, and other corporate interests.

Governor Hogg: 1891–1895

Attorney General James Hogg was an important reformer in Texas politics and developed a reputation as the champion of common people. Railroad interests dominated most western states' governments, prompting Hogg to run for governor with the objective of regulating railroads. Although he faced strong opposition from powerful corporate interests that viewed him as a threat, Hogg won the nomination in the 1890 Democratic State Convention.

A commission to regulate railroads was authorized in the subsequent election. The Railroad Commission was eventually given the power to regulate rubber-tired vehicles used in Texas commerce and the production and transportation of oil and natural gas.

Politics in the early 1900s distinguished Texas as one of the most progressive states in the nation. Texas pioneered the regulation of monopolies, railroads, insurance companies, and child labor. It reformed its prisons and taxes, and in 1905, replaced nominating conventions with direct primaries.

Farmer Jim: 1914–1918

James E. Ferguson entered the Texas political scene in 1914 and was a controversial and powerful force in Texas politics for the next 20 years. Ferguson owned varied business interests and was the president of the Temple State Bank. Although sensitive to the interests of the business community, Ferguson called himself "Farmer Jim" to emphasize his rural background.

The legislature was unusually receptive to Ferguson's programs, which generally restricted the economic and political power of large corporations and tried to protect the common people. It also enacted legislation designed to assist tenant farmers, improve public education and colleges, and reform state courts.

The legislature also established a highway commission to manage state highway construction. Texas's county governments had been given the responsibility of constructing state roads within their jurisdictions. The result was that road quality and consistency varied widely between counties. The agency's authorization to construct and maintain Texas's intrastate roadways standardized the system and facilitated motorcar travel.

Rumors of financial irregularities in Ferguson's administration gained credibility, but his declaring war on The University of Texas would prove fatal. Ferguson vetoed the entire appropriation for the university, apparently because the board of regents refused to remove certain faculty members whom the governor found objectionable. This step alienated politically powerful graduates who demanded that he be removed from office. Farmer Jim was impeached, convicted, removed, and barred from holding public office in Texas.

World War I, the Twenties, and the Return of Farmer Jim: 1919–1928

Texas saw a boom during World War I. Its favorable climate and the Zimmerman Note, in which Germany allegedly urged Mexico to invade Texas, prompted the national government to station troops in the state. Texas became and continues to be an important training area for the military.

Crime control, education, and the Ku Klux Klan, a white supremacist organization, were the major issues of the period. Progressive measures enacted during this period included free textbooks for public schools and the beginning of the state park system. The 1920 legislature also ratified the Eighteenth Amendment to the U.S. Constitution establishing national Prohibition.

The strongest anti-Klan candidate in 1924 was Miriam A. "Ma" Ferguson, wife of the impeached Farmer Jim. She ran successfully on a platform of "Two Governors for the Price of One," becoming the first female governor of Texas. Detractors alleged that she was only a figurehead and that Farmer Jim was the real governor. Nonetheless, Ma's election indicated that Texas voters had forgiven Farmer Jim for his misbehavior. She was successful in getting legislation passed that prohibited wearing a mask in public, which resulted in the end of the Klan as an effective political force.

National politics became an issue in Texas politics in 1928. Al Smith, the Democratic nominee for president, was a Roman Catholic, a "wet," and a big-city politician. Herbert Hoover, the Republican nominee, was a Protestant, a "dry," and an international humanitarian. Hoover won the electoral votes from Texas—the first Republican ever to do so.

The Great Depression: 1929–1939

The stock market crashed in 1929 and Texas, along with the entire nation, was economically crushed. Prices dropped, farm products could not be sold, mortgages and taxes went unpaid, jobs evaporated, and businesses and bank accounts were wiped out.

In 1932, Ma Ferguson, using economy in government as her campaign issue, was reelected governor. The 1933 ratification of the Twenty-first Amendment to the U.S. Constitution brought an end to nationwide Prohibition. Prohibition ended in Texas two years later with the adoption of local-option elections, although selling liquor by the drink was still forbidden statewide.

POLITICS AND GOVERNMENT AFTER WORLD WAR II: 1948–TODAY

The 1948 senatorial campaign attracted several qualified candidates. The runoff in the Democratic primary pitted former governor Coke Stevenson against U.S. Congressman Lyndon Johnson.

The election was the closest statewide race in Texas history. At first, the election bureau gave the unofficial nomination to Stevenson, but the revised returns favored Johnson. The final official election results gave Johnson the nomination by a plurality of 87 votes. Both candidates charged election fraud.

Box 13 in Jim Wells County, one of several *machine*-controlled counties dominated by political boss George Parr (the Duke of Duval), was particularly important in the new figures. This box revised Johnson's vote upward by 202 votes and Stevenson's upward by only one. Box 13 was also late in reporting, thereby tainting Johnson's victory. About the election, historian T. R. Fehrenbach wrote, "There was probably no injustice involved. Johnson men had not *defrauded* Stevenson, but successfully *outfrauded* him."

The 1950s: Shivercrats and the Seeds for a Republican Texas

Allan Shivers became governor in 1949, and in 1952 the national election captured the interests of Texans. Harry Truman had succeeded to the presidency in 1945 and was reelected in

1948. Conservative Texas Democrats became disillusioned with the New Deal and Fair Deal policies of the Roosevelt–Truman era and wanted change.

Another major concern for Texans was the tidelands issue. With the discovery of oil in the Gulf of Mexico, a jurisdictional conflict arose between the government of the United States and the governments of the coastal states. Texas claimed three leagues (using Spanish units of measure, equal to about 10 miles) as its jurisdictional boundary; the U.S. government claimed Texas had rights to only three miles. At stake were hundreds of millions of dollars in royalty revenue.

Both Governor Shivers and Attorney General Price Daniel, who was campaigning for the U.S. Senate, attacked the Truman administration as being corrupt, soft on communism, eroding the rights of states, and being outright thieves in attempting to steal the tidelands oil from the schoolchildren of Texas. State control of the revenue would direct much of the oil income to the Permanent School Fund and result in a lower tax burden for Texans. The Democratic nominee for president, Adlai Stevenson of Illinois, disagreed with the Texas position.

The Republicans nominated Dwight Eisenhower, a World War II hero who was sympathetic to the Texas position on the tidelands. Eisenhower was born in Texas (but reared in Kansas), and his supporters used the campaign slogan "Texans for a Texan." The presidential campaign solidified a split in the Texas Democratic Party that lasted for 40 years. The conservative faction, led by Shivers and Daniel, advocated splitting the ticket, or voting for Eisenhower for president and Texas Democrats for state offices. Adherents to this maneuver were called Shivercrats. The liberal faction, or Loyalist Democrats of Texas, led by Judge Ralph "Raff" Yarborough, campaigned for a straight Democratic ticket.

Texas voted for Eisenhower, and the tidelands dispute was eventually settled in its favor. Shivers was reelected governor and Daniel won the Senate seat. Shivers, Daniel, and other Democratic candidates for statewide offices were also nominated by the Texas Republican Party. Running as Democrats, these candidates defeated themselves in the general election.

The 1960s

Lyndon B. Johnson, majority leader of the U.S. Senate and one of the most powerful men in Washington, lost his bid for the Democratic presidential nomination to John F. Kennedy in 1960. He then accepted the nomination for vice president. By the grace of the Texas legislature, Johnson was on the general election ballot as both vice-presidential and senatorial nominee. When the Democratic presidential ticket was successful, he was elected to both positions, and a special election was held to fill the vacated Senate seat. In the special election, Republican John Tower was elected and became the first Republican since Reconstruction to serve as a U.S. senator from Texas.

The 1970s

In 1979, William P. Clements became the first Republican governor of Texas since E. J. Davis was defeated in 1874. The election of a Republican governor did not affect legislative–executive relations and had limited impact on public policy because Clements received strong political support from conservative Democrats.

The 1980s: Education Reform

Democratic Attorney General Mark White defeated incumbent governor Bill Clements in 1982. Teachers overwhelmingly supported White, who promised salary increases and expressed support for education. The first comprehensive educational reform since 1949 became law in 1984. House Bill 72 increased teacher salaries, made school district revenue somewhat more equitable, and raised standards for both students and teachers.

In 1986, voter discontent with education reform, a sour economy, and decreased state revenue were enough to return Republican Bill Clements to the governor's office. In 1988, three Republicans were elected to the Texas Supreme Court and one to the Railroad Commission—the first Republicans elected to statewide office (other than governor or U.S. senator) since Reconstruction.

In 1989, the Texas Supreme Court unanimously upheld an Austin district court's ruling in *Edgewood* v. *Kirby*[5] that the state's educational funding system violated the Texas constitutional requirement of "an efficient system" for the "general diffusion of knowledge." After several reform laws were also declared unconstitutional, the legislature enacted a complex law that kept the property tax as the basic source for school funding but required wealthier school districts to share their wealth with poorer districts. Critics called the school finance formula a "Robin Hood" plan.

The 1990s: Texas Elects a Woman Governor and Becomes a Two-Party State

In 1990, Texans elected Ann Richards as their first female governor since Miriam "Ma" Ferguson. Through her appointive powers, she opened the doors of state government to unprecedented numbers of women, Latinos, and African Texans. Dan Morales was elected the first Latino to statewide office in 1990, and Austin voters elected the first openly gay legislator in 1991. Texas elected Kay Bailey Hutchison as its first female U.S. senator in 1992. She joined fellow Republican Phil Gramm as they became the first two Republicans to hold U.S. Senate seats concurrently since 1874.

When the smoke, mud, and sound bites of the 1994 general election settled, Texas had become a two-party state. With the election of Governor George W. Bush, Republicans held the governor's office and both U.S. Senate seats for the first time since Reconstruction. Republicans won a majority in the Texas Senate in 1996, and voters ratified an amendment to the Texas Constitution that allowed them to use their *home equity* (the current market value of a home minus the outstanding mortgage debt) as collateral for a loan.

The 1998 general election bolstered Republican political dominance as the party won every statewide elective office, positioning Governor George W. Bush as the frontrunner for the Republican nomination for president. Legislators deregulated electric companies, the legal blood-alcohol level for driving drunk was reduced to 0.08 percent, and the state's city annexation law was made more restrictive. Public school teachers received a pay raise but were still paid below the national average. Taxpayer-funded vouchers to pay for children's private school education failed. And Texas adopted a program to provide basic health insurance to some of the state's children who lacked health coverage, although over 20 percent of Texas's children remained uninsured.

The 2000s: Texas Becomes a Republican State, Controversy and Conflict

The 2001 legislature enacted a hate crimes law that strengthened penalties for crimes motivated by a victim's race, religion, color, gender, disability, sexual orientation, age, or national origin. The legislature also criminalized open alcohol containers in most motor vehicles, established partial funding for health insurance for public school employees, and made it easier for poor children to apply for health care coverage under Medicaid. The legislature also increased subsidies to corporations by agreeing to reimburse school districts that give corporations reduced taxes.

Republicans swept statewide offices and both chambers of the legislature in the 2002 elections, returning Texas to a one-party status. A nonpartisan policy, however, remained in effect in the legislature because the lieutenant governor and speaker appointed Democrats to some committee chair and vice-chair positions.

A projected $10 billion budget deficit created an uncomfortable environment for Republicans. Politically and ideologically opposed to new taxes and state-provided social services, the legislature and the governor chose to reduce funding for most state programs; expenditures for education, health care, children's health insurance, and social services for the needy were sharply reduced.

Meanwhile, attempts to effectively close tax loopholes failed. For example, businesses and professions of all sizes continued to organize as partnerships to avoid the state corporate franchise tax. The legislature placed limits on pain-and-suffering jury awards for injuries caused by physician malpractice and hospital incompetence and made it more difficult to sue the makers of unsafe, defective products.

The legislature's social agenda was ambitious. It outlawed civil unions for same-sex couples and barred recognition of such unions from other states. A 24-hour wait to be "educated" about the fetus was also required before a woman could have an abortion.

Although the districts for electing U.S. representatives in Texas had been redrawn by a panel of one Democratic and two Republican federal judges following the 2000 Census, Texas Congressman and U.S. House Majority Leader Tom DeLay was unhappy that more Republicans were not elected to Congress. Governor Rick Perry agreed and called a special session to redraw the redrawn districts to increase Republican representation. Democrats argued that the districts had already been established by the courts and that Perry and DeLay only wanted to increase the number of Republican officeholders. The legislature adopted the Republican proposal and the U.S. Supreme Court affirmed that states could redistrict more than once each decade and rejected the argument that the redistricting was either illegal or partisan.

The Texas government in 2007 waged almost continuous battle with itself. Conflict between the house and the speaker, the senate and the lieutenant governor, the senate and the house, and the legislature and the governor marked the session. Legislators did restore eligibility of some needy children for the Children's Health Insurance Program.

The 2009 legislature seemed almost placid after the unprecedented house revolt against Speaker Tom Craddick and election of Joe Straus as new speaker. However, consideration of the contentious voter identification bill caused conflict in the last days of the session and resulted in a parliamentary shutdown. The house adjourned without resolution of a voter identification bill and postponed other important matters to be resolved by a special session. The legislature passed new laws, including limited restrictions on using a cell phone when driving through a school zone and a tax increase on smokeless tobacco.

In 2010, much of the state's political attention was focused on disputes about Texas's acceptance of federal funds. Texas accepted federal stimulus money to help balance the state's budget but turned down more than $500 million in federal stimulus money for unemployed Texans. The state declined to apply for up to $700 million in federal grant money linked to Race to the Top, a program to improve education quality and results. Governor Perry believed the money would result in a federal takeover of Texas's schools. Texas also joined Alaska as the only two states refusing to participate in a National Governors Association effort to rewrite national curriculum standards.

ENDNOTES

[1]See David Montejano, *Anglos and Mexicans in the making of Texas, 1836–1986* (Austin: University of Texas).

[2]The information in this and subsequent sections depends heavily on Seymour V. Connor, *Texas: A History* (New York: Thomas Y. Crowell, 1971); Rupert N. Richardson, *Texas: The Lone Star State*, 3rd ed. (Englewood Cliffs, NJ: Prentice Hall, 1970); T. R. Fehrenbach, *Lone Star: A History of Texas and the Texans* (New York: Collier Books, 1980).

[3]The Annexation of Texas, Joint Resolution of Congress, March 1, 1845, *U.S. Statutes at Large*, *Vol. 5.*

[4]See *A Declaration of the Causes Which Impel the State of Texas to Secede from the Federal Union*, http://avalon.law.yale.edu/19th_century/csa_texsec.asp.

[5]777 S.W.2d 391 (Tex. 1989).

Chapter 1

Texas Culture and Diversity

LEARNING OBJECTIVES

★ Analyze the relationships among political culture, public opinion, and public policy in Texas.

★ Describe the social and cultural groups that migrated to Texas, including early European settlers through modern-day migration from other states and other countries.

★ Describe the distinctive social, economic, and political characteristics of major Texas regions.

★ Distinguish among moralistic, traditionalistic, and individualistic cultures.

★ Trace the struggle for equal rights in Texas.

★ Describe the social and cultural changes that are likely to define Texas's political future.

Broaden your cultural and political experiences. Sample ethnic, religious, and ideological groups that are different from your own to get a perspective on the rich diversity of modern Texas political life at representative websites:

★ **Ideological Politics Sites**

Engage conservative political views at the Right Side of Austin website **therightsideofaustin. wordpress.com/** and liberal political perspectives at the *Texas Observer* website **www. texasobserver.org/**.

★ **Ethnic Politics Sites**

Check out a major Latino organization, the Texas League of United Latin American Citizens at **tx-lulac.org/** and a major African Texan site, Texas's National Association of Colored People at **texasnaacp.org/**.

★ **Gender Politics Sites**

Explore the Texas chapter of the National Organization for Women at **www.nowtexas .org/**, the Texas Eagle Forum at **www.texaseagle .org/**, and a gay, lesbian, bisexual, and transgender group's website at **www.equalitytexas.org/**.

Get involved and learn about your own culture. Talk to grandparents, parents, uncles, and aunts to learn what they know about your culture and family history. Record as much oral history as you can about their personal lives, experiences, and political recollections as well as family myths and traditions. You may find this information priceless as you talk to your own children and grandchildren about their culture.

Go to the library and log onto the Internet to research the background and richness of your family culture. Pick a hero who shares your culture. Here are a few reliable sources:

★ Institute of Texan Cultures: **www .texancultures.com/**

★ Texas State Library and Archives Commission: **www.tsl.state.tx.us**

★ Texas State Historical Association and Center for Studies in Texas History: **www.tshaonline.org**

Political Culture

The dominant political values and beliefs in a nation or state.

Ideology

A pattern of political beliefs about how society and the economy operate, including policy orientations consistent with that pattern; a set of beliefs consistent with a particular political perspective.

Conservative

A political ideology marked by the belief in a limited role for government in taxation, economic regulation, and providing social services; conservatives support traditional values and lifestyles, and are cautious in response to social change.

A **political culture** reflects the political values and beliefs of a people. It explains how people feel about their government—their expectations of what powers it should have over their lives and what services it should provide. A political culture is largely developed through agents of socialization such as family, religion, peer group, and education and is characterized by its levels of ethnic and religious diversity and political tolerance. Shaped by culture, individual participation in the political system depends on how people view their place within it.

TEXAS POLITICAL CULTURE AND REGIONS

We will begin by exploring Texas's dominant political culture and its **ideology** and how each influences public policy. Then we will look at other aspects of the state's political culture and examine the subtle variations in the state from one region to another.

Political Culture, Public Opinion, and Public Policy

Texas's political culture is **conservative**. Figure 1.1a shows that in a recent public opinion survey, 52 percent of Texas registered voters rate themselves as slightly to extremely conservative, while only 22 percent label themselves as slightly to extremely liberal.

Ideology The Texas brand of conservative is skeptical of state government involvement in the economy. Most Texans favor low taxes, modest state services, and few business regulations. Because they support economic individualism and free-market capitalism, Texans generally value profit as a healthy incentive to promote economic investment and individual effort, while they see social class inequality as the inevitable result of free-market capitalism. For them, an individual's quality of life is largely a matter of personal responsibility rather than an issue of public policy.

Some conservatives accept an active role for the government in promoting business. They are willing to support direct government subsidies and special tax breaks for businesses to encourage economic growth. They may also support state spending for infrastructure, such as transportation and education that sustains commercial and manufacturing activity. These conservatives often advocate vigorous state regulation of labor unions.

Social conservatives support energetic government activity to enforce what they view as moral behavior and traditional cultural values. For example, they usually champion vigorous law enforcement, drug control, and immigration enforcement. Social conservatives, who often are Christian fundamentalists, usually advocate the use of state power to restrict gambling, pornography, abortion, and same-sex relationships.

> **Did You Know?** About half of Texas Christians consider themselves to be "born again."

A distinct minority in Texas, **liberals** believe that state government can be used as a positive tool to benefit the population as a whole. Most Texas liberals accept private enterprise as the state's basic economic system but believe excesses of unregulated capitalism compromise the common good. They endorse state policies to abate pollution, to enforce the rights of workers and consumers, and to protect ethnic and sexual minorities.

Liberals often believe that a great deal of social inequality results from the institutional and economic forces that are often beyond a single individual's control. As a result, they support the use of government power to balance these forces and to promote a better quality of life for middle- and lower-income people. For example, liberals argue that it is fair to tax those with the greatest ability to pay and to provide social services for the community as a whole.

A significant number of Texans have mixed views. On some issues, they take a liberal position, but on others they have a conservative perspective or no opinion at all. Others have moderate views—Figure 1.1a shows that 25 percent of Texans say that they are "in the middle"; that is, their beliefs are between conservative and liberal viewpoints. The "Get Active" features in later chapters will give you the tools to explore Texans' policy differences in greater depth and to engage with various ideological groups in Texas.

Liberal
A political ideology marked by the advocacy of positive government action to improve the welfare of individuals, government regulation of the economy, support for civil rights, and tolerance for social change.

Partisanship Texans' conservative political views are reflected in their political party affiliation. Figure 1.1b shows that 49 percent of Texas's registered voters self-identify either as Republicans or as independents who lean Republican. Only 37 percent of registered voters call themselves either Democrats or independents who lean toward the Democrats. In practice, polling research confirms that independents who lean toward one or the other of the two parties usually behave as partisans, and the only true swing voters are independents who refuse to admit a leaning toward either party; they make up 13 percent of Texans who are registered to vote. Polling and actual election results prove the dominance of the more conservative Republican Party in Texas. We will examine the ideological and policy differences between the two parties in greater depth in Chapter 5.

Public Opinion Table 1.1 shows that when Texans are asked about their specific policy opinions on state taxes and social policies they do, indeed, have conservative views.

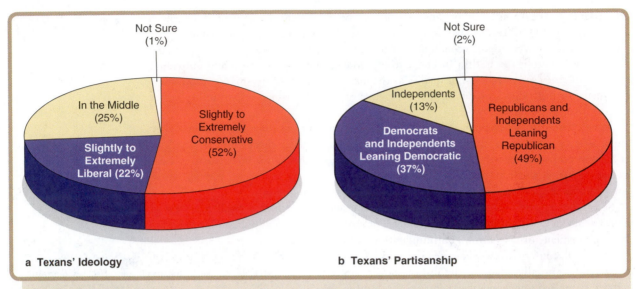

a Texans' Ideology

b Texans' Partisanship

Figure 1.1

Texans' Ideology and Partisanship

Public opinion polling confirms that the majority of Texans identify themselves as conservative and that the Republican Party has a 12-point advantage in party identification.

Source: University of Texas/Texas Tribune, *Texas Statewide Survey*, Survey of 800 registered voters conducted October 19-26, 2011 with a margin of error (MOE) +3.46%, published at http://d2o6nd3dubbyr6.cloudfront.net/media/documents/uttt201110.summary-all.pdf .

Explain the differences between conservative and liberal ideologies. Why is it difficult for Democrats to win statewide office even with the support of independents?

TABLE 1.1 Public Opinion and Public Policy in Texas

Public Policy Option	Percent Supporting	Percent Opposing
Tax Policies		
Increase the state tax on business.[b]	18	82
Increase the state sales tax rate.[b]	12	88
Implement a state income tax on individuals.[b]	6	94
Spending Policies		
Cut funding for elementary and secondary education.[b]	15	85
Cut funding for higher education.[b]	27	73
Cut funding for children's health program.[b]	10	90
Close one or more adult prisons.[b]	30	70
Cut funding for new highways.[b]	28	72
Social Policies		
Provide a pathway to citizenship for illegal aliens.[a]	39	51*
Use the death penalty for those convicted of violent crime.[a]	74	21*
Always allow abortion as a matter of personal choice.[a]	36	59*

TABLE 1.1 Public Opinion and Public Policy in Texas, *continued*

Public Policy Option	Percent Supporting	Percent Opposing
Require a sonogram (ultrasound) as a condition for abortion.[c]	62	37*
Legalize marijuana.[c]	33	65*

*Some results may not total 100 percent because "no opinion" responses are not reported here.

[a]University of Texas/Texas Tribune, *Texas Statewide Survey,* 800 registered voters, October 19–26, 2011, at http://d2o6nd3dubbyr6.cloudfront.net/media/documents/uttt201110.summary-all.pdf

[b]University of Texas/Texas Tribune, *Texas Statewide Survey,* 800 registered voters, May 11–18, 2011, at http://d2o6nd3dubbyr6.cloudfront.net/media/documents/uttt-201105-summary-all.pdf

[c]Texas Lyceum Poll, *Texas Statewide Survey,* 707 adults, May 24–31, 2011, at www.texaslyceum.org/media/staticContent/PubCon_Journals/2011/2011_Texas_Lyceum_Poll_Results.pdf

Sources: Although responses may vary from one survey to the next depending on how questions are phrased, three recent surveys indicate Texans have conservative opinions about selected taxing policies and social issues. However, Texans support major state spending programs.

▲ **On which public policy issues would conservatives favor increased state control? On which issues would liberals favor smaller government? Explain how Texans' support for spending and opposition to taxes complicate policy making.**

However, that pattern is not as clear regarding state spending. During the state budget crisis of 2011, when voters were asked whether they supported spending cuts in various state services to balance the budget, a large majority of Texas voters refused to support cuts in a single major state program. In fact, 53 percent believe Texas spends too little on elementary and secondary education.

Political scientists were not surprised by these survey results. Numerous national and state surveys conducted over several decades indicate that many voters subscribe to a conservative label and voice general support for cutting the size of government, but when they are asked about cuts to specific programs, voters balk. There is a paradox in public opinion—many voters identify themselves as conservatives and they favor spending cuts in the abstract, but they support spending for most government programs in practice. This paradox creates the potential for decision-making gridlock, and it presents an enormous dilemma for policy makers. Texas officials have resolved this conflict in favor of modest public spending.

Public Policy Conservative opinions have been translated into most public policies. Compared to other states, taxes in Texas are very low, and, despite the public's ambiguous attitudes about spending, the state has committed far fewer financial resources to public services than in most other states. Texas takes in less per capita revenue than all but four states and, per capita, it spends less than 46 other states.

Texas, however, has not been reluctant to use the power of the state to enforce certain traditional values, to restrict abortions, to limit same sex-relationships, and to impose relatively severe penalties on lawbreakers. We will analyze Texas public policy in considerable depth in Chapter 13.

We now turn to some other approaches to describe the Texas political culture, including Elazar's classical model for classifying state political cultures and a discussion of regional cultural differences within the state. We will conclude with a sketch of Texas's rich ethnic and demographic diversity.

Moralistic, Traditionalistic, and Individualistic Cultures

A number of different approaches have been used to study diversity in nations, regions, states, and communities. One popular approach is that of Daniel J. Elazar, who depicted American political culture as a mix of three distinct subcultures, each prevalent in at least one area of the United States.

HOW DOES TEXAS COMPARE?
How Texas Ranks among the 50 States: Public Policy and Quality of Life

Public Policy	Texas's Rank*
Revenue and Spending	
Tax revenue per capita	46th
Tax expenditure per capita	47th
Public Education Spending	
Average public school teacher salary	33rd
State and local spending per student	44th
High school graduation rate	43rd
Health Care	
Per capita spending on Medicaid	49th
Per capita spending on mental health	50th
Public Safety	
Rate of incarceration	9th
Number of executions	1st
Quality of Life	
Percent of adults (over age 25) with a high school diploma	50th
Average SAT scores	45th
Percent of population without health insurance	1st
Percent of children living in poverty	4th
Mortgage foreclosure rates	10th
Amount of atmospheric carbon dioxide emissions	1st
Amount of toxic emissions released into water	1st
Income inequality between rich and poor	9th
Home ownership rate	44th
Percent living below federal poverty level	4th
Teenage birth rate	7th

*First is highest and fiftieth is lowest.

Source: The Texas Legislative Study Group, *Texas on the Brink: How Texas Ranks Among the 50 States,* 5th edition, February, 2011, texaslsg.org/texasonthebrink/texasonthebrink.pdf

FOR DEBATE

1. Texas's various ranks among the 50 states are often used to make a political point or further a political agenda. How would liberals use these rankings? Which of these rankings would conservatives tout with pride?

2. Looking only at the public policy matters, explain how these rankings show that Texas public policy is conservative by comparison to other states.

3. Looking at quality-of-life issues, explain how liberals would see these rankings as a call to government action. Discuss how conservatives, with their limited-government philosophy of self-reliance, would see these quality-of-life issues as a matter of individual personal responsibility and not within the proper purview of state government action.

Elazar used the term *moralistic* to describe a culture whose adherents are concerned with "right and wrong" in politics. **Moralistic culture** views government as a positive force, one that values the individual but functions for the benefit of the general public. Discussion of public issues and voting are not only rights but also opportunities to better the individual and society alike. Furthermore, politicians should not profit from their public service. Moralistic culture is strongest in New England and, although historically a product of Puritan religious values, today it is associated with more secular (nonreligious) attitudes.

Individualistic culture embodies the view that government is practical; its prime objective should be to further private enterprise, yet its intervention into people's lives should be strictly limited. Blurring the distinction between economic and political life, individualistic culture sees business and politics as appropriate avenues by which an individual can advance her or his interests. Accordingly, business interests play a very strong role, and running for office is difficult without their support. Conflicts of interest are fairly commonplace, and political corruption may be expected as a natural political activity. The individualistic culture predominates in the commercial centers of the Middle Atlantic states, moving west and south along the Ohio River and its tributaries.

Widespread throughout America, **traditionalistic culture** in Texas derives primarily from the plantation society of the Old South and the patrón system of northern Mexico and South Texas. Government is seen to have an active role but primarily to maintain the dominant social and religious values. Government should also help maintain accepted class distinctions and encourage the beliefs of the dominant religion. Traditionalistic culture views politics as the special preserve of the social and economic elite—as a process of maintaining the existing order. Believing in personal rather than public solutions to problems, it views political participation as a privilege and accepts social pressure and restrictive election laws that limit participation.[1]

Moralistic culture

A political subculture that views government as a positive force; one that values the individual but functions to benefit the general public.

Individualistic culture

A political subculture that views government as a practical institution that should further private enterprise but intervene minimally in people's lives.

Traditionalistic culture

A political subculture that views government as an institution to maintain the dominant social and religious values.

Political Culture and Political Participation

Elazar considered Texas a mix of traditional and individualistic cultures. The traditional overrides the individualistic in East Texas, which was initially settled by immigrants from the Upper Old South and Mexican border areas, where the patrón system dominated early Texas. The individualistic supersedes the traditional throughout the rest of the state. As a result, in Texas, participation in politics is not as highly regarded as in those states with a moralistic culture. Voter turnout in Texas is, in fact, well below the national average. Texans see politics largely as the domain of economic interests, and most tend to ignore the significance of their role in the political process and how it might benefit them.[2]

Did You Know? Voter turnout in Texas is consistently counted among the lowest of the 50 states.

Texas Cultural Regions

D. W. Meinig found that the cultural diversity of Texas was more apparent than its homogeneity and that no unified culture has emerged from the various ethnic and cultural groups that settled Texas. He believed that the "typical Texan," like the "average American," does not exist but is an oversimplification of the more distinctive social, economic, and political characteristics of the state's inhabitants.[3]

---

[1]Daniel J. Elazar, *American Federalism: A View from the States*, 3rd ed. (New York: Harper & Row, 1984).
[2]Ibid.
[3]Information for this section is adapted from D. W. Meinig, *Imperial Texas: An Interpretive Essay in Cultural Geography* (Austin, TX and London: University of Texas Press, 1969).

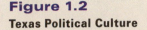

Texas Political Culture

Maxwell's original figure is based on Elazar and Meinig concepts.

In which political cultural area do you reside? Do you agree with the author's description of your area? Construct your own cultural description of the area in which you live.

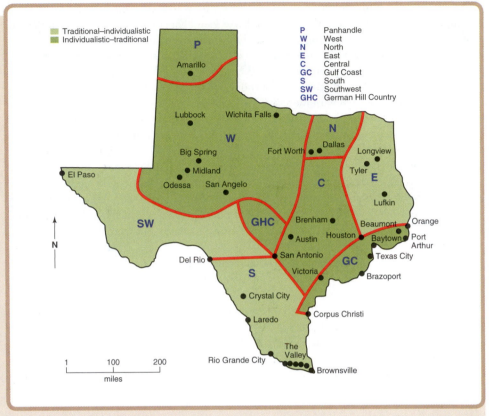

Both Meinig and Elazar see modern regional political culture as largely determined by migration patterns because people take their culture with them as they move geographically. Meinig believed that Texas had evolved into nine fairly distinct cultural regions. However, whereas political boundaries are distinct, cultural divisions are often blurred and transitional. For example, the East Texas region shares political culture with much of the Upper South, whereas West Texas shares a similar culture with eastern New Mexico, and so forth (Figure 1.2).

The effects of mass media, the mobility of modern Texans statewide and beyond, and immigration from Mexico also blur the cultural boundaries within Texas, between its bordering states, and with Mexico. Although limited because they do not take into account these modern-day realities, both Meinig's and Elazar's explanations are useful guides to a general understanding of contemporary Texas culture, attitudes, and beliefs.

East Texas East Texas is a social and cultural extension of the Old South. It is basically rural and biracial. Despite the changes brought about by civil rights legislation, African-American "towns" still exist alongside Anglo-American "towns," as do many segregated social and economic institutions, such as churches, fraternal lodges, and chambers of commerce.

East Texas counties and towns are often dominated by old families, whose wealth is usually based on real estate, banking, construction, and retail merchandising. Cotton—once "king" of agriculture in the region—has been replaced by beef cattle, poultry, and timber. As the result of a general lack of economic opportunity, young East Texans migrate to metropolitan areas, primarily Dallas–Fort Worth and Houston. Seeking tranquility and solitude, retiring urbanites have begun to revitalize some small towns and rural communities that lost population to the metropolitan areas. Fundamentalist Protestantism dominates the region spiritually and permeates its political, social, and cultural activities.

The Gulf Coast Texas was an economic colony before 1900; it sold raw materials to the industrialized North and bought northern manufactured products. However, in 1901, an oil well named Spindletop drilled near Beaumont ushered in the age of Texas oil, and the state's economy began to change. Since the discovery of oil, the Gulf Coast has experienced almost continuous growth, especially during World War II, the Cold War defense buildup, and the various energy booms of the late-twentieth and early-twenty-first centuries.

In addition to being an industrial and petrochemical center, the Gulf Coast is one of the most important shipping centers in the nation. Out-of-state investors, largely from the northeastern states, backed Spindletop, and its success stimulated increased out-of-state investment. Local wealth was also generated and largely reinvested in Texas to promote long-range development. Nevertheless, much of the economy is still supported by the sale of raw materials.

A Boom Based in Houston Through boom and bust, the petrochemical industry, which is concentrated on the Gulf Coast, has experienced unprecedented growth, creating a boomtown psychology. Rapid growth fed real estate development and speculation throughout the region. The Houston area especially flourished, and Harris County (Houston) grew to become the third-most-populous county in the United States.

Houston's initial growth was fueled by the influx of job seekers from East Texas and other rural areas of the state after World War II. This influx gave the Gulf Coast the flavor of rural Texas in an urban setting. Houston's social and economic elite were generally composed of second- and third-generation rich whose wealth came from oil, insurance, construction, land development, or banking—see the Texas Insiders feature.

Houston's rural flavor diminished over the years as the transformation of the U.S. economy from industrial to a service basis drove migration to Texas from the Frost Belt (Great Lakes and Mid-Atlantic states). This migration included both skilled and unskilled workers and added large numbers of well-educated young executives and professionals to the Houston elite pool.

The Gulf Coast economy also attracts heavy immigration from the Americas, Africa, Europe, and Asia, giving modern Houston an international culture comparable to Los Angeles or New York. In fact, modern Houston has street signs in Vietnamese, Chinese, and English in areas with large Vietnamese and Chinese populations.

The collapse of the oil boom and drastic declines in the price of oil and other petroleum products in the 1980s and 1990s struck especially hard at the Gulf Coast economy, which relies heavily on the petrochemical industry. Conversely, rising prices in the 2000s have resulted in another oil-based boom for the region.

The implosion of Houston-based Enron Corporation in the early 2000s affected financial markets and political attitudes nationwide, but it was especially damaging to Houston's economy, labor force, and national image. Enron was intertwined with the fabric of Houston's political, social, cultural, and financial existence to an extent rarely seen in corporate America. A dynamic corporate citizen, Enron made significant contributions to almost every aspect of Houston life. Its collapse left many Houstonians with dramatically decreased retirement incomes and investments. Despite the Enron collapse, the Gulf Coast continues to be a remarkably vibrant and energetic region. Houston, the worldwide oil and gas capital, boasts many corporate headquarters.

Texas INSIDERS

The Suite 8F Crowd: The Power of Economic Ties and Personal Loyalties

The embodiment of the Texas insider lived in Suite 8F of the Lamar Hotel in Houston. In this suite, meetings were attended by corporate executives, power brokers, newspaper publishers, attorneys, and politicians who determined political futures, public policies, and corporate wealth. The group, a quintessential clique, was so powerful that its very existence could only be imagined to exist in the paranoid mind of a left-wing conspiracy theorist writing a fictional exposé on insatiable capitalism.

But it was real. Between the late 1930s and 1960s, some of the wealthiest men in Texas met with some of the most powerful politicians to walk the halls of power in Houston, Austin, and Washington, D.C. As a group, they mapped political strategy to determine government contracts, political contributions, potential candidates, committee assignments, and administrative appointments.

Suite 8F was where deals were made. A partial membership list included Jesse H. Jones, George and Herman Brown, Gus Wortham, James Abercrombie, and James Elkins Sr. All had established corporations and amassed great wealth in construction, oil and gas, lumber, publishing, insurance, and the law.

Politicians were either invited into the group because of their power or became powerful because of their association with the group. Among them were John Nance Garner, Sam Rayburn, Lyndon Johnson, and Albert Thomas from the national government. From the state government came Allan Shivers, William Hobby, Ed Clark, Ben Ramsey, Otis Loch, and Wardlow Lane. These politicians were known as the East Texas Group and yielded considerable power in Austin.

As time passed, younger politicians were added, corporations changed management, and membership evolved to reflect new realities. But the group never lost sight of its original purposes: to use power to determine government policy, to direct government expenditures to increase corporate wealth, and to determine the rulers of the nation and the state.

Thinking about the role of elites in Texas politics The power of the 8F crowd was possible because of the economic ties and personal connections enabled by the single-industry dominance of the oil industry and the social networks that it established. In today's diverse economy and multicultural society, the number of power centers has grown, and it is no longer possible to set the state's destiny in a storied smoke-filled room and to settle on public policy with a handshake. While economic ties and personal loyalties still play a major part in political decisions, the power elites now also acquire power by manipulating information, by capitalizing on the state's political culture, and by acting on shared ideology. As we describe Texas's political insiders in later chapters, note how the state's power brokers assert their influence.

Sources: Bob Bowman, "The 8F Crowd; Lamar Hotel's Suite 8-F, 'Unofficial Capital of Texas,'" www.texasescapes.com/AllThingsHistorical/8-F-Crowd-Lamar-Hotel-Houston-Texas-BB606.htm and Nate Blakeslee, Paul Burka, and Patricia Kilday Hart; "Power"; *Texas Monthly*, Volume 32, number 2, Feb. 2011, p.8.

Although negatively affected, Texas's economy weathered the 2008 economic and financial meltdown much better than other urban states. Texas real estate also suffered fewer home foreclosures, primarily because the state did not experience a housing boom comparable to the West Coast, East Coast, or Nevada and Arizona.

South Texas
The earliest area settled by Europeans, South Texas developed a **ranchero culture** on the basis of livestock production that was similar to the feudal institutions in faraway Spain. **Creoles**, who descended from Spanish immigrants, were the economic, social, and political elite, whereas the first Texas cowboys, the **Mestizos** and the Native Americans, did the ranch work. Anglo Americans first became culturally important in South Texas when they gained title to much of the real estate in the region following the Texas Revolution of 1836. However, modern South Texas still retains elements of the ranchero culture, including some of its feudal aspects. Large ranches, often owned by one family for several generations, are prevalent; however, wealthy and corporate ranchers and farmers from outside the area are becoming common.

Because of the semitropical South Texas climate, **The Valley** (of the Rio Grande) and the Winter Garden around Crystal City became major producers of vegetable and citrus products. These areas were developed by migrants from the northern United States in the 1920s and continue to be important multi-use agricultural assets. The development of citrus and vegetable enterprises required intensive manual labor, which brought about increased immigration from Mexico. Modern South Texas Latinos can usually trace their U.S. roots to the 1920s or later because many of the original Latino settlers had been driven south of the Rio Grande after the Texas Revolution.

Southwest Texas
Southwest Texas exhibits many of the same **bicultural** characteristics as South Texas. Its large Mexican-American population often maintains strong ties with relatives and friends in Mexico. The Roman Catholic Church strongly influences social and cultural attitudes on both sides of the border.

Southwest Texas is a major commercial and social passageway between Mexico and the United States. El Paso, the "capital city" of Southwest Texas and the sixth-largest city in Texas, is a military, manufacturing, and commercial center. El Paso's primary commercial partners are Mexico and New Mexico. The economy of the border cities of Southwest Texas, like that of South Texas, is closely linked to Mexico and has also benefited from the economic opportunities brought about by NAFTA. The agricultural economy of much of the region depends on sheep, goat, and cattle production, although some irrigated row-crop agriculture is present. Most of the labor on ranches, as well as in manufacturing and commerce, is Latino.

The Texas Border
South and Southwest Texas comprise the area known as the "Texas Border." A corresponding "Mexico Border" includes parts of the Mexican states of Chihuahua, Coahuila, Nuevo León, and Tamaulipas. It can be argued that the Texas Border and the Mexico Border are two parts of an economic, social, and cultural region with a substantial degree of similarity that sets it off from the rest of the United States and Mexico. The Border region, which is expanding in size both to the north and to the south, has a **binational**, bicultural, and bilingual subculture in which **internationality** is commonplace and the people, economies, and societies on both sides constantly interact.[4]

Ranchero culture
A quasi-feudal system whereby a property's owner, or patrón, gives workers protection and employment in return for their loyalty and service. The rancher or ranchero and workers all live on the *rancho*, or ranch.

Creole
A descendant of European-Spanish (or in some regions, French) immigrants to the Americas.

Mestizo
A person of both Spanish and Native American lineage.

The Valley
An area along the Texas side of the Rio Grande River known for its production of citrus fruits.

Bicultural
Encompassing two cultures.

Binational
Belonging to two nations.

Internationality
Having family and/or business interests in two or more nations.

---

[4]"Texas Border Region," July 1998, p. 3; Jorge Bustamante, "A Conceptual and Operative Vision of the Population. Problems on the Border," in *Demographic Dynamics on the U.S.-Mexico Border*, eds. John R. Weeks and Roberto Ham Chande (El Paso, TX: Texas Western Press, 1992).

Maquiladora

A factory in the Mexican border region that assembles goods imported duty-free into Mexico for export. In Spanish, it literally means "twin plant."

North American Free Trade Agreement (NAFTA)

A treaty among Canada, Mexico, and the United States that calls for the gradual removal of tariffs and other trade restrictions. NAFTA came into effect in 1994.

South and Southwest Texas are "mingling pots" for the Latino and Anglo-American cultures. Catholic Latinos often retain strong links with Mexico through extended family and friends in Mexico and through Spanish-language newspapers. Many Latinos continue to speak Spanish; in fact, Spanish is also the commercial and social language of choice for many of the region's Anglo Americans.

The Texas Border cities are closely tied to the Mexican economy on which their prosperity depends. Although improving economically, these regions remain among the poorest in the United States.

The economy of the Texas Border benefits economically from **maquiladoras**, which are Mexican factories where U.S. corporations employ inexpensive Mexican labor for assembly and piecework. Unfortunately, lax environmental and safety standards result in high levels of air, ground, and water pollution in the general area. In fact, the Rio Grande is now one of America's most ecologically endangered rivers.

The ongoing **North American Free Trade Agreement (NAFTA)**, which has helped remove trade barriers between Canada, Mexico, and the United States, is an economic stimulus for the Texas Border because it is a conduit for much of the commerce with Mexico.

Immigration and National Security Poverty, military conflicts, crime, political disorder, and suppression of civil liberties in Central America and Mexico have driven hundreds of thousands of immigrants into the border regions of the United States. This flow of immigrants continues but has begun to level off because of the economic turndown, tightened security measures, and fence construction. The Texas Border is a major staging ground for the migration of both legal and illegal immigrants as well as human traffickers into the interior of Texas and the rest of the United States. The government's immigration control expenditures economically benefit the regions. Military expenditures by the U.S. government are also important to the economy of the region. Six military bases are located in the Texas Border regions. The craving of some Americans for illegal, mind-altering, addictive chemicals provides a steady flow of American capital through the Texas Border into Mexico and South America. Basically, the drug traffic is uncontainable as long as its U.S. market exists, but newspapers and other media virtuously trumpet feel-good headlines about "record drug busts" and arrests while the drug trade continues unabated.

This "invisible trade," because of its illegal status, inevitably results in violence as surely as did the failed American experiment prohibiting the sale and consumption of alcoholic beverages from 1919 to 1933. The collateral damage of the drug trade is readily visible and all too common as stories of death and destruction are lead stories for evening news and provide villains and endless plots for movies and television detective programs. Although the worst of the violence is confined to the border areas of Mexico and the United States, the political, economic, lawless, and violent geographic extension of the drug trade is increasingly evident throughout both countries.

Collateral to the drug traffic and its companion violence is a reverse cash flow from Mexico to the United States for weapons purchases. The illegal weapons traffic moves easily obtained weapons, ammunition, and explosives from Texas and other states into Mexico and South America. However, the incoming cash from weapons is far less than the amount of money leaving the United States for drug purchases in Mexico and South America.

When the expenditures by the Mexican, Texas, and U.S. governments for narcotics agents and immigration agents, prison construction and operation, equipment purchases, related military operations, and increased police employment are combined with the expenses, wages, and bribe money spent by drug, weapon, and human traffickers, the result is increased employment and a significant but unwholesome economic infusion to both sides of the border. Immigration, illegal trafficking in humans, drugs, and weapons, and border security will continue to be major political issues for both Democrats and Republicans in the foreseeable future.

German Hill Country The Hill Country north and west of San Antonio was settled primarily by immigrants from Germany but also by Czech, Polish, and Norwegian immigrants. Although the immigrants mixed with Anglo Americans, Central European culture and architecture were dominant well into the twentieth century. Skilled artisans were common in the towns; farms were usually moderate in size, self-sufficient, and family owned and operated. Most settlers were Lutheran or Roman Catholic, and these remain the most common religious affiliations for modern residents.

The German Hill Country is still a distinct cultural region. Although its inhabitants have become "Americanized," they still cling to many of their Central European cultural traditions. Primarily a farming and ranching area, the Hill Country is socially and politically conservative and has long been a stronghold of the Texas Republican Party.

Migration into the region, primarily by Anglo Americans and Latinos, is increasing. The most significant encroachment into the Hill Country is residential growth from rapidly expanding urban areas, especially San Antonio and Austin. Resorts, country homes, and retirement villages for well-to-do urbanites from the Gulf Coast and Dallas–Fort Worth area are beginning to transform the cultural distinctiveness of the German Hill Country.

West Texas The defeat of the Comanches in the 1870s opened West Texas to Anglo-American settlement. Migrating primarily from the southern United States, these settlers passed their social and political attitudes and southern Protestant fundamentalism on to their descendants.

Relatively few African Americans live in modern West Texas, but Latinos migrated into the region in significant numbers, primarily to the cities and the intensively farmed areas. West Texas is socially and politically conservative, and its religion is Bible Belt fundamentalism. West Texas voters in the past supported conservative Democrats and today favor the Republican Party. Indeed, this is true of most conservative Texans throughout the state.

The southern portion of the area emphasizes sheep, goat, and cattle production. In fact, San Angelo advertises itself as the "Sheep and Wool Capital of the World." Southern West Texas, which is below the Cap Rock Escarpment, is the major oil-producing area of Texas. The cities of Snyder, Midland, and Odessa owe their existence almost entirely to oil and related industries.

Northern West Texas is part of the Great Plains and High Plains and is primarily agricultural, with cotton, grain, and feedlot cattle production predominating. In this part of semiarid West Texas, the outstanding agricultural production is due to extensive irrigation from the Ogallala Aquifer. The large amount of water used for irrigation is gradually depleting the Ogallala. This not only affects the present economy of the region through higher costs to farmers but also serves as a warning signal for its economic future.

The Panhandle Railroads advancing from Kansas City through the Panhandle brought Midwestern farmers into this region, and wheat production was developed largely by migrants from Kansas. Because the commercial and cultural focus of the region was Kansas City, the early Panhandle was basically Midwestern in both character and institutions. The modern Texas Panhandle shares few cultural attributes with the American Midwest. Its religious, cultural, and social institutions function with little discernible difference to those of northern West Texas. The Panhandle economy is also supported by production of cotton and grains, the cultivation of which depends on extensive irrigation from the Ogallala Aquifer. Feedlots for livestock and livestock production were established because of their proximity to the region's grain production but are major economic enterprises in their own right. Effective conservation of the Ogallala Aquifer is critical to the economic future of both northern West Texas and the Panhandle.

North Texas North Texas is located between East and West Texas and exhibits many characteristics of both regions. Early North Texas benefited from the failure of the French socialist colony of La Réunion, which included many highly trained professionals in medicine, education, music, and science. (La Réunion was located on the south bank of the Trinity River, across from modern downtown Dallas.) The colonists and their descendants helped give North Texas a cultural and commercial distinctiveness. North Texas today is dominated by the Dallas–Fort Worth **Metroplex**. Dallas is a banking and commercial center of national importance, and Fort Worth is the financial and commercial center of West Texas.

Metroplex
The greater Dallas–Fort Worth metropolitan area.

When railroads came into Texas from the North in the 1870s, Dallas became a rail center, and people and capital from the North stimulated its growth. Fort Worth became a regional capital that looked primarily to West Texas. The Swift and Armour meatpacking companies, which moved plants to Fort Worth in 1901, became the first national firms to establish facilities close to Texas's natural resources. More businesses followed, and North Texas began its evolution from an economic colony to an industrially developed area.

North Texas experienced extraordinary population growth after World War II, with extensive migration from the rural areas of East, West, and Central Texas. The descendants of these migrants are now third- and fourth-generation urbanites and tend to have urban attitudes and behavior. Recent migration from other states, especially from the North, has been significant. Many international corporations have established headquarters in North Texas. Their executive and support staffs contribute to the region's diversity and cosmopolitan environment.

Although North Texas is more economically diverse than most other Texas regions, it relies heavily on banking, insurance, and the defense and aerospace industries. Electronic equipment, computer products, plastics, and food products are also produced in the region.

Central Texas Central Texas is often called the "core area" of Texas. It is roughly triangular in shape, with its three corners being Houston, Dallas–Fort Worth, and San Antonio. The centerpiece of the region is Austin, one of the fastest-growing metropolitan areas in the nation. Already a center of government and education, the Austin metropolitan area has become the "Silicon Valley" of high-tech industries in Texas. Although the worldwide downturn in the high-tech sector after 2000 dealt a serious blow to the area's economy, high-tech industries still make a major economic contribution.

Austin's rapid growth is a result of significant migration from the northeastern United States and the West Coast, as well as from other regions in Texas. The influx of well-educated persons from outside Texas has added to the already substantial pool of accomplished Austinites, making it the intellectual and governmental capital of the state, as well as the economic center of Central Texas. The cultural and economic traits of all the other Texas regions mingle here, with no single trait being dominant. Although the Central Texas region is a microcosm of Texas culture, the city of Austin itself stands out as an island of liberalism in a predominantly conservative state.

POLITICS AND CULTURAL DIVERSITY

The politics of cultural regions have begun to lose their distinctive identities as Texas has become more metropolitan in outlook and as it became more economically and ethnically diverse. With these changes, a number of groups have begun to aspire toward greater cultural, political, social, and economic equality.

Texans Struggle for Equal Rights

Anglo male Texans initially resided atop the pyramid of status, wealth, and civil rights in organized Texas society. They wrote the rules of the game and used those rules to protect their position against attempts by females, African Americans, and Latinos to share in the fruits of full citizenship. Only after the disenfranchised groups organized and exerted political pressure against their governments did the doors of freedom and equality open enough for them to slip inside.

Female Texans Women in the Republic of Texas could neither serve on juries nor vote, but unmarried women retained many of the rights that they had enjoyed under Spanish law, which included control over their property. Married women retained some Spanish law benefits because, unlike Anglo-Saxon law, Texas marriage did not join the married couple into one legal person with the husband as the head. Texas married women could own inherited property, share ownership in community property, and make a legal will. However, the husband had control of all the property, both separate and community (including earned income), and an employer could not hire a wife without her husband's consent.[5]

Texan Minnie Fisher Cunningham was a champion for women's suffrage in the state.

Describe legal restrictions on women before the suffrage movement. What explains the opposition to women's right to vote?

Divorce laws were restrictive on both parties, but a husband could win a divorce for the wife's "amorous or lascivious conduct with other men, even short of adultery," or if she had committed adultery only once. He could not gain a divorce for concealed premarital fornication. On the other hand, a wife could gain a divorce only if "the husband had lived in adultery with another woman." Physical violence was not grounds for divorce unless the wife could prove a "serious danger" that might happen again. In practice, physical abuse was tolerated if the wife behaved "indiscreetly" or had "provoked" her husband. Minority and poor wives had little legal protection from beatings because the woman's "station in life" and "standing in society" were also legal considerations.[6]

Governor Jim Ferguson unwittingly served as a springboard for the Women's Suffrage movement in the World War I period. Led by Minnie Fisher Cunningham, Texas suffragists organized, spoke out, marched, and lobbied for the right to vote during the Ferguson years but were unable to gain political traction because of Ferguson's opposition. When he became embroiled in political controversy over funding for the University of Texas, women joined in the groundswell of opposition. Suffragists effectively lobbied state legislators "through the back door," and organized rallies advocating Ferguson's impeachment.[7]

Texas women continued to actively participate in the political arena although they lacked the right to vote. They supported William P. Hobby for governor as "The Man Whom Good Women Want." Hobby was considered receptive to women's suffrage. The tactic was ultimately successful and women, with some delays, won the legislative battle and gained the right to vote in the 1918 Texas primary.[8]

National suffrage momentum precipitated a proposed constitutional amendment establishing the right of women to vote throughout the United States. Having endured more than five years of "heavy artillery" from Cunningham and the Texas Equal Suffrage Association, legislative opposition crumbled, and Texas became one of the first southern states to ratify the Nineteenth Amendment. Texas women received full voting rights in 1920.[9]

Women were given the right to serve on juries in 1954. Texas's voters' ratification of the Equal Rights Amendment in 1972 and the passage of a series of laws titled the Marital Property Act amounted to major steps toward women's equality and heralded the beginning of a more enlightened era in Texas. The Act granted married women equal rights in insurance,

---

[5]Elizabeth York Enstam, "Women and the Law," *Handbook of Texas Online*, www.tshaonline.org/.
[6]Ibid.
[7]Women of the West Museum, "Western Women's Suffrage—Texas," theautry.org/research/women-of-the-west.
[8]Ibid.
[9]Ibid.

banking, real estate, contracts, divorce, child custody, and property rights. This was the first such comprehensive family law in the United States.[10]

Until 1973, abortion in Texas, as in many states, was illegal. In that year, Sarah Weddington argued a case before the Supreme Court that still stands at the center of national debate—*Roe* v. *Wade*. The *Roe* decision overturned Texas statutes that criminalized abortions and in doing so established a limited, national right of privacy for women to terminate a pregnancy. *Roe* followed *Griswold* v. *Connecticut*, a 1965 privacy case that overturned a state law criminalizing the use of birth control.[11]

African Texans

Africans from other areas of the United States were brought to Texas as slaves and served in that capacity until the end of the Civil War. They first learned of their freedom on June 19, 1865. During Reconstruction, African Texans both voted and served in numerous political positions, but the end of Reconstruction and Anglo-Texan opposition eventually ended African Texans' effective political participation.

Civil rights were an increasingly elusive concept for racial minorities following Reconstruction. African Texans were legally denied the right to vote in the Democratic **white primary**. Schools and public facilities such as theaters, restaurants, beaches, and hospitals were legally segregated by race. Segregation laws were enforced by official law enforcement agents as well as by Anglo-Texan cultural norms and unofficial organizations using terror tactics. Although segregation laws were not usually directed at Latinos, who were legally white, such laws were effectively enforced against them as well. The **Ku Klux Klan (KKK)**, local law officers, and the Texas Rangers actively participated in violence and intimidation of both Latinos and African Texans to keep them "in their segregated place." Lynching was also used against both groups, often after torture.[12]

The KKK was first organized in the late 1860s to intimidate freed African slaves. A modified version was reborn in the 1920s with a somewhat-altered mission. The new Klan saw itself as a patriotic, Christian, fraternal organization for native-born white Protestants. Its members perceived both a general moral decline in society, precipitated by "modern" young people, and a basic threat to the Protestant white Christian "race" and its values by African Texans, Jews, Catholics, Latinos, German Texans, and other "foreigners." Acting on its paranoia, the 1920s Klan set out to force society to comply with its version of fundamentalist Christian morality. It used intimidation, violence, and torture that included hanging, tarring and feathering, branding, beating, and castration as means of coercion. As many as 80,000 Texans may have joined the "invisible empire" in an effort to make the world more to their liking. Many elected officials—U.S. and state legislators as well as county and city officials—were either avowed Klansmen or friendly neutrals. In fact, the Klan influenced Texas society to such an extent that its power was a major political issue from 1921 through 1925.[13]

In response to this racially charged atmosphere, a number of organizations committed to civil rights were founded or grew larger during the 1920s. These included the National Association for the Advancement of Colored People (NAACP), established in 1909, and the

White primary

The practice of excluding African Americans from Democratic Party primary elections in Texas. First enforced by law and later by party rules, this practice was found unconstitutional in *Smith* v. *Allwright*, 321 U.S. 649 (1944).

Ku Klux Klan (KKK)

A white supremacist organization. The first Klan was founded during the Reconstruction era following the Civil War.

---

[10]Enstam, "Women and the Law."

[11]*Roe* v. *Wade*, 410 U.S. 558 (1973); *Griswold* v. *Connecticut*, 381 U.S. 479 (1965); Sarah Weddington, "Roe v. Wade," *Handbook of Texas Online*, www.tshaonline.org/handbook/online/articles/jrr02. The 2011 Texas legislature passed a law that a woman must have both a sonogram (ultrasound) and the fetal image described by the physician prior to terminating a pregnancy. The law also requires a 24-hour waiting period before the actual procedure.

[12]Texas State Historical Association, *Handbook of Texas Online*, www.tshaonline.org/handbook/online/.

[13]Christopher Long, "KU KLUX KLAN," *Handbook of Texas Online*, published by the Texas State Historical Association at www.tshaonline.org/handbook/online/articles/vek02.

League of United Latin American Citizens (LULAC), which was formed in Corpus Christi in 1929.

When Dr. L. H. Nixon, an African American citizen of El Paso, was denied the right to vote in the Democratic primary, the NAACP instituted legal action and the U.S. Supreme Court found in *Nixon* v. *Herndon* (1927) that the Texas White Primary law was unconstitutional. However, the Texas legislature transferred control of the primary from the state to the Democratic State Executive Committee and the discrimination continued. Dr. Nixon again sought justice in the courts, and the U.S. Supreme Court in 1931 also ruled the new scheme unconstitutional. Texas Democrats then completely excluded African Texans from party membership. In *Grovey* v. *Townsend* (1935), the U.S. Supreme Court upheld this ploy, and the Texas Democratic primary remained an all-white organization. Although it had suffered a temporary setback in the episode, the NAACP had proven its potential as a viable instrument for African Texans to achieve justice.[14]

The Texas branch of the NAACP remained active during the World War II period and served as a useful vehicle for numerous legal actions to protect African-Texan civil rights. African Texans eventually won the right to participate in the Texas Democratic primary when the U.S. Supreme Court ruled in *Smith* v. *Allwright* (1944) that primaries were a part of the election process and that racial discrimination in the electoral process is unconstitutional. Twenty years later, the first African Texans since Reconstruction were elected to the Texas legislature.

World War II veteran Heman Sweatt applied for admission to The University of Texas Law School, which by Texas law was segregated. State laws requiring segregation were constitutional so long as facilities serving blacks and whites were equal. Because Texas had no law school for African Texans, the legislature hurriedly sought to establish a law school for Sweatt and for his convenience located in his hometown of Houston. Although officially established, the new law school unfortunately lacked both faculty and a library, and as a result, the NAACP again sued the state. The U.S. Supreme Court ruled that Sweatt's new law school indeed was not equal to the University of Texas Law School and ordered him admitted to that institution. It is worth noting that "separate-but-equal" facilities remained legal after this case because the court did not overturn *Plessy* v. *Ferguson*, which granted the constitutional sanction for legal segregation. Instead, the court simply ruled that the new law school was not equal to The University of Texas.[15] Segregation was not outlawed until the 1954 Brown decision.

The political and social fallout from the U.S. Supreme Court's *Brown* v. *Board of Education* (1954) public school desegregation decision did not bypass Texas.[16] When the Mansfield school district, just southeast of Fort Worth, was ordered to integrate in 1956, angry whites surrounded the school and prevented the enrollment of three African-Texan children. Governor Allan Shivers declared the demonstration an "orderly protest" and sent the Texas Rangers to support the protestors. Because the Eisenhower administration took no action, the school remained segregated. The Mansfield school desegregation incident "was the first example of failure to enforce a federal court order for the desegregation of a public school." Only in 1965, when facing a loss of federal funding, did the Mansfield ISD desegregate.[17]

Joseph Scherschel/Time Life Pictures/Getty Images

Heman Sweatt successfully integrated Texas public law schools after the U.S. Supreme Court began to chip away at the "separate-but-equal" doctrine in the landmark case Sweatt v. Painter, 339 U.S. 629 (1950).

The Fourteenth Amendment to the U.S. Constitution says that no state shall deny any person the equal protection of the laws. Why did the Supreme Court hold that state laws requiring racial segregation violate this provision?

---

[14]*Seymour* v. *Connor*, Texas: *A History* (New York: Thomas Y. Crowell, 1971), pp. 378–379.

[15]*Sweatt* v. *Painter*, 339 U.S. 629 (1950); *Plessy* v. *Ferguson*, 163 U.S. 537 (1892).

[16]*Brown* v. *Board of Education of Topeka*, 347 U.S. 483 (1954).

[17]George B. Green, Mansfield School Desegregation Incident," *Handbook of Texas Online*, published by the Texas State Historical Association at www.tshaonline.org/handbook/online/articles/jcm02.

Federal District Judge William Wayne Justice in *United States* v. *Texas* (1970) ordered the complete desegregation of all Texas public schools. The decision was one of the most extensive desegregation orders in history and included the process for executing the order in detail. The U.S. Fifth Circuit Court largely affirmed Justice's decision but refused to extend its provisions to Latino children.[18]

The 1960s is known for the victories of the national civil rights movement. Texan James Farmer was cofounder of the Congress of Racial Equality (CORE) and, along with Dr. Martin Luther King Jr., Whitney Young, and Roy Wilkins, was one of the "Big Four" African Americans who shaped the civil rights struggle in the 1950s and 1960s. Farmer, who followed the nonviolent principles of Mahatma Gandhi, initiated sit-ins as a means of integrating public facilities and freedom rides as a means of registering African Americans to vote. The first sit-in to protest segregated facilities in Texas was organized with CORE support by students from Wiley and Bishop Colleges. The students occupied the rotunda of the Harrison County courthouse in Marshall.[19]

Did You Know? CORE founder James Farmer was a member of the 1935 national champion debate team at Wiley College that inspired the critically renowned movie *The Great Debaters* starring Denzel Washington.

Latino Texans Like most African Americans, Latinos were relegated to the lowest-paid jobs as either service workers or farm workers. The Raymondville Peonage cases in 1929 tested for the first time the legality of forcing vagrants or debtors to repay farmers by requiring them to work off debts and fines as labor on private farms. The practice violated federal statutes but was commonplace in some Texas counties. The Willacy County sheriff stated in his defense that Mexicans often sought arrest to gain shelter and that "peonage was not an unknown way of life for them." The trials resulted in the arrest and conviction of several public officials and private individuals. The outcome of the trials was unpopular in the agricultural areas and contrary to the generally accepted belief that farmers should have a means of collecting debts from individual laborers.[20]

World War II Latino-Texan veterans, newly returned from fighting to make the world safe for democracy, found discrimination still existed in the homeland. A decorated veteran, Major Hector Garcia settled in Corpus Christi and became convinced by conditions in the Latino-American community in South Texas that still another battle was yet to be fought—and in his own backyard. Garcia, a medical doctor, found farm laborers enduring inhuman living conditions; deplorable medical conditions in slums; disabled veterans starving, sick, and ignored by the Veterans Administration; and an entrenched unapologetic Anglo-Texan culture continuing public school segregation.

To begin his war, Dr. Garcia needed recruits for his "army." With other World War II veterans, Dr. Garcia organized the American GI Forum in a Corpus Christi elementary school

AP Photo

Texas Southern University students stage a sit-in at a Houston supermarket lunch counter, 1950.

Why did students risk arrest in protests that focused national attention on segregation? Why do minorities use tactics other than voting to achieve their strategic goals?

---

[18]Frank R. Remerer, "*United States* v. *Texas*" (1970) *Handbook of Texas Online.* Accessed November 18, 2011.
[19]For more information, see CORE-online.org.
[20]Alicia A. Garza, Raymondville Peonage Cases," *Handbook of Texas Online,* published by the Texas State Historical Association at www.tshaonline.org/handbook/online/articles/pqreq.

classroom in March 1948. This organization spread throughout the United States and played a major role in giving Latino Americans full citizenship and civil respect.[21]

One of the incendiary sparks that ignited Latino Texans to fight for civil rights was Felix Longoria's funeral. Private Longoria was a decorated casualty of World War II whose body was returned to Three Rivers for burial in the "Mexican section" of the cemetery, which was separated from the white section by barbed wire. But an obstacle developed—the funeral home's director refused the Longoria family's request to use the chapel because "whites would not like it." Longoria's widow asked Dr. Hector Garcia for support, but the funeral director also refused his request. Dr. Garcia then sent a flurry of telegrams and letters to Texas congressmen protesting the actions of the director. Senator Lyndon B. Johnson immediately responded and arranged for Private Longoria to be buried at Arlington National Cemetery.[22]

The fight to organize into labor unions was the primary focus for much of the Latino civil activism in the 1960s and 1970s. In rural areas, large landowners controlled the political as well as the economic system and were united in opposition of labor unions. The United Farm Workers (UFW) led a strike against melon growers and packers in Starr County in the 1960s, demanding a minimum wage and resolution of other grievances. Starr County police officers, the local judiciary, and the Texas Rangers were all accused of brutality as they arrested and prosecuted strikers for minor offenses.

On February 26, 1977, members of the Texas Farm Workers Union (TFWU), strikers, and other supporters began a march to Austin to demand a $1.25 minimum wage and other improvements for farm workers. Press coverage intensified as the marchers slowly made their way north in the summer heat. Politicians, members of the American Federation of Labor–Congress of Industrial Organizations (AFL–CIO), and the Texas Council of Churches accompanied the protestors. Governor John Connally, who had refused to meet them in Austin, traveled to New Braunfels with then House Speaker Ben Barnes and Attorney General Waggoner Carr to intercept the march and inform strikers that their efforts would have no effect. Ignoring the governor, the marchers continued to Austin and held a 6500-person protest rally at the state capitol. The rally was broken up by Texas Rangers and other law enforcement officers. The Union took legal action against the Rangers for their part in the strike and the protest. The eventual ruling of the U.S. Supreme Court held that the laws the Rangers had been enforcing were in violation of the U.S. Constitution. The Rangers were subsequently reorganized and became a part of the Texas Department of Public Safety.[23]

One of the first successful legal challenges to segregated schools in Texas was *Delgado* v. *Bastrop ISD* (1948). The suit by Gustavo C. (Gus) Garcia charged that Minerva Delgado and other Latino children were denied the same school facilities and educational instruction available to other white races. The battle continued until segregated facilities were eventually prohibited in 1957 by the decision in *Herminca Hernandez et al.* v. *Driscoll Consolidated ISD*.[24]

Important to Latinos and, ultimately, all others facing discrimination was *Hernandez* v. *State of Texas* (1954). Pete Hernandez was convicted of murder in Edna, Jackson County, Texas, by an all-Anglo jury. Latino attorneys Gustavo (Gus) Garcia, Carlos Cadena, John Herrera, and James DeAnda challenged the conviction, arguing that the systematic exclusion of Latinos from jury duty in Texas violated Hernandez's rights to equal protection of the law guaranteed by the Fourteenth Amendment of the U.S. Constitution. Texas courts

---

[21]www.justiceformypeople.org/drhector2.html.

[22]V. Carl Allsup, "Felix Longoria Affair," *Handbook of Texas Online*, published by the Texas State Historical Association at www.tshaonline.org/handbook/online/articles/vef01.

[23]See Robert E. Hall, "Pickets, Politics and Power: The Farm Worker Strike in Starr County," *Texas Bar Journal*, Volume 70, number 5, 2007.

[24]V. Carl Allstrop, "*Delgado* v. *Bastrop ISD*," *Handbook of Texas Online*, published by the Texas State Historical Association at www.tshaonline.org/handbook/online/articles/jrd01.

Gus Garcia, legal advisor for the American G.I. Forum, is shown during a visit to the White House. Garcia was the lead attorney in the U.S. Supreme Court decision Hernandez v. Texas, 347 U.S. 475 (1954).

Why is it unconstitutional to deny a person the right to serve on a jury because of ethnicity?

had historically ruled that Latinos were white, so excluding them from all-Anglo (white) juries could not be legal discrimination. To change the system, the Latino team of lawyers would have to change the interpretation of the U.S. Constitution. The stakes were high. If they failed, Latino discrimination throughout the southwestern United States could legally continue for decades. Garcia argued before the U.S. Supreme Court that Latinos, although white, were "a class apart" and suffered discrimination on the basis of their "class." The U.S. Supreme Court agreed, overturned the Texas courts, and ruled that Latinos were protected by the Constitution from discrimination by other whites. The Hernandez decision established the precedent of Constitutional protection by class throughout the United States and was a forerunner for future decisions prohibiting discrimination by gender, disability, or sexual preference.[25]

Gay, Lesbian, and Transgendered Texans Discrimination against gay, lesbian, and transgendered Texans has long been considered a God-given right by some Texas heterosexuals. Neither workplace, school, nor church has provided sanctuary from prejudice for gay, lesbian, and transgendered Texans. Furthermore, state law has criminalized certain intimate sexual conduct by two persons of the same gender.

A Harris County sheriff's deputy discovered two men having intimate sexual conduct in a private residence and the men were arrested and convicted for violating a Texas anti-sodomy statute. Their conviction was appealed and eventually reached the U.S. Supreme court in the case *Lawrence* v. *Texas*. In Justice Kennedy's opinion for the court, he stated that the Texas law violated the due process clause of the Fourteenth Amendment, which does not protect sodomy but does protect personal relationships. The Texas statute intended to control the most intimate of all human activity, sexual behavior, in the most private of places, the home. Citizens of Texas are able to legally have personal relationships without fear of punishment or criminal classification. The decision also invalidated sodomy laws in 13 other states, thereby protecting same-sex behavior in every state and territory in the United States.[26]

The right to marry is the current frontline of the gay, lesbian, and transgendered battle for equal rights. The Defense of Marriage Act (DOMA) complicates the battle. DOMA defines marriage as a legal union between a man and a woman and further stipulates that hostile states do not have to recognize same-gender marriage contracts from other states.[27] The definition of "marriage" is at the center point of the conflict. Is marriage a religious ceremony or is it a secular contract? If religious, there should not be an issue except between the couple and their higher power. If secular, religious beliefs should not restrict the union, and "it's my life" would be the guiding principle. The problem is that governments have piled bundles of baggage onto marriage, including Social Security benefits, tax filings, family insurance benefits, and community property, thereby affecting both lives immediately following the kiss and prior to cutting the cake.

Texans, by the overwhelming majority of 76 percent, added an amendment to the Texas Constitution in 2005 banning both gay and lesbian marriage and civil unions. The amendment also prohibits hospital visitation rights, community property rights, and survivors' benefits for gay and lesbian couples. The authority to make medical decisions for an incapacitated loved one is also prohibited. The couple also faces discrimination in employment, housing, and public accommodations, and gay or lesbian children often lack protection in the state's schools.

---

[25]V. Carl Allstrop, "*Hernandez* v. *State of Texas*," 347 U.S. 475 (1954) *Handbook of Texas Online.* Published by the Texas State Historical Association.
[26]*Lawrence* v. *Texas* (539 US 558 (2003).
[27]Defense of Marriage Act, enacted September 21, 1996.

TABLE 1.2 Key U.S. Supreme Court Decisions Protecting Texans' Rights to Equality and Privacy

Unconstitutional Texas Practice	U.S. Constitutional Violation	Landmark Supreme Court Case
Texas laws permitting the Democratic Party to to conduct whites-only primaries. Also used in other Southern states.	No state shall deny any person the right to vote on account of race—Fifteenth Amendment.	*Smith* v. *Allright* (1944)
Texas law requiring racially segregated law schools. Professional schools were segregated throughout the South.	No state shall deny any person the equal protection of the law—Fourteenth Amendment.	*Sweatt* v. *Painter* (1950)
Texas practice of denying Latinos the right to serve on juries.	No state shall deny any person the equal protection of the law—Fourteenth Amendment.	*Hernandez* v. *State of Texas* (1954)
State laws mandating statewide segregation of public schools and most facilities open to the public. Texas was among the 17 mostly Southern states with statewide laws requiring segregation at the time of the decision.	No state shall deny any person the equal protection of the law—Fourteenth Amendment.	*Brown* v. *Board of Education of Topeka* (1954)
Texas law making abortion illegal; 30 states outlawed abortions for any reason in 1973.	No state shall deny liberty without due process of law—Fourteenth Amendment.	*Roe* v. *Wade* (1973)
Texas law making homosexual conduct a crime; 14 mostly Southern states made homosexual conduct a crime at the time of the decision.	No state shall deny liberty without due process of law—Fourteenth Amendment.	*Lawrence* v. *Texas* (2003)

This table shows the important U.S. constitutional decisions that have expanded minority rights in Texas and nationwide.

▲ **How has Texas's Southern conservative political culture resisted social change? Why have ethnic and sexual minorities sought remedy for discrimination in the U.S. Supreme Court, an institution outside the control of state politics?**

CULTURAL DIVERSITY TODAY

Texas is one of the fastest-growing states in the nation. No longer predominantly rural and agrarian, Texas is becoming more culturally diverse as immigrants from other nations and migrants from other states continue to find it a desirable place to call home. The 2010 census showed a significant trend toward greater ethnic diversity. Figure 1.3 shows that the growing

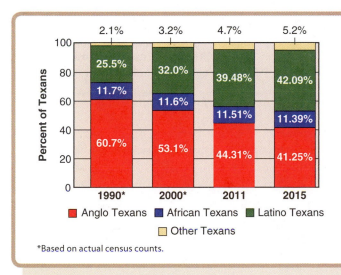

Figure 1.3

Texas Ethnic Populations, Past, Present, and Future, 1990–2015.

This figure shows the changing demographics of Texans.

Source: Adapted from "Projections of Texas and Counties in Texas by Age, Sex and Race/Ethnicity for 1990, 2000, 2011, and 2015," Texas State Data Center, Office of the State Demographer; and Census Bureau, Census 2000 and 2010.

What implications does Texas's changing ethnic makeup have for the state's political future?

diversity of Texas's population is projected to continue, and Texans now have the opportunity to continue to build on their already-rich cultural pluralism. Increasing diversity could also have a significant impact on Texas's politics and culture.

Voter participation in Texas is historically low, ranking 45th among the states in voter turnout. Social scientists argue that this is attributable to political conditioning as well as social and economic reality. Latino participation is low even by Texas standards, but because Latinos are predicted to become the largest plurality in Texas by 2015, there could be significant political impact if this sleeping political giant arises.

Demographics

Population characteristics, such as age, gender, ethnicity, employment, and income, that social scientists use to describe groups in society.

Equally important, changes in the ethnic makeup of the state's population will present decision makers with enormous challenges. Figure 1.4 shows that income inequality parallels ethnic divisions in Texas. Poverty rates are higher and overall incomes are lower among African Texans and Latinos. Lower incomes are associated with limited educational opportunity, lack of health insurance, and lower rates of participation in the state's civic life. Poverty drives up the cost of state social services and is a factor that contributes to crime, family break-ups, and illegitimate births even as it drives up the cost of social services. How Texas deals with changes in the state's **demographics** is likely to be the focus of political controversy for years to come.

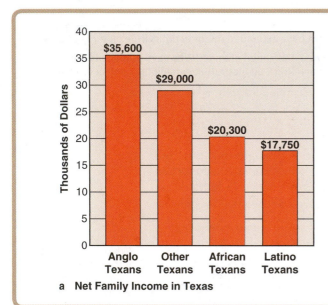

a   **Net Family Income in Texas**

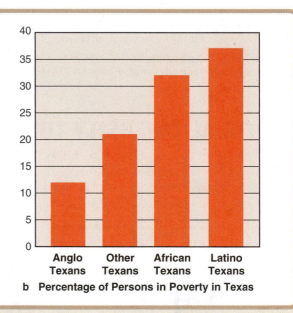

b   **Percentage of Persons in Poverty in Texas**

Figure 1.4

Ethnicity, Income, and Poverty in Texas

Today, inequality among ethnic groups is no longer so much reflected by overt official legal discrimination as by unequal wealth, income, and access to health care.

Source: The Henry J. Kaiser Family Foundation, "State Health Facts Online," http://www.statehealthfacts.kff.org

Why do ethnic minorities earn less that Anglo Texans? How do income inequality and increasing ethnic diversity challenge policy makers in Texas?

The Texas Political Culture: Shaped by the Old South's Traditionalism and the Frontier Experience's Individualism

by Dr. Brian K. Dille,
Odessa College

Most Americans are familiar with Texans' bravado, bragging about their state and being "a Texan." The Texas swagger and drawl are often depicted by the media as "typically Texan." Bumper stickers such as "Everything is bigger and better in Texas" and "I wasn't born in Texas, but I got here as fast as I could" are a common sight in the state. "If you pray and live a good life, when you die you will go to Texas" is another refrain frequently seen and heard. Many Texans view their state as special, unique, and superior to other states. Where did these "Texanisms" and "Texas attitude" come from? They were shaped by Texas's unique historical experience and political culture.

Is Texas a southern or western state? Many people believe it to be a typical southern state. Others disagree, arguing that Texas exhibits more traces of the West and the frontier experience. The truth is somewhere between the two. The Texas political culture is a mix of the traditionalistic subculture from its Old South heritage, the individualistic subculture from the frontier experience, and the Midwestern and German influences. East Texas is strongly traditionalistic and has the "Old South" atmosphere, whereas the individualistic

culture is more dominant in the Panhandle, West Texas, and Southwest Texas.

The traditionalistic political subculture is found primarily in the South and Border States, particularly in the former Confederate states. Anglos from the lower South and Hispanics, reflecting the patrón culture, contributed to the strong presence of traditionalistic beliefs and practices. The impact of the Old South occurred when over 20,000 American immigrants, most from the American South, flooded into Texas from 1824–1830 to take advantage of Mexico's offer of free land under the impresario land grant program. Those southern immigrants, settling in what is now East Texas, brought southern practices, beliefs, traditions, institutions, and the traditionalistic political subculture into Texas. To this day, East Texas still has the "feel" of the Old South.

The preservation of the status quo was a key component of the traditionalistic political subculture. The dominant planter class generally viewed change as a threat to the institution of slavery. The primary function of government was seen as maintaining the status quo. The slogan, "If it ain't broke, don't fix it" is an accurate description of many Texans' world view. The continuing failure to rewrite and adopt a new state constitution to replace the outdated state constitution of 1876 is indicative of this persistent, antichange attitude. No serious attempt at constitutional revision has occurred since voters overwhelmingly rejected a proposed new state constitution in 1975.

Participation in this traditionalistic environment was confined to a small elite group, the planter class. Texas's past use of restrictive voting requirements such as the poll tax, the white primary, an annual registration requirement, and restrictions on the military vote were all a reflection of the Old South's elitism and its aim to limit political participation to the "right people," the Anglo elite. Mass voter participation, particularly by African Americans, Hispanics, and the uneducated nonelites was often discouraged. Those barriers to suffrage fell only when declared unconstitutional by the United States Supreme Court. Although the barriers have been removed, the impact is still evident today: Texas ranks 43rd in the percentage of voting-age population registered to vote and 45th in the percentage of the voting-age population that votes.[28] Even today, the Texas public often has only limited power and influence.

The traditionalistic subculture advocated the enactment of policies to benefit the elite and was maintained by a class-based social structure. This is still reflected in the Texas tax structure and the laissez faire attitude on the role of government. Texas, one of six states that have no state income tax, relies solely on regressive taxes. A 2009 study named Texas's tax system as one of the 10 most regressive in the nation.[29] This results in poorer Texans paying a much larger portion of their income in taxes than do the wealthy. The laissez faire attitude toward the role of government is reflected in the comparatively low funding of social programs, weak environmental regulations, and weak regulations on business. Texas's funding and provision of social services typically ranks in the bottom 10 in comparison with the other 49 states.[30]

---

[28]U.S. Census Bureau, Voting and Registration in the Election of November 2008, Table 4b, Reported Voting and Registration of the Voting-Age Population, by Sex, Race and Hispanic Origin, for States: November 2008. Online. Available at www.census.gov/hhes/www/socdemo/voting/publications/p20/2008/tables.html.

[29]Institute on Taxation and Economic Policy, *"Who Pays? A Distributional Analysis of the Tax Systems of All 50 States,"* (November 2009). Online. Available at www.itepnet.org/whopays3.pdf.

[30]Texas Legislative Study Group, *"Texas on the Brink,"* (February 2011). Available at texaslsg.org/texasonthebrink/texasonthebrink.pdf.

Texas's state constitution even limits welfare spending to one percent of the state budget. The result of weak environmental regulations is that Texas ranks number one in each of the following: the amount of carbon dioxide emissions;[31] the amount of volatile organic compounds released into the air;[32] the amount of toxic chemicals released into the water;[33] the amount of recognized carcinogens released into the air;[34] and the amount of hazardous waste generated.[35] Texas Governor Rick Perry often promotes these "reasonable regulations" as proof of Texas's "business-friendly environment."[36]

Texas's long experience with segregation and race discrimination was a product of the Old South's traditionalism and southern race relations. Many Texas communities and school districts continued to practice segregation long after the *Brown* v. *Board of Education* U.S. Supreme Court decision of 1954 declared segregated public schools unconstitutional. President Lyndon Johnson was reportedly angered and frustrated by continued news stories reporting that blacks were still being turned away from public accommodations in the state capital of Austin during his presidency in the mid- to late-1960s. Despite substantial progress made in the fight to end all forms of race discrimination, the dragging death of a black man, James Byrd, Jr., by three white men in Jasper, Texas, in June of 1998 was another indication that pockets of old racial attitudes, prejudices, and practices still exist.

The Old South's traditionalistic culture was also characterized by a dominant conservative political philosophy and a one-party Democratic political system. Initially, conservatism and the Democratic Party's embrace of popular sovereignty during the battle over the expansion of slavery into the West pushed the antebellum South, including Texas, into the arms of the Democratic Party. The role of the Republican Party during the Civil War, the abolition of slavery, and Reconstruction simply reinforced the allegiance to the Democratic Party. After the Civil War, the Republican Party became, to most Southerners, the party of the North, the party that freed the slaves and defeated the Confederacy, and the party responsible for the "abuses of Reconstruction." In the twentieth century, as the Republican Party became more conservative and pro-business, Texas continued to support the Democratic Party, voting for Franklin D. Roosevelt four times and supporting Democratic President Lyndon B. Johnson over conservative icon Barry Goldwater in the 1964 presidential election. However, charismatic Ronald Reagan, extremely popular in Texas, slowly began to change the perception of the Republican Party in the 1980s from an "elitist, country-club party to a more

populist one."[37] This political realignment continued under the governorship and presidency of Texan George W. Bush, making Texas a truly "red state." The shift to the Republican Party has merely reinforced Texans' conservatism. Today, more Texans (44.8 percent) still consider themselves conservative rather than moderate (33.3 percent) or liberal (17.5 percent).[38]

For most of American history, the South, including Texas, has been rural and agrarian. As recently as the 1940s, Texas was still primarily a rural and agricultural state. The oil industry and World War II led to the growing urbanization and industrialization of Texas. Today, Texas is an urban, industrial megastate, containing three of the ten most populous cities in the nation. However, urban, industrial Texas is still the number two agricultural state in the nation,[39] and the vast, open spaces of much of West Texas and the Panhandle continue to give the state a "rural feel."

The second political subculture, the individualistic subculture, is found throughout much of the United States, but particularly in the Mid-Atlantic States, the Midwest, the West, and Southwest. Midwestern and German settlers and immigrants from the Upper South brought these individualistic beliefs into Texas. This subculture viewed the democratic order as a marketplace, advocated minimal government in the private sector, and believed participation was a necessary evil. Politics was seen as a less-than-honorable career and as a profession better left to those willing to dirty their hands. Political participation was generally seen as a necessary evil rather than a citizen's obligation. Government was not to be concerned with the creation of a "good society."

Texas's frontier experience further shaped this individualistic subculture. It is true that at one time all states were on the frontier. However, Texas, because of its large size and geographical location, was on the frontier longer than any other state, with the possible exception of Alaska. The Spanish established the first permanent settlements in Texas in the first two decades of the eighteenth century, and the first large number of American immigrants arrived in Texas in the 1820s. The Native American "threat" in Texas was not ended until the summer of 1875 when the last band of Comanches were defeated and transferred to a reservation. In addition, Texans dealt with the border bandits until March of 1916 when the U.S. Army under General John J. Pershing was sent into Mexico in response to Pancho Villa's raids on the border communities of Texas. This "frontier atmosphere" was something Anglo Texans dealt with for almost a century and Hispanic Texans even longer. That long frontier experience had a strong impact on the individualistic culture in Texas.

[31]U.S. Environmental Protection Agency, Energy CO2 Emissions by State (2005). Online. Available at www.epa.gov/climatechange/emissions/downloads/CO2FFC_2005.xls.

[32]Scorecard: The Pollution Information Site, Rankings of States by Air Pollutants Emissions. Online. Available at scorecard.org/env-releases/cap/rank-states-emissions.tcl.

[33]Scorecard: The Pollution Information Site, States with Reported Releases of Toxics Release Inventory: Water Releases. Online. Available at scorecard.org/ranking/rankstates. tcl?how_many=100&drop_down_name=Water+releases.

[34]Scorecard: The Pollution Information Site, States with Reported Releases of Recognized Carcinogens to Air. Online. Available at scorecard.goodguide.com/env-releases/state.tcl?fips_state_code=48.

[35]U.S. Environmental Protection Agency, National Biennial Resource Conservation and Recovery Act (RCRA) Hazardous Waste Report: Based on 2009 Data (November 2010), Exhibit 1.2. Online. Available at www.epa.gov/osw/inforesources/data/br09/national09.pdf.

[36]members.texasone.us/site/PageServer?pagename=TexasAdvantageLegislativeAccomplishments.

[37]Interview with Cunningham, Sean P. Accessed at voices.washingtonpost.com/political-bookworm/2010/03/modern_conservatism_texas-styl.html

[38]www.bizjournals.com/austin/stories/2009/08/17/daily28.html.

[39]State of the States. Accessed at www.gallup.com/poll/125066/State-States.aspx?ref=interactive.

"Frontier justice" was practiced in this frontier environment. Outlaws and criminals were often found guilty and then hanged because the frontier lacked the resources for much of a jail or prison system. This frontier justice mentality is still seen in Texas today in its frequent use of the death penalty and its strong opposition to gun control. Texas, by far, leads the nation in executions.[40] With only eight percent of the nation's population, Texas executes over one-third of those executed in the entire nation. Most Texans are proud, rather than ashamed, of that number one ranking. In the words of Texas comedian Ron White, "If you come to Texas and kill someone, we will kill you back" and "Other states are trying to abolish the death penalty . . . [Texas is] putting in an express lane."[41]

The frontier experience also shaped attitudes toward gun ownership and gun control. On the frontier, Texans needed guns to protect themselves from Native Americans, outlaws, rattlesnakes, and coyotes. Texans, to this day, are notoriously opposed to stringent gun controls. Many Texans view the right to own a gun "as essential as the right to life itself."[42] Many fathers in Texas teach their daughters how to shoot, a practice much less common in other parts of the nation. Today, Texas has more gun owners than any other state. Texans own approximately 51 million firearms, almost a quarter of all arms in the United States![43] As of 2009, the NRA had approximately 250,000 members in Texas. What is surprising is that Texas is actually third rather than first in terms of NRA membership nationwide.[44] Texans, however, are working on improving that ranking. Currently, the "Support Project One Million: Texas" is engaging in an effort to increase NRA membership in Texas to one million members.[45]

People living on the frontier grew accustomed to a strong spirit of self-reliance. Texans learned to rely on themselves rather than look to government because there was little government on the frontier. This strong belief in self-reliance and pulling oneself up by the bootstraps is still reflected in Texas today. Texas's comparatively low levels of funding to social programs illustrate this. In education, Texas ranks 38th on current expenditures per student,[46] 44th on state and local expenditures per pupil in public schools,[47] and 47th on state aid per pupil in average daily attendance.[48] In health care, Texas ranks 50th on per capita state spending on mental health,[49] 49th on per capita state spending on Medicaid,[50] and 47th in average monthly WIC benefits per person.[51] Despite the dangerous work environment in the oil fields, Texas ranks 50th in workers' compensation coverage.[52] It is not that Texas lacks the resources to spend more on these programs—Texans choose not to.

With little government on the frontier, people became accustomed to minimal regulation on business. This reinforced Texans' strong belief in free enterprise. Texas has historically been a weak-regulation, business-friendly state. Today, Texas Governor Perry and other Texas political and business leaders consistently promote Texas as that business-friendly state, with low taxes, "reasonable regulations," and right-to-work laws. Although these weak regulations and "business-friendly" policies have led to atrocious environmental rankings (cited earlier in this essay), many Texans strongly believe these are the primary factors responsible for the booming Texas economy over the last three to four decades.

Land was vitally important on the frontier. It provided a livelihood for farmers and ranchers. The accumulation of land also became a path to political, social, and economic power. Today, land ownership is still considered important in Texas. When Texans come into money, they often purchase land. It is telling that in the last fifty years only three presidents, all westerners, vacationed on their ranches: Ronald Reagan, a Californian; and two Texans—Lyndon Baines Johnson and George W. Bush.

Life on the frontier was tough, and settlers learned to rely on others, often helping neighbors raise a log cabin, harvest a crop, or nurse sick family members back to health. Visitors and travelers were often welcomed with open arms because they brought news from back East and provided a welcome break from the isolation of frontier life. That strong spirit of helpfulness and friendliness is still evident in Texas today. Travelers, tourists, and new residents to Texas consistently comment on the friendliness of Texans to ordinary strangers.

The hard life of the frontier produced a spirit of pride in those who survived and "made it." That pride has been accentuated by Texas's unique historical experience as an independent republic. The feeling that Texas is somehow unique,

---

[40]Death Penalty Information Center, Number of Executions by State and Region Since 1976. Online. Available at www.deathpenaltyinfo.org/number-executions-state-and-region-1976.

[41]www.brainyquote.com/quotes/authors/r/ron_white.html#ixzz1mD66IsQn.

[42]learnarms.com/texas-gun-control-revolution/.

[43]Ibid.

[44]www.projectonemilliontexas.com/.

[45]Ibid.

[46]National Education Association, Rankings & Estimates (December 2009). Online. Available at www.nea.org/assets/docs/010rankings.pdf.

[47]Texas Legislative Budget Board, 2010 Texas Fact Book. Online. Available at www.lbb.state.tx.us/Fact_Book/Texas_FactBook_2010.pdf.

[48]Ibid.

[49]The Henry J. Kaiser Family Foundation, State Health Facts Online, State Mental Health Agency Per Capita Mental Health Services Expenditures, FY2005. Online. Available at www.statehealthfacts.org/comparemaptable.jsp?ind=278&cat=5.

[50]The Henry J. Kaiser Family Foundation, State Health Facts Online, Total Medicaid Spending, FY2008. Online. Available at www.statehealthfacts.org/comparecat.jsp?cat=6&rgn=6&rgn=1.

[51]U.S. Department of Agriculture, Food and Nutrition Services, WIC Program: Average Monthly Benefit Per Person, FY 2009. Online at www.fns.usda.gov/pd/25wifyavgfd$.htm.

[52]Corporation for Enterprise Development, Assets and Opportunity Scorecard, 2009-2010, Workers Compensation Coverage. Online. Available at scorecard2009.cfed.org/main.php?page=scorecard_policies.

special, and one of a kind is evident in the pride displayed throughout the state: the common practice of flying the state flag on farms, ranches, and in many yards; the Texas chain stores in many malls (in addition to many online companies) selling nothing but products celebrating Texas and its heritage; and the prevalent "we-are-the-best" attitude that some non-Texans have interpreted as arrogance.

The influences of these two subcultures reinforce each other and can still be seen today in the structure of government and the policies pursued. Both political subcultures share common political views, advocating a limited role for government and discouraging mass participation. Government should only do that which individuals cannot do for themselves, leaving the rest to the private sector. Taxes should be low, social services limited, and the advancement of civil rights minimal. Texas state government is limited with a weak governor, a part-time legislature ("the less time they are in Austin, the less damage they can do"), and power divided among many elected officials. State regulations on business and the environment are kept to a minimum and voter participation in Texas is still relatively low. Texas consistently ranks near the bottom (47th) of the 50 states on government expenditures[53]

and relies on a regressive tax system with a comparatively low (46th) tax burden.[54] "The best government is the government that governs least" could easily be the bumper sticker expression best describing Texans' philosophy on government today. It is now the twenty-first century and the antebellum South and frontier are long gone. However, Texans still continue to support the conservative, laissez faire policies and limited government promoted by the traditionalistic and individualistic political culture of the state. Long live the Old South and the frontier environment!

JOIN THE DEBATE

1. Evaluate the impact of the Old South and frontier experience on Texas. Has it been more positive or negative? Provide specific examples of Texas state government and policies today to support your position.

2. How did the Old South and frontier experience shape the choices the Texas Legislature made in the Spring 2011 session when they faced a predicted state deficit of more than $20 billion?

---

[53]The Henry J. Kaiser Family Foundation. Total State Expenditures per Capita, SFY2008. Online. Available at www.statehealthfacts.org/comparemaptable.jsp?ind=32&cat=1.

[54]The Henry J. Kaiser Family Foundation. State Government Tax Collections per Capita, 2009. Online. Available at www.statehealthfacts.org/comparemaptable.jsp?ind=30&cat=1.

CHAPTER SUMMARY

★ A political culture reflects the political values and beliefs of people. It explains how people feel about their government—their expectations of what powers it should have over their lives and what services it should provide. Texans' predominantly conservative political culture is reflected in voters' Republican affiliation and in the state's conservative public policies.

★ Texas can be divided into a series of cultural regions with differing characteristics and traditions: (1) East Texas, (2) the Gulf Coast, (3) South Texas, (4) Southwest Texas, (5) the German Hill Country, (6) West Texas, (7) the Panhandle, (8) North Texas, and (9) Central Texas. These regions display varying combinations of moral, traditionalistic, and individualistic cultures.

★ Women were not legally equal to men in early Texas and their path to equality has been a winding and occasionally hesitant one. Activists finally won the long battle for the right to vote in 1918. It was not until 1972 that women won equal rights in real estate, contracts, divorce, child custody, and property rights. The judicial decision in *Roe* v. *Wade*

that further clarified the right of women to control their reproductive functions is still at the center of a national controversy. Civil rights have always been an issue, and the dominant Anglo Texans once believed that the primary purpose for Africans and Latinos being in Texas was to supply sources of cheap labor. Modern Texans can take no pride in the historical treatment of both these groups, who were undereducated and exploited for their labor and lived under a state-enforced caste system. The enduring consequences of discrimination are still evident in Texas, as is illustrated by lower levels of health care, education, and income.

★ African Texans' struggle for legal equality reflected similar struggles being simultaneously waged in other southern states. The battle to vote in the Democratic primary and admission to public accommodations and public schools were settled only by national courts or congressional intervention.

★ The Latino struggle in Texas was similar to that of African Texans and was resolved only by national action. Several Latino rights organizations were founded in Texas, and the judicial decision in *Hernandez* v. *Texas* (1954) that established the constitutional concept of a "class apart" became important throughout the United States. The right to form labor unions occupied much of the Latino Movement in the 1960s and 1970s.

★ Gays, lesbians, and transgendered Texans are now waging similar battles for legal equality. *Lawrence* v. *Texas* (1973) gained national significance by decriminalizing sexual activity between consenting persons of the same gender.

★ Projections of population growth and immigration predict a shift in Texas's population away from an Anglo-Texan plurality to a Latino-Texan plurality. Increased political clout can come with increased population, and Latino Texans could begin to challenge the political and economic dominance of Anglo Texans. Regardless of the political outcome of population shifts, Texas is becoming more culturally diverse and now has an opportunity to build on its already-rich cultural pluralism.

HOW TEXAS COMPARES

★ Beginning in the 1820s, Texas's settlers came from the "Anglo" political culture of the Old South, and Texas political history can best be compared to that of other southern states. Like those states, the Texas political culture is considered both traditionalistic and individualistic.

★ Texas public policies are conservative. Per capita, only four states have lower taxes, and no state spends less on public services than Texas. The state has more business-friendly economic policies and culturally traditional social policies than most states.

★ Texas spends less on public schools than 17 other states, but none has a larger percentage of the population without high school diplomas.

★ Only five states score lower than Texas on the Scholastic Assessment Test (SAT) scores.

★ Texas's economy has become more industrialized than that of most states but continues to maintain the lax environmental standards of the past. Texas ranks first among the states in emission of greenhouse gases into the air and toxins released into the water. Texas ranks first in the amount of cancer-causing chemicals released into the air and ranks seventh in those released into water. Overall, Texas ranks first in the amount of hazardous waste generated.

★ With three of America's ten largest cities, Texas has become the second-most populous state and one of the most metropolitan. Texas ranks among the top ten states in population growth, and today it has twice the percentage of Latinos in its population as the nation as a whole.

KEY TERMS

bicultural, *p. 11*
binational, *p. 11*
conservative, *p. 2*
Creole, *p. 11*
demographics, *p. 22*
ideology, *p. 2*

individualistic culture, *p. 7*
internationality, *p. 11*
Ku Klux Klan (KKK), *p. 16*
liberal, *p. 3*
maquiladora, *p. 12*
Mestizos, *p. 11*

Metroplex, *p. 14*
moralistic culture, *p. 7*
North American Free Trade Agreement (NAFTA), *p. 12*
political culture, *p. 2*

ranchero culture, *p. 11*
traditionalistic culture, *p. 7*
The Valley, *p. 11*
White primary, *p. 16*

REVIEW QUESTIONS

1. Describe the policy differences between Texas conservative and liberal ideologies. How does public opinion and public policy in the state reflect the dominant values and beliefs of the state's voters?

2. Describe the general cultural characteristics of Texas's regions. Does the description fit your home area?

3. What do the terms *moralistic*, *traditionalistic*, and *individualistic* signify? Why do Texas's regions differ on these criteria? How would you classify yourself as an individual on these criteria? Why?

4. Describe the major developments in the struggle of Texas women, African Texans, Latinos, gays, and lesbians to achieve social and political equality? Why do you think there was opposition?

5. How will Texas's population growth and its changing demographics affect the state's political landscape? What challenges does a more diverse population present for policy makers?

LOGGING ON

Welcome to cyberpolitics in Texas. The Internet creates unprecedented opportunities for research, communication, and participation in Texas politics. Today, students can easily communicate with the authors of their textbooks, government leaders, and fellow students all across Texas. To facilitate this, Wadsworth, Cengage Learning has developed a companion website available at **www.cengagebrain.com**.

Use reports on public opinion at national polling data sites like **www.gallup.com/**, **www.pollster.com/polls/**, and **pollingreport.com/** to show how public opinion in Texas compares with that of the nation as a whole.

The *Handbook of Texas Online* is a great source for information on Texas history, culture, and geography. A project of the Texas State Historical Association, it is an encyclopedia of all things Texan at **www.tshaonline.org/**. Use it to sketch the historical changes in the status of one or more of the ethnic or gender groups discussed in the civil rights section in this chapter. Then search census data at **www.census.gov** to evaluate their income, education, and quality of life in today's Texas.

Compose four or five "Did You Know? features like the ones in this chapter from factual information and statistics found in Legislative Budget Board, *Texas Fact Book 2010,* **www.lbb.state.tx.us/Fact_Book/Texas_FactBook_2010.pdf**. Explain the significance of the factoids that you select and how they could impact Texas politics and public policy.

Select examples of Texas rankings on public policy and quality-of-life issues to show Texas's conservative political culture. Use *Texas on the Brink,* a report by the liberal-leaning Texas Legislative Study Group that focuses on where the state of Texas stands compared to other states in the United States at **texaslsg.org/texasonthebrink/?m=201102**. Compare state tax rankings with those of other states at the conservative-oriented Tax Foundation website **www.taxfoundation.org**.

Chapter 2

Texas in the Federal System

LEARNING OBJECTIVES

- ★ Demonstrate an understanding of the state political system and its relationship with the federal government.

- ★ Define the concept of federalism.

- ★ Compare the different parts of the U.S. Constitution that formulate the current understanding of federalism.

- ★ Identify the three types of powers found in the U.S. federal system.

- ★ Differentiate among dual federalism, cooperative federalism, and coercive federalism.

- ★ Identify factors that contribute to tension between state and federal governments.

- ★ Explain the importance of the Tenth Amendment in the current federalism debate.

- ★ Explain how the Elastic Clause and the Commerce Clause have been used to expand federal powers.

- ★ Analyze the strengths and weaknesses of the U.S. federal system.

- ★ Explain the impact of the Fourteenth Amendment on the states.

- ★ Analyze the amount of Texas revenue coming from the federal government.

Interested in learning more about the debates over federalism? Consider joining the *American Constitution Society for Law and Society* or the *Federalist Society*. Student membership rates are affordable. You may consider attending meetings, and, if possible, presenting student research papers at those meetings. Joining may also give your résumé a little more cachet. Be aware that the *American Constitution Society* is a progressive organization, and the *Federalist Society* is a conservative and libertarian organization. To learn more and join, explore the following:

★ Visit the American Constitution Society at **www.acslaw.org/** and read more about them. Then click on *Join ACS*. Rates are $10 for students.

★ View the Federalist Society at **www .fed-soc.org/** and read more about them. Then click on *membership*. Student rates are $5.

★ Watch YouTube videos from the American Constitution Society and the Federalist Society. They will provide you with the types of issues that continue to inform the political debate.

The relationship between the state of Texas and the federal government has been tense in recent years. Texas policy makers have increasingly viewed the federal government as encroaching on the state's sovereignty, while the federal government has attempted to enforce new laws, rules, and regulations in the state. From health care reform to immigration to environmental policy, Texas and the federal government disagree on the proper role of each in the creation, enactment, and enforcement of public policy. Tension between the national government and the states is nothing new and has constantly redefined our concepts of federalism. Today's conflicts between the two levels of government may once again change our understanding of the federal system.

We will begin by defining federalism and discussing how the concept has evolved through time. Then we will turn our attention to Texas and how federalism specifically affects the state's policies and politics.

WHAT IS FEDERALISM?

Unitary system

A system of government in which one central government has ultimate authority; any regional or local governments are subordinate to the central government.

Governmental systems are often classified into three types based on their degree of centralization—unitary, confederal, and federal. Most nations in the world are governed by a **unitary system** in which the national government has ultimate authority. Unitary governments may be democratic like those in Japan or Denmark, or they may be undemocratic like those in China or Saudi Arabia. These are all unitary governments simply because one government governs the entire nation. Unitary governments may choose to create local or regional governments for administrative purposes, but the local governments are creations of the national government and have only whatever powers the national government chooses to give them. Britain had such a centralized system at the time of the American Revolution, and it was what the colonists regarded as excessive centralization that sparked our independence movement.

After independence, Americans overreacted to their experiences with an excessively centralized government by creating one that was so decentralized as to be unworkable. Under the Articles of Confederation, all power was placed in the hands of the state governments, and the central government had only the power that states had chosen to give it. Such a system in which regional governments have all authority with central institutions subordinate to the state or regional governments is called a confederacy or **confederal system**. Because this form is unstable, as were the U.S. Articles of Confederation, there are no real examples of confederal forms in the modern world, though some might argue that the European Union has many characteristics of a confederacy.

Because Americans had learned from their colonial experiences that a unitary government can be remote and abusive, they turned to a confederal form, which proved to be simply impractical. As a result, at the U.S. Constitutional Convention in 1787, Americans invented an entirely new form of government never before seen in the history of the world—a federal system. Federalism represents an attempt to combine the advantages of a unitary government (national unity and uniformity where they are necessary) with the advantages of a confederacy (local control and political diversity from state to state where they are possible). The concept of federalism has flourished and has been widely adopted, especially in nations with large areas and diverse populations to govern. Today, Mexico, Canada, Australia, and Brazil are among the largest nations to use federal systems.

A **federal system** of government is one in which governmental power is divided and shared between a national or central government and state or regional governments. In the United States, governmental power is shared among the national government, state governments, and local governments.

When the framers of the U.S. Constitution set out to revise the Articles of Confederation in 1787, they opted to give more authority to the central government. One of their critical challenges was the creation of a representative government for a large nation with a diverse population. The framers of the U.S. Constitution wanted to achieve a balance between parochial interests and broader national concerns. The federal system was the solution to this challenge. James Madison wrote in Federalist 10:

> By enlarging too much the number of electors, you render the representative too little acquainted with all their local circumstances and lesser interests; as by reducing it too much, you render him unduly attached to these, and too little fit to comprehend and pursue great and national objects. The federal Constitution forms a happy combination in this respect; the great and aggregate interests being referred to the national, the local and particular to the state legislatures.[1]

The federal system would help create a balance between the local concerns and the national concerns.

In the nation's history, the shift in power has been from one where the states reserved many of their powers to one where the federal government has become more dominant. According to some scholars, a new shift in the balance of power seems to be occurring, but the direction of this new shift in power is not entirely clear. Is the United States becoming more centralized or more decentralized? At this point, the answer is not entirely clear, but it is certain that Texas political figures have been pushing for a shift in power away from the federal government.

Types of Powers in Federal System

In the U.S federal system, there are three types of powers—delegated, reserved, and concurrent. **Delegated Powers** are those that the constitution gives to the national government.

Confederal system
A system of government in which member state or regional governments have all authority and any central institutions have only the power that regional governments choose to give them; also known as confederacies.

Federal system
A system of government in which governmental power is divided and shared between a national or central government and state or regional governments.

Delegated powers
Those powers that the constitution gives to the national government. These include those enumerated powers found in Article I, Section 8 of the U.S. Constitution as well as a few other powers that have evolved over time.

[1]Madison, James, *Federalist 10*, November 23, 1787.

Texas INSIDERS

The Koch Brothers and George Soros: Out-of-State Conspirators or Public-Spirited Citizens?

The framers of the Constitution intended that federalism should balance national and local concerns, and as a part of a federal political system, Texas and its politics are often influenced by high-profile players on the national political stage. Some of them have contributed directly to candidates for state office, while others have helped set the agenda for political debate by contributing to organizations that promote political causes that have an impact on the state.

Charles and David Koch, according to *Forbes,* tied as the fourth-wealthiest Americans with $25 billion each, made their fortunes in oil, paper, and lumber. They have generously funded various Republican, conservative Christian, and Tea Party causes as well as research supporting climate change skepticism. In addition, they have donated to conservative organizations like Americans for Prosperity, the Heritage Foundation, and the Federalist Society for Law at George Mason University. Charles Koch co-founded

Charles G. Koch (along with his brother David) has contributed $700,000 to conservative candidates in Texas between 2003 and 2011.

What are the paths to becoming part of the political elite besides personal wealth?

Billionaire investor George Soros has funded organizations that impact the web of liberal opinion leadership in Texas and throughout the nation.

Do campaign contribution and lobby disclosure laws prevent wealthy individuals from implementing hidden agendas?

(*continued*)

the Cato Institute, a libertarian think tank, and supports the libertarian Reason Foundation.

In Texas, the Koch brothers have funded the Texas Public Policy Foundation, and Koch Industries affiliates contributed more than $285,289 to 64 candidates for state office, including Gov. Rick Perry, Lt. Gov. David Dewhurst, and Attorney General Greg Abbott in 2010 alone.

In contrast, George Soros, the seventh-wealthiest American with $22 billion, has supported mostly liberal causes such as civil rights, transparent government, environmental protection, and marijuana legalization. He has financed Democratic-leaning groups and liberal organizations such as the Center for American Progress, MoveOn.org, and the Open Society Institute, which provided a research grant to the open-government organization Texans for Public Justice.

Liberals often paint the Koch brothers as sinister conspirators controlling the conservative movement, and conservatives portray George Soros as a secret puppet master pulling the strings of liberal organizations. These images may result from a natural suspicion of political elites, but neither of them is remotely accurate. While the Koch brothers and Soros have significant influence, they share power with numerous other political elites, and their agendas are hardly secret.

Thinking about the role of elites in Texas politics Name the state issues that would interest national political elites. What are the techniques that national political elites use to affect state politics in Texas?

Sources: "The Forbes 400: The Richest People in America," *Forbes*, September 21, 2011, at www.forbes.com/forbes-400/; National Institute on Money in State Politics at www.followthemoney.org/database/; Open Secrets.org at www.opensecrets.org/news/2010/09/opensecrets-battle---koch-brothers.html; Jane Mayer, "Covert Operations: The Billionaire Brothers Waging War Against Obama," *The New Yorker*, August 30, 2010; Byron York, "America Coming Together Comes Apart," *National Review*, August 3, 2005; Texans for Public Justice, *Press Release*, December 20, 2001.

These include those enumerated powers found in Article I, Section 8 of the U.S. Constitution as well as a few other powers that have evolved over time. Note that there are three types of delegated powers—expressed, implied, and inherent. **Expressed powers** are those found in Article I, Section 8 and are explicitly listed in the U.S. Constitution. **Implied powers** are those delegated powers that are necessary and proper for the government to perform the functions that are expressly delegated. **Inherent powers** are delegated powers that come with an office or position—generally the executive branch. While the U.S. Constitution does not clearly specify powers granted to the executive branch, over time, inherent powers have evolved as part of the powers needed to perform the functions of the executive branch.

A second group of powers in the federal system is known as **reserved powers**. Reserved powers are those powers that belong to the states. The legitimacy of these powers comes from the Tenth Amendment. Lastly, there are **concurrent powers**, which are those powers shared by both the national government and the states. Examples of these powers are listed in Table 2.1.

THE U.S. CONSTITUTION AND FEDERALISM

The U.S. Constitution addresses the sharing of power between the state and federal government in various sections. Article I, Section 8, for instance, lists the enumerated powers "expressly" granted to Congress by the Constitution. Article VI, Section 2 stipulates the Supremacy Clause, which reads:

This Constitution, and the Laws of the United States which shall be made in Pursuance thereof; and all Treaties made, or which shall be made, under the Authority of the United States, shall be

Expressed powers
Those delegated powers that are found in Article I, Section 8 and are clearly listed in the U.S. Constitution.

Implied powers
Those delegated powers that are assumed to exist in order for the federal government to perform the functions that are expressly delegated. These powers are granted by the necessary and proper clause in Article I, Section 8.

Inherent powers
Those delegated powers that come with an office or position—generally the executive branch. While the U.S. Constitution does not clearly specify powers granted to the executive branch, over time inherent powers have evolved as part of the powers needed to perform the functions of the executive branch.

TABLE 2.1 Examples of Major State and Federal Powers

Delegated Powers—Federal Government Powers	Reserved Powers—Exclusive to the States Government	Concurrent Powers—Shared by Federal and State Government
Declare war	Conduct elections	Borrow money
Raise armies	Provide for the public health and safety	Levy taxes
Enter into treaties	Ratify constitutional Amendment	Make and enforce the law
Coin money	Establish and provide for local governments	Establish courts
Regulate international and interstate commerce	State police powers	Charter banks

Among these examples of national powers, the power to provide for the common defense and to regulate commerce, since the 1930s, have been interpreted broadly to allow the national government to expand dramatically.

▲ **Give examples of national programs that have been rationalized as a regulation of interstate commerce.**

Reserved powers

Those powers that belong to the states. The legitimacy of these powers comes from the Tenth Amendment.

Concurrent powers

Those powers that are shared by both the national government and the states.

Supremacy Clause

Article VI, Section 2 of the U.S. Constitution, which states that the U.S. Constitution, as well as laws and treaties created in accordance with the U.S. Constitution, supersede state and local laws.

Tenth Amendment

Section of the U.S. Constitution that reserves powers to the states. It reads as follows: "The powers not delegated to the United States by the Constitution, nor prohibited by it to the States, are reserved to the States respectively, or to the people."

Commerce clause

An enumerated power in Article I, Section 8 of the U.S. Constitution that gives Congress the power to regulate commerce.

Necessary and proper clause

The last clause in Article I, Section 8 of the U.S. Constitution that gives Congress implied powers.

the supreme Law of the Land; and the Judges in every State shall be bound thereby, any Thing in the Constitution or Laws of any State to the Contrary notwithstanding.[2]

In the event that conflict should arise between federal and state law, the **Supremacy Clause** states that federal law must be followed. The **Tenth Amendment** to the U.S. Constitution also helps define the balance of power in the federal system. The Tenth Amendment reads as follows: "The powers not delegated to the United States by the Constitution, nor prohibited by it to the States, are reserved to the States respectively, or to the people." Some read the Tenth Amendment as limiting the federal government, shifting greater power to the states. The Fourteenth Amendment also affects the balance of power in the federal system.

Article I, Section 8

Conflicts between the national government and states have arisen on a number of occasions, in part because of different understandings of two sections of the U.S. Constitution—Article I, Section 8 (see Table 2.2) and the Tenth Amendment. Article I, Section 8 of the U.S. Constitution enumerates the powers granted to Congress, including the power to regulate interstate commerce. It is this "**commerce clause**" in Article I that was used to justify the Patient Protection and Affordable Care Act as well as several other broad national government actions.

More important for a discussion on federalism, however, is the last clause on the list, "To make all Laws which shall be necessary and proper for carrying into Execution the foregoing Powers, and all other Powers vested by this Constitution in the Government of the United States, or in any Department or Officer thereof."[3] This is known as the **necessary and proper clause**, or the elastic clause of the U.S. Constitution, and was given a very expansive meaning early in the nation's founding.

McCulloch v. *Maryland* and the Necessary and Proper Clause

In 1819, the U.S. Supreme Court expanded the power of the U.S. Congress. In *McCulloch* v. *Maryland*, the state of Maryland, in a desire to limit competition with banks chartered by the state of Maryland, attempted to tax the Second Bank of the United States, a bank created by the federal government. The head of the Baltimore Branch of the Second Bank

---

[2]"The Constitution of the United States," Article VI, Section 2.
[3]"The Constitution of the United States," Article I, Section 8, Necessary and Proper Clause.

TABLE 2.2 Powers Granted to Congress under Article I, Section 8:

The Congress shall have Power To lay and collect Taxes, Duties, Imposts and Excises, to pay the Debts and provide for the common Defence and general Welfare of the United States; but all Duties, Imposts and Excises shall be uniform throughout the United States;

To borrow money on the credit of the United States;

To regulate Commerce with foreign Nations, and among the several States, and with the Indian Tribes;

To establish an uniform Rule of Naturalization, and uniform Laws on the subject of Bankruptcies throughout the United States;

To coin Money, regulate the Value thereof, and of foreign Coin, and fix the Standard of Weights and Measures;

To provide for the Punishment of counterfeiting the Securities and current Coin of the United States;

To establish Post Offices and Post Roads;

To promote the Progress of Science and useful Arts, by securing for limited Times to Authors and Inventors the exclusive Right to their respective Writings and Discoveries;

To constitute Tribunals inferior to the supreme Court;

To define and punish Piracies and Felonies committed on the high Seas, and Offenses against the Law of Nations;

To declare War, grant Letters of Marque and Reprisal, and make Rules concerning Captures on Land and Water;

To raise and support Armies, but no Appropriation of Money to that Use shall be for a longer Term than two Years;

To provide and maintain a Navy;

To make Rules for the Government and Regulation of the land and naval Forces;

To provide for calling forth the Militia to execute the Laws of the Union, suppress Insurrections and repel Invasions;

To provide for organizing, arming, and disciplining, the Militia, and for governing such Part of them as may be employed in the Service of the United States, reserving to the States respectively, the Appointment of the Officers, and the Authority of training the Militia according to the discipline prescribed by Congress;

To exercise exclusive Legislation in all Cases whatsoever, over such District (not exceeding ten Miles square) as may, by Cession of particular States, and the acceptance of Congress, become the Seat of the Government of the United States, and to exercise like Authority over all Places purchased by the Consent of the Legislature of the State in which the Same shall be, for the Erection of Forts, Magazines, Arsenals, dock-Yards, and other needful Buildings; And

To make all Laws which shall be necessary and proper for carrying into Execution the foregoing Powers, and all other Powers vested by this Constitution in the Government of the United States, or in any Department or Officer thereof.

The meaning of these powers, especially the "necessary and proper" clause, is subject to political and legal interpretation.

▲ **Give examples of national programs that are the result implied powers.**

of the United States refused to pay the tax. The state of Maryland argued that the U.S. Constitution did not give the national government the power to create a national bank, and thus the Bank of the United States was unconstitutional. Chief Justice John Marshall argued that, while it was true that the creation of a bank was not an enumerated power under Article I, Section 8, the Supremacy Clause of the Constitution, and the necessary and proper clause, gave Congress authority to create the bank. Justice Marshall wrote, "The Government of the Union, though limited in its powers, is supreme within its sphere of action, and its laws, when made in pursuance of the Constitution, form the supreme law of the land."[4] The Court further concluded that if the end or goal is legitimate, then the act is constitutional. If Congress has the power to regulate commerce, for instance, then Congress can enact legislation that will help it carry out that end.[5] *McCulloch* v. *Maryland* broadly expanded the powers of the federal government.

---

[4] *McCulloch* v. *Maryland*, 17 U.S. 316 (1819).
[5] Ibid.

The Early View: Dual Federalism and the Tenth Amendment

Even with the broad powers granted to the federal government by *McCulloch* v. *Maryland*, the relationship between the federal government and state governments was one that left clear demarcations between the two levels of government. Through the nineteenth century and the early part of the twentieth century, scholars have dubbed the type of federalism that existed during this time as **dual federalism**. The dominant concept of federalism until the 1930s, dual federalism is characterized by four features that indicate demarcations between the states and the national government.

1. The national government is one of enumerated powers only.
2. The purposes which the national government may constitutionally promote are few.
3. Within their respective spheres the two centers of government are "sovereign" and hence "equal."
4. The relation of the two centers with each other is one of tension rather than collaboration.[6]

These four characteristics were postulated by Edward S. Corwin in his 1950 eulogy to the concept of dual federalism.[7] Corwin argued that, "what was once vaunted as a Constitution of Rights, both State and private, has been replaced by a Constitution of Powers."[8] While this claim may be debated, it was clear that a new understanding of the relationship between federal and state governments was underway.

The Tenth Amendment was the bulwark for dual federalism. It ensured that states like Texas retained those powers that were not given to the federal government. The Tenth Amendment was written to limit the powers of the national government to those stipulated in Article I, Section 8. But, as early as 1789, supporters of the federal system worked to weaken the Tenth Amendment. In the process of writing the Tenth Amendment, Representative Thomas Tudor Tucker proposed adding the term *expressly* so that the amendment would read, "The powers not *expressly* delegated to the United States."[9] He believed that adding the term would limit the powers of the federal government to those *expressly* stated in the Constitution. James Madison and others argued against the proposal, and it was rejected.

As a result, the Tenth Amendment was left to be interpreted as limiting national powers either a little or a lot. After the replacement of Chief Justice John Marshall with Chief Justice Roger Taney, the Supreme Court began to rein in the national government. When faced with a case that pitted the federal government's power to regulate commerce on the one hand, and the states' internal police power, on the other, the court would side with the states.[10] This would be the dominant concept of federalism until the 1930s.

The Development of Cooperative Federalism

The exclusion of the term *expressly* made it much easier for the national government to expand its powers, but a new set of national and global challenges served as the trigger that contributed to the shift in power from state governments to the federal government. Two world wars, the Great Depression, advances in technology, the civil rights movement, and the Cold War

Dual federalism

The understanding that the federal government and state governments are both sovereign within their sphere of influence.

---

[6]Edward S. Corwin, "The Passing of Dual Federalism," *Virginia Law Review*, Vol. 36, No. 1. (1950) p. 4.

[7]Ibid.

[8]Ibid.

[9]*Annals of Congress. The Debates and Proceedings in the Congress of the United States.* "History of Congress." 42 vols. Washington, DC: Gales & Seaton, 1834–56.

[10]See *New York* v. *Miln*, 36 US 11 Pet. 102 (1837).

with the former Soviet Union contributed to a greater need for centralizing power. Edward Corwin surmises, "The Federal System has shifted base in the direction of a consolidated national power, while within the National Government itself an increased flow of power in the direction of the President has ensued."[11] Corwin's concept of dual federalism would be replaced by **cooperative federalism**, a relationship where "the National Government and the States are mutually complementary parts of a *single* government mechanism all of whose powers are intended to realize the current purposes of government according to their applicability to the problem in hand."[12] Cooperative federalism used the power of the national government to encourage the states to pursue certain public policy goals. When the states cooperated, they would receive matching funds or additional assistance from the national government. When the states did not cooperate, funds could be withheld from the states.

The development of the concept of cooperative federalism was largely the result of a vast expansion of federal grants-in-aid. The evolution of federal grants to state and local governments has a long and controversial history. Although some grants from the national government to the states began as early as 1785, the adoption of the income tax in 1913 drastically altered the financial relationship between the national and state governments by making possible extensive aid to state and local governments.

The Great Depression of the 1930s brought with it a series of financial problems more severe than state and local governments had previously experienced. Increased demand for state and local services, when revenues were rapidly declining, stimulated a long series of New Deal grant-in-aid programs, ranging from welfare to public health and unemployment insurance.

Most of these early grant-in-aid programs were **categorical grants**. Under such aid programs, Congress appropriates funds for a specific purpose and sets up a formula for their distribution. Certain conditions are attached to these grant programs:

1. The receiving government agrees to match the federal money with its own, at a ratio fixed by law (between 10 and 90% of the cost of the program).
2. The receiving government administers the program. For example, federal funds are made available for Medicaid, but it is the state that actually pays client benefits.
3. The receiving government must meet minimum standards of federal law. For example, states are forbidden to spend federal money in any way that promotes racial segregation. Sometimes additional conditions are attached to categorical grants, such as regional planning and accounting requirements.

Most federal aid, however, now takes the form of newer **block grants** specifying general purposes such as job training or community development but allowing the state or local government to determine precisely how the money should be spent. Conditions may also be established for receipt of block grants, but state and local governments have greater administrative flexibility than with categorical grants. Federal transportation, welfare, and many other grants have been reformed to allow for significant **devolution** of power to the states through block grants.

Civil Rights Versus States' Rights

Heated civil rights battles developed during the nation's transition from dual federalism to cooperative federalism. During this period, states, especially southern states, claimed that the

Cooperative Federalism

A relationship where "the National Government and the States are mutually complementary parts of a *single* government mechanism all of whose powers are intended to realize the current purposes of government according to their applicability to the problem in hand."[13]

Categorical grants

Federal aid to state or local governments for specific purposes, granted under restrictive conditions and often requiring matching funds from the receiving government.

Block grants

Federal grants to state or local governments for more general purposes and with fewer restrictions than categorical grants.

Devolution

The attempt to enhance the power of state or local governments, especially by substituting more flexible block grants instead of restrictive categorical grants in aid.

---

[11]Corwin, "The Passing of Federalism," p. 2.
[12]Ibid, p. 19.
[13]Ibid.

national government was encroaching on states' rights, and no public policy area garnered more opposition from the southern states than civil rights issues.

During the period of dual federalism, the U.S. Supreme Court created the **separate-but-equal doctrine** in *Plessey* v. *Ferguson* (1896). The court used a novel interpretation of the Fourteenth Amendment to protect "states' rights" when it held that segregation did not violate the constitutional requirement that no state shall deny any person the equal protection of the laws. It held that state and local governments could pass laws requiring racial segregation because, so long as physical facilities are equal for both races, blacks are as separate from whites as whites are from blacks. This interpretation ignored the intent in segregation laws to communicate a sense of social inferiority to blacks by making it a crime for them to associate with whites. The court also ignored the fact that African-American facilities were either clearly inferior or nonexistent.

The Plessy decision allowed continued discrimination against African Americans and it became pervasive throughout the South as states enacted **Jim Crow laws** that required racial segregation of almost every aspect of life.

After World War II, the separate-but-equal doctrine would slowly be weakened, and Texas contributed to the weakening of the doctrine by producing the setting for the Supreme Court case *Sweatt* v. *Painter* (see Chapter 1). After graduating from Jack Yates High School in Houston and Wiley College in Marshal Texas, Heman Marion Sweatt, an African-American student, hoped to attend law school in his home state of Texas. But the law school at the University of Texas at Austin did not matriculate African Americans. African-American students from Texas who wanted to attend law school were encouraged to go out of state to attend law school. The Supreme Court ruled that in shifting its responsibilities to other states, the State of Texas was not providing separate accommodations—a requirement under the doctrine of separate but equal.

Sweatt v. *Painter* led to the creation of what are now Texas Southern University and the Thurgood Marshall School of Law. The Thurgood Marshall School of Law is the top producer of African-American attorneys to the Texas Bar. But perhaps more significantly, Heman Marion Sweatt helped to further weaken the doctrine of separate but equal, paving the way for *Brown* v. *Board of Education*, which eventually reversed *Plessy* v. *Ferguson*.

Brown v. *Board of Education* would lead to the desegregation of schools (see Chapter 1). The Twenty-fourth Amendment (which outlawed the poll tax), Civil Rights Act of 1964, Voting Rights Act of 1965, and many other laws that promoted equality would follow. Southern states saw such legislation as an encroachment on their sovereignty—or states' rights. To this day, Texans are engaged in debates over states' rights. When the "American Idol" pop singer Kelly Clarkson tweeted that she loved the Texas congressman and Republican presidential candidate Ron Paul because, "he believes in states having their rights," she was harshly criticized by those for whom "states rights" is coded language that speaks to a racist element in society. Republican commentator David Azerrad has recommended that Republicans, "speak of Federalism, not 'States' Rights.'"[14] For many, the language of states' rights continues to be loaded with meaning that harkens back to a time when segregation was enforced by the states. Members of minority communities see their fears of states' rights manifested in efforts that could reduce minority political participation, a reduction in access to public goods, and more stringent law enforcement that leads to higher incarceration rates among minorities.

Separate-but-equal doctrine

Doctrine that resulted from Supreme Court ruling in *Plessey* v. *Ferguson* that legalized segregation.

Jim Crow laws

State and local laws that promulgated racial segregation.

---

[14]Allen G. Breed, "US candidates' talk of states' rights raises issue," NECN.com, http://www.necn.com/01/26/12/US-candidates-talk-of-states-rights-rais/landing_politics.html?&apID=b5b2026aa30e4894a69d21d0e64e433e.

TEXAS AND THE FEDERAL SYSTEM

Some interpret the emphasis on states' rights as an effort to thwart civil rights for racial and gender minorities. However, other more conservative Texans see states' rights as reflecting a more genuine concern with a growing federal government that they believe has simply become too powerful and now performs more functions that states could perform better, or that individuals can or should do for themselves. They are especially concerned with the coercive power of the federal government over both state governments and individuals.

So far, we have been looking at the U.S. Constitution and how the national political and legal climates have changed our concepts of the relative powers of the national and state governments. Now we will look at federalism from the Texas perspective, how the national government's powers have affected the state, and how political leaders have coped with the changing nature of federalism.

Coercive Federalism and Texas

Many Texans would argue that a shift away from cooperative federalism has been underway since the late 1970s. This new form of federalism has been referred to as **coercive federalism**. Coercive federalism is defined as a relationship between the national government and states in which the former directs the states on policies they must take. In this shift to coercive federalism, the federal government centralizes more power and has increasingly obstructed the states. As evidence of this shift, the U.S. Advisory Commission on Intergovernmental Relations reported that more than half of all preemption laws—going back to the nation's founding—were enacted between the 1970s and 1980s.[15] Such encroachment on states was not one-sided. The federalism scholar John Kinkaid writes, "Liberals, lacking revenue for major reductions in equity programs, and conservatives, lacking public support for major reductions in equity programs, switched from fiscal to regulatory tools."[16] Because neither liberals nor conservatives had the political support to expand or contract programs that promoted equity, lawmakers in Congress and the White House opted to enact new rules.

During Governor Rick Perry's 2011–2012 presidential bid, he invoked the Tenth Amendment frequently. Governor Perry argues that the federal government has increasingly taken

JIM WATSON/AFP/Getty Images

Governor Rick Perry meets President Obama at an airport in August, 2010, to present him with a list of grievances against the federal government.

Why would conservative Texans object to federal policies so strenuously?

Coercive Federalism

A relationship between the national government and states in which the former directs the states on policies they must take.

[15]U.S. Advisory Commission on Intergovernmental Relations, *Federal Preemption of State and Local Authority* (Washington, D.C.: Advisory Commission on Intergovernmental Relations, draft report, 1989).

[16]John Kinkaid, "From Cooperative to Coercive Federalism," *Annals of the American Academy of Political and Social Sciences*, Vol. 509, 1990, pages 139–152.

AP Photo/Harry Cabluck

Anxious about the growth of national government power, some Texas Tea Party protestors have been sympathetic to secessionist rhetoric.

What drives such antifederalist sentiments?

over more activities of the state governments. The governor's website reports the following as his governing principle:

> States are best positioned to deal with state issues, a fact the founding fathers had in mind when they included the 10th Amendment in the Bill of Rights. Over the years, that right has been clouded by ongoing federal encroachments that are reflected in a recent series of attempts by Washington to seize even more control over numerous Texas programs, including some of the most successful initiatives of their kinds in the country.[17]

Governor Perry sees the health care reform legislation, Environmental Protection Agency regulations, and cap-and-trade legislation efforts as recent examples of the national government placing undue burdens on Texas.

The Texas Legislature followed Governor Perry's lead. In 2011, Texas House Speaker Joe Straus created the Select Committee on State Sovereignty to address bills that attempted to limit the federal government's activities in health care reform, manufacture of ammunitions and firearms, and water resources. One bill also urged the president to support the Defense of Marriage Act, while others called for changes that would allow states to reject federal laws. The committee gave Texas lawmakers an opportunity to express their objection to national government activities, in general, and support for the Tenth Amendment of the U.S. Constitution. Of the twenty-eight bills referred to the Select Committee on State Sovereignty, only one concurrent resolution, which called for a balanced budget amendment, was signed by the governor.

Supporters of federal efforts see the national government as requiring the state to do what it has been reluctant to do. As an example, they point to the high level of Texans without health care insurance. Currently, Texas has one of the largest percentages of uninsured residents of any state.[19]

Supporters of federal involvement also point to the Texas Commission on Environmental Quality's (TCEQ) efforts to enforce air and water quality standards. The Alliance for a Clean Texas reported that TCEQ "seems incapable of meeting many challenges in a straightforward and efficient enough manner to effectively protect the health of our citizens and the environmental integrity of our state's natural resources." If the state does not meet air quality standards as called for by the federal government, then the state could lose federal funds for transportation projects.

[17]Office of the Governor Rick Perry. "Governor's Initiatives," June 2010, page 3, http://governor.state.tx.us/initiatives/10th_amendment/.

[18]*Texas* v. *White*, 74 U.S. 700 (1869).

[19]Centers for Disease Control. "National Health Statistics Report: State, Regional, and National Estimates of Health Insurance Coverage for People Under 65 Years of Age: National Health Interview Survey, 2004–2006." Number 1, June 19, 2008, www.cdc.gov/nchs/data/nhsr/nhsr001.pdf.

HOW DOES TEXAS COMPARE?
How Texas's Environment Ranks among the 50 States: A Question of States' Rights

The Office of the Governor believes so firmly in protecting states' rights that he made the Tenth Amendment to the Constitution a central element of his bid for the Republican nomination for the presidency. On Governor Perry's website (governor.state.tx.us/initiatives/10th_amendment/), two of the three action items that he lists are in the environmental arena. Governor Perry believes that the national Environmental Protection Agency (EPA) and proposed cap and trade policies encroach on states' rights and will cost Texas jobs.

Cap-and-trade is a proposed market-driven environmental policy that sets limits (or caps) on the amount of pollution that industry can produce. These limits are set by selling a limited number of permits to pollute. Factories that produce less pollution could trade some of their permits to industries that pollute more, thus making it costlier for those industries that pollute more to do business. The expectation is that industries will develop innovative technologies that would cut down on pollution.

The Environmental Protection Agency is also caught in the governor's crosshairs. The EPA, under the Obama administration, has pushed to regulate pollution in Texas. The governor's website reports the following:

> The Obama administration has taken yet another step in its campaign to harm our economy and impose federal control over Texas. With their efforts to take control of a permitting process that the Clean Air Act allows to be delegated to the states, the EPA is on the verge of killing thousands of Texas jobs and derailing a program that has effectively cleaned Texas' air. An increasingly activist EPA is ignoring the progress Texas has made to clean its air over the last decade, and should instead look to our state's successful approach to issues concerning energy and the environment.[20]

The state of Texas has certainly taken the lead in several key environmental areas. But it has some major weaknesses as well. So, how does Texas compare?

Environmental Quality Measure	Texas's Rank (50th = Lowest, 1st = Highest)	Did you know?
Wind Power[21]	1st	In 2010, Texas produced enough wind energy to power 2.7 million Texas homes.
Clean Water[22]	38th	According to the Environmental Working Group; Arlington, Fort Worth, and Austin have the top-rated water utilities, while Houston has one of the lowest-rated water utilities.

(continued)

---

[20]Office of the Governor Rick Perry. *Initiatives 10th Amendment.* http://governor.state.tx.us/initiatives/10th_amendment/.

[21]American Wind Energy Association. "Wind Energy Facts: Texas," January 2012. www.awea.org/learnabout/publications/upload/4Q-11-Texas.pdf.

[22]Water Department.

Environmental Quality Measure	Texas's Rank (50th = Lowest, 1st = Highest)	Did you know?
The number of days when monitored concentrations of a criteria pollutant exceed a National Ambient Air Quality Standard (NAAQS) multiplied by the total number of people living in the affected area.[23]	2nd	When you multiply the number of days Texans are exposed to unhealthy air quality by the number of people exposed to unhealthy air quality, you get the number 1,135,690,880.
Pollution in areas where cancer risk exceeds 1 in 1,000, looking at all sources of pollution.[24]	6th	You can go to the Good Guide Scorecard website (http://scorecard.goodguide.com/env-releases/) to find out about pollution where you live and work.
The number of people exposed to levels of hazardous air pollutants from industry that exceed the Clean Air Act's noncancer risk goal.[25]	1st	3,489,874 people are exposed to levels of hazardous air pollutants from industry that exceed the Clean Air Act's noncancer risk goal.

Texas has led the nation in developing alternative sources of energy that produce clean energy. From El Paso to the Texas Panhandle, thousands of wind turbines have been installed and are generating enough energy to power over two million homes. Wind energy usage diminishes our reliance on other sources of energy that pollute the environment, namely coal-powered power plants. Texas has taken some positive steps to address air quality while at the same time addressing energy efficiency.

Texas is also headquarters to the world's petrochemical industry, which, on top of producing many jobs for Texans, also produces a significant amount of pollution. The national government sees a cap-and-trade program as a way of getting industry to invest in technology that will produce less pollution. For Texans living near polluting industries, that may be welcome news. Texas ranks at, or near, the top of the list among states that produce hazardous air pollutants. Some of these come from dry cleaners, gas stations, and auto body paint shops. Some pollution is produced by automobiles, airplanes, ships, tractors, and other such machines. A third source of pollution comes from chemical plants, petroleum refineries, power plants, and other major industries. It is this third category that would be most impacted by a cap-and-trade system. It is also one that is increasingly being regulated by the Environmental Protection Agency.

Because Texas has so many of these industries, some of its political and business leaders fear that the federal government would regulate a major segment of the state's economy excessively. The fear of job loss and profits are of major concern for Texans. Policy makers must weigh those concerns against the health of its citizens. Cancer-causing pollution is a major threat to Texans and one that policy makers want to balance with job and economic security.

FOR DEBATE

Should the federal government regulate air quality if the state fails to meet deadlines for reaching certain benchmarks toward cleaner Texas air? Recall that the governor believes the Tenth Amendment is on his side. Is regulating air quality a federal question or a question of states' rights?

---

[23]Source: Good Guide Scorecard: The Pollution Information Site. *States With Health Risk from HAPs*, http://scorecard.goodguide.com/env-releases/hap/rank-states.tcl?how_many=100&drop_down_name=Population+in+areas+where+hazard+index+exceeds+1&rank_source_type=point.
[24]Ibid.
[25]Ibid.

Federal Grants-in-Aid in Texas

The federal government is the largest source of revenue for the state of Texas. Table 2.3 shows the source of state revenue, the amount, the percentage of the total, and the percentage change from 2010. These are listed from the largest amount to the smallest amount. Of the $183 billion in state revenue, $71.2 billion came from the federal government—38.9 percent of the total state revenue.

© Mira/Alamy

Federal air pollution regulations have been a major source of conflict between Texas and the national government.

How does the national government assert a positive role in solving nationwide problems? What might motivate Texas leaders to assert state powers on environmental issues?

TABLE 2.3 Texas Revenue by Source for 2012–13 Biennium			
Source	**Amount in Millions**	**Percent of Total**	**Percent Change from 2010–11**
Tax collection	80,576.1	44	8.6
Federal income	71,247.8	38.9	(5.4)
Fees, fines, licenses, and penalties	14,987.3	8.2	1.7
Interest and investment income	1,799.0	1	(14.1)
Lottery	3,390.8	1.9	2.5
Land income	1,408.7	.8	(36.6)
Other revenue sources	9,682.1	5.3	(.07)
Total net revenue	183,091.7	100	.8

Source: Comptroller of Public Accounts 2012-13 Certification Revenue Estimate. December 2011.

This table shows the sources of all types of Texas state revenues. Notice that federal funds account for almost as large a share of those revenues as state taxes.

▲ **How has the national government used federal funding to shape state policies?**

The latest expansion of federal grants was a temporary response to the economic collapse that began in 2007. In an attempt to stem the effects of the Great Recession, Congress passed a series of massive economic stimulus and bailout bills. Among them was the American Recovery and Reinvestment Act of 2009 that pumped $12.1 billion of mostly temporary federal funds into Texas's treasury during the 2010–2011 budget period. More than one-half of these stimulus grants were spent on education, with much of the remainder going to state programs such as transportation, Medicaid, and unemployment benefits.

Although the infusion of these funds allowed the Texas legislature to balance the state's budget despite plummeting state tax revenues, the temporary stimulus grants of recent years were extremely controversial. Governor Perry took a high-profile stance against several grants that he believed placed too many restrictions on the state. For example, the state refused approximately $500 million in unemployment aid because the funds were conditioned on the state expanding eligibility for the program. Although resistance to stimulus funds was particularly intense, the tension between federal and state power will continue to be a feature of the American federal system, as it has been throughout the nation's history.

The percentage of the state's revenue coming from the federal government has grown. In 1978, about a quarter of the state's revenue was provided by the federal government. During the most recent years of the Great Recession, the percentage of federal funds has exceeded 40 percent. Figure 2.1 shows the percentage of state revenue coming from the federal government from 1978 to 2011. This growth can be explained by the formulas the federal government uses to calculate need. The state's growing population, combined with a large low-income population and a growing elderly population, has contributed to this growth.

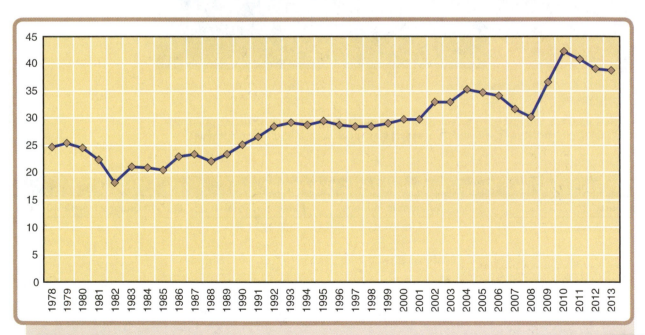

Figure 2.1

Percentage of Texas revenue coming from Federal Government (1978–2011)

This figure shows that Texas, like most states, has become increasingly reliant on federal funding to finance state programs like health services, highways, and education.

Analyze the kinds of changes Texas could expect if federal funds were cut or eliminated.

HOW DOES TEXAS COMPARE?
How Federal Grants to Texas Rank among the 50 States

From 2000–2009, Texas and its local governments received $240 billion in federal aid, making it the third-largest recipient of federal dollars for the past decade. But Texas has a large population.

Federal Grants-in-Aid to Texas	Texas's Rank (50th = Lowest, 1st = Highest)	Did you know?
Federal aid to state and local governments 2000–2009[26]	3rd	While Texas accounts for 8 percent of the U.S. population, it received 6 percent of the federal dollars for that time period.
Federal aid to state and local governments, per capita 2000–2009[27]	44th	
Federal aid to state and local governments, per capita for 2009 only[28]	43rd	
Federal aid to state and local governments, per capita in 2006 when Texan was in the White House[29]	37th	When the former Texas Governor George W. Bush was in the White House, Texas ranked 37th in per capita federal aid.
For every dollar spent, share Texas get back.[30]	37th	The Legislative Budget Board reported that in fiscal year 2008, for every dollar Texans paid in federal taxes, Texans received 89 cents.

While Texas may have been the third-largest recipient of federal dollars for the past decade, it ranks 44th in the dollars it receives per capita. In the last decade, while the average state received $12,292 per person, Texas received $9,682 per person. For 2009 alone, Texas received $1,426 per person, while the national average for that year was $1,798 per person, placing Texas in 43rd place for federal dollars received per capita. The Legislative Budget Board reports that in 2008, Texas received 89 cents for every dollar it paid in federal taxes, ranking it in 37th place among the states.[31]

FOR DEBATE

Should Texas lawmakers fight for a greater slice of the federal pie? Texas has a large poor population with real needs for government services, but it also has a political culture that eschews big government.

---

[26]Source: U.S. Census Bureau. Table 433. Federal Aid to State and Local Governments by State 2000–2009.
[27]Ibid
[28]Ibid
[29]Ibid
[30]Legislative Budget Board. *Top 100 Federal Funding Sources In the Texas State Budget*, October 2010, page 1.
[31]Ibid.

Unfunded Mandates

Unfunded mandates are those obligations that the federal government imposes on state governments with little or no funds to help support the program. Even with the passage of the Unfunded Mandates Reform Act of 1995, which President Bill Clinton signed, the federal government has found ways of getting around the law. Loopholes and exemptions have made it possible for Congress to obligate Texas and other states to implement certain policies or risk losing federal funds. Governor Rick Perry has been critical of unfunded mandates, even criticizing President George W. Bush's No Child Left Behind Act for obligating states to make changes to their educational system without providing the needed federal funds to implement the program.[32] These laws allow the lawmakers who create the laws the opportunity to take credit for creating legislation without necessarily having to raise the revenue that funds the programs.

The federal government is not the only government that enacts unfunded mandates for lower levels of government. The State of Texas has also enacted a fair number of unfunded mandates that require local governments to take certain actions without providing local governments adequate funds to implement the requirements. The Texas Association of Counties, which works on behalf of the state's 254 counties, had been critical of the state's unfunded mandates. It reports, "Unfunded mandates impose costs on Texas counties and their taxpayers into the millions of dollars statewide and force counties to increase local property tax rates to pay for edicts from above."[33] The state has required county governments to provide legal services, health services, and children's protective services; while also requiring the counties to provide the funding.

In 2011, the Texas Legislature attempted to address the issue, but was unable to get a bill through the legislature. Governor Rick Perry entered the fray by creating the Task Force on Unfunded Mandates, which was charged with identifying unfunded mandates that the state passes on to local governments. The Task Force also offers recommendations on how to limit those mandates. It remains to be seen whether the rate and cost of unfunded mandates will decline for both Texas and local governments within its jurisdiction.

Health Care Reform: A Challenging Case in Federalism

Probably no controversy better illustrates the competing visions of our federal system than the recent saga of national health care reform. Shortly after the passage of the Patient Protection and Affordable Care Act, Texas Attorney General Greg Abbott joined 25 other states' attorneys general in opposing the new health care law. At issue was the new law's requirement that individuals purchase health insurance. This would mean that many employed individuals, and young adults in particular, would no longer be able to choose between being covered and not being covered.

While states like Texas have frequently required individuals to purchase other types of insurance, such as automobile liability insurance, the national government has never mandated that individuals "buy any good or service as a condition of lawful residence in the United States."[34] The "individual mandate," as it has come to be known, would require individuals who can afford insurance, but are uninsured, to purchase health insurance.

[32]Dunham, Richard, "George W. Bush Defends No Child Left Behind reform from attacks by Rick Perry, others," *Houston Chronicle,* January 12, 2012, http://blog.chron.com/txpotomac /2012/01/george-w-bush-defends-no-child-left-behind-reform-from-attacks-by-rick-perry-others/

[33]Texas Association of Counties. *Unfunded Mandates Initiatives.* Updated February 25, 2011, www.county.org/ resources/legis/ufm.asp

[34]Texas Attorney General Greg Abbott interviewed by Paul Burka, *Burkablog*, March 30, 2010, "Abbott on the legal case against health care," www.texasmonthly.com/blogs/burkablog/?p=6652

The $2.5 trillion health care industry accounts for 17 percent of the United States Gross Domestic Product (GDP). Millions of Americans have no health insurance, but doctors and hospitals are required to treat those seeking emergency medical treatment. Critically ill patients cannot be turned away because they are not insured or cannot afford treatment. The costs of covering the uninsured, therefore, are shared by those who can afford coverage. It is estimated that the uninsured cost the average American family and their employer "$1,017 in health care premiums."[35] This added cost paid by the insured is often referred to as a hidden tax on the American people.

In Texas, 25 percent of residents, or 6.2 million Texans, do not have health insurance coverage.[36] Nationally, 16 percent of Americans are uninsured.[37] Children account for 1.3 million of the uninsured in the state of Texas.[38] According to Families USA, the new health care reform law will lead to 4.2 million newly insured.[39] This would reduce the number of uninsured by roughly two-thirds. Families USA also estimates that 31,700 lives will be saved and 222,500 businesses will be helped by health care reform.[40] The need to improve coverage in Texas is evident, but the new Patient Protection and Affordable Care Act raised some interesting questions about the power of the federal government.

The limits on what Congress can do are stipulated in Article 1, Section 8 of the U.S. Constitution. Among Congress's powers is the power to regulate commerce. It is this power that Congress used to justify the Patient Protection and Affordable Care Act. Congress argued that because it has the power to regulate commerce, and the buying of health insurance is a commercial activity, then Congress has the power to regulate health care coverage.

Some disagreed that the Act regulated commerce and concluded that it infringed on states' rights. While it is the case that some powers are shared between the states and the federal government, others are exclusive to either one or the other. For example, the power to regulate commerce is granted to Congress. The power to provide for the public health and safety is deemed a power reserved to the state by the Tenth Amendment.

Attorney General Greg Abbott argued that the Act does not regulate commerce, but rather that it created policing authority that is generally the purview of the states. He argued, "Because Congress does not have the authority to impose the individual mandate, it violates the Tenth Amendment by straying into a sphere of state sovereignty. This falls into the area of the police power, or the general health and safety of the people."[41] Given that different federal court circuits arrived at different conclusions, the Supreme Court weighed in to determine whether the Act regulates commerce or whether the Act regulates the refusal to buy insurance. After setting aside three days of hearings in March of 2012, the Supreme Court was asked to decide whether Congress has the power to require an individual to buy insurance, which in turn could lead to a broader interpretation of the commerce clause; or whether the Supreme Court agrees with Texas and the 25 other states' claim that the Act infringes on the states' power to promote the general health and safety of the people. In doing so, the U.S. Supreme Court was asked to determine the constitutionality of the individual mandate. The Supreme Court, led by Chief Justice John Roberts, rejected the federal government's claim that the commerce clause allowed congress to create the individual mandate. But,

[35]Kim, Seung Min. "Study: Insured pay 'hidden tax' for uninsured health care," *USA Today*, May 29, 2009, http://www.usatoday.com/money/industries/insurance/2009-05-28-hiddentax_N.htm

[36]Statehealthfacts.org. *Texas: Health Insurance Coverage of the Total Population, States (2009–2010), U.S. (2010).* www.statehealthfacts.org/profileind.jsp?ind=125&cat=3&rgn=45

[37]Ibid.

[38]Ibid.

[39]Families USA, "Health Reform Central: From the States" www.familiesusa.org/health-reform-central/from-the-states/from-the-states.html

[40]Ibid.

[41]Texas Attorney General Greg Abbott interviewed by Paul Burka, *Burkablog*, March 30, 2010, "Abbott on the legal case against health care," www.texasmonthly.com/blogs/burkablog/?p=6652

Justice Roberts argued, the "penalty," which the law required be paid to the IRS, is in actuality a "tax," which congress has the power to levy. As a result, the most controversial aspect of the law—the individual mandate—is deemed constitutional.

The controversy surrounding the Patient Protection and Affordable Care Act is an excellent example of the conflicts that can arise between the federal government and the states. The conflict revolves around the proper balance of power between the federal government and the states, and that balance is determined by the Constitution, statutes, and the interpretation of the Constitution by the men and women who make up our various political and legal institutions. We can now see that Texas has played an active role in the constant redefining of the concept of federalism.

Garcia v. San Antonio Metropolitan Transit Authority

It would be a Texas case that would further refine, and, some may argue, broaden, the powers of the federal government. In 1983, the Supreme Court was tasked with answering the question, "Did the principles of federalism make the San Antonio Metropolitan Transit Authority immune from the Fair Labor Standards Act?"[42] To understand this case, one must go back to 1938, the year Congress enacted the Fair Labor Standards Act. The Fair Labor Standards Act was signed during the Great Depression by President Franklin D. Roosevelt, outlawing child labor, establishing a minimum wage, limiting the workweek to 40 hours, and mandating overtime pay. Congress had the authority to establish this law under the Commerce Clause of the U.S. Constitution. The law, however, exempted state and local governments from the requirements. That would change in the 1970s, when Congress amended the Fair Labor Standards Act to include state and local governments in the minimum wage, maximum hour, and overtime pay provisions.

In 1976, the Supreme Court ruled on a case known as *National League of Cities* v. *Usery*. This case would famously be reversed nine years later. At issue was whether the federal government had the authority to regulate the labor market of state and local government employees. In *National League of Cities* v. *Usery*, the U.S. Supreme Court concluded that the amendment to the Fair Labor Standards Act would "interfere with the *integral* [italics added] government functions of" state and local governments.[43] The amended Fair Labor Standards Act, the Court concluded, violated the Tenth Amendment of the Constitution. As a result, cities could ignore the minimum wage and maximum hour provisions of the Fair Labor Standards Act.

In *Garcia* v. *San Antonio Metropolitan Transit Authority*, however, the Supreme Court would reverse itself. In this decision, the Supreme Court ruled that the Commerce Clause did in fact give Congress the power to extend the Fair Labor Standards Act requirements to the states and local governments. *Garcia* v. *San Antonio Metropolitan Transit Authority* further moved the balance of power from the states to the national government, limiting the role of the Tenth Amendment and the powers reserved to the states. In the process, the court decision expanded the reach of the Commerce Clause into increasingly tangential connections to interstate commerce. The limits of the Commerce Clause may not yet be fully known because the Supreme Court continues to review federal laws that receive their authority from the Commerce Clause.

States as Policy Laboratories and the AMBER Alert System

One of the great values of a federal system is that states are able to experiment with public policy. With 50 different states, the nation has 50 different laboratories that can produce a variety of possible solutions to common problems. If a state solution fails, at least the whole

---

[42]Oyez: U.S. Supreme Court Media, IIT Chicago-Kent College of Law, *Garcia* v. *San Antonio Metropolitan Transit Authority*, www.oyez.org/cases/1980-1989/1983/1983_82_1913#sort=vote
[43]*National League of Cities* v. *Usery* 426 U.S. 833.

nation is not committed to the policy, but if these solutions work, they can then be expanded to other jurisdictions. The AMBER Alert System is a good example of a successful policy solution that was expanded nationwide.

In 1997, Dallas area child advocates asked the local police department and broadcasters to implement the AMBER Alert System—a law enforcement tool that would employ the community in the search for missing children. The request was spurred on after a nine-year-old child named Amber Hagerman was abducted and murdered in Arlington, Texas. AMBER Alerts are shared with the community using a variety of broadcasting tools. One common method has been the use of electronic signs on major thoroughfares to announce the more serious missing children and missing persons cases to the broader community, in the hope that the community might assist in locating these missing persons.

The AMBER Alert System was very effective at helping find missing children, so the federal government considered implementing it nationwide. In 2003, the federal government passed the AMBER Alert Act, creating a nationwide system for finding abducted children. The federal government would give states that chose to implement the program funds as well as assist with establishing voluntary standards. The program has expanded across all 50 states. Because child abductors attempt to flee the states where they committed the abduction, the national coordination assists in ensuring that the alert is shared across state borders. In 2010, 25 percent of the cases nationwide "had recoveries out of the state/territory of the original activation."[44] A system that allows for communication among law enforcement authorities across states lines is useful. Interestingly, Texas is second only to Michigan in the number of alerts issued in 2010.[45]

The AMBER Alert System and many other policies were initially created at the state level. The states serve as public policy laboratories that allow policy makers the opportunity to experiment with policy that is right for the state, that may be borrowed by other states, or that may produce data that helps other states refine their own public policy.

The Fourteenth Amendment and Incorporation of the Bill of Rights

The Reconstruction Era was a period in which the "Radical Republicans" in Congress took control of public policy. They enfranchised the recently freed male population and limited political and voting rights for those who fought against the Union. During this period in Texas history, Republicans (the party of Lincoln) would govern the state of Texas. The governorship of Edmund Davis and other Republicans proved to be very unpopular with Texans, however. While this period in Texas history witnessed the election of a number of African Americans to the state legislature, the corrupt practices of Governor Edmund Davis proved to be too much for Texans. Nevertheless, the Reconstruction Era did witness a period in which the federal government encroached more on state governments, particularly Confederate states.

One outcome of the Civil War was the enactment of the Fourteenth Amendment. While the Fourteenth Amendment makes a variety of significant contributions that are still being debated today, one of its more important contributions is found in the **incorporation doctrine**. The incorporation doctrine states that certain rights found in the Bill of Rights in the U.S. Constitution are rights that cannot be encroached upon by the states. Before the enactment of the Fourteenth Amendment, the protections found in the Bill of Rights were protections from federal intervention—not state intervention. But the enactment of the

Incorporation doctrine
Certain rights found in the Bill of Rights are rights that cannot be encroached upon by the states.

[44]National Center for Missing & Exploited Children, "Analysis of Amber Alert Cases in 2010," p. 24, www.amberalert.gov/pdfs/10_amber_report.pdf.
[45]Ibid., p. 9.

Fourteenth Amendment changed this understanding. The relevant section of the Fourteenth Amendment reads as follows:

> No State shall make or enforce any law which shall abridge the privileges or immunities of citizens of the United States; nor shall any State deprive any person of life, liberty, or property, without due process of law; nor deny to any person within its jurisdiction the equal protection of the laws.

This clause was interpreted to mean that the protections found in the Bill of Rights could not be denied by the states. While not all rights found in the Bill of Rights have been incorporated by the U.S. Supreme Court, many have been, as we shall see in Chapter 3. Texas has contributed several cases to the Supreme Court that have further expanded the number of rights from which we now receive protections from the state. *Aguilar* v. *Texas*, for instance, helped to further clarify the incorporation of the Fourth Amendment, which provides protections against unreasonable searches and seizures.[46] *Pointer* v. *Texas* also helped incorporate the Sixth Amendment, which grants the accused the right to confront the witnesses against the accused.

The Fourteenth Amendment further expanded the powers of the federal government over state governments, and it proved to be a very powerful change, one that we are debating to this day. In recent years, Texas lawmakers have raised challenges to the Fourteenth Amendment of the U.S. Constitution on the question of citizenship. Among its provisions, the amendment begins by defining a U.S. citizen as being, "All Persons born or naturalized in the United States and subject to the jurisdiction thereof, are citizens of the United States and of the State wherein they reside," so it recognizes anyone born in the United States as a citizen.

Furthermore, Article I, Section 8 gives Congress the power, "to establish an uniform Rule of Naturalization."[47] This power gives the U.S. Congress the authority to create rules for immigration and naturalization. The enforcement of immigration law is the purview of the federal government and not the states.

In recent years, Texas lawmakers, growing frustrated that the federal government has been unable to take on the issue of the undocumented population, have attempted to address the issue at the state level. In recent legislative sessions, lawmakers have attempted to circumvent the Fourteenth Amendment by sponsoring legislation that would deny the rights of citizenship to babies born in the United States to undocumented parents. It is argued that because the parents of these infants have broken the law, the infants should not receive the benefits of citizenship.[48] If such bills were to become law in Texas, the U.S. Supreme Court would have to settle the conflict between the state and federal government. Representative Leo Berman, who introduced such a bill in the Texas House of Representatives, said, "We want to be sued into federal court where our attorney general can take this all the way to the U.S. Supreme Court."[49] In introducing such bills, Texas is challenging well-established interpretations of the U.S. Constitution.

Same-Sex Marriage and the Full Faith Credit Clause of the U.S. Constitution

In 1996, the federal government enacted the Defense of Marriage Act (DOMA), which some believe violated the right of states to determine their own civil laws. DOMA would allow states to reject marriages between members of the same gender that occurred in other states.

---

[46]It should be noted that *Wolf* v. *Colorado* (1949) and *Mapp* v. *Ohio* (1961) first incorporated the Fourth Amendment.

[47]"The Constitution of the United States," Article I, Section 8.

[48]Another question worth pondering in this discussion is the clause in the Constitution, which states that "no Attainder of Treason shall work Corruption of Blood" (Article III Section 2). The Constitution outlaws the punishment of offspring for the crimes committed by the parents. It has generally been understood that the blood of the child is not corrupted by the sins of the father or the mother.

[49]David Rauf, "Berman: 14th Amendment does not 'apply to foreigners,'" *Houston Chronicle*, log.chron.com/ texaspolitics/2009/02/berman-14th-Amendment-does-not-apply-to-foreigners/

Several states have legalized marriage between same-sex couples. Whether other states must recognize those marriages under the "full faith and credit" clause of the Constitution is still a matter of legal dispute.

Why would socially conservative Texans support a national law (DOMA) that exempts Texas from recognizing such marriages?

Currently, some states allow same-sex marriages. When asked about the state of New York allowing same-sex marriages, Governor Rick Perry, seeing the issue of same-sex marriage as a states' rights issue, said, "Well you know what, that's New York and that's their business, and that's fine with me." But in Texas, gay marriages are outlawed. Texans amended the state constitution in 2005, defining a marriage as being a union between a man and a woman.

The U.S. Constitution is not silent on this matter, however. Article IV, Section 1 of the U.S. Constitution requires states to recognize "the public acts, records, and judicial proceedings of every other state."[50] This is known as the Full Faith and Credit Clause of the U.S. Constitution. The Full Faith and Credit Clause contributes to the federalism question because it mandates that Texas recognize the official documents and court rulings from other states. The Full Faith and Credit Clause seems to require that marriages occurring in New York be recognized in Texas. Currently, the issue has not been fully reconciled by the political institutions or the courts. President Barack Obama announced in 2011 that the Justice Department would not defend the Defense of Marriage Act (DOMA) because it deemed key provisions of the act unconstitutional. Congress has also attempted to repeal DOMA, but such efforts have not succeeded. The courts have also weighed in on the issue, and a number of cases are working their way up the courts.

Some believe that if the courts outlaw DOMA, states with bans on same sex marriage will be required to honor same-sex marriages that occur in other states. Others believe that the Full Faith and Credit Clause would not require that states recognize same-sex marriages, or, if so, only in a limited capacity.[51] The coming years will provide a clearer picture to this debate.

[50]"The Constitution of the United States," Article IV, Section 1.
[51]Joseph W. Singer, "Same sex marriage, Full Faith and Credit, and the evasion of obligation," *Stanford Journal of Civil Rights and Civil Liberties*. vol. 1. 2005.

ArrowStudio, LLC/Shutterstock

"Texas Won't Forget These Federal Bureaucracies!"

Dr. Neal Coates
Abilene Christian University

INTRODUCTION

In this chapter, we have discussed Texans' leadership in a nationwide movement to limit the role of the national government. In fact, limiting the role of the national government was the central focus of Governor Perry's campaign for the Republican nomination for president. This article shows that, with their predominantly antifederal political culture, many Texans may be overlooking the positive contributions the national government makes in the state.

During the 2012 presidential campaign, candidate and Texas Governor Rick Perry made headlines for forgetting during a debate the name one of the three federal agencies he wanted to eliminate if elected president. He remembered the departments of Commerce and Education, but not Energy.[52] Unfortunately for the conservative Texans and others across the nation who were supporting his bid for the nation's highest office, this mistake came at a crucial moment before the Iowa Caucus and was a factor in the governor's drop in the polls and his eventual withdrawal from the race, even prior to the South Carolina primary.[53]

What a disappointment for those voters who believe the federal government should be reigned in and that states should have more power! The strong desire by the governor to eliminate some federal agencies is based on what he sees as government waste, duplication of efforts by the states,

or, more precisely, the view that the federal government has expanded too much during prior decades into the areas of oversight that have been traditionally and constitutionally reserved to the states.[54]

The spotlight on these three large agencies during the 2012 campaign was, however, also a reminder to Texans that a large number of United States bureaucracies regularly operate in the Lone Star State. These agencies employ a sizable number of persons, upwards to 30,000 in the Metroplex alone. Do Texans really know what federal bureaucracies are found here and what they do? Or have we perhaps forgotten about some of them? We must remember that, in the realm of federalism, national-level bureaucracies work alongside state agencies to make a difference by providing basic services and affecting our everyday quality of life.

BORDER PATROL

Perhaps the first federal agency that comes to mind for any border state, especially one next to Mexico, is Customs and Border Protection. CBP is one of the Department of Homeland Security's largest and most complex bureaucracies, with a priority now of keeping terrorists out of the country. It is also involved in facilitating trade and travel while enforcing hundreds of regulations, including immigration and drug laws.[55] Due to the great pressure to combat illegal immigration and the importation of illegal narcotics, Governor Perry has several times called on the federal government to bolster the number of CBP agents and to construct a barrier along high-traffic areas of the border.[56] But the efforts to safeguard the nation's boundaries due to terrorism threats, immigration woes, and drugs have slowed legitimate traffic for inspections between the United States and Mexico, hurting the trade economy. It is safe to say that this federal agency's role in Texas will continue to be a subject of scrutiny for years.

MILITARY BASES

We regularly hear about the role the Department of Defense plays around the world, but we are not always aware of the number of military bases in this state and their economic impact. More Texans have historically volunteered for the military than from other states, and since World War II, Texas has hosted a number of bases to help protect the nation. They range from Dyess Air Force Base in Abilene, which hosts the B-1 bomber, to the huge Ft. Hood Army base, the largest active-duty U.S. military base in the world.[57] There are

[52]"Rick Perry's Debate Lapse: 'Oops'—Can't Remember Department of Energy," *ABC News*, November 9, 2011, http://abcnews.go.com/blogs/politics/2011/11/rick-perrys-debate-lapse-oops-cant-remember-department-of-energy

[53]"Rick Perry Drops Out of 2012 Presidential Race Ahead of South Carolina Primary," *Huffington Post*, January 19, 2012, www.huffingtonpost.com/2012/01/19/rick-perry-drops-out-2012-_n_1214032.html

[54]See, for example, Rick Perry's campaign website at "Issues—10th Amendment and the Fighting Intrusive Washington Policies," www.rickperry.org/issues/tenth-amendment.

[55]"About CBP," www.cbp.gov/xp/cgov/about

[56] "Where Rick Perry Stands on Issues of Import to Latino Voters," *Fox News Latino*, January 10, 2012, http://latino.foxnews.com/latino/politics/2012/01/06/where-rick-perry-stands-on-issues-import-to-latino-voters.

[57]"Fort Hood: The Largest US Military Base in the World," *The Telegraph*, November 6, 2009, www.telegraph.co.uk/news/uknews/defence/6511138/Fort-Hood-The-largest-US-military-base-in-the-world.html

twenty-three bases in Texas (five Army, seven Air Force, one Navy, and ten Coast Guard facilities).[58]

In short, the Defense Department budget plays a huge role in Texas's economy. Fort Hood alone has an economic impact of over $11 billion on the Texas economy. This includes military and civilian payrolls, contracts and purchases, construction costs, and school district expenditures. Over the years, much growth has occurred in nearby businesses, ranging from hotels and restaurants to dry cleaners and retail outlets, that service these military personnel and their families. There are 53,000 soldiers at Fort Hood, and the base employs 5,100 civilians and 9,200 service and contract workers.[59]

The U.S. Census Bureau reports that statewide there are more than 131,500 active-duty military and 48,000 civilian employees. Texas officials believe the impact of the military payroll to be more than $77 billion. For the state as a whole, contracts for the military totaled $60 billion.[60]

Since the 2005 BRAC, the base realignment and closure process, Texas has actually benefitted even though three were shuttered in Corpus Christi, San Antonio, and Texarkana. Texas has gained thousands of soldiers compared to most states. Fort Sam Houston in San Antonio, the Army's headquarters for many medical services, has grown by 8,000 jobs, and officials expect a $2.9 billion yearly impact. Ft. Bliss is gaining 24,000 soldiers from the U.S. Army's 1st Armored Division in Germany, and in 2011 had $286 million in construction; in 2012, it is $214 million. In addition, the Texas Department of Transportation agreed to build a $350 million loop to connect the base to El Paso's freeways and another $1 billion for transportation throughout the city. Although President Obama has proposed two rounds of base closures as the Pentagon withdraws from the wars in Iraq and Afghanistan, the federal budget for FY 2013 contains $450 million in military construction projects in Texas.[61]

When you consider the number of retirees who choose to live in the Lone Star State after their military career is finished, the impact on the economy is multiplied. They also rely on medical services from various hospitals and other facilities operated by the Department of Veterans Affairs.

AGRICULTURE

We all like to eat, of course, and the Texas Department of Agriculture (TDA) works with the U.S. Department of Agriculture (USDA) to provide crucial services to ensure that what people consume is safe and nutritious. The USDA also helps market the wheat, cotton, and other products grown in this state around the world, and it works with TDA to promote billions of dollars of sales of Texas food, fiber, wine, livestock, horticulture, and forestry products.

Federal government support for agriculture has existed for a many years. In fact, 2012 marks the 150th anniversary of the founding of the USDA under President Lincoln. The Homestead Act of 1862 then opened lands to settlement—160 acres were given to any family who staked a claim, built a home, and farmed for five years. Today, programs annually provide billions of dollars to farmers and reduce risks associated with farming such as from weather loses. In 2008, Congress passed a five-year, $300 billion farm bill, and at present federal subsidies account for more than a fourth of net agricultural income.[62] Of the many services provided by the USDA, many Texans do not know about the Natural Resources Conservation Service. NRCS conservationists, rangeland management specialists, soil scientists, biologists, geologists, engineers, and foresters work with landowners who volunteer to develop conservation plans, create and restore wetlands, and prevent erosion. In addition, all 217 soil and water conservation districts in Texas—including five elected officials—regularly give input to NRCS.[63]

CONCLUSION

This description of some of the U.S. agencies here in Texas just scratches the surface. There are many others, such as the departments of Health and Human Services, Treasury, the Federal Bureau of Investigation, and Transportation. In fact, according to the U.S. Census Bureau (another federal agency!), 284,371 federal employees work here, complementing the 1,351,298 state and local employees.[64] In short, every major bureaucracy of the federal government has a presence in Texas and provides services and employment. Even the college students who enjoy the trails and campgrounds of Big Bend and Guadalupe Mountains national parks are using property overseen by the Department of the Interior. We all gain, even if we grumble from inconveniences at the airport amid safety checks by the Transportation Safety Administration. Citizens even complain loudly about the cost overruns of agencies such as the Federal Emergency Management Agency, but they clamor to be in line to apply for FEMA assistance after a natural disaster like Hurricane Ike.

We must remember that the United States of America has a federal system—powers are shared between the national and the state governments—and that everyone benefits. In this vein, conservative Texans will continue to question the growth

[58]"U.S. Military Major Bases and Installations: Texas," http://usmilitary.about.com/library/milinfo/statefacts/bltx.htm

[59]"Fort Hood Impacts Texas Economy by $10.9 Billion," Press Release, Texas Comptroller's Office, May 13, 2008, www.hotda.org/Articles%20of%20Interest/Economic%20Impact%20Press%20Release.pdf

[60]Gary Martin, "Federal Budget Cuts Will Likely Hit Texas Military Bases," *Houston Chronicle*, February 19, 2012, www.chron.com/news/houston-texas/article/Federal-budget-cuts-will-likely-hit-Texas-3341836.php

[61]Rachel Craft, "Military Base Closures Impact Texas Cities," *The Texas Tribune*, May 5, 2010; Gary Martin, "Federal Budget Cuts Will Likely Hit Texas Military Bases," *Houston Chronicle*, February 19, 2012, www.chron.com/news/houston-texas/article/Federal-budget-cuts-will-likely-hit-Texas-3341836.php

[62]U.S. Department of Agriculture, www.usda.gov/wps/portal/usda/usdahome; Texas Department of Agriculture, http://texasagriculture.gov

[63]See www.tx.nrcs.usda.gov

[64]2010 Federal Government Employment & Payroll, www.census.gov/govs/apes, www2.census.gov/govs/apes/10stltx.txt; "Federal Employees by State," National Treasury Employees Union, www.theyworkforus.org/documents/FedEmployeesStats.pdf

of the national government, and all of us will attempt to hold accountable our elected officials and the bureaucrats they employ, but federalism is certainly here to stay.

JOIN THE DEBATE

1. Generally, conservatives support the national government bolstering its national security functions while cutting back on social services, environmental protection, and education programs. Why do critics of national government power favor retrenchment in some federal functions but actually support expansion of its power in other areas of public policy?

2. What is the "proper" role for the national government? Is the part it plays determined solely by the U.S. Constitution, or is it ultimately determined by the political process?

CHAPTER SUMMARY

★ Federalism is a system of governments in which power is constitutionally divided between a national government and state or regional governments. The constitution expressly and implicitly gives the national government delegated powers in Article I, Section 8 and reserves powers to the state in the Tenth Amendment.

★ Exclusive powers are given to the national government only; reserved powers belong only to the states, and concurrent powers are shared between both levels of government.

★ The view of how much power should be granted to each level of government has changed dramatically with the changing national political climate. During the earliest constitutional period, Chief Justice John Marshall took a broad view of national powers. By the 1830s, a concept of dual federalism developed in which the national government was limited and distinctly separate from the states, but that view changed in the 1930s when the New Deal began to offer

extensive grants-in-aid to the states to help finance common national programs—the basis for a cooperative federalism. Since the 1970s, some states, especially conservative ones, have come to resent national government mandates and conditions necessary to receive federal grants—they view today's federal-state relationship as coercive federalism.

★ Texas has contributed to shaping this concept of federalism not only by bringing key Supreme Court cases to the debate, but also because its current political leadership has contributed to the debate. Governor Rick Perry and the Texas Legislature have raised concerns about the impact that the federal government may have on Texas. The debates presented by Governor Rick Perry and the Texas Legislature have focused on the Tenth Amendment and powers reserved to the states. It remains to be seen whether a new balance will be struck between federal and state governments. In the coming months and years, Texans will continue to see the understanding of the concept of federalism evolve.

HOW TEXAS COMPARES

★ As one of the nation's more conservative states, Texas has resisted the expansion of federal power more than most, and as a result, its policies have been more frequently challenged in the courts. Texas has led the way in an effort to redefine the nature of federalism.

★ Texas's environmental controls have been quite lax compared to those of other states, and this has resulted in ongoing conflict with the national government and the Environmental Protection Agency.

★ Although federal grants-in-aid account for a hefty share of state revenues, Texas receives less per capita in federal grants-in-aid than most other states and gets back a smaller share in the form of grants than it pays to the federal government in the form of taxes. Most federal grants are based on state spending effort, and Texas simply spends less for public services than most other states.

KEY TERMS

block grants, *p. 37*
categorical grants, *p. 37*
coercive federalism, *p. 39*
confederal system, *p. 31*
Commerce Clause, *p. 34*
concurrent powers, *p. 34*

cooperative federalism, *p. 37*
delegated powers, *p. 31*
devolution, *p. 37*
dual federalism, *p. 36*
expressed powers, *p. 33*
federal system, *p. 31*

implied powers, *p. 33*
incorporation doctrine, *p. 49*
inherent powers, *p. 33*
Jim Crow laws, *p. 38*
necessary and proper clause, *p. 34*
reserved powers, *p. 34*

separate-but-equal doctrine, *p. 38*
Supremacy Clause, *p. 34*
Tenth Amendment, *p. 34*
unfunded mandates, *p. 46*
unitary system, *p. 30*

REVIEW QUESTIONS

1. Define federalism. Explain the difference between delegated and reserved powers and give examples of each. What is the importance of Article I, Section 8 and the Tenth Amendment in the Constitution?

2. Define and give examples of exclusive and concurrent powers. What is the significance of the implied powers clause or the necessary and proper clause? Explain how the national government has used the necessary and proper clause and the Commerce Clause to expand the scope of its power.

3. Explain how the dominant concepts of federalism have changed as the political and legal climate has changed. Describe the differences between the concepts of dual federalism and cooperative federalism. What historical developments led to the expansion of national government power? Explore the role the national government has played in the advancement of civil rights, public health, and environmental protection.

4. Define grants-in-aid and their scope in the modern federal system. What are the major types of grants-in-aid? How has the national government used its financial powers to shape state policies?

5. Evaluate arguments for states' rights and the argument that the national government's powers should be limited. Evaluate the argument that states serve as policy laboratories in a federal system. What role has Texas played in the efforts to limit national government power?

LOGGING ON

Explore the role of the U.S. Supreme Court in serving as an umpire between the national government and the states at Scotus Blog at **www.scotusblog.com/**.

Follow Texas's disputes with the federal government over such issues as abortion, environmental protection, voter ID laws, health care reform, and immigration at the state attorney general's website at www.oag.state.tx.us/. Use the *Texas Tribune's* interactive site to keep up with the state's legal battles with the national government at **www.texastribune.org/library/about/texas-versus-federal-government-lawsuits-interactive/**. Keep up with health care reform issues at the Kaiser Family Foundation site at **www.kff.org/**.

Discover problems that state governments face and the kinds of innovative solutions that they have developed at Pew Center for the States at **www.pewstates.org/**. Find examples of the states serving as "laboratories for democracy."

Analyze conservative arguments for states' rights and a limited national government at the Tea Party Patriots site at **www.teapartypatriots.org/** or at the Freedom Works site at **www.freedomworks.org/**. Contrast these views with groups who see a positive role for the national government, for example, the Center on Budget and Policy Priorities at **www.cbpp.org/**.

Chapter 3

The Texas Constitution in Perspective

LEARNING OBJECTIVES

★ Explain the origin and development of the Texas Constitution.

★ Identify Texas's historic constitutions and the cultural and political forces that shaped each of their distinctive features.

★ Identify the rights protected by the Texas Bill of Rights and distinguish those that are also protected by the U.S. Constitution.

★ Describe separation of powers and checks and balances in both theory and practice.

★ Describe the major constitutional structures, functions, and limits of Texas's legislative, executive, and judicial branches.

★ Describe the constitutional functions and limits of the three major types of local government.

★ Identify Texas voter qualifications and restrictions on the right to vote.

★ Explain the process of amending and revising the Texas Constitution and the reasons that amendments are frequently necessary.

GET *Active*

Link up with groups active in supporting your view of constitutional rights.

Conservative Groups

★ The National Rifle Association supports a broader right to keep and bear arms: **www.nra.org/**

★ Students for Concealed Carry on Campus at concealedcampus.org/ fights to repeal restrictions on campus firearms.

★ Texas Alliance for Life at **www .texasallianceforlife.org/** is a pro-life group.

★ Texas Eagle Forum at **texaseagle.org/** and the Federalist Society at **www.fed-soc.org/** broadly advocate conservative views of personal liberties.

Liberal Groups

★ Texas Freedom Network at **www.tfn.org/** and the Anti-Defamation League at **www .adl.org/** focus on religious liberty.

★ NARAL Pro-Choice America at **www.naral .org/** supports abortion rights.

★ The Brady Campaign at **www.bradycampaign .org/** advocates gun control.

★ Texas Coalition to Abolish the Death Penalty at **www.tcadp.org/** fights capital punishment.

★ Texas Civil Liberties Union at **www.aclutx .org/** supports liberal positions on civil liberties.

★ Tune in to the continual rewriting of the state's fundamental law by voting in Texas elections to ratify state constitutional amendments. Note that proposals are sometimes detailed and confusing, and beware of biased special-interest group television and newspaper ads describing them. Good amendment summaries and analyses are available in news sections of local papers and the websites of The League of Women Voters at **www.lwvtexas .org** and The Legislative Council at **www .tlc.state.tx.us.**

The real character of a government is determined less by the provisions of its constitution than by the minds and hearts of its citizens. Government is a process of decision making conditioned by its history, its people, and pressures exerted by citizens, interest groups, and political parties.

Still, our national, state, and local governments would be vastly different were it not for their constitutions. Although the exact meaning of constitutional provisions may be disputed, there is general agreement that constitutions should be respected as the legal basis controlling the fundamentals of government decision making. Constitutions serve as a rationalization for the actions of courts, legislatures, executives, and the people themselves. Indeed, the very idea of having a written constitution has become part of the political culture—the basic system of political beliefs in the United States.

Constitutions establish major governing institutions, assign them power, and place both implicit and explicit limits on the power they have assigned. And, because Americans respect constitutions, they promote **legitimacy**, the general public acceptance of government's "right to govern."

Legitimacy

General public acceptance of government's right to govern; also, the legality of a government's existence conferred by a constitution.

TEXAS CONSTITUTIONS IN HISTORY

Like all constitutions, early Texas constitutions reflected the interests and concerns of the people who wrote and amended them. Many of their elements parallel those of other state constitutions; others are unique to Texas.

Early Texas Constitutions

The constitutions of the Texas Republic and the first state constitutions of Texas are products of the plantation culture of Anglo-protestant slaveholders. These early constitutions adopted some institutions from Texans' experiences during Mexican rule and forthrightly rejected others.

Republic of Texas Constitution
The first Texas Constitution after independence from Mexico was written in 1836 for the Republic of Texas. In reaction to the influence of the Catholic Church during Mexican rule, largely protestant Texans wrote a constitution with careful separation of church and state, forbidding clergymen of any faith from holding office. It changed the antislavery policies of the old Mexican government by forbidding masters to free their own slaves without consent of the Republic's congress and denied citizenship to descendants of Africans and Indians. Remembering the abuses of Mexican President Santa Anna, Texans limited the terms of their presidents to three years and prohibited them from being elected to consecutive terms.

The Republic of Texas Constitution did adopt some provisions from Spanish-Mexican law, including **homestead** protections, protection for a wife's property rights, and the concept of **community property**, meaning that property acquired during marriage would be owned equally by husband and wife. These elements of Mexican law would later be absorbed into American political culture as other states adopted similar provisions.

Still, the Republic's constitution was mostly a product of the political culture of the Anglo-American southern planters. It incorporated English **common law** and lifted many provisions almost word-for-word from the U.S. Constitution and from southern states like Tennessee from which many Texas settlers had come.

Acting in haste because of the fear of attack from the Mexican cavalry, the Republic's constitutional convention wrote a concise document establishing a *unitary* form of government (see Chapter 2), free of many of the detailed restrictions that would later come to limit Texas government.

Constitution of 1845
A new constitution was written in 1845 in preparation for Texas's admission to the United States. It is interesting to note that it required a two-thirds vote in the Texas House to establish any corporation and made bank corporations illegal altogether. Although the 1845 Constitution contained many provisions similar to the Republic's constitution, it also began to introduce features recognizable in today's state constitution. For example, it was almost twice as long as the Republic of Texas's Constitution and included restrictive language on the legislature, which was allowed to meet only once every two years. The statehood constitution limited state debt to $100,000 except in cases of war, insurrection, or invasion, and it established the Permanent School Fund. The only amendment to the 1845 Constitution was adopted to limit the power of the governor by providing for the election of some of the officers that governors previously were allowed to appoint, thereby establishing the beginnings of a **long ballot** with which Texans are familiar today.

Constitution of 1861
The 1861 Constitution was basically the same as that of 1845 except it reflected that Texas had become one of the Confederate states at war with the Union—it increased the debt ceiling and prohibited the emancipation of slaves.

Homestead
An owner-occupied property protected from forced sale under most circumstances.

Community property
Property acquired during marriage and owned equally by both spouses.

Common law
Customs upheld by courts and deriving from British tradition.

Long ballot
A ballot that results from the election of a large number of independent executive and judicial officers; giving the chief executive the power to appoint most executive and judicial officers results in a short ballot.

Reconstruction Constitutions and Their Aftermath

While earlier constitutions contained a number of elements still found in today's Texas Constitution, it was the aftermath of the Civil War—the political reaction to Reconstruction—that affirmed Texans' fear of government and set the stage for the writing of today's state constitution.

Constitution of 1866 After the Civil War, Texans wrote the 1866 Constitution, which they thought would satisfy the Unionists and permit the readmission of Texas under President Andrew Johnson's mild Reconstruction program. This document nullified secession, abolished slavery, and renounced Confederate war debts. Under its terms, a civilian government was elected and operated for several months despite some interference from the Freedmen's Bureau.

The 1866 Constitution soon became void because the Radical Republicans in Congress passed the Reconstruction Act of 1867 that required Confederate states to adopt constitutions that met with the approval of the U.S. Congress and, under its authority, the military deposed civilian elected officials and effectively restored military rule.

Constitution of 1869 With most whites either barred from the election or boycotting it, voters elected members to a constitutional convention in 1868. It produced a document that centralized state power in the hands of the governor, lengthened the chief executive's term to four years, and allowed the governor to appoint all major state officers, including judges. It provided annual legislative sessions, weakened planter-controlled local government, and centralized the public school system. The convention in 1868 reflected little of the fear of centralized government power that was later to become the hallmark of Texas government. The proposed constitution was ratified in 1869.

The 1869 Constitution served as the instrument of government for an era that most Texans and traditional historians would regard as the most corrupt and abusive in the state's history. Under Republican Governor E. J. Davis, large gifts of public funds were made to interests such as railroads, tax rates skyrocketed to pay for ambitious and wasteful public programs, landowners refused to pay high property taxes (amounting to as much as one-fifth of personal income), many Texans simply refused to pay these exorbitant taxes, and government accumulated what was for that time an incredible public debt. Law and order collapsed, and much of the state fell prey to desperados and Native-American attacks on white settlers. Instead of using the state police and militia to maintain the peace, Governor Davis made them a part of his powerful political machine and a symbol of tyranny. He took control of voter registration, intimidated unsupportive newspapers, and arrested several political opponents. In 1874, his handpicked supreme court used the location of a semicolon in the state constitution as a pretext for invalidating the election of Democrat Richard Coke, and he wired President Grant to send federal troops to thwart the overwhelming Democratic victory. Grant refused, and Democrats slipped past guards at the capitol and gathered in the legislative chambers to form the new government.

According to legend, Davis, determined not to give up his office, surrounded himself with armed state police in the capitol. Only when a well-armed group of Coke supporters marched toward the capitol singing "The Yellow Rose of Texas" did Davis finally vacate his office. For most Texans, Reconstruction left a bitter memory of a humiliating, corrupt, extravagant, and even tyrannical government.

Revisionist historians argue that Governor Davis was not personally corrupt and that Reconstruction brought progressive policies and built roads, railroads, and schools while protecting the civil and political rights of former slaves. Some see it as a period in which an activist government attempted to play a positive role in people's lives. The period that followed was characterized by a conservative white reaction to these policies.

The Constitutional Convention of 1875

Whichever historical view is more accurate, it is clear that most Texans of the day were determined to strip power away from state government by writing a new constitution. The Texas Grange, whose members were called Grangers, organized in 1873. Campaigning on a platform of "retrenchment and reform," it managed to elect at least 40 of its members to the constitutional convention of 1875. Like most of the 90 delegates, they were Democrats who were determined to strike at the heart of big government, which had served Reconstruction minority rule.

> **Did You Know?** Only 15 of the 90 elected convention delegates were Republicans; however, during the course of the convention, one of the Republican delegates was declared insane and replaced by a Democrat.

To save money, the convention did not publish a journal—reflecting the frugal tone of the final constitution. The convention cut salaries for governing officials, placed strict limits on property taxes, and restricted state borrowing; it was also miserly with the power it granted government officials. It stripped most of the governor's powers, reduced the term of office from four to two years, and required that the attorney general and state judges be elected rather than appointed by the governor.

Nor did the legislature escape the pruning of the convention. Regular legislative sessions were to be held only once every two years, and legislators were encouraged to limit the length of the sessions. Legislative procedure was detailed in the constitution, with severe restrictions placed on the kinds of policies the legislature might enact. In fact, a number of public policies were written into the constitution itself.

Local government was strengthened, and counties were given many of the administrative and judicial functions of the state. Although the Grangers had opposed the idea of public education, they were persuaded to allow it if segregated schools were established by local governments.

The convention largely reacted to the abuse of state power by denying it. When the convention ended, some of the money appropriated for its expenses remained unspent. Despite opposition from blacks, Republicans, most cities, and railroad interests, voters ratified the current state constitution of 1876.

THE TEXAS CONSTITUTION TODAY

Many students begin their examination of state constitutions with some kind of ideal or model constitution in mind. Comparisons with this ideal then leave them with the feeling that if only this or that provision were changed, state government would somehow find its way to honesty, efficiency, and effectiveness. In truth, there is no ideal constitution that would serve well in each of the uniquely diverse 50 states, nor is it possible to write a state constitution that could permanently meet the dynamically changing needs and concerns of citizens. Further, because government is much more than its constitution, honest and effective government must be commanded by the political environment—leaders, citizens, parties, interest groups, and so forth—constitutions cannot guarantee it. Scoundrels will be corrupt and unconcerned citizens apathetic under even the best constitution.

However, this pragmatic view of the role of state constitutions should not lead to the conclusion that they are only incidental to good government. A workable constitution is necessary for effective government even if it is not sufficient to guarantee it. Low salaries may discourage independent, high-caliber leaders from seeking office, constitutional restrictions may make it virtually impossible for government to meet the changing needs of its citizens, and institutions may be set up in such a way that they will operate inefficiently and irresponsibly.

The events preceding the adoption of the 1876 Texas Constitution did not provide the background for developing a constitution capable of serving well under the pressures and

Delegates to the constitutional convention of 1875 substantially limited the power of state government.

What did delegates consider abuses of state power that needed to be prevented in the future?

changes that would take place in the century to follow. The decade of the 1870s was an era of paranoia and reaction, and the constitution it produced was directed more toward solving the problems arising from Reconstruction than toward meeting the challenges of generations to follow—it was literally a reactionary document.

TABLE 3.1 Basic Rights in the Texas and U.S. Constitutions		
Basic Right	**Texas Constitution**	**U.S. Constitution**
Religious Liberty	Article 1, Sections 4–7	First and Fourteenth Amendments
Freedom of Expression	Article 1, Sections 8 and 27	First and Fourteenth Amendments
Right to keep and bear arms	Article 1, Section 23	Second and Fourteenth Amendments
Against quartering troops	Article 1, Section 25	Third Amendment
Against unreasonable search and seizure	Article 1, Section 9	Fourth and Fourteenth Amendments
Right to grand jury indictment for felonies	Article 1, Section 10	Fifth Amendment
Right to just compensation for taking property for public use	Article 1, Section 17	Fifth and Fourteenth Amendments
Right to due process of law	Article 1, Section 19	Fifth and Fourteenth Amendments
Right against double jeopardy	Article 1, Section 14	Fifth and Fourteenth Amendments
Right against forced self-incrimination	Article 1, Section 10	Fifth and Fourteenth Amendments
Right to fair trial by jury	Article 1, Section 10	Sixth and Fourteenth Amendments
Rights against excessive bail or cruel and unusual punishment	Article 1, Sections 11 and 13	Eighth and Fourteenth Amendments

These rights are guaranteed by both national and state constitutions.

▲ **Explain how states can set higher standards than the national government does for applying these provisions. What rights does Texas's constitution protect that the U.S. Constitution does not?**

Bill of Rights and Fundamental Liberty

Although the Texas Constitution has been the target of much criticism, it contains a Bill of Rights (Article 1) that is often held in high regard because it reflects basic American political culture and contains provisions that are similar to those found in other state charters and the U.S. Constitution.

The Fourteenth Amendment to the U.S. Constitution provides that no state shall deny any person life, liberty, or property without the due process of law. As the U.S. Supreme Court has interpreted this Amendment, it has ruled that states must respect most of the U.S. Bill of Rights because its provisions are essential to "liberty" and "due process." As a result, many individual rights are protected by both the state and federal courts. If the state courts fail to protect an individual's rights, that person can also then seek a remedy in the federal courts. Table 3.1 shows important basic rights protected by both the U.S. and Texas Constitutions.

State constitutional guarantees are not redundant, however, because the U.S. Constitution establishes only *minimum* standards for the states. Texas's courts have interpreted some state constitutional provisions to broaden basic rights beyond these minimums. Although the U.S. Supreme Court refused to interpret the Fourteenth Amendment as guaranteeing equal public school funding,[1] Texas's Supreme Court interpreted the efficiency clause of Texas's Constitution (Article 7, Section 1) as requiring greater equity in public schools.[2] By using Texas's constitutional and **statutory law** (passed by the legislature), Texas courts have struck down polygraph tests for public employees, required workers' compensation for farm workers,

Statutory law

Law passed by legislatures and written into code books.

---

[1]*San Antonio Independent School District* v. *Rodriguez,* 411 U.S. 1 (1973).
[2]*Edgewood* v. *Kirby,* 777 S.W. 2d 391 (Tex. 1989).

expanded free-speech rights of private employees, and affirmed free-speech rights at privately owned shopping malls.

The Texas Bill of Rights guarantees additional rights not specifically mentioned by the U.S. Constitution. Notably, Texas has adopted an amendment to prohibit discrimination based on sex. A similar guarantee was proposed as the Equal Rights Amendment to the U.S. Constitution, but it was not ratified by the states. The Texas Constitution also guarantees victims' rights and access to public beaches. It forbids imprisonment for debt or committing the mentally ill for an extended period without a jury trial. It also prohibits monopolies and the suspension of the **writ of habeas corpus** under any circumstances. Article 16 protects homesteads and prohibits garnishment of wages except for court-ordered child support.

Although the state constitution forbids same-sex marriages, the Texas Bill of Rights and other provisions guarantee the average citizen a greater variety of protections than most other state constitutions. We will extensively discuss Texans' basic rights in Chapter 12.

Separation of Powers

Like the state bill of rights, Article 2 of the Texas Constitution limits government. To prevent the concentration of power in the hands of any single institution, the national government and all states have provided for a **separation of powers** among three branches—legislative, executive, and judicial. The function of the legislative branch is to make laws, and it is by law that governments define crime, establish the basis of civil suits, determine who will pay how much in taxes, and set up government programs and the agencies that administer them. The function of the executive branch is to carry out the law, to arrest criminals, to collect taxes, to provide public services, to hire government employees and to supervise their day-to-day conduct. The function of the judicial branch is to interpret the law as it applies to individuals and institutions.

Despite the separation of powers, there is still the potential for any of these three branches to abuse whatever powers they have been given. The Texas Constitution also follows American tradition in subsequent constitutional articles—it sets up a system of **checks and balances**. Table 3.2 illustrates that, under certain circumstances, a function normally assigned to one branch of government can be influenced by another. For example, the veto power that deals with lawmaking (a legislative function) is given to the governor (an executive). Impeachment and conviction, which deal with determining guilt (a judicial function), are given to the legislature. The state senate (a house of the legislature) confirms appointments the governor makes in the executive branch. Although there is a separation of powers, the checks-and-balances system requires that each branch must have the opportunity to influence the others. The three branches specialize in separate functions, but there is some sharing of powers as well. In Chapters 7 through 12, you will see how extensively these three branches of government interact.

Legislative Branch

The legislative article (Article 3) is by far the longest in the Texas Constitution. It assigns legislative power to a **bicameral** (two-house) legislative body consisting of the 31-member senate and the 150-member house of representatives. Elected for a four-year term from single-member districts, each senator must be at least twenty-six years old, a citizen, and must have resided in the state for five years and in the district for one year. A representative serves only two years and must be at least twenty-one years old, a citizen, and a resident of the state for two years and of the district for one year.

Although populous industrialized states are usually much more generous, the Texas Constitution sets annual salaries at $7200 unless the Texas Ethics Commission

Writ of habeas corpus

A court order requiring that an individual be presented in person and that legal cause be shown for confinement; it may result in release from unlawful detention.

Separation of powers

The principle behind the concept of a government with three branches—legislative, executive, and judicial.

Checks and balances

The concept that each branch of government is assigned power to limit abuses in the others, for example, the executive veto could be used to prevent legislative excesses.

Bicameral

Consisting of two houses or chambers; applied to a legislative body with two parts, such as a senate and a house of representatives (or state assembly). Congress and 49 state legislatures are bicameral. Only Nebraska has a one-house (unicameral) legislature.

TABLE 3.2 Texas's Constitutional Checks and Balances

Checks on the Legislature	*Checks on the Executive Branch*	*Checks on the Judicial branch*
★ The governor may veto bills passed by the legislature subject to a two-thirds vote to override.	★ Texas's House of Representatives may impeach an executive by a majority vote.	★ The governor appoints judges to fill vacancies in district and higher courts until the next election.
★ The governor may use the line item veto on appropriations bills.	★ Texas's Senate may convict and remove an executive by a two-thirds vote.	★ The House may impeach and the Senate may remove state judges.
★ The governor may call special legislative sessions and set their agenda.	★ The Senate confirms official appointments of the governor by a two-thirds vote.	★ The legislature sets judicial salaries.
★ The governor may address the legislature and designate emergency legislation that can be considered in the first 30 days of the session.	★ The legislature creates nonconstitutional executive agencies, assigns them their powers, and appropriates their funds.	★ The legislature establishes many lower courts by statute.
		★ The legislature may pass new laws if they disagree with court interpretation of existing ones.
★ The courts use *judicial review* to declare legislative acts unconstitutional.	★ The courts may declare actions of the governor or state agencies unconstitutional or illegal.	★ Two-thirds of the legislature may propose constitutional amendments to overturn court decisions.

This table shows the major checks and balances in the Texas Constitution. In practice, the political environment determines how effectively they limit each branch of government.

▲ How effective are these checks when, as in Texas, all three branches are controlled by the same party with shared political goals and philosophies? Do these checks lead to gridlock when control of the three branches is divided between two parties?

Biennial regular session

Regular legislative sessions are scheduled by the constitution. In Texas, they are held once every two years; hence they are biennial.

Special session

A legislative session called by the Texas governor, who also sets its agenda.

recommends an increase and voters approve it. The Ethics Commission has made no such recommendation but has exercised its power to increase the per diem (daily) allowance while the legislature is in session. No other large state sets legislative salaries so low (see Figure 3.1).

Texas restricts the legislature to **biennial regular sessions** (convened once every two years). Because sessions are also limited to 140 days, important legislation may receive inadequate consideration, and many bills are ignored altogether. The 2011 legislature introduced an incredible 10,889 bills and resolutions and passed only 5,974 (55 percent) of them, while spending about $1 billion for every day in session.

Except to deal with rare matters of impeachment, Texas's legislature may not call itself into **special sessions** or determine the issues to be decided. Lasting no more than 30 days, the governor convenes special sessions to consider only the legislative matters he or she presents. Special sessions are more restricted in Texas than in any other state.

Did You Know? In the rush of its short 1971 regular session, the Texas House of Representatives passed a resolution to honor Albert De Salvo, otherwise known as the "Boston Strangler," for "pioneering efforts in population control techniques."

HOW DOES TEXAS COMPARE?
Limits on Legislative Terms, Salaries, and Sessions

Terms Like 34 other states, Texas does not limit the number of terms legislators may serve. Voters are left to decide whether to retain experienced incumbents or replace them with fresh legislators.

Salaries Figure 3.1 shows that the Texas Constitution is much more restrictive than most states with respect to legislative salaries and sessions. Although New Hampshire pays its legislators only $200, no other populous state sets legislative pay as low as Texas. Most larger states pay their legislators in the salary range of middle-class employees, and many allow legislators to set their own salary by statute.

Sessions Most states provide annual regular legislative sessions and 14 states place no limit on their length. Texas is among only five states with biennial legislative sessions. Unlike most legislatures, the Texas legislature may not call itself into special session or determine agendas. Low salaries and limited sessions make it difficult for the Texas legislature to function as a professional institution and may make members more dependent on interest groups for income and research on public policy. Recent research indicates that more-professional legislatures—those with higher salaries, longer sessions, and better staffs—are significantly more responsive to public opinion and enact policies that are more congruent with public preferences.*

FOR DEBATE

1. Should Texas limit the number of terms legislators serve? Or, would term limits also restrict legislators' experience and, therefore, make them more vulnerable to the influence of lobbyists?

2. Should Texas consider increasing legislative salaries and the length of their sessions? Or, would doing this give legislators too much power?

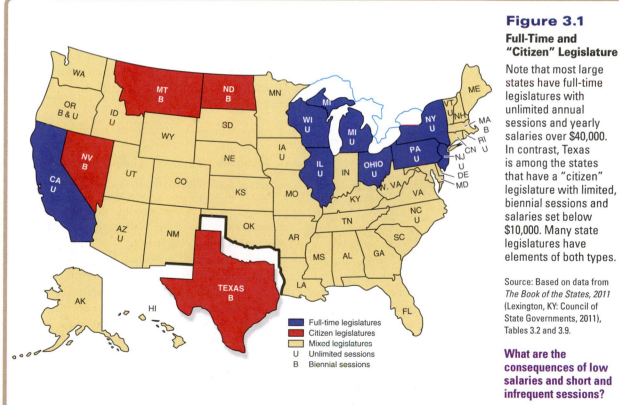

Figure 3.1

Full-Time and "Citizen" Legislature

Note that most large states have full-time legislatures with unlimited annual sessions and yearly salaries over $40,000. In contrast, Texas is among the states that have a "citizen" legislature with limited, biennial sessions and salaries set below $10,000. Many state legislatures have elements of both types.

Source: Based on data from *The Book of the States, 2011* (Lexington, KY: Council of State Governments, 2011), Tables 3.2 and 3.9.

What are the consequences of low salaries and short and infrequent sessions?

Legend:
- Full-time legislatures
- Citizen legislatures
- Mixed legislatures
- U Unlimited sessions
- B Biennial sessions

---

*Lax, Jeffrey R. and Justin H. Phillips, "The Democratic Deficit," Unpublished paper, Midwestern Political Science Association meeting 2010.

The Texas Constitution establishes more specific procedural requirements than most other state constitutions. Although the provision is often suspended, the constitution requires that a bill must be read on three separate days unless four-fifths of the legislature sets aside the requirement. It stipulates when bills may be introduced and how they will be reported out of committee, signed, and entered in the journal once enacted. It even specifies how the enacting clause will read.

Although most states legally require a balanced budget, Texas's constitutional restriction seems more effective than most. Article 3, Section 49, strictly limits the legislature in authorizing state debt except under rare conditions. The comptroller of public accounts is required to certify that funds are available for each appropriations measure adopted. Although specific constitutional amendments have authorized the sale of bonds for veterans' real estate programs, student loans, parks and water development, and prison construction, Texas's per capita state debt remains among the lowest in the nation.

Constitutional detail further confines the legislature by making policies on subjects that normally would be handled by legislative statute. Much of the length of Article 3 results from its in-depth description of state policies such as the Veterans' Land Program, Texas park and water development funds, student loans, welfare programs, a grain warehouse self-insurance fund, and the municipal donation of outdated firefighting equipment. The constitution establishes the design of the great seal of Texas, authorizes the legislature to pass fence laws, and even explains how the state must purchase stationery! Article 16 authorizes the legislature to regulate cattle brands; Article 11 permits the building of seawalls. By including such **statute-like details** in the Texas Constitution, its framers guaranteed that even relatively unimportant decisions that could easily be handled by the legislature must be changed only by constitutional amendment.

Events may outstrip detailed constitutional provisions, leaving **deadwood** (inoperable provisions) that voters must constantly approve amendments to remove. For example, Article 9, Section 14, provides for the establishment of county poorhouses. The basic distrust of the legislature, however much it may have been deserved in 1876, put a straitjacket on the state's ability to cope with the challenges of the twenty-first century.

Executive Branch

Article 4 establishes the executive branch, with the governor as its head. The governor must be a citizen, at least thirty years of age, and a resident of the state for five years immediately preceding his or her election to a four-year term. The constitution no longer limits the governor's salary, and, according to statute, it is $150,000.

Provisions for terms, qualifications, and salary may be somewhat less restrictive than in most states, but the power of the office has much more severe constitutional restrictions. Although the constitution provides that the governor shall be the chief executive, it actually establishes a **plural executive** by dividing executive powers among a number of independently elected officers—the governor, lieutenant governor, attorney general, comptroller of public accounts, commissioner of the general land office, and three railroad commissioners. There are also provisions for a state board of education to be either elected or appointed. The constitution stipulates that the governor appoint the secretary of state.

In the tradition of the constitutional plural executive, the legislature by statute has also established an elected commissioner of agriculture and has exercised its option to make the state board of education elected independently of the governor. The result of electing so many state executive officers is a long ballot that voters find confusing because it is difficult for them to assign responsibility in a system of diffused power.

Statute-like detail

Detailed state constitutional policies of narrow scope, usually handled by statutes passed by legislative bodies.

Deadwood

State constitutional provisions voided by a conflicting U.S. constitutional or statutory law; also provisions made irrelevant by changing circumstances.

Did You Know? Although no county elected an inspector of hides and animals in modern times, the position remained a constitutional office until 2007.

Plural executive

An executive branch with power divided among several independent officers and a weak chief executive.

Most of the remaining agencies that the legislature establishes to administer state programs are headed by appointed multimember boards with substantial independence from the governor. Generally, the governor appoints only supervisory boards to six-year staggered terms with the approval of two-thirds of the state senate. The board in turn appoints its agency's director. The governor usually does not appoint the agency administrator directly—the board does. Furthermore, Texas is one of seven states that lacks a formal cabinet.

The governor has limited **removal powers** to supplement these **indirect appointive powers**. The governor may fire his or her own staff and advisors at will, but removal of state officers is more difficult. The governor may fire appointed officers only if two-thirds of the senators agree that there is just cause for removal, making firing almost as difficult as impeachment and conviction. Furthermore, the governor may not remove anyone appointed by a preceding governor. **Directive authority** (to issue binding orders) is still quite restricted, and **budgetary power** (to recommend to the legislature how much it should appropriate for various executive agencies) is limited by the competing influences of the Legislative Budget Board.

Removal powers

The authority to fire appointed officials. The Texas governor has limited removal powers; they extend only to officials he or she has appointed and are subject to the consent of two-thirds of the state senators.

Indirect appointive powers

Texas governor's authority to appoint supervisory boards but not operational directors for most state agencies.

Directive authority

The power to issue binding orders to state agencies; the directive authority of Texas's governor is severely limited.

HOW DOES TEXAS COMPARE?
Governors and the Organization of the Executive Branch

Governors' Qualifications, Terms, Term Limits, and Salaries

The Texas governor's salary is typical among the states. Although qualifications to be governor are similar to most states, Texas does not impose term limits on its chief executive. Many states limit the governor to a maximum of two consecutive terms.

In most states, Governor Rick Perry would not have been allowed to run for reelection in 2010. It is precisely Governor Perry's long tenure in office that allowed him to become an extremely powerful governor despite limitations in Texas's constitution and statutes. Governor Perry has been able to put his political allies on all state boards even though members serve six-year overlapping terms. During this same period, he was also able to put his brand on the judiciary by filling frequent vacancies on the bench resulting from early retirements.

Constitutional Provisions For Chief Executives' Qualifications			
Provisions	**Texas Governor**	**U.S. President**	**The 50 States Governors**
Age	30 years	35 years	34 states set the minimum age at 30
Residence	5 years	14 years	5 years or fewer in 37 states
Terms	4 years	4 years (limited to 2 terms or 10 years)	48 states allow a 4-year term, but unlike Texas, 36 states also impose term limits

Source: Data from *The Book of the States*, 2011 (Lexington, KY: Council of State Governments, 2009), Tables 4.2 and 4.9

Hierarchical *versus* Plural Executives

Like the national government, Alaska, Hawaii, and Maine have hierarchical executive systems in which the chief executives appoint important executive officers as subordinates. Most other states have a plural executive system in which several major executives are independently elected and are not answerable to the governor. However, few states elect as many executive officers as Texas. Seven states have abolished the office of lieutenant governor as an executive elected statewide, and some have made offices as important as the attorney general appointed rather than elected. Rarely are comptrollers or land, educational, or agricultural officers elected as they are in Texas. Critics charge that electing so many executives confuses voters about lines of administrative responsibility and about whom they should hold accountable for problems in state government.

The Texas Constitution mentions even public notaries, thereby making them constitutional officers even though they are not elected.

FOR DEBATE

1. Should Texas follow the lead of the national government and most states and impose constitutional term limits on its chief executive? Or, should voters be left the right to decide how many terms their governor may serve when they decide to reelect or defeat the incumbent?

2. Does a hierarchical executive system allow for streamlining, coordination, and efficiency by a highly visible chief executive's office that the public can easily hold accountable? Or, does a centralized executive system concentrate too much power in the hands of the governor and allow the chief executive to appoint officers that the public should be allowed to elect?

Budgetary power

The power to propose a spending plan to the legislative body; a power limited for Texas's governor because of the competing influences of the Legislative Budget Board.

Item veto

Executive authority to veto sections of a bill and allow the remainder to become law.

Reduction veto

The power of some governors to reduce amounts in an appropriations bill without striking them out; Texas's governor does not have this power.

Pocket veto

Chief executive's power to kill legislation by simply ignoring it after the end of the legislative session; this power is not available to Texas's governor.

The statutes and the constitution combine to make the governor a relatively weak executive, but the veto gives the governor effective influence over legislation. Texas's legislature has not mustered the necessary two-thirds vote to override a governor's veto in more than 40 years. The Texas legislature often lacks the opportunity to override a veto because major legislation may be adopted during the last days of the session. The Texas Constitution allows the governor 10 days to act during the session and 20 days after it adjourns. During the final 10 days, the governor may avoid the threat of an override by simply waiting until the legislature adjourns before vetoing the bill.

Texas is among 43 states that give the governor the **item veto** power to strike out particular sections of an appropriations bill without vetoing the entire legislation. Several states also allow their governors to item veto matters other than appropriations, but Texas does not. The governor of Texas lacks both the **reduction veto** (to reduce appropriations without striking them out altogether) and the **pocket veto** (to kill bills simply by ignoring them after the end of the session). To become effective, Texas's governor must maximize influences within the majority party, access to publicity, appointive powers, the veto, and the power to call special sessions. Otherwise, a governor can become hemmed in by constitutional and statutory restraints.

Courts

Just as the constitution limits the power of the chief executive, Article 5 also fragments the court system. Texas is the only state other than Oklahoma that has two courts of final appeal—the highest court for civil matters is the nine-member Texas Supreme Court; the other, for criminal matters, is the nine-member Texas Court of Criminal Appeals. Leaving some flexibility as to number and jurisdiction, the constitution also creates courts of appeals, as well as district, county, and justice of the peace courts. The same article describes the selection of grand and trial juries and such administrative officers as sheriff, county clerk, and county and district attorneys.

The number and variety of courts are confusing to the average citizen, and coordination and supervision are minimal. State courts have also come under attack due to the lack of qualified judges. The constitution specifies only general qualifications for county judges and justices of the peace, who need not be lawyers. There may have been good reasons for lay-people to serve as judges in a simple, rural setting, but today many Texans regard them as an anachronism.

The manner of selecting judges is another factor that affects their qualifications, in that Texas judges are chosen in **partisan elections**, in which they run as Democrats or Republicans. Trial judges are elected to serve for four years and appeals court judges for six, but judges traditionally leave office before the end of their last term. The governor has the power to fill most vacancies until the next election—a power that gives the governor enormous influence over the makeup of the courts because, once in office, judges are usually returned to office without serious challengers in the next election.

Partisan elections

General elections in which candidates are nominated by political parties, and their party labels appear on the ballot.

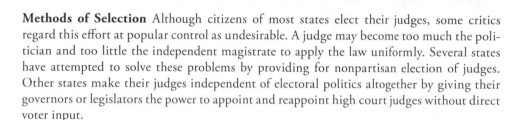

HOW DOES TEXAS COMPARE?
Selecting Judges

Methods of Selection Although citizens of most states elect their judges, some critics regard this effort at popular control as undesirable. A judge may become too much the politician and too little the independent magistrate to apply the law uniformly. Several states have attempted to solve these problems by providing for nonpartisan election of judges. Other states make their judges independent of electoral politics altogether by giving their governors or legislators the power to appoint and reappoint high court judges without direct voter input.

Appointive-Elective Plans Many states have attempted to combine the advantages of appointment with the benefits of election. In some states, the governor appoints a judge for the first term, after which the judge must run for reelection against candidates who may file for the office. Different states use some variation of the **merit plan** (also known as the Missouri Plan), in which the governor must make an appointment from a list nominated by a judicial qualifying commission for an initial term after which voters decide whether to retain the appointed judge based on his or her record.

Merit Plan

A method of selecting judges based on the candidate's qualifications rather than politics. Under this system, the governor fills court vacancies from a list of nominees submitted by a judicial commission, and these appointees later face retention elections. Also known as the Missouri Plan.

Life Terms Like the founders of the U.S. Constitution, two of the original thirteen states continue to strive for complete judicial independence by setting no term length at all for their supreme court judges. Rhode Island and Massachusetts allow high court judges to serve for terms of good behavior until retirement with no need to be reappointed or reelected. Figure 3.2 shows the methods used to select supreme court judges in various states.

FOR DEBATE

1. Should Texas consider adopting a merit plan in an effort to focus the judicial selection process on qualifications and reduce the effects of special interest campaign contributions? Or, should voters be allowed to elect judges in partisan elections just as they elect other officials?

2. How would Texans react to lifetime terms for its highest court judges? Why?

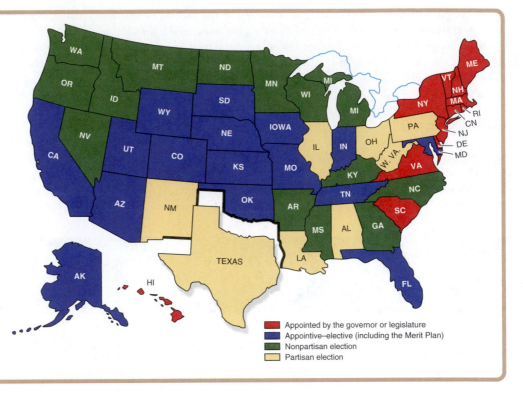

Figure 3.2
State-by-State Selection of Supreme Court Judges

Sources: Based on data from Bureau of Justice Statistics, *State Court Organization, 2004* NCJ 212351, National Center for State Courts, February 2011; *The Book of the States, 2011* (Lexington, KY: Council of State Governments, 2011), Table 5.6.

What are the advantages of partisan election of judges? Why would some reformists support a merit plan for judge selection?

Legend:
- Appointed by the governor or legislature
- Appointive–elective (including the Merit Plan)
- Nonpartisan election
- Partisan election

Local Government

Texas's constitution subordinates local governments to the state, and it decentralizes government power by assigning many state responsibilities to local governments, especially counties. As a result, the constitution describes a rigid organizational structure for counties in Articles 9 and 16, and voters of the entire state were once required to approve amendments so individual counties could abolish unneeded offices like treasurer, weigher, or surveyor. The constitution now authorizes county voters to abolish certain offices, but there is no provision for county home rule. As in state government, the constitution divides and diffuses county powers through a plural executive system.

The legislature has the power to set up structures for city governments and offers municipalities several standard alternative *general-law charters*. Cities with populations of more than 5000 may adopt *home-rule charters* that establish any organizational structure or program that does not conflict with state law or the constitution (see Chapter 14).

Generally, the legislature has the power to provide for the establishment of limited-purpose local governments known as special districts. Numerous special districts are also established by the constitution itself, and to eliminate one of these requires an amendment. Many of them have been created to perform functions that general-purpose local governments, such as counties and cities, cannot afford because of constitutional tax and debt limits. Arising out of constitutional restrictions, *special districts* have multiplied taxing and spending authorities and, except for school districts, operate largely outside the public's view.

Suffrage

Suffrage
The legal right to vote.

A major function of the state and local governments is to determine the character of democracy in America as they set requirements for **suffrage** (the legal right to vote) and administer elections. Article 6 of the Texas Constitution deals with suffrage requirements. It denies the right to vote to persons under age 18, certain convicted felons, and individuals found mentally incompetent by a court of law. We will extensively discuss the development of Texans' suffrage rights in Chapter 4.

Although constitutional restrictions on their qualifications are now as minimal as any in the nation, Texas voters still lack certain opportunities to participate in state government. **Initiative** (registered voters proposing statutory or constitutional changes by petition), **referendum** (voters approving changes in law by election), and **popular recall** (citizens petitioning for a special election to remove an official before his or her term expires) are available in many other states and even in some Texas cities, but not for statewide issues in Texas.

Texas permits voters to decide directly on only three matters: constitutional amendments, the state income tax, and legislative salaries. Texas's political parties sometimes place referenda on their primary ballots, but the results are not legally binding.

AMENDING AND REVISING THE TEXAS CONSTITUTION

Given the level of detail in the Texas Constitution, it is frequently necessary to amend it to reflect changing realities. The number of amendments indicates that Texans understand the need to amend the constitution, even though they have steadfastly resisted any attempts to systematically revise it.

Amendment Procedures

Article 17 of the Texas Constitution provides that the **proposal of constitutional amendments** must be by two-thirds of the total membership of each house of the legislature (at least 21 senators and 100 representatives). **Ratification** of constitutional amendments requires approval by a majority of those persons voting on the amendment in either a general or a special election. Because such an extraordinary majority of legislators must agree merely to propose constitutional amendments, a number of them are relatively uncontroversial. Historically, voters have approved more than 70 percent of proposed constitutional amendments.

Initiative

An election method that allows citizens to place a proposal on the ballot for voter approval. If the measure passes, it becomes law (permitted in some Texas cities but not in state government).

Referendum

An election that permits voters to determine if an ordinance or statute will go into effect.

Popular recall

A special election to remove an official before the end of his or her term, initiated by citizen petition (permitted in some Texas cities but not in state government).

Proposal of constitutional amendments

In Texas, the proposal of a constitutional amendment must be approved by two-thirds of the total membership of each house of the Texas legislature.

Ratification

Approval of a constitutional amendment by a majority of voters.

Texas INSIDERS

James Leininger and the Battle to Ban Same-Sex Marriage in the Texas Constitution

After the 2005 Texas legislature mustered the necessary two-thirds vote to propose the constitutional amendment to ban same-sex marriage in the Texas Constitution, Dr. James Leininger became the driving financial force in the campaign to persuade a majority of Texas voters to ratify it. Numerous pastors formed the Texas Restoration Project to attempt to register religious voters, and other ministers used their pulpits to support the amendment. Given Texans' conservative social attitudes, it was no real surprise when voters approved the ban on gay marriage with 76 percent of the vote, even though its opponents outspent its supporters 3 to 1. Today, 31 states have constitutional

(continued)

provisions that either forbid same sex-marriage or authorize the legislature to do so.

The battle to adopt a same-sex marriage ban resulted in an astonishingly easy victory for its supporters. Realizing the usual political tilt of Texans' public opinion, the ban's supporters made no futile effort to change voters' basic beliefs or their fundamental values. By presenting gay marriage as a threat to traditional marriage, the amendment's supporters sought to "spin" perspectives on the issue, tailoring their message to correspond to voters' preexisting attitudes. They targeted specific groups of potential voters who already shared their goals and mobilized sympathetic voters to turn out and vote. Especially in low-turnout elections, successful "get-out-the-vote" efforts to motivate latent supporters often determine the election outcome.

Thinking about the role of elites in Texas politics Explain, from this example, how Texas's political culture enables elites like Leininger to become a dynamic force in developing and implementing state policy.

Sources: National Conference of State Legislatures (www.ncsl.org/IssuesResearch/HumanServices/SameSexMarriage/tabid/16430/Default.aspx); Texans for Public Justice, "Sexual Persuasion: In Gay-Marital Amendment Spat, Tolerant Give More Than Intolerant," *Lobby Watch*, October 24, 2006 (info.tpj.org/Lobby_Watch/10-24-05_gaymarriage.html); Texans for Public Justice, "Rick Perry's Heavenly Host," August 2011 (http://info.tpj.org/reports/pdf/PerryLeiningerHeavenlyHost.pdf), "Who Is James Leininger?" *Texas Tribune*, August 26, 2011.

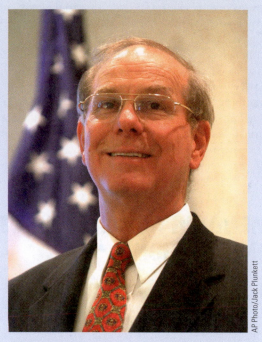
AP Photo/Jack Plunkett

Dr. James R. Leininger makes his money in the medical-device industry and spends much of it supporting numerous conservative and fundamentalist Christian causes. A co-founder of the Texas Public Policy Foundation, which has had much influence on Texas's tax and education policies, Leininger has also fought for conservative Christian candidates for the Texas State Board of Education, has battled to divert public funds to parochial and private schools (vouchers), and has become a major sponsor of Governor Perry's political career.

Explain why Leininger has been such a major force in Texas politics.

Criticisms of the Texas Constitution

The Texas Constitution is one of the longest, most detailed, and most frequently amended state constitutions in the nation. With 90,000 words, it is the second longest after Alabama's; with 474 amendments, it is the fourth-most-amended state constitution because Texans have often responded to emerging challenges by further amending their constitution. The constitution, reformers charge, is poorly organized and confusing to most of the state's citizens.

Critics argue that the state must resort to the amendment process often because the Texas Constitution is badly written. One sentence rambles on for 765 words, and several approach 300 words in length. The content is ambiguous and overlapping. For example, provisions dealing with local government are scattered throughout Articles 3, 5, 8, 9, 11, and 16. This poor draftsmanship has led to a restrictive interpretation of its provisions, public ignorance of its contents, and uncertainty as to its intentions.

Although only two state constitutions (along with the U.S. Constitution) contain fewer than 10,000 words, few are as restrictive as the Texas Constitution. The continuing need to amend detailed and restrictive state constitutions means that citizens are frequently called on to pass judgment on proposed amendments. Although some of the constitution's defenders maintain that giving Texas voters the opportunity to express themselves on constitutional amendments reaffirms popular control of government, voters display little interest in amendment elections. Faced with trivial, confusing, or technical amendments, often only 10 to 15 percent of the voting-age population votes on constitutional amendments, and, lately, turnout has been dropping into the single digits.

Attempts to Revise the Texas Constitution

Attempts to revise the constitution have met with successive failures. Ironically, in 1972, Texas voters had to amend the constitution to provide for its revision. Under the provisions of that amendment, the legislature established a constitutional revision commission of 37 members appointed by the governor, lieutenant governor, speaker of the house, attorney general, chief justice of the supreme court, and presiding judge of the court of criminal appeals. The commission made several proposals. Meeting in 1974, the legislature acted as a constitutional convention and agreed to many of these recommendations. However, the convention divided over the issue of a right-to-work provision to restrict organized labor, and the final document could not muster the two-thirds vote needed to submit the proposal to the electorate.

In the 1975 regular session, the legislature proposed eight constitutional amendments to the voters. Together, the proposed amendments were substantially the same as proposals the legislature had previously defeated. If they had been adopted, the amendments would have shortened the constitution by 75 percent through reorganization and by eliminating statute-like detail and deadwood. The legislature would have been strengthened by annual sessions, and a salary commission would have set the legislators' salary. Although limited to two terms, the governor would have been designated as the chief planning officer and given removal powers and certain powers of fiscal control. The court system would have been unified and its administrative procedure simplified. Local governments would have operated under broader home-rule provisions, and counties would have been authorized to pass general ordinances and to abolish unneeded offices.

Opponents' chief arguments were against more power for the legislature, greater government costs, and the possibility of an income tax—all of which are serious issues for many Texans. Because the legislature had written the proposals, it was easy for the Texas voter to see such things as annual sessions and flexibility concerning their salaries as a "grab for power" that would substantially increase government expenditures. Despite an emotional campaign, only 23 percent of registered voters cast ballots in the election, and they overwhelmingly rejected the proposed amendments.

HOW DOES TEXAS COMPARE?
Constitutions' Length, Detail, and Their Need for Amendments

As of 2013, the U.S. Constitution had been in effect for 224 years but had been formally amended only 27 times. It has endured mammoth and fundamental changes in government and society largely because it does not lock government into a rigid framework. Because the U.S. Constitution addresses only the most basic elements of government and leaves much to Congress, the president, and the courts, few formal amendments have been necessary.

The U.S. Constitution provides for a basically representative government; however, it was hardly democratic in the early years. During the Jeffersonian and Jacksonian eras, however, government became more democratic as political parties developed, states lowered suffrage requirements, and voters were allowed to choose electors in the electoral college.

The nineteenth century saw the growth of the new nation from 13 fledgling agricultural states on the Atlantic coast to a vast industrial and commercial nation stretching across a continent. In the twentieth century, America moved from the position of a third-rate international power to a dominant role in the world. Since the New Deal of the 1930s, government has been further transformed into a highly developed welfare state. Much of the nature of the national government is determined by statute, executive order, and court interpretation, so these changes did not require changing the language of the U.S. Constitution.

Although there is considerable variation among state constitutions (see Figure 3.3), most are much longer than the national constitution, and they frequently deal with details of both structure and policy. Consequently, as changing political and social conditions require changes in government structure and policy, formal constitutional amendments are necessary. The details of and the frequent amendments to state constitutions occur for several reasons:

1. Public officials, interest groups, and voters seem to view their state constitutions as more than the basic law of the state. They fail to make a clear distinction between *what ought to be* and *what ought to be in the constitution.* Thus all sorts of inappropriate details are included in the documents. A constitution is fundamental law; it deals with the basic principles of government. It is organic law—the superior law that establishes governing institutions and organizes their formal power relationship. Accordingly, constitutions ideally should describe how decisions will be made but not actually establish policies, which must change with political and social conditions.

2. States have added detailed amendments to overturn the effects of controversial court interpretations of general constitutional provisions. For example, supreme courts in Hawaii, Massachusetts, Iowa, New Jersey, and Vermont found that denying the benefits of marriage to same-sex couples was a violation of their state constitutions. As a result, Hawaii added a constitutional amendment to overturn the court decision that had allowed same-sex marriage, and a majority of other states (including Texas) have now added amendments to define marriage as an exclusively heterosexual right.

3. Institutions and interest groups frequently feel safer when their interests are protected in a constitution (which is more difficult to change than ordinary law). This has caused many state constitutions to become long lists of protections for vested interests.

4. State governments have a peculiar position in the federal system. They are presumed to have all the powers that have not been explicitly prohibited them. Thus citizens who are wary of strong governments have felt the need to impose detailed constitutional restrictions.

5. When state governments misuse their powers, the response is usually to place constitutional limitations and restrictions on those powers. The result is a longer constitution but probably not a more responsible government. A government bound by a rigid constitution cannot respond effectively to changing needs. Excessive restrictions may actually guarantee unresponsive and hence irresponsible government.

Most state constitutions are poorly written and arranged. Some provisions are so poorly drafted that they are interpreted to be even more restrictive than the constitution's framers intended and as a result, new amendments must be added to authorize states to perform vital functions in a modern society.

Although the process of amending the Texas Constitution is about as difficult as in other states, Texans have amended their constitution 474 times since 1876, resulting in more than three times as many amendments as the average state. Only three state constitutions—those of South Carolina (497), California (525), and Alabama (854)—have more amendments than Texas.

THE 50 STATES' CONSTITUTIONS COMPARED

Characteristic	Texas Constitution	U.S. Constitution	50-State Average
Length (words)	90,000	7,575	38,427
Amendments	474	27	147
Age (years)	137	224	111
Frequency of amendment	3.5 per year	Once every 8 years	1.3 per year

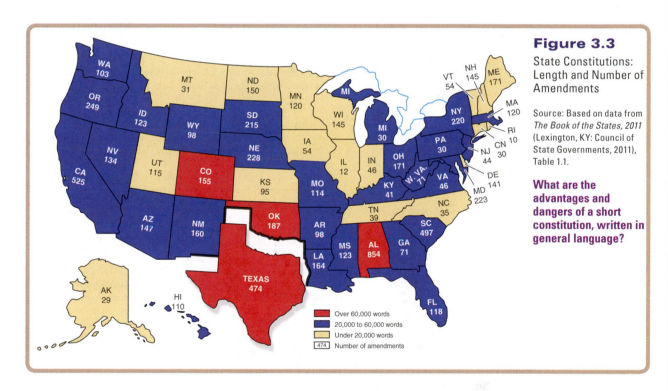

Figure 3.3
State Constitutions: Length and Number of Amendments

Source: Based on data from *The Book of the States, 2011* (Lexington, KY: Council of State Governments, 2011), Table 1.1.

What are the advantages and dangers of a short constitution, written in general language?

Legend:
- Over 60,000 words
- 20,000 to 60,000 words
- Under 20,000 words
- 474 Number of amendments

FOR DEBATE

1. Critics argue that Texas's constitution should be written in general language, details should be omitted, and day-to-day decisions should be left to the legislature, the governor, and the courts. Would shortening the constitution give too much power to state government?

2. Does the frequent need to amend the state's constitution empower the people?

Reconstituting Texas: E. J. Davis and His Legacies

By Timothy Hoye,
Texas Woman's University

E. J. Davis remained loyal to the United States, and his service in the Union army was a bitter reminder of Texas's defeat in the Civil War.

INTRODUCTION

During the decade that followed the Civil War, Texas went from a period of Reconstruction to one of reconstitution. In the aftermath of the war, the drive to guarantee former slaves their political and civil rights created racial resentment among many white Texans, and the centralization of state power at the same time created an antigovernment political environment that resulted in the writing of Texas's current constitution. The restrictiveness in the state constitution is a direct result of the attitudes of those who wrote and ratified it.

Louis Menand begins his Pulitzer Prize–winning study of post–Civil War America by observing the "remarkable fact" that the United States fought a civil war "without undergoing a change in its form of government."[3] The same cannot be said of Texas.

After the war, Texans faced the daunting task of reconstituting themselves in the shadow of defeat and occupation by Union forces. When Union troops began to occupy Texas in May and June of 1865, a four-year period began of military rule punctuated by clashes between former secessionists and Unionists. Early postwar attempts to reestablish order were frustrated by conflicting agendas between and among the Union army, the newly established Freedmen's Bureau, President Andrew Johnson, a resurgent Democratic Party in Texas, and Radical Republicans in both the United States Congress and in Texas.

Clear Reconstruction policies would be established when, on March 2, 1867, the Radical Republicans in Washington prevailed among the contending postwar factions. With passage of the First Reconstruction Act, military rule was strengthened, many local officials were removed from office by order of the military, and their replacements were required to take a Test Oath that they had never borne arms against the United States. Radical Reconstruction also required former

How did resentments against Governor Davis lead to the writing of the current Texas Constitution?

Confederate states to ratify the Thirteenth, Fourteenth, and Fifteenth Amendments to the U.S. Constitution, and Texas was required to write a constitution to replace the one it had ratified in 1866.

In 1867, Texas held its election to select delegates for a state constitutional convention—the first statewide election in which African Americans could vote in Texas.[4] From June 1868 to February 1869 delegates met in convention at Austin. Eventually, in July 1869, Texas voters ratified a new constitution. With support from President Ulysses S. Grant, Edmund J. Davis was elected governor in December 1869 and assumed office the following January. The 12th Texas Legislature was also elected and, in February 1870, the new legislature voted to adopt the Fourteenth and Fifteenth Amendments to the U.S. Constitution, chose two United States senators, and completed requirements for readmission to the Union. On March 30, 1870, President Ulysses S. Grant signed an act restoring Texas to the Union.

E. J. Davis, the 1869 Constitution, and Ex Parte Rodriguez

The implementation of the new constitution and Governor Davis's actions under it would create much resentment within more traditional circles in Texas and, in time, lead to considerable reaction and, by most readings, a considerable reactionary reconstituting of Texas in the mid-1870s. Much of the resentment was race based and "violence against blacks was both widespread and brutal."[5]

[3]Louis Menand, *The Metaphysical Club: A Story of Ideas in America* (New York: Farrar, Straus, and Giroux, 2001), p. ix.
[4]James Alex Baggett, "Origins of Early Texas Republican Party Leadership," *The Journal of Southern History* 40 (August 1974), 450.
[5]Gregg Cantrell, "Racial Violence and Reconstruction in Texas, 1867–1868," *Southwestern Historical Quarterly* 93 (July 1989–April 1990), 335.

Texas State Library and Archives Commision

The previous 1866 Constitution had denied African Americans the right to vote, to hold office, and to serve on juries and provided for segregated schools. The 11th Texas legislature, meeting in the fall of 1866, passed laws denying African Americans the right to testify in court cases involving whites, denied them service in the state militia, created a separate insane asylum for freedmen, and established segregation on the railroads.

The 1869 Constitution, by comparison, provided that "all freemen" have "equal rights" (Article 1, Section 2), and that no citizen will "ever be deprived of any right, privilege, or immunity, nor be exempted from any burdens, or duty, on account of race, color, or previous condition" (Article 1, Section 21). In fact, although African-American Republicans outnumbered white Republicans after 1867, they "did not dominate the party" in leadership positions. No African Americans received a cabinet post in the Davis administration.[6] Of the 90 delegates at the constitutional convention of 1868/1869, only nine were African American. In addition, the highest government position achieved by African-American Republicans during this time was to the office of state senator, and only three were elected.[7]

Other resentments derived from the Davis administration's response to the problem of increased violence and lawlessness in Texas. The legislature created both a state militia and a state police force, with the former often assisting the latter. Complaints of inappropriate police behavior were numerous, such as using police to protect and promote Republican candidates and voters while neglecting the opposition. Governor Davis, similarly, used martial law to enforce order in Madison, Hill, Walker, Limestone, and Freestone counties.

The creation of a "highly centralized" system of public schools was also heavily criticized. The state selected teachers, shaped the curriculum, made attendance compulsory, and included the education of African Americans. Other actions of the Republican-dominated legislature delayed the first election to be held after the readmission of Texas to statehood, gave the governor numerous additional appointive powers at the local level, provided considerable subsidies to railroad interests, raised taxes, encouraged immigration, made homesteads easier to obtain, and tended to be soft regarding Indian policies.[8]

Opponents regarded these policies as excessive, and they saw the root problem as a constitution that granted too much power to the legislature, the executive branch, the judiciary, and to government in general. The constitution of 1869 provided for annual sessions of the legislature and gubernatorial appointment of the attorney general, the secretary of state, and all judicial positions, including appointments to the supreme court, a detail that would become especially important in the Ex Parte Rodriguez case that will be discussed in this section. Most important, for critics, the 1869 Constitution was the product of pressure from Washington and those who were perceived by many to be "radical" Republicans more concerned with punishing than reconstructing the southern states.

Growing opposition to the centralization of power established by a constitution of questionable legitimacy and to actions of a legislature counter to antebellum sentiments in Texas led to a coalition of moderate Republicans and Democrats who managed to gain control of the Texas House after the 1872 elections. The following year, on December 2, Texas voters elected Democrat Richard Coke governor by a two-to-one margin. Governor Davis, however, refused to step down, claiming that the election had been ruled unconstitutional by the Texas Supreme Court and that he was duty bound to enforce the court's decision.

The case in question was Ex Parte Rodriguez, better known to history as the semicolon case. The 1869 Constitution, in Article 3, Section 6, provided that elections "shall be held at the county seats of the several counties, until otherwise provided by law; and the polls shall be opened for four days.… " The state's position, supported by the newly elected Democrats, was that the legislature had "provided by law" new places and new times, both within the legislature's power under the constitution's language. Lawyers for Rodriguez, who was accused of voting twice in Harris County, argued that their client was not guilty because the election was illegal. The semicolon in the constitutional language, they argued, set the requirement for "four days" apart from the previous section and thereby beyond the legislature's power to change. The court sided with the Rodriguez claim and voided the election.

All of this became a moot point, however, when newly elected Democrats, in defiance of the court, took control of the legislative chambers under the protection of guards sent by Governor Davis to arrest them and declared the election valid. Governor Coke was sworn in on January 15, 1874, and Governor Davis resigned four days later. Democrats would control state government for the next hundred years.

The 1876 Reconstitution of Texas

For the better part of the last 137 years, it has been commonplace to see the present Texas Constitution as a reaction to the failings and outright corruption of Governor E. J. Davis and his radical Republican friends. Among the first tasks of the new Democrat-controlled legislature was to begin preparations for the rewriting of what nearly everyone in Austin thought a disastrous 1869 Constitution. In the summer of 1875, Texas voters approved a constitutional convention, which began deliberations on September 6. Ninety delegates, three from each of the existing thirty senatorial districts, gathered in Austin. Seventy-five of the delegates were Democrats and fifteen were Republicans, including six African Americans.

What resulted from the convention was the 1876 Constitution, a constitution routinely criticized as being too long, poorly organized, badly written, and containing too much statutory material. It has been amended more than 450 times, most recently with the addition of 7 amendments in November 2011. The biggest criticism, however, is that it is the product of reaction rather than proaction, of avoiding past errors rather than planning for the challenges of a modern Texas.

The Texas Constitution provides for a biennial legislature (Article 3), a weak chief executive (Article 4), an elected plural

---

[6]Merline Pitre, "A Note on the Historiography of Blacks in the Reconstruction of Texas," *Journal of Negro History* 66 (Winter 1981–1982), 341.

[7]Baggett, *The Journal of Southern History* 40, p. 442.

[8]Carl H. Moneyhon, "Reconstruction," *Handbook of Texas Online*, www.tshaonline.org/handbook/online/articles/mzr01

executive (Article 4), and elected judges (Article 5), none of which contributes to efficiency of government for a diverse, complex, and dynamic environment such as one finds in twenty-first-century Texas. All of this suggests that the challenge of reconstituting Texas continues to the present day and that a closer look at the constitutional legacy of E. J. Davis might be in order.

Numerous revisionist and postrevisionist scholars have "demonstrated nuances that need to be considered" in evaluating Governor E. J. Davis and his legacy.[9] A more complex picture has emerged of Davis's impact on the Texas political landscape during the Reconstruction period. Traditionally, his legacy is one of tyranny and corruption, the legacy of an ambitious, overreaching governor. Increasingly, he is less the vilified governor and more a leader in the attempt to reconstitute Texas with a modern constitution providing strong institutions of government.

JOIN THE DEBATE

1. Which state government policies led to the antigovernment sentiment that dominated the political environment during the writing of Texas's constitution of 1876? Which constitutional provisions reflect these antigovernment sentiments today?

2. How can a constitution balance fear of excessive government power with the need for responsible government action?

3. If Texans were to reconstitute the state political system today, how would it differ from the one established in 1876? Would Texans agree with Governor E. J. Davis's vision of a modern state?

[9]Barry A. Crouch, "'Unmanacling' Texas Reconstruction: A Twenty-Year Perspective," *Southwestern Historical Quarterly* 93 (July 1989–April 1990), p. 282.

CHAPTER SUMMARY

★ Constitutions are always the result of a political process in which framers reflect their values, hopes, and fears. The current Texas Constitution was written in the period following Reconstruction after the U.S. Civil War. Most white Texans viewed the Reconstruction state government as extravagant, tyrannical, and abusive. In 1875, an elected state constitutional convention reacted to the Reconstruction regime by limiting state government in almost every imaginable way. Voters overwhelmingly approved the convention's work in 1876.

★ The Texas Constitution includes a bill of rights that is more expansive than those in most state constitutions, including protections for homesteads, debtors, and the mentally ill. The Texas Constitution includes an Equal Rights Amendment to forbid discrimination by sex.

★ The Texas Constitution follows the national pattern by establishing a separation of powers between legislative, executive, and judicial branches.

★ The Texas Constitution strictly limits the sessions and salaries of state legislators and includes many statute-like details that the legislature cannot change without a constitutional amendment. Special sessions are especially restricted, and procedures in both regular and special sessions are circumscribed.

★ The governor of Texas is limited in his or her role as chief executive because Texas has a plural executive system that includes many independently elected executives over which the governor has no control. The governor lacks most of the powers of typical executives to hire, fire, direct, and budget. Although Texas has had some powerful governors, such as Allan Shivers, John Connally, and Rick Perry, they became effective despite the constitution—not because of it.

★ The power of the courts to interpret the Texas Constitution is limited by the document's detail. Texas divides its final courts of appeal into two bodies—the Court of Criminal Appeals and the Texas Supreme Court—and also establishes intermediate courts of appeals and district, county, and justice of the peace courts. Judges are chosen in partisan elections. Critics say that judges elected in this way may become too concerned with political matters.

★ County and special district governments are particularly limited by constitutional and statutory requirements. Only larger cities have the considerable flexibility of home rule and some allow citizen participation by initiative, referendum, or recall. All local governments face debt and tax restrictions.

★ A constitution sets forth fundamental law that establishes essential governing principles and structures. Some state constitutions, like that of Texas, also go beyond those essentials to establish many details of routine government and require frequent amendment to reflect new realities. It is difficult for the state government to develop effective programs without first amending the constitution. Numerous amendments dealing with minor issues are added, like patches, to the constitution.

★ Critics find the Texas Constitution confusing. It contains not only the fundamentals of government but also detailed provisions concerning matters that might better be left to the ongoing institutions of government. It is long, it contains much deadwood, and many say that it is poorly drafted and disorganized. Reformers argue that a constitution should include only organic law; that is, it should organize responsible institutions of government. If it goes beyond fundamentals, it becomes a rigid legislative code that is difficult to change and can be baffling to voters.

HOW TEXAS COMPARES

Texas has one of the longest, most detailed, and most frequently amended state constitutions in the United States. More than most state constitutions, the Texas Constitution reflects a political culture that is skeptical of government.

★ Most large state legislatures meet annually for longer sessions, have more flexibility in passing statutes and budgets, and receive higher salaries than in Texas.

★ Most states have a stronger chief executive who can appoint, remove, direct, and budget more effectively than can the Texas governor.

★ Most top state judges are selected using either nonpartisan elections or some type of merit plan rather than the Texas system of partisan election.

★ Many states allow initiative, referendum, and popular recall; these are unavailable to Texas voters at the state level.

KEY TERMS

bicameral, *p. 63*
biennial regular session, *p. 64*
budgetary power, *p. 68*
checks and balances, *p. 63*
common law, *p. 58*
community property, *p. 58*
deadwood, *p. 66*
directive authority, *p. 67*

homestead, *p. 58*
indirect appointive powers, *p. 67*
initiative, *p. 71*
item veto, *p. 68*
legitimacy, *p. 57*
long ballot, *p. 58*
Merit Plan, *p. 69*
partisan elections, *p. 69*

plural executive, *p. 66*
pocket veto, *p. 68*
popular recall, *p. 71*
proposal of constitutional
    amendments, *p. 71*
ratification, *p. 71*
reduction veto, *p. 68*
referendum, *p. 71*

removal powers, *p. 67*
separation of powers, *p. 63*
special session, *p. 64*
statute-like details, *p. 66*
statutory law, *p. 62*
suffrage, *p. 70*
writ of habeas corpus, *p. 63*

REVIEW QUESTIONS

1. How does the Texas Constitution differ from the constitutions of other states and the U.S. Constitution?

2. What are the historical reasons for restrictions in Texas's constitution? What benefits did the state constitution's writers hope to achieve by limiting state government?

3. Describe the constitutional organization of each of the three branches of Texas government. How is the state's constitution amended?

4. Discuss the major constitutional provisions that restrain each branch of state government. What are the consequences of such restrictions?

5. What are the strengths and weaknesses of the Texas Constitution? Should it be revised? Why or why not?

LOGGING ON

The complete text of the Texas Constitution, all 17 articles, is at **www.constitution.legis.state.tx.us/**. In the index, click on Article 3, "Legislative Department." Click on Section 29 and notice that even the enacting clause for legislation is included in the constitution. Click on Article 16, Section 6, and notice the level of detail. Read the deadwood provision in Article 9, Section 14. Contrast the legislative and executive articles (3 and 4) of Texas's constitution with those of Illinois (Articles 4 and 5) at **www.ilga.gov/**.

Read constitutional amendments that have been recently proposed by the Texas legislature and a history of state constitutional amendments among publications at **www.tlc .state.tx.us/**.

Article 16, Section 50, of Texas's constitution protects homesteads against forced sale to collect on mortgages and other liens that exceed 80 percent of fair market value at the time the loan was made. Many believe this provision discouraged risky lending and borrowing and saved Texas from the worst of the real estate meltdown that affected much of the rest of the country. Compare Texas's foreclosure rates at **www.realtytrac.com/ trendcenter/** to see if the evidence supports this conclusion.

Article 3, Section 59 of Texas's constitution severely limits state debt. Research how effective these restrictions have been by comparing per capita debt among the 50 states at **www .taxfoundation.org/research/show/268.html**.

Chapter 4

Voting and Elections

LEARNING OBJECTIVES

★ Analyze the state election process.

★ Identify the leading predictors of whether a person votes.

★ Describe different forms of political participation.

★ Describe some of the ways that politicians have restricted the right to vote in Texas over the years.

★ Explain why voter turnout is low in Texas.

★ Describe the historical importance of the primary in Texas politics.

★ Describe how open and closed primaries differ.

★ Explain how candidates get on the ballot.

★ Identify the factors that provide the most advantages to candidates in Texas state elections.

★ Discuss why it is so difficult to control spending in Texas election campaigns.

© Glowimages / Getty Images, Inc.

GET *Active*

- ★ Act out, join the movement, start a street team, and register to vote at the Rock the Vote website: **www.rockthevote.com/home.html**.
- ★ Register to vote at the Texas Secretary of State's website: **www.sos.state.tx.us/elections/voter/reqvr.shtml**.
- ★ Check candidates' positions and find out which interest groups support them at the searchable website for Project Vote Smart at **votesmart.org/index.htm**.
- ★ Follow the money in Texas election campaigns at the excellent searchable website for the National Institute on Money in State Politics at **www.followthemoney.org/index.phtml**.
- ★ Check out election results at **www.sos.state.tx.us/elections/historical/index.shtml**.
- ★ Keep up with public opinion in Texas at **www.pollingreport.com/** and **www.rasmussenreports.com/public_content/politics/general_state_surveys/texas/**.
- ★ Follow Professor Rick Hasen's popular and well-respected election law blog at **http://electionlawblog.org/**.

One of the distinguishing features of Texas politics is the number and variety of elections held in the state. Texas elects a large number of officials to do different things at different levels of government. See for yourself: go to your county website and locate a sample ballot. To find your county's URL, go to **www.state.tx.us**. On this home page, under "Living," click on "Texas Cities and Counties," and then open the "County Directory."

Once you have located your county website, find a sample ballot. Ballots are usually stored on the county clerk's section of the site. You may be able to click on a link marked "Elections" or "County Clerk," although a site's structure is sometimes not so straightforward. In some instances, you may find that your county simply does not post a sample ballot. You might mention this in an email to the county clerk. Perhaps the clerk's office will send you one.

If your county website does not have a sample ballot, try another county's, such as Bexar, Dallas, Denton, El Paso, Harris, Jefferson, or Travis, all of which include a full sample ballot before primary and general elections. Examine the ballot from top to bottom, keeping in mind that it may take some time. Indeed, in some areas, people may be asked to vote for more than 100 different offices, from governor to railroad commissioner, from state representative to city council members, from state judges to county judges, justices of the peace, and constables. There are other offices as well, and often a constitutional amendment or two is included.

Learn about current elections at **www.localvoter.com**. Here you will find information about candidates and issues in your community, learn how to get involved, and get links to other resources.

Fact check Texas politicians' claims at **www.politifact.com/texas**.

Democracy makes demands on its citizens, in terms of both time and money. A sacrifice of time is required if voters are to inform themselves of the qualifications of the large number of candidates who compete in the spring for nomination in the party primaries. Then, in November, roughly 4,200 of these party nominees ask the voters to elect them in the general election to numerous local, state, and national offices.

POLITICAL PARTICIPATION

Voting in elections is the most basic and common form of political participation. Many people take part in other ways, such as discussing political issues with friends and co-workers, writing letters to local representatives or to newspaper editors, distributing campaign literature or contributing money to a campaign, and placing bumper stickers on cars. Some people are members of interest groups, whether neighborhood or trade associations, serve on political party committees, or act as delegates to conventions. Yet others participate in demonstrations or sit-ins, such as the flurry of Tea Party protests.

The Participation Paradox and Why People Vote

Elections, of course, are the defining characteristic of representative democracies. It is through our votes that we hold elected officials accountable. After all, votes are what matter to politicians, at least those interested in winning and holding office. If we vote—and reward and punish elected officials for what they do while in office—politicians have an incentive to do what we want. If we do not vote, elected officials are largely free to do what they want. Clearly, voting is important in a representative democracy.

The problem is that a single individual's vote is rarely decisive because few elections are decided by a single vote. This fact begs the question: Why do people vote? Among political scientists, this is known as the **participation paradox**. The point of this paradox is not to suggest that people should not vote but rather to highlight that they vote for other reasons.

Participation paradox

The fact that citizens vote even though a single vote rarely determines an election.

WHO VOTES?

Over the years, political scientists have learned quite a lot about why people go to the polls. It is now clear that a relatively small number of demographic and political variables are especially important.[1] The most important demographic variables are education, income, and age. The more education a person has, the more likely the person is to vote. The same is true for income, even controlling for education. Age also matters. As people grow older, they are more likely to vote, at least until they become very old. Why do these factors matter? The answer is straightforward: people who are educated, have high incomes, and are older are more likely to care about and pay attention to politics. Thus, they are more likely to vote.

In addition to demographic factors, certain political factors influence the likelihood of voting, especially one's expressed interest in politics and intensity of identification with political parties. The more a person is interested in politics, the more likely the person is to vote.

The effect is fairly obvious but nevertheless quite important. A person who does not have a lot of education or income is still very likely to vote if the person has a strong interest in politics.

Identification with either of the major political parties also makes a person more likely to vote. This pattern reflects the fact that strong partisan identifiers, on average, care a lot more about who wins than people who do not identify with the parties. It also reflects the mobilization of identifiers by the political parties—that is, the more one identifies

Did You Know? Although voting is the most common form of political participation, a much smaller number of Americans participate in other ways. In 2008, surveys indicate that 20 percent wore a button or displayed a bumper sticker, 13 percent donated money to a political party or campaign, 9 percent attended a political meeting or rally, and 5 percent worked for a political party or candidate.[2]

---

[1]Raymond E. Wolfinger and Steven Rosenstone, *Who Votes?* (New Haven, CT: Yale University Press, 1980). Also see Sydney Verba and Norman H. Nie, *Participation in America* (New York: Harper & Row, 1972).

[2]American National Election Studies, University of Michigan, www.electionstudies.org. Note that these numbers may overstate the actual levels of participation because they are difficult to verify, and we know that survey respondents tend to exaggerate turnout.

with a party, the more likely it is that the person will be contacted by the party and its candidates during election campaigns.

In one sense, deciding to vote is much like deciding to attend a sporting event, for example, a professional baseball game. We do not go to a game to affect the outcome. We go for other reasons, because we like baseball and care about it. The same is true for voting; education, income, age, interest, and party identification are important indicators of our desire to participate.

Of course, other factors are also important for explaining electoral participation, but the small set of demographic and political variables tells us quite a lot. With this information, we can pretty much determine whether a person will or will not vote in a particular election. We also can account for most of the differences in turnout among different groups, such as African Americans, Asian Americans, Latinos, and whites.

The Practice of Voting

The legal qualifications for voting in Texas are surprisingly few and simple. Anyone who is (1) a citizen of the United States, (2) at least 18 years of age, and (3) a resident of the state is eligible to register and vote in Texas. The only citizens prohibited from voting are those who have been declared "mentally incompetent" in formal court proceedings and those currently serving a sentence, parole, or probation for a felony conviction.

Establishing residence for voting is no longer a matter of living at a place for a specified time. Residence is defined primarily in terms of intent (that is, people's homes are where they intend them to be). No delay in qualifying to vote is permitted under U.S. Supreme Court rulings except for a short period of time in which the application is processed and the registrant's name is entered on the rolls. In accordance with the Court's ruling, that delay in Texas is fixed at 30 days.

Meeting these qualifications does not mean that a person can simply walk into the voting booth on election day. In order to vote, a person must be registered. As a result of the Voting Rights Acts of 1965 and 1970, a number of U.S. Supreme Court rulings, and congressional action, the registration procedure is almost as simple as voting itself. (This was not always true—see the Legal Constraints section.)

A person may register in person or by mail at any time of the year up to 30 days before an election. Since the passage of federal "motor voter" legislation, a person can also register when obtaining or renewing a driver's license; indeed, every person renewing a driver's license is asked whether he or she wants to register to vote. The secretary of state makes postage-free registration applications available at any county clerk's office and at various other public offices. Spouses, parents, or offspring also can register the applicant, provided that they are qualified voters.

Once they register, voters are automatically sent renewals at their address of record by January 1 in even-numbered years, but these renewals cannot be forwarded to new addresses. Thus voters are permanently registered unless their nonforwardable certificate is returned by mail to the voter registrar.

Names on returned certificates are stricken from the eligible voters list and placed on a strike list. The strike list is attached to the list of voters for each precinct; for three months, the previously registered voters whose names are on the strike list can vote in their old precincts if they have filled out a new voter registration card for the new residence. They can vote, however, only for those offices that both residences have in common. Thus, the person who has moved can vote on at least a portion of both the first and runoff primary ballots.

Coroners' reports, lists of felony convictions, and adjudications of mental incompetence are also used to purge the list of eligible voters. Anyone can purchase the computer-generated voter list for each county in the state. Political parties and candidates make extensive use of voter lists when trying to identify likely voters during election campaigns.

The present Texas registration system is as open and modern as that of any other state that requires advanced registration. A number of states, including Maine, Minnesota, and Wisconsin, permit election-day registration, and North Dakota has no registration at all. There, one just walks in, shows identification, and votes.[3]

Once registered, voting in Texas is fairly easy. Consider that in counties with a 5 percent or greater language minority, Texas requires that all ballots and election materials be printed in other languages in addition to English. Texas also was one of the first states to institute early voting, which allows people to vote at a number of different sites before election day. Indeed, many people who are unable to vote on election day can vote in advance by mail.

Recent decisions have halted the trend of making voting easier in Texas. Most notably, the legislature enacted a voter identification (ID) requirement in 2011. This law requires voters to show one of five forms of identification when they go to vote: a driver's license, military ID, a passport, a concealed handgun license, or a voter ID card that the state provides for free. There are arguments in favor of having a voter ID requirement and also arguments against it, though most observers expect it to dampen turnout, particularly among minorities. (It thus is more likely to hurt Democratic candidates.) In March, 2012, the U.S. Department of Justice raised an objection to the law (and a similar one in South Carolina), which puts the policy on hold. The federal courts will resolve the issue.

Voter Turnout in the United States and in Texas

Voter turnout

The percentage of people who are eligible to vote that actually vote.

Voting-age population (VAP)

The total number of persons in the United States who are 18 years of age or older, regardless of citizenship, military status, felony conviction, or mental state.

Making registration and voting easier was expected to result in increased **voter turnout**— the proportion of eligible Americans who vote. Such has not been the case; indeed, the reverse has been true. Since 1960, turnout has actually declined. This is not to suggest that the actual number of voters has diminished. In fact, the number has steadily increased, from 70.6 million votes for president in 1964 to an estimated 129 million votes in 2012— an increase of 83 percent. However, the number of voting-age Americans increased from 114.1 million to 231 million during the same period—an increase of more than 100 percent. Thus the **voting-age population (VAP)** has grown at a much faster rate than the actual voting population.[4]

Figure 4.1 shows voter turnout in presidential elections from 1932 to 2012. Voter turnout peaked in 1960 and has not reached that all-time high since. In 2012, turnout among the VAP was approximately 55 percent.[5] There are two main reasons for the decrease in voter turnout in the United States after the 1960s. The first reason can be traced to the Twenty-sixth Amendment, which lowered the voting age from 21 to 18 in 1972. The amendment was passed at the height of the Vietnam War, with proponents arguing that a person who could be drafted and sent off to war should be able to vote.

---

[3]*Do* note that some Republican-controlled legislatures have tried to repeal election-day registration and were successful in Montana and Maine, though voters in the latter overturned the decision in a referendum. Efforts to repeal still are under way in Wisconsin. In Democrat-controlled Connecticut, conversely, there are moves to institute election-day registration.

[4]The VAP is an imperfect measure of the voting-eligible population (VEP) because it includes people who cannot vote (noncitizens and felons) and excludes people who can (eligible citizens living overseas). Because the number of noncitizens and felons is large and the sum of these far exceeds the number of overseas eligibles, the VAP tends to exaggerate the actual VEP. In 2008, for example, the difference was substantial (approximately 18 million people). The VAP measure will therefore understate rates of participation. Unfortunately, reliable measures of VEP over long stretches of time are not readily available, particularly at the state level, which is why VAP is used here. For more information on measuring turnout, see the United States Elections Project at http://elections.gmu.edu.

[5]When the VEP is used (see footnote 4), the estimated turnout in 2012 was 60 percent, 5 points greater than estimated with the VAP.

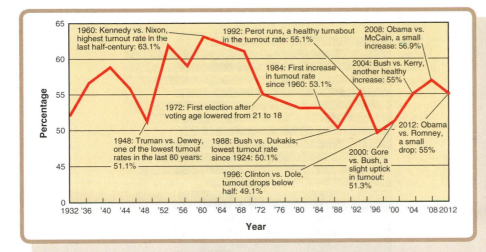

Figure 4.1

How Many People Vote in the United States? Presidential Election Turnout, 1932–2012

Here we see that turnout declined in the early 1970s but has not changed much during the last 30 years. Only a little more than 50 percent of the voting-age population now vote in presidential elections.

Describe the groups that are most likely to vote. Does one party or the other benefit more when there is a high turnout of voters?

By extending the vote to 18- to 20-year-old citizens, the amendment expanded the eligible voting population. As we have already seen, however, these young people are less likely to vote than are older persons—since they were given the right to vote, citizens in the 18- to 20-year-old age group have rarely posted turnout rates as high as 40 percent, even in presidential elections. Thus, adding the age group to the lists of eligible voters in 1972 slightly reduced the overall turnout rate. Second, identification with the two major political parties dropped substantially after the 1960s, and approximately one-third of all Americans now consider themselves *independents*, though the percentage has declined in recent years.[6] (The proportion is greater for younger voters.) As noted earlier, these voters are less likely to vote than are partisans.[7]

Turnout in American general elections is significantly lower than that in other industrialized democracies of the world. Figure 4.2 shows that in most comparable nations, voter turnout is approximately 20 percent higher than in the United States. Interestingly, American political attitudes seem more conducive to voting than those in countries with far higher turnouts. Low voter turnout in the United States is caused by other factors, including institutional structures (primarily the strength of political parties) and the fact that we require voters to register—in some nations, citizens are automatically registered to vote when they meet age requirements.[8]

---

[6]See Paul R. Abramson and John H. Aldrich, "The Decline of Electoral Participation in American," *American Political Science Review* 76 (June 1982), pp. 502–521.

[7]Some scholars attribute part of the decline in turnout to the increasing tendency toward divided government at the national level, where the president is from one political party and the majority in Congress is from the other. The argument is that divided government makes it more difficult for voters to assign responsibility for policy decisions and that, as a result, voters cannot easily reward or punish specific elected officials at the polls. See Mark N. Franklin and Wolfgang P. Hirczy de Mino, "Separated Powers, Divided Government, and Turnout in U.S. Presidential Elections," *American Journal of Political Science Review* 42 (January 1998), pp. 316–326.

[8]G. Bingham Powell, Jr., "American Voter Turnout in Comparative Perspective," *American Political Science Review* 80 (March 1986), pp. 17, 23. Switzerland, the only country studied where turnout is lower than in the United States, was not included in this computation.

Figure 4.2

Voter Turnout from around the World

The United States is most similar to India, Russia, and Tunisia.

Source: International Institute for Democracy and Electoral Assistance, www.idea.int

Why is turnout so far below what we observe in other established, industrialized democracies?

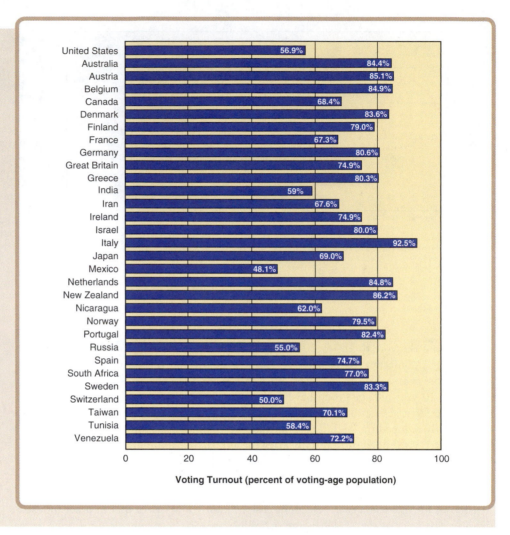

Voting Turnout (percent of voting-age population)

United States	56.9%
Australia	84.4%
Austria	85.1%
Belgium	84.9%
Canada	68.4%
Denmark	83.6%
Finland	79.0%
France	67.3%
Germany	80.6%
Great Britain	74.9%
Greece	80.3%
India	59%
Iran	67.6%
Ireland	74.9%
Israel	80.0%
Italy	92.5%
Japan	69.0%
Mexico	48.1%
Netherlands	84.8%
New Zealand	86.2%
Nicaragua	62.0%
Norway	79.5%
Portugal	82.4%
Russia	55.0%
Spain	74.7%
South Africa	77.0%
Sweden	83.3%
Switzerland	50.0%
Taiwan	70.1%
Tunisia	58.4%
Venezuela	72.2%

HOW DOES TEXAS COMPARE?
Voter Turnout in the State and Nation

Although national turnout declined somewhat after 1960, Table 4.1 shows that voter turnout in Texas (as in most of the South) has remained fairly stable at levels far below the national average. In the presidential elections of 2012, for example, Texas voter turnout was 41.9 percent, or 13 percent below the rest of the nation. That year, Texas had the lowest turnout rate of any state in the nation.

TABLE 4.1 Percentage of the Voting-Age Population Casting Ballots in Presidential General Elections, 1960–2012

	1960	1964	1968	1972	1976	1980	1984	1988	1992	1996	2000	2004	2008	2012
United States	62.8	61.9	60.6	55.5	53.3	52.6	53.1	50.1	55.2	49.1	51.3	55.4	56.9	55
Texas	41.8	44.4	48.7	45.3	46.2	44.9	47.2	45.5	49.1	41.3	43.1	45.5	45.6	41.9
Difference (Texas vs. United States)	21.0	17.5	11.9	10.2	7.1	7.7	5.9	4.7	6.1	7.8	8.2	10.0	10.3	13
Rank of Texas among the 50 states	44th	48th	43rd	43rd	44th	44th	45th	46th	46th	48th	48th	49th	49th	50th

Sources: Lester Milbrath, "Participation in the American States," in Herbert Jacob and Kenneth N. Vines (eds.), *Politics in the American States,* 2nd ed. (Boston: Little, Brown, 1971), pp. 38–39; *Statistical Abstract of the United States, 1976, 1979, 1983, 1986, 1989, and 1993* (Washington, DC: U.S. Government Printing Office); Federal Election Commission, "Voter Registration and Turnout," www.fec.gov; United States Elections Project, http://elections.gmu.edu/Turnout_2004G.html, http://elections.gmu.edu/Turnout_2008G.html. For 2012, turnout estimates are based on data from the Texas Secretary of State and VAP numbers are from the United States Elections Project.

In midterm elections, Texas's turnout has bounced around a lot from election to election but is consistently lower than in most other states (see Table 4.2). The turnout rate typically has been between 20 and 30 percent, and only Louisiana has consistently vied with Texas for the dubious honor of the lowest turnout in the nation.[9] In 2010, voter participation was 27.3 percent, lower than any other state.

TABLE 4.2 Percentage of the Voting-Age Population Casting Ballots in Nonpresidential General Elections, 1962–2010

	1962	1966	1970	1974	1978	1982	1986	1990	1994	1998	2002	2006	2010
United States	45.4	45.4	43.5	36.1	35.3	38.0	33.4	33.1	36.0	36.4	36.2	37. 1	37.8
Texas	25.8	20.9	27.5	18.4	24.1	26.2	25.5	26.8	31.3	6.1	28.8	25.8	26.7
Difference (Texas vs. United States)	19.6	24.5	16.0	17.7	11.2	11.8	7.9	6.3	4.7	10.3	7.4	11.3	11.1
Rank of Texas among the 50 states	43rd	50th	47th	49th	46th	48th	45th	42nd	45th	47th	49th	50th	50th

Sources: *Statistical Abstract of the United States, 1976, 1979, 1983, 1989,* and *1996* (Washington, DC: U.S. Government Printing Office); Federal Election Commission, "Voter Registration and Turnout," http://www.fec.gov; United States Elections Project, http://elections.gmu.edu/Turnout_2002G.html; http://elections.gmu.edu/Turnout_2006G.html; http://elections.gmu.edu/Turnout_2010G.html.

FOR DEBATE

1. What factors explain why Texas has such a low voter turnout compared to other states?

2. How would a higher voter turnout affect election results in Texas?

3. Should government take steps to encourage more people to vote? Why or why not?

[9]In Louisiana, the state and local contests are decided before the general election, so the motivation for voting is low. Louisiana's "blanket primary" ballot lists all candidates from all parties. If no one receives a majority of the votes in a given race, the top two vote recipients compete in a runoff primary, irrespective of political party affiliation, and the winner of the primary is elected.

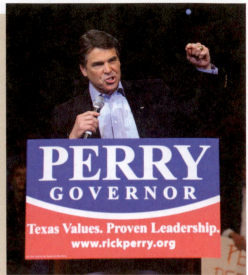

When former Houston Mayor Bill White challenged incumbent Governor Rick Perry in the 2010 election, only 27 percent of the voting age population turned out to vote.

Why do so few voters turn out in nonpresidential elections in Texas? Would a larger number of Texans cast their ballots for governor if the election were held at the same time as the presidential election?

Reasons for Low Voter Turnout in Texas

Most Texans probably think that Texas is in the mainstream of American society. Why, then, is there such a difference between Texas and other urbanized and industrialized states in its political behavior? Why does Texas compare more closely with states of the Deep South in voter turnout? The answer may lie in its laws, socioeconomic characteristics, political structure, and political culture.

Legal Constraints Traditionally, scholars interested in the variation in turnout across the American states have focused on laws regulating registration and voting. Clearly, the most important of these laws were the restrictions on who may vote, such as the poll tax, property ownership requirements, or the outright exclusion of African Americans and women.

Although these restrictions disappeared some time ago, other barriers to registration and voting persisted, and some remain in effect today.[10] One can ask: Does a state promote political participation by setting the minimum necessary limitations and making it as convenient as possible for the citizen to vote? Or, does a state repeatedly place barriers on the way to the polls, making the act of voting physically, financially, and psychologically as difficult as the local sense of propriety will allow? There is no doubt into which category Texas once fell—the application has been uneven, but historically Texas was among the most restrictive states in its voting laws.

---

[10]See Glenn Mitchell, II and Christopher Wlezien, "The Impact of Legal Constraints on Voter Registration, Turnout, and the Composition of the American Electorate," *Political Behavior* 17 (June 1995), pp. 179–202.

However, nearly all of these restrictions have been changed by amendments to the U.S. Constitution, state and national laws, rulings by the U.S. Department of Justice, and judicial decisions. Even a cursory examination of these restrictions and the conditions under which they were removed makes one appreciate the extent to which Texas's elections were at one time closed. Consider these changes in Texas voting policies:

1. *Poll tax.* The payment of a poll tax as a prerequisite for voting was adopted in 1902. The cost was $1.75 ($1.50 plus $0.25 optional for the county) and represented more than a typical day's wages for some time. Many poor Texans were kept from voting. When the Twenty-fourth Amendment was ratified in 1964, it voided the poll tax in national elections. Texas and only one other state kept it for state elections until it was held unconstitutional in 1966 (*United States* v. *Texas,* 384 U.S. 155).

2. *Women's suffrage.* An attempt was made to end the denial of the ballot to women in 1917, but the effort failed by four votes in the Texas legislature. Women were allowed to vote in the primaries of 1918, but not until ratification of the Nineteenth Amendment in 1920 did full suffrage come to women in Texas.

3. *White primary.* African Americans were barred from participating when the first party primary was held in 1906. When movement toward increased participation seemed likely, Texas made several moves to avoid U.S. Supreme Court rulings allowing African Americans to vote. Not until 1944 were the legislature's efforts to deny African Americans access to the primaries finally overturned (*Smith* v. *Allwright*, 321 U.S. 649).

4. *Military vote.* Until 1931, members of the National Guard were not permitted to vote. Members of the military began to enjoy the full rights of suffrage in Texas in 1965, when the U.S. Supreme Court voided the Texas constitutional exclusion (*Carrington* v. *Rash*, 380 U.S. 89).

5. *Long residence requirement.* The Texas residence requirement of one year in the state and six months in the county was modified slightly by the legislature to allow new residents to vote in the presidential part of the ballot, but not until a 1972 ruling of the U.S. Supreme Court were such requirements abolished (*Dunn* v. *Blumstein*, 405 U.S. 330).

6. *Property ownership as a requirement for voting in bond elections.* Texas held to this requirement until the U.S. Supreme Court made property ownership unnecessary for revenue bond elections in 1969 (*Kramer* v. *Union Free District No. 15*, 395 U.S. 621), and for tax elections in 1969 (*Cipriano* v. *City of Houma*, 395 U.S. 701), and in 1975 (*Hill* v. *Stone*, 421 U.S. 289).

7. *Annual registration.* Even after the poll tax was voided, Texas continued to require voters to register every year until annual registration was prohibited by the federal courts in 1971 (*Beare* v. *Smith,* 321 F. Supp. 1100).

8. *Early registration.* Texas voters were required to meet registration requirements by January 31, earlier than the cutoff date for candidates' filings and more than nine months before the general election. This restriction was voided in 1971 (*Beare* v. *Smith,* 321 F. Supp. 1100).

9. *Jury duty.* Texas law provided that the names of prospective jurors must be drawn from the voting rolls. Some Texans did not like to serve on juries, and not registering to vote ensured against a jury summons. (Counties now use driver's licenses for jury lists.)

Texas used almost every technique available except the literacy test and the grandfather clause[11] to deny the vote or to make it expensive in terms of time, money, and aggravation. This is not the case today. Most barriers to voting in Texas have been removed, and as was mentioned previously, the legislature has instituted a number of provisions that make voting

---

[11]The grandfather clause gave white citizens who were disenfranchised by poll tax or literacy requirements the right to vote if they had been eligible to vote before the passage of the restricting legislation. These laws were found unconstitutional by the U.S. Supreme Court in *Guinn* v. *United States*, 238 U.S. 347 (1915).

easier than in most states. Thus, the laws in Texas may help us understand why turnout was low in the past and, with the relaxing of restrictions, why turnout has increased somewhat since 1960. The current laws do not help us understand why turnout in Texas remains low today. For this, we need to look elsewhere.

Socioeconomic Factors Texas is known as the land of the "big rich" cattle barons and oil tycoons. What is not so well known is that Texas is also the land of the "big poor" and that more than 4 million persons—more than in any other state—live in poverty here. Although nationally the proportion of people living below the poverty level in 2010 was 15.3 percent, in Texas the proportion was 17.9 percent. For African-American and Latino Texans, almost 25 percent have incomes below this level. Of the more than 4 million individuals in Texas living in poverty, more than one-third are children. Understandably, formal educational achievement is also low. Of Texans older than 25 years of age, one in four has not graduated from high school. Among African Americans, the ratio is just less than one of three, and among Latinos, it is almost one of two.[12]

Given that income and education are such important determinants of electoral participation, low voter turnout is exactly what we should expect in Texas. Because income and education levels are particularly low among African Americans and, especially, Latinos, turnout is particularly low for these groups. Voting by Texas minorities is on the rise, however, and this has led to much greater representation of both groups in elected offices, as we will see. These trends should continue as income and education levels among minorities increase.

Signing petitions and attending rallies are important forms of political participation. Although people are less likely to vote in the United States and especially in Texas, by comparison with people in other countries, they are more likely to take part in other ways.

Identify forms of participation other than voting. Which forms of participation have the greatest impact on Texas's

---

[12]U.S Census Bureau, http://www.census.gov/prod/2011pubs/acsbr10-01.pdf and http://www.census.gov/hhes/www/poverty/data/threshld/thresh10.xls. The definition of *poverty* depends on the size and composition of the family. For a family of four (two adults and two children), the threshold in 2010 was an annual income of $22,314 or less.

Political Structure Another deterrent to voting in Texas is the length of the ballot and the number of elections. Texas uses a long ballot that provides for the popular election of numerous public officers (whom some people believe should be appointed). In an urban county, the ballot may call for the voter to choose from as many as 150 to 200 candidates vying for 50 or more offices. The frequency of referendums on constitutional amendments contributes to the length of the ballot in Texas. Voters are also asked to go to the polls for various municipal, school board, bond, and special-district elections. Government is far more fragmented in Texas than in other states, and the election of so many minor officials may be confusing and perhaps a lot more frustrating for voters.

Political Culture Insights into voter participation levels have been derived from the concept of political culture, which, as defined in Chapter 1, describes the set of political values and beliefs that are dominant in a society. Borrowed from social anthropologists, this concept has been found to be applicable to all political systems, from those of developing countries to modern industrial democracies. It has been especially useful in the study of American politics, where federalism has emphasized the diversity among regions, states, and communities—a diversity that cries out for some approach that can effectively explain it.

As we saw in Chapter 1, the American political culture is actually a mix of three subcultures, each prevalent in at least one area of the United States.[13] The *moralistic culture* is a product of the Puritan era and is strongest in New England. The *traditionalistic culture* comes to us via the plantation society of the Deep South. The *individualistic culture* was born in the commercial centers of the Middle Atlantic states, moving west and south along the Ohio River and its tributaries. It is the mix as well as the isolation of these cultures that gives American politics its flavor.

Important to students of electoral politics is that "the degree of political participation (i.e., voter turnout and suffrage regulations) is the most consistent indicator of political culture."[14] The moralistic culture perceives the discussion of public issues and voting as not only a right but also an opportunity that is beneficial to the citizen and society alike. In contrast, the traditionalistic culture views politics as the special preserve of the social and economic elite and a process of maintaining the existing order. Highly personal, it views political participation as a privilege and uses social pressure as well as restrictive election laws to limit voting. The individualistic culture blurs the distinction between economic and political life. Here business and politics are both viewed as appropriate avenues by which an individual can advance his or her interests, and conflicts of interest are fairly common. In this culture, business interests can play a very strong role, and running for office is difficult without their support.

Low voter turnout in Texas may be due in part to the state's political culture, which is a mix of the traditionalistic and the individualistic. The traditionalistic aspect is especially characteristic of East Texas, settled primarily by immigrants from the Deep South in the years prior to the Civil War. The individualistic aspect predominates throughout the rest of the state. As a result, participation in politics is not as highly regarded as it is in other states, particularly those with a moralistic culture, and politics in Texas is largely the domain of business interests. People may be less likely to vote in Texas because they do not value political participation itself and because they tend to think that they play only a little role in politics.

---

[13]Daniel J. Elazar, *American Federalism: A View from the States*, 3rd ed. (New York: Harper & Row, 1984).
[14]David C. Saffel, *State Politics* (Reading, MA: Addison-Wesley, 1984), p. 8.

ELECTIONS IN TEXAS

Winning an office is typically a two-stage process. First, the candidate must win the Democratic or Republican Party nomination in the primary election. Second, the candidate must win the general election against the other party's nominee. It is possible for a candidate to get on the general-election ballot without winning a primary election (as will be discussed shortly), but this is rare. As in most other states, elections in Texas are dominated by the Democratic and Republican parties.

Primary Elections

Three successive devices for selecting political party nominees have been used in the history of this country, each perceived as a cure for the ills of a previously corrupt, inefficient, or inadequate system. The first was the caucus, consisting of the elected political party members serving in the legislature. The "insider" politics of the caucus room motivated the reformers of the Jackson an era to throw out "King Caucus" and to institute the party convention system by 1828. In this system, ordinary party members select delegates to a party convention, and these delegates then nominate the party's candidates for office and write a party platform. The convention system was hailed as a surefire method of ending party nominations by the legislative bosses. By 1890, the backroom politics of the convention halls again moved reformers to action, and the result was the **direct primary**, adopted by most states between 1890 and 1920. Texas's first direct primary was held in 1906, under the Terrell Election Law passed in 1903. It enables party members to participate directly in their party's selection of a candidate to represent them in the general election.

Direct primary
A method of selecting the nominees from a political party where party members elect the candidates who represent them in the general election.

Traditionally regarded as private activities, primaries were at one time largely beyond the concern of legislatures and courts. Costs of party activities, including primaries, were covered by donations and by assessing each candidate who sought a party's nomination. Judges attempted to avoid suits between warring factions of the parties as much as they did those involving church squabbles over the division of church property. This was the perception on which the U.S. Supreme Court upheld in 1935 the Texas Democratic Party convention's decision barring African Americans from participating in the party primary.[15] Because political party activities were increasingly circumscribed by law, the Court reversed itself in 1944 and recognized the primary as an integral part of the election process.[16]

It argued that in a one-party state, which Texas was at the time, the party primary may be the only election in which any meaningful choice is possible. Because the Democratic Party seldom had any real opposition in the general election, winning the nomination was, for all practical purposes, winning the office. The party balance in Texas has changed quite a lot in recent years, however. The Republicans have overtaken the Democrats and now hold every statewide elected office.

Who Must Hold a Primary?
Any party receiving 20 percent of the gubernatorial vote must hold a primary, and all other parties must use the convention system.[17] New parties must meet additional requirements if their nominees are to be on the general-election ballot. In addition to holding a convention, these parties must file with the secretary of state a list of supporters equal to 1 percent of the total vote for governor in the last general election. The list may consist of the names of those who participated in the party's convention, a

---

[15]*Grovey* v. *Townsend*, 295 U.S. 45 (1935).
[16]*Smith* v. *Allwright*, 321 U.S. 649 (1944).
[17]The La Raza Unida Party challenged this limitation. The Justice Department and federal courts sustained the challenge but only as it applied to La Raza Unida, which was permitted to conduct a primary in 1978. Otherwise, the law stands as written.

nominating petition, or a combination of the two. Persons named as supporters must be registered voters who have not participated in the activities (primaries or conventions) of either of the two major parties. Each page (although not each name) on the nominating petition must be notarized. Such a requirement is, as intended, difficult to meet and therefore inhibits the creation of new political parties.[18]

Financing Primaries Party primaries are funded partly by modest candidate filing fees, but most of the primaries' costs come from the state treasury. The parties' state and county executive committees initially make the expenditures, but the secretary of state reimburses each committee for the difference between the filing fees collected and the actual cost of the primary. To get on the party primary ballot, a candidate needs only to file an application with the state or county party chair and pay the prescribed fee. The categories of fees, applicable also for special elections, are summarized in Table 4.3.

So that no person is forced to bear an unreasonable expense when running for political office, the legislature provided that a petition may be submitted as an alternative to the filing fee. Such petition must bear the names of at least 5,000 voters for candidates seeking nomination to statewide office. For district and lesser offices, the petition must bear the signatures of voters equal to 2 percent of the vote for the party's candidate for governor in the last election, up to a maximum of 500 required signatures.

Administering Primaries In the county primaries, the chair and county executive committee of each party receive applications and filing fees and hold drawings to determine the order of names on the ballot for both party and government offices. They then certify the ballot, select an election judge for each voting precinct (usually the precinct chair), select the voting devices (paper ballots, voting machines, or punch cards), and arrange for polling places and printing. After the primary, the county chair and executive committee canvass the votes and certify the results of their respective state executive committees.

TABLE 4.3 Fees for Listing on the Party Primary Ballot in Texas, Selected Offices

Office	Fee
U.S. Senator	$5,000
U.S. Representative	$3,125
Texas Statewide Officers	$3,750
State Senator	$1,250
State Representative	$750
County Commissioner	$750–$1,250
District Judge	$1,500–$2,500
Justice of the Peace, Constable	$375–$1,000
County Surveyor	$75

How much do filing fees limit candidates' access to the state ballot? Should election laws attempt to discourage frivolous candidates?

---

[18]The necessity of notarizing the pages increases the difficulty. The application of technical aspects of the law and adverse interpretations are but a part of the harassment that minor parties and independents have traditionally encountered in their quest for a place on the ballot. For example, in 1976, the secretary of state interpreted the law as requiring that each signature must be notarized. The next year, the legislature specified that a notary need sign only each part of the petition. See Richard H. Kraemer, Ernest Crain, and William Earl Maxwell, *Understanding Texas Politics* (St. Paul, MN: West, 1975), pp. 155, 157.

In the state primary, the state party chair and the state executive committee of each political party receive applications of candidates for state offices, conduct drawings to determine the order of names, certify the ballot to the county-level officials, and canvass the election returns after the primary.

The Majority Rule

In Texas, as in other southern states (except for Tennessee and Virginia) that were once predominantly Democratic, nominations are by a majority (50% plus 1) of the popular vote. If no candidate receives a majority of votes cast for a particular office in the first primary, a **runoff primary** is required in which the two candidates receiving the greatest number of votes are pitted against each other. Outside the South, where the balance between the two major parties has traditionally been more equal, only a plurality of the votes (more votes than for anyone else) is required, and consequently no runoff is necessary.

Primary elections in Texas are held on the first Tuesday in March of even-numbered years. The runoff primary is scheduled for the fourth Tuesday in May or more than two months after the initial party primary election. Although there are earlier presidential primaries, no other state schedules primaries to nominate candidates for state offices so far in advance of the general election in November.

Turnout in Texas primaries is much lower than in general elections. Take 2010, for example: Despite competitive gubernatorial nomination contests, particularly in the Republican primary, only 2.1 million Texans voted, approximately 12 percent of the 18 million people who were 18 years of age or older. The people who do vote in primary elections are hardly representative of the population—they tend to be better educated, more affluent, and more ideologically extreme.

Closed Primary

Party primaries are defined as either *open* or *closed*. These terms relate to whether or not participation is limited to party members. Because the purpose of a primary is to choose the party's nominee, it may seem logical to exclude anyone who is not a party member. However, not every state recognizes the strength of that logic. Texas and 15 other states have an **open primary** in which voters decide at the polls (on election day) in which primary they will participate. Of course, a person is forbidden to vote in more than one primary on election day, and once she has voted in the first primary cannot switch parties and participate in the runoff election or convention of any other party. In contrast, the typical **closed primary** requires that a person specify a party preference when registering to vote. The party's name is then stamped on the registration card at the time of issuance. Each voter may change a party affiliation at any time up to 30 days (usually) before participating in a primary or a convention. Voters are limited, however, to the activities of the party they have formally declared as their preference. If the individual registers as an independent (no party preference), that person is excluded from the primaries and conventions of *all* parties. Twenty states have closed primaries.

Some states have a semiclosed (or semiopen) system, in which independents are allowed to vote in either primary. Five other states have a mixed system, where one party has an open and the other a closed (or semiclosed) primary. Another three states use a top-two primary, in which candidates from different parties compete in a single primary and the top two vote-getters proceed to the general election. Primary elections clearly differ quite a lot across states, but those differences have little bearing on the general election. Whether voters participate in a party primary or not, they are completely free to vote for any party candidate, the Democrat, the Republican, or another candidate in the general election in November.

Crossover Voting

The opportunity always exists in Texas for members of one political party to invade the other party's primary. This is called **crossover voting**. It is

---

Runoff primary

A second primary election that pits the two top vote-getters from the first primary, where the winner in that primary did not receive a majority. The runoff primary is used in states such as Texas that have a majority election rule in party primaries.

Open primary

A type of party primary where a voter can choose on election day in which primary they will participate.

Closed primary

A type of primary where a voter can participate only in the primary for the party of which they are a member.

Crossover voting

When members of one political party vote in the other party's primary to influence the nominee that is selected.

HOW DOES TEXAS COMPARE?
Term Limits in the States

Twenty-one states have instituted term limits for state legislative offices since 1990, though six of these states later repealed the limits. Thirty-six states have gubernatorial limits. Texas does not limit the terms of either legislators or the governor, but most neighboring states limit both, including Arkansas, Colorado, Louisiana, and Oklahoma. The remaining neighbor, New Mexico, only has gubernatorial term limits.

FOR DEBATE

Why do states institute term limits? What benefits do they have? What costs? Would the Texas public better represented with term limits? Why or why not?

designed to increase the chances that the nominee from the other party will be someone whose philosophy is like that of the invader's own party. For example, Democrats might cross over to vote for the more moderate candidate in the Republican primary, or Republicans might cross over into the Democratic primary to support the candidate who is least objectionable from their viewpoint.

General Elections

The purpose of party primaries is to nominate the party's candidates from the competing intra-party factions. General elections, in contrast, are held to allow the voters to choose from among the competing political party nominees and write-in candidates—the people who will actually serve in national, state, and county offices. General elections differ from primaries in at least two other important ways. First, general elections are the official public elections to determine who will take office; thus, they are administered completely by public (as opposed to party) officials of state and county governments.[19] Second, unlike Texas's primaries, in which a majority (50% plus 1) of the vote is required, the general election is decided by a **plurality vote**, whereby the winning candidate needs to receive only the largest number of the votes cast for all the candidates for that office.

Plurality vote
An election rule in which the candidate with the most votes wins regardless of whether it is a majority.

General elections in Texas are held every other year on the same day as national elections—the first Tuesday after the first Monday in November of even-numbered years. In years divisible by four, we elect the president, vice president, all U.S. representatives, and one-third of the U.S. senators. In Texas, we elect all 150 members of the state house during these years and roughly half (15 or 16) of the 31 senators. We also elect some board and court positions at the state level as well as about half of the county positions. However, most major state executive positions (governor, lieutenant governor, attorney general, and so forth) are not filled until the midterm national election, when the U.S. representatives and one-third of U.S. senators (but not the president) again face the voters. Of course, all state representatives and half of the senators are elected in these years. Some board members, judges, and county officers are, too.

Holding simultaneous national and state elections has important political ramifications. During the administration of Andrew Jackson, parties first began to tie the states and the national government together politically. A strong presidential candidate and an effective

---

[19]County officials help administer general elections on behalf of the state.

candidate for state office can benefit significantly by cooperating and campaigning under the party label. This usually works best, of course, if the candidates are in substantial agreement with respect to political philosophy and the issues.

In Texas, which is more politically conservative than the average American state, fundamental agreement is often lacking. This has been especially true for Democratic candidates. Popular Democrats in the state often disassociate themselves from the more liberal presidential nominees of the party. As Democratic candidate for governor, Bill White played down his connections to national Democrat Bill Clinton and rarely mentioned Democratic President Barack Obama.

When the Texas Constitution was amended in 1972 to extend the terms (from two years to four years) for the governor and other major administrative officials, the elections for these offices were set for November of midterm election years. This change had two main effects. First, although candidates are also running for Congress in midterm elections, separation of presidential and state campaigns insulates public officials from the ebb and flow of presidential politics and allows them to further disassociate themselves from the national political parties. Elections for statewide office now largely reflect Texas issues and interests. Second, the separation reduces voting in statewide elections and makes the outcomes much more predictable. As was shown earlier, turnout in midterm elections is much lower than in presidential election years, when many people are lured to the polls by the importance of the office and the visibility of the campaign. The independent and the marginal voters are active, and election results for congressional and state-level offices are less predictable. In midterm election years, however, the less-informed and the less-predictable voters are more likely to stay home, and the contest is largely confined to political party regulars. Most incumbent state politicians prefer to cast their lot with this more limited and predictable midterm electorate.

Special Elections

As the name implies, special elections are designed to meet special or emergency needs, such as ratification of constitutional amendments or filling vacant offices. Special elections are held to fill vacancies only in legislative bodies that have general (rather than limited) lawmaking power. Typical legislative bodies with general power are the U.S. Senate and U.S. House of Representatives, state legislatures, and city councils in home-rule cities. (All other vacancies, including judgeships and county commissioners, are filled by appointment.) Runoffs are held when necessary. The elections provide for the filling of a vacancy only until the end of the regular term or until the next general election, whichever comes first.

Because special elections are not partisan, the process of getting on the ballot is relatively easy and does not involve a primary.[20] All that is required is the filing of the application form in a timely and appropriate manner and the payment of the designated filing fee. Unlike general elections, the winner of a special election must receive a majority of the votes. Thus a runoff special election may be necessary when no candidate wins outright the first time around. The runoff requirements have been enacted in piecemeal fashion—an illustration of how public policy is often enacted only for political advantage. Those in control of the legislature can and do change the rules of the game to benefit those who share their political views.

Before 1957, all special elections required only a plurality vote, but when candidates identified as "liberals" began to win elections under the plurality requirement, the legislature acted quickly to require a majority. During the special election in 1957, the liberal candidate, Ralph Yarborough, appeared likely to win, so the Texas House (then controlled by conservative

---

[20]The nonpartisan nature relates only to the fact that the party label does not appear on the ballot and certification by the party is not necessary. Special elections are, in fact, often partisan because regular party supporters work for "their" candidates.

Democrats) quickly passed a bill requiring a runoff in any election to fill a vacated U.S. Senate seat. However, a few liberal legislators were able to delay the bill in the state senate until after the election, in which Yarborough led the field of 23 candidates. Because he received only 38 percent of the popular vote, it is possible that Yarborough would have lost in a runoff. Sixteen days later, the senate passed the bill, and it was signed into law by the governor—too late to affect Yarborough's election. Once in office, Senator Yarborough was able to capitalize on his incumbency and served for 13 years.

The Conduct and Administration of Elections

Texas's secretary of state is the state's chief elections officer and interprets legislation and issues guidelines. The secretary of state has the responsibility of disbursing funds to the state and county executive committees to pay for the primary elections and is the keeper of election records, both party and governmental. The secretary of state also receives certificates of nomination from parties that have conducted primaries and conventions and uses these certificates to prepare the ballot for statewide offices. Along with the governor and a gubernatorial appointee, the secretary of state sits on the three-member board that canvasses election returns for state and district offices.

County-Level Administration
Except for the preparation of the statewide portion of the ballot, county-level officials actually conduct general elections. Counties may choose from three options for the administration of general elections. The first option is to maintain the decentralized system that the counties have used for decades. Under this system, the major portion of responsibility rests with the county clerk. By the time the clerk receives the state portion of the ballot from the secretary of state, he or she will have constructed the county- and precinct-level portion by having received applications and certified the candidates' names. The board of elections (consisting of the county judge, sheriff, clerk, and chair of the two major parties' executive committees) arranges for polling places and for printing ballots. The county tax assessor–collector processes all voter applications and updates the voting rolls. The county commissioners' court draws precinct voting lines, appoints election judges, selects voting devices, canvasses votes, and authorizes payment of all election expenses from the county treasury.

The two other options available are designed to promote efficiency. One is for the county commissioners' court to transfer the voter registration function from the tax assessor–collector's office to that of the county clerk, thus removing the assessor–collector from the electoral process. The other option represents more extensive reform. It calls for all election-related duties of both the assessor–collector and the county clerk to be transferred to a county election administrator. This officer is appointed for a term of two years by the County Elections Commission, which, in those counties that choose the election administrator option, replaces the board of elections. (Membership is the same, except that in the use of the commission, the county clerk serves instead of the sheriff.)

Ballot Construction
Like so many other features of an election system, ballot construction reflects both practical and political considerations. Two basic types of general-election ballots are available—the party-column ballot and the office-block ballot. On the **party-column ballot**, the names of all the candidates of each party are listed in parallel columns under the party label. This type traditionally has been used in Texas. The ballot itemizes the offices as prescribed by law in descending order of importance, and the candidates are listed in each row. Beside each name is a box (on paper ballots) or a lever (on voting machines) that the voter must mark or pull if the voter wishes to vote a split ticket. At the top of each column is the party's name and a box or lever. To vote a straight-party ticket, the voter need only mark the box or pull the lever for the party of his or her choice.

Party–column ballot
A type of ballot used in a general election where all of the candidates from each party are listed in parallel columns.

On the **office-block ballot**, the names of the parties' candidates are randomly listed in under each office (Figure 4.3). To vote a straight-party ticket, the voter must pick that party's candidates in each of the blocks. Several states use the office-block ballot, which is also called the "Massachusetts ballot" because it originated there. Minor parties in Texas and independent voters advocate the use of this ballot type because it makes straight-ticket voting for the major parties more difficult.

Office-block ballot

A type of ballot used in a general election where the offices are listed across the top, in separate blocks.

The Politics of Ballot Construction   Understandably, supporters of the major Texas political parties strongly support the use of the party column ballot. It enables

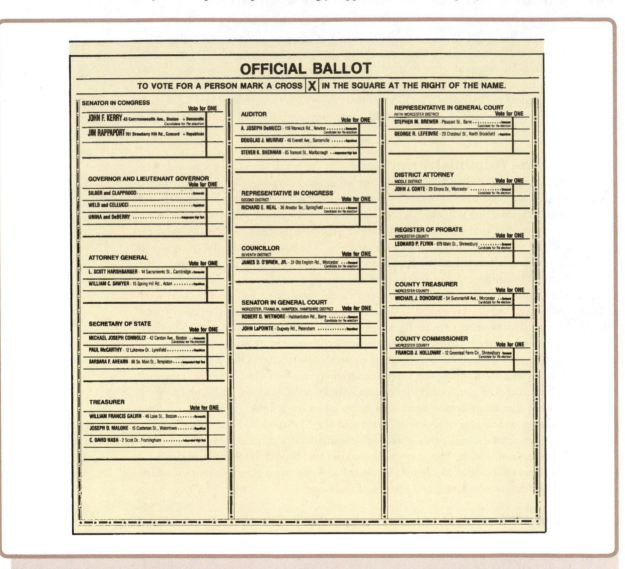

Figure 4.3

Example of the Office Block Ballot Used in Massachusetts

In contrast with the party-column ballot, which lists candidates of each party in parallel columns, the office-block ballot lists candidates in rows underneath each office. Notice also that voters cannot easily vote a straight-party ticket.

Compared to the party-column ballot, how would this office block arrangement encourage ticket splitting?

lesser-known candidates to ride on the coattails of the party label or a popular candidate running for major office. There may also be an extra payoff in the use of this type of ballot when a party is listed in the first column. The parties are slated from left to right on the ballot according to the proportion of votes that each party's candidate for governor received in the most recent gubernatorial election. Thus, the majority party (Republicans) benefits by occupying the coveted first column on the ballot. Democrats usually come second; next come third-party candidates and candidates of parties that were not on the ballot in the last election; and last come the independents.

Most Texas counties have moved away from a strict party-column ballot. Partly because of the adoption of electronic voting machines (discussed later in this chapter), ballots in these counties combine features of both the office-block and party-column designs (Figure 4.4). As with the office-block ballot, candidates are listed underneath each office. As with the party-column ballot, however, one can vote a straight-party ticket with a single mark; that is, before turning to specific offices, voters are first given the option to vote a straight ticket. Republican candidates are consistently listed first, Democrats come next, followed by other candidates.

Getting on the Ballot

For a name to be placed on the general-election ballot, the candidate must be either a party nominee or an independent. For any party that received at least 5 percent of the vote for any statewide office in the previous general election, the full slate of candidates is placed on the ballot automatically. Thus, the Democratic and Republican parties have no problem submitting candidate names, and certification by the appropriate party officials for primary or convention winners is routine.

Minor parties have a more difficult time. For instance, in 2010 the Green Party again broke the 5 percent barrier and, along with the Libertarians, earned a place on the 2012 ballot—any other minor parties must petition for a ballot position. Independent candidates for president have the most difficult challenge because they must present a petition signed by 1 percent of the total state vote for president in the last election. In 1992, Ross Perot's supporters presented 54,275 signatures, which qualified him to appear on the ballot.

For all other offices except president, the total vote for governor is the basis for determining the required number of signatures for both independents and third-party candidates. For statewide office, signatures equaling 1 percent of the total gubernatorial vote are needed; for multicounty district offices, 3 percent; and for all other district and local offices, 5 percent. Although the number of signatures is relatively small for some offices (a maximum of 500 at the local level), the process of gaining access to the ballot by petition is difficult.[21]

> **Did You Know?** Getting off a ballot can be as difficult as getting on. Take the case of Tom DeLay, the former member of the U.S. House of Representatives. After he resigned from Congress in June of 2006, the Republican Party tried to have him replaced on the general-election ballot. U.S. District Judge Sam Sparks ruled that he must remain on the ballot, and the Fifth Circuit Court of Appeals upheld the decision.

Write-In Candidates

Write-in candidates are not listed on the ballot—voters must write them on the ballot. These candidates often are individuals who have entered and lost in a party primary. A different type of write-in candidacy developed in 1976 when Charles W. Barrow, Chief Justice of the Fourth Court of Civil Appeals in San Antonio, was thought to be virtually unopposed for the Democratic nomination for associate justice of the Texas Supreme Court. The legal establishment was stunned when Don Yarbrough, a young Houston attorney involved in a number of legal entanglements, upset Barrow in the quest for the Democratic nomination. Apparently, the voters had confused the young attorney's name with former gubernatorial candidate Don Yarborough. No one had filed in the Republican primary.

---

[21]Signers must be registered voters and cannot have participated in the selection of a nominee for that office in another party's primary.

Straight Party
(Partido Completo)
- ○ **Republican Party (REP)**
  (Partido Republicano)
- ○ **Democratic Party (DEM)**
  (Partido Democratico)
- ○ **Libertarian Party (LIB)**
  (Partido Libertario)
- ○ **Green Party (GRN)**
  (Partido Verde)

FEDERAL
(FEDERAL)

United States Representative, District 20
(Representante de los Estados Unidos, Distrito Núm. 20)
- ○ **Clayton Trotter (REP)**
- ○ **Charles A. Gonzalez (DEM)**
- ○ **Michael "Commander" Idrogo (LIB)**

United States Representative, District 21
(Representante de los Estados Unidos, Distrito Núm. 21)
- ○ **Lamar Smith (REP)**
- ○ **Lainey Melnick (DEM)**
- ○ **James Arthur Strohm (LIB)**

United States Representative, District 23
(Representante de los Estados Unidos, Distrito Núm. 23)
- ○ **Francisco "Quico" Canseco (REP)**
- ○ **Ciro D. Rodriguez (DEM)**
- ○ **Martin Nitschke (LIB)**
- ○ **Ed Scharf (GRN)**
- ○ **Craig T. Stephens (IND)**

United States Representative, District 28
(Representante de los Estados Unidos, Distrito Núm. 28)
- ○ **Bryan Underwood (REP)**
- ○ **Henry Cuellar (DEM)**
- ○ **Stephen Kaat (LIB)**

STATE
(ESTADO)

Governor
(Gobernador)
- ○ **Rick Perry (REP)**
- ○ **Bill White (DEM)**
- ○ **Kathie Glass (LIB)**
- ○ **Deb Shafto (GRN)**
- ○ **Write-in***(Voto Escrito)*

Lieutenant Governor
(Gobernador Teniente)
- ○ **David Dewhurst (REP)**
- ○ **Linda Chavez-Thompson (DEM)**
- ○ **Scott Jameson (LIB)**
- ○ **Herb Gonzales, Jr. (GRN)**

Attorney General
(Procurador General)
- ○ **Greg Abbott (REP)**
- ○ **Barbara Ann Radnofsky (DEM)**
- ○ **Jon Roland (LIB)**

Comptroller of Public Accounts
(Contralor de Cuentas Públicas)
- ○ **Susan Combs (REP)**
- ○ **Mary J. Ruwart (LIB)**
- ○ **Edward Lindsay (GRN)**

Commissioner of the General Land Office
(Comisionado de la Oficina General de Tierras)
- ○ **Jerry Patterson (REP)**
- ○ **Hector Uribe (DEM)**
- ○ **James L. Holdar (LIB)**

Commissioner of Agriculture
(Comisionado de Agricultura)
- ○ **Todd Staples (REP)**
- ○ **Hank Gilbert (DEM)**
- ○ **Rick Donaldson (LIB)**

Railroad Commissioner
(Comisionado de Ferrocarriles)
- ○ **David Porter (REP)**
- ○ **Jeff Weems (DEM)**
- ○ **Roger Gary (LIB)**
- ○ **Art Browning (GRN)**

Justice, Supreme Court, Place 3
(Juez, Corte Suprema, Lugar Núm. 3)
- ○ **Debra Lehrmann (REP)**
- ○ **Jim Sharp (DEM)**
- ○ **William Bryan Strange, III (LIB)**

Justice, Supreme Court, Place 5
(Juez, Corte Suprema, Lugar Núm. 5)
- ○ **Paul Green (REP)**
- ○ **Bill Moody (DEM)**
- ○ **Tom Oxford (LIB)**

Justice, Supreme Court, Place 9
(Juez, Corte Suprema, Lugar Núm. 9)
- ○ **Eva Guzman (REP)**
- ○ **Blake Bailey (DEM)**
- ○ **Jack Armstrong (LIB)**

Judge, Court of Criminal Appeals, Place 2
(Juez, Corte de Apelaciones Criminales, Lugar Núm. 2)
- ○ **Lawrence "Larry" Meyers (REP)**
- ○ **J. Randell Stevens (LIB)**

Judge, Court of Criminal Appeals, Place 5
(Juez, Corte de Apelaciones Criminales, Lugar Núm. 5)
- ○ **Cheryl Johnson (REP)**
- ○ **Dave Howard (LIB)**

Judge, Court of Criminal Appeals, Place 6
(Juez, Corte de Apelaciones Criminales, Lugar Núm. 6)
- ○ **Michael E. Keasler (REP)**
- ○ **Keith Hampton (DEM)**
- ○ **Robert Ravee Virasin (LIB)**

Member, State Board of Education, District 3
(Miembro de la Junta Estatal de Educación Pública, Distrito Núm. 3)
- ○ **Tony Cunningham (REP)**
- ○ **Michael Soto (DEM)**
- ○ **Dean Kareem Higley (LIB)**
- ○ **Write-in***(Voto Escrito)*

Member, State Board of Education, District 5
(Miembro de la Junta Estatal de Educación Pública, Distrito Núm. 5)
- ○ **Ken Mercer (REP)**
- ○ **Rebecca Bell-Metereau (DEM)**
- ○ **Mark Loewe (LIB)**

State Senator, District 19
(Senador Estatal, Distrito Núm. 19)
- ○ **Dick Bowen (REP)**
- ○ **Carlos Uresti (DEM)**
- ○ **Mette A. Baker (LIB)**

State Senator, District 25
(Senador Estatal, Distrito Núm. 25)
- ○ **Jeff Wentworth (REP)**
- ○ **Arthur Maxwell Thomas, IV (LIB)**
- ○ **Write-in***(Voto Escrito)*

State Representative, District 116
(Representante Estatal, Distrito Núm. 116)
- ○ **Trey Martinez Fischer (DEM)**

State Representative, District 117
(Representante Estatal, Distrito Núm. 117)
- ○ **John V. Garza (REP)**
- ○ **David McQuade Leibowitz (DEM)**

State Representative, District 118
(Representante Estatal, Distrito Núm. 118)
- ○ **Joe Farias (DEM)**

State Representative, District 119
(Representante Estatal, Distrito Núm. 119)
- ○ **Michael E. Holdman (REP)**
- ○ **Rolando Gutierrez (DEM)**

State Representative, District 120
(Representante Estatal, Distrito Núm. 120)
- ○ **Ruth Jones McClendon (DEM)**

State Representative, District 121
(Representante Estatal, Distrito Núm. 121)
- ○ **Joe Straus (REP)**

State Representative, District 122
(Representante Estatal, Distrito Núm. 122)
- ○ **Lyle Larson (REP)**
- ○ **Masarrat Ali (DEM)**

State Representative, District 123
(Representante Estatal, Distrito Núm. 123)
- ○ **Mike Villarreal (DEM)**

State Representative, District 124
(Representante Estatal, Distrito Núm. 124)
- ○ **José Menéndez (DEM)**
- ○ **Douglas P. Hanson (LIB)**

State Representative, District 125
(Representante Estatal, Distrito Núm. 125)
- ○ **Joaquin Castro (DEM)**
- ○ **Jeffrey C. Blunt (LIB)**

Justice, 4th Court of Appeals District, Place 2 Unexpired Term
(Juez, Corte de Apelaciones, Distrito Núm. 4, Lugar Núm. 2, Duración Restante del cargo)
- ○ **Marialyn Barnard (REP)**
- ○ **Rebeca C. Martinez (DEM)**

Justice, 4th Court of Appeals District, Place 6
(Juez, Corte de Apelaciones, Distrito Núm. 4, Lugar Núm. 6)
- ○ **Sandee Bryan Marion (REP)**

District Judge, 45th Judicial District
(Juez del Distrito, Distrito Judicial Núm. 45)
- ○ **Barbara Hanson Nellermoe (DEM)**

Figure 4.4

A Typical Texas Ballot from Bexar County

Recall from the text that Republican candidates were listed first in 2010 because their candidate (Rick Perry) received the most votes in the previous gubernatorial election. Notice that voters are able to vote for all of the candidates of a single party—that is, vote a *straight ticket*—by making a single mark on the ballot. It is in midterm elections, like this one in 2010, that state executives are elected.

Why would party leaders prefer such a ballot arrangement?

Embarrassed, the legal establishment sought to have the primary winner disqualified from the ballot. Failing that, they mounted a write-in campaign supported strongly by the leaders of both political parties. Playing the name game themselves, they chose as their candidate District Judge Sam Houston Jones. The write-in campaign failed miserably. Don Yarbrough's victory was short-lived, however. Under threat of removal by the legislature, he resigned after serving approximately six months. He was replaced through gubernatorial appointment by Judge Charles W. Barrow, his opponent in the Democratic primary.

Write-in candidates have had an easier time as a result of a law subsequently passed by the legislature, though it still is not easy. A candidate must file a declaration of candidacy with the secretary of state 70 days before election day. With the declaration the candidate must include either the filing fee or a nominating petition with the required number of signatures. The names of write-in candidates must be posted at the election site, possibly in the election booth. A candidate not properly registered cannot win, regardless of the votes he or she receives. Even when registered, write-in candidates are seldom successful—recall the earlier discussion of the race to replace Tom DeLay in 2006, when circumstances for the write-in seemed unusually favorable.

The Secret Ballot and the Integrity of Elections

The essence of the right to vote is generally viewed as the right to cast a ballot in secret, have the election conducted fairly, and have the ballots counted correctly. The **Australian ballot**, adopted by Texas in 1892, includes names of the candidates of all political parties on a single ballot printed at the public's expense and available only at the voting place.[22] Given a reasonably private area in which to mark the ballot, the voter was offered a secret ballot for the first time.

Australian ballot
A ballot printed by the government (as opposed to the political parties) that allows people to vote in secret.

Although there are legal remedies such as the issuance of injunctions and the threat of criminal penalties, Texas has looked primarily to "political" remedies in its effort to protect the integrity of the electoral process. Minor parties have reason to be concerned that irregularities in elections administered by members of the majority party may not be observed or, if observed, may not be reported. Even in the absence of wrongdoing, the testimony of the correctness of an election by individuals with opposing interests helps ensure public faith in the process.

Traditional practice has been that in general and special elections, the county board of elections routinely appoints as election judges the precinct chair of the political party whose members constitute a majority on the elections board. Each election judge is required to select at least one election clerk from a list submitted by the county chair of each political party. Moreover, law now recognizes the status of poll watchers, and both primary candidates and county chairs are authorized to appoint them.

Candidates can ask for a recount of the ballots. The candidate who requests a recount must put up a deposit—$60 per precinct where paper ballots were used and $100 per precinct using electronic voting—and is liable for the entire cost unless he or she wins or ties in the recount. In a large county, a recount can be quite costly. Consider Dallas County, which has almost 700 precincts. Despite this drawback, the current practice marks a real improvement over the days when often ineffective judicial remedies were the only recourse.

Multilingualism

Ballots in most Texas counties are printed in English. In more than 100 counties, the ballot is printed in both English and Spanish. In 2002, the U.S. Department of Justice ordered Harris County, which includes Houston, to provide ballots (and voting material) in Vietnamese as well (Figure 4.5). It is the only county in Texas to be included in the order and the only county outside California to do so. In some parts of the country, other languages are required, including Chinese, Eskimo, Filipino, Japanese, and Korean. In Los Angeles County alone, ballots are printed in seven different languages. This all is due to the Voting

---

[22]Optional at first, the Australian ballot was made mandatory in 1903.

SAMPLE BALLOT   LÁ PHIẾU MẪU

Harris County – November 6, 2012 – General and Special Elections

Quận Harris – 6 tháng Mười Một, 2012 – Các Cuộc Tổng Tuyển Cử và Bầu Cử Đặc Biệt

Straight Party
Bỏ phiếu cho các ứng cử viên của cùng một đảng

☐ Republican Party
Đảng Cộng Hòa

☐ Democratic Party
Đảng Dân Chủ

☐ Libertarian Party
Đảng Tự Do

☐ Green Party
Đảng Xanh

President and Vice President
Tổng Thống và Phó Tổng Thống

☐ Mitt Romney / Paul Ryan
Republican Party *Đảng Cộng Hòa*

☐ Barack Obama / Joe Biden
Democratic Party *Đảng Dân Chủ*

☐ Gary Johnson / Jim Gray
Libertarian Party *Đảng Tự Do*

☐ Jill Stein / Cheri Honkala
Green Party *Đảng Xanh*

☐ Write-in
Bầu chọn ứng cử viên không có tên trong lá phiếu

United States Senator
Thượng Nghị Sĩ Hoa Kỳ

☐ Ted Cruz
Republican Party *Đảng Cộng Hòa*

☐ Paul Sadler
Democratic Party *Đảng Dân Chủ*

☐ John Jay Myers
Libertarian Party *Đảng Tự Do*

☐ David B. Collins
Green Party *Đảng Xanh*

United States Representative, District 2
Dân Biểu Hoa Kỳ Khu vực số 2

☐ Ted Poe
Republican Party *Đảng Cộng Hòa*

☐ Jim Dougherty
Democratic Party *Đảng Dân Chủ*

☐ Kenneth Duncan
Libertarian Party *Đảng Tự Do*

☐ Mark A. Roberts
Green Party *Đảng Xanh*

United States Representative, District 7
Dân Biểu Hoa Kỳ Khu vực số 7

☐ John Culberson
Republican Party *Đảng Cộng Hòa*

☐ James Cargas
Democratic Party *Đảng Dân Chủ*

☐ Drew Parks
Libertarian Party *Đảng Tự Do*

☐ Lance Findley
Green Party *Đảng Xanh*

United States Representative, District 8
Dân Biểu Hoa Kỳ Khu vực số 8

☐ Kevin Brady
Republican Party *Đảng Cộng Hòa*

☐ Neil Burns
Democratic Party *Đảng Dân Chủ*

☐ Roy Hall
Libertarian Party *Đảng Tự Do*

United States Representative, District 9
Dân Biểu Hoa Kỳ, Khu vực số 9

☐ Steve Mueller
Republican Party *Đảng Cộng Hòa*

☐ Al Green
Democratic Party *Đảng Dân Chủ*

☐ John Wieder
Libertarian Party *Đảng Tự Do*

☐ Vanessa Foster
Green Party *Đảng Xanh*

United States Representative, District 10
Dân Biểu Hoa Kỳ, Khu vực số 10

☐ Michael McCaul
Republican Party *Đảng Cộng Hòa*

☐ Tawana W. Cadien
Democratic Party *Đảng Dân Chủ*

☐ Richard Priest
Libertarian Party *Đảng Tự Do*

United States Representative, District 18
Dân Biểu Hoa Kỳ Khu vực số 18

☐ Sean Seibert
Republican Party *Đảng Cộng Hòa*

☐ Sheila Jackson Lee
Democratic Party *Đảng Dân Chủ*

☐ Christopher Barber
Libertarian Party *Đảng Tự Do*

United States Representative, District 22
Dân Biểu Hoa Kỳ Khu vực số 22

☐ Pete Olson
Republican Party *Đảng Cộng Hòa*

☐ Kesha Rogers
Democratic Party *Đảng Dân Chủ*

☐ Steve Susman
Libertarian Party *Đảng Tự Do*

☐ Don Cook
Green Party *Đảng Xanh*

United States Representative, District 29
Dân Biểu Hoa Kỳ, Khu vực số 29

☐ Gene Green
Democratic Party *Đảng Dân Chủ*

☐ James Stanczak
Libertarian Party *Đảng Tự Do*

☐ Maria Selva
Green Party *Đảng Xanh*

United States Representative, District 36
Dân Biểu Hoa Kỳ, Khu vực số 36

☐ Steve Stockman
Republican Party *Đảng Cộng Hòa*

☐ Max Martin
Democratic Party *Đảng Dân Chủ*

☐ Michael K. Cole
Libertarian Party *Đảng Tự Do*

Railroad Commissioner
Ủy Viên Ngành Hỏa Xa

☐ Christi Craddick
Republican Party *Đảng Cộng Hòa*

☐ Dale Henry
Democratic Party *Đảng Dân Chủ*

☐ Vivekananda (Vik) Wall
Libertarian Party *Đảng Tự Do*

☐ Chris Kennedy
Green Party *Đảng Xanh*

Railroad Commissioner, Unexpired Term
Ủy Viên Ngành Hỏa Xa, Nhiệm Kỳ Vô Thời Hạn

☐ Barry Smitherman
Republican Party *Đảng Cộng Hòa*

☐ Jaime O. Perez
Libertarian Party *Đảng Tự Do*

☐ Josh Wendel
Green Party *Đảng Xanh*

Justice, Supreme Court, Place 2
Chánh Án, Tối Cao Pháp Viện, Vị Trí số 2

☐ Don Willett
Republican Party *Đảng Cộng Hòa*

☐ RS Roberto Koelsch
Libertarian Party *Đảng Tự Do*

Justice, Supreme Court, Place 4
Chánh Án, Tối Cao Pháp Viện, Vị Trí số 4

☐ John Devine
Republican Party *Đảng Cộng Hòa*

☐ Tom Oxford
Libertarian Party *Đảng Tự Do*

☐ Charles E. Waterbury
Green Party *Đảng Xanh*

Justice, Supreme Court, Place 6
Chánh Án, Tối Cao Pháp Viện, Vị Trí số 6

☐ Nathan Hecht
Republican Party *Đảng Cộng Hòa*

☐ Michele Petty
Democratic Party *Đảng Dân Chủ*

☐ Mark Ash
Libertarian Party *Đảng Tự Do*

☐ Jim Chisholm
Green Party *Đảng Xanh*

Presiding Judge, Court of Criminal Appeals
Chánh Án Chủ Tọa, Tòa Kháng Án Hình Sự

☐ Sharon Keller
Republican Party *Đảng Cộng Hòa*

☐ Keith Hampton
Democratic Party *Đảng Dân Chủ*

☐ Lance Stott
Libertarian Party *Đảng Tự Do*

Judge, Court of Criminal Appeals, Place 7
Chánh Án, Tòa Kháng Án Hình Sự, Vị Trí số 7

☐ Barbara Parker Hervey
Republican Party *Đảng Cộng Hòa*

☐ Mark W. Bennett
Libertarian Party *Đảng Tự Do*

Judge, Court of Criminal Appeals, Place 8
Chánh Án, Tòa Kháng Án Hình Sự, Vị Trí số 8

☐ Elsa Alcala
Republican Party *Đảng Cộng Hòa*

☐ William Bryan Strange, III
Libertarian Party *Đảng Tự Do*

Member, State Board of Education, District 4
Hội Viên, Hội Đồng Quản Trị Giáo Dục Tiểu Bang, Khu Vực số 4

☐ Dorothy Olmos
Republican Party *Đảng Cộng Hòa*

☐ Lawrence Allen, Jr.
Democratic Party *Đảng Dân Chủ*

Rights Act of 1965 and its subsequent amendment in 1992. According to Section 203 of the act, a political subdivision (typically, a county) must provide language assistance to voters if significant numbers of voting-age citizens are members of a single-language minority group and do not speak or understand English "well enough to participate in the electoral process." Specifically, the legal requirement is triggered when more than 5 percent of the voting-age citizens or 10,000 of these citizens meet the criteria. The 2010 Census shows that more than 80,000 people living in Harris County identify themselves as Vietnamese, and the U.S. Department of Justice determined that at least 10,000 of them are old enough to vote but are not sufficiently proficient in English, thereby triggering the requirement. Given the levels of immigration into the United States, the number of ballot languages is almost certain to increase.

Early Voting All Texas voters can now vote before election day.[23] Some voters can vote by mail, specifically those who plan to be away from the county on election day, those who are sick or disabled, anyone who is 65 years or older, and people who are in jail but are otherwise eligible to vote. The rest of us can only vote early in person. Generally, early voting begins the 17th day before election day and ends the 4th day before election day. In addition to traditional election-day voting sites, such as schools and fire stations, there are several other more familiar places to vote early, including grocery and convenience stores. This innovation has clearly made voting easier in Texas, and people are using it. In the 2010 midterm election, more than 53 percent of the votes were cast before election day, and in 2012, early votes were 63 percent of the total. Although people are voting earlier, they are not voting in greater numbers, as we noted earlier in the chapter. The growing tendency toward early voting may still have important implications for when and how politicians campaign.

Early voting

The practice of voting before election day at traditional voting locations, such as schools, and other locations, such as grocery and convenience stores.

HOW DOES TEXAS COMPARE?
Early Voting in the States

Early voting is allowed in 32 states, two of which permit it only by mail. In Texas and four other states—Indiana, Louisiana, Maryland, and Tennessee—voters may only vote early in person unless they will be absent on election day or have special needs. In 27 states, voters can choose whether to vote early in person or by mail. At least 30 percent of all votes nationwide in 2008 were cast before election day. In 11 states, more than half were cast early: Arizona, Colorado, Florida, Georgia, Nevada, New Mexico, North Carolina, Oregon, Tennessee, Texas, and Washington.[24]

FOR DEBATE

Early voting is supposed to make voting easier, but it is not clear that it has much effect on turnout. Why is this the case? What does this tell us about electoral participation? What other things can lawmakers do to increase turnout in Texas?

---

[23]For a nice description of early voting and a preliminary assessment of its effects, see Robert M. Stein and Patricia A. Garcia-Monet, "Voting Early But Not Often," *Social Science Quarterly* 78 (December 1997), pp. 657–671. For a more recent review and assessment, see Paul Gronke, Eva Galanes-Rosenbaum, and Peter A. Miller, "Early Voting and Turnout," *PS: Political Science and Politics* 40 (December 2007), pp. 639–645.
[24]National Council of State Legislatures, www.ncsl.org/default.aspx?tabid=16604; United States Election Project, http://elections.gmu.edu/Early_Voting_2008_Final.html; Election Reform Information Project, www.electionline.org.

Counting and Recounting Ballots

We take for granted that when we vote, our votes count. As we learned in Florida in the 2000 presidential election, this is not true. The first machine count of ballots in Florida showed George W. Bush with a 1,725-vote lead. In a mandatory machine recount of the same ballots, the same machines cut his lead to 327. We were also told that some 2 to 3 percent of the ballots were not counted at all. How could this happen? What does this mean? The answer is simple: Machines make mistakes. Some ballots are not counted. Some may even be counted for the wrong candidate. This shocked most Americans.

Experts have known for a long time that vote counting contains a good amount of error. By most accounts, the error rate averages 1 to 2 percent, although it can be higher depending on the ballot and the machines themselves. The error rate is largest for punch-card ballots, which have been commonly used in big cities in Texas and other states. To vote, one inserts the ballot into a slot in the voting booth and then uses a stylus to punch holes corresponding to candidates' names that are printed on separate lists, usually in the form of a booklet. There are two sources of error associated with these ballots. First, some voters do not fully punch out the pieces of paper from the perforated holes. That is, these pieces of paper, which are called **chad**, remain attached to the ballot. Second, even where the chad are completely detached, machines do not read each and every ballot. This is of importance to voters. It is typically of little consequence for election outcomes, however. Counting errors tend to cancel out, meaning that no candidate gains a much greater number of votes. Thus, the errors are important only when elections are very close, within a half percentage point, which is not very common. When it does happen, the losing candidate can request a recount.

Texas has fairly specific laws about recounts. A candidate can request a recount if he or she loses by less than 10 percent. This is a fairly generous rule compared to other states. The candidate who requests the recount does have to pay for it, however, which means that most candidates do not request a recount unless the margin is much closer, say, one percentage point or less. As for the recount itself, the Texas Election Code states that "only one method may be used in the recount" and "a manual recount shall be conducted in preference to an electronic recount." The procedures are fairly detailed. What may be most interesting is the set of rules for how chad should be interpreted. Indeed, canvassing authorities are allowed to determine whether "an indentation on the chad from the stylus or other object is present" and whether "the chad reflects by other means a clearly ascertainable intent of the voter to vote."[25] This leaves a lot of room for discretion on the part of canvassing authorities in the various Texas counties.

Chad

The small pieces of paper produced in punching data cards, such as punch-card ballots.

© tom carter/Alamy

Voters cast their votes electronically by touching screens.

Does electronic voting solve the problems with paper ballots? How can we tell?

[25]Texas Code 127.130. Also see Carlos Guerra, "Texas Is Far Friendlier to *All* Our Chad," *San Antonio Express-News,* November 25, 2000, p. B-1.

Electronic Voting Partly in response to the events in Florida—and the seeming potential for similar problems in Texas—a number of counties introduced **electronic voting** in the 2002 midterm elections. Instead of punching holes in ballots or filling in bubbles on scannable sheets, most voters today cast ballots by touching screens. The technology is similar to what is used in automated teller machines (ATMs) and electronic-ticket check-ins at many airports and promises an exact count of votes. It is now used for voting throughout much of Texas and the United States. As with the introduction of any new technology, problems have occurred.[26]

Electronic voting
Voting using touch screens similar to e-ticket check-ins at most airports.

ELECTION CAMPAIGNS IN TEXAS

The ultimate aim of party activity is to nominate candidates in the party primary or convention and get them elected in the general election. The campaign for the parties' nomination is often more critical in one-party areas of the state—Democrats in South Texas and in some large urban areas and Republicans in many rural and suburban areas. For local and district offices in these areas, the key electoral decision is made in the primaries because the dominant parties' nominee is almost certain to win the general election. In statewide elections, the crucial electoral decision is often made in the Republican primary where the party's nominee is chosen. The Republican candidate then has a relatively clear path to winning office.

Candidates seeking their parties' nomination in a primary pursue a different sort of campaign strategy than they do when they later run in the general election. The primary electorate is usually much smaller and made up of more-committed partisans. As a result, primary candidates are likely to strike a more ideological or even strident approach that appeals to activists. Once they have won their primaries, candidates will often moderate their views to win over swing voters and independents in the general election. For little-known candidates, money and the endorsement of party elites are more crucial in the primary than in the general election. Little-known candidates can frequently count on the party label to sweep them into office in general elections.

The General Election Campaign

To a large extent, election outcomes are predictable. Despite all the media attention paid to the conventions, the debates, the advertising, and everything else involved in election campaigns, certain things powerfully structure the vote in national and state elections.[27] In state elections, two factors predominate: party identification and incumbency.

First, where more people in a state identify with one political party than with the other, the candidates of the preferred party have an advantage in general elections. For instance, when most Texans identified with the Democratic Party, Democratic candidates dominated elected offices throughout the state. As Texans have become more Republican in their identification, Republican candidates have done very well; indeed, as was mentioned earlier, Republicans now hold every statewide elected office. Identification with the political parties varies a lot within Texas, however, and this has implications for state legislative elections. In some parts of the state, particularly in the big cities, more people identify with the Democratic Party, and Democratic candidates typically represent those areas in the state house and senate

---

[26]Rachel Konrad, "Reports of Electronic Voting Trouble Top 1,000," *USA Today,* November 4, 2004.
[27]Most of the research has focused on presidential elections. See Robert S. Erikson and Christopher Wlezien, *The Timeline of Presidential Elections: How Campaigns Do (and Don't) Matter.* (Chicago: University of Chicago Press, 2012). Some research has also been done on state gubernatorial and legislative elections. See, for example, Mark E. Tompkins, "The Electoral Fortunes of Gubernatorial Incumbents," *Journal of Politics* 46 (May 1984), pp. 520–543; Ronald E. Weber, Harvey J. Tucker, and Paul Brace, "Vanishing Marginals in State Legislative Elections," *Legislative Studies Quarterly* 16 (February 1991), pp. 29–47.

(see Chapter 7). Thus party identification in the state and in districts themselves tells us a lot about which candidates win general elections.

Second, incumbent candidates—those already in office who are up for reelection—are more likely to win in general elections. This is particularly true in state legislative elections, where the districts are fairly homogeneous and the campaigns are not very visible, but incumbency is also important in elections for statewide office. Incumbents have a number of advantages over challengers, the most important of which is that they have won before. To become an incumbent, a candidate has to beat an incumbent or else win in an open-seat election, which usually involves a contest among a number of strong candidates. By definition, therefore, incumbents are good candidates. In addition, incumbents have the advantage of office. They are in a position to do things for their constituents and thus increase their support among voters.

Although party identification and incumbency are important in Texas elections, they are not the whole story. What they really tell us is the degree to which candidates are advantaged or disadvantaged as they embark on their campaigns. Other factors ultimately matter on election day.[28]

Mobilizing Groups

Mobilizing Groups Groups play an important role in elections for any office. A fundamental part of campaigns is getting out the vote among groups that strongly support the candidate. To a large extent, candidates focus on groups aligned with the political parties.[29] At the state level, business interests and teachers are particularly important. Republican candidates tend to focus their efforts on the former and Democratic candidates on the latter. Candidates also mobilize other groups, including African Americans and Latinos. Traditionally, Democratic candidates emphasized these minority groups, though Governor Bush broke somewhat with this tradition and focused substantial attention on the Latino community in Texas. Mobilizing groups does not necessarily involve taking strong public stands on their behalf, especially those that are less mainstream. Indeed, the mobilization of such groups is typically conducted very quietly, often through targeted mailings and phone calls.

Choosing Issues

Choosing Issues Issues are important in any campaign. In campaigns for state offices, taxes, education, immigration, and religious issues are very salient, and abortion matters a lot. Just as they target social groups, candidates focus on issues that reflect their party affiliations, but they avoid unpopular positions like higher taxes or budget cuts for education or law enforcement. Where candidates do differ is in their emphasis on particular issues and their policy proposals. These choices depend heavily on carefully crafted opinion polls. Through polls, candidates attempt to identify the issues that the public considers to be important and then craft policy positions to address those issues. The process is ongoing, and candidates pay close attention to changes in opinion and, perhaps most important, to the public's response to the candidates' own positions. Public opinion polling is fundamental in modern election campaigns in America, and campaign messages are often presented in advance to focus groups, test groups of selected citizens to help campaign strategists tailor their messages in a way that will appeal to particular audiences.

---

[28]For a detailed analysis of election campaigns in Texas in a single election year, see Richard Murray, "The 1996 Elections in Texas," in Kent L. Tedin, Donald S. Lutz, and Edward P. Fuchs (eds.), *Perspectives on American and Texas Politics*, 5th ed. (Dubuque, IA: Kendall/Hunt, 1998), pp. 247–286.

[29]For an analysis of how membership in various demographic groups influences voting behavior, see Robert S. Erikson, Thomas B. Lancaster, and David W. Romero, "Group Components of the Presidential Vote, 1952–1984," *Journal of Politics* 50 (May 1988), pp. 337–346. For an analysis of how identification with various social groups influences voting behavior, see Christopher Wlezien and Arthur H. Miller, "Social Groups and Political Judgments," *Social Science Quarterly* 78 (December 1997), pp. 625–640.

The Campaign Trail Deciding where and how to campaign are critical elements in campaign strategy. Candidates spend countless hours "on the stump," traveling about the state or district to speak before diverse groups. In a state as large as Texas, candidates for statewide office must pick and choose areas so as to maximize their exposure. Unfortunately for rural voters, this means that candidates spend most of their time in urban and suburban areas where they can get the attention of a large audience through the local media.

Nowadays, no candidate gets elected by stumping alone. The most direct route to the voters is through the media. There are 20 media markets in Texas. These include approximately 200 television and cable stations and more than 500 radio stations. In addition, 79 daily newspapers and many more weekly newspapers are dispersed throughout the state's 254 counties.[30] Candidates hire public relations firms and media consultants, and advertising plays a big role. These days, a successful campaign often relies on **negative campaigning**, in which candidates attack opponents' issue positions or character. As one campaign consultant said, "Campaigns are about definition. Either you define yourself and your opponent or [the other candidates do]. … Victory goes to the aggressor."[31] Although often considered an unfortunate development in American politics, it is important to keep in mind that negative campaigning can serve to provide voters with information about the candidates and their issue positions.

Timing The timing of the campaign effort can be very important. Unlike presidential elections, campaigns for state offices, including the governorship, begin fairly late in the election cycle. Indeed, it is common to hear little from gubernatorial candidates until after Labor Day and from candidates for the legislature not until a month before the election.

Candidates often reserve a large proportion of their campaign advertising budget for a last-minute media "blitz." However, early voting may affect this strategy somewhat. Recall that in 2012, approximately 63 percent of the votes in Texas were cast early, during the weeks leading up to the election, which means that the final campaign blitz came too late to have any effect on more than half of all voters. Consequently, candidates in the future may be less likely to concentrate their efforts so tightly on the final days of the campaign.

Money in Election Campaigns

Election campaigns are expensive, which means that candidates need to raise a lot of money to be competitive. Indeed, the amount of money a candidate raises can be the deciding factor in the campaign. Just how much a candidate needs depends on the level of the campaign and the competitiveness of the race. High-level campaigns for statewide office are usually multimillion-dollar affairs.

In recent years, the race for governor has become especially expensive. In 2002, Tony Sanchez spent nearly $70 million, a striking sum and mostly his own funds, but lost handily to incumbent Governor Rick Perry, who spent just less than $30 million. In 2006, the four candidates vying spent a much smaller amount, about $46 million in total, with Perry leading the way at $23 million. In 2010, Perry spent $40 million to Bill White's $25 million and won yet again.

Although lower-level races in Texas are not usually million-dollar affairs, they can be expensive as well. This is certainly true if a contested office is an open seat, where the incumbent is not running for reelection, or if an incumbent is from a marginal district—one in

Negative campaigning

A strategy used in election campaigns in which candidates attack opponents' issue positions or character.

---

[30]*Gale Directory of Publications and Broadcast Media*, 148th ed. (Detroit, MI: Gale Research, 2012).
[31]Quoted in Dave McNeely, "Campaign Strategists Preparing Spin Systems," *Austin American-Statesman*, October 21, 1993, p. A11.

which the incumbent won office with less than 55 percent of the vote. It is not unusual for a candidate in a competitive race for the state house to spend between $100,000 and $200,000.

Where does this money come from? Candidates often try to solicit small individual contributions through direct-mail campaigns. However, to raise the millions required for a high-level state race, they must solicit "big money" from wealthy friends or business and professional interests that have a stake in the outcome of the campaign; see some examples in the Texas Insiders feature. Another source of big money is loans—candidates often borrow heavily from banks, wealthy friends, or even themselves.[32]

Banks, corporations, law firms, and professional associations, such as those representing doctors, real estate agents, or teachers, organize and register their **political action committees (PACs)** with the secretary of state's office. PACs serve as the vehicle through which interest groups collect money and then contribute it to political candidates.

Political action committees (PACs)

Organizations that raise and then contribute money to political candidates.

Where Does the Money Go?

In today's election campaigns, there are many ways to spend money. Newspaper ads, billboards, radio messages, bumper stickers, yard signs, and phone banks are all staples in traditional campaigns. Candidates for statewide and urban races must rely on media advertising, particularly television, to get the maximum exposure they need in the three- or four-month campaign period. Campaigns are becoming professionalized, with candidates likely to hire consulting firms to manage their campaigns. Consultants contract with public opinion pollsters, arrange advertising, and organize direct-mail campaigns that can target certain areas of the state.

We can get some idea about spending in campaigns from what candidates pay for advertising and political consultants in Harris County, which includes Houston:[34]

Did You Know? During the 2009–2010 election cycle in Texas, over 1,300 PACs were active and spent over $130 million. Consider a small sampling of the PACs that organizations have established: AQUAPAC (set up by the Water Quality Association), BEEF-PAC (Texas Cattle Feeders Association), SIX-PAC (National Beer Wholesalers Association), WAFFLEPAC (Waffle House, Inc.), and WHATAPAC (Whataburger Corporation of Texas).[33]

★ A 30-second TV "spot" costs about $1,500 for a daytime ad, $2,000 to $5,000 for an ad during the evening news, and $5,000 to $20,000 during prime time (8:00 P.M. to 11:00 P.M.), depending on the show's popularity rating; for some popular programs such as CSI, the cost can be as much as $25,000.

★ Prime time for most radio broadcasting is "drive time" (5:00 A.M. to 10 A.M. and 3:00 P.M. to 8:00 P.M.), when most people are driving to or from work. Drive-time rates range from $250 to $2,000 per 60-second spot.

★ Billboards can run from $600 to $15,000 a month, depending on the location (billboards on busy highways are the most expensive).

★ Newspaper ads cost around $250 per column inch ($300 to $500 on Sunday). In 2008, a half-page ad in the *Houston Chronicle* run on the day before the election cost about $15,000. Advertising rates for election campaigns are actually higher than standard rates because political advertisers do not qualify for the discounts that regular advertisers receive.

★ Hiring a professional polling organization to conduct a poll in Harris County costs $15,000 to $30,000.

★ Hiring a political consulting firm to manage a campaign in Harris County runs up to $50,000 plus a percentage of media buys. (Technically, the percentage is paid by the television and radio stations.) Most firms also get a bonus ranging from $5,000 to $25,000 if the candidate wins.

---

[32]For a comprehensive treatment of money in election campaigns, see Frank J. Sorauf, *Inside Campaign Finance: Myths and Realities* (New Haven, CT: Yale University Press, 1992).

[33]Federal Election Commission, www.fec.gov

[34]Nancy Sims of Pierpont Communications, with offices in Austin and Houston, graciously provided this information.

Texas **INSIDERS**

Profiles of Texas Campaign Megadonors

AP Photo/Houston Chronicle/Melissa Phillip, File

Daemmrich Photography, Inc.

Texas homebuilder Bob Perry (no relation to the governor), one of the nation's largest political contributors, donated more than $2.5 million to Governor Rick Perry's campaigns and more than $60 million to other Republican causes. He has become one of the most powerful behind-the-scenes movers and shakers both in Texas politics and in the nation as a whole. He has sought to limit Texas homeowners' right to sue builders for shoddy construction, and he has been a major supporter of pro-business conservatives.

Is the right to contribute to election campaigns an essential element of freedom of expression? Campaign contributors usually give money to candidates who are already sympathetic to their general viewpoints, but can these contributions also be used as a tool to manipulate specific decisions?

Trial lawyer Steve Rostyn has donated at least $7 million to various failed Democratic campaigns. Rostyn has also had little success in fighting caps on policyholders' awards when they sue insurance companies for claims such as those resulting from windstorm damage.

Most observers agree that campaign contributions open doors, giving contributors access to public officials to argue the case for their interests. What factors determine if donors actually succeed in persuading decision makers to support policies that benefit them?

Thinking about the role of elites in a democracy Do large campaign contributions skew public policy toward wealthier individuals and groups? Do other forms of public participation balance the influence of large contributors?

TABLE 4.4 Profiles of Texas Campaign Mega-Donors

Donor	Candidate	Donor's Special Interest
Republican Governors' Association	Republican	Election of Republican governors
Bob and Doylene Perry	Republican	Protection of homebuilders against liability; opposition to business regulation
Harold Simmons	Republican	Protection of chemical plants against regulation; building nuclear waste facility in Texas; limiting lawsuits
AT&T, Inc. PAC	Republican	Favorable regulation and low taxes on the communications industry

(continued)

TABLE 4.4 (continued)

Donor	Candidate	Donor's Special Interest
Lonnie A. "Bo" Pilgrim	Republican	Pilgrim's Pride chicken processing; limits on workers' compensation
TXU PAC	Republican	TXU Energy; permitting coal-fired generating plants
Texas Association of Realtors PAC	Republican	Real estate industry; property rights
T. Boone Pickens	Republican	Oil and gas industry; support for natural gas to fuel motor vehicles
Ray L. Hunt	Republican	Oil and gas industry
Koch PAC	Republican	Koch Industries; conservative and libertarian causes; limits on public employee unions and benefits
James R. and Cecilia Leininger	Republican	Use of public funds to support private schools; fundamentalist values
Associated General Contractors of Texas	Republican	Heavy construction, including highways
Democratic Governors Association	Democrat	Election of Democratic governors
American Federation of State, County and Municipal Employees	Democrat	Protection of public employee jobs, salaries, and benefits
Provost Umphrey Law Firm, LLP	Democrat	Personal injury lawyers; representing injured clients against insurance companies and other businesses
Service Employees International Union	Democrat	Workers rights, wages, and benefits, especially for lower-paid occupations
Communications Workers of America	Democrat	Worker benefits for a wide range of members

This table shows a sampling of mega-donors who have contributed a total of at least $100,000 to Texas gubernatorial campaigns in the last three elections. It illustrates who gives, to whom, and in which kinds of public policy decisions they have an interest.

Sources: Texas Ethics Commission data compiled by Texans for Public Justice, *Governor Rick Perry's $100,000-plus Mega-Donors*, July 13, 2011, Matt Stiles, "Prolific Donor Has Given $66 Million Since 2000," *The Texas Tribune*, March 29, 2010, (http://info.tpj.org/reports/PerryJuly2011Update/Perry100kContributorsJuly2011.html), and Influence Explorer, *Bill White Contributions 2009–2010* (http://influenceexplorer.com/politician/billwhite/2ae6d79176f74c38877161544e650d84?cycle=2010).

Clearly, money is important in election campaigns. Although the candidate who spends the most money does not always win, a certain amount of money is necessary for a candidate to be competitive. Speaking with his tongue partly in his cheek, one prominent politician noted, in regard to high-level statewide races in Texas, that, even if "you don't have to raise $10 million, you have to raise $8 million."[35]

Control over Money in Campaigns Prompted by the increasing use of television in campaigns and the increasing amount of money needed to buy it, the federal government and most state governments passed laws regulating the use of money in the early 1970s. The Federal Elections Campaign Act of 1972 established regulations that apply only to federal elections: president, vice president, and members of Congress. It provided for public financing of presidential campaigns with tax dollars, limited the amount of money that individuals and PACs could contribute to campaigns, and required disclosure of campaign donations. In 1976, the Supreme Court declared that it was unconstitutional to set spending

---

[35]"The Senate Can Wait," interview with Jim Hightower, *Texas Observer*, January 27, 1989, p. 6.

limits for campaigns that were not publicly funded; this means there are no spending limits for congressional races.[36]

Not surprisingly, expenditures in election campaigns continue to increase. The Federal Election Commission reported that $211.8 million was spent in the 1976 election of the president and members of Congress, with $122.8 million spent in the presidential race alone. Of the $60.9 million spent in the elections of the 435 House members, more money was spent on behalf of the candidates in Texas ($4.5 million) than on those of any other state except California.[37] Such expenditure levels (only $140,000 per seat) appear modest by today's standards. By 2010, the average was nearly $1.7 million per U.S. House seat and substantially larger for U.S. Senate elections—at least $27 million. The level of campaign spending is likely to continue to rise.

Later amendments to the Federal Elections Campaign Act made it legal for national political parties to raise and spend unlimited amounts of **soft money**, funds spent by political parties on behalf of political candidates. Party funds could be used to help candidates in a variety of ways, especially through voter registration and get-out-the-vote drives. The U.S. Supreme Court further opened up spending in 1985 by deciding that **independent expenditures** could not be limited.[38] As a result, individuals and organizations could spend as much as they want to promote a candidate as long as they were not working or communicating directly with the candidate's campaign organization. The 2002 Campaign Reform Act limited independent expenditures by corporations and labor unions, but this was overturned by the Supreme Court in its 2010 decision in *Citizens United* v. *Federal Election Commission*.[39] This may have implications for state and local races that have bans on corporate spending, including Texas. The 2002 Act also deprived the parties of their soft money resources, but activists simply set up nonparty organizations to collect and disperse such funds. Understandably, it has been difficult to effectively control money in election campaigns.

FEC regulations apply only to candidates for national office. For candidates running for state offices, the most important provisions of Texas law regarding money in campaigns are as follows:

★ Candidates may not raise or spend money until an official campaign treasurer is appointed.

★ Candidates and PACs may not accept cash contributions for more than an aggregate of $100, but checks in unlimited amounts are permitted.

★ Direct contributions from corporations and labor unions are prohibited, though this may change in the wake of the recent Supreme Court decision, *Citizens United* v. *Federal Elections Commission*, 558 U.S. 50 (2010).

★ Candidates and treasurers of campaign committees are required to file sworn statements listing all contributions and expenditures for a designated reporting period to the Texas secretary of state's office.

★ Both criminal and civil penalties are imposed on anyone who violates the law's provisions.

★ Primary enforcement of campaign regulations is the responsibility of the Texas Ethics Commission.

Although these provisions may sound imposing, the fact is that raising and spending money on Texas campaigns still is pretty much wide open. For example, corporations and

Soft money
Money spent by political parties on behalf of political candidates, especially for the purposes of increasing voter registration and turnout.

Independent expenditures
Money individuals and organizations spend to promote a candidate without working or communicating directly with the candidate's campaign organization.

---

[36]*Buckley* v. *Valeo*, 424 U.S. 1 (1976).

[37]*Congressional Quarterly Almanac, 1977* (Washington, DC: CQ Press, 1977), p. 35A; *Congressional Quarterly Weekly Report*, March 5, 1989, p. 478. Since 1976, the federal government has actually expanded the role of money in elections.

[38]Federal Election Commission, www.fec.gov

[39]*Citizens United* v. *Federal Election Commission*, 558 U.S. 50 (2010).

labor unions may not give directly to a candidate, but they may give via their PACs. Note also that there are no limits on the amount a candidate may spend. Probably the most important effect of the campaign finance law in Texas comes from the requirement of disclosure. How much money a candidate raises, who makes contributions, and how campaign funds are spent are matters of public record. This information may be newsworthy to reporters or other individuals motivated to inform the public.

Who Gets Elected

It is useful to think of elected offices in Texas as a pyramid. At the bottom of the pyramid are the most local of offices; at the top is the governor. Moving from bottom to top, the importance of the office increases and the number of officeholders decreases. It thus gets more and more difficult for politicians to ascend the pyramid, and only the most effective politicians rise to the top. This tells us a lot about candidates and elections in Texas and elsewhere.

In local elections, the pool of candidates is diverse in many ways, including educational background, income, and profession. As we move up the pyramid, however, candidates become much more homogeneous. For statewide office, the typical candidate is middle or upper class, from an urban area, and has strong ties to business and professional interests in the state. Most elected state officers in Texas, including the governor, lieutenant governor, and attorney general, must be acceptable to the state's major financial and corporate interests and to its top law firms. These interests help statewide candidates raise the large amounts of money that are critical to a successful race.

Successful candidates for statewide office in Texas have traditionally been white Protestant males. Prior to 1986, when Raul Gonzalez was elected to the state supreme court, no Latino or African American had been elected to statewide office, though these two ethnic groups combined represent one-half of the state's population. The only female governor until that time was Miriam A. "Ma" Ferguson, who in the 1920s served as surrogate for her husband, Jim. In 1982, Ann Richards was elected state treasurer, becoming the second woman ever to be elected to statewide office in Texas.

Women and minorities have made substantial gains in statewide offices. Ann Richards became the first woman elected governor in her own right. Kay Bailey Hutchison captured the state treasurer's office and in 1993 won a special election to become the first woman from Texas elected to the U.S. Senate. Dan Morales was the first Latino to win a state executive office when he captured the attorney general's office. More history was made when Morris Overstreet of Amarillo won a seat on the Texas Court of Criminal Appeals and became the first African American elected to a statewide office.

Women and ethnic groups are starting to make inroads in other elected offices in Texas. In the 83rd Legislature (2013–2014), 31 women were elected to the 150-member house and 6 to the 31-member senate. Women have also held the post of mayor in five of the state's largest cities: Houston, Dallas, San Antonio, El Paso, and Austin. Latinos hold 40 seats in the state legislature, and African Americans occupy 20. Among the state's 36 U.S. congressional representatives, there are 3 women, 6 Latinos, and 4 African Americans. Clearly, Texas politics has changed a lot over a short time.

The New Media and Texas Politics

Laura K. De La Cruz
El Paso Community College

INTRODUCTION

The media have played an important role in politics since our nation's birth, but the system is shifting from the "news" media to the "new" media. In the early 1800s, politicians campaigned via letter writing and newspaper articles, reaching hundreds. In the early 1900s, politicians campaigned via train tours and press coverage, reaching thousands. In the early 2000s, politicians campaigned via the new media of viral politics and social networking sites, reaching millions. Texas is becoming a leader in new media politics.

TRADITIONAL MEDIA

Historically, political news coverage was dominated by broadcast television and daily newspapers. Throughout Texas's quest for independence and statehood, newspapers were used to promote those goals and solicit support from the United States. William Travis's letter of appeal for support from February 24, 1836, was published in newspapers across the United States, garnering American support for the Texas War of Independence (www.lsjunction.com/docs/appeal.htm).

The *Galveston County Daily News* is Texas's oldest continuously published newspaper and debuted on April 11, 1842. It is not, however, the first newspaper published in Texas. That honor goes to the *Gaceta de Texas,* which was published on May 25, 1813 in Nacogdoches. However, the reach of newspapers was fairly limited, and print media remained the primary source of Texas political news until the advent of radio.

In 1911, radio broadcasting began at The University of Texas (UT) and Texas A&M campuses, and by the 1920s radio stations were broadcasting across Texas. Radios played an important role in Texas politics by offering news reports, covering campaigns, and broadcasting inaugurations. Like other radio stations across the nation, Texas stations were regulated by the Federal Communications Commission (FCC) and were required to offer equal time to candidates from different parties to present their views. After 1949,

they were also required to comply with the FCC's Fairness Doctrine and avoid promoting a particular party or viewpoint over another.

Television appeared in Texas on September 27, 1948, when a Fort Worth station broadcast a speech by President Harry Truman. In 1954, Spanish television debuted in the El Paso–Juarez, Mexico area. Television quickly supplanted both radio and newspapers as people's primary source of political news with its ability to broadcast live events in dramatic fashion.

NEW MEDIA

During the past 30 years, and particularly the last 10, attention has shifted to new forms of media such as cable programs, talk radio/podcasts, websites/social networking sites, blogs/RSS feeds, and phone applications.

An event instrumental to this shift was the FCC's elimination of the Fairness Doctrine in the 1980s. Like radio stations, television stations initially were required to comply with the Fairness Doctrine. The advent of cable television and the increasing number of television channels convinced the FCC that there was no longer limited access to news and, therefore, no longer a need for the Fairness Doctrine. Television and radio both responded to this change by creating programming specifically tailored to liberal and conservative audiences.

Cable Television Cable television channels have provided viewers with a growing variety of news programs—programs that have become increasingly partisan during the past 10 years. Many, such as Fox News and MSNBC, purposely slant their news toward their viewers' political ideologies and only cover items their viewers want to hear about.

The future: Webcams are allowing viewers to create their own television programming, with ready access by millions via You Tube and other video sites. Organizations such as Texas Tech (www.youtube.com/texastech) have already created their own channels on YouTube, with politicians soon to follow. Politicians will create their own programming for the Internet and YouTube in order to reach larger audiences.

Talk Radio/Podcasts There are dozens of talk radio stations in Texas, broadcasting in both English and Spanish. They cover a diverse range of topics, including local events, tourism, entertainment, and politics. Talk radio stations, like cable television channels, are providing partisan political news targeting specific audiences.

The future: Online talk radio programs are cheap and easy for individuals to create and provide via the Internet. Sites like www.blogtalkradio.com give people the opportunity to offer their own version of the news, particularly local news. Conservative programs such as "Conservative Latino Talk Radio" and progressive programs such as "Capitol Annex Radio" broadcast regularly.

Websites Websites are used by almost every government agency in Texas, from state to local. Politicians have also adopted websites, both incumbents and challengers. The Texas governor's office, for example, provides the incumbent with a site sponsored and maintained by the state of Texas (www.governor.state.tx.us/). This is an added benefit for the incumbent, who can use the site to promote his/her agenda and enhance their image. Personal websites allow politicians and candidates the opportunity to campaign, find volunteers, and fund-raise. For example, when Governor Rick Perry was running for reelection in 2010, he had the double benefit of his personal website (www.rickperry.org/) and the state's website as vehicles to highlight his successes.

The future: Politicians will continue to use websites, but these will remain a fairly passive vehicle for politics. Their potential is limited as politicians look for more active ways to reach voters and to target specific audiences. In many ways, websites are becoming like newspapers. They can offer personalized videos, blogs, and minute-by-minute news, but these are politician-driven. Nevertheless, their potential for fund-raising remains strong.

Blogs Anyone with an Internet connection can start a blog and thousands have on topics ranging from cooking to politics. Technology allows for RSS feeds whereby readers subscribe and blog posts are automatically delivered to their email. Phone applications now allow blog posting to be delivered via cell phone.

Blogs in Texas range from grassroots such as Burnt Orange (www.burntorangereport.com), started by students from UT Austin in 2004 to blogs such as the *Houston Chronicle's* Texas Politics blog (http://blogs.chron.com/texaspolitics/).

The future: Blogs are a time-consuming method of presenting a message, and politicians are looking for media that get their message out faster. These methods tend to require a message that is brief and direct. Nevertheless, blogs will continue to be used by politicians who want to provide more extensive coverage of an issue.

Social Networking Sites Social networking sites such as Facebook, MySpace, Twitter, and MeetUp can be credited with changing politics in 2008 when President Obama used social networking sites to campaign and fund-raise in unprecedented ways. These sites have been used to stream video, solicit feedback via like/dislike selections, and to provide postings in real time.

These sites are being used in 2012 by Texas politicians such as Governor Rick Perry (www.twitter.com/governorperry and www.facebook.com/GovernorPerry), candidates for the Texas Senate such as Wendy Davis (www.myspace.com/wendydavisforsenate), and political groups looking for potential members (http://conservative-and-libertarian-politics.meetup.com/).

The future: As social networking sites themselves network with each other (Facebook links with Flickr, Digg, Delicious, Pinterest, Technorati, YouTube, and others), more information about users becomes available in order to target their message. This will be particularly helpful for politicians who can then reach voters quickly and efficiently.

Phones Cell phones have opened up a whole new way of connecting with potential voters and supporters. Text messages about running mate selection, video streaming of press events, and video capture of news events via phone cameras have changed politics in ways unheard of prior to 2005. Universities such as UT Austin already have phone applications or apps (www.utexas.edu/iphoneapp/) so students, alumni, and supporters can keep up with the latest news.

The future: Phone apps will change politics in ways unimaginable today. Already apps exist that provide conservative talking points, offer *New York Times* opinion pieces, or provide copies of various political books and documents from throughout history. Potential uses include locator apps that allow users to find others who share a similar ideology—a "liberal or conservative finder" type application, bill-tracking applications, video streaming of legislative meetings, and GPS tracking of politicians and candidates.

Pros and Cons of the New Media The new media is a change from the traditional media in that it is viewer-driven (or voter-driven) as opposed to media-driven (or politician-driven). In many ways, it is democracy at its best. Voters can pick and choose what they see and hear as well as provide instant feedback to express their views. Ultimately, however, voices may get lost in the din, creating mob rule online.

Another bonus of the new media is that viewers and readers now have a greater selection of news from which to choose and can share news with others. News becomes viral and spreads quickly across the world. It is the ultimate in free speech but may cause information overload (resulting in too much free speech, if there is such a thing!).

The new media also creates more points of history as individuals can now save history via technology. Pictures, video, and recordings will preserve larger and larger amounts of history, thus preserving politics for posterity—or will they? The sheer amount of material may keep relevant history from being recorded. Politicians may be haunted by videos that are decades old and no longer relevant. Furthermore, history could potentially be deleted. For example, Twitter postings may be deleted if someone later regrets their posting, thus depriving historians of important artifacts.

Ultimately, the most significant consequence of the new media is that distance becomes irrelevant, and as a result, national and international news now becomes Texas news and vice versa. The old saying, "All politics is local" now becomes "All political news is local."

JOIN THE DEBATE

1. How do consumers of the new media evaluate their sources? Will a highly competitive, worldwide new media environment replace traditional journalistic standards and editorial review?

2. How will the new media finance costly fact gathering and investigative journalism? Will advocacy journalism replace fact-based reporting?

3. In what ways does the development of the new media enhance democracy? Is there a danger that the fragmentation of the media will cause voters to become more polarized into hostile political camps?

CHAPTER SUMMARY

Elections are the defining characteristic of representative democracy. It is through our votes that we hold elected officials accountable.

★ A small number of demographic and political variables are important in predicting who will vote. The most important demographic variables are education, income, and age. Certain political factors also influence the likelihood of voting, especially a person's level of interest in politics and intensity of identification with a political party. Other factors are important as well, but with this small set of demographic and political variables, we can make a good prediction as to whether a person will vote in a particular election.

★ Voting in Texas (and most other states) is a two-stage process. Before you can vote, you must first register. Traditionally a barrier for women and minorities, the registration procedure today is as simple as voting itself—perhaps even simpler. Since the passage of federal "motor voter" legislation, a person can register when obtaining or renewing a driver's license. Once registered, voting in Texas is easy, though the passage of voter identification requirements may make things harder for some people, particularly minorities.

★ National turnout in presidential elections has fluctuated between 50 and 55 percent in recent years. In midterm elections, turnout is around 40 percent. These numbers are lower than what we find in most other advanced democracies. Voter turnout in Texas is even below the U.S. national average.

★ Low voter turnout in Texas may be due in part to the state's socioeconomic characteristics. A comparatively large percentage of the population lives below the poverty level. An even larger percentage has not graduated from high school, and these people are not very likely to vote. Income and education levels are low for African Americans and Latinos, so turnout is particularly low for these groups. Political factors, such as political structure and political culture, may also play a role in low turnout.

★ In Texas, as in other southern states that once were predominantly Democratic, a majority rule is used in primary elections. If no candidate receives a majority of the votes cast for a particular office in the first primary, a second, runoff primary is used to determine the winner. Outside the South, only a plurality of the votes is typically required.

★ Ballot design is an important factor in elections. Texas traditionally has used the party-column ballot, in which the names of all the candidates of each party are listed in parallel columns. The main alternative is the office-block ballot, in which the names of candidates are listed underneath each office. Many Texas counties have now adopted electronic voting systems, which combine features of the office-block and party-column designs.

★ Texas is a diverse state, and the pool of candidates for local offices reflects this diversity. As we move up the pyramid of elected offices, however, the candidates become much more homogeneous—successful candidates for statewide office traditionally have been white male conservatives. While this remains true today, women and minorities have made substantial gains, and these gains are likely to continue as more women and minorities enter politics.

★ In a state as large as Texas, media advertising, political consultants, and polling are required for any candidate seeking to win statewide office or the most competitive state legislative and local elections. These services are expensive.

★ Without a certain amount of funding, it is impossible to be competitive in Texas elections. The high, and still rising, costs of campaigns mean that serious candidates must collect contributions from a variety of sources. Most candidates must rely on PACs and wealthy individuals. Although the Texas legislature has passed laws regulating campaign finance in state races, raising and spending funds is still fairly wide open.

HOW TEXAS COMPARES

★ Texas traditionally has had very restrictive voting rules, and voter turnout has been among the lowest of the 50 states. In the 2012 election, no state had a lower rate of voter turnout than Texas.

★ It now is much easier to register and vote in the state. Texas was among the first states to institute early voting, and turnout has since come more in line with what we see in other states, though it still is below average.

★ Texas does not limit the terms of states legislators or governors, but twenty-one states do, including all of the neighboring states.

KEY TERMS

Australian ballot, *p. 101*
chad, *p. 104*
closed primary *p. 94*
crossover voting *p. 94*
direct primary *p. 92*
early voting *p. 103*

electronic voting *p. 105*
independent expenditures
   p. 111
negative campaigning *p. 107*
office-block ballot *p. 98*
open primary *p. 94*

participation paradox *p. 82*
party-column ballot *p. 97*
plurality vote *p. 95*
political action committees
   (PACs) *p. 108*
runoff primary *p. 94*

soft money *p. 111*
voter turnout *p. 84*
voting-age population (VAP)
   p. 84

REVIEW QUESTIONS

1. What explains why some people are more likely to vote than others?

2. Why is voter turnout in Texas lower than it is in most other states?

3. How will the new voter identification law impact turnout in Texas?

4. What is the majority election rule, and why do we use it in Texas primaries?

5. Why are some candidates more likely than others to win elections in Texas?

6. What have elected officials in the United States and Texas done to control money in election campaigns? Have these measures been effective?

LOGGING ON

There are many websites related to voting, elections, and campaigns. The political parties have websites, as do most political candidates, and there are several independent sites. For a wide-ranging list of political resources on the Web, try the American Political Science Association site at **www.apsanet.org/content_2775.cfm?navID=9**. For a virtual warehouse of national and state public opinion data, go to **www.pollingreport.com**. For current election polling data, go to **www.pollster.com**. For specific information about U.S. voting behavior in every national election year, go to the National Election Studies home page at **www.electionstudies.org**. For specific information about voting and elections in Texas, go to the secretary of state's election page at **www.sos.state.tx.us/elections**.

For information about particular issues, go to the League of Women Voters at **www.lwvtexas.org**. To find out more about youth voter turnout, visit CIRCLE at **www.civicyouth.org**. CIRCLE has conducted research on civic and political engagement by youth since 2001. At this site, you can find information specifically about Texas voting.

One of the critical issues discussed in this chapter is money in elections. To do some research on this issue, go to **www.fec.gov**, the Federal Election Commission (FEC) site. Click on "Campaign Finance Reports and Data" and then on "Search the Disclosure Database." This gives you access to the campaign spending data collected by the FEC. For instance, you can see how much candidates received and spent and where the contributions came from. To start, follow the link "Candidate and PAC/Party Summaries." Once there, pick "Texas" in the state list and then "Send Query" and you will see what different candidates spent. You will also see what different PACs contributed. The names and numbers may surprise you!

Chapter 5

Political Parties

LEARNING OBJECTIVES

★ Evaluate the role of political parties in Texas.

★ Describe the features that characterize American political parties.

★ Explain why Texas politics were dominated by the Democratic Party until the early 1990s.

★ Analyze the differences between liberal and conservative views.

★ Classify the types of people and groups who generally support Texas Republicans and Texas Democrats.

★ Name the geographical areas of Texas that generally support the GOP and those areas where the Democratic Party is stronger.

★ Explain the difference in temporary versus permanent party organization in Texas and give an example of each.

★ Define realignment and describe the reasons a majority of Texas voters have gradually come to identify with the Republican Party.

★ Predict why more Texas voters may identify with the Democratic Party in the future.

© Glowimages / Getty Images, Inc.

GET Active

Decide where you stand on the ideological spectrum. Sample conservative and liberal opinion:

Liberal/Progressive Groups

★ Link up with the *Texas Observer* at **www.texasobserver.org/**.

★ Plug into **www.offthekuff.com/** and **www.texaskaos.com/**.

★ Nose around Brains and Eggs at **brainsandeggs.blogspot.com/**.

Conservative Groups

★ Tune into The Right Side of Austin at **http://therightsideofaustin.wordpress .com/**.

★ Sound out the *Texas Conservative Review* at **www.texasconservativereview.com/ index.html**.

★ Team up with your political party. On-campus organizations usually include the Young Democrats (**www.texasyds .com**) and Young Republicans (**texasyoungrepublicans.com/**).

Help select your party's nominee. Register and vote in your party's primary election. To vote in the primary, you must be registered at least 30 days in advance. In Texas, you simply decide which party you prefer and vote to select that party's nominee. The only real restriction is that you must choose one party or the other.

Go to your party's precinct convention or caucus. If you vote in your party's primary, you are eligible to attend your party's precinct convention (or caucus, as it is referred to in presidential election years). The convention begins a few minutes after the polls close and is usually in the same location as the primary. Attendance is often sparse, which means you have a good chance of being heard and even being elected as a delegate.

Attend your party's county- or district-level convention. Delegates selected at the precinct level go on to attend their party's county or district convention. Delegates to these conventions pass resolutions and elect candidates to the state convention, which is held every two years in June. If you are selected as a delegate to the state convention, you have become a serious party activist. For more information on the Texas party conventions and events, leaders, rules, and issue positions, check the websites of the state political parties, listed in "Logging On."

The Founders created our complicated system of federal government and provided for the election of a president and Congress. However, the U.S. Constitution makes no mention of political parties. Indeed, these early leaders held negative attitudes about parties. George Washington warned of the "baneful effects of the spirit of party" in his farewell address. James Madison, in Federalist Paper 10, criticized parties or "factions" as divisive but admitted that they were inevitable. Madison and others thought that parties would encourage conflict and undermine consensus on public policy. Yet despite their condemnation of parties, these early American politicians engaged in partisan politics and initiated a competitive two-party system.

Parties, then, are apparently something we should live neither with nor without. They have been with us from the start of this country and will be with us for the foreseeable future, influencing our government and public policy. It is important, therefore, to gain an understanding of what they are all about.

What is a political party? This question conjures up various stereotypes: smoke-filled rooms where party leaders or bosses make important behind-the-scenes decisions; activists or regulars who give time, money, and enthusiastic support to their candidates; or voters who proudly identify themselves as Democrats or Republicans. Essentially, though, a political party is simply a broad-based coalition of interests whose primary purpose is to win elections. Gaining control of government through popular elections is the most important goal for political parties, and most of the activities parties pursue are directed toward this purpose. Parties recruit and nominate their members for public office. They form coalitions of different groups and interests to build majorities so that they can elect their candidates.

Political parties are vital to democracy in that they provide a link between the people and the government. Parties make it possible for the ordinary citizen and voter to participate in the political system; they provide the means for organizing support for particular candidates. In organizing this support, parties unify various groups and interests and mobilize them behind the candidate who supports their preferred positions.

FUNCTIONS OF POLITICAL PARTIES

Political parties developed and survived because they perform important functions. The first function of parties is to nominate and elect their members to public office. Except for most Texas local elections, in which parties are forbidden by law to participate, candidates are nominated by political parties, and parties run the election process. The second function of political parties is to simplify the issues for voters so that people understand the alternative positions on questions of public policy. In other words, parties educate the public. They help make sense of the issues and provide voters with cues on how to vote.

The third function of parties is to mobilize voters by encouraging participation in the electoral process. Citizens are persuaded to become active in support of party candidates. Contributing money to campaigns, telephoning, and door-to-door canvassing are all examples of how parties mobilize supporters. The more organized the party, the more effective it becomes in getting out the vote for its candidates.

Finally, the fourth function of parties is to run the government at whatever level they are active. The president, members of Congress, governors, state representatives, and Texas state judges are all elected to public office under the party label. Once elected, these officials try to push forward the positions of their party. However, in our political system, it is often difficult for parties to manage government because separate branches of government may not be under the control of the same party.

CHARACTERISTICS OF AMERICAN POLITICAL PARTIES

American political parties have three distinct characteristics not always found in parties elsewhere in the world: (1) pragmatism, (2) decentralization, and (3) the two-party system.

Pragmatism

Pragmatism in politics means that ideas should be judged on the basis of their practical results rather than on the purity of their principles.[1] In other words, a pragmatist is interested

Pragmatism
The philosophy that ideas should be judged on the basis of their practical results rather than on an ideological basis. American political parties are pragmatic because they are more concerned with winning elections than with taking clear, uncompromising stands on issues.

---

[1]Marjorie Randon Hershey, *Party Politics in America*, 14th edition (New York: Longman, 2011), p. 289.

in what works on a practical basis. American parties are sometimes willing to compromise principles to appeal successfully to a majority of voters and gain public office. They willingly bargain with most organized groups and take stands that appeal to a large number of interests to build a winning coalition. In other words, American parties are much less programmatic than many Western European parties. The latter possess a consistent commitment to a particular ideology and their supporters are firmly committed to programmatic goals.

Pragmatism often means taking clear-cut positions only on issues where there is broad agreement. A campaign strategy designed to attract all groups and to repel none fails to bring the party's ideology into sharp focus. But taking clear stands on controversial issues may alienate potential members of the party's electoral coalition. Political parties and their candidates, including those in Texas, therefore, prefer to deemphasize issues and instead attempt to project a positive but vague image. Broad, fuzzy campaign themes that stress leadership potential, statesmanship, activities, family life, and personality often take precedence over issues.

Although the broad electoral coalitions that comprise American parties make it difficult for them to achieve ideological consistency, it would be a mistake to assume that parties in America do not differ from one another. Indeed, most observers think that American parties have become more programmatic and more polarized in recent years. To succeed, they must satisfy their traditional supporters: voters, public opinion leaders, interest groups, and campaign contributors. The candidates are not blank slates but have their own beliefs, prejudices, biases, and opinions. In most elections, broad ideological differences are apparent. Voters in Texas who participated in the presidential election of 2012 could easily differentiate between the conservative orientation of Mitt Romney and the more liberal philosophy of his opponent, Barack Obama.

Decentralization

At first glance, American party organizations may appear to be neatly ordered and hierarchical, with power flowing from the national to state to local parties. In reality, however, American parties are not nearly so hierarchical. They reflect the American federal system, with its **decentralization** of power to national, state, and local levels. Political party organizations operate at the precinct, or **grassroots**, level; the local government level (city, county, or district); the state level (especially in elections for governor); and the national level (especially in elections for president).

Figure 5.1 illustrates the nature of power in American political parties. State and local party organizations are semi-independent actors who exercise considerable discretion on most party matters. The practices that state and local parties follow, the candidates they recruit, the campaign money they raise, the innovations they introduce, the organized interests to which they respond, the campaign strategies they create, and most important, the policy orientations of the candidates who run under their label are all influenced by local and state political cultures, leaders, traditions, and interests.[2]

Compared with party systems in other countries, the American party system is quite decentralized. However, Figure 5.1 also illustrates how power has shifted to the national party organizations in recent years. Both the Democratic and Republican national parties have become stronger and more involved in state and local party activities through various service functions. By using new campaign technologies—computer-based mailing lists, direct-mail solicitations, and the Internet—the national parties have raised millions of dollars. Thus, the national party organizations have assumed a greater role by providing unprecedented levels of assistance to state parties and candidates. This assistance includes a variety

Decentralization

Exercise of power in political parties by state and local party organizations rather than by national party institutions.

Grassroots

The lowest level of party organization. In Texas, the grassroots level is the precinct level of organization.

---

[2]Norman J. Ornstein, Andrew Kohut, and Larry McCarthy, *The People, the Press, and Politics: The Times Mirror Study of the American Electorate* (Washington, DC: Times Mirror Center for the People and the Press, 1988).

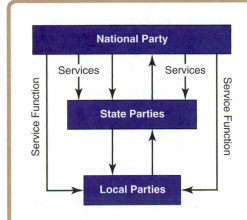

Figure 5.1

The Decentralized Nature of American Political Parties and the Importance of the National Party's Service Function

The diagram shows the semi-independent relationship that exists among national, state, and local party organizations and the increasingly important services and funds provided by the national party organization.

As national party organizations grow stronger, how much influence should they have over state and local parties and candidates? Should the latter pay close attention to the positions of the national party platform? Should voters hold state and local candidates accountable for the performance of national leaders?

of services—candidate recruitment, research, public opinion polling, computer networking, production of radio and television commercials, direct mailing, consultation on redistricting issues, and the transfer of millions of dollars worth of campaign funding. Not surprisingly, as national parties provide more money and services to state and local parties, they exercise more influence over state and local organizations, issues, and candidates.[3]

Two-Party System

In a majority of states, political competition usually comes down to competition between the two major parties, the Democrats and the Republicans. Third parties have tried to gain office but with little success, primarily because the pragmatic major parties make a conscientious effort to absorb them by adopting their issues (for example, the Populist Party of the 1890s was absorbed by the Democratic Party). Voters, potential campaign contributors, and political activists also behave pragmatically; they tend to avoid supporting a losing cause. Our electoral system, the **single-member district system**, encourages this pragmatic behavior. If only one representative can be elected in a district, voters will cast their ballots for the major-party candidates that have the best chance of winning.

In Texas, third parties such as the Libertarian Party or Green Party must receive at least 5 percent of the vote in the previous election to gain automatic ballot status. Failure to gain this 5 percent means that third parties can get on the ballot only by launching petition drives that gather the signatures of registered voters who did not vote in either party's primary. Independent candidates must also meet this standard. For example, in the 2006 gubernatorial election, independent candidates Carole Keeton Strayhorn and Kinky Friedman were forced to collect 45,000 signatures from eligible voters who had not voted in the March 7 primary to compete against incumbent governor Rick Perry in the November election.

DEVELOPMENT OF THE TEXAS PARTY SYSTEM

Although for most of its existence, the United States has had a **two-party system**, many states and localities—including Texas—have been dominated by just one party at various times in history. Texas was formerly a one-party Democratic state, but in recent years the

Single-member district system

A system in which one candidate is elected to a legislative body in each election district.

Two-party system

A political system characterized by two dominant parties competing for political offices. In such systems, minor or third parties have little chance of winning.

---

[3]Margaret Randon Hershey, *Party Politics in America*, 14th ed. (New York: HarperCollins, 2011), pp. 71–74.

state parties have become competitive in congressional and state-level races. To understand political parties in Texas, it is necessary to examine the historical predominance of the Democratic Party, the emergence of two-party competition in the state, and the reality of Republican Party domination at present.

The One-Party Tradition in Texas

Under the Republic of Texas, there was little party activity. Political divisions were usually oriented around support of, or opposition to, Sam Houston, a leading founder of the Republic. After Texas became a state, however, the Democratic Party dominated Texas politics until the 1990s. This legacy of dominance was firmly established by the Civil War and the era of Reconstruction, when Yankee troops, under the direction of a Republican Congress, occupied the South. From the time that the Republican and former Union soldier Edmund J. Davis's single term as governor ended in 1873 until the surprising victory of the Republican gubernatorial candidate Bill Clements in 1978, the Democrats exercised almost complete control over Texas politics.

The Democratic Party was at times challenged by the emergence of more liberal third parties. The most serious of these challenges came in the late nineteenth century with the Populist revolt. The Populist Party grew out of the dissatisfaction of small farmers who demanded government regulation of rates charged by banks and railroads. These farmers—joined by sharecroppers, laborers, and African Americans—mounted a serious election bid in 1896 by taking 44.3 percent of the vote for governor. Eventually, however, the Democratic Party defused the threat of the Populists by co-opting many of the issues of the new party. The Democrats also effectively disenfranchised African Americans and poor whites in 1902 with the passage of the poll tax.

Two events in the early twentieth century solidified the position of the Democrats in Texas politics. The first was the institution of party primary "reforms" in 1906. For the first time, voters could choose the party's nominees by a direct vote in the party primary. Hence, the Democratic primary became the substitute for the two-party contest: the general election. In the absence of Republican competition, the Democratic primary was the only game in town, and it provided a competitive arena for political differences within the state.

The second event to help the Democrats was the Depression. Although the Republican presidential candidate, Herbert Hoover, carried Texas in 1928, Republicans were closely associated with the Great Depression of the 1930s. The cumulative effect of this association, the Civil War, and Reconstruction ensured Democratic dominance in state government until the early 1990s.

Ideological Basis of Factionalism: Conservatives and Liberals

Although members of a political party may be similar in their views, factions or divisions within the party inevitably develop. These conflicts may involve a variety of personalities and issues, but the most important basis for division is ideology.

To understand the ideological basis for factionalism in political parties in Texas, it is necessary to define the terms conservative and liberal—a difficult task because the meanings change with time and may mean different things to different people.

Conservatives Conservatives believe that individuals should be left alone to compete in a free market unfettered by government control; they prefer that government regulation of the economy be kept to a minimum. They extol the virtues of individualism, independence, and personal initiative. However, conservatives support government involvement and funding to promote business. They favor construction of highways, tax incentives for investment, and other government aids to business. The theory is that these aids will encourage economic development and hence prosperity for the whole society (the trickle-down theory). On the other hand, conservatives are likely to oppose government programs that involve large-scale redistribution of wealth such as welfare, health care aid, or unemployment compensation.

Some conservatives view change suspiciously; they tend to favor the status quo—things as they are now and as they have been. They emphasize traditional values associated with the family and close communities, and they often favor government action to preserve what they see as the proper moral values of society. Because conservatives hold a more skeptical view of human nature than liberals do, they are more likely to be tougher on perceived threats to personal safety and the public order as well as to traditional and religious values. For example, conservatives are more likely to favor stiffer penalties for criminals, including capital punishment. Conservatives may combine support for the free market with support for traditional values, or they may adopt only one of these views.

One particular form of conservatism is libertarianism. In recent years, the Libertarian Party has become an active, if not always influential, force in Texas politics. The Libertarian Party has a hands-off philosophy of government that appeals to many Texas conservatives. The party's general philosophy is one of individual liberty and personal responsibility. Applying their doctrine to the issues, Libertarians would oppose Social Security, campaign finance reform, gun control, and many foreign policies. They consider programs like Social Security to be "state-provided welfare" and believe that regulating campaigns promotes too much government involvement. They also oppose U.S. intervention in world affairs. The Libertarian Party faces the same hurdles as other third parties: poor financing, a lack of media coverage, and in some states, getting access to the ballot.

Liberals Liberals believe that it is often necessary for government to regulate the economy and to promote greater social equality. They point to great concentrations of wealth and power that have threatened to control government, destroy economic competition, and weaken individual freedom. Government power, they believe, should be used to protect the disadvantaged and to promote equality. Consequently, liberals are generally supportive of the social welfare programs that conservatives oppose. Liberals champion wage and hour laws, the right to form unions, unemployment and health insurance, subsidized housing, and improved educational opportunities. They are also more likely to favor progressive taxes, which increase as incomes increase. The best example of a progressive tax is an individual income tax.

Liberals possess a more optimistic view of human nature than conservatives. They believe that individuals are essentially rational and therefore that change will ultimately bring improvement in the human condition. Liberals want government to protect the civil rights and liberties of individuals and are critical of interference with any exercise of the constitutional rights of free speech, press, religion, assembly, association, and privacy. They are often suspicious of conservatives' attempts to "legislate morality" because of the potential for interference with individual rights.

Conservative and Liberal Factions in the Democratic Party

For many years, factions within the Texas Democratic Party resembled a two-party system, and the election to select the Democratic Party's nominees—the primary—was the most important election in Texas. Until the 1990s, conservative Democrats were much more successful than their liberal counterparts in these primaries, in part because Republican voters, facing no significant primary race of their own, regularly crossed over and supported conservative Democratic candidates. Voters in the general elections, facing a choice between a conservative

Ted Cruz (left) debates Lieutentant Governor David Dewhurst during the 2012 Republican primary. With strong support from more ideological conservatives such as the Club for Growth and Tea Party activists, Cruz won the party's nomination to the U.S. Senate by successfully characterizing Dewhurst as the "establishment" candidate.

Explain why winning the high-stakes Republican primaries is so critical in Texas, where the Republican nominee can expect to win the general election.

© Bob Daemmrich/Alamy

Did You Know? In 1952, conservative Democratic Governor Allan Shivers was nominated by both the Democratic and Republican parties for the same office.

Democrat and a conservative Republican, usually went with the traditional party—the Democrats. These Republican crossover votes enabled conservative Democrats, with few exceptions, to control the party and state government until the late 1970s.

Conservative Democrats in Texas provided a very good example of the semi-independent relationship of national, state, and local party organizations illustrated in Figure 5.1. Texas conservatives traditionally voted Democratic in state and local races but often refused to support the national Democratic candidates for president. Indeed, the development of the conservative Democratic faction in Texas was an outgrowth of conservative dissatisfaction with many New Deal proposals of Franklin D. Roosevelt in the 1930s and Fair Deal proposals of Harry Truman in the 1940s. Conservative Democrats in Texas continued their cool relationship with the national party when many of them supported Republican presidential candidates: Dwight Eisenhower in 1952 and 1956, Richard Nixon in 1968 and 1972, and Ronald Reagan in 1980 and 1984.

Several factors accounted for the historical success of conservative Democrats, but the most important were the power and resources of the conservative constituency. Conservatives have traditionally made up the state's power elite, representing such interests as the oil, gas, and sulfur industries; other large corporations; bigger farms and ranches (agribusiness); owners and publishers of many of the state's major daily newspapers; and veterans. In other words, the most affluent people in the state are able and willing to contribute their considerable resources to the campaigns of like-minded politicians. These segments of the population are also the most likely to turn out and vote in elections. This was a significant advantage to conservative Democrats competing in the party primary, in which turnout in the past has been particularly low.

Liberals in the Texas Democratic Party consist of groups who have supported the national party ticket and its presidents (Roosevelt, Truman, Kennedy, Johnson, Carter, Clinton, and Obama). These groups include the following:

★ Organized labor, in particular the American Federation of Labor–Congress of Industrial Organizations (AFL-CIO)

★ African-American groups, such as the National Association for the Advancement of Colored People (NAACP)

★ Latino groups, such as the American G.I. Forum, League of Latin American Citizens (LULAC), Mexican American Democrats (MAD), and Mexican American Legal Defense and Educational Fund (MALDEF)

★ Various professionals, teachers, and intellectuals
★ Small farmers and ranchers, sometimes belonging to the Texas Farmers Union
★ Environmental groups, such as the Sierra Club
★ Abortion rights groups, such as the Texas Abortion Rights Action League
★ Trial lawyers—that is, lawyers who represent plaintiffs in civil suits and defendants in criminal cases

The success of liberal Democratic politicians in Texas was infrequent and rarely persisted for more than a few years. In recent years, liberal Texas Democrats have had more success in capturing their party's nomination, largely because conservatives are voting in the Republican primary. Lately, liberal or moderate Democrats have been routinely nominated for all the statewide races. This last point illustrates the irony for liberal Democrats: although they have gained control of the Democratic party as conservatives have defected from their ranks, these very defections have left the Democrats in the minority and made the Republicans dominant in Texas.

Rise of the Republican Party

Before the presidential election of November 1988, only three contemporary Republicans had won statewide races in Texas: Senator John Tower (1961–1985), Governor Bill Clements (1979–1983 and 1987–1991), and Senator Phil Gramm (1985–2003). Why had the Republican Party failed to compete in Texas in the past? The most important reason is the bitter memory left by Texas's experience in the Civil War and during Reconstruction. The Republican administration of Governor E. J. Davis under the Texas Constitution of 1869 was considered the most corrupt and abusive period of Texas history. Only in the past few years has the Republican Party been able to shake its image as the party of Reconstruction.

The Republicans Become Competitive   The revival of the Republican Party was foreshadowed in the 1950s by the development of the so-called presidential Republicans (people who vote Republican for national office but Democratic for state and local office). Conservative Democrats objected to the obvious policy differences of the state and national Democratic parties and often voted for Republican presidential candidates.

The first major step in the rejuvenation of the Republican Party in Texas came in 1961, when John Tower, a Republican, was elected to the U.S. Senate. Tower won a special nonpartisan election held when Lyndon Johnson gave up his Senate seat to assume the vice presidency. Tower initially won with the help of many liberal Democrats and was reelected until he retired in 1984. His seat was retained by the Republicans with the election to the Senate of former Representative Phil Gramm over his liberal Democratic opponent Lloyd Doggett in 1984. In November 2002, John Cornyn, a Republican and the state's former attorney general, was elected to replace Gramm.

In November 1978, the Republicans achieved their most stunning breakthrough when Bill Clements defeated John Hill in the race for governor. After losing the governor's seat to moderate-conservative Mark White in 1982, Republicans regained their momentum in 1986, when Clements turned the tables on White and recaptured the governor's chair.

Developments in the 1990s and early 2000s transformed Texas into "Republican country." With the election in 1992 of U.S. Senator Kay Bailey Hutchison, Republicans held both U.S. Senate seats for the first time since Reconstruction. In 1994, Republican George W. Bush defeated incumbent Democratic governor Ann Richards.

By far the most impressive gains for the GOP came in the November 1998 elections, when incumbent Governor George W. Bush led a sweep of Republicans to victory in every

TABLE 5.1 Changes in the Number of Republican and Democratic Officeholders in Texas

Body	1973		2013	
	Democrats	Republicans	Democrats	Republicans
Texas House of Representatives	132	17	55	95
Texas Senate	28	3	12	19
U.S. House of Representatives	20	4	12	24
U.S. Senate	1	1	0	2

▲ **What explains the Republicans' dominance of the Texas political scene today? To what extent will demographic changes affect the future success of the party?**

By permission of Gary Markstein and Creators Syndicate Creators Syndicate, Inc., Gary Markstein, November 10, 2004

This cartoon highlights the underdog status of the Democratic Party in Texas in recent years.

What strategies should the Democrats employ to become more competitive in state elections? How do changing state demographics give the Democrats hope for the future?

statewide election. For the first time in living memory, no Democrats occupied any statewide executive or judicial office. Republicans have continued to maintain their monopoly on statewide offices. In 2004, after a successful effort at congressional redistricting, the GOP captured a majority in Texas's congressional delegation.

The Republican Party is also extremely competitive in lower-level offices in the state, where Democrats were once most firmly entrenched. In 1974, the GOP held only 53 offices at the county level; they now hold more than 2,000 county offices. In 1996, the GOP gained a majority of seats in the state senate, the first time in 126 years that Republicans held a majority in either house of the legislature, and in 2002, they captured the state house of representatives.

Table 5.1 shows the dramatic increases by Republicans in the Texas legislature and the Texas delegation to the U.S. House of Representatives. The extent to which these gains signal a Republican-dominated party system in Texas is discussed later in this chapter.

Sources of Republican Strengths and Weaknesses Republican voting strength in recent years has been concentrated in several clusters of counties (see Figure 5.2):

* Houston suburbs
* Fort Worth area
* Midland–Odessa area
* Northern Panhandle
* East Texas rural counties
* Hill Country–Edwards Plateau area

Results from the 2012 presidential election reveal that the Republican Party is weaker in the following areas:

* South and South Central Texas
* Central cities of Austin, Dallas, El Paso, Houston, and San Antonio
* Far West Texas

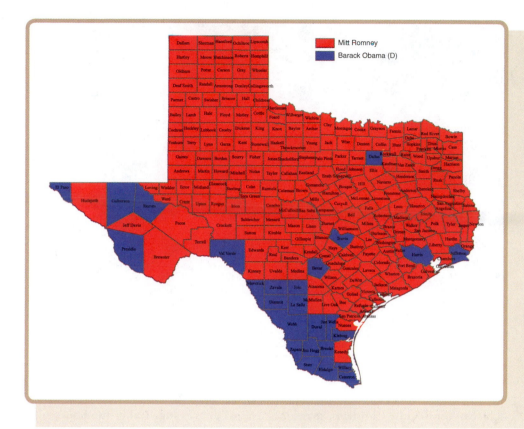

Figure 5.2

Results of the 2012 Presidential Election

The map shows the only 26 counties won by Barack Obama. Note that Obama carried more populous counties like Bexar, Dallas, Harris and Travis, and Mitt Romney carried the smaller counties outside of South and Southwest Texas.

Source: Office of the Texas Secretary of State.

What does this mean for the future of the Democratic Party in Texas? Speculate on the strategy Republicans may use to maintain their electoral dominance.

The Republican Party seems to appeal primarily to the following groups:

★ Middle- and upper-class individuals in suburban communities
★ Rural areas and small towns
★ White Anglo-Saxon Protestants
★ German Americans whose ancestors were strong supporters of the Union during the Civil War
★ Active and retired military officers
★ Traditional conservatives who find themselves in a new urban setting

The party has benefited from the economic growth and prosperity that occurred in Texas from the end of World War II to the early 1980s. During this period, newcomers from more Republican parts of the country were lured to the state by a sympathetic business climate or by the promise of jobs. These transplanted Texans joined more prosperous native Texans to provide a political climate more conducive to Republican Party politics.

Did You Know? In the 1890s, the journalist O. Henry wrote, "We only had two or three laws [in Texas], such as against murder before witnesses, and being caught stealing horses, and voting the Republican ticket."

Conservative and Moderate Factions within the Republican Party

As the Republican Party becomes dominant in Texas politics, it is experiencing some of the factional differences that characterized the Democratic Party in Texas for years. For example,

Delegates attending state party conventions, like this 2010 Republican convention in Dallas, are highly partisan activists.

Explain the role of state conventions in internal party affairs. Are the parties' candidates bound by the platforms that the state conventions write?

Evangelical (fundamentalist) Christians

A number of Christians, often conservative supporters of the Republican Party, who are concerned with such issues as family, religion, abortion, gay rights, and community morals.

Party platform

The formal issue positions of a political party; specifics are often referred to as planks in the party's platform

a bloc of conservative Christians, sometimes referred to as **evangelical** or **fundamentalist Christians,** have increasingly dominated the Texas Republican Party. This group is concerned with such issues as family, religion, and community morals, and it has been effective in influencing the **party platform**. Associated with a broad spectrum of Protestant Christianity that emphasizes salvation and traditional values, evangelical voters are likely to support culturally conservative politics.

Since 1994, the Republican state party chair and a majority of the members of its state executive committee have been conservative Christians. This dominance of leadership positions has given the conservative Christians a degree of control of the party machinery that continues today.

The control of the state's Republican Party by the conservative, or right, wing is opposed by the more moderate, or centrist, wing. Many of these moderates fear that the radicalism of the right will interfere with the party's ability to win elections. Many moderates represent business interests and are more concerned with keeping taxes low and limiting the government's interference in business decision making than with moral issues.

Another group that has been associated with the Republican Party is the Tea Party. The latter is a conservative grassroots movement that generally favors lower government spending and involvement. The movement began in opposition to President Obama's health care initiative. Although Tea Party members deny a formal association with either political party, they have been responsible for the nomination and election of a number of conservative Republicans.

In general, the Republican Party has failed to generate much support among the state's minority voters. African-American identification with the GOP consistently hovers around 5 percent. And party strategists have made no great effort to attract African Americans because they are unlikely to switch parties.

Texas ***INSIDERS***

Inside the Republican Party: Republican Elites Square Off over Immigration

In recent years, the Republican Party has developed two factions with two different styles of leadership. One group might be called the "true believers." They staunchly adhere to conservative principles by fighting government spending, business regulation, and taxation but usually favor vigorous government action to prevent abortion and illegal immigration. Tea Party activists, values voters, and Christian conservatives are usually more ideological and steadfast in their beliefs because their political beliefs are a matter of personal identity. Among the foremost leaders of this wing of the party are leaders such as Senator Dan Patrick.

In contrast, the more pragmatic elements of the Republican Party are

Once a radio talk show host and now a state senator, Dan Patrick formed the "Tea Party" caucus in the Texas legislature and has been a vocal advocate of making it a state crime to be an undocumented alien in Texas.

How does the "Tea Party" leadership style differ from more "pragmatic" Republicans?

Bill Hammond is president of the Texas Association of Business (TAB), known as the voice of Texas business. The TAB has long supported a comprehensive approach to illegal immigration, including a path to citizenship.

On which issues do the "pragmatists" differ from more ideological Republicans?

(continued)

moderately conservative, but because they are often focused on business interests, their approach to politics is more entrepreneurial—they are willing to bargain. Unlike the ideological wing, they support government spending for infrastructure and education that will benefit business. And, they are not usually very engaged on cultural issues, like abortion and same-sex marriage, that do not directly affect their economic interests. TAB President Bill Hammond is probably the preeminent leader among this group of Republicans.

Usually, these two wings of the Republican Party have been able to work harmoniously, but their differences over immigration came into focus when Governor Perry declared the "sanctuary cities" bill an emergency during the 2011 legislative session. The bill would have denied state funding to cities that did not require police to ask suspects about their immigration status.

Pragmatic business leaders Bob Perry (see the "Texas Insiders" feature in Chapter 4) and Charles C. Butt of H.E.B. grocery stores hired the prestigious lobby firm HillCo (see "Texas Insiders" in Chapter 6), and together they successfully blocked the bill. Both business leaders depend on low labor costs and consumer demand that immigrants bring to Texas.

Thinking about the role of political elites in Texas politics The function of elections is to offer voters a choice between competing elites. For Republicans, the party primary offers a choice between different styles and policies as voters select the party's nominees. Is it more important for Republicans to select leaders who stand by their principles or those willing to compromise to get things done?

Sources: Jim Henson, "Immigration, Perry, and a Divided GOP," *The Texas Tribune,* July 27, 2011, at www.texastribune.org/texas-politics/2012-presidential-election/immigration-gop-vs-gop-and-perry/; Patricia Kilday Hart, "Business Opposition Puts 'Sanctuary Cities Bill at Risk," *Houston Chronicle,* June 25, 2011.

ORGANIZATIONAL BASIS OF PARTY MACHINERY IN TEXAS

To better understand how political parties are organized in Texas, we can divide the party machinery into two parts: the temporary, consisting of a series of short-lived conventions at various levels; and the permanent, consisting of people elected to continuing leadership positions in the party (see Figure 5.3).

Temporary-Party Organization

Consisting of precinct, county or district, and state conventions, the temporary party organizations select delegates to higher conventions that ultimately write party rules, approve the state party platforms, and select the permanent party structures that manage party affairs between conventions.

Precinct Convention

The voting precinct is the starting point of party activity because it is the scene of the **precinct convention**, a gathering of the faithful that is open to all who voted earlier in the day in that party's **primary**. It is also the key to getting involved in politics. (See Get Active!) Usually on the first Tuesday in March in even-numbered years, both the Democratic and Republican parties hold conventions in almost all the voting precincts in the state. The ticket of admission is usually a voter registration card stamped to indicate that one has voted in the party's primary earlier in the day. The agenda of the precinct

Precinct convention

A gathering of party members who voted in the party's primary for the purpose of electing delegates to the county or district convention.

Primary

An election held by a political party to nominate its candidates. Texas party primary elections are usually held in the spring.

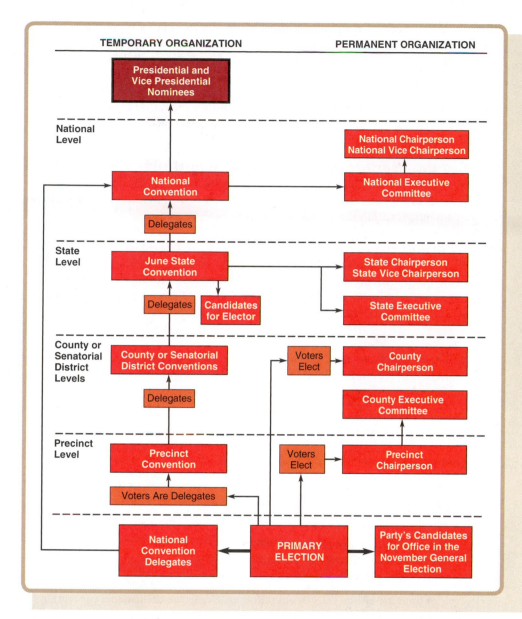

TEMPORARY ORGANIZATION   PERMANENT ORGANIZATION

Figure 5.3

Texas Political Party Organization.

The chart shows the three levels of state party organization in Texas and the ties of the state organization to the national party organization.

Describe how voters are involved in both the temporary and permanent state organizations. How does the process of selecting delegates ensure that many of the delegates who attend the national convention have been "grassroots" supporters of the party?

convention includes adoption of resolutions to be passed on to the county or senatorial district convention and selection of delegates to the county or senatorial district convention.

Although eligibility for participation in this grassroots level of democracy is open to all who vote in the first primary election, attendance is minimal—usually only 2 percent to 3 percent of those who vote. This low attendance makes it possible for a small, determined minority of the electorate to assume control of the precinct convention and dominate its affairs.

A precinct convention normally starts with the signing in of those present and certifying that they voted in the party's primary. In presidential years, those signing in also indicate their preference for a presidential candidate; in nonpresidential years, other designations may be used, such as "conservative caucus" or "moderate-progressive caucus." The preferences are used to evaluate the relative strength of support for each candidate or caucus. The factions with the largest numbers present dominate the selection of delegates to the county convention.

If contending factions in a precinct are evenly divided, a walkout is possible if one side or the other loses a key vote and claims that a grave injustice was done. Such a group will conduct its own convention, called a "rump convention," going through the same procedures; then both precinct groups will appeal to a credentials committee appointed by the county executive committee. The credentials committee will decide which set of rival delegates is officially seated at the county convention. Although fairness and justice sometimes intervene, the decision on which group to seat usually depends on which faction is in the majority on the credentials committee.

County and Senatorial District Conventions In the weeks after the primary and the precinct conventions, county and state senatorial district conventions are held. In the most populous counties, the county convention has given way to state senatorial district conventions within those counties. Delegates vote on adoption of resolutions to be considered at the state convention and select delegates and alternates to attend that convention.

As with the precinct convention, liberal or conservative factions or those representing different presidential candidates will seek to dominate the selection of delegates. Walkouts followed by rump conventions may occur at the county or even the state level. In Texas, bitter intra-party conflict has historically characterized the Democratic Party more than the Republican Party, but that has changed as Republican primaries and conventions have grown in importance.

State Convention Both the Democratic and Republican parties in Texas hold state conventions in June of even-numbered years. The major functions of these biennial state conventions are to do the following:

★ Elect state party officers.
★ Elect 62 members to the state executive committee, two from each senatorial district.
★ Adopt a party platform (see Table 5.2 for examples of recent Texas party platform planks).
★ Certify to the secretary of state the candidates nominated by the party in its March primary.

In addition, in presidential election years, the state convention also will do the following:

★ Elect the party's nominees from Texas to the national committee of the party.
★ Select the state's 38 potential presidential electors.
★ Elect some delegates to the party's national nominating convention, held in July or August (the number of delegates selected is determined by national party rules).

The role of state convention delegates in selecting delegates to the national convention has diminished in recent years. Most of the delegates for both parties are now selected on the basis of the party's presidential preference primary. A **presidential preference primary** allows voters in the party primary to vote directly on the party's presidential nominee.

Presidential preference primary

A primary election that allows voters in the party to vote directly for candidates seeking their party's presidential nomination.

Political parties in Texas select delegates to the national nominating convention using both the primary and the caucus system. In a process nicknamed the "Texas Two-Step," Texans in both parties first vote in the primary election. Those who participate in the primary are then eligible to attend the party caucuses later that evening after the polls close. Texas Democrats choose delegates based on votes in both the primaries and caucuses, while most Republican delegates are selected in a winner-take-all vote in the primaries. The GOP caucuses are used almost exclusively to select delegates to the state party convention.

Permanent-Party Organization

The permanent structure of the party machinery consists of people selected to lead the party organization and provide continuity between election campaigns.

TABLE 5.2 Excerpts from the 2012 Texas Democratic and Republic Party Platforms

Texas Democrats	Texas Republicans
Believe a democratic government exists to help us achieve as a community, state, and nation what we cannot achieve as individuals, and that it must serve all citizens	Believe in personal responsibility and accountability; a free enterprise society unencumbered by government; self sufficient families, founded on the traditional marriage of a natural man and a natural woman.
Believe government should "provide multi-language instruction, beginning in elementary school, to make all students fluent in English and at least one other language …"	Support "American English as the official language of Texas" and "encourage non-English speaking students to transition to English within three years."
Enact a constitutional amendment to prevent extending the sales tax to food and medicine and oppose efforts to impose a national sales tax	Support a national sales tax collected by the states once the IRS is abolished and the Sixteenth Amendment to the U.S. Constitution is repealed
Support abortion by trusting "the women of Texas to make personal and responsible decisions about when and whether to bear children … rather than having these personal decisions made by politicians"	Oppose abortion because "all innocent human life must be respected and safeguarded from fertilization to natural death; therefore, the unborn child has a fundamental individual right to life …"
Would abolish the death penalty in Texas and replace it with the punishment of life imprisonment without parole.	Believe "that properly applied capital punishment is legitimate, is an effective deterrent, and should be swift and unencumbered"
Believe "the state should establish a 100% equitable school finance system with sufficient state revenue to allow every district to offer an exemplary program"	Oppose "teaching of Higher Order Thinking Skills (values clarification), critical thinking skills and similar programs" that "have the purpose of challenging the students fixed beliefs…. We support reducing taxpayer funding to all levels of education institutions."
Support "a path for children of undocumented parents, who were brought here as minors, to earn legal status and future citizenship by going to college or serving in the military."	Support limiting citizenship by birth "to those born to a citizen of the United States with no exceptions."
Believe "the minimum wage must be raised, enforced, and applied meaningfully across-the-board …"	Believe "the Minimum Wage Law should be repealed"

Source: Texas Democratic Party, http://www.txdemocrats.org/, and Republican Party of Texas, http://www.texasgop.org/.

Precinct-Level Organization At the lowest, or grassroots, level of the party structure is the precinct chair, who is chosen by the precinct's voters in the primary for a two-year term. Often the position is uncontested, and in some precincts, the person can be elected by write-in vote. The chair serves as party organizer in the precinct, contacting known and potential party members. The chair may help organize party activities in the neighborhood, such as voter registration drives. The precinct chair is also responsible for arranging and presiding over the precinct convention and serving as a member of the county executive committee.

County-Level Organization A much more active and important role is that of the county chair. The voters choose who will hold this office for a two-year term in the party primary. The chair presides over the county executive committee, which is composed of all precinct chairs. With the later concurrence of the county commissioners' court, the county chair determines where the voting places will be for the primary and appoints all primary election judges. Accepting candidates for places on the primary ballot, the printing of paper ballots, and the renting of voting machines are also the chair's responsibilities. Finally, the chair, along with the county executive committee, must certify the names of official nominees of the party to the secretary of state's office.

The county executive committee has three major functions: assemble the temporary roll of delegates to the county convention, canvass the returns from the primary for local offices, and help the county chair prepare the primary ballot, accept filing fees, and conduct a drawing to determine the order of candidates' names on the primary ballot. This is an important consideration if "blind voting" may be a problem (in that ill-informed voters tend to opt for the first name they come to on the ballot).

State-Level Organization Delegates to the state convention choose the state chair—the titular head of the party—at the state convention for a two-year term. The duties of the chair are to preside over the state executive committee's meetings, call the state convention to order, handle the requests of statewide candidates on the ballot, and certify the election runoff primary winners to the state convention.

The 64-member state executive committee has a chair and a vice chair of the opposite sex. In addition, the Democratic and Republican state convention delegates choose one man and one woman from each of the 31 state senate districts. Unlike Republicans, the Democrats also include several members from various special caucuses on their state executive committee. The main legal duties of the state executive committee are to determine the site of the next state convention—sometimes a crucial factor in determining whose loyal supporters can attend because the party does not pay delegates' expenses—canvass statewide primary returns, and certify the nomination of party candidates.

The state executive committee also has some political duties, including producing and disseminating press releases and other publicity, encouraging organizational work in precincts and counties, raising money, and coordinating special projects. The state committee may work closely with the national party. These political chores are so numerous that the executive committees of both parties now employ full-time executive directors and staff assistants.

A NEW ERA OF REPUBLICAN DOMINANCE

The Republican Party continues its dominance in Texas state politics. Republicans hold a majority of seats in the Texas House, the Texas Senate, and the Texas congressional delegation. They have also made significant gains in local offices. Clearly, the old pattern of Texans voting Republican at the top of the ticket and Democratic at the bottom of the ticket is no longer true.

Party realignment

The transition from one dominant-party system to another. In Texas politics, it refers to the rise and possible dominance of the Republican party in recent years.

Partisan identification

A person's attachment to one political party or the other.

Most observers now agree that Texas has experienced **party realignment**, the transition from one stable party system to another. After more than a century of Democratic Party domination after the Civil War, the pendulum has swung to the Republican Party. Realignment involves more than just casting a vote for a Republican Party candidate; it refers to a shift in **partisan identification**. Evidence that Texas is becoming a Republican-dominated state comes from public opinion polls that show that more Texans are identifying with the Republican Party than in the past. As Table 5.3 indicates, in 1952, an overwhelming percentage of Texans who identified with a political party were Democrats. Fifty years later, polls show that identification with the Republican Party now exceeds that of the Democratic Party; and while many Texans consider themselves independents, more of them "lean" to the Republicans when pollsters press them about their preferences.

Several reasons account for the rise of Republican Party dominance in Texas. The first is the shift among existing voters as conservative middle- and upper-class white Democrats slowly but surely switch their allegiance to the Republican Party. After years of voting Republican in presidential elections but identifying themselves as Democrats, these conservatives began thinking of themselves as Republicans. Many white voters defected to the Republican Party because they were alienated by the national Democratic Party's emphasis on civil rights in the 1960s and 1970s. The existence of popular and powerful Democratic leaders from Texas such as President Lyndon B. Johnson (1963–1968) may have slowed the transition briefly but could not stop it.

This shift in partisan identification was also spurred, in part, by the election of an extremely popular Republican president. Ronald Reagan, elected in 1980 and reelected in 1984, combined clear conservative positions with a charismatic personality that attracted conservative Democrats into the Republican camp. The impact of Reagan's leadership was reinforced by the election of George W. Bush to the presidency in 2000 and 2004. Bush had been a very popular governor, and his election to the presidency helped solidify the Republican realignment in Texas.

Party switching by native Texans has not been the only cause of realignment. Another factor involves newcomers to the state. A majority of recent migrants to Texas from other states have been Republicans or independents. These newcomers, who came to Texas in large numbers in the 1970s and 1980s, have helped break down traditional partisan patterns.

Finally, long-term economic trends have provided opportunities for political change. Texas has slowly become an industrialized and urbanized state—a pattern that accelerated after the 1940s. Industrialization, urbanization, and the rise of an affluent middle class have created a new environment for many Texans, who have adopted a new party as part and parcel of their new lives. In some parts of the country, urbanization and affluence have been associated with support for the Democratic Party, but in Texas these phenomena may have benefited the Republicans.

HOW DOES TEXAS COMPARE?
Party Competition in the 50 States

Research in political science has shown that states with higher levels of party competition for control of government tend to spend more on social programs and have higher levels of voter turnout. Although all 50 states have some competition between the two parties, some states are much more competitive than others. The Party Competition map indicates states in which the Democratic or Republican parties are dominant and states that are more evenly matched; it emphasizes voting patterns in state elections and does not necessarily reflect familiar electoral college maps for presidential elections

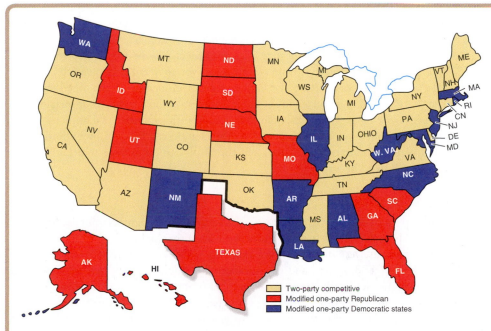

Two-party competitive
Modified one-party Republican
Modified one-party Democratic states

Figure 5.4

Party Competition in the Fifty States: How Texas Compares

The map illustrates the level of party competition in the American states.

Sources: Thomas M. Holbrook and Raymond J. La Raja, "Parties and Elections," in Virginia Gray and Russell L. Hanson (eds.), *Politics in the American States*, 9th ed. (Washington, DC: CQ Press, 2008). The authors recalculate a measure of interparty competition, the Ranney Index, developed by Austin Ranney, "Parties in State Politics," in Herbert Jacob and Kenneth Vines (eds.), *Parties in the American States*, 3rd ed. (Boston: Little, Brown, 1976).

FOR DEBATE

How would party competition make a state's political system more responsive to residents' needs and values? Based on demographic changes in Texas, is the state likely to become more or less competitive in the future?

TABLE 5.3 Percentage of Voters Indicating a Major Party Identification

Year	Democrats	Republicans	Total
1952	66	6	72
1972	57	14	71
1990	34	30	64
2002	25	37	62
2008	35	36	71
2012	31	33	64

Sources: Polls conducted by Belden and Associates (1952 and 1972), Harte-Hanks Communications (1990), and American National Election Studies (2002), The University of Texas *Austin/Texas Tribune* Polls (2008 and 2012).

Can the Democrats Still Be Competitive?

Some observers believe that Texas will emerge as a competitive two-party state. They note that Democrats still have considerable resources in many local governments, especially in some central cities and South and Southwest Texas.

Democratic strategists are also encouraged by the state's growing population of ethnic minorities, particularly Latinos. These voters tend to support Democratic candidates. Ethnic minorities now make up a majority of the state's population. The growing number of Latinos could cause the phenomenon of **tipping**—that is, growing numbers of a demographically significant group cause significant changes in the electorate. If Latino voters' energy and commitment to politics continue, a significant Democratic resurgence would probably occur.

Republican party strategists argue that Hispanic voters may be induced to support the GOP. The latter feels it is more in tune with Latino voters' identification with conservative social positions such as abortion and family values. Democrats, on the other hand, still believe that Latinos will be attracted to the party for its traditional support for social welfare programs and civil rights. Observers note that a substantial number of Latino voters are **swing voters** not bound by party identification. The Democratic Party cannot afford to take this portion of the electorate for granted, and the GOP cannot assume that Latino party identification will trend its way.

Dealignment

There is some speculation that what is occurring in Texas is not realignment but **dealignment**, meaning that the voters are refusing to identify with either political party and are more inclined to call themselves "independents." Table 5.3 shows a realignment occurring as the number of Democrats decreased and the number of Republican identifiers increased. But there is also evidence for dealignment as the number of independent voters increased in the 1990s. Dealignment comes from evaluating the percentage of **ticket splitters**, who are willing to vote for candidates of both parties in the general election, and straight-ticket voters. Increased numbers of ticket splitters indicate that dealignment is occurring.

Tipping

A phenomenon that occurs when a group that is becoming more numerous over time grows large enough to change the political balance in a district, state, or county.

Swing Voters

People who cast their ballots on the basis of personality and other factors rather than strictly on the basis of party affiliation; swing voters are often those "independents" who are persuadable by either party's campaign.

Dealignment

The situation that arises when large numbers of voters refuse to identify with either of the two parties and become increasingly independent of party affiliation.

Ticket splitters

People who vote for candidates of more than one party in a given election.

Where the Parties Stand

Malcolm L. Cross
Tarleton State University

INTRODUCTION

A political party's platform formally presents the party's principles and public policy prescriptions. The platforms of the Texas Democratic and Republican parties are adopted at the parties' biennial conventions, held the summer before a general election, following extensive discussions within each party's respective platform committee and sometimes lengthy debates and floor fights at the parties' convention.[4]

The platforms are not binding on either the parties' nominees for public office or on officeholders elected with the parties' labels. Indeed, party nominees are selected in primary elections months before the conventions meet to debate and adopt their platforms.

Yet a party's platform is important for what it tells about the party that produced it. The issues stressed and the programs proposed reflect the respective values of the different segments of society supporting the party, as well as the governing philosophies of the most politically involved party activists—the citizens who vote in the primaries and attend parties' precinct, county, and state conventions, the volunteers who serve in the network of party committees, and the officeholders elected under their parties' banners. To study the platforms is to learn more about the differences between the Democratic and Republican parties, and therefore to understand the consequences of supporting one party over the other.

The respective platforms the Texas Republicans and Democrats adopted in 2010 differ markedly in issues raised or ignored, in programs proposed, and in overall tone. The platform of the Republican Party of Texas proclaims that "[t]he embodiment of the conservative dream in America is Texas," and that "[t]he Republican Party of Texas unequivocally defends that dream," through promoting limited government, free enterprise, and traditional values derived from the Bible.[5] The Democratic Party's platform does not, on the other hand, explicitly advocate any version of liberalism, yet it asserts a more optimistic view of government's potential to do good, and therefore a greater acceptance of activist government, proclaiming the Democrats' belief that "[D]emocratic government exists to achieve as a community, state, and nation what we cannot achieve as individuals …"[6] But although the Democratic platform says the party has "faith that democracy, built on the sacred values of family, freedom, and fairness, can afford every Texan, without exception, the opportunity to achieve their God-given potential,"[7] it otherwise lacks the explicit religiosity characteristic of much of the Republican platform. No doubt the difference in tone reflects the overwhelming support of conservative Christians for the state GOP, and the power they have thereby gained.

These differing themes, set out in the respective principles in each party's platform, are especially apparent in the proposals each party makes concerning education, which is noteworthy because Texas spends more money on education—public and higher combined—than on any other policy.[8] The Democrats, for example, support public education through independent school districts under the supervision of a "reformed" State Board of Education after it has been liberated from "right-wing Republican extremists,"[9] and more federal aid to education. The Republicans, however, want to strengthen local control of independent school districts and eliminate the federal Department of Education and the No Child Left Behind Act. Moreover, reflecting their skepticism of government and their desire to promote traditional religious values, they support alternatives to the public schools as means of educating children, advocating more freedom—and more financial aid—for parents who want to homeschool their children or send their children to private or parochial schools. The Democrats denounce this as a desire to "siphon off limited public education funds for inequitable, unaccountable voucher and privatization schemes," which they say are "attempts to destroy our public schools."[10]

The platforms show sharp differences between the Democrats and Republicans on a wide variety of other issues, especially—but not exclusively—cultural issues. For example, both Democrats and Republicans stress the need to strengthen

---

[4]As a delegate to numerous precinct, county, and state party conventions, this writer has participated in the drafting and adopting of party platforms at all three levels.

[5]The 2010 platform of the Republican Party of Texas can be accessed through a link on the party's official website at www.texasgop.org/about-the-party. The quote is from p. 7.

[6]The 2010 platform of the Texas Democratic Party can be accessed through a link on the party's official website at www.txdemocrats.org/issues/platform. The quote is from p. 2.

[7]Ibid.

[8]Education is discussed on pp. 4–9 of the Democratic platform, and pp. 18–22 of the Republican Platform.

[9]Democratic Platform, p. 6.

[10]Democratic Platform, p. 5.

and protect families, yet again differ sharply on how to do so.[11] The Democratic platform stresses strengthening a wide variety of government programs, including those to promote a "Children's Bill of Rights" for children placed in foster care, to reform Child Protective Services through caseload reduction and greater "compliance with federal requirements for caseworker meetings with clients," to strengthen child support collection efforts, better nutrition for "low income children, as well as elderly and disabled Texans,"[12] to develop more affordable housing, and to promote more effective utility regulation and consumer protection. Each program, they say, will relieve stress on families. They denounce Republican efforts to privatize social welfare services.

The Republican approach puts far less emphasis on government programs, and far more focus on the promotion of traditional values. The Republican platform "support[s] the definition of marriage as a God-ordained, legal and moral commitment only between a natural man and a natural woman, which is the foundational unit of a healthy society. ..."[13] It opposes efforts "to force acceptance, affirmation and normalization of homosexual behavior," and "would make it a felony to issue a marriage license to a same-sex couple and ... to perform a marriage ceremony for such."[14]

The Democrats make little mention of abortion, other than perfunctory remarks about freedom of choice, perhaps to avoid a debate which, at least in Texas, they cannot win.[15] The Republicans, however, devote far more space in their platform to express their opposition to abortion under almost all circumstances, to denounce partial-birth abortion and fetal tissue harvesting, and to support stronger parental notification laws and the proposed Human Life Amendment to the U.S. Constitution, which would make abortion under most circumstances not only illegal but also unconstitutional.[16]

The Democrats likewise make little mention of stem cell research, other than to endorse it as a means of finding cures to currently incurable illnesses.[17] But the Republicans explicitly denounce embryonic stem cell research, while supporting research with stem cells from other sources.[18]

Reflecting their sympathy for organized labor, Democrats oppose right-to-work laws, which prohibit contracts between unions and employers that require employees either to join unions or to pay dues; support the Employee Free Choice Act, which allows unions to organize a workforce using sign-up cards rather than requiring secret ballots; and support higher minimum wage laws.[19] Republicans, showing their alliance with business, support right-to-work laws, oppose the Employee Free Choice Act, and seek the abolition of the government-mandated minimum wage.[20]

The Democrats favor more government action to help create jobs.[21] The Republicans are silent on the issue of job creation, while stressing overall deregulation of economic activity.[22]

The Democrats support the current Social Security system,[23] while the Republicans seek its privatization with individual retirement accounts.[24]

The Democrats support Obamacare,[25] but the Republicans want it eliminated and replaced with more reliance on market-based solutions to the health insurance dilemma.[26]

The Democrats support American efforts to cooperate with other nations in the maintenance of world peace, and to withdraw our armed forces from the wars in the Middle East.[27] The Republicans want the United States out of the United Nations and oppose timetables for troop withdrawals.[28]

The Democrats want a moratorium on executions while the death penalty is analyzed;[29] the Republicans want to retain it.[30]

Yet not all issues produce such sharp disagreements. Neither party advocates a state income tax, or—despite the Democrats' consistent support for strengthening government programs—truly significant measurable increases in expenditures. The Democrats apparently accept the fiscal conservatism the Republicans so ardently support.[31]

Moreover, if the Democrats and Republicans agree on anything, it is on the need to unrelentingly promote the best interests of Texans and Texas. The party platforms may present different visions of what is best for Texas. But the effort each party devotes to producing its platform shows the seriousness with which it takes the challenges confronting Texas and the determination to use its values to meet those challenges and make Texas better for the effort.

JOIN THE DEBATE

1. Where do Democrats agree with Republicans? Where do they differ? Which party better reflects your positions on policy issues and values?

2. Do you think a candidate for office should be required to support his party's platform?

---

[11]See the Democratic Platform, pp. 18–23, and the Republican Platform, pp. 13–14.
[12]Quotes are from p. 19 of the Democratic Platform.
[13]Republican Platform, p. 10.
[14]Ibid., p. 13.
[15]Ibid., p. 18.
[16]Republican Platform, p. 14.
[17]Democratic Platform, p. 17
[18]Republican Platform, p. 15.
[19]Democratic Platform, p. 10.
[20]Republican Platform, p. 25.
[21]Democratic Platform, pp. 9–12.
[22]Republican Platform, pp. 25–26.
[23]Democratic Platform, pp. 20–21.
[24]Republican Platform, p. 17.
[25]Democratic Platform, pp. 14–15.
[26]Republican Platform, p. 18.
[27]Democratic Platform, p. 41.

CHAPTER SUMMARY

★ Despite the hostility of the founders, political parties have become an important part of American political life. Parties perform critically important functions in a democracy. They nominate and elect their members to public office, educate and mobilize voters, and provide them with cues on how to vote and run the government at whatever level (local, state, or national) they are active.

★ In discussing political parties in the United States, we must look at three fundamental characteristics: (1) pragmatism, (2) decentralization, and (3) the effects of the two-party system. Pragmatism follows from the major goal of American parties, which is to build majority coalitions and win elections. This means that both Republican and Democratic Party candidates are sometimes fuzzy on issues. Recently, however, American parties (including those in Texas) have become more programmatic. That is, Democrats and Republicans have become easier to distinguish.

★ Parties are relatively decentralized, with much of the control of the nominating process (the primary) and party machinery in the hands of state and local voters and their leaders. In the recent past, however, both the Democratic and Republican national party organizations have increased their control over state and local parties because of their capacity to raise large amounts of money and provide various services.

★ For much of its history, Texas was a one-party Democratic state. Until recently, one-party dominance meant that the election to select the Democratic Party's nominees—the

Democratic primary—was the most important election in Texas. Moderate and conservative factions within the Democratic Party became the key political players.

★ After years of domination by the Democratic Party, Texas began to experience a strong two-party competition. As a result, both parties strengthened their party machinery and made aggressive appeals to their traditional constituencies. By the late 1990s, the Republicans had become the dominant party in Texas. The transition from a party system in which the Democrats were overwhelmingly dominant to a new system in which the Republicans have a clear edge can be described as a political realignment. After the 1960s, the Republicans slowly but surely gained strength at the state level. In 1978, they gained the governorship. By 2002, they controlled both chambers of the state legislature, and in 2004, Republicans captured a majority in the state's congressional delegation. The Republicans will no doubt remain dominant in the near future.

★ Republicans have attracted voters in the expanding suburban areas of the state and have increased their appeal to white voters in rural areas. Democrats have attracted votes in inner cities and among ethnic minorities. The state's increasing ethnic diversity could thus augur well for the Democratic Party in the long run.

★ A second political mechanism that may be at work, in addition to realignment, is political dealignment. In this process, voters become detached from both political parties and begin to see themselves as independents.

HOW TEXAS COMPARES

★ Although Texas has a unique and colorful political history, its broad outlines parallel the pattern of other southern states. As in many other southern states, conservatives within the Democratic Party dominated state politics between the Reconstruction era and the 1960s. And like many other southern states, Texas underwent a general partisan realignment toward the Republican Party during the latter part of the twentieth century.

★ Today, Texas has become one of the most reliably conservative Republican states in the nation in both state and national elections. In fact, Texas's loyalty to the Republican Party stands out as unique among the largest states. In recent presidential elections, such large diverse states as Illinois, Ohio, Pennsylvania, Michigan, and Florida have been "swing states" in which the Democrats and

Republicans are competitive. Among the most populated states, only Texas has consistently supported the Republican nominee in all of the last nine presidential elections.

★ While Texas's historic and current politics reflect political dynamics similar to other southern states, its future is likely to follow the patterns of the southwestern states along the Mexican border. Like California, New Mexico, Arizona, and Nevada, Texas has a large and increasing Latino population. Already, Texas has the second-largest Latino population among the 50 states, and Texas Latinos are projected to become the majority within the next 20 years. This growing minority has given heavy support to the Democratic Party in most states (except Florida), and it has the potential to change the future direction of politics in Texas as well as many other states.

KEY TERMS

dealignment, *p. 136*
decentralization, *p. 120*
evangelical (fundamentalist) Christians, *p. 128*

grassroots, *p. 120*
partisan identification, *p. 134*
party platform, *p. 128*

REVIEW QUESTIONS

1. Explain why the Democratic Party dominated Texas politics until the 1970s.

2. Discuss what it means to be a conservative or a liberal.

3. Describe the development of conservative and liberal factions within the Democratic Party and later within the Republican Party.

4. Discuss the reasons for and describe the events that led to the rise of the Republican Party in Texas.

5. Define *realignment*. Analyze to what extent realignment has occurred in Texas politics. Has Texas become a state that is dominated by the Republican Party, or is competition between the parties to be the norm in the future?

LOGGING ON

The two major political parties have websites both in Texas and nationally:

Democrats in Texas at **www.txdemocrats.org**
Democrats nationally at **www.democrats.org**
Republicans in Texas at **www.texasgop.org**
Republicans nationally at **www.rnc.org**

The website for the Texas Ethics Commission has information about campaign finance, forms to be filed for office seekers, and reports on expenditures of the two political parties. Visit it at **www.ethics.state.tx.us/index.html**.

Examine the liberal or progressive point of view with the *Texas Observer* at **www.texasobserver.org**.

Review conservative ideas on the site Born Conservative at **bornconservative.com/**.

Chapter 6

Interest Groups

LEARNING OBJECTIVES

- ★ Evaluate the role of interest groups in Texas politics and policy formulation.
- ★ Explain the role of the First Amendment in protecting the rights of interest groups.
- ★ Define *interest groups* and explain what they do.
- ★ Know the differences among types of interest groups.

- ★ Describe what lobbyists must report as well as what they do not report.
- ★ Describe the work of lobbyists.
- ★ Know the different actors that lobbyists attempt to influence.
- ★ Differentiate between iron triangles and issue networks.

© Glowimages / Getty Images, Inc.

GET Active

Go to the Texas Ethics Commission's website to discover which people, corporations, labor unions, and nonprofit organizations are lobbying Texas state government. The address is **www.ethics.state.tx.us**.

Learn how to lobby. Go to the Texas State Teachers Association website at **www.tsta.org/**. Click on the Issues & Action tab and then click on Guide to Lobbying under the Take Action at the State Level! Menu.

Identify a state or local interest group related to your career or professional ambitions. Research this group—an easy way to start is to type the name of the group into a search engine such as Yahoo! or Google—and identify the officers, membership dues, size of membership, issues being promoted, and name and frequency of any publications. To go further, consult the Texas Ethics Commission's reports on campaign contributions or lobbyists at **www.ethics.state.tx.us** to see how active the group is in Texas.

Using a search engine such as Yahoo! or Google, type in the name of a major corporation, a labor union, a professional organization, a nonprofit organization, or a public interest group. See what public policy issues each is promoting in Texas and in the nation.

You can find out who spent the most money lobbying Texas's decision makers at **http://info.tpj.org/reports/pdf/AustinOldest2011.pdf**.

When Texas billionaire Harold Simmons was told by the Texas Commission on Environmental Quality that he could not import radioactive waste from other states, he did it anyway. His company, Waste Control Specialists, planned to bury the waste at its waste dump near Andrews, Texas. This site sits in close proximity to two water tables, including sections of the Ogallala Aquifer—an important source of water for the High Plains region of the United States. The Texas Commission on Environmental Quality warned that "groundwater is likely to intrude into the proposed disposal units and contact the waste from either or both of two water tables near the proposed facility."[1] After permission to bring in the waste was initially rejected, the company put its lobbyists to work. The team included the former executive director of TCEQ, Jeff Saitas. The company lobbied TCEQ's executive director, Glenn Shankle, who overruled the technical team. Shortly thereafter, Waste Control Specialists was given permission. A few months later, Glenn Shankle followed Jeff Saitas to become a lobbyist for Waste Control Specialists. The revolving-door problem, in which policymakers and regulators leave government positions only to return as lobbyists for the industries they once regulated, is a challenge in a pro-business, anti-regulation state like Texas.

---

[1]TCEQ Interoffice Memo to Susan Jablonski, Director, Radioactive Materials Division from TCEQ RML Team, regarding groundwater intrusion into proposed LLRW facility, August 14, 2007, http://texasnuclearsafety.org/downloads/TCEQ_interoffice_memo_81407.pdf.

THE STAKES IN THE POLICY-MAKING PROCESS

The introductory anecdote illustrates what is at stake in the political process. The state of Texas regulates one of the most productive economies in the world; it has an annual gross state product worth $1.3 trillion.[2] The state's total spending is $173.5 billion.[3] Special interest groups often depend on government spending and lobby policy makers for a piece of the government largess. Road construction companies can ask the governor for support to increase spending on infrastructure projects. Schoolteachers can lobby the legislature for minimal cuts to public education. And advocates for the infirm can ask lawmakers to improve spending for health care. Because the state spends so much money on the many public goods, interest groups want a piece of government spending. Many interest groups lobby the government either to spend more, or, if under threat from cutbacks, at least to maintain current spending levels.

Although agriculture and energy make up a large sector of the Texas economy, the state has diversified its economy significantly since the mid-1980s. The state's population is almost 26 million people and is growing fast. The racial and ethnic makeup of the state is one of the most diverse in the country. Texas attracts people from a variety of religious backgrounds, has a highly dispersed age demographic, and is becoming more tolerant of gay and lesbian populations. The state has both a large poor and middle-income population. Texas is diverse in a variety of ways, and this diversity brings with it a greater variety of special interest groups. Citizens with special interests organize around their concerns, **lobbying** the government for fair and equal treatment, for protections from more powerful groups, and for protection of liberties.

Some states have such huge markets that they are in a position to enact legislation that determines what entire industries produce and how they produce it, and Texas is such a state. Manufacturers wanting to sell in Texas modify their products to meet the specifications set by state regulations and they lobby Texas officials to set standards that are favorable to their industries.

Citizens organize into interest groups to protect themselves, their interests, and their values. The structure of state government provides groups many different avenues to influence state policy. Not only can special interest groups lobby the 150 members of the Texas House and 31 members of the Texas Senate, special interest groups can also petition officers in the Texas executive branch—the thousands of executive branch appointees and bureaucrats. Special interest groups can bring lawsuits before the courts and they can also rally the public's support.

Lobbying
Direct contact between an interest group representative and an officer of government.

WHAT ARE INTEREST GROUPS?

Citizens may act alone to influence government, and millions do. When citizens join with others into an organizational structure designed to express their preferences to government, they act as an **interest group**. The media frequently speak of the interests of women, minorities, employers, Texans, and others, but interests must unite in a cooperative effort to promote some policy objective before they may be thought of as interest groups.

Interest groups are collections of private citizens with shared interests that pursue public-policy goals on behalf of their members. Their interests are narrower than those of political parties. Unlike political parties, they do not nominate candidates for office and may work with officials of both parties to secure their goals. Although they sometimes endorse

Interest group
An organization that expresses the policy desires of its members to officers and institutions of government; also known as a *pressure group*.

---

[2]Texas Comptroller of Public Accounts. "Winter 2011–2012 Economic Forecast: Economic Summary through Fiscal Years 1991 through 2041," www.texasahead.org/economy/indicators/ecoind/ecoind5.html#product .
[3]Legislative Budget Board. *2012: Texas Fact Book*, p. 46 at www.lbb.state.tx.us/Fact_Book/Fact%20Book%202012.pdf.

Bob Daemmrich/The Image Works

Lobbying is when agents of interest groups make direct face-to-face contact with public officials in an effort to affect public policy.

What techniques do lobbyists use to influence government officials?

Pressure group

See *interest group.*

Lobbyist

In state law, a person who directly contacts public officials to influence their decisions. Registered lobbyists are paid to represent the interests of their employers.

and support candidates for office, their primary purpose is to influence government decision makers.

Interest groups are also called **pressure groups**. This second name derives from the fact that interest groups apply pressure on decision makers when seeking policy outputs favorable to them. Pressure is inherent in any situation in which policy makers must select one particular course of action from among several choices. Officeholders are sensitive to interest-group pressure because of groups' potential voting power, the value of their potential endorsements, the size of their campaign contributions, and the number of their members who may volunteer in the next election campaign. Groups employ **lobbyists** to express their policy positions to public officials.

TYPES OF INTEREST GROUPS

Interest groups can be classified in a multitude of ways. The simplest is to categorize them according to their primary purpose—economic, noneconomic, or both.

Economic Interest Groups

The traditional categories of economic interests operating at the state level are business and the professions, education, local government, agriculture, and labor. Groups in each category seek financial advantages for their members. Business and agriculture are always interested in keeping their taxes low, securing subsidies, avoiding regulation, and receiving government contracts to increase profits. Education and local government groups want greater state support for their governments and increased salaries and benefits for their public employees. Local government groups try to block unfunded state mandates and obtain more local control or less state control over their affairs. Labor unions seek legislation to make it easier to organize (unionize) labor and to obtain generous workers' compensation and workplace safety regulations.

Agencies of government also lobby each other. They are not generally recognized as interest groups, but they are affected by what other political institutions and jurisdictions decide. The governors' staffs promote their political agendas in the legislature. Cities, school districts, and other local governments are seriously affected by legislative decisions on finances and local government authority. They are also affected by rules set by state executive-branch agencies. Therefore, they must protect and/or promote their interests by employing lobbyists or reassigning employees to be lobbyists as needed.

In recent years, the public has been critical of governmental agencies for hiring lobbyists. Critics argue that the public elects representatives, not lobbyists, to represent their interests; hiring lobbyists is simply an added cost to taxpayers. But cities, universities, and other public agencies respond that they are at a tremendous disadvantage when they do not have the additional assistance of lobbyists. When the Texas Department of Transportation hired a lobbyist, Robert Black, a spokesman for Governor Rick Perry defended the action by saying, "The fact of the matter is the transportation bureaucracy in Washington, DC, is incredibly extensive and to have people on the ground who can traverse that bureaucratic maze is highly valuable."[4] Cities and other local governments that do not hire lobbyists to represent their interests can find themselves at a disadvantage.

[4]Michelle Mittelstadt, "Democrats Rip State Agency for Hiring DC Lobbyists," *Houston Chronicle,* 2 February 2007, Sec. A. 1.

Noneconomic Interest Groups

Noneconomic groups seek the betterment of society as a whole or the reform of the political, social, or economic systems in ways that do not directly affect their members' pocketbooks. Such groups are difficult to form because the groups work for goods that benefit everyone. This creates an incentive for individuals who will benefit from the work of a noneconomic interest group to become what Mancur Olson calls a *free rider*.[5] A free rider is an individual who benefits from the work of an interest group but who does not participate in the collective actions that made the benefits possible. Environmental and political reformers maintain that the beneficiaries of their programs are the members of society. Clean air, water, and elections are said to promote the well-being of all. Many individuals who join noneconomic interest groups are motivated to participate by three things—intense passion, selective incentives, and social pressures. Individuals who join the Texas Right to Life movement are motivated by strong beliefs about conception and when life begins. The intensity of passion a citizen possesses motivates him or her to join. Other organizations recruit members by offering selective incentives like t-shirts, coffee mugs, and newsletters as a way to attract members.

Other noneconomic interest groups rely on social pressure to attract members to join. Neighborhood organizations can pressure neighbors to join the local civic association because failing to join a neighborhood group makes one auspiciously absent from civic life in the community. The threat of ostracism leads many to join such groups. Noneconomic interest groups benefit from large memberships because they translate into greater political clout in Texas's legislature. Group members can write letters, call, and even vote for or against members of the legislature. What some noneconomic interest groups lack in financial resources they make up for in group membership.

Mixed-Interest Groups

Many groups do not fit neatly into the economic or noneconomic classification because they pursue social goals that have clear economic effects. Discrimination in any form—on the basis of age, disability, ethnicity, gender, or native language—is a social problem that has negative consequences on wages and promotions in the workplace. Groups pursuing social equality and economic goals are classified as mixed or hybrid organizations. Few, if any, demands on the political system affect all classes of citizens equally. Some benefit, some suffer inconvenience, and others experience economic loss from any policy adopted. Table 6.1 gives some examples of Texas interest groups in all three categories.

WHY PEOPLE JOIN INTEREST GROUPS

People join interest groups for many reasons. To influence government, one needs to become a joiner. Most individuals lack the status, knowledge, political skills, and money to succeed on their own. Joining together creates a network of like-minded people who can pool their talents and other resources to pursue their political ends. Furthermore, work and family obligations leave little time for one to become an expert on the complexities of policy issues. The solution is to create or hire an **advocacy** organization to protect one's economic, recreational, social, or political interests. The organization can monitor activities in the capitol and alert its members to the need to call or write public officials and influence the decisions relevant to them. Working as a group with many members contacting officials at the same time increases the organization's chances of achieving favorable results.

Advocacy
Promotion of a particular public policy position.

---

[5]Olson, Mancur, *The Logic of Collective Action: Public Goods and the Theory of Groups* (Revised edition, Boston: Harvard University Press, 1971).

TABLE 6.1 Interest Group Classifications and Selected Examples

Classification	Sector	Examples
Economic	Agriculture	Texas Farm Bureau
	Business	Texan Association of Business and Chambers of Commerce
	Labor	Texas AFL-CIO; American Federation of State and County Municipal Employees
	Occupations and professions	Texas Association of Realtors; Texas Trial Lawyers Association
Noneconomic	Patriotic	American Legion
	Public interest	Texas Common Cause; Texans for Public Justice
	Religious	Texas Christian Life Commission
Mixed	Education	Texas State Teachers' Association
	Environment and recreation	Texas Nature Conservancy; Citizens Environmental Coalition
	Race and gender	League of United Latin American Citizens; NAACP; Women's Health and Family Planning Association of Texas
	Local government	Texas Municipal League; Texas County Judges and Commissioners' Association

This table shows the types of interest groups and examples of each.

▲ **Use our Logging On feature to find out which public policies each of these groups advocate. What is the difference between economic and noneconomic interest groups?**

Joining groups also advances career and social goals. Certainly, belonging to a collective organization that meets periodically increases one's circle of friends and business contacts. Getting to know others in your trade or profession can certainly lead to job offers, exchanges of knowledge, and enjoyment of others who share your interests. Hence active membership leads to networking that has economic, social, and political benefits.

The culture of a profession may require membership—that is, it is regarded as unprofessional not to be a member. People are expected to stay current in their field. All organizations exist to disseminate information or knowledge, but an organization may also have other tangible benefits that make the dues very reasonable. For example, malpractice insurance is available to teachers, attorneys, and medical providers through their professional organizations. A monthly or quarterly magazine or newsletter may be the factor that attracts members to a group. Publications of nature and conservation groups are invariably so beautiful that one might join simply to enjoy the magazine. Whatever the principal reason for joining, one should not be surprised to learn that these groups actively engage in the practice of influencing government. After all, the government regulates our occupations and professions. It decides who pays how much in taxes and who receives the benefits of those tax dollars through public spending programs. No aspect of life is untouched by the political system. Those who do not pay attention to what is going on in Washington and Austin and their local city hall sooner or later feel the effects of what occurs there. Government is a process of determining who gets what and who pays for it; it is a process of determining whose values will prevail. As Congresswoman Barbara Jordan famously said, "Government is too important to be a spectator sport."

WHAT INTEREST GROUPS DO

The primary goal of each interest group is to influence all branches of government at all levels to produce policies favorable to its members and to block policies that might be harmful to their interests. Interest groups are instrumental in drawing *selected* citizens into political participation to influence public policies, most often in a way that encourages the promotion of narrow, selfish interests. Indeed, critics focus on the harm that can result from powerful groups demanding that public policy reflect their values. Critics of the system of influence also worry about corruption and intimidation of public officials by what they call "special interests." The need for campaign contributions, they believe, makes elected officials especially vulnerable to pressure. The bottom line for critics is their concern that special interests will prevail over the interests of the general public.

Interest groups, however, have the ability to draw citizens into the political processes. Democracy calls for politically attentive and active citizens. From this perspective, interest groups educate their members about issues and mobilize them to participate in constitutionally approved ways. Simultaneously, interest groups inform and educate public officials.

Interest groups provide policy makers valuable information both as they lobby individual government officials and as they testify before legislative committees. Because state law makes it a crime to knowingly share false information with state lawmakers,[6] most special interest groups are careful to provide truthful, albeit one-sided, information. The information provided by interest groups can be costly to gather both in terms of time and money. However, because interest groups provide the information free of cost, taxpayers are spared the expense.

The number and variety of interest groups also ensure that no one group will be dominant. States like Texas, which have a diverse and complex economic system, tend to produce a greater diversity of interest groups. This wide diversity of interest groups in Texas makes it difficult for any one special interest group to dominate the state's politics. As a result, the public may sometimes be protected from public policy that benefits one group at the expense of the many. Agricultural, energy, legal, banking, medical, religious, racial, ethnic, and educational interest groups are just a few organized interests in Texas, and all compete with one another for favorable legislation. Because Texas has so many interest groups, no one group is able to completely dominate the political process. Table 6.2 summarizes some of the positive and negative effects of interest-group activity.

Now we will tap into the process to learn how interest groups use both direct and indirect means to achieve their political ends.

Direct Means of Influencing Government

Interest groups employ several tactics to directly influence policy makers, including lobbying office holders, filing suit in court, getting their advocates appointed to state boards, testifying before legislative committees, and organizing public demonstrations.

TABLE 6.2 Positive and Negative Side Effects of Interest Group Activity	
Positive	**Negative**
Increased political representation	Narrow interests represented
Political participation and mobilization	Secret communications with officials
Education of their members	Corruption or intimidation of public officials
Shared information and data	Biased information for decision makers
Representation based on voluntary association and free speech	Unequal representation based on financial resources and organizational skills

This table shows some of the benefits and disadvantages resulting from interest group representation.

▲ **What regulations can mitigate the costs of interest group activity without compromising freedom of expression and the rights to assemble and petition government officials?**

---

[6]Texas Government Code, 305.021.

Lobbying the Legislative and Executive Branches

Lobbying is direct contact between an interest group representative and a legislative or executive branch official or employee for the purpose of influencing a specific public policy outcome. Most people seem to understand that legislatures create, finance, and change government programs, and many individuals and groups affected by these legislative decisions try to influence the process. The average voter may not be aware that enormous sums of money, privilege, and prestige are also at stake in the executive decision-making process as well.

The executive branch or administration is charged with the **implementation** (carrying out) of legislative policy. The legislature delegates a great deal of **discretion** to executive agencies, both directly and indirectly. The legislative branch **delegates** power to the executive branch to select the means to carry out law. The administrative agencies finish the policy-making process by promulgating rules or regulations that specify how the law shall be applied to actual situations. Organized interest groups have a real interest in shaping the regulations that will apply to them. In short, because what government does is not simply the result of legislative decisions, lobbyists must actively monitor and seek to influence executive-branch rule making and enforcement as well.

Filing Suit in Court

Organized interests use the courts to further their causes for several reasons. One is that a lack of funds or public support dictates that their resources be spent on litigation. Lawsuits are less expensive than trying to influence the legislature, and public opinion is supposed to be irrelevant to judicial outcomes.

A second reason for using the courts is that they may be a last resort when an interest group has not prevailed in the legislative or executive decision-making process. Courts can declare legislation unconstitutional or rule that executive decisions are illegal. Interest groups may find that the courts may apply an interpretation of the law that is more beneficial to their interests than rulings by an administrative agency.

A third purpose is to delay the implementation of the law or rules. Courts often stay implementation of a law or rule while a case is pending. The members of the group can continue to operate as before, in the more profitable and unrestrained manner. Filing suit, even when one expects to lose, serves to delay application of costly rules.

A fourth reason to file suit is to gain public attention. Media coverage of the suit brings public attention to the case and may also bring pressure on decision makers to change their policies or to negotiate with the filer to settle on a more favorable public policy.

Advising and Serving the State

State law in Texas generally requires that appointed boards be composed of members, a majority of whom come from the profession, occupation, business, or activity the state agency is regulating. The mere existence of such laws is testimony to the power of special interest groups to institutionalize their influence on government. These board members and commissioners are part-time officials and full-time practitioners of the occupation that they have the power to regulate. They personally exercise power as state officials even as they represent a special interest group that lobbies the agency and provides it with information. This blurring of the line between the state and the special interest is called **co-optation**. The **public interest** is endangered when state officials act as agents for the group the agency regulates. A **conflict of interest** exists when the decision maker is personally affected by the decision being made.

Organizing Public Demonstrations

Marches and demonstrations are used periodically to obtain publicity for a cause. Press coverage is all but guaranteed. This sort of *theater* is especially suited for television news. When the legislature is in session, demonstrations are plentiful. During the 82nd legislative session, public school teachers, immigrants' rights groups, Tea Party members, and countless others rallied in Austin to express support or opposition to a whole host of bills.

Implementation
Carrying out by members of the executive branch any policy made by the legislature and judiciary.

Discretion
The power to make decisions on the basis of personal judgment rather than specific legal requirements.

Delegate
To legally transfer authority from one official or institution to another.

Co-optation
The capturing of an institution by members of an interest group. In effect, in such a situation, state power comes to be exercised by the members of the private interest.

Public interest
The good of the whole society, without bias for or against any particular segment of the society.

Conflict of interest
The situation that exists when a legislator, bureaucrat, executive, official, or judge is in a position to make a decision that might result in personal economic benefit or advantage.

One challenge for interest groups using this kind of tactic is to enlist enough members to be impressive and at the same time keep control of the demonstration. Violating the law, forging signatures on letters sent to lawmakers, blocking traffic, damaging property, and using obscenities do not win support from fellow citizens or public officials with the power to change the conditions the group is protesting. A recently developed variation of public demonstrations is **astroturf lobbying**—fabrication of public support for issues supported by industry and special interest groups but which gives the impression of widespread public support.

Indirect Means of Influencing Government

Besides trying to directly influence state policymakers, interest groups endeavor to shape the political environment in which policy decisions are made. They engage in political campaigns and other public relations efforts to create a favorable political climate in which to pursue their groups' agenda.

Electioneering Although interest groups do not nominate candidates for office, one candidate for an office may be more supportive of their cause than another. The organization may decide to endorse and recommend that its members vote for the candidate more disposed to support their values.

The organization's newsletter or magazine will be used to carry this message. A second means of helping candidates favorable to the group's interests is to create a political action committee (PAC). As explained in Chapter 4, the sole purpose of a PAC, which is legally separate from the interest group, is funneling money to candidates for office.

Special interest groups are powerful enough to influence the outcome of elections. Interest groups are in a position to make significant campaign contributions that will elect candidates who hold positions that affect their interests. In some cases, interest groups are powerful enough to have their own employees selected for public office. Several of the state's major law firms, which also have powerful lobbying arms in Texas government, boast members of the Texas legislature and executive branch as current or former members. Similarly, senior administrators with powerful corporations or special interest groups tend to be successful in being selected to serve on government boards and commissions.

Educating the Public There is wisdom in providing the general public with messages that build a positive image. Well-funded interest groups employ the services of public relations firms to build reputations for honesty, good products and services, concern for the well-being of the customers, and good citizenship. Interest groups may use the organizations' magazines, annual reports for stockholders, and press releases to newspapers as vehicles for building their own reputation and educating the public about the wisdom of policy proposals supported by the organization. They may purchase print and broadcast advertisements to shape and mobilize public opinion on behalf of the interest or to neutralize opposition to their cause.

It is very important for a group or individual that wants government to take action to articulate the need or problem in exactly the right language to stay in control of the issue and to evoke a positive official response. Interest groups usually prefer to influence public officials before the issue becomes public. Once an issue becomes public, every opponent will try to redefine the issue in a negative light. For example, people who want to promote school vouchers that may be used in religious schools must emphasize the responsibility of the state to assist all children to learn. Opponents will seek to convince the majority that such aid is

State employees such as these teachers become an economic interest group when they demonstrate in support of their job benefits.

Is a public demonstration an effective interest group tactic?

Astroturf lobbying
The fabrication of public support for issues supported by industry and special interest groups but which give the impression of widespread public support.

a violation of the "separation of church and state." Words are the weapons of political battle, and most new political struggles are group-against-group battles.

Socializing Interest groups know that friendships can be formed at social functions. Informal occasions allow people to interact in comfortable settings. A lobbyist may invite a public official to lunch or to a party to establish a positive relationship. Formal occasions designed to honor a person can also serve to build positive relationships. Invitations to speak before a group are a way to cultivate friendships. The purpose of all social invitations is to establish an impression that pays off when public officials take favorable votes or make other kinds of policy decisions friendly to the interest group. Thus, socializing is seen as a good investment for interest groups, regardless of an immediate need for the public official's support.

Access to public officials is the prerequisite for influencing public decisions. Getting in the door to discuss a matter of concern in time to shape the public policy outcome is the goal. Indirect means of influencing government often pave the way for direct lobbying. Groups that have established good reputations with public officials do not have to engage in demonstrations, but even the most successful groups can expect to lose sometimes.

THE CRAFT OF LOBBYING

Whether they work for a single client or have a massive client list to serve, lobbyists use a variety of strategies to influence different branches of government. Their techniques of persuasion and the kinds of resources that they employ vary with the kind of policy they are trying to influence and the size and skill of their lobby operation. Now we go inside lobbying operations to explore some of their most effective techniques of persuasion.

> **Did You Know?** In 2011, Texas special interests hired 1,836 lobbyists and spent at least $169 million to influence state policies.

Before the Legislature

It is obvious that anyone who directly contacts public officials to influence their behavior should be extroverted and enjoy socializing. The lobbyist's first job is to become known and recognized by members of the legislature and any executive officials relevant to the interest he or she represents. Before a legislative session begins, a lobbyist must have successfully completed several tasks: (1) learn who is predisposed to support the cause, who is on the other side, and which members can be swayed, (2) memorize the faces of the members, their non-legislative occupation, the counties they represent, and a little about their family, (3) establish rapport through contact with the members of the legislature, (4) get to know the staffs of legislators because through them the member can be influenced, and (5) know the legislative issues, including the arguments of opponents. To maintain a relationship, the lobbyist must provide the legislator with sound, accurate information about the legislation the lobbyist's group is supporting or opposing. This includes "off-the-record" admission of the pluses and minuses of the legislation. Honesty is, in fact, the best policy for a lobbyist when dealing with a public official.

A lobbyist can befriend a legislator in several ways that may eventually pay off. Lobbyists have information that may be valuable to a legislator, and they may be able to help draft an important piece of legislation for the official. Providing an occasional free meal or acknowledging a helpful legislator at a banquet in the legislator's honor also has merit from the lobbying perspective. All these actions are necessary to create and maintain goodwill, without which nothing is possible.

How does a lobbyist approach a member of the legislature or the leadership? How do you get in the door, and what do you say when you get in? How important is the staff of a legislator to a lobbyist? Is it necessary to see all 181 members of the legislature, the lieutenant governor, and the governor? Because a session has only 140 days, it should be clear that lobbying must precede the convening of the legislature. The 18-month period between regular sessions leaves ample time to work on relationships, learn what proposals have a chance of receiving favorable response, draft legislation, and line up sponsors to introduce bills in the house and senate at the beginning of the next session.

Not all members of the legislature are equal. Establishing rapport and obtaining feedback from the very powerful presiding officers—the speaker of the house and lieutenant governor—is especially useful. No endorsement is more important to an interest group than that of the presiding officers. If an endorsement for the group's legislative proposal is not forthcoming, the lobbyist must persuade the presiding officers to be neutral in the legislative struggle. Securing the endorsement of the chair of each committee through which the legislation must pass before it can go to the floor for a vote is an advantage second only to that of securing the support of the presiding officers. Legislation sought by local governments must have the endorsement of community leaders or it is doomed to fail. Our Texas Insiders feature puts a face on one of the most successful lobby operations in Texas; HillCo has numerous clients and primarily represents business interests.

Texas INSIDERS

HillCo: Texas's Premier Lobbying Outfit and Its Influence in Texas

In some years, lobbyists registered with the Texas Ethics Commission outnumber legislators ten to one. Many lobbyists represent only one or two clients, but a few of them conduct sufficient lobby business to qualify as true Texas insiders. Among them is the powerful HillCo.

Headed by Neal "Buddy" Jones and Bill Miller, HillCo has been involved in almost every big legislative fight in the last 15 years. When Bob Perry and Charles C. Butt saw their business interests threatened, they hired HillCo to block the "sanctuary cities" bill in the legislature. (See Texas Political Insiders in Chapter 5.) One of the most popular and gregarious figures in the Capitol, HillCo partner Bill Miller helped manage Tom Craddick's races for the speakership in the House of Representatives and later helped finance Lt. Gov. David Dewhurst's expensive, but ill-fated, campaign for the U.S. Senate in 2012.

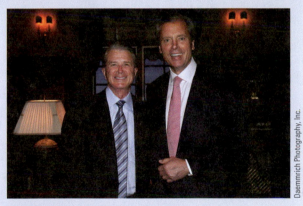

Daemmrich Photography, Inc.

Shown with Lt. Gov. Dewhurst (right), Neal T. "Buddy" Jones learned the inside game in the Texas legislature while working as the executive assistant to former Democratic Speaker Gib Lewis. Later, he learned the ropes as an independent lobbyist for the well-connected Bass brothers, billionaire investors. Jones went on to found the prestigious HillCo lobby partnership with Bill Miller.

How can personal relationships, developed through years of contacts with policymakers, affect the decision-making process?

(continued)

Among its notable clients, HillCo partners have represented the following:

- Alcoa
- AT&T
- Continental Airlines
- Farmers Insurance
- General Motors
- H-E-B Grocery
- Koch Industries
- Microsoft
- Perry Homes
- Pharmaceutical Research and Manufacturers of America (known as "big PhRMA")
- Pfizer
- Wyeth Pharmaceuticals

As its website boasts, "Wherever government touches private business, HillCo is there." HillCo Partners have also organized a political action committee. HillcoPAC donated $3.1 million to political candidates between 2004 and 2010. Houston

homebuilder Bob Perry and Dallas Cowboys owner Jerry Jones also gave some of their money to candidates through the HillCo PAC.

Thinking about the role of elites in Texas politics As salespersons for their groups' ideas, lobbyists perform the same kinds of intermediary functions that any salesperson provides. They provide information vital to decision making and facilitate a final deal. But like the salesperson, lobbyists provide selective information, rely on personal persuasion, and use techniques of influence that do not always promote fact-based decisions. What techniques do lobbyists use to sell their clients' ideas to legislators and other policymakers?

Sources: National Institute on Money in State Politics at www.followthemoney.org/database/lobbyist.phtml?l=179932 and www.followthemoney.org/database/search.phtml?searchbox=hillCo; Nate Blakeslee, Paul Burka, and Patricia Kilday Hart, "Power Company: Who Are the Most Influential People Determining the Fate of Texas—and What Do They Want?" *Texas Monthly*, Volume 32, number 2, February, 2011, p. 165.

Before Administrative Agencies

Both administrators and interest-group representatives seek each other out to provide and obtain information. For example, if the Texas Educational Diagnosticians Association and colleges of education want to know whether the examination for certification is scheduled for revision, they contact the State Board for Educator Certification to find out. The issue is important to the Texas Educational Diagnosticians Association because the content and difficulty of the examination affect the number of recruits to the profession. The faculties of education know that changes in the examination by the state mean changes in the curriculum. The inquiry about the examination also allows the interest groups to communicate their professional opinion about the current examination and make suggestions about any changes.

Administrators seek to discover the impact of their programs and rules on the clientele they serve. They may seek input from those they serve about current and planned programs. Thus, they surrender some of their power to the profession to maintain the political support for their agency necessary to retain support from the legislature and governor.

An agency's clients are especially interested in influencing the rules and guidelines that control how they do business because the rules of doing business directly affect profits. Guidelines are issued by agencies to govern the actions of their employees (bureaucrats) in applying the law. The agency also issues formal rules that prescribe the standards of conduct followed by citizens subject to the law. The rule-making process in Texas gives all interested parties an opportunity to influence the agency's decision. Notice of intent to make a rule is required to be published in the ***Texas Register***. A time for written public comment on the proposed rule is established. At the close of the comment period, the agency analyzes the public's views. It then publishes a "final rule" that has the same force as law.

Texas Register
The official publication of the state that gives the public notice of proposed actions and adopted policies of executive branch agencies.

Although all citizens have the right to participate in the rule-making process, it is obvious that only those aware of and interested in a proposed rule participate. Ordinary citizens do not subscribe to the *Texas Register*. Corporations, labor unions, law firms, and interest groups do. Hence they know when to mobilize their members to influence decision making. Interest groups contact members by mail, e-mail, or phone and ask them to call or write the agency about the rule. Sometimes preaddressed cards with the desired message are distributed to members to sign and mail to the agency.

A natural linkage exists from agency to clientele and clientele to agency. Most state agencies are headed by boards and commissions drawn from the industry, trade, profession, or activity the agency regulates. Those who govern and those who are governed know each other because they usually share the same occupations or business interests. State board or commission members are recruited from the businesses or occupations that they regulate, and upon retirement from government service, they return to the very industries that they regulated while they were in office. The age-old questions are asked: Can the interests of the larger society be protected with such a blurring of roles? Can someone regulating an economic activity that he or she has been engaged in and to which he or she intends to return be an objective public servant? Does a system in which the regulators are chosen from the ranks of the regulated have a built-in bias? One might argue that such arrangements endanger the public interest and benefit only special interests. At least one observer has concluded that "the state's business and political elites are hopelessly intertwined."[7] Such crony capitalism has for generations characterized the relationship between major industries in Texas and the state's political leadership.

Before the Courts

Filing suit is not lobbying or pressure politics. It is using a long-established set of legal procedures to challenge the substance of law, administrative rules, or other government action.

Only persons licensed to practice law can handle cases in the state's major trial courts. Anyone negatively affected by a law, administrative rule, or government action may seek relief from the courts. The challenge may be that the agency failed to follow proper procedures in making the rule or that it misinterpreted the law in writing guidelines or rules. Applying the law or rules unfairly is another basis for suit. The use of the courts is the last resort. Major corporations, labor unions, and interest groups employ attorneys on their staffs to protect their interests. Small and less-wealthy organizations may keep attorneys on retainer or use attorneys on their board of directors to represent their interests as needed. As with everything else in life, money makes a difference in what one can do.

In a state that elects judges, the question arises as to whether wealthy corporations, interest groups, and unions can influence judicial decisions through campaign contributions. Twice in the past 15 years, CBS has run programs about "justice for sale" on *60 Minutes*, alleging that the Texas Supreme Court overwhelmingly identifies with specific interests. These reports have led to demands for campaign finance regulations to reduce any possible conflicts of interest caused by justices accepting campaign contributions. In the 2008 elections for the Texas Supreme Court, the incumbents and their challengers "took approximately two-thirds of their political funds from contributors with business before the court."[8] Thus far, the legislature has resisted enactment of anything but voluntary compliance standards for judicial campaigns.[9] The U.S. Supreme Court steered clear of restricting

---

[7]"The Future Is Texas," *Economist*, December 19, 2002, p. 29.

[8]Texans for Public Justice, "Courtroom Contributions Stain Supreme Court Campaigns: October 2008," http://info.tpj.org/reports/courtroomcontributions/index.html.

[9]Clay Robison, "Campaign '96: 'Justice for Sale' Charges Leveled Anew," *Houston Chronicle*, September 22, 1996, p. 1A.

campaign contributions in the 2009 *Caperton* v. *A.T. Massey Coal Company* case. In this case, the Supreme Court ruled:

> We conclude that there is a serious risk of actual bias—based on objective and reasonable perceptions—when a person with a personal stake in a particular case had a significant and disproportionate influence in placing the judge on the case by raising funds or directing the judge's election campaign when the case was pending or imminent. The inquiry centers on the contribution's relative size in comparison to the total amount of money contributed to the campaign, the total amount spent in the election, and the apparent effect such contribution had on the outcome of the election.[10]

Although the decision begins to set parameters for the most egregious examples of conflicts of interest, *Caperton* v. *A.T. Massey* does not ban campaign contributions made by litigants or attorneys (see Texas Insiders Chapter 11). If greater restrictions are to be established, it will be up to the Texas legislature to set those restrictions.

Large campaign contributions to judicial candidates are newsworthy because judges are held to a higher standard than elected legislators and executives. Legislators and elected executives are expected to be highly partisan. Judges must be as impartial as human imperfection allows. Texas is one of 8 states that elect their judges in partisan elections. Although most voters do not know who the judicial candidates are, they prefer to elect their judges rather than allow an independent commission or some other body to nominate nonpartisan judges. Political parties and campaign consultants also have a vested interest in maintaining the status quo. Reformers, however, will continue to seek changes in the method of selecting judges, even when they do not advocate changes in the other branches of government.

The Regulation of Lobbying

Of course, a danger always exists that well-organized, well-financed, narrow special interest-group influence will dominate over the general public good. Although bribery is illegal, other forms of interest-group influence are not only legal but also are protected by the Texas and U.S. Constitutions. Our constitutions guarantee citizens the right to political participation through voting, speaking, writing, and petitioning government "for redress of grievances." To peaceably assemble for political expression is likewise a clearly protected right. The Texas constitution says it very well:

> The citizens shall have the right … to … apply to those invested with the powers of government for redress of grievances or other purposes, by petition, address or remonstrance (Article 1, Section 27).

The First Amendment to the United States Constitution spells out our freedoms of expression:

> Congress shall make no law … abridging the freedom of speech, or of the press; or the right of the people peaceably to assemble, and to petition government for redress of grievances.

In these constitutional provisions, free speech, a free press, and the right to join together in political parties and interest groups are guaranteed; these guarantees, along with the right to vote, are essential to the very existence of a democracy.

---

[10]*Caperton* v. *A.T. Massey* 129 U.S. 2264 (2009).

However, representative democracy also creates dangers. The liberty that comes with representative democracy requires that citizens must sufficiently inform themselves about political issues and involve themselves in the choices to be made. Extreme behaviors in either direction—zealousness or apathy—can endanger democracy. Highly organized and active groups can threaten the well-being of the unorganized majority. The organized and zealous can be expected to triumph over the apathetic or unorganized. Hence small self-interested groups may gain control of policy making at the expense of the broader public interest.

Fearing the influence of powerful organizations asserting influence behind the scenes, reformers have supported laws that they believe respect basic rights while requiring that lobbyists' efforts be made public. The rationale for these laws is that the public should at least know who backs which policy choices and who stands to gain from them.

Who Registers and Reports Lobbying Costs

Not all lobbyists are required by state law to register and report their activities. Classes of lobbyists not required to register and report include state officials and state employees who lobby, even as their principal function. Also exempt are individuals from the private sector who are not paid for their services and do not directly spend any money to influence legislative or administrative action.

Those who do have to register and report are private-sector lobbyists who cross through the compensation threshold of $1,000 salary per calendar quarter or the expenditure threshold of $500 per quarter-year. These rules seem simple and straightforward, but an examination of the law reveals that not all compensation and expenditures are counted as lobbying. The registration form requires the lobbyist to report the following:

* For whom the person lobbies, including information about these clients
* The policy areas of their concern
* The compensation category into which the salary or reimbursement received falls
* The identity of, and information about, anyone who assists the principal lobbyist through direct contact with public officials
* Expenditures for broadcast or print advertisements, mass mailings, and other communications designed to support or oppose legislation or administrative actions
* Expenditures on members of the state legislature in excess of $50 a day on food, drink, transportation, or lodging or in the form of a gift must be reported by name, date, place, and purpose.

Activity reports must be filed by the tenth day of each month for any lobbyist who foresees expending more than $1,000 per year. Those who spend less need file only annually.[11]

A firm or entity often represents multiple clients before the state legislature or administrative agencies. For many years, those who wanted anonymously to influence legislative and executive officials could simply hire someone else to lobby on their behalf. Now, the reporting law requires the lobbyist working for a lobbying firm to reveal the identity of their actual clients and to report when their clients may have policy interests that conflict with each other.

Exempted from reporting are the following:

* Compensation received to prepare for lobbying
* Office expenses, including telephone, fax, copying, office supplies, postage, dues and subscriptions, transportation, and the costs of clerical help
* Costs associated with events to which all members of the legislature are invited
* Campaign contributions to public officials are not reported as lobbying expenses but as campaign contributions at different times from as lobbying expenses.

---

[11]Texas Ethics Commission, "Chapter 34: Regulation of Lobbyists," www.ethics.state.tx.us/legal/ch34.html.

These and other exemptions in the law mean that the public gets a very incomplete picture of the investments that interests groups make in lobbying.

Critics of the law maintain that some provisions leave the public ill-informed because lobbyists' compensation and expenditures are reported in broad categories rather than in specific amounts. For example, one report filed with the Texas Ethics Commission by Electronic Data Systems Corporation (EDS) of Dallas in 1995 identified 42 lobbyists; 31 were paid from $0.00 to $9,999.99; two received $50,000 to $99,999.99; seven were paid $150,000 to $199,999.99; and one was paid $200,000 to $999,999.99. Merely reporting by category obscures a great deal; EDS spent somewhere between $1,400,000 and $3,008,990, but the exact amount is unknown.[12] In 2005, Southwestern Bell, renamed AT&T, reported having 129 lobbyists paid between $4 and $7 million.[13]

Reporting on which policy a lobbyist seeks to influence similarly requires only checking the appropriate box on the form. Reformers charge that those requirements provide very little information that the public can use. To reveal what one lobbied about would enable the public to see where corporations, trade associations, labor unions, and individuals spend their political capital and would require lobbyists to list the specific bill numbers on which they worked or the rule-making hearings at which they testified. The lobby industry has sufficient power to prevent changes in the reporting law to require reporting the exact nature and extent of interest-group influence in the Texas political system. Although critics fault the Texas Ethics Commission for not vigorously enforcing reporting laws except in high-profile cases, it serves as a comprehensive repository of campaign financial statements, lists of registered lobbyists, campaign contributions and campaign expenditures. One critic admitted the Texas Ethics Commission is "a pretty darn good library" even if "it's not a good cop."[14] The members of the Texas legislature are provided a list of registered lobbyists and their clients by February 1 of each legislative session and the public may obtain copies of registration and activity reports from the Ethics Commission website.

> **Did You Know?** The Texas Ethics Commission fined Sharon Keller, the controversial presiding judge of the Texas Court of Criminal Appeals, $100,000 for failing to disclose $2.4 million in assets.[15]

Thanks to Texas Ethics Commission records and the research of Texans for Public Justice, several interesting facts about the lobby industry in Texas are clear: Special interests entered into 8,716 lobby contracts with 1,836 lobbyists in 2011. These contracts are estimated to be worth between $169 and $345 million. Thirty lobbyists earned more than $1.5 million for their services; 14 identifiable "industry" groupings spent more than $5 million each to have their interests protected or advanced; and most lobbyists are affiliated with law firms in Texas.[16] Table 6.3 provides details of the 14 identifiable interests spending the most money to influence Texas state government and the number of contracts each entered into.

---

[12]Texas Ethics Commission, "List of Employers and Clients, 1995," pp. 63–65.

[13]Texans for Public Justice, "Austin's Oldest Profession: Texas' Top Lobby Clients and Those Who Service Them," at www.tpj.org/reports/austinsoldest06/clients.html.

[14]Kelley Shannon quoting Craig McDonald, Executive Director of Texans for Public Justice, in "Texas: The Story behind the Score," *State Integrity Investigation*, www.stateintegrity.org/texas_story_subpage.

[15]Steve McGonigle, "Sharon Keller plans to appeal $100,000 fine levied by state ethics panel," *The Dallas Morning News*, May 1, 1010, www.dallasnews.com/news/politics/state-politics/20100501-Sharon-Keller-plans-to-appeal-8011.ece.

[16]Texans for Public Justice, "Austin's Oldest Profession: Texas's Top Lobby Clients and Those Who Service Them, Analyzing the 2011 Lobby Contracts," http://info.tpj.org/reports/pdf/AustinOldest2011.pdf.

TABLE 6.3 Number and Maximum Value of Contracts Signed by Selected Lobby Industry Groups: 2011

Industry Group	Contracts	Maximum Value of Contracts
Energy/natural resources	1,357	$64,124,000
Health	1,239	$53,230,000
Ideological/single issue	1,559	$43,675,002
Miscellaneous business	1,024	$40,785,001
Communications	399	$22,950,000
Finance	479	$18,390,000
Lawyers and lobbyists	366	$17,200,000
Computers and electronics	334	$14,475,000
Insurance	316	$14,100,000
Transportation	360	$13,105,000
Construction	305	$12,675,000
Real estate	321	$10,355,000
Agriculture	142	$6,900,000
Other	186	$6,445,000
Labor	130	$6,265,000
TOTALS:	**8,716**	**$345,430,004**

Source: Texans for Public Justice, "Austin's Oldest Profession: Texas's Top Lobby Clients and Those Who Service Them, Analyzing the 2011 Lobby Contracts," http://info.tpj.org/reports/pdf/AustinOldest2011.pdf.

This table shows the magnitude of efforts to influence Texas policymakers.

▲ **Why do interest groups spend this much money trying to influence public policy? Explain why lobby tactics are so expensive.**

THE BALANCE OF POLITICAL POWER IN TEXAS

Do interest groups dominate the state's political system? Contemporary wisdom says they do. Look at the money poured into the system by corporate Texas and other special interests. The average person cannot compete. Every serious attempt to secure campaign finance reform has failed. Voting and political attentiveness is so low in Texas that the public is easily fooled. Several economic interests, such as insurance companies, oil and gas companies, and certain utilities, usually have their way with the state.

Indeed, sitting members of the legislature themselves are known to represent special interests before state agencies and courts and many have economic ties with enterprises that have interests in pending legislation. Governor Rick Perry, the speaker of the house, and members of both the Texas Senate and House have arranged for special benefits for their campaign contributors or clients.[17]

---

[17]Matt Stiles and Brian Thevenot, " Perry's Appointed Regents are Big Donors," *The Texas Tribune*, August 24, 2010, www.texastribune.org/texas-state-agencies/governors-office/perrys-appointed-regents-are-big-donors; Texans for Public Justice, "How Politicians Got Fat on a Risky Weight-Loss Stimulant," October 21, 2002, http://info.tpj.org/Lobby_Watch/ephedra.html; "Revolving-Door Lobbyist Adopts So-Craddick Method," November 22, 2002, http://info.tpj.org/Lobby_Watch/caprock.html; "Companies Paid Craddick a Big Income While Claiming His 1999 Energy Tax Cut," December 17, 2002, http://info.tpj.org/page_view.jsp?pageid=236&pf=1; Formby, Brandon and Gromer Jeffers Jr., "Questions Raised About Rep. Linda Harper-Brown's use of a Mercedes," *The Dallas Morning News*, June 18, 2010.

Others argue that the structure of government is designed to make it hard for any group to dominate the state. The structure of government is characterized by (1) the separation of powers, (2) checks and balances, (3) elected officials responsible to different constituencies at the ballot box at different times, (4) appointed officials with fixed terms, and (5) career bureaucrats. These structures make the political system difficult to capture by any one interest. The house and senate and the governor must agree to create law. The implementation of law is placed in the hands of elected and appointed executive officers and the unelected bureaucrats below them.

Texas is too pluralistic or diverse for the whole governmental enterprise to be dominated by one interest. Special interests do, of course, sometimes come into conflict with each other. Matters involving large amounts of money or important changes in existing policy invite crowds. In such situations, for anything to happen, some compromise among competing interests must occur, resulting in a mix of values incorporated into the policy decision.

The computer age gives citizens access to information never before possible and it offers a political tool that invites inputs from underrepresented, new voices who otherwise lack the financial and other resources to have a serious impact on policymaking. Furthermore, interest groups are limited because they operate in an environment where the general public is critical, if not cynical, of the political process.

Despite these checks on the power of interest groups, many Texans believe that special interests control government and perceive that as bad; their prevailing view is that the little guy has no chance of being heard or heeded. Their cynicism seems to be driven by scandal-centered news media coverage.

These same Texans may not realize that if they belong to a rod or gun club, teach school, drive a truck, or practice carpentry, they are members of a group that lobbies the legislature and executive agencies in Austin. A story about a lobbyist helping a legislator by supplying needed information or assisting in the actual writing of a bill useful to the people back home seldom makes the news.

HOW DOES TEXAS COMPARE?
Corruption Risk Among the 50 States

Using several broad measures to evaluate how well state regulations and procedures guard against the potential for corruption, the Center for Public Integrity found that Texas ranks 27th among the 50 states on its *Corruption Risk Report Card*. In the report assembled by The Center for Public Integrity, Public Radio International, and Global Integrity, Texas received a D+ for its performance on 14 different measures of risk for corruption. While Texas receives good marks for internal audits, state pension fund management, and procurement, it receives failing marks for public access, executive accountability, state civil service management, the state insurance commission, and redistricting. It receives a D- for political financing and a D+ for legislative accountability.

In 1991, Texans voted in favor of creating the Texas Ethics Commission, which should have contributed to minimizing the risk of political corruption. The Texas Ethics Commission, however, has been limited in what it can actually do. Its enforcement functions have mostly been limited to minor cases of failing to submit campaign contribution reports on time. Caitlin Ginley of the Center for Public Integrity reports, "The Texas Ethics Commission is comprised of appointees by the governor and legislature, which not only presents an inherent conflict but often leads to gridlock. Commissioners are typically split along party lines, but

Texas Corruption Risk Report Card Categories and Grades

Public Access to Information	F	Political Financing	D–
Executive Accountability	F	Legislative Accountability	D+
Judicial Accountability	C	State Budget Process	C
State Civil Service Management	F	Procurement	B–
Internal Auditing	A	Lobbying Disclosure	C–
State Pension Management	B–	Ethics Enforcement Agencies	C+
State Insurance Commission	F	Redistricting	F

in order to pursue an investigation, at least six of the eight commissioners must agree." The structure of the commission severely limits its ability to regulate ethical violations.

Texas law does not limit individual campaign contributions; it allows lawmakers to retire and become lobbyists the next day; it allows bureaucrats to retire and become consultants for the very industry they had been hired to regulate, and the law leaves "significant loopholes" in financial disclosure requirements. These issues contribute to the low mark for the state of Texas.

FOR DEBATE

Should the State of Texas regulate ethical violations among lawmakers more stringently? If so, how? As you read lobby and campaign finance disclosure requirements, look for practical ways to limit potential conflicts of interest among policymakers.

Sources: The Center for Public Integrity, Public Radio International, and Global Integrity, 2011. *State Integrity Investigation: Keeping Government Honest*, http://www.stateintegrity.org/your_state; Caitlin Ginley, "Grading the nation: How accountable is your state?" *Center for Public Integrity*. March 19, 2012, www.iwatchnews.org/2012/03/19/8423/grading-nation-how-accountable-your-state; Kelley Shannon, "Texas: The story behind the score," *Center for Public Integrity*. *State Integrity Investigation: Keeping Government Honest*, www.stateintegrity.org/Texas_story_subpage.

Factors That Affect Interest Group Power

Interest groups assert political influence throughout the nation, but several factors make Texas especially vulnerable to their influence.

Culture of Nonparticipation One hundred and fifty years of one-partyism (see Chapters 4 and 5) created less incentive for average Texans to participate in political affairs than citizens living in states with competitive parties. The absence of two competitive political parties also helped establish a history of elitist rule and strong special interests. Indeed, the conservative Texas political elites used their control of state government to enact laws that discouraged mass political participation, including the poll tax, annual voter registration, the white primary, and recently, the passage of voter ID laws (see Chapter 4). These barriers to participation promoted a government by elites and a traditionalistic culture of nonparticipation by the masses.

Party Competition Studies of the power of interest groups consistently show that where political parties are weak, interest groups are strong. States with a long history of two-party competition have weaker interest groups than states in the early stages of party development.[18] Parties in competitive states must appeal to the majority of the population to

[18]Ronald Hrebenar and Clive Thomas, "Who's Got Clout? Interest Group Power in the States," *State Legislatures*, April 1999, pp. 30–34.

have a chance of winning elections. They cannot focus on a single issue or a limited number of issues, as interest groups do, and win a majority of the vote. During the past 30 years, Texas has transformed from a one-party Democratic state to a one-party Republican state passing through only a brief phase of genuine party competition. The one-party Republican state today is just as vulnerable to interest group domination as was the once one-party Democratic state.

A Part-Time Legislature Texas, with a population of nearly 26 million, is the second-largest state in the Union, but it is the only big state with short, infrequent legislative sessions. Legislative pay is below poverty level, and legislator turnover is fairly high. Texas legislators must depend on outside sources of income to earn a living, making them vulnerable to the temptations of special interest groups. Some lawmakers work in occupations whose clients include the very interests groups that also lobby these lawmakers. Texas legislators have limited staffs to provide them with independent information; Texas representatives' average staff number about three people, whereas senators have an average staff of a little more than seven. The result is a legislative body that is easily influenced by special interest groups. Professor Cal Jillson put it this way: "If you meet only occasionally, get paid little and have weak staffs, you are at the disposal of the [lobbyists] because you have to go to them to get information."[19]

Many Texans have argued that a part-time legislature is better because it governs less, but in Texas, this is not always the case. In the 140 days of the 82nd Legislature Session, more than 1,485 bills became law.[20] The 111th Congress, by contrast, produced 383 laws between January 2009 and January 2011.[21] With fewer resources and less time, the Texas legislature produces many more pieces of legislation than the U.S. Congress. Although the Texas legislature is certainly not governing less (as measured by legislative activity), the Texas legislature passes far more bills in a much shorter period of time than Congress.

> **Did You Know?** The Texas legislature passed more than 10 laws for every day it was in session in 2011.

As it stands, legislators rely on lobbyists to write many of the bills that lawmakers then introduce. As an example, the American Legislative Exchange Council (ALEC) has been criticized for writing the language for the voter ID law, which some believe will cut down on voter fraud, yet others believe is voter suppression legislation. Because of time constraints, lawmakers rely on interest groups like ALEC to write the bills they then claim as their own. Legislators cannot become familiar with all of the legislation on which they vote, and instead depend on interest-group sources for information and advice.

The Revolving Door and the Texas Legislature High turnover is another consequence of an understaffed, low-paid legislature that meets infrequently. As legislators retire and move on to other occupations, a peculiar practice—referred to as the **revolving door**—has developed. Many ex-lawmakers become lobbyists for the very interest groups they once regulated. To be certain, few people would be better suited to serve as lobbyists than ex-lawmakers. Former legislators are intricately familiar with the legislative process, many are policy experts, and they often have friendships with lawmakers who are still in office. Their familiarity with the policy-making process, their policy expertise, and their

Revolving door
The interchange of employees between government agencies and the private businesses with which they have dealings.

---

[19]Quoted in Clay Robison, "Weak State Government Paved Way for Lobbyists," *Houston Chronicle,* December 29, 2002, p. A24.

[20]Texas Legislature Online. "Texas Legislature: Bills Signed by the Governor" 82nd Legislature Regular Session, www.legis.state.tx.us/Reports/Report.aspx?LegSess=82R&ID=signedbygov; Texas Legislature Online. "Texas Legislature: Bills Filed Without the Governor's Signature" 82nd Legislature Regular Session, www.legis.state. tx.us/Reports/Report.aspx?LegSess=82R&ID=filedwogovsign.

[21]Library of Congress. "Search Bill Summary and Status: 111th Congress," http://thomas.loc.gov/home/ LegislativeData.php?&n=BSS&c=111.

friendships with lawmakers make them very attractive candidates for special interest groups seeking to hire lobbyists.

The revolving door may create opportunities for retiring legislators, but it also creates the potential for conflict of interest. Lawmakers, planning their next career move, might feel compelled to reward their future employers with favorable public policy choices. Lawmakers might author bills that help the industries on whose behalf they hope to lobby, once they leave office. Although it is difficult to gauge the extent to which *quid pro quo* occurs, the coincidences can be troubling. In 2003, state representative Jamie Capelo co-authored a bill that capped medical liability lawsuits. Shortly after leaving office, Capelo became a lobbyist for interest groups that benefited from his bill. Such connections between public policy and the interest-group beneficiaries that would later employ the sponsors of the public policy are common.

Many are critical of unscrupulous lawmakers using public service as a stepping-stone to a more lucrative career as a lobbyist. "[P]eople rightfully wonder when did they stop being a lawmaker and when did they start to become a special-interest lobbyist," states Andrew Wheat, with Texans for Public Justice.[22] Public service should be its own reward. Most public servants do not enter public service because it is lucrative, but because they care about creating good public policy. Banning retired legislators from lobbying would limit their career paths, but it would also reduce the potential for conflict of interest while they are still legislators.

Unlike the federal government and many other states, Texas does not ban retiring government officers from becoming lobbyists. Although 26 other states have some ban on lobbying immediately after leaving office, Texas has no such restrictions. Texas legislators, whose poor pay does not compare to the salaries of successful lobbyists, have an incentive to leave public service for the attractive pay available to lobbyists. One study conducted by the Center for Public Integrity found 70 former members of the Texas legislature working as lobbyists—the largest number of any state. California and New York, which have full-time legislative bodies, only reported 35 and 19 ex-lawmakers-turned-lobbyists, respectively.[23]

However, temporary moratoriums on former officials lobbying for one or two years after leaving office do not entirely solve the problem of conflict of interest. The Center for Public Integrity data for 2005 indicates that states with no ban on lobbying produced an average of 29 ex-lawmakers who became lobbyists, states with a one-year ban averaged 22 lawmakers who became lobbyists, and the six states with a two-year ban averaged 28 lawmakers who became lobbyists.[24] The differences among the states are even smaller when one takes into account that some states have much smaller legislative bodies, thus producing fewer ex-lawmakers.

Decentralization of the Executive Branch

Yet another institutional feature of Texas government may enhance the power of interest groups—its plural executive system. Power is divided among numerous independently elected executives: governor, lieutenant governor, attorney general, comptroller, agricultural commissioner, land commissioner, and the multimember Railroad Commission and State Board of Education. The **fragmentation**, or division of power, within the executive branch is intensified by the use of independent boards and commissions to supervise state agencies. The governor appoints all members of nearly every unelected board and commission, usually one-third of the members every two years, but has little power to remove them during their six-year terms. If each agency were headed by a single executive, appointed and removable by the governor, agencies would theoretically be more responsive to the governor's agenda than to the agencies' clientele interest groups.

Fragmentation
Division of power among separately elected executive officers. A plural executive is a fragmented executive.

---

[22]Grissom, Brandi, "Ex-Lawmaker's Lobbying looks bad, group says," *El Paso Times*, May 21, 2009.
[23]Center for Public Integrity, "Statehouse Revolvers," October 12, 2006, www.publicintegrity.org/2006/10/12/5900/statehouse-revolvers.
[24]Ibid.

The plural executive, together with a fragmented board and commission system, means no strong central authority exists with the legal power to control the executive branch. As a result, interest groups find numerous points of access in the executive branch, increasing agencies' vulnerability to their influence. In fact, state laws require that many boards and commissions must include members who are engaged in the profession, business, or occupation that the board regulates, further adding the potential for conflicts of interest.

Weak Interest Group Regulations While Texas laws require lobbyists to file extensive reports with the Texas Ethics Commission, Texas has little power to enforce restrictions on conflicts of interest between public officials and lobbyists as they seek special favors from government. State laws define lobbying and require reporting of information about the lobbyist, the lobbyist's employer, and the expenses associated with trying to influence government decisions; candidates must also report most of their campaign contributions and other gifts. The Texas Ethics Commission simply accepts these reports from officeholders, candidates, and lobbyists and makes them public, but it has relatively weak powers to establish standards of conduct for officeholders, candidates, and lobbyists. Instead, Texas ethics laws primarily depend on publicity to enforce high standards of conduct among lobbyists and public officials; this approach to lobby regulation places a special responsibility on the public and the press to examine these reports and act on them. The ethic commission's website and various public-interest watchdog groups have organized the reports in searchable form useful to the public.

The Media One of the institutions essential to the survival of democracy is the media. Radio, television, Internet, and print journalists serve as watchdogs of government. Public officials and bureaucrats know that every decision they make, as well as their general conduct, is fair game for the news media. The public has a right to know what its public servants are doing, and the media are committed to telling it. But the media communicate in two directions: They not only relay the activities of government to the people but also transmit the people's moods and messages to the halls of state. The media are thus a link between people and government—but not a neutral one.

The media are allies of the people in their demands that the government's business be conducted in public view. They work to promote open meetings, open records, and recorded votes on policy decisions in the legislature and in administrative boards and commissions. Openness is the enemy of corruption, bribery, conflicts of interest, and other forms of unethical conduct, and the press delights in exposing such to the public. Thus the interaction of lobbyists and public officials is a matter of interest to the media.

The self-imposed restraints on reporting what the state of Texas is doing remind us that newspapers, newsmagazines, and radio and television stations are also businesses concerned with making a profit. Austin, the state capital, is not home to the major newspapers or broadcasting channels in the state. It is expensive to employ journalists and station them in Austin for your hometown news industry. Most Texas media outlets subscribe to wire services (Associated Press and Reuters) to get the news from Austin, even when the legislature is in session. Many newspapers are parts of chain-of-information companies that keep an office in Austin and feed all their papers and radio and TV stations in the state. Cox, Scripps Howard, Hearst, and A. H. Belo each maintain staff in Austin. In addition, hundreds of Texas radio stations subscribe to the Texas State Network, which maintains an office in the capital city. The media presence in Austin probably helps keep the government honest and responsive to the public.

Constituent Influence The constant forces affecting interest-group strength on any policy issue are constituent values, attitudes, and beliefs. No elected official can consistently ignore the "folks back home." Most state representatives and senators have lived in their district for a long time and know the culture of the region. Serving in Austin only 140 days every other year, legislators spend most of their time at home with their constituents and, on most major issues, they know what the voters would have them do.

Although it is unlikely that an elected representative vote contrary to clear-cut constituent opinion to please a special interest, constituents are often divided on major issues and probably have no opinion at all on the many intricate details of policy decisions that affect interest groups. It is on these issues that interest groups, fellow legislators, the governor, and the party struggle for influence.

Interest Groups as Checks on Interest Groups

On issues of major public importance, interest groups have conflicting views and compete with each other to achieve different policy outcomes. Many interest groups and individuals take an interest in broad issues like tax policy, education, campaign finance reform, gun control, and abortion. And, as the number of participants in any political debate increases, the potential for conflict increases and the influence of each particular interest group diminishes.

When a special interest is seeking a change in policy that affects the balance of power in the political, social, or economic system, much greater participation occurs because group will be pitted against group, and the general public will get the opportunity to participate because the media will transmit stories of conflict to their readers, listeners, and viewers. The challenge for the public officials involved in high-profile policy decisions is to lead the warring groups to a compromise if any policy decision is to be made at all.

On more obscure or narrow issues, a single group may find itself without political opposition. Under such circumstances, the interest group must persuade only a few key people, such as legislative committee chairs and presiding officers, to win a floor vote in the legislature. And because many administrative agencies deal with policies that are narrow in scope, a few interest groups frequently dominate agency policies. Whether many special interests are involved in the policy-making process or only one, the status, resources, size, reputation, and lobbying skills of any group affect its access to agency heads and legislators. These factors, along with the political environment, shape policy outcomes.

Campaign Contributions

Money in politics is the hot topic of the day. The amount of money raised and spent by candidates for elective office at all levels has increased to a startling degree. Most campaign contributions for the state legislature and the statewide offices come from large donors. These donors represent banks, insurance companies, the petrochemical industry, physicians, trial lawyers, real estate agents, teachers, and others who, through political action committees, funnel money to candidates. These campaign contributors give large amounts because the state legislature, the governor, the Railroad Commission, and other elected officials make decisions that affect these donors' economic well-being. Donors contribute to gain **access** to public officials, which means getting in the door to sit down and talk about their needs. A substantial contribution seems to create an obligation on the part of an elected official to listen when a contributor calls. Ordinary citizens find access more difficult.

Access
The ability to contact an official either in person or by phone. Campaign contributions are often used to gain access.

> **Did You Know?** The average winning candidate for the Texas legislature spent $371,890[25] in 2010 to win an office that pays $7,200 a year!

According to Texans for Public Justice, legislative candidates raised $98.4 million in the 2010 election cycle. An estimated $76.9 million was raised by the 271 major candidates vying for a seat in the Texas House, and an estimated $21.5 million was raised by the 44 candidates vying for seats on the Texas Senate.[26] Sixty-seven percent of the dollars raised by

---

[25] Texans for Public Justice, "Money in PoliTex: A Guide to Money in the 2010 Texas Elections," at http://info.tpj.org/reports/politex2010/SenateSummary.html.
[26] Ibid.

AP Photo/Harry Cabluck

Rep. Sylvester Turner, center, is approached by lobbyists outside the Texas House of Representatives chamber.

What is the evidence that campaign contributions influence public policy making?

Late-train contributions

Campaign funds given to the winning candidate after the election up to 30 days before the legislature comes into session. Such contributions are designed to curry favor with individuals the donors may not have supported originally.

Did You Know? Texans for Lawsuit Reform, the largest single interest-group contributor to 2010 legislative campaigns, had enormous success in getting its legislative agenda adopted.

house candidates went to incumbents, and 46 percent of money raised by senate candidates went to incumbent senators.[27] Even when candidates face little or no opposition, they raise large amounts of money. Their success in raising campaign contributions is indicative of the state's economic and political importance.

One of the biennial rituals in Austin occurs after each election when special interest groups hold fund-raising events to honor selected legislators. State law forbids giving and accepting campaign contributions 30 days before the start of a legislative session and throughout the session, causing a rush of fund-raising activity in the five weeks after election day. These lobbyist fund-raising parties occur after the election, not before. The reason, as one lobbyist said, is to "pay the price of admission" or to obtain good access to legislators. These so-called **late-train contributions** are commonly given to the winning candidates in the executive branch as well. Losers are rarely the beneficiaries of such largess.

Does money buy sponsorship of bills and special favors? The public and the press think it does. Lobbyists and legislators claim it does not.[28] The increasing amounts of campaign contributions and the 18 percent increase in the number of lobbyists from 1998 to 2011 hardly lead to any other conclusion.[29] Records of the 2011 session of the legislature show lobbyists spending as much as $345 million trying to influence decisions of the Texas House and Senate.[30]

Anecdotal evidence that contributions buy public policy is mixed, but cases have been identified, which leaves the casual observer with the perception that conflicts of interest do arise. An example of such a case was brought to national attention during a Republican presidential debate in Tampa Florida, when candidate Michele Bachmann blasted fellow candidate Rick Perry for mandating a vaccine for cervical cancer for girls. The controversy began February 2, 2007, when Governor Rick Perry issued an executive order to vaccinate preteen girls against the sexually transmitted human papilloma virus, which causes cervical cancer in women. Fearing opposition from members of his own party, Governor Perry circumvented the Texas legislature with the executive order. He took this action, expecting opposition from conservative groups that believe such a vaccine would give young girls tacit consent to have sex.

Shortly after he issued the executive order, it was revealed that Governor Perry's chief of staff Deirdre Delisi met with other members of the governor's team for an "HPV Vaccine for Children Briefing," October 16, 2006.[31] That same day, Merck and Company's political action committee contributed $5,000 to the Perry campaign. Merck is the only manufacturer of Gardasil, the vaccine against the virus. One of Merck's lobbyists at the time was Mike Toomey, Rick Perry's former chief of staff and Deirdre

---

[27]Ibid.

[28]James Gibbons, "Officials Come and Go; the Lobby Rules," *Houston Chronicle*, January 27, 2003.

[29]The Texas Ethics Commission listed 1561 registered lobbyists in 1999. In 2011, the number of registered lobbyists increased to 1837. See: *Texas Ethics Commission*," Lobby Lists and Reports," www.ethics.state.tx.us/dfs/loblist.htm; *Austin American-Statesman*, May 5, 1999, p. B2; Michael Holmes, "Lobbyists Paying Plenty for Attention, Study Finds," *Austin American-Statesman*, May 24, 1999, p. B2; Texans for Public Justice, "Austin's Oldest Profession: Top Lobby Clients and Those Who Service Them," 2005, at www.tpj.org/reports/austinsoldest06/facts.html.

[30]Texans for Public Justice, "Austin's Oldest Profession: Texas's Top Lobby Clients and Those Who Service Them, (Analyzing the 2011 Lobby Contracts)," http://info.tpj.org/reports/pdf/AustinOldest2011.pdf.

[31]Liz Austin Peterson, "Perry's staff discussed vaccine on day Merck donated to campaign," *Associated Press*, February 22, 2007.

Delisi's predecessor. In early March of 2007, the Texas legislature passed a bill rescinding the executive order, which
Governor Perry grudgingly allowed to become law without
his signature.

Although the governor's office claims that the connec-
tion between the campaign contribution and the meeting held by his chief of staff was
merely a coincidence, candidate Michele Bachmann reminded Americans, "We cannot forget that in the midst of this executive order, there was a big drug company that made millions of dollars because of this mandate."[32] Critics contend that the coincidence, at the very
least, sheds light on the conflicts of interest that can occur between elected officials in need
of raising campaign contributions and the need of special interest groups for public policy
that provides them direct benefits.

Texas's Most Powerful Interest Groups

Twenty-five years ago, business and the professions tended to be the most powerful interests in the states. They still are, despite a mushrooming of several other groups. Generally
speaking, the newer interests, such as the environmentalists, have not supplanted the
old. In conservative pro-business Texas, that's not surprising. For many corporations,
the power of interest groups waxes and wanes depending on the political environment. If
an industry believes that it stands to gain or lose from government action, it will lobby
the legislature. Although it is not only measure of an interest group's influence, one can
gauge the strength of its lobbying effort by the amount of money it spends to lobby state
officials.

Table 6.4a lists the 27 clients that spent $1 million or more on lobbying in 2011, and
Table 6.4b shows the percentage of total lobby contracts coming from each category of
interest groups. Note how frequently groups from the energy and natural resources sector
appear. Nineteen percent (or up to $64 million) of all lobbying contracts in 2011 were made
on behalf of the energy and natural resources sector of the economy.[33] While some energy
companies were lobbying for relief from falling natural gas prices, others were hoping for
permission to build nuclear reactors in Texas. The tsunami that wiped away the Fukushima
II Nuclear Power Plant also wiped away the support to build more nuclear power plants in
Texas anytime soon.[34] The power of interest groups is in part a function of the lobbying
campaigns they organize.

That said, in the past, politicians have identified the most powerful interests in Texas as
the Texas Association of Business, Texans for Lawsuit Reform, Texas Medical Association,
Texas Realtors' Association, and the Texas State Teachers' Association. Other groups with
more than average influence are the Texas Motor Truck Association, Texas Trial Lawyers
Association, Texas AFL-CIO, Independent Oil and Gas Producers Association, and the Texas
Municipal League.[35]

These groups have the money to maintain permanent headquarters in Austin and employ
clerical and research staffs as well as lobbyists to make their prominence known. These
resources, when competently managed, literally allow some interest groups to create a need

---

[32]Bachmann, Michele, CNN-Tea Party Republican Debate in Tampa Florida, September 12, 2011. Tran-
scripts available at www.nytimes.com/2011/09/13/us/politics/cnn-tea-party-republican-debate-in-tampa-fla.
html?pagewanted=all.

[33]Texans for Public Justice, "Austin's Oldest Profession: Texas's Top Lobby Clients and Those Who Service Them
(Analyzing the 2011 Lobby Contracts)," http://info.tpj.org/reports/pdf/AustinOldest2011.pdf.

[34]Ibid.

[35]Hrebenar and Thomas, "Who's Got Clout?" *Interest Group Politics in the Southern States*, ed. Ronald Hrebenar
and Clive Thomas (Tuscaloosa: University of Alabama Press, 1992), pp. 58–162.

TABLE 6.4a The Biggest Spenders on Lobbyists in Texas

Client	Maximum Value of Lobbying Contract	Industry
AT&T Corp.	$10,560,000	Communications
Energy Future Holdings Corp.	$2,640,000	Energy/natural resources
American Electric Power	$1,950,000	Energy/Natural Resources
CenterPoint Energy	$1,805,000	Energy/Natural Resources
McGinnis, Lochridge & Kilgore	$1,650,000	Lawyers/Lobbyists
Global Gaming, LSP	$1,600,000	Miscellaneous Business
Texas Association of Home Health Care	$1,565,000	Health
Oncor Electric Delivery Co.	$1,525,000	Energy/Natural Resources
TX Medical Assn.	$1,480,000	Health
TX Assn. of Realtors	$1,420,000	Real Estate
Assn. of Electric Companies of TX	$1,395,000	Energy/Natural Resources
TXU Energy Retail Co.	$1,495,000	Energy/Natural Resources
Linebarger Heard Goggan Blair	$1,335,000	Lawyers/Lobbyists
TX Cable & Telecom. Assn.	$1,320,000	Communications
Luminant Holding Co.	$1,255,000	Energy/Natural Resources
TX Trial Lawyers Assn.	$1,250,000	Lawyers/Lobbyists
Waste Control Specialists	$1,190,000	Energy/Natural Resources
Verizon	$1,185,000	Communications
Entergy Corp.	$1,155,000	Energy/Natural Resources
NRG Energy	$1,140,000	Energy/Natural Resources
City of Houston	$1,095,000	Ideological/Single Issue
Baker Botts	$1,050,000	Lawyers/Lobbyists
City of Austin	$1,030,000	Ideological/Single Issue
Ryan and Company	$1,020,000	Finance
Atmos Energy Corp.	$1,020,000	Energy/Natural Resources
Altria-Philip Morris	$1,005,000	Agriculture
Henderson Global Investors	$1,000,000	Finance

TABLE 6.4b Interest Group Sector Lobby Spending as a Percentage of Total Contracts

Interest Group Sector	Percent of Total Lobbying Contracts, 2011
Energy/Natural Resources	19
Health	15
Miscellaneous Business	12
Insurance and Finance	9
Transportation and Construction	8
Communications	7
Lawyers and Lobbyists	5
Computers and Electronics	4
Real Estate	3
Agriculture	2
Labor	2
Ideological and Single issue	13

Source: Texans for Public Justice, "Austin's Oldest Profession: Texas's Top Lobby Clients and Those Who Service Them, Analyzing the 2011 Lobby Contracts," http://info.tpj.org/reports/pdf/AustinOldest2011.pdf.

Table 6.4a shows which clients spent the most on lobbying, and Table 6.4b shows the percentage of total lobby contracts representing each major interest group sector.

▲ **Search out the policy goals of these big spenders. How many of them represent consumers, workers, or environmentalists? Do these interests reflect the needs of the general public?**

for themselves within the halls of government. Research shows that the number-one element determining the political power of a group is how much public officials need the group. This need may be for any expertise the group has to help the state solve problems. It may be dependence on the group for campaign contributions. Perhaps it is dependence on the economic health of the sector of the economy the group represents. A public official's need for a particular interest can have many explanations.[36]

Most registered lobbyists represent business. Business is a huge category, encompassing both the powerful and the weak. Not everyone in business shares the same viewpoint. Independent and small businesses frequently seek policy outcomes opposed by larger enterprises. Business should not be thought of as monolithic.

Unfortunately, unraveling the lobbyist registration report to determine the number of lobbyists representing a trade group, business association, or other interest is challenging. A number of organizations may be listed, supported by the same benefactors, representing the same industry, business, or activity. It is easier to identify the lobbyists representing a particular company, profession, union, or employee association. Fifty-seven percent of the business interests are associated with an identifiable company. However, many companies are also represented in **umbrella organizations**, in which industries, wholesalers, producers, retailers, and others join together to promote their collective interests. In other words, one may employ lobbyists directly through the firm and also through these umbrella organizations.

Whether the interest is one of the elite and powerful or one of the relatively unknown groups, it usually attempts to inform its members through newsletters or other means about important matters likely to come before the legislature and executive agencies. An interest group may also seek to organize its membership into telephone or mail chains. When a "hot" issue is about to come to a vote, the group may dispatch an "action alert" asking members to contact public officials expressing the group's position on the issue. The group's intent is to apply outside (grassroots) pressure while its lobbyists work with public officials inside the halls of state government in Austin.

What seems logical is that special interests having full-time staffs, multiple lobbyists, and the ability to disburse sizable campaign contributions achieve more than resource-poor groups. However, additional factors are involved. The media can sway the opinion of the people and public officials on many issues. The governor may intervene in affairs before executive agencies or in legislative issues and change the outcome. Access and good-will "bought" by campaign contributions can be nullified by media exposure, public opinion, and the countervailing power of rival interest groups. Thus, the so-called powerful groups may win more than they lose, but they do not own the government and are not guaranteed success.

Interest Group Alliances and the Dynamics of Power

Ernest Griffin observed in the 1930s that the relationships and interactions among members of the legislature are generally weaker than the relationships between the legislators and lobbyists, academics, and high-ranking bureaucrats who interact to address specific needs and solve specific problems.[37] These alliances among interest groups, legislators, and bureaucrats can develop such a long-standing relationship held together by mutual self interest that they become a subsystem in the legislative and administrative decision-making processes. Called **iron triangles**, these alliances operate largely outside public view because they dominate a narrow range of routine decisions that are of marginal interest to the general public but are of

Umbrella organization

An organization created by interest groups to promote common goals. Several interest groups may choose to coordinate their efforts to influence government when they share the same policy goal. The organization may be temporary or permanent.

Iron triangle

A working coalition among administrative agencies, clientele interest groups, and legislative committees that share a common interest in seeing either the implementation or the defeat of certain policies and proposals.

---

[36]Ibid.
[37]Ernest Griffin, *The Impasse of Democracy* (New York: Harrison-Hilton Books, 1939), p. 182.

critical importance to the interest groups and bureaucrats involved. For example, the oil interests have formed a close association with the Texas Railroad Commission, whose members they help elect, while the agriculture industry forms a similar symbiotic relationship with the commissioner of agriculture and agriculture committees in the state legislature. Highway contractors form a similar alliance with the Texas Department of Transportation and interested legislators. We will illustrate these alliances more extensively in Chapter 10 as we discuss the state's bureaucracy.

Whereas iron triangles are more or less permanent alliances between legislators, bureaucrats, and interest groups controlling narrow issues of mutual self interest, other broader public issues like health care, abortion, and environmental protection activate wider-ranging coalitions among interest groups, career bureaucrats, academic researchers, think tanks, political bloggers, editors, neighborhood leaders, radio talk show hosts, and other community activists who form **issue networks**. These issue-network alliances are dynamic—different activists and interest groups organize around different public issues.[38]

Iron triangles are most likely to control rather routine decisions. Economic concerns dominate their agenda as they seek subsidies, tax breaks, and regulations favorable to their economic interests. Issue networks have broader policy interests and hence have more participants, but these alliances are still relatively small and often temporary. However, issue networks have the potential to blossom into a larger **political movement**. When the web of opinion leaders in issue networks taps into a large set of issues important to the masses of people, they may develop a large following with a fairly stable membership. One such political movement is the Tea Party.

Beginning among a relatively small network of activists opposing the federal bailouts of the financial industry, the Tea Party movement gained strength with the passage of the stimulus bill (The American Recovery and Reinvestment Act of 2009) and finally evolved into a full-fledged antigovernment movement by the time health care reform was passed (the Patient Protection and Affordable Care Act of 2010). A small alliance of interested groups had transformed into a mass political movement.

In Texas, the Tea Party movement has had enormous success. Their support led to strong Republican showing in the 2010 elections, and a Republican supermajority in the Texas legislature, receptive to the conservative agenda, enacted several bills popular with Tea Party and pro-business groups. During the 82nd legislative session, pro-life groups lobbied successfully for two major pieces of legislation that would restrict a woman's right to choose an abortion—the sonogram bill and the bill restricting funding for Planned Parenthood. These laws serve as a testament to how interest group alliances can become powerful forces both in elections and in the policy-making process.

Issue network

Fluid alliances of individuals and organizations who are interested in a particular policy area and join together when policy-making topics affect their interests.

Political movement

A mass alliance of like-minded groups and individuals seeking broad changes in the direction of government policies.

---

[38]Hugh Heclo, "Issue Networks and the Executive Establishment," in *The New American Political System*, ed. Anthony King (Washington, DC: American Enterprise Institute, 1978), pp. 87–124.

God, Gays, Guns, and Immigration in Texas

John Osterman
San Jacinto College

Interest groups seek to influence the government at the national, state, and local levels. Unlike political parties, they do not seek to control the government. Interest groups are the product of a pluralistic society, and society is the aggregate of the ideals, values, and beliefs of the individuals that comprise it. Given these truths, a study of interest groups is also a study of the ideology that is the foundation of society. The source of these beliefs is found in families and institutions, and the process of adopting them is called socialization. What makes Texas different from other states in terms of ideology is what is taught or practiced in homes and institutions throughout the state.

At least four issues get a lot of attention in Texas: God, gays, guns, and immigration. Specific groups may not be organized for just these issues; however, plenty of interests compete to influence the government at all levels as well as the society as a whole. Organized interests typically lobby elected and unelected government officials for changes in the law, policy, or constitutional interpretation. They also mobilize voters through e-mail campaigns and get media attention with marches and demonstrations. Of course, a changing culture can bring about policy changes as well, and the issues that impact Texas also impact the nation.

GOD

When one thinks of Texas, one often thinks of tradition and religion—they go hand in hand. From "one nation under God" to "God bless Texas," from the Texas pledge to the moment of silence, God is alive and well in Texas. This can be witnessed by looking at the many mega-churches in Texas such as Lakewood Church in Houston led by Joel Osteen with the largest average attendance in the nation. Osteen's message reaches far and wide. He has preached at both Dodger and Yankee stadiums to sold-out crowds. The Second Baptist Church of Houston led by Ed Young is

another example and is ranked as the fifth-largest church in the country. The Catholic Church also has an enormous presence in Texas with two archdioceses. More than 1.5 million Catholics live within archdiocesan boundaries of the Archdiocese of Galveston-Houston, the largest in the state of Texas and the eleventh-largest in the United States. These institutions and the families who frequent them shape the values that define the culture.

Recently, the Texas State Board of Education (SBOE) debated the issue of God in textbooks, among other things. For example, changes were proposed to remove Christmas from the Texas Essential Knowledge and Skills (TEKS) exam. In addition, recommendations were made to require classroom analysis of the Founding Fathers' intent in the First Amendment rather than merely use the expression "separation of church and state." The fifteen-member SBOE chooses the next generation of history textbooks for Texas children. The board has ten Republicans and five Democrats, many of whom are social conservatives. The board writes the curriculum standards for subject areas such as English, science, and social studies. This has been a controversy in part because liberals and conservatives have different ideas about history and the influence of religion in history. On the liberal side are such groups as American Atheists, Americans United for Separation of Church and State, and the American Civil Liberties Union (ACLU). On the conservative side is the Liberty Institute.

GAYS

Houston recently elected its first openly gay mayor, Anise Parker. Many were shocked and surprised that such a conservative city in a conservative state could elect someone from the gay, lesbian, bisexual, transgender (GLBT) community to the highest political position in the fourth-largest city in the nation. However, it was no surprise to many in Houston. Parker, a Rice University graduate, had been the comptroller for the city and a city council member while never hiding her sexual preferences. She was recently named to *Time*'s list of the "World's Most Influential People." That influence includes the power to appoint judges who are also from the GLBT community. She recently named Municipal Court Judge Barbara E. Hartle to be the chief presiding judge of the municipal courts in Houston.

Another aspect of sexual preference that has received attention is same-sex marriage. In 2004, Texas Baptists passed a resolution affirming that marriage is between a man and a woman. Such groups mobilized voters to support an amendment to the Texas Constitution defining marriage in the same way; this is a result of the culture. This view was reinforced when the SBOE asked publishers to rewrite textbooks to reflect the same language when defining marriage. However, in 2010, a same-sex couple from Massachusetts filed for divorce in Texas, and an Austin judge granted it. Greg Abbott, Attorney General for the State of Texas, argued against granting the divorce because the state does not recognize same-sex marriage.

GUNS

Texas is no stranger to guns. Recently, the legislature voted to give every college student and their teachers the right to carry weapons on campus. The bill was ultimately defeated; however, it shows the degree to which Texans believe in the Second Amendment. In a related story, a person was detained at the state capitol after discharging a weapon outside. After such an event, it is natural to expect an immediate call for changes in security policy, but no such call came. It seemed like just another day in the Lone Star State. On another typical day in Texas, Governor Rick Perry shot and killed a coyote while jogging using a .308 laser-sighted Ruger pistol with hollow-point bullets. From the classroom to the capitol, guns are a way of life in Texas.

Texas is a right-to-carry state, which requires a concealed weapon permit. With that right in mind, the school board in the Harrold Independent School District voted to allow teachers and staff to carry weapons on campus. Along the same lines, the Castle Doctrine in Texas is also a product of the culture. It states that Texans have a legal right to defend themselves with deadly force in their homes, cars, and workplaces if a person unlawfully enters or attempts to enter, and the property owner has no duty to retreat. Although the Second Amendment to the U.S. Constitution guarantees every American the right to keep and bear arms, the battle to preserve the right wages on in Texas. Obviously, the National Rifle Association (NRA) plays a role in Texas and across the nation.

IMMIGRATION

In light of Arizona's recent law allowing state and local law enforcement to ask for proof of citizenship or residence when detaining someone for allegedly committing a crime, Texas became the focus of attention when it advocated adopting a similar law. In 2008, Texas State Representative Debbie Riddle (R-District 150) filed a bill allowing state and local law enforcement officers to arrest those who are in the country illegally. Although the bill did not pass, it is likely to be reconsidered as a result of the passage of the Arizona law.

Clearly, the League of Latin American Citizens (LULAC) and the Mexican American Legal Defense and Educational Fund (MALDEF) are the most prominent interest groups supporting illegal immigrants in Texas, followed closely by the Roman Catholic Church. On the other side are groups such as the Federation for American Immigration Reform (FAIR) and Texans for Immigration Reform (TFIR). FAIR, a national organization with over a quarter-million members, seeks to improve border security. Rather than just lobby members of Congress, FAIR publishes research for academics and government officials. TFIR, on the other hand, focuses on Texas and legislative efforts that will stop illegal immigration in the state. They also collect information about the services illegal immigrants use that are provided by taxpayers. In an effort to bring information to voters about immigration reform efforts, TFIR joined with Citizens for Immigration Reform (CIR) out of Dallas and the Austin Townhall Conservatives – Immigration Reform Committee. This coalition is the foundation for the Immigration Reform Coalition of Texas (IRCOT). Collectively, these groups promote their ideals, values, and beliefs by disseminating information and building social networks.

The Minuteman Project received abundant media attention for several years during the Bush administration but has not been covered much since then. The project describes itself as a multi-ethnic immigration law enforcement advocacy group, and law enforcement appears to be the driving concern of conservative groups. One factor contributing to the lack of border security groups in Texas might be the size of the Hispanic population. Hispanics make up over 30 percent of the population in Texas, resulting in ongoing socialization due to the integration of Hispanics and non-Hispanics in public schools and other social institutions. There is unmeasured influence from groups that disseminate information pertaining to these issues via websites and blogs that provide readers with an opportunity to educate themselves in the absence of coverage by the mainstream media. One such group is the Texas Public Policy Foundation, a nonpartisan research institute or think tank.

CONCLUSION

Interestingly, each of these issues and the groups that debate these issues coincide on many levels. For instance, many immigrants in Texas are Hispanic and Catholic. Immigrants to Texas bring their culture with them. Texas holds true to the death penalty, while Catholics do not, and the Catholic Church does not support gay marriage; however, Mexico recently allowed gay marriages. The conflict between groups over law-and-order issues as well as religious and privacy issues is often described as a culture war. This war is witnessed in the public square where cultures meet. Moreover, families, schools, and churches teach their culture to new generations. The future of interest groups and the policies they promote are found in the ever-changing culture.

JOIN THE DEBATE:

1. Examine your own ideals, values, and beliefs and discuss whether or not you would have these views if you had been raised differently or in a state other than Texas.

2. Underlying each of these issues is a concern for freedom. How might your freedom be challenged by groups that have views different from your own?

CHAPTER SUMMARY

★ Interest groups are organizations of people who agree on policy issues that affect their members. Interest groups do not nominate candidates for office but do care about the ideologies of those who stand for election. They therefore may form political action committees to support candidates favorable to their causes.

★ The constitutions of the United States and Texas promote political expression. The right to organize to petition officials is explicit. This right recognizes that representatives of the people can represent their constituents only when they are informed of their wishes. Interest groups are therefore constitutionally protected.

★ Groups with sufficient resources employ staff to monitor the government. They proactively bring issues before decision makers and reactively move into the political process to stop or alter proposals that negatively affect their membership.

★ Business groups are among the strongest interests. Large corporations lobby decision makers through umbrella organizations and directly. It is not uncommon for large interests to have more than 20 paid lobbyists working for them during a legislative session. Between sessions, groups conduct research, draft proposed legislation for the next session, and monitor and influence the executive branch, which writes the rules to carry out laws.

★ Interest groups have been powerful in Texas due to the historical absence of competitive two-party politics, restrictive election laws, low voter turnout, and the below-average educational attainment of many citizens.

★ As happens at the national level, iron triangles often form in Texas. These triangles unite interest groups that represent a particular industry or activity with the bureaucracy that regulates the activity and with the members of the legislative committee that oversees the bureaucracy. Iron triangles are especially potent in Texas because regulatory boards and commissions are required to have members who actively participate in the regulated activity. This requirement almost guarantees conflicts of interest. Looser alliances called issue networks also form. These may consist of legislators, legislative staff members, interest group leaders, bureaucrats, journalists, scholars, and others who support a particular policy position on a given issue.

★ The media, a few nonprofit and officially nonpartisan special interests, and the Texas Ethics Commission are the sources of most of the information we have about the relationships among interest groups and public officials in Texas. Most lobbyists are required to file reports with the Ethics Commission, which, in turn, publishes the names, addresses, employers, expenditures, and salaries (in broad categorical ranges) of lobbyists. The media and the nonpartisan interests blow the whistle about conflicts of interest and official behavior that is suspect.

HOW TEXAS COMPARES

★ Special interest groups seem to have more influence in Texas than in many other states because part-time legislators with low salaries and limited staffs are unable to develop independent information about pending public policy; instead, they depend on lobbyists for information. Fragmentation in the executive branch leaves many access points for interest-group influence, and press coverage of interest-group influence at the capitol is weak.

★ The Center for Public Integrity uses a variety of measures to rate Texas's risk for corruption, and it finds the Texas Ethics Commission's enforcement powers particularly weak regarding both lobbying and campaign finance practices, compared to similar institutions in other states.

KEY TERMS

access, *p. 163*
advocacy, *p. 145*
astroturf lobbying, *p. 149*
conflict of interest, *p. 148*
co-optation, *p. 148*
delegate, *p. 148*

discretion, *p. 148*
fragmentation, *p. 161*
implementation, *p. 148*
interest group, *p. 143*
iron triangles, *p. 167*
issue networks, *p. 168*

late-train contributions, *p. 164*
lobbying, *p. 143*
lobbyist, *p. 144*
political movement, *p. 168*
pressure group, *p. 144*
public interest, *p. 148*

revolving door, *p. 160*
Texas Register, *p. 152*
umbrella organization, *p. 167*

REVIEW QUESTIONS

1. What are interest groups? What do they do? How do they do what they do?

2. Interest groups are not political parties. What is the difference between these two political institutions in scope and purpose?

3. What are the two major classifications of interest groups? What are the subcategories? Identify an interest group in each subcategory.

4. What characteristics of the people of Texas affect the influence of interest groups?

5. Where political party competition is strong, interest-group power is weakened. Why?

6. Interest groups attempt to influence the decisions of all three branches of government, but not by the same methods. Explain.

7. What is lobbying? What does a lobbyist do?

8. Which interests are the most powerful in Texas? Why?

9. Define *conflict of interest*. Cite some hypothetical instances of such conflicts. How can the state regulate legislators and groups to minimize them? Can the public interest be balanced with the need for expertise on the boards and commissions of Texas?

10. Reformers are seriously concerned about the methods of financing judicial elections. What kinds of interest groups are involved in this issue? Specifically, what groups favor and oppose change? What are the stated and real reasons?

LOGGING ON

Use these websites of major Texas interest groups to list the major policy focuses that each promotes. Explain whether these policy positions benefit the group's self-interest or whether the group is a public-interest group that simply promotes a vision of good government as it members see it. To access the websites of some of the leading economic interest groups in Texas, go to the following addresses:

  Texas Association of Business: **www.txbiz.org/**
  Texans for Lawsuit Reform: **www.tortreform.com**
  Texas Trial Lawyers Association: **www.ttla.com/tx**
  Texas Farm Bureau: **www.txfb.org**
  Texas AFL-CIO: **www.texasaflcio.org**
  Texas State Teachers' Association: **www.tsta.org**
  Texas Association of School Boards: **www.tasb.org**

To access the websites of some leading noneconomic interest groups in Texas, go to the following addresses:

  National Organization for Women: **www.now.org**
  NAACP: **www.naacp.org**
  Center for Public Integrity: **www.publicintegrity.org**
  Texans for Public Justice: **www.tpj.org**
  Texas Common Cause: **www.commoncause.org**

To access the websites of some think tanks in Texas, go to the following addresses:

  Center for Public Policy Priorities: **www.cppp.org**
  Center for Responsive Politics: **www.opensecrets.org**
  Texas Public Policy Foundation: **www.texaspolicy.com**

Chapter 7

The Legislature: Organization and Structure

LEARNING OBJECTIVES

★ Describe the membership and organization of the Texas legislature.

★ Summarize the redistricting process and explain its significance.

★ Describe the significance of *Reynolds* v. *Sims*.

★ Describe the differences between formal and informal qualifications for service in the Texas legislature.

★ Evaluate the concept of a "citizen legislature" and analyze the consequences of poor compensation, short legislative sessions, and small staffs.

★ Assess the role of campaign contributions in legislative elections.

★ Define *descriptive representation* and evaluate the extent to which members of the legislature should reflect the state's population as a whole.

★ Identify the presiding officers of the Texas House and Texas Senate and their functions.

★ Distinguish among the different types of legislative committees.

★ Evaluate the significance of legislative staff sizes.

GET Active

Volunteer on a political campaign or intern for a member of the Texas House or Texas Senate. Here's how to identify candidates running for public office:

★ Visit the Texas Secretary of State's website at **www.sos.state.tx.us/** and click on Elections and Voter Information.

★ View the list of candidates on the Texas Democratic and Republican Party websites at **www.txdemocrats.org/** and **www .texasgop.org/**.

★ Try the League of Women Voters of Texas in your community at **www .lwvtexas.org/** for a source of valuable information on candidates.

You also might explore these legislative internship opportunities for Texas students:

★ Investigate the Texas Legislative Internship Program at **www.rodneyellis.com/tlip/**.

★ Try the Moreno Rangel Legislative Leadership Program, which provides internship opportunities to Latino/Latina undergraduate and graduate students, at **http://mallfoundation.org/morenorangel-legislative-leadership-program/**.

★ Consider the Senator Gregory Luna Legislative Scholar Fellows Program at **http://tshrc.org/luna-scholars-fellows-program/**.

★ Check with your own university. Many universities have their own legislative internship programs.

★ Call your representative in the Texas House or Senate for additional internship opportunities. For a listing of Texas House members, check **www.house.state.tx.us/welcome.php**, and for a listing of Texas Senate members, check **www.senate .state.tx.us/**.

© AP Photo/Harry Cabluck

The Texas House and Senate meet in separate wings of the Capitol building in Austin.

What are the advantages and disadvantages of a bicameral (two-house) legislature?

The Texas legislature is bicameral—it consists of two houses, the 31-member Texas Senate and the 150-member Texas House of Representatives. On most matters, the two houses share equal powers and both of them must agree on a proposed bill for it to become law. The Senate does have the special power to confirm or approve the governor's appointments of state officers. By establishing a bicameral legislature, framers of the Texas Constitution followed the pattern set for the national Congress and used in every state other than Nebraska, which has a unicameral, or one-house, legislature.

The chief argument for the use of bicameral legislative bodies is that one house can serve as a check on the other so that legislation will not be passed hastily without adequate reflection, and every proposed law must be considered twice by two separate institutions. Because it slows legislative action, bicameralism can also mean that the two houses might gridlock as one house passes good or needed policy changes and the other house balks.

SELECTING LEGISLATORS

The one hundred and fifty members of the Texas House are all elected for two-year terms when the state holds its general election in even-numbered years. At that time, only half of the state senators are usually elected because they serve four-year staggered terms. All legislators are elected from single-member districts. We now look at the factors that affect selection of the members of the Texas legislature, including the politics of districting as well as their legal, or formal, qualifications and political considerations that amount to informal qualifications necessary to win office.

Geographic Districts

In Texas, like in other states, the Texas legislature used the 2010 Census data to draw the geographic boundaries for the districts of the Texas House, Texas Senate, and other elected positions. Because Texas has experienced dramatic population growth, its many district lines must be redrawn to reflect the change. The 150 members of the Texas House of Representatives, like the 31 members of the Texas Senate, are elected from the districts for the 83rd Legislative Session, found in Figures 7.1 and 7.2, respectively. These districts are approximately equal in population size, as required by the U.S. Supreme Court decision in *Reynolds* v. *Sims*. In this court case, the Supreme Court ruled, "Simply stated, an individual's right to vote for state legislators is unconstitutionally impaired when its weight is in a substantial fashion diluted when compared with votes of citizens living in other parts of the State."[1] Known as "one person, one vote," this decision mandated **reapportionment**, or the requirement that each legislator should represent approximately the same number of people. Redistricting, or redrawing the district lines, is required following each census to maintain equal representation.

Should the Texas legislature fail to redistrict, the state constitution provides for the function to be performed by the Legislative Redistricting Board. The board is **ex officio**, which means that its members hold other offices. It is made up of the lieutenant governor, the speaker of the house, the attorney general, the comptroller, and the commissioner of the General Land Office.

The average population of an electoral district for the Texas House of Representatives in 2011 was 171,165. In 2011, House members represented 32,000 more people than they did a decade earlier. Representing approximately 828,216 residents, Texas Senators served an estimated 156,000 more people in 2011 than they did in 2000. Members of the Texas Senate represent more people than the Texas delegation to the U.S. House of Representatives. These House and Senate seats must be drawn to be as evenly matched as possible. Legislative districts can deviate plus or minus 5 percent from the mean, but not much more. In instances in which districts deviate too much from the mean, the state of Texas must justify these deviations to the U.S. Justice Department. The once-per-decade redistricting ritual goes more or less unnoticed by the casual observer of politics. For the political practitioner and the political activist, however, it may resemble a life-or-death struggle.

The way districts are drawn at any level of government determines, to a large extent, the political, ideological, and ethnic makeup of the legislative body. With redistricting, political careers may be made or broken, public policy determined for at least a decade, and the power of ethnic or

Reapportionment

The redrawing of district and precinct lines following the national census to reflect population changes.

Ex officio

Holding a position automatically because one also holds some other office.

Did You Know? Drawing district lines for partisan political advantage got the name *gerrymandering* in 1812 when the Massachusetts legislature and Governor Elbridge Gerry, wishing to preserve a Republican majority, redrew a district in such a convoluted shape that a political cartoonist portrayed it as a salamander and dubbed it the "Gerrymander." The shapes of several current Texas congressional districts exceed the oddity of the original gerrymander.

---

[1] *Reynolds* v. *Sims*, 377 U.S. 533 (1964).

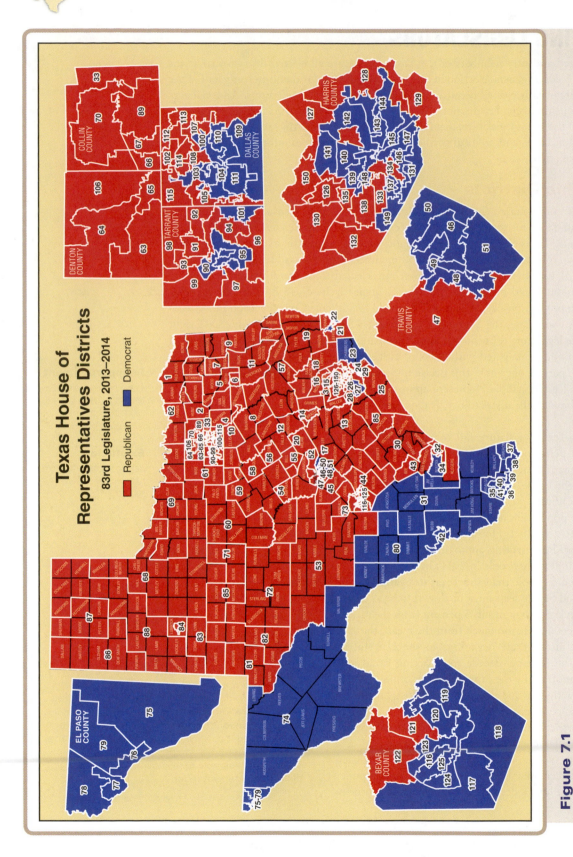

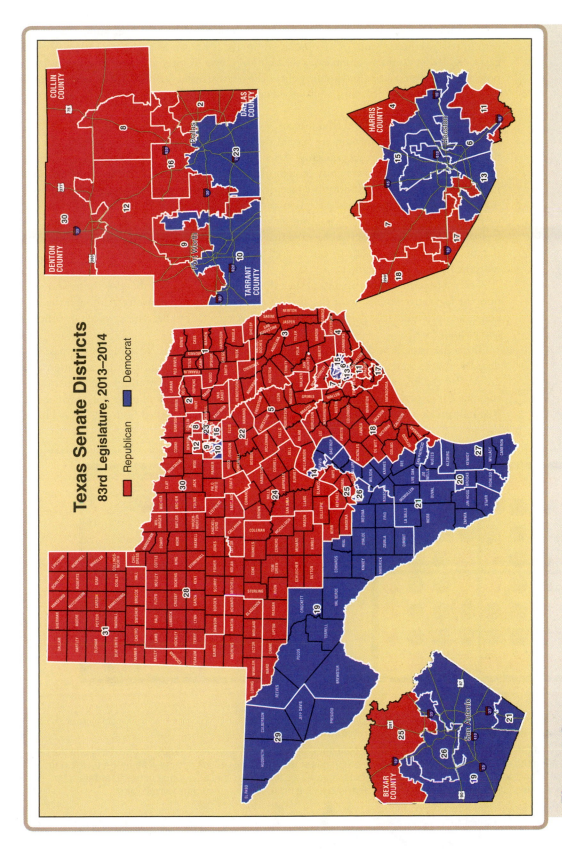

Texas Senate Districts
83rd Legislature, 2013–2014

- Republican
- Democrat

Figure 7.2
Texas Senate Districts, 83rd Legislature, 2013–14.

Source: Texas Legislative Council, Plan S172.

Gerrymander
A district or precinct that is drawn specifically to favor some political party, candidate, or ethnic group.

Cracking
A gerrymandering technique in which concentrated political or ethnic minority groups are split into several districts so that their votes in any one district are negligible.

Packing
Gerrymandering technique in which members of partisan or minority groups are concentrated into one district, thereby ensuring that the group will influence only one election rather than several.

Pairing
Placing two incumbent office-holders in the same elective district through redistricting. This is usually done to eliminate political enemies.

Incumbent
The current holder of an office.

political minorities neutralized. A district drawn in such a way as to give candidates from a certain party, ethnic group, or faction an advantage is known as a **gerrymander**. Because gerrymandering decreases or increases the political power of specific groups of voters, it has a powerful effect on politics and public policy. The relative influence of political parties, ethnic groups, ideological combatants, and individual politicians in the political process is at stake. (See Figure 7.3.)

Three basic gerrymander techniques are generally used. One is to diffuse a concentrated political or ethnic minority among several districts so that its votes in any one district are negligible. This is known as **cracking**. A second tactic, known as **packing**, is used if the minority group's numbers are great enough when diffused to affect the outcome of elections in several districts—the minority is concentrated, or packed, in one district, thereby ensuring that it will influence only one election and that its influence in the whole legislature will be minimal. A third tactic is a **pairing** technique that redistricts two or more **incumbent** legislators' residences or political bases so that both are in the same district, thereby ensuring that one will be defeated. Pairing can be used to punish legislators who have fallen from grace with the legislative leadership.

Gerrymandering is also used to protect the "right kind" of incumbents—those who support the legislative leadership or the agenda of powerful special interests. Although the federal courts prohibit racial gerrymandering, they are reluctant to become involved in political gerrymandering.

Texas has experienced some very contentious debates over redistricting in the past few decades. As the state's minority population grows, demand for political representation also grows. But the minority population is not the only group growing in influence. Increasingly, the state has grown more and more Republican. In doing so, more and more policymakers are Republicans as well. After the 2010 elections, Republicans controlled both the Texas House

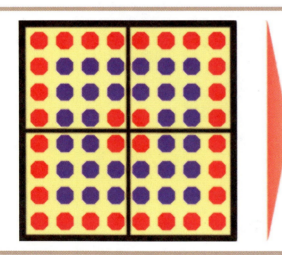 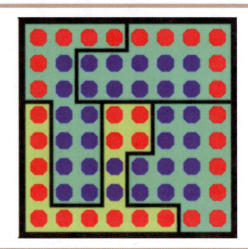

Figure 7.3
A Schematic to Illustrate the Process of Gerrymandering

The schematic on the left shows an example with the blue dots representing a number of people in one party and the red dots representing the same number of persons in the other in four equally competitive districts. The figure on the right shows how the same population can be gerrymandered to guarantee a three-to-one advantage in representation for the blue voters. You could try your hand at drawing districts with a three-to-one advantage for the reds.

Explain the types of gerrymandering strategies.

and Texas Senate with much larger majorities than they held previously. As a result, Republicans were able to redraw district boundaries that were favorable to the Republican Party. Groups representing minority groups sued the state, charging that new district boundaries ignored the growth in the Latino population. Latino groups and Republicans were able to come to an agreement on the Texas Senate maps. The Texas House and congressional district maps were not settled in time for the regularly scheduled Texas primary.

Because Texas has a history of discrimination, it is one of nine states covered under the federal Voting Rights Act, so Texas is required to receive preclearance for its newly drawn districts. Texas had two options: it could expedite the approval process by asking the U.S. Justice Department for approval, or it could go through the United States District Court for the District of Columbia. Early in 2012, the U.S. Supreme Court also became involved in the redistricting battle.

Both the federal courts and the Justice Department agreed that the Republican-drawn maps violated the Voting Rights Act. As a result, interim district boundaries were drawn by the federal district courts in San Antonio so that primary elections would not be delayed any further. Typically, Texas primaries are usually held in early March; but in 2012, they were held May 29th. Figure 7.4 shows U.S. Congressional districts in Texas.

During the heat of the redistricting controversy in the winter of 2012, Texans were asked what they felt were the state's most pressing problems. While the expected issues of the economy, unemployment, and border security were at the top of the list, surprisingly, five percent of Texans polled pointed to legislative redistricting as one of the state's most important problems.[2] It ranked in seventh place, ahead of gas prices and water supply.[3] A sizeable number of Texans—42 percent—supported the creation of an independent redistricting commission to redraw legislative district lines. Twenty-nine percent of Republicans, 43 percent of independents, and 70 percent of Democrats supported the creation of an independent, nonpartisan redistricting commission to reduce political considerations in the drawing of legislative district boundaries.

This support for creating a redistricting commission can be explained in part by the lack of fairness that Democrats and members of minority groups see in the process. As word of the new district boundaries trickled out, it was Democrats, and many of their Hispanic and African-American constituents who believed that the new district boundaries could lead to a loss of political representation. Support for a redistricting commission may also be favored by those who feel that legislative redistricting efforts lead to less competitive races. As districts are drawn to elect a member from one party or the other, viable electoral opposition is greatly diminished. Partisan gerrymandering contributes to a lack of competition, which, in turn, leads to the election of policymakers who are either more liberal or more conservative than the population they represent. The support for the creation of a redistricting commission indicates that the way in which district lines are drawn is less than optimal for Texans.

Qualifications for Membership

Although legal, or formal, qualifications must be met before anyone can serve in the state legislature, rarely do these requirements prohibit serious candidates from seeking legislative seats. In fact, the criteria are broad enough to allow millions of Texas residents to run for the legislature.

Formal Qualifications To be a Texas state senator, an individual must be a U.S. citizen, a qualified voter, at least 26 years of age, and must have lived in the state for the previous five years and in the district for one year prior to election. Qualifications for House

---

[2]University of Texas/Texas Tribune Poll, February 2012, http://texaspolitics.laits.utexas.edu/11_5_0.html.
[3]Ibid.

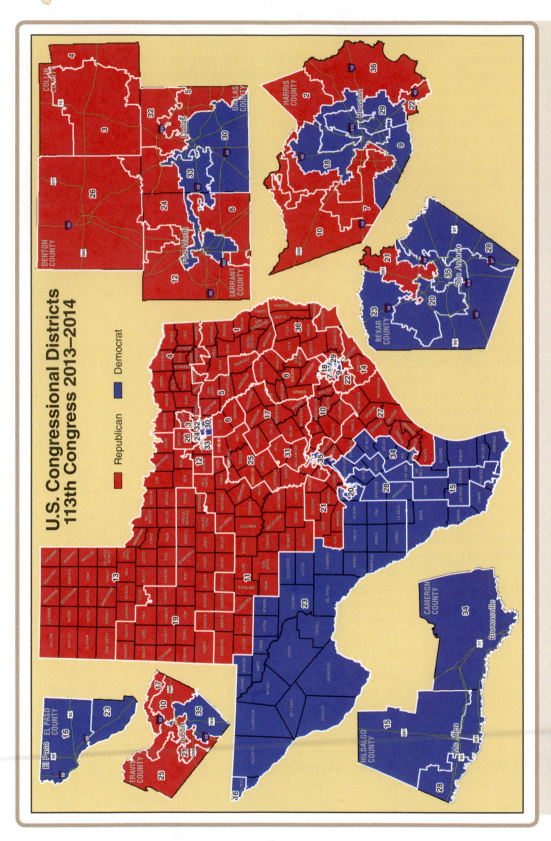

Figure 7.4
U.S. Congressional Districts, 113th Congress, 2013–14.

Source: Texas Legislative Council, Plan C235

membership are even more easily met. A candidate must be a U.S. citizen, a qualified voter of the state, at least 21 years of age, and have lived in Texas for the two previous years and in the district for one year prior to being elected.

Informal Qualifications The most important requirements for holding legislative office in Texas are not the legal limitations but the informal ones. Certain political, social, and economic criteria determine who is elected not just to the state legislature but also to offices at all levels of government—national, state, county, city, and special district.

Party Until the 1990s, the Democratic Party was the dominant legislative party in Texas. However, the resurgence of the Republican Party has made Texas a strongly Republican state. By the end of 2004, Republicans had established dominance over all three branches of state government, with two Republican U.S. senators and a Republican majority in the U.S. House of Representatives. Figure 7.5 shows that it is increasingly advantageous to be a Republican candidate in Texas electoral politics.

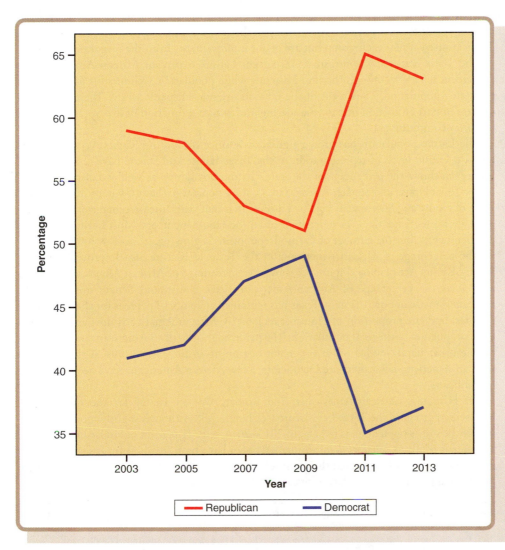

Figure 7.5

Partisanship in the Texas House of Representatives

This figure shows the percentage of Democratic and Republican house members since Republicans gained control of the lower House in 2003.

Why is it important which party controls the legislature? Give examples of differences between the parties on districting, setting the legislative agenda, and making public policy.

Descriptive representation

The idea that legislative bodies should represent not only voters' political views but also the demographic and geographic characteristics that affect their political perspectives.

Demographics   Although not a majority, the plurality of Texans are Anglo American and Protestant and they elect legislators who share these characteristics, just as a predominantly Latino district usually elects a Latino legislator and voters in an African-American district usually elect an African-American representative. When the people in legislative districts elect representatives that "look like" the people they represent, the legislative body is said to achieve **descriptive representation**. The state of Texas has one of the most diverse populations in the United States. It is one of the few states with a majority-minority population, meaning that the majority of the population is a member of a minority group.[4] Currently, 45 percent of the population is non-Hispanic white, 38 percent is Hispanic, 12 percent is African American, 4 percent is Asian American, and the remaining 1 percent is of some other racial or ethnic group.[5] Much of this diversity is also found in the Texas House, although there are differences among the makeup of the various racial and ethnic groups in the state and in the makeup of the representatives in the Texas House and Texas Senate.

Minority populations in Texas have experienced significant improvements in their respective levels of descriptive representation. In the 83rd Legislative Session, 22 percent of the members of the Texas House were Latino, 12 percent were African American, and 2 percent (or 3 representatives) were Asian American. Women, who account for slightly more than one-half of the state's population, account for 21 percent of the representatives in the Texas House. The differences between the makeup of the state's population and the members of the Texas House vary for each group but are major improvements from the recent past.

The Texas Senate, by contrast, is 23 percent Latino, 6 percent African American, and 19 percent female. Although the non-Hispanic white population accounts for 45 percent of the state's population, 71 percent of the senators are non-Hispanic white. These discrepancies are in part a function of gerrymandering and in part a function of low voter turnout in minority communities.

The Latino population has grown significantly since the Voting Rights Act of 1965. As a result, Latino levels of representation in the Texas House and Senate have also increased. Figure 7.6 shows the percentage of the state's Latino population as well as Latino members of the Texas House and Senate. As the state's Latino population has grown, so, too, have the share of House and Senate seats held by Latinos. In recent years, the percentage of Latino senators has been greater than the percentage of Latino House members. Most Latino legislators are Democrats, but the number of Latino Republicans is growing.

The percentage of African Americans in the Texas legislature also improved since the Voting Rights Act of 1965. Figure 7.7 shows the percentage of African Americans in Texas as well as the percentage of African-American Texas House and Senate members. The African- American population in Texas has remained at about 12 percent for the last several decades, and the proportion of House seats held by African-Americans now approximates their proportion of the total population. The percentage of African Americans in the Senate, on the other hand, leveled off at 6 percent beginning in the early 1990s. Although most African-American lawmakers are Democrats, a few African Americans have been elected as Republicans.

Of Hispanics, African Americans, and women, women are by far the most underrepresented group in the Texas Legislature (see Figure 7.8). Although slightly more than one-half of the state's population is female, in 2013–2014, only 21 percent of House members and 19 percent of Texas senators were women. Women have been involved in Texas politics for quite some time. Texans elected their first female governor in 1925, and they have been sending women to the Texas legislature since the women's suffrage movement. In the mid-1970s,

---

[4]Robert Bernstein. "Texas Becomes Nation's Newest 'Majority-Minority' State," Census Bureau Announces." *US Census Bureau News*, 11 August 2005.

[5]U.S. Census Bureau. *State and County QuickFacts*, http://quickfacts.census.gov/qfd/states/48000.html.

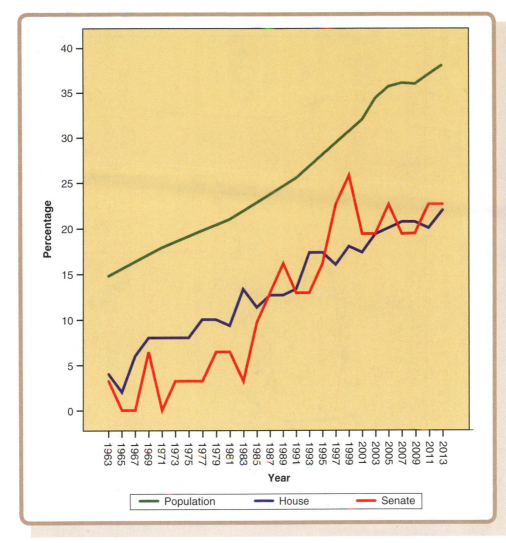

Figure 7.6

Latino Population and Latino Representation in the Texas House and Senate

This figure shows that as Latinos have increased in population so has their representation in both houses of the legislature, but they are still under-represented.

How much of the Latino representation is the result of districting, and how much of it is the result of Latinos' youth and lower voter turnout?

women began to win House seats with greater frequency, and in the Senate a similar pattern is seen beginning in the mid-1980s. In recent years, women have continued to make improvements.

Asian Americans account for a little more than 4 percent of the state's population.[6] Nevertheless, three Asian-American members of the Texas House serve in the 83rd Legislative Session—Dallas Republican Angie Chen Button, Houston Democrats Hubert Vo and Gene Wu.

Although Hispanics, African Americans, Asian Americans, and women are underrepresented in the Texas legislature relative to their percentages in the general population, the numerical representation of these groups in the legislature should increase dramatically during the next decade. As ethnic minority populations increase and as more women run

---

[6]U.S. Census Bureau. *State and County QuickFacts*, http://quickfacts.census.gov/qfd/states/48000.html.

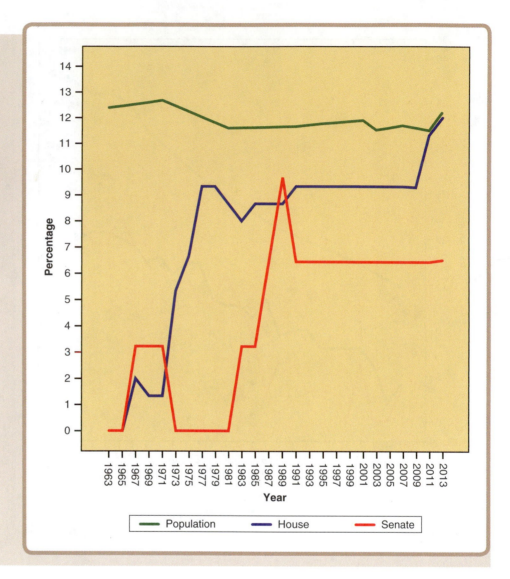

Figure 7.7

African-American Population and African-American Representation in the Texas House and Senate

This figure shows that African Americans are represented in the Houses of the legislature in approximate proportion to their population, but they are still underrepresented in the Senate.

How could senate district size explain African-American underrepresentation in the upper house?

for public office, these groups will experience greater descriptive representation in the Texas House and Senate. However, because the Anglo-American ethnic group is currently overrepresented, where the legislative lines are drawn will determine how equitable the representation will be following the 2020 Census.

Occupation Law is the most frequently represented profession in U.S. legislative bodies. In other democratic countries, the percentage of lawyers in legislative bodies is far smaller, and lawyers are viewed as just another professional group that might seek to advance its own interests. In the United States, however, the expectation that politicians be lawyers is so woven into our political fabric that people who want political careers often become lawyers as a step toward that goal.

Increasingly, however, legislative bodies are becoming more diverse in the occupations and training of their members. The number of lawyers serving in state legislative bodies has decreased somewhat. The reasons for this include the professionalized nature of state legislative assemblies. One study has determined that as legislative bodies enact ethics reform,

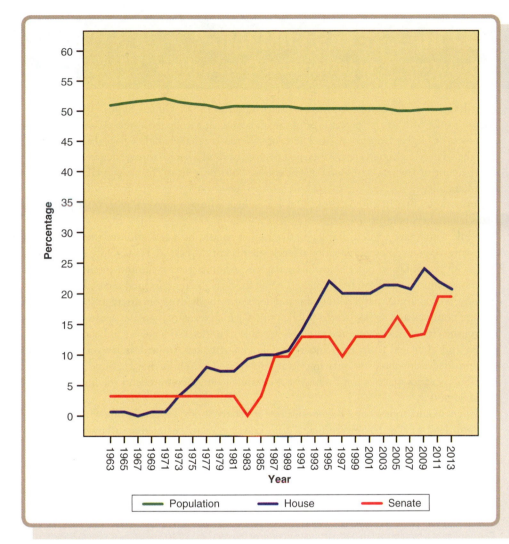

Figure 7.8

Female Population and Female Representation in the Texas House and Senate

This figure shows women are one of the most underrepresented social groups on the legislature compared to their population.

Explain the underrepresentation of women in legislative positions.

the number of lawyers in the legislature diminishes.[7] Others report that lawyers are much more common in southern states.[8] In Texas, lawyers account for 30.4 percent of the lawmakers.[9] In the 81st Texas Legislative Session, 29 percent of House members and 39 percent of senators were lawyers.[10] Lawyers are being joined by lawmakers from other occupations. This diversity of elected officials further contributes to descriptive representation. Lawmakers are not only looking more like their constituents in their race, ethnicity and gender, they are also representing a greater diversity of occupations.

[7]Beth A. Rosenson, "The Impact of Ethics Laws on Legislative Recruitment and the Occupational Composition of State Legislatures," *Political Research Quarterly* 59 (2006), 626.

[8]Peverill Squire, "Legislative Professionalization and Membership Diversity in State Legislatures," *Legislative Studies Quarterly* 17, no. 1 (Feb. 1992): 75.

[9]*Chronicle of Higher Education*. "How educated are state legislators?" June 12, 2011, http://chronicle.com/article/Degrees-of-Leadership-/127797/.

[10]Data for the Texas House was obtained from the Chief Clerk's Office, Joe Straus Speaker, *Biographical Data House of Representatives 81st Legislature* (June 1, 2010), www.house.state.tx.us/members/. The data for the Texas Senate was obtained from the Texas Senate website, www.senate.state.tx.us/75r/senate/members.htm#members.

HOW DOES TEXAS COMPARE?
Legislators' Education and Occupation

Texas has one of the better-educated legislative bodies in the United States. The Texas legislature ranks fifth in the percentage of lawmakers with a college degree. According to the Chronicle of Higher Education, 86.2 percent of Texas lawmakers hold a baccalaureate degree or higher. Forty-eight percent have earned degrees beyond a baccalaureate degree. Nationally, 74.7 percent of lawmakers hold college degrees. Four percent of Texas lawmakers have not attended college.

Texas ranks first in the percentage of lawmakers who are lawyers, with 30.4 percent of Texas lawmakers holding law degrees.

While some have argued that legislative bodies should be a reflection of the people they represent, when it comes to educational levels, that is not the case in Texas. Only 26 percent of Texans 25 years old and older hold college degrees. And, in spite of the anti-intellectual rhetoric among some lawmakers, policymakers come from the better-educated segments of society.

Some would argue that a better-educated legislative body can contribute to the enactment of more complex and sophisticated public policy, which leads to a greater sense of alienation among the citizenry. Because the public is less able to understand its laws, it becomes disconnected and alienated from its democracy. Clever lawmakers trained as lawyers are able to build in special loopholes or bury important public policy in bills that are hundreds of pages long. Such tactics make it impossible for the public to fully comprehend the intent or effect of public policy.

Others would argue that a better-educated legislative body, especially one with many lawyers, will lead to a better government. Who knows the law better than a lawyer, they may argue. Furthermore, we are living in a complex society, and so complexity is called for in public policy. They would argue that poorly educated Texans would be unable to fully comprehend the complexity of the issues today.

Education Category	Rank	Percentage
Percentage of lawmakers with baccalaureate degree or higher	5th	86.2%
Percentage of lawmakers with law degrees	1st	30.4%

Sources: *Chronicle of Higher Education*. "How educated are state legislators?" http://chronicle.com/article/Degrees-of-Leadership-/127797/; U.S. Census Bureau, 2012, *State and County QuickFacts,* http://quickfacts.census.gov/qfd/states/48000.html.

FOR DEBATE

1. Can legislators understand the needs and viewpoints of the general population, even if they are better educated than the average resident?

2. Do well-educated lawmakers help or hurt our democracy?

3. What problems might result from the overrepresentation of lawyers in Texas's legislature?

Money The primary qualification for winning legislative office is access to money. Many competent, motivated citizens who want to serve are excluded because they are unable to raise the money necessary to finance an adequate campaign. Thus, the voters' pool of potential candidates is initially reduced by the economic special interests that make most campaign contributions. Securing office space, printing campaign literature, buying postage stamps, building a campaign organization, and purchasing advertisements are all among the necessary ingredients for a successful campaign.

In 2010, the National Institute on Money in State Politics found that the 332 candidates who ran for the Texas House raised an average of $236,392 for their campaigns. In 2008, the candidates raised an average of $197,415 for their campaigns. In two years, the average amount raised increased by more than $38,978. The 56 Texas Senate candidates raised an average of $377,692 for their campaigns.[11] Candidates raised more than $99.6 million for their campaigns in the House and Senate races.[12]

Winners for the house seats raised an average of $378,416, compared to $119,999 for the losing House candidates. Among the senators, the winners raised an average of $656,908, compared to an average of $22,730 for the losers.[13] The amount of money needed to win an election is growing and increasingly becoming out of reach for many would-be candidates. Our Texas Insiders feature puts a face on the organizations and individuals who dominate the funding of legislative campaigns.

> **Did You Know?** After making $65,000 in inappropriate campaign contributions, Dallas billionaire Harold Simmons asked 18 lawmakers to give the money back.

Texas ✦✦ INSIDERS

Following the Money: Campaign Contributors in Texas Legislative Elections

This table shows the total amount of campaign contributions raised by all Texas legislative candidates in 2010 and the average amount they raised. Along with candidates' incumbency and their party affiliation, campaign funding is an outstanding predictor of general election victory—the legislative candidates who outspent their opponents won 92 percent of the time.

Large contributors pursue several strategies: In closely contested races, some contributors may be trying to help elect candidates who best represent their interests and viewpoints. In other instances, their pattern of giving does not seem to be directed at affecting election outcomes but, instead, seems to represent an attempt to influence the legislative process itself. For example,

TABLE 7.1a Campaign Contributions to Candidates for the Texas Legislature

Office	Total	Number of Candidates	Average
Senate	$21,149,989	56	$377,678
House	$78,482,292	332	$236,392

(continued)

[11]National Institute On Money in State Politics; "Texas 2010 Candidates" www.followthemoney.org/database/StateGlance/state_candidates.phtml?s=TX&y=2010&f=S.
[12]Ibid.
[13]Ibid.

TABLE 7.1b Top Five Campaign Contributors in Texas House Races

Contributor	Total	Percentage of Total	Sector
Texans for Lawsuit Reform	$5,176,786	6.60%	General business
Texans for Insurance Reform	$2,591,865	3.30%	Ideology/single issue
Associated Republicans of Texas	$2,133,555	2.72%	Ideology/single issue
House Democratic Campaign Committee	$1,953,247	2.49%	Party
Perry, Bob J.	$1,733,500	2.21%	Construction

TABLE 7.1c Top Five Campaign Contributors in Texas Senate Races*

Contributor	Total	Percentage of Total	Sector
Perry, Bob J.	$544,500	2.57%	Construction
Border Health	$486,750	2.30%	Health
Texas Association of Realtors	$426,548	2.02%	Finance, insurance & real estate
Texas Medical Association	$255,741	1.21%	Health
Time Warner	$251,075	1.19%	Communications & electronics

*Excludes self-financed Senate candidate Ben Bius.

Source: National Institute on Money in State Politics at www.followthemoney.org/database/. The institute's searchable database relies on Texas Ethics Commission reports.

Tables 7.1b and 7.1c show the largest campaign contributors in all candidates' campaigns for the Texas Senate and Texas House of Representatives. In some instances, organizations themselves did not donate. Rather, their money came from the organizations' PACs, their individual members, employees, or owners.

▲ **Whatever their motivations, large donors usually have considerable success with their legislative agendas. In Chapter 12, we discuss the stunning legislative successes of Texans for Lawsuit Reform, the largest funder of House campaigns and the sixth-largest funder of Senate campaigns.**

contributors may target their giving to incumbents in safe districts, especially those who hold powerful legislative offices such as committee chairs and the speaker; even those who are unopposed for reelection often have huge campaign accounts. Occasionally, a single contributor will give to both candidates in the same closely contested race. Contributors frequently give money to the winner even after election day—so-called "late train" contributions.

Thinking about the role of elites in Texas politics What indicates when a campaign contribution might be intended to influence a legislator's vote? How can voters, small contributors, and poorly groups balance the political influence of large contributors?

THE "CITIZEN LEGISLATURE"

Texas has "citizen legislators" who meet for only 140 days every other year and receive most of their income from outside sources. It is only reasonable to expect them to be more focused on their full-time careers and outside sources of income than on the public interest. Limited sessions, low salaries, higher turnover rates, and limited staffing result in a nonprofessional legislature. As we saw in Chapter 3, Texans seem unwilling to follow the lead of other larger states by professionalizing their legislature.

Terms and Turnover

Texas senators are elected for four-year staggered terms and representatives for two-year terms. That means that the entire House and half the Senate are elected every two years. All senators were elected in the first election following redistricting (2012). At the beginning of the session, the senators drew lots to determine which senators will serve a two-year term. The unlucky senators must run for reelection in 2014, whereas the lucky senators will not face another reelection campaign until 2016. All senators will then serve four-year terms until the 2022 election. The relative competitiveness of the senators' districts determines whether the decision of the lottery is only an inconvenience or an incident of major significance. Texas legislators experience a more rapid turnover than their counterparts in the U.S. Congress, where seniority brings political power.

Low salaries, short sessions, heavy workloads, and inadequate staff and clerical assistance all diminish the Texas legislators' effectiveness. Frustrated by the inability to achieve legislative goals not supported by "The Lobby" or the presiding officers, many legislators leave office to pursue full-time careers or to seek higher political office. The generally more prestigious senators tend to serve longer than their House counterparts.

The argument in favor of retaining experienced legislators conflicts with growing public support for limiting the number of terms legislators may serve. Texas legislators do not have limits on the number of terms they may serve, but the idea of legally mandated **term limits** is quite popular; it reflects an increasing frustration with government, especially the legislative branch, which seems more and more to be the captive of organized special interests. Supporters of term limit legislation assume that the election of new legislators will disrupt established working relationships between legislators and interest groups. However, the new legislators would be immediate "lame ducks" with legally mandated tenure and be even more vulnerable to influence by expert lobbyists and career bureaucrats.

Term limits
Restrictions on the number of times that a politician can be reelected to an office or the number of years that a person may hold a particular office.

Compensation

Legislators received an annual salary of $7,200 plus $150 per day during both regular and special sessions in 2011. They also have a travel allowance on a reimbursement basis when the legislature is in session. The Texas Ethics Commission is constitutionally empowered to establish the per diem allowance, which it regularly increases, but the Ethics Commission can only propose a salary increase because voters must approve any increase. Lawmakers have not received a salary increase since 1975, and voters rejected the last attempt to increase their pay in 1991. Texas lawmakers are among the worst paid large-state legislators in the country, but they have found ways to benefit from their contacts with special interest groups to offset their living expenses.

A legislator has little motivation to seek or keep the position solely for the salary. Present legislative salaries are so low that legislators must obtain their primary income from other sources. Legislators who are lawyers accept **retainer** fees from a variety of clients, including those who have lawsuits against state agencies. Lawyers and nonlawyers alike receive consulting fees from business clients and act to invest based on information that they gain from lobbyists and "insider information" that they gain from their own specialized knowledge about the prospects for pending legislation. Texans thus oblige their legislators to seek additional income yet ask few questions about the nature or sources of this income. People tend to be loyal to those who pay them, and it is not the public that furnishes most of the legislators' incomes.

Retainers
Fees charged by lawyers. Some special interest groups place lawyer-legislators on retainer with the intent of legally compromising their objectivity on important matters of public policy.

Some reformers believe that legislators' pay should be increased and their outside income strictly limited. In the present system, the potential for conflict between the public interest and the interests of lawmakers' private businesses or their employers is obvious. And while higher pay would not guarantee honest legislators, it would enable the conscientious ones to perform their legislative duties without turning to sources of outside income that compromise their ability to represent the constituents who elected them.

The Limited Session

The Texas legislature meets on the second Tuesday in January in odd-numbered years for a 140-day session. It is the only legislature in the ten most populous states to meet only every two years. In these short, infrequent sessions, the volume of legislation can be overwhelming. Most bills are passed or killed with little consideration, but they still consume valuable time that could be used for more practical purposes. Conversely, many important bills are never granted a legislative hearing.

The short biennial sessions and the increasingly complex problems of a modern society make 30-day special sessions, which can be called only by the governor, more probable. They are, however, unpopular with both the general public and the legislators. The public views their $1.2 million price tag as wasteful, and legislators are put out by being called away from their homes, families, and primary occupations. Furthermore, opponents often kill legislation by intentional neglect in the regular session and they will strongly fight a special session to reconsider its corpse.

Because most of the legislative work is performed during the regular session, time becomes critical. Legislators find it increasingly difficult to maintain even rudimentary knowledge of the content of much of the legislation that must be considered, whether in committee or on the floor. These time constraints dictated by the limited session, combined with inadequate staff support and weak legislative research institutions like the Office of House Bill Analysis, serve to isolate individual legislators and deepen their reliance on the information provided by lobbyists, administrators, and the legislative leadership.

Bills of limited scope or on trivial matters are a further drain on legislative time. For example, bills regulating the size of melon containers or minnow seining in a specific county do affect public policy, but they could easily be delegated to an executive department or agency responsible for their administration.

Other bills are introduced as a favor to an interested constituent or interest group by a friendly legislator. When these bills lack legislative, interest group, or administrative support, they have no chance of passage or even serious committee consideration.

The limited biennial session tends to work against deliberative, orderly legislative practice and ultimately against the public interest. Texas legislators cannot possibly acquaint themselves in only 140 days with the immense volume of legislation presented to them. Few legislators have personal knowledge of any particular subject under consideration unless they are employed, retained, or hold investment interests in the particular field.

Although 45 states have annual sessions to conduct state business, Texans refuse to accept annual regular sessions. Texans' general belief is that the legislature does more harm than good when it is in session and a longer session will simply give legislators more time for legislative mischief. Unfortunately, evidence supports this position. Historically, much of the most odious legislation was passed in the final days of the session. Because of the shortness of the session and procrastination and delaying tactics by legislators, the end-of-session flow of legislation became a deluge. Under these conditions, legislators simply did not have time for even the most rudimentary review of important last-minute legislation.

In 1993, the House adopted new rules to deal with the end-of-session legislative crunch. During the last 17 days, the House may consider only bills that originated in the Senate or that received previous House approval. The new rules also gave House members 24 hours to study major legislation before floor action. These reforms diminished the volume of last-minute legislation and gave legislators time to become better acquainted with bills.

Resolutions by legislators to congratulate a distinguished constituent, a winning sports team, or a scout troop for some success or other are common. Legislators usually pay little attention to this legislation, but it is important to the honorees. Demonstrating the lack of legislative scrutiny, one such resolution was passed unanimously by the Texas House on April Fools' Day 1971—a congratulatory recognition of Albert De Salvo for his "noted activities and unconventional techniques involving population control and applied psychology." The House later withdrew this recognition when it discovered that De Salvo was in fact the "Boston Strangler," an infamous serial murderer.

ORGANIZATION OF THE TEXAS LEGISLATURE

The legislature has organized several institutions that affect its operations during and after the session—its presiding officers, standing committees, and the legislative staff.

Presiding Officers

Among the Texas legislature's institutions, the most visible individuals are the two presiding officers—the lieutenant governor in the Senate and the Speaker of the House of Representatives. Each exercises tremendous power.

Lieutenant Governor
The presiding officer in the Texas Senate is the lieutenant governor, who serves as the Senate president. Although not officially a senator, the lieutenant governor is in the unique position of being a member of both the legislative branch and the executive branch. The lieutenant governor is elected in a statewide, partisan election and can have a party affiliation that is different from that of the governor or other members of the Texas executive branch. In the event the office becomes vacant through death, disability, or resignation, the Senate elects one of its members to serve as lieutenant governor until the next regular election. The senators have adopted rules that grant the lieutenant governor extensive legislative, organizational, procedural, administrative, and planning authority.

This statewide election, for a four-year term, attracts far less public attention than the power of the office merits; the lieutenant governor is one of the most powerful officials in Texas government. Organized interests are aware of the importance of the office, however, and contribute sizable sums to influence the election.

Lieutenant governors in most other states, like the vice president in the federal government, are neither strong executives nor strong legislative officials. Some states have either eliminated the office or have the governor and lieutenant governor run as a team. In other states, the governor and other executives monopolize the executive function, and the upper house, where the lieutenant governor usually presides, is often too protective of its legislative powers to include him or her in the real power structure. Although many lieutenant governors exercise a hybrid executive-legislative function, their actual powers do not approach those enjoyed by the lieutenant governor of Texas.

Speaker of the House
The Texas House of Representatives, in a recorded majority vote of its members, chooses one of them to serve as its presiding officer. The campaign for

AP Photo/Harry Cabluck

Texas Lt. Gov. David Dewhurst, center, talks with Sen. Rodney Ellis, D-Houston, right, and Sen. Bob Deuell, R-Greenville, left, during a meeting of the Senate Committee of the Whole Thursday, May 13, 2004, in Austin, Texas. Dewhurst worked the floor in an attempt to move a school finance bill out of the committee.

How do the Texas Lieutenant Governor's powers compare with those of other states?

A bipartisan coalition in the Texas House of Representatives first elected Joe Straus in 2009, but his moderate image created political problems among more conservative Republicans.

How is the speaker's bargaining position affected by the need to win a majority of fellow representatives to get reelected?

this post can be very competitive and may attract candidates from all parts of the ideological spectrum. Because the vote for speaker is not secret, the winning candidate often takes punitive action against opponents and their supporters. As a result, incumbent speakers, until recently, faced almost no opposition. In 2002, Republicans gained a majority in the Texas House, and with it came the ousting of the Democratic incumbent and the election of its first Republican speaker since Reconstruction, Tom Craddick. When the Republicans took control of the Texas House in 2002, they enjoyed an 88-to 62-seat majority and held on to a fairly narrow majority until their 2010 landslide victory gave them overwhelming dominance in the House. During this period, Republicans continued to elect one of their own as speaker.

That is not to say, however, that incumbent Republican speakers have not gone unchallenged from within their own party; in fact, recent Republican speakers have experienced challenges from both the left and right. During the 80th Legislative Session, Republican Speaker Tom Craddick was harshly criticized for his autocratic style; after Republicans lost seats in the House, many of his fellow Republicans turned on him, and in 2009, Republicans and Democrats joined together to elect Joe Straus as their new speaker.

Then, during the 82nd Legislative Session, Speaker Joe Straus himself faced an open challenge from members of his own party who were critical that he was not conservative enough. Joe Straus is a more moderate Republican from San Antonio, whom some members of his own party have called a RINO (Republican in Name Only).[14] Although speakers generally do not attract a lot of opposition, Speaker Straus's moderate views have continued to attract opposition from within his own party. After the 2010 Republican state convention, Speaker Straus was challenged by several more conservative members of Republican Party for being too cozy with Democrats.[15] So far, House Republicans' attempts to oust the speaker have failed because the speaker has apparently built a successful coalition of Republicans and Democrats to retain the leadership position.

The threats to Joe Straus's speakership came on the heels of a truly impressive Republican sweep. The 82nd Legislative Session witnessed a 102 to 48 Republican seat advantage in the Texas house. With such growth in Republican seats, Straus could have anticipated greater support. But, because most of the gains came from a highly energized Tea Party movement, it was difficult for Straus to savor his party's gains. Instead, a more conservative coalition of Republicans joined the house, and they did not necessarily agree with Joe Straus's moderate positions. As a result, in an effort to placate the growing conservative wing of his own party, Joe Straus has moved further to the right. This did not stop Tea Party Republicans from recruiting a challenger against the speaker for his San Antonio district in 2012.

---

[14]Leo Berman, in a television interview, claimed that the Republican Party had been "taken over by 11 people last session that we call RINOs, Republicans in Name Only." Representative Berman counts Speaker Straus as one of the 11 RINOs. Watson, Brad (2010, June 20). *Inside Texas Politics* (television broadcast), Dallas/Fort Worth, WFAA News 8, www.wfaa.com/video?id=96754954&sec=552937.

[15]Jason Embry, "Former Party Leader Tries to Rally Republican Against Straus," *Austin American Statesman*, www.statesman.com/blogs/content/shared-gen/blogs/austin/politics/entries/2010/06/12/former_party_leader_tries_to_r.html?cxntfid=blogs_postcards.

Typically, house members or candidates who support the winning candidate can become a part of the speaker's "team," even if they are members of the opposition party. Team status may include membership on a prestigious committee or even a committee chair or vice chair appointment. During the 2009 legislative session, Republican Speaker Joe Straus relied on Democrats to chair or vice chair committees. Of 34 standing committees at the time, house Democrats chaired 18, and another 15 were vice chairs. But in the next session in 2011, under threat to his leadership, Straus reduced the number of Democratic committee chairs on his team from 18 to 11, and many of these were for the less influential committees.

Team members also may attract campaign contributions and other assistance for their own political campaigns and may gain lobby support for legislative programs. This team policy is known as the "no-party" philosophy. Representatives are elected as party members but achieve leadership status by supporting the winning candidate for speaker. In an attempt to curtail abuses of power, candidates who use threats or promises of important appointments are guilty of "legislative bribery." The law is difficult to enforce, though, and the speaker's supporters are usually appointed to important committees.

Funds raised and spent for a campaign to become speaker are part of the public record. Candidates for speaker are required to file a complete statement of loans, campaign contributions, and expenditures with the secretary of state. No corporation, labor union, or organization may contribute, and individual contributions are limited to $100. All expenditures greater than $10 must be reported. These requirements are an attempt to reduce the influence of lobbyists and interest groups on the speaker's race by limiting and making public their campaign contributions. However, the support of **The Lobby** (major Texas economic interests) is necessary for a representative to become speaker.

The Lobby

The collective characterization of the most politically and economically powerful special interest groups in the state.

Legislative Committees

Legislative committees are necessary for any orderly consideration of proposed legislation. Because of the volume of legislative proposals offered each session, legislators cannot possibly become familiar with all bills—not even all the major ones. They therefore organize themselves into committees for the division of labor necessary to ensure that at least someone knows something about each piece of proposed legislation. Committees serve as the workhorses of the Texas legislature.

The numerous types of legislative committees in the Texas House and Texas Senate include standing, conference, joint, and select committees. **Standing committees** are permanent committees that initially consider most legislation after it is introduced; they hold hearings on some bills and mark them up or rewrite them to meet the wishes of the committee majority. However, most bills lack significant support and simply die in standing committee for lack of action; for most bills, standing committees are the place bills go to die. Thus, standing committees act as screening mechanisms to filter out bad bills or bills that have little or no political support.

Standing committees

Permanent committees that function throughout the legislative session.

The two types of standing committees are substantive and procedural. Substantive standing committees consider bills and monitor administrative behavior in a specific subject matter such as taxing, education, and agriculture. The Texas House also has several *procedural* standing committees that regulate the flow of legislation, pass resolutions, conduct investigations, and so forth.

Many of the standing committees have been further divided into **subcommittees** to further specialize in particular categories of legislation. The subcommittees are usually the first to become familiar with a bill. Made up of a smaller number of standing committee members, subcommittees hold initial hearings, mark up legislation, and then report their work to the whole standing committee.

Subcommittees

Divisions of a committee that consider specific subtopics of a committee's primary jurisdiction.

TABLE 7.2 Types of Committees in the Texas Legislature

	Types of Committees			
	Standing	**Conference**	**Joint**	**Select**
Function	Lawmaking authority	Lawmaking authority	Advisory	Advisory
Longevity	Permanent	Temporary	Permanent	Temporary
Membership	From one chamber only	From both the House and Senate	From both the House and Senate	May include members of one chamber, members of both chambers, or members of the legislature and nonlegislators
Examples	House: Agriculture and Livestock Committee Senate: Criminal Justice Committee		Legislative Budget Board	House Select Committee, Emergency Preparedness

This table shows the various types of committees in the Texas legislature.

▲ **How do the various types of committees differ? Explain why committees do so much of the legislative work and how they act as tools of the presiding officers.**

A chair and a vice chair head every committee. Each legislator serves on at least one committee, and some serve on several. When a committee's membership is further divided into subcommittees, each has its own chairs and vice chairs as well.

In addition to standing committees and their subcommittees, a variety of special committees can be classified based on function, membership, and longevity (see Table 7.2). Whereas the function of standing and conference committees is to draft legislation, other committees are charged with a specific purpose such as studying a problem and making recommendations to the legislature. The Select Committee on Federal Legislation created by Speaker Joe Straus to monitor the activities of the federal government in January of 2010 is an example of this type of committee.

Conference committees are temporary committees appointed to compromise House and Senate versions of a bill. A separate conference committee is appointed to resolve differences between each bill passed by the two houses in different form.

Interim committees meet when the legislature is not in session to consider proposed legislation for the next legislative session or to study a particular problem that has arisen since the last session.

Standing and select committees usually include members from only one chamber, whereas conference and **joint committees** consist of members from both chambers. Some special committees may even include members of the public. Conference and select committees tend to be temporary or **ad-hoc committees**, whereas others are more long lasting (standing and joint committees).

Legislative Staff

The legislature provides only minimal funds for hiring competent staff. Monthly staff allotments are $11,925 for House members and $35,625 for senators, who are also reimbursed for other "reasonable and necessary" office expenses. This money is for staff salaries and office expenses, not personal use. House members have about three or four staff people, whereas in the Senate, the average staff size is slightly more than seven. Some senators have as many as 14 staff members, while others have as few as four.[16]

Conference committee

An ad-hoc committee that meets to resolve differences between Senate and House versions of the same legislation.

Interim committee

Committee that meets between legislative sessions.

Joint committee

Committee that includes members of both houses.

Ad-hoc committee

A temporary committee.

---

[16]The data was calculated using the following report of the House Research Organization: "Legislative Staff: 80th Legislature," *Focus Report No. 80-4*. 1, March 2007, at www.hro.house.state.tx.us/focus/staff80.pdf.

Neither individual legislators nor legislative committees have professional staff comparable with that of special interest groups. With minimal staff support, "expert" testimony and arguments of interest group lobbyists and agency liaisons can mislead ill-informed legislators and committees. Powerful interests and administrative agencies have a distinct advantage when they monopolize the available information and expertise and thus force legislators to remain dependent on them for research data, advice, and other services.

Both legislative houses have established nonpartisan institutions to provide information to legislators. Former house speaker Pete Laney created the House Bill Analysis Department as part of legislative operations. Continued and renamed the House Research Organization by Speaker Craddick, it provides bill analyses, floor reports, issue focus reports, and interim news to legislators and the public.[17]

"The Lobby" plays an important role in the selection of the speaker of the house.

Do special interest groups compromise the independent judgment of the legislature? Or do they provide a vital link between government and the public?

The Senate Research Center was formed in 1979 as the Senate Independent Research Group. It currently provides research and bill analysis to the Texas Senate and the lieutenant governor's office. The center's staff also attend meetings and conferences of other governmental entities and report to the senators on their content.

Whenever the legislature considers increasing appropriations to hire competent staff for individual legislators and, even more important, for committees, both the general public and special interests voice strong opposition—the former out of ignorance, the latter out of self-interest.

Ironically, legislators who report a surplus in their expense accounts are acclaimed by the press and their constituents as conscientious guardians of the public treasury, whereas, in fact, their ignorance of proposed legislation may cost taxpayers millions of dollars in wasted revenues. By contrast, legislators who use their allotted money to become informed about pending legislation are often suspected of wasting the money—or stealing it.

Texas legislative committees lack year-round professional staffs, which could give the legislators sources of information and services independently of those provided by interest groups, administrators, and the legislative leadership. Texas senators have enough staff to research some legislation each session, but House members are not as fortunate. Texas spends less than 0.3 percent of total state expenditures on legislative staff salaries, services, and accommodations.

---

[17]The public can access much of the House Research Organization data by visiting its website, www.hro.house.state.tx.us/; the Senate Research Center can be found at www.senate.state.tx.us/SRC/Index.htm.

Redistricting in Texas: The Jaybirds and Wood-peckers Are at It Again

Robert Glen Findley
Odessa College

INTRODUCTION

Paraphrasing Benjamin Disraeli, politics simply defined is the pursuit, and exercise, of power. And nothing is more political, or more partisan, than the reapportionment/redistricting process, especially in Texas. The dominant party claims that gerrymandering the district lines is nothing more than a reflection of the wishes of the voters, while the party out of power screams, "disfranchisement." However, recent events in Texas have taken this process to a whole new level. What needs to be examined is why this is the case. Why has this process become so contentious? Why all of the drama? After all, the process is pretty straightforward ... well, sort of.

Reapportionment/redistricting is required by both the U.S. and Texas Constitutions. In Article I, Section 2 of the U.S. Constitution, we find that a count must be taken every decade, "Representatives ... shall be apportioned among the several states ... which shall be determined by adding to the whole number of free persons.... . The actual enumeration shall be made ... every subsequent term of ten years... ." The Texas State Constitution goes on to say in Article 3, Section 28 that, "the legislature shall, at its first session after the publication of each United States decennial census, apportion the State into senatorial and representative districts... ." In other words, the voting districts for Congress and the Texas legislature are to be redrawn every 10 years. However, Texas (along with many other states) usually ignored redistricting. In fact, for the first half of the twentieth century, little effort was made by the legislature to address the issue, resulting in an imbalance that tilted heavily toward the more rural districts where growth had stagnated (contributing to overrepresentation),

while the more urban areas exploded in population (leading to underrepresentation). Malapportionment of districts was the result; underpopulated rural districts elected more legislators than overpopulated urban ones.

These inequities finally led to the proposal (in 1948) and ratification (in 1949) of an amendment to create an agency to examine the issue of over/underrepresentation. What grew out of this was the Legislative Redistricting Board (LRB). An *ex officio* agency consisting of the lieutenant governor, the House speaker, the attorney general, the comptroller, and the land commissioner, the LRB was designed to take up the issue of redistricting for the state legislature when the legislature itself fails to come up with an appropriate plan or the legislature's plan is invalidated.

While the legislature did draw new voting districts following the 1950 and 1960 Censuses, the rural/urban inequities continued. At this point, the federal courts got involved. In *Baker* v. *Carr* (1962), the Supreme Court determined that these unbalanced districts could be challenged utilizing language in the Fourteenth Amendment to the U.S. Constitution, and in *Reynolds* v. *Sims* (1964), the Court determined that the houses of a bicameral state legislature must be apportioned on the basis of the state's population and that the state's citizens must have equal political influence regardless of their address, hence the expression, "one man, one vote."

During this same time frame, Congress also addressed the issue of minority disfranchisement by passing the Voting Rights Act of 1965, essentially eliminating the literacy test as a requirement for voter registration. The act also required that redrawn voting districts be blessed off by the U.S. Justice Department (a.k.a. preclearance). This affected states that had used discriminatory measures to keep minorities from participating in the electoral process. Ironically, because Texas did not use literacy tests, it did not initially fall under the VRA umbrella. However, in 1975, Texas became subject to preclearance requirements that mandated that redrawn districts had to be preapproved.

It is also important to note that during the 1950s and 60s, the political winds were shifting in Texas as it began to transition from one-party Democrat to something (briefly) resembling a two-party state. The GOP began to make inroads into the Texas political system. Texas Republicans also benefitted from the changes in the redistricting process. Whereas prior to the 1970s, redistricting mostly benefitted incumbents (who were usually white-male Democrats), the growth of the GOP influence, combined with the corresponding decline in Democratic power, led to the contentiousness between the parties that exists today. What was once a process to protect incumbents has shifted to a battle for partisan control (or in the case of the Democrats, to try and remain relevant).

Following the 1990 Census, the districts were redrawn. The Democrats still had a majority on both chambers and also controlled the executive branch. As they drew new districts, they tried to balance two competing goals of trying to increase representation of ethnic minority Democrats while trying to protect Anglo Democratic incumbents. The resulting legislative map drew federal scrutiny and, as a result, was adjusted in 1993. Still, Republicans in Texas were not pleased, so they sued the state. The Texas House of Representatives negotiated with the plaintiffs, and some of the urban districts were redrawn. The Justice Department and federal courts approved the plan, and Republicans had some gains in the legislature.

However, these disputes paled in comparison to what followed the 2000 Census. Neither party had a large enough majority to control the redistricting process. As a result, the 2001 session ended without a redistricting plan. At that point, the responsibility for redrawing the legislative districts fell to the LRB, while redrawing the Congressional districts went to the federal courts. The LRB was tilted four to one in favor of the GOP, and its legislative districting plan, with some alterations by a federal court, allowed the GOP to control both chambers of the legislature following the 2002 elections.

Congressional redistricting was another matter. Because the LRB has jurisdiction only over redistricting the legislature, the job of redrawing the lines for Congress fell to the federal courts. The initial map satisfied the Democrats but did not please the Republicans. As a result, the issue of redistricting surfaced again toward the end of the 2003 legislative session. Probably due to the influence of U.S. House Majority Leader Tom DeLay of Sugarland, Governor Perry and Texas House Speaker Tom Craddick decided to push for midterm redistricting. This was unusual in that unless a court order compels action, state legislatures traditionally do not redistrict more than once per decade. Moreover, this led to three special sessions (the House Democrats walked out of one, and the Senate Democrats walked out of another) and a number of court challenges, with *LULAC* v. *Perry,* 548 U. S. 399 (2006) as the most prominent case. Ultimately, the Justice Department and the courts approved the plan and the Supreme Court found no reason to prevent mid-decade redistricting or to rule that partisan redistricting was in any way unconstitutional. And the new district plan resulted in even more GOP gains.

Yet, still no one is happy. The results of the 2010 Census were made even more interesting because Texas picked up four additional Congressional seats as the result of dramatic population growth (approximately 4 million from 2000 to 2010). However, the bickering began even before the census was completed, and multiple lawsuits were filed at both the state and federal level. This culminated in December of 2011 as the U.S. Supreme Court determined that the interim map drawn by the San Antonio Federal Court could not be used. As a result of this ruling, the primary elections for 2012 were delayed from their original March date to April and then to May 29, 2012. The voting maps are still under scrutiny. It is also worthy to note that this is the first redistricting effort since the 1960s to take place under a Democratic administration in Washington, DC. This, of course, has led to additional distrust because most Texas Republicans have little use for President Obama and what they perceived as a partisan Justice Department.

Without a doubt, the redistricting process in Texas is particularly quarrelsome, and this does not appear likely to change in the near future. It is unlikely that Texas's legislature will pass a law to create a citizen redistricting commission (like those in Iowa or California) to make the process less politically charged, and it is likely that the contentious redistricting process will continue. Texas has a bit of a reputation for feuding anyway, from the Regulator-Moderator War in the 1840s to the competitions found any fall Friday night on any high school football field in the state. As a result, two characteristics of the redistricting will remain evident. The process will continue to be political in the pursuit and exercise of power and it will to continue to be bitterly divisive.

JOIN THE DEBATE

1. What is at stake in the redistricting process? Why do the high political stakes in the process produce contentious and polarized political battles?

2. What kinds of reforms might reduce bitter legislative and legal battles over the redistricting maps? Why is it unlikely that the legislature will turn its precious political power of redistricting over to a nonpartisan citizen commission?

CHAPTER SUMMARY

★ The Texas legislature meets on odd-numbered years for 140 days. Texas alone, among the large states, has such a restricted period of time in which to conduct legislative business. The Texas legislator tends to be a white male Protestant businessperson or lawyer with enough personal wealth or interest group support to adequately finance a campaign.

★ Most Texans are skeptical of professional politicians and prefer a part-time "citizen legislature" to a full-time professional legislature. Critics, however, argue that short biennial sessions, low salaries, high turnover rates among members, and limited staffing hamper the legislature's ability to effectively analyze public policy and make them dependent on lobbyists for information and advice.

★ Texas has 31 senators and 150 representatives. The Texas two-chamber legislature is presided over by the lieutenant governor in the Senate and the speaker in the House of Representatives. Actual power in the legislative process rests with these presiding officers. Through appointive, jurisdictional, and other procedural powers, they are able to strongly influence state policy.

★ Historically, Texas government has been dominated by a coalition of conservative Democrats and Republicans. This coalition dominated the legislature through ideology rather than using party membership as the basis for control. Under Republican control of the legislature, the no-party system of legislative organization remains superficially intact, and Democrats continue to be appointed to chair committees under Republican leadership. The viability of the no-party system may be nearing its end as state politics becomes more partisan.

★ Legislative action is based on the committee system. The presiding officers appoint the committee chairs and many of the committee members who initially consider legislation. The officers assign bills to committees and have discretion over which committee to use. If a committee does not report on a bill (but instead pigeonholes or tables it), the measure is most likely dead for the session.

KEY TERMS

ad-hoc committees, *p. 194*
conference committees, *p. 194*
cracking, *p. 178*
descriptive representation, *p. 182*
ex officio, *p. 175*

gerrymander, *p. 178*
incumbent, *p. 178*
interim committees,
      p. 194
joint committee, *p. 194*

The Lobby, *p. 193*
packing, *p. 178*
pairing, *p. 178*
reapportionment,
      p. 175

retainers, *p. 189*
standing committees,
      p. 193
subcommittees, *p. 193*
term limits, *p. 189*

REVIEW QUESTIONS

1. What are the formal and informal qualifications for holding office in the Texas legislature?

2. What are geographic single-member districts? What are some of the advantages and disadvantages of this system?

3. Who are the presiding officers of the Texas legislature, and how are they each chosen? What are their duties and powers?

4. What is legislative amateurism, and how does it affect the legislative process?

5. Describe the several types of legislative committees. What is the function of each?

LOGGING ON

The *Texas Legislature Online* has all the information on the Texas legislature at **www.capitol.state.tx.us**. Be sure to check out the "Presiding Officer" pages. The lieutenant governor is at **www.senate.state.tx.us/75r/ltgov/ltgov.htm**. The speaker of the house is at **www.house.state.tx.us/members/speaker/**. The Legislative Budget Board, which helps the legislature prepare the budget, is at **www.lbb.state.tx.us**.

The Texas State Library is a source for legislative, administrative, and judicial research as well as general information about many political, economic, and social aspects of Texas. The library can be accessed at **www.tsl.state.tx.us**.

The Legislative Reference Library of Texas is another good source of information about the Texas legislature, and it offers an option to allow you to search the status of bills in past legislative session. The address is **www.lrl.state.tx.us**.

Compare the structure, organization, salaries, and sessions of the Texas legislature using the legislative chapter of *The Book of the States* at the Council of State Government Website, **www.csg .org/**, and find out about new policy initiatives in other states at the National Conference of State Legislatures at **www.ncsl.org/**.

Several citizen and consumer lobbies act as legislative watchdogs as they report on Texas legislative and political activities.

Texas Common Cause works to make government more responsive to citizens. Its site is **www.commoncause .org**. To follow the money in state politics, the Center for Public Integrity provides details of campaign financing at **www .publicintegrity.org**. Texans for Public Justice is a nonpartisan, nonprofit policy and research organization that tracks the influence of money in politics. It is located at **www.tpj.org**.
The Texas Public Policy Foundation is the premier think tank for conservative political policies and initiatives and has had a great deal of influence on the Texas legislature. Find it at **www .texaspolicy.org**.

Many good sites are available to find out about civil rights. Go to the Senate Hispanic Research Council Inc. site at www .tshrc.org. You may also want to visit the Texas Civil Rights Project at **www.texascivilrightsproject.org**. To learn about Latino Civil Rights and advocacy organizations in Texas, visit the National Council of La Raza at **www.nclr.org** and click on NCLR Affiliates.

Other sources of political information that researchers may find interesting include **www.selectsmart.com**, **http:// votesmart.org/**, **www.opensecrets.org**, and the Texas Public Interest Research Group at **www.texpirg.org**.

Chapter 8

The Legislative Process

LEARNING OBJECTIVES

- ★ Identify the presiding officers of the Texas House and Senate and identify their powers.
- ★ Assess the role of committees in the Texas legislature.
- ★ Define the different types of committees and know their functions.
- ★ Explain the impact of the calendars on bill passage.
- ★ Explain the two-thirds rule in the Texas Senate.

- ★ Know the difference between a *recorded vote* and a *voice vote*.
- ★ Identify procedural tools at the disposal of senators in their efforts to block or pass bills.
- ★ Describe how a bill becomes a law.
- ★ Identify and describe the various legislative boards and committees at the disposal of the legislative leadership.

Check your legislators' voting record in the 82nd Legislative Session. See how interest groups rate them on a conservative/liberal scale at websites such as **http://texasconservativeroundtable.com/2012-scorecards, www.empowertexans.com/82nd-session-index/**, and **www.txbiz.org/advocacy/2011_voting_record.aspx**. For a political scientist's analysis of legislators' ideology, see Mark P. Jones, "Republican Candidates Side-by-Side," *Texas Tribune*, May 7, 2012 at **www.texastribune.org/texas-politics/2012-legislative-election/guest-column-republican-candidates-side-side/**.

Adopt a bill of your own on a topic in which you have an interest. (Or visit the website of an organization that you support or admire and choose a bill that they support.)

Find out which interest groups favored or opposed your bill. Why did they take the positions they took? Use the Internet to follow the bill through the legislative process. Did your bill pass, or was it killed in the process? If it was killed, where did it die? What action did the governor take on the bill?

Your best place to start the exercise is Texas Legislature Online at **www.capitol.state.tx.us/**. To get legislative process information, click on Legislation. You will also find help at the Legislative Reference Library website at **www.lrl.state.tx.us/**. Information about the governor's role and other topics can be found at **www.governor.state.tx.us/**.

To understand how the Texas legislature works, you must understand the powers of the lieutenant governor in the Texas Senate and the speaker in the Texas House of Representatives. Their powers are roughly divided into two general categories: procedural powers, which are directly related to the legislative process; and institutional powers, which are used to affect administrative policy and management of Texas government.

Lieutenant Governor David Dewhurst and House Speaker Joe Straus look over the House calendar. These presiding officers drive much of the legislative process and are at the center of negotiation among legislators and interest groups.

How might the calendar be used as a tool of power? What other powers allow the presiding officers to dominate the legislative process?

POWERS OF THE PRESIDING OFFICERS

The rules of each house, formal and informal, give the presiding officers the procedural power to appoint most committee members and committee chairs, assign bills to committees, schedule legislation for floor action, recognize members on the floor for amendments and points of order, interpret the procedural rules when conflict arises, and appoint the chairs and members of the conference committees. Furthermore, statutes grant the presiding officers nonprocedural, institutional power to appoint the members and serve as joint chairs of the Legislative Budget Board and Legislative Council and determine the members of the Legislative Audit Committee and the Sunset Advisory Commission. Power in the Texas legislature is thus concentrated in the offices of the lieutenant governor and the speaker of the house.

LEADERSHIP IN THE LEGISLATIVE PROCESS

The presiding officers dominate every step from initial committee consideration to scheduling and floor debate and finally to negotiation of differences between the senate and house versions of a bill.

The Standing Committees

Standing committees do much of the legislative work in both chambers of the Texas legislature. The presiding officers' power to appoint their members and chairs gives the speaker and lieutenant governor considerable influence over their work and, therefore, considerable influence over policy decisions.

House Committee Membership
The speaker appoints the total membership as well as the chair and vice chair of all house procedural committees such as calendars, rules, ethics, and redistricting committees. One such committee, the House Calendars Committee, controls the flow of most legislation from the committees to the house floor. The speaker uses his or her influence with the Calendars Committee to determine when or whether bills are heard on the house floor.

The speaker also appoints the total membership as well as the chair and vice chair of the powerful 27-member Appropriations Committee and the chairs of the five subcommittees into which the Appropriations Committee is divided. The Appropriations Committee strongly influences all state spending and has important budget and oversight functions as well.

For nonprocedural committees other than appropriations, a limited seniority system in the house determines up to one-half of a committee's membership; the speaker appoints the other half. The speaker also appoints the committee's chair and vice chair, which ensures that the committee leadership as well as a numerical majority of each substantive committee will be speaker appointees. Besides controlling the Calendars and Appropriations committees, it is important for the speaker to have strong allies on the powerful Ways and Means and State Affairs Committees.

Senate Committee Membership
The lieutenant governor officially appoints all members and the chairs of all senate committees. In practice, an informal seniority system allows senators to choose their preferred committee until one-third of the committee's positions are filled. This ensures that senior senators will serve on some of the more powerful committees such as the Finance, Jurisprudence, and State Affairs Committees. The chairs of the standing committees, at their discretion, may appoint subcommittees from the committee membership.

Standing Committees as Tools of the Presiding Officers
The appointive power of the presiding officers means that the action of a committee on specific legislation is usually predictable. The presiding officers can also use the power of appointment to reward friends and supporters as well as to punish opponents. Interest groups often attempt to influence the presiding officers to assign sympathetic legislators to standing committees that have jurisdiction over legislation vital to their interests.

Because the relative power of a committee varies, a legislator's committee assignment directly affects the legislator's influence in the legislature. Serving on an important committee, especially as its chair, gives a legislator a strong bargaining position with administrators, lobbyists, and other legislators. Legislators negotiate intensely to get choice committee assignments, and they join in various coalitions, compromises, and bargains to get them. Conflict in the process is unavoidable and Texas legislators have resolved it by concentrating power over committee selection in the presiding officers.

Selection of Committee Chairs

Owing to the chair's power over the committee's organization, procedure, and the jurisdiction of its subcommittees, the fate of much public policy is determined when the chair is selected. As a result, ambitious legislators and powerful interest groups compete for these positions, and the conflict over their selection must be resolved. In some states, the majority of each committee selects its chair; others use a seniority system. In Texas, the presiding officers make these decisions.

The presiding officers' power to appoint committee chairs is a tool that works like a magnet to attract legislators to their team. If legislators want to "get along," they "go along" with the presiding officers. Their influence over other legislators also increases the bargaining position of the presiding officers relative to interest groups. The lobbyist who can help get a sympathetic legislator appointed as chair of an important committee has earned the salary that the interest group employer pays. At the same time, the lobbyist owes the presiding officer a real favor for appointing the "right" committee chair.

The appointive power of the presiding officers, although significant, is not absolute; they often appoint as chairs key committee people who have political power in their own right, such as members with close ties to a powerful special interest group. The presiding officers may then have the support of some of the more powerful members of the legislature in a reciprocally beneficial relationship. The presiding officers can usually count on the loyalty of the chairs, who can in turn, usually depend on the presiding officer's support.

The No-Party System

The Texas legislature has historically been organized on the basis of ideology, rather than political party, with a coalition of conservative Republicans and a few moderate Democrats usually in control. Under this no-party system, party affiliation has less significance than ideology and interest group ties. Political party caucuses do not fill positions of power as they do in the U.S. Congress; instead members of the minority party may join the presiding officers' teams, serve on important committees, and occasionally even chair minor committees in the Texas legislature.

In recent years, however, the parties are becoming more intensely polarized about public policy issues, and as a result, the legislature is becoming more partisan. Under threat to his leadership, Speaker Joe Straus reduced the number of Democratic committee chairs in his team from 18 in 2009 to 11 in 2011, and many of the Democratic chairs were assigned to the less influential committees.

Committee Jurisdiction

The presiding officers in the Texas legislature assign bills to particular standing committees, and they have considerable discretion when making these assignments because committee jurisdiction in the Texas legislature is often poorly defined. Texas's presiding officers do not hesitate to assign a bill they oppose to a committee they know will kill it, and likewise, they assign bills they support to a committee that will report favorably on it. Because the presiding officers can stack the committees to their liking, this is simple to do.

Presiding officers may press committees to kill a specific bill for several reasons:

★ The backers and financial supporters of the presiding officer may view the bill as a threat to their economic or political well-being.
★ The presiding officer and his or her team may feel that the bill's legislative and interest-group supporters have been uncooperative in the past and should be punished.
★ The supporters of the bill may either refuse or be unable to match the bargaining level of the bill's opponents.
★ The presiding officer and his or her supporters may feel that the bill, if it became law, would take funds away from programs that they favor.
★ The presiding officer thinks the bill is simply bad public policy.

Committee members may negotiate with the presiding officers by promising substantial changes in the bill, supporting legislation that the leadership team favors, or opposing a bill that the leadership wants to defeat. A politically knowledgeable leadership that astutely uses this power can help consolidate committee support for its policies.

Standing Committees' Powers and Functions

Committees are often called **little legislatures** because they normally conduct the real legislative business of compromise and accommodation. Standing committees may totally rewrite a bill, **pigeonhole** it (bury it in committee), or **mark up** the bill by substantially altering it by adding or deleting major provisions. Rarely does a committee report a bill out in the form in which it was originally introduced.

Division of Labor Because several thousand bills are introduced into the Texas legislature each session, a division of labor is necessary. Every bill introduced during the legislative session is referred to a committee, which conducts public hearings where witnesses—both for and against—may be heard, debates held, and bills marked up. Because standing committees do the basic legislative work, the general membership relies heavily on them for guidance in deciding how to vote on a bill being considered on the floor.

Competency Where a seniority system is used, committee members and chairs are usually returned to the same committee posts each session, and legislators can thus become reasonably informed, if not expert, in a given subject. This expertise is important because committee members must first hear interest group representatives and administrative officials and evaluate their arguments concerning the merits of proposed legislation.

Because Texas legislators operate under only a limited seniority system, the expertise of committee members may be gained outside the formal structures of government. State legislators are seldom politicians to the exclusion of other occupations, and these other endeavors can result in conflicts of interest for committee members. For example, if the primary occupation of a legislator is banking, that particular lawmaker may be more sensitive to interests of the banking industry than to those of the public interest. The same problem arises with regard to any occupation—oil, real estate, the law, insurance, and so on. Although legislators may not be initially involved in an occupation that benefits from their committee activity, they often become investors, employees, or attorneys for those business interests relating to their committee's jurisdiction.

The Pigeonhole Standing committees act as a screening system as they bury bills. A legislator may introduce a bill as a favor to some group or constituent, knowing full well that it will be killed in committee (and that the committee will take the blame). The presiding officers assign bills to hostile committees with the intent that they will be totally rewritten if not pigeonholed. Legislators not serving a particular standing committee may bargain with its members to pigeonhole a bill because they are ideologically opposed to it, because their interest-group supporters oppose it, or simply because they want to avoid voting on a controversial bill.

AP Photo/Harry Cabluck

Standing committees do much of the legislative work of ignoring or pigeonholing bills lacking significant support, gathering information in public hearings, and rewriting or marking up legislation to make essential political compromises that make a bill's passage possible.

Explain how the presiding officers influence the work of standing committees.

Little legislatures
Another name for standing committees because most of the work of legislation occurs in committees.

Pigeonhole
To kill a bill in standing committee usually by setting it aside without taking any action at all.

Mark up
Rewrite of a bill in standing committee, usually substantially altering it by adding or deleting major provisions.

Discharge process
A rarely used legislative process for rescuing a bill pigeonholed in standing committee.

Tagging
A senate rule that allows a senator to demand a 48-hour advance notification before a standing committee holds hearings on a particular bill.

Bureaucratic oversight
The legislative function of monitoring administrators to make sure they are administering the laws according to legislative intent.

Calendar
The list of bills reported out of committee and ready for consideration by the house or the senate.

Bills that are pigeonholed may be extracted from reluctant committees, but it is usually difficult to so. Legislators are reluctant to press for discharging a bill from committee even when they support it; they see the **discharge process** as a threat to the privileges of the whole committee system—privileges that they, too, enjoy.

In the Texas Senate, a single senator may use another tactic to delay committee hearings for up to 48 hours by **tagging** a specific bill. If a senator notifies the chair of a senate committee that he or she wants 48 hours' advance notice before hearings are held on a bill, the committee may take no action on the bill within that period. Tagging delays the legislative progress on the bill and is effective only because of the short legislative session. A senator may use the tagging privilege only once, but it enables a single senator effectively to kill a bill late in the session or to demand negotiations with the bill's sponsors in exchange for removing the tag.

Bureaucratic Oversight In the United States, legislatures function as watchdogs over the executive branch—that is, the legislature "oversees" administrative agencies as they execute the law and implement public programs. The vehicle for **bureaucratic oversight** is usually legislative committee hearings where legislators investigate the activities of bureaucrats to determine whether they are administering the laws as the legislature intended or whether new or revised legislation is needed.

Ostensibly, the committees are watching out for the public good by checking on whether the bureaucrats perform their duties in ways consistent with the public interest. More often than not, committees serve as the legislative advocates for the bureaucrats' interests and viewpoints. As part of the iron-triangle power structure described in Chapter 6, legislative committees often lack any incentive to put state agencies under critical scrutiny and short, infrequent legislative sessions make continuous legislative oversight of state agencies impossible.

Scheduling the Legislative Process

The flow of legislation from the standing committees to debate and final vote in the entire house or senate is scheduled on a **calendar**. Scheduling is important in any legislative body, but in Texas, it is paramount because of the legislature's short biennial sessions. Timing is also of strategic importance because, in the process of negotiation, any of the following situations may develop:

★ Supporters may want floor consideration of a bill delayed until they can muster the necessary votes to get it passed.
★ Opponents think they have the necessary votes to defeat the bill but think that the votes could erode if the supporters are given time to consolidate their forces.
★ Conversely, supporters may want an early consideration of a bill because the opposition appears to be gaining strength.

Because of these political calculations, the presiding officers can use their influence over scheduling to expedite or to hinder the progress of legislation and to reward allies or punish enemies.

House Calendars The House Committee on Calendars or the House Committee on Local and Consent Calendars schedule legislation by placing it on one of the house calendars—the Emergency Calendar, Major State Calendar, Constitutional Amendments Calendar, General State Calendar, Local, Consent and Resolutions Calendar, Resolutions Calendar, and Congratulatory and Memorial Resolutions Calendar.

While the speaker exercises no direct formal control over house calendars, the speaker is careful to appoint members and chairs of the two calendars committees who can be persuaded to accommodate the speaker's wishes. Unimportant or trivial bills are placed on special schedules and are usually disposed of promptly with little debate on the house floor, but the process is not so automatic for major or controversial legislation. When or whether such legislation is scheduled is a decision largely determined by the speaker and the House Calendars Committee chair.

Senate Calendar Officially, the senate has a calendar system that advances bills systematically. A senate rule requires that bills be placed on the calendar and then considered on the senate floor in the same chronological order in which they were reported from the committees. In practice, bills are taken off the calendar for senate floor consideration by a **suspension of the rule**, which requires a two-thirds majority vote of the entire membership of the senate. The process goes something like this: The first bill placed on the senate calendar each session is called a **blocking bill**, usually a bill dealing with a trivial matter that senators have no interest in passing (see the chapter essay for examples). The blocking bill is never taken up on the senate floor; its only purpose is to stop floor consideration of any other bills except by the two-thirds vote to suspend the rule requiring chronological consideration of bills.

This time-honored practice affects the senate's entire legislative process because it allows just 11 senators to block a bill. The irony is that although only a simple majority is necessary for final passage in the senate, a two-thirds majority is necessary to get the bill to the floor for consideration by the entire senate. The two-thirds rule is designed to protect the minority from the majority.

The two-thirds rule is also a means whereby the senate can kill a bill without having a floor vote for or against—it just fails to reach the floor and thus dies on the calendar. Although lobbyists are keenly interested in this action, the general public is usually unaware that a vote even occurred or where the individual senators stood on the issue. It is also a tool that can be used to enhance the powers of the presiding officer. By using this two-thirds vote requirement, the lieutenant governor may keep a bill from reaching the floor of the senate by simply persuading 11 members to vote against it. The bill would then lack the necessary two-thirds majority to reach the floor. Any coalition of 11 senators can, of course, achieve the same result—occasionally against the wishes of the lieutenant governor.

Realizing that 11 senators were prepared to block passage of a bill to establish a new voter ID requirement during the 2011 session, the lieutenant governor and a majority of senators adopted a rule to specifically exempt from the two-thirds requirement the bill requiring voters to show state-issued picture identification before voting. In 2011, the senate passed the voter identification bill (S.B. 14) by a simple majority over the strong objections of opponents who believed the ID requirement would disparately impact the elderly and minorities in voting because members of those populations are less likely to have a photo identification card.

Floor Action

Floor action refers to action by the entire house or the entire senate to debate, amend, and pass or defeat legislation. To take official action, each house requires a **quorum** of two-thirds of its membership to be present. On several occasions, a determined minority opposed to a scheduled action have used quorum-busting tactics by deliberately absenting themselves to deny their chamber the quorum necessary to proceed on any legislation.

During floor action, the Texas Constitution requires that bills must be "read on three consecutive days in each house."

Suspension of the rule
The setting aside of the rules of the legislative body so that another set of rules can be used.

Blocking bill
A bill placed early on the senate calendar that will never be considered by the full senate. Its purpose is to require two-thirds of the senators to vote to suspend the senate rule that requires bills to be considered in the order they are reported out of committee. The effect is that any bill appearing later on the calendar must have the support of two-thirds of the senate if it is to be allowed to come up for debate and passage.

Floor Action
The entire senate or house acting as a whole to debate, amend, vote on, enact, pass, or defeat proposed legislation.

Quorum
The number of members that the rules require to be present to conduct official business. In the Texas Senate and House, two-thirds of the total membership is necessary to take most floor actions.

Did You Know? In 1979, Lt. Governor Hobby ordered the Texas Rangers to find 12 senators, dubbed the "Killer Bees," who were hiding out to deny the senate a quorum to pass a split primary bill. In their quorum-busting efforts, house Democrats, known as the "Killer D's," fled to Oklahoma escape the reach of Texas law enforcement during the 2003 gerrymandering battle; senate Democrats, known as the "Texas Eleven," later took up the cause and fled to New Mexico for 46 days.

Floor leaders

The legislators who are responsible for getting legislation passed or defeated. Their job is to negotiate, bargain, and compromise because they are in the center of political communication.

Point of order

A formal objection that rules of procedure are not being followed on the house floor. Successfully raising a point of order can result in the postponement or defeat of a bill.

Chubbing

Slowing the legislative process by maximizing debate, amendments, and points of order on minor bills to prevent ultimate consideration of a more controversial bill further down on the calendar.

The purpose of the requirement was to ensure that laws would not be passed without adequate opportunity for debate and understanding. Bills are read once upon being introduced and prior to being assigned to a committee by the presiding officer. In practice, though, the entire bill is seldom read at this time. Instead, a caption or a brief summary is read to acquaint legislators with the subject of the bill. The bill is read the second time before floor debate in each house, and if an entire bill is to be read, it is usually on this second reading. The third reading occurs at least one day after initial floor passage.

The constitution allows bills that are "cases of imperative public necessity" as so stated in the bill, to be read for the third time on the same day as floor passage, as long as four-fifths of the membership agrees. All bills now routinely contain this provision and usually pass the third reading immediately following floor passage. A simple majority is required for final passage on the third reading, but amendments must have a two-thirds majority.

House Floor Action

As bills reach the floor of the house of representatives, a loudspeaker system allows the members and visitors to follow the debate on the floor. The **floor leaders** are the representatives who take center stage attempting to rally support or opposition to a bill during floor action. They usually stand at the front of the chamber, answer questions, and lead debate on the bill. Microphones located elsewhere in the house chamber serve other lawmakers who wish to speak or ask questions. Representatives are each allotted 10 minutes to speak, but few of them utilize even this limited privilege.

The consideration of bills on the floor of the house would seem to be a study in confusion and inattention. Throughout the process, members of the house may be laughing, talking, reading papers, or sleeping at their desks. Often, however, because many members may know very little about the bill under consideration, floor debate should be an excellent opportunity for both proponents and opponents of the legislation to convince fellow legislators to vote for or against the bill.

Actually, eloquent speeches seldom change votes on major legislation because most legislators already have well-defined positions developed long before the bill reaches the floor. Many legislators know little of the specific content of specialized legislation that has generated little statewide interest, and sometimes they vote for or against it based on the advice of lobbyists or fellow legislators and only ask what the bill was about after the votes are tallied.

Presided over by the speaker, floor action is usually routine, but it can become quite dramatic and debate can become intense when major legislation is brought up for a vote. Representatives opposing legislation may bring up points of order requiring rulings by the speaker. A **point of order** is a representative's objection that the rules of procedure are not being followed during floor action. If the speaker sustains the point of order late in the session, there may not be time to correct the error, and the bill dies. In 1997, one legislator raised points of order that killed some 80 bills at the end of the session.

Late in the session, opponents may attempt to delay action on a bill in an effort to run out the clock on the session. Unlike state senators, representatives do not have the privilege of unlimited debate, but they have developed other strategies to forestall legislative action. For example, knowing that a bill they oppose is scheduled to come up for debate, opponents may engage in **chubbing** by slowing down the whole legislative process, debating preceding bills for the

Representative Jim Keffer urges an "aye" vote on the floor of the Texas House of Representatives. The electronic tote board in the background is used to tally votes. Floor debate rarely determines how legislators will vote on a major bill; they usually decide how they will vote long before the bill reaches the floor.

AP Images/Harry Cabluck

What political factors affect legislators' decisions to support or oppose legislation?

maximum allotted time, peppering the bill's sponsors with trivial questions, and proposing so many amendments and raising so many points of order that the house does not get around to the bill to which they ultimately object.

House members then insert cards that allow them to push buttons to record a "aye," "no," or "present" vote on a large electronic scoreboard by means of green, red, and white bulbs next to each legislator's name. As votes are cast, the bill's supporters and opponents walk up and down the aisles pleading with either one finger (vote "yes") or two fingers (vote "no").

Until recently, lawmakers decided many bills by **voice vote** only, which meant that many of their votes were not recorded and voters had no way of knowing how their representatives voted on many bills. A state constitutional amendment passed in November 2007 ended this practice by requiring **recorded votes** on final passage of all bills.

The use of recorded votes, which became a political issue in the 79th (2005) and 80th (2007) Legislative Sessions, can be viewed from several legitimate perspectives. The most important argument is that voting records are necessary for constituents to know how their representatives and senators voted on the issues. Without this information, voters cannot make informed decisions on election day—and democracy itself can become reduced to choosing political leaders on the basis of television image, mudslinging, and trivialities.

On the other hand, recorded votes can become political weapons wielded unfairly against legislators in campaigns. A legislator may be strongly opposed to one provision in an important bill and may unsuccessfully work, lobby, and argue against this measure in committee and on the floor of the chamber. Yet if the bill contains other provisions that the legislator views as important and worthwhile, he or she may vote for the entire bill despite the objectionable provision. Political opponents may then pluck this provision from the total bill and use it as a campaign issue to defeat the legislator. These rivals know that the legislator cannot deny having voted for the objectionable provision, but they conveniently fail to point out that it was a small part of a much larger bill. This is an unfair but effective campaign tactic.

Also, the final recorded vote may or may not be a measure of the legislator's efforts for or against the legislation. Test votes on amendments or procedural issues are often more important and more informative regarding where legislators actually stand. Under Proposition 11, these more important votes, which occur in the second reading, may continue to be obfuscated with voice votes unless the chamber provides exceptions to the rules.

Senate Floor Action

The senate scene may be similar to that in the house in one sense—usually few members are paying attention to the debate. Although debate time is not limited in the senate as it is in the house, debates on even important bills are usually much shorter in the senate. The fact that legislation is brought up for senate debate by a two-thirds vote means that most major compromises have been made before the legislation reaches the senate floor and that there is widespread support for its passage.

Only rarely does a senator opposing a bill resort to a **filibuster**—a prolonged debate—on the senate floor. Senators may use a filibuster either to attract public attention to a bill that

Did You Know? In 2009, House Democrats chubbed to death a bill to require voters to present valid ID at the polls because they feared that it would keep low-income and elderly citizens from voting.

Did You Know? Ghosts appear to participate in the legislative process. On August 7, 1991, three votes were cast on Representative Larry Evans's (D-Houston) electronic voting machine after his death! Actually, legislators sometimes illegally hand their key cards to fellow representatives to cast votes for them.

Did You Know? A bill's general subject and its supporters may determine how legislators vote. In 1965, for example, 22 members of the Texas House of Representatives voted against the U.S. Bill of Rights when it was introduced as "an act to protect our fundamental liberties" by Representative Jake Johnson, a liberal from San Antonio.

Voice vote
An oral vote cast by lawmakers that is not recorded in the official record.

Recorded votes
Votes in which the names of those who cast the vote are recorded in the house journal.

Filibuster
An attempt by a senator to delay a bill by unlimited debate.

is sure to pass without the filibuster or to delay legislation in the closing days of the session. In fact, just the *threat* of a filibuster may be enough to compel a bill's supporters to change the content of the bill to reach a compromise with the dissatisfied senator. If a filibuster does occur, it means it was impossible to reach a compromise, usually because a sufficient number of senators strongly favor the bill and refuse to be intimidated by the threat of a filibuster. Democratic Senator Wendy Davis from Fort Worth used the filibuster to protest the billions of dollars in spending cuts to public education that resulted from the 82nd Legislative Session. The filibuster is credited with forcing Governor Rick Perry to call a special session to address education spending.

Filibusters, however, are far less important in the Texas Senate than in the U.S. Senate, where many major bills are blocked by the threat of partisan filibusters. The difference in the Texas Senate is that a member may not yield the floor to another senator who wants to continue the filibuster. In the Texas Senate, the floor is controlled by the lieutenant governor, so only one senator may filibuster as long as he or she can physically last, and then the vote is taken.

Did You Know? Former Texas Senator Bill Meier set the world record for a filibuster in May 1977 by talking for 43 hours, breaking Senator Mike McKool's old record of 42 hours and 33 minutes.

In the U.S. Senate, a minority of senators may pass debate back and forth unless 60 senators agree to invoke

Cloture

A parliamentary move to stop legislative debate and force a floor vote; also known as *closure*.

cloture to limit debate. Filibusters are so frequent in the U.S. Senate that it is often simply assumed that 60 votes will be required to pass a bill.

Usually after a modest amount of debate, the Texas Senate takes a vote without the benefit of an electronic scoreboard. Senators plead for votes by holding up a single finger for a "yes" vote and two fingers for a "no" vote. A clerk records the vote, and only a simple majority is necessary for passage.

Conference Committees

A unique by-product of bicameralism is the need to resolve differences in similar bills passed by the two houses. A temporary or ad-hoc committee known as a **conference committee** is appointed for each bill to resolve these differences. To determine the acceptability of proposed compromises, the members of this committee remain in contact with interested legislators, lobbyists, administrators, and the presiding officers as they deliberate.

Conference committee

An ad-hoc committee that meets to resolve differences between senate and house versions of the same legislation.

In Texas, conference committees consist of five members from each house, appointed by their respective presiding officer. The compromise proposal must win the support of a majority of the committee members from each house to be reported out of the committee. Because the members of the conference committee may strengthen, weaken, or even kill a bill, the attitudes of the legislators appointed to the committee are of crucial concern to the various interests involved. This affords the presiding officers, as well as the conference committee members, enviable bargaining positions. Bargaining before the selection of the committee is common, and it continues within the committee during deliberations.

After a bill has been reported from the conference committee, it may not be amended by either house but must be accepted or rejected as it is written or sent back to the conference committee for further work. In practice, due to the volume of legislation that must be considered in the limited time available, the Texas legislature tends to accept **conference committee reports** on most legislation.

Conference committee report

A compromise between the house and senate versions of a bill reached by a conference committee. It may not be amended by either house but must either be rejected, accepted, or sent back to the committee for more work.

How a Bill Becomes a Law

Bills may be introduced in either house or, to speed the process, in both houses at the same time. Let us consider the example of a bill that is introduced in the senate before it is sent to the house of representatives. The numbers in Figure 8.1 correspond to the numbers in the following discussion.

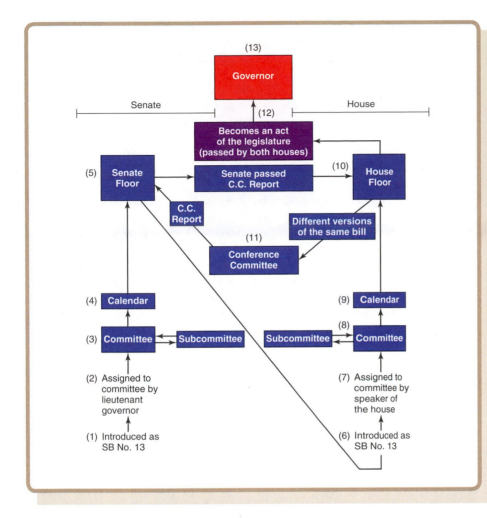

Figure 8.1
How a Bill Becomes a Law

This diagram takes a bill step by step through the legislature from introduction in the Texas House to signing by the governor. Bills may also originate in the Texas Senate.

As a bill works its way through the legislative process, what factors determine whether a bill becomes a law?

1. *Introduction to the senate.* Only a senator may introduce a bill in the senate, and only a representative may do so in the house. It is not difficult to find a legislator who is willing to perform this somewhat clerical function. More difficult is finding a sponsor who will devote political skill and bargaining prowess to help get the bill through the intricacies of the legislative process. Upon introduction, the bill is assigned a number, for example, Senate Bill 13 (SB 13). The first bill introduced in the house of representatives would be styled as HB 1.

2. *Assignment to a committee.* The lieutenant governor assigns bills to committees in the senate and for many bills will have to choose from two or more committees. It is very important to proponents of a bill that the chosen committee does not oppose the spirit of the bill. If possible, proponents of the bill and their allies will gain the lieutenant governor's support and get a friendly committee assignment in exchange for their support of or opposition to a bill of particular interest to the lieutenant governor.

3. *Senate committee action.* As noted earlier, committees are often called "little legislatures" because of the power they have over bills. In both the committee and the subcommittee, the supporters and the opponents of the bill are allowed to testify. Witnesses are often lobbyists or concerned bureaucrats affected by the bill. The subcommittee then marks up the

bill (makes changes) and sends it to the committee, where it may be further marked up. Some senate committees do not have subcommittees; in that case, the entire committee initially hears testimony and marks up the bill. The committee may then report on the bill favorably or unfavorably or may refuse to report on it at all.

4. *Senate calendar.* As described earlier, the senate has only one calendar of bills, and it is rarely followed. In the usual procedure, a senator makes a motion to suspend the regular calendar order and consider a proposed bill out of sequence. For this parliamentary maneuver to succeed, prior arrangements must be made for the lieutenant governor to recognize the senator who will make the motion. If two-thirds of the senators agree to the motion, the bill, with the blessings of the lieutenant governor, is ready for action on the senate floor.

5. *Senate floor.* The president of the senate (the lieutenant governor) has the power to recognize senators who wish to speak, to vote in the event of a tie, and to interpret rules and points of order. Rarely do members of the senate overrule these interpretations.

    The Texas Senate permits unlimited debate, but this policy is not meant to imply that the Texas Senate is a deliberative body, for it is not; such a luxury is prevented by the short legislative session. Unlimited debate could, however, lead to a filibuster—an attempt to "talk the bill to death" or force a compromise. If a bill is successful in reaching the senate floor, it has already cleared its major obstacle (the two-thirds majority necessary for senate consideration) and will usually be passed in some form. Only a simple majority is necessary for a bill to pass.

    The senate may also form itself into a **committee of the whole**, at which time the lieutenant governor appoints a senator to preside. Only a simple majority rather than the usual two-thirds is necessary to consider legislation, and the lieutenant governor may debate and vote on all questions, but otherwise the senate rules are observed. No journal is kept of the proceedings.

6. *Introduction to the house.* After the senate passes a bill, the bill is sent to the house of representatives. A procedure similar to that in the senate is followed there.

7. *Assignment to a committee.* It is the responsibility of the speaker of the house to assign each bill to a committee. The speaker, like the lieutenant governor, has some freedom of choice because the vague jurisdiction of house committees over specific kinds of legislation.

8. *House committee action.* Committee action in the house of representatives is similar to that in the senate. Each bill is assigned to a committee and then to a subcommittee, which may want to hold public hearings. The subcommittee as well as the committee may amend, totally rewrite, pigeonhole, or report favorably or unfavorably on a bill.

9. *House calendars.* A bill that is either reported favorably by the committee or receives a favorable minority report by the required number of committee members is placed on one of the house calendars by one of the committees on calendars. This establishes the approximate order in which the whole house will consider the legislation. If the calendars committees fail to assign the bill to a calendar, they may be forced to do so by the action of a simple majority of the house. However, if a bill has the blessing of the speaker, it is sure to be promptly placed on the appropriate calendar.

10. *House floor.* The speaker of the house has the power to recognize representatives on the house floor and also to interpret the rules and points of order. Although the speaker may be overruled, he or she seldom is. The size of the house necessitates that debate be more limited than in the senate—usually 10 minutes for each member. Bills may be amended, tabled (which usually kills the measure), killed outright, or sent back to committee. "Yes" votes of only a simple majority of members present and voting are necessary for a bill to be passed.

Committee of the whole

The entire senate acting as a committee. Its purpose is to allow the senate to relax its rules and thereby expedite legislation.

11. *Conference committee.* If the house of representatives makes a change in the senate-passed version of a bill, a conference committee is necessary to resolve the differences between the two houses. The lieutenant governor appoints five senators, and the speaker appoints five representatives to sit on the committee. The compromise bill must be approved by a majority of both the senators and the representatives before it can be reported out of the conference committee.

12. *Final passage.* The bill is sent first to the chamber where it originated and then to the other chamber for final approval. Neither one may amend the reported bill but rather must accept it, reject it, or send it back to the conference committee. The conference report is sent to the governor after it passes both houses.

13. *The governor.* The governor has several options concerning an act arriving on his or her desk. First, the governor may sign it into law. Second, the governor may choose not to sign, in which case it becomes law in 10 days if the legislature is in session or in 20 days if the legislature is not in session. Third, the governor may choose to veto the act, but the veto can be overridden by a two-thirds vote in each house. The governor must either accept or veto the complete act if it does not contain provisions for appropriating funds. In appropriations acts, the governor may strike out an item of appropriation, but the governor does not have a reduction veto to reduce spending for an item. Also, the governor may not veto riders on appropriations bills that do not authorize state spending.

The governor may use the veto late in the legislative session without fear of the legislature's overriding it because a veto cannot be overridden in a subsequent session. If the governor signs an act of the legislature, it will become law in 90 days—sooner if it appropriates funds or the legislature has designated it as emergency legislation. If the act requires the expenditure of funds, the comptroller of public accounts must certify that adequate revenue is available for its implementation. If revenue is lacking, the act goes back to the legislature, where either adequate funds are provided or it is approved by a four-fifths majority in each house. If neither option is successful, it cannot be implemented.

INSTITUTIONAL TOOLS OF LEADERSHIP

Taken as a whole, the procedural tools of leadership give the presiding officers enough authority, both formal and informal, to exercise fundamental control over the legislative process. Complementing their procedural powers, institutional powers give the lieutenant governor and speaker influence over the actual policy implementation, further enhancing their bargaining position with economic and political players who seek to influence the state's public policy.

The Legislative Budget Board

Most states, the U.S. government, and most countries have only one budget. Texas has two. Each agency in state government presents its budget requests to both the governor's office and the powerful **Legislative Budget Board (LBB)**. The board then provides the governor and the legislature with a draft of the appropriations bill. The LBB has broad authority for strategic, long-range planning, bill analyses, and policy-impact analyses of education, criminal justice, and financial policies.

The LBB consists of 10 members, including the lieutenant governor and the speaker, who serve as joint chairs. The remainder of the board is composed of the chairs of the Senate Finance Committee and the House Ways and Means and Appropriations Committees,

Legislative Budget Board (LBB)

The body responsible for proposing the legislature's version of the proposed biennial budget. The governor also proposes a budget to the legislature.

who serve as automatic members, and two house members and three senate members appointed by their respective presiding officer. The LBB operates continuously, even when the legislature is not in session, under the management of an administrative director appointed by the board.

Control of the board gives the two presiding officers strong influence over state spending from the budgeting stage through the final appropriating stage. LBB staff assist appropriating committees and their chairs and serve as watchdogs overseeing to some extent the expenditures of the executive agencies and departments.

HOW DOES TEXAS COMPARE?
The State Legislatures: Cutting State Budgets And Raising State Employee Health Costs

At a time when health care costs continue to climb and budget shortfalls are making it difficult for states to meet their obligations, some states are turning to their state employees to share more of the sacrifice. That has been the case with health care.

National Public Radio reported that "Premiums in Texas's unregulated health insurance industry have soared by 105 percent over the past 10 years, according to the federal Agency for Health Care Research and Quality." And, during the 82nd Legislative Session, lawmakers continued to look at increasing state employee contributions to health insurance premiums as a way of dealing with their health insurance costs.

Recently, the National Conference of State Legislatures assembled a report comparing the monthly premium health care costs for state employees. Of the 42 states that responded to the survey, Texas had premiums that were lower than the national average, but the state also required that employees themselves pay a larger share of the premium cost.

The National Conference of State Legislatures collected data on what they describe as lowest-cost insurance options and standard policy options for family coverage. The low-cost insurance options include plans that require high annual deductions and are connected to health savings accounts. The standard plans included managed care and cover a broad array of health services.

The average premium for the low-cost plans is $1,101.28, with states paying $974.66, or 88 percent of the cost. Texas's low-cost premium was $1,047.62, with the state covering $703.92 or 67 percent of the cost and state employees paying the remainder. Of the 42 states that participated in the analysis, Texas had a below-average cost—$53.66 less than the national average. Texas, however, required the state employee to pay a significantly larger share of the premium. Only five other states required their state employees to pay a larger share of the cost.

A similar finding was true for the standard plans. The average premium for the states was $1,377.03, with the states contributing an average $1,096.63, or 80 percent of the cost. In Texas, the cost was $1,202.46, with the state paying only $807.86, or 67 percent of the cost. Only eight other states required a higher employee contribution from their state employees than is required of Texas state employees.

Only two states cover the entire premium for the standard family insurance policy, and nine states cover the entire premium for the lowest-cost family insurance policies.

	Low-cost Premium				Standard Plans		
State	Premium	Employee Contribution	State Ranking	State	Premium	Employee Contribution	State Ranking
MS	$949	$593	1	MS	$1,041	$685	1
NC	$901.14	$490.34	2	NC	$991.24	$580.44	2
ME	$1,810.70	$419.92	3	IN	$1,646.80	$578.08	3
MO	$1,616.00	$381	4	WY	$1,661.16	$559.80	4
LA	$971.32	$377.24	5	LA	$1,251.40	$486.04	5
TX	$1,047.62	$343.70	6	MO	$1,688.	$453	6
				AZ	$2,229.24	$448.62	7
				ME	$1,810.70	$419.92	8
				TX	$1,202.46	$394.60	9

Sources: Wade Goodwyn, "Gov. Perry Cut Funds For Women's Health in Texas", *National Public Radio,* September 20, 2011, www.npr.org/2011/09/20/140449957/gov-perry-cut-funds-for-womens-health-in-texas; National Conference of State Legislatures, "2011 State Employee Health Benefits: Monthly premium costs (family and individual coverage)," September 2011, http://www.ncsl.org/Portals/1/documents/health/StateEHBenefits2011.pdf.

FOR DEBATE

Explain how Texas legislative policies for state employees reflect the state's conservative ideology of limited government spending and individual responsibility. Facing declines in state revenues, where should the state legislature impose cutbacks and fiscal austerity policies? Does cutting state employee benefits affect recruitment of qualified public servants?

The Legislative Council

Another instrument of influence is the 14-member **Legislative Council**, made up of six senators, the chair of the House Administration Committee, five other representatives, and the lieutenant governor and speaker, who serve as joint chairs. The lieutenant governor appoints the senate members, and the speaker appoints the house members. With the exception of the speaker and lieutenant governor, the terms of the appointees end with the beginning of the regular legislative session. The presiding officers govern the council during the regular session.

The Legislative Council, its director, and staff function as a source of information and support to the legislature, state agencies, and other governmental institutions. It also provides research, computing, and printing support for legislators and helps them draft legislative proposals. The council staff plays a key role in the redistricting process.

Legislative Council
The body that provides research support, information, and bill-drafting assistance to legislators.

Legislative Audit Committee
The body that performs audits of state agencies and departments for the legislature.

The Legislative Audit Committee

The **Legislative Audit Committee** appoints and supervises the state auditor, who with the consent of the senate, heads the State Auditor's Office. The six-member Legislative Audit Committee is composed of the lieutenant governor, the chair of the Senate Finance Committee, one senator chosen by the lieutenant governor, the house speaker, and the chairs of the house Appropriations Committee and Ways and Means Committee.

The authority of the Office of the State Auditor is both broad and deep. Under the direction of the committee, state agencies and departments, including colleges and universities, as well as any entity receiving funds from the state can be audited. The auditor's office may conduct financial, compliance, efficiency, effectiveness, and special audits as well.

The Sunset Advisory Commission

The Texas Sunset Act reevaluates the need for more than 150 statutory state agencies on a 12-year cycle to determine the need for their continuance. Because they are automatically terminated, the "sun sets" on those agencies not specifically renewed by the legislature, and many of those that are reauthorized by legislation are given altered scope and authority.

Sunset Advisory Commission

A body that systematically evaluates most government agencies and departments and may recommend restructuring, abolishing, or altering the jurisdiction of an agency.

The 12-member **Sunset Advisory Commission** enforces the act. The lieutenant governor appoints five senators and one public member, and the speaker appoints five representatives and one public member to the commission. Public members are appointed for two-year terms and legislators for four-year staggered terms. The commission chair is appointed by the presiding officers and alternates between senate and house members. The agency's chief executive officer is appointed by the commission.

In the Sunset Advisory Commission's more than 35-year history, the commission has abolished more than 52 state agencies, saving taxpayers hundreds of millions of dollars. In recent years, however, abolishing state agencies has proven politically unpopular. As a result, the Sunset Advisory Commission has worked to improve and reorganize state agencies, rather than abolish them completely.

RESTRAINTS ON THE POWERS OF THE PRESIDING OFFICERS

Although the aggregate of the organizational, procedural, and institutional powers of the speaker and the lieutenant governor seems to be—and at times is—overwhelming, certain restraints curtail arbitrary and absolute use of these powers.

Personality

The personalities of the individual presiding officers and the way they view the role of their offices determine their approach to legislative leadership. They may use their powers to develop strong, aggressive leadership, ruthlessly overpowering opposition, or they may be accommodating and compromising, accomplishing the desired results with only the implied threat of reprisal.

The Team

The presiding officers require a strong coalition of legislative support to accomplish their aims despite the concentration of powers they enjoy. Support from other legislators may be based on personal friendship, shared ideology, or political convenience. More likely, legislators may feel that it is in the best interest of their constituents and supporters for them to be team players and back the presiding officers. The speaker and the lieutenant governor are usually able to build and add cohesiveness to this support through the use of their powers to reward or punish.

The Lobby and Bureaucracy

The relationship between the presiding officers, the lobby, and their bureaucratic allies is of great importance in determining the chance of success for specific legislation. When the lieutenant governor, speaker, bureaucrats, and lobby all agree and work together toward a common goal, legislative victory is almost assured.

In the event of conflict between the lobby–bureaucracy coalition and the speaker or the lieutenant governor—the presiding officer's agenda may be either diluted or defeated, depending on such complex factors as the amount of support that can be mustered from the governor, interest groups, and legislators.

Against a strong coalition between an interest group and the bureaucracy, all of a presiding officer's formal and informal powers may not be enough to control the legislation. The officer would simply be confronted by too much combined political power. A conflict of this nature is unusual. Generally, the presiding officers are in basic agreement with the more powerful interests, which have often given political and financial support to their campaigns.

The Governor

The Texas Constitution gives the governor a considerable role in the legislative process. The governor may veto any bill and can use the item veto on appropriations. These formal powers place the governor in a strong bargaining position, and the governor's support for or opposition to specific programs is an important factor. The governor's influence with the lobby and the threat to veto constitute the most useful instruments to achieve changes in the substance of a bill while it is still in the legislature. Of course, the governor has lost a battle with the legislative leadership if forced to veto a bill after attempting to influence it.

In fact, a coalition of the governor, the lieutenant governor, and the speaker is the norm, with each sharing influence over the legislative process. The governor also has the support of friendly interest groups that can often be enlisted to influence the presiding officers and other legislators. A governor who tends toward activism can exercise substantial influence over legislation. If the governor chooses a passive legislative role, however, his or her influence is significantly decreased; inaction or restraint affects public policy as profoundly as activist leadership does.

Political Climate

The general public is seldom aware of events in Austin. Rare exceptions are when a climate of scandal spreads over the state, as in the veterans' land scandals of the 1950s, the Sharpstown Bank scandal of the 1970s, or the delinquent property tax scandal of the 1990s. Although public involvement is stimulated by a scandal, it seems confined to finding guilty parties rather than making serious inquiries into the need for reform of basic government procedures. Scandal does have the benefit of making the presiding officers aware of public scrutiny and therefore more responsive to criticism. In fact, the political climate following the Sharpstown and delinquent property tax scandals resulted in ethics reform legislation. Without scandal, the legislative leadership is all but freed from public attention, with only interest groups, administrators, a few concerned citizens, some members of the press, and the governor exhibiting awareness of legislative activity.

Occasionally, a political wave sweeps across the state, as happened in the 2010 Texas elections. The conservative Republican landslide that year swept numerous social conservatives into office and shifted state leaders' political calculations. In response, the presiding officers were compelled to respond, enabling the passage of dramatic new social legislation. Our How Does Texas Compare feature illustrates the impact of this changed political calculus.

HOW DOES TEXAS COMPARE?
Legislatures, Women's Health, And Abortion Politics

The Texas legislature was among several state legislatures controlled by social conservatives that adopted policies to reduce funding for women's health clinics. A number of legislative leaders called these clinics "abortion clinics," even though no clinics receiving state or federal funds perform abortions. Texas lawmakers cut spending for these clinics, and instead, increased spending by $8 million to help fund crisis pregnancy centers that counsel pregnant women against abortion.

Even before this recent bout on women's health clinics, the state of Texas did not have a very good track record when it came to women's health. According to the Centers for Disease Control, Texas had the third-highest rate of teen pregnancy in the country after Mississippi and New Mexico. Texas even has the distinction of producing the third-highest rate of 10- to 14-year-old mothers.

Critics expect that the recent round of budget cuts and lawmakers' decisions on reproductive health will have some dire consequences for the state. Wade Goodwyn reports, "The budget cuts to family planning clinics won't in the end save Texas money. The state estimates nearly 300,000 women will lose access to family planning services, resulting in roughly 20,000 additional unplanned births."

When it comes to sexually transmitted diseases, Texas women suffer greatly. Texas ranks 9th in the number of cases per 100,000 who suffer from chlamydia and 13th in the number per 100,000 who suffer from HIV AIDS.

Texas women do not rate any better on receiving mammogram or Pap smear tests. Texas women 50 years of age and older are less likely to receive a mammogram test than women in other states. Texas ranks 10th in the percentage of women who do not receive a mammogram test. Texas ranks 11th in the percentage of women who have not received a Pap smear. On general health measures, Texas ranks 2nd in the percentage of women who suffer from diabetes and 7th in the percentage of women who suffer from cardiovascular disease.

FOR DEBATE

How does the state's political climate affect the legislature's policy choices? How do women's health and reproductive policies reflect both social and economic conservatism in Texas? Do Texas's low rankings on women's health reflect public policy, or do they reflect the state's high rates of poverty?

Sources: Goodwyn, Wade, "Gov. Perry Cut Funds For Women's Health in Texas," *National Public Radio*, September 20, 2011, www.npr.org/2011/09/20/140449957/gov-perry-cut-funds-for-womens-health-in-texas; Joyce A. Martin, Brady E. Hamilton, Stephanie J. Ventura, Michelle J. K. Osterman, Sharon Kirmeyer, T. J. Mathews, and Elizabeth C. Wilson, "Births: Final Data for 2009," *National Vital Statistics Report* Vol. 60, Number 1, 2011, www.cdc.gov/nchs/data/nvsr/nvsr60/nvsr60_01.pdf; Centers for Disease Control and Prevention, "2010 Sexually Transmitted Disease Surveillance," Tables 4 and 5, www.cdc.gov/std/stats10/tables.htm#chlam; Centers for Disease Control and Prevention, Division of HIV/AIDS Prevention-Surveillance and Epidemiology, Special Data Request, December 2011; Centers for Disease Control and Prevention (CDC), "Behavioral Risk Factor Surveillance System Survey Data," at http://apps.nccd.cdc.gov/brfss/list.asp?cat=WH&yr=2010&qkey=4427&state=All; Kaiser Family Foundation, "Women's Health Disparities," www.statehealthfacts.org/women.jsp.

Political or Economic Ambition

Through effective management of the press, accumulation of political credits to be cashed in at some future date, and consolidation of interest group support, the offices of the speaker and lieutenant governor can serve as stepping-stones for both advancement in politics and future economic comfort. Because interest group support, campaign finances, and the support of established politicians are all necessary, the presiding officers must play their political cards right if they want to build an economic and political base solid enough to attain future political or economic success. The presiding officers must not, therefore, antagonize powerful economic and political forces in the process. Consequently, political and economic ambition can serve as a very real restraint on their independence.

Other Legislators

Many committee chairs and other legislators exercise a great deal of influence in their own right through their mastery of the intricacies of legislative rules and procedures, strong support of powerful interest groups, and the respect or fear they can generate in other legislators.

Because of the ties that these individuals have built over the years with administrators, interest groups, and other legislators, the presiding officers may need to solicit their support on key legislation. Generally, however, these individuals are the exception in an environment heavily influenced by the lieutenant governor or speaker.

Our Texas Insiders feature explains how interest groups can influence legislators' decision-making.

Texas **INSIDERS**

The Revolving Door: Legislators Becoming Lobbyists

As we pointed out in Chapter 6, it is not unusual for former legislators to become lobbyists—a practice referred to as the revolving door. In recent years, former representatives Michael Krusee and Fred Hill and former senators Kyle Janek and Kipp Averitt have reported at least $300,000 in lobby contracts to the Texas Ethics Commission. At least 65 former legislators have filed as lobbyists in 2010. Low legislative salaries may very well explain why legislators might

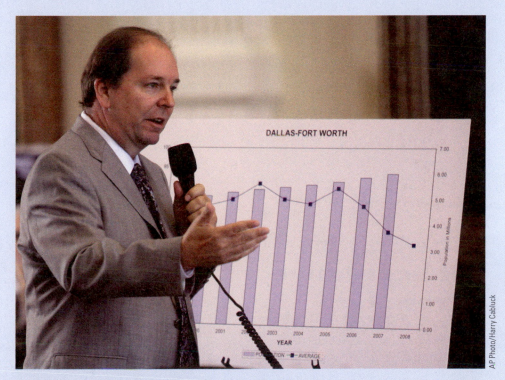

Less than a week after winning the Republican nomination for another term in the Texas Senate, Kipp Averitt resigned his Senate seat and became a lobbyist representing health care, natural gas, and bingo interests. By 2011, he had landed more than $345,000 in lobby contracts.

Why might legislators prefer an occupation as a lobbyist to that of legislator? Why might special interests seek out former legislators to become their lobbyists?

(continued)

retire and seek more lucrative occupations such as lobbying.

Meanwhile, interest groups might find it to their advantage to recruit lobbyists who have previously served in the legislature—former legislators have made contacts while serving in the legislature and know how legislators decide on public policy. Former legislators have been schooled in the legislature's procedures and know where its levers of power are located. For example, a dozen local governments and local government advocacy groups may have considered his legislative contacts when they hired former representative Fred Hill as their lobbyist in 2009—he had been chair of the House Local Government Ways and Means Committee.

Numerous other examples show interest groups seeking out former legislators to be their lobbyists. AT&T had at least five former legislators on its payroll when it lobbied for legislation to require the state to pay for relocation of communications lines to make way for road construction projects. Tobacco giant Reynolds American, Inc. had seven former lawmakers on its payroll as it fought tobacco-control measures, including a statewide ban on smoking in public.

Thinking about the role of elites in Texas politics Critics of revolving-door practices argue that current legislators are overly receptive to the lobbying of their former colleagues and that legislators may give certain interest groups favorable treatment in hopes of winning lobbying contracts from them after they retire from the legislature. Should Texas, like many states and the federal government, ban former legislators from lobbying for a specified time after they leave office? Would such a ban limit freedom of expression guaranteed by the Constitution?

Sources: "More Lawmakers Hit Lobby: Democrats work for Food," *Lobby Watch*, April 7, 2011, http://info.tpj.org/Lobby_Watch/pdf/Revolvers2011.pdf; Ross Ramsey, Legislature Is a Training Ground for Lobbyists," *Texas Tribune*, June 10, 2010; "Ten New Lawmaker Retreads Merge Into the 2009 Lobby," *Lobby Watch*, May 20, 2009, at http://info.tpj.org/Lobby_Watch/05-20-09_revolvers.html; "Tobacco Firms' 40 Lobbyists Put Popular Legislature Proposals At Risk," *Dallas Morning News*, May 11, 2009.

The Politics of Legislative Procedure

John David Rausch, Jr.
Teel Bivins Professor of Political Science, West Texas A&M University

INTRODUCTION

Many citizens fail to understand that the intricacies of legislative procedure have a direct impact on the kinds of policies that have a chance to become law. Like the filibuster in the U.S. Senate, the two-thirds rule in the Texas Senate protects the minority against abuse by an overbearing majority, but it also allows the minority to thwart the will of the majority with uncompromising obstructionism. Balancing minority rights and majority rule is a difficult problem in a representative democracy.

The Texas legislature experienced something of a role reversal during the opening days of the 81st Legislature in January 2009. Usually, legislative watchers expect to see raucous partisan debate over the rules in the house of representatives. This time it was partisan division in the Texas Senate that was on display. The *Austin American-Statesman* described the senate as "an upper chamber long known for its decorum and reluctance to publicly air its dirty laundry." To start the new legislative session, the paper opened with an article describing the debate over the rules as "a dramatic display of partisan bloodletting."[1] The *Dallas Morning News* reported, "The usually harmonious Senate began its year with discord."[2] The cause of the discord was the senate's two-thirds rule and the way Republicans in the senate wanted to alter the rule to allow for a vote on proposals to advance voter identification legislation.

The rule is officially known as the two-thirds rule and it is unique among the legislative procedures used by state legislatures in the United States. I will consider below the various other names applied to the rule such as the "blocker" bill and the "Rosebush" bill. Most properly, it is the two-thirds rule. Under the rules of the Texas Senate, "senators are required to take up bills and resolutions for debate according to the 'regular order or business.'" The regular order of business in the Texas Senate is governed by Rules 5.09 through 5.12. "Bills and resolutions shall be considered on second reading and shall be listed on the Daily Calendar and Resolutions on the President's table in the order in which the committee report was received by the Secretary of the Senate."[3] Bills and resolutions on third reading are considered in the order in which they received the second reading. Rule 5.13 establishes a procedure for getting around the regular order of business requirement: "A bill, joint resolution, or resolution affecting a state policy may be considered out of its regular calendar order if two-thirds of the members present vote to suspend the regular order of business."[4] The two-thirds rule has been a part of legislative procedure in the Texas Senate since the 1870s.

A little clarification is in order. One term often used in a discussion of the politics of the two-thirds rule is the "blocker bill" or "blocking bill." A "blocker bill" is that piece of legislation that is reported out of committee first to require suspension of the rules. Usually, this piece of legislation is a minor bill. In the 81st Legislature, the blocker bills were SB 621, relating to the creation, purpose, implementation, and funding of the County Park Beautification and Improvement Program, and SJR 19, authorizing the state to accept gifts of historical value. Both measures died in the senate. Sometimes one reads about the Rosebush bill, specifically in Republican opinion pieces critical of the practice.[5] I have not been able to identify the origin of the "Rosebush" bill.

This two-thirds rule seems to violate the idea of majority rule because 11 senators working together can defeat any piece of legislation by blocking the bill from reaching the senate calendar. Writing in the *Temple Daily Telegram* in January 1956, reporter Stuart Long documented the history of the two-thirds rule and how procedures developed to use the rule to defeat legislation. Following the rules, each morning the calendar clerk prepared the list of bills to be considered that day in the order specified by the rules. However, near the middle of the twentieth century, senate leadership changed the procedure, making the calendar meaningless. Long writes, "For, in the last eight years, there has been a gradual abandonment of the use of the calendar, as called for in the rules. The abandonment became complete in the 1951 session."[6]

Instead of following the calendar, all important bills are brought up for consideration by a "motion to suspend the regular order in order to take up Senate Bill xxx." The motion requires a two-thirds majority of the senators present to carry, in legislative parlance. Because the senate has 31 members, 11 senators can vote "no" on the motion to suspend the rules, and, therefore, prevent a bill from being considered on the floor.[7]

According to Long's research, the lieutenant governor determined the order of business, a practice in effect today. The lieutenant governor chooses to recognize a senator to make a motion to suspend the rules. If the motion is successful, then that senator is allowed to "run" with his or her bill. If the motion is defeated because it did not have the support of 21 senators, then that senator must wait for another opportunity to bring up his or her legislation. The practice began gradually while Governor Allan Shivers was lieutenant governor (1947–1949) and expanded under the leadership of Lieutenant Governor Ben Ramsey (1951–1963; the post was vacant from 1949 to 1951).[8]

Commentators and senators have decried the practice as undemocratic because it places significant power in the hands of the lieutenant governor, acting as president of the senate. If a senator is not on the lieutenant governor's favored list, the senator could find that he or she is not recognized to make a motion to suspend. A small minority working together could prevent important legislation from being enacted by banding together and voting not to accept the motion to suspend the rules. In 1956, Senator A. M. Aiken Jr., Democrat of Paris, announced that he was running for lieutenant governor, telling his senate colleagues that he would return to using the senate calendar if elected.[9]

Why did the two-thirds rule spur such heated partisan conflict in the Texas Senate at the beginning of the 81st Legislature? It would appear as though many senators would

---

[1] Mike Ward, "Texas Senate Adopts Rules Change to Allow Voter ID Vote," *Austin American-Statesmen*, January 15, 2009.

[2] Terrence Stutz, "Texas Senate at Odds over Voter ID Legislation, Two-Thirds Rule," *Dallas Morning News*, January 14, 2009.

[3] Legislative Reference Library, "The Two-Thirds Rule," www.lrl.state.tx.us/citizenResources/twoThirds.html.

[4] Legislative Reference Library.

[5] Jared Woodfill, "Time to Kill the Blocker Bill," *Harris County Republican Party Online Newsletter,* January 10, 2009, www.harriscountygop.com/eblast/eb011009.asp.

[6] Stuart Long, "With 11 Senators for You, Kill Any Bill You Want To," *Temple Daily Telegram*, January 21, 1956.

[7] Ibid.

[8] Ibid.

[9] Ibid.

find the procedural tradition hurts their ability to represent their constituents, especially if they are not part of the lieutenant governor's team. The Legislative Reference Library offers the following justification for maintaining the tradition: "Among other things, it is generally acknowledged that the senate's two-thirds rule fosters civility, a willingness to compromise, and a spirit of bipartisanship."[10]

The Republican Party of Texas wants the senate to end the use of the blocker rule. The party's 2008 platform clearly states, "Rosebush–Blocker Rule—We oppose the Rosebush–Blocker Rule in the Texas Senate."[11] Many Republicans argue that conservative legislation has to be watered down in order to pass a bill. Opponents of the blocker bill point out that legislation important to conservatives in Texas was killed by the blocker bill. These bills include a Voter Photo ID Bill in 2007 and a 2003 bill calling for a reduction in the property tax appraisal cap. Senator Dan Patrick, a Republican from Houston, emphasizes the elimination of the blocker bill in his campaign materials and public speeches. If the senate must maintain a super-majority requirement, Senator Patrick would prefer a three-fifths majority, or at least 19 senators.[12] In 2009, 19 Republicans were serving in the Texas Senate.

Not all Texas Republicans agree that the two-thirds rule has outlived its usefulness. Senator Robert Duncan, a Republican from Lubbock, argued in January 2009, "The conservative position should be to protect the two-thirds rule." The rule prevents "bad legislation and too much government in the state of Texas." "Only in very rare and specific situations, such as voter identification laws that are being prevented from passing based on pure partisan grounds, should we consider exceptions to the two-thirds rule."[13]

Texas Republican Party Chair Cathie Adams also spoke out in support of the theory behind the two-thirds rule. She did not want to see the two-thirds rule abolished completely for all senate issues. Getting rid of the two-thirds rule might make it easier to enact pro-gambling measures, for example.[14]

The partisan rancor that marked the start of the Texas Senate's regular session in January 2009 was settled by a rules change. The change provided that an exemption from the two-thirds rule be allowed for the voter ID legislation. The passage of this bill would require that voters present photo identification before voting at a polling place. Democratic senators argued that other important pieces of legislation also be exempted from the rule. Senator Kirk Watson, a Democrat from Austin, wanted to include children's health care, affordable college tuition, relief from rising utility costs and insurance bills, environmental protection, and job creation, on the list of bills exempt from the two-thirds rule. According to Watson, the only bills worthy of being in the special class of exempt legislation were "the most political, partisan bills that protect the powerful."[15] None of Watson's proposed bills were exempted.

The rule change, with the exemption, was adopted by a vote of 18 to 13. Senator John Carona, a Republican from Dallas, was the only Republican to vote against the change.

JOIN THE DEBATE

1. Should the two-thirds rule be abolished? Is the rule a useful tradition or an obstacle that can kill legislation important to all Texans? Should it be replaced with a lower threshold for having legislation considered and voted on in the senate? If so, what should that lower threshold be?

2. Does the two-thirds rule grant too much power to a political minority?

3. Is Senator Watson correct in arguing that the senate's list of bills worthy of exempting from the two-thirds rule do not include those that would help the greatest number of Texans?

4. Does the two-thirds rule work?

[10]Legislative Reference Library, www.lrl.state.tx.us/citizenResources/twoThirds.html.

[11]Woodfill, "Time to Kill the Blocker Bill."

[12]Stutz, "Texas Senate at Odds over Voter ID Legislation, Two-Thirds Rule."

[13]Senator Robert Duncan, "Rare Amendment to the Senate's Two-Thirds Rule," January 22, 2009, www.duncan.senate.state.tx.us/pdf/012209.Duncan.pdf.

[14]Ward, "Texas Senate Adopts Rules Change to Allow Voter ID Vote."

[15] Kirk Watson, "Watson Wire: Two-Thirds of a Wrong Isn't Right," January 19, 2009, www.kirkwatson.com/watson-wire/two-thirds-of-a-wrong-isnt-right.

CHAPTER SUMMARY

★ To reach the floor of the house, a bill must also be placed on a calendar by one of the two calendar committees. These committees are firmly under the control of the speaker. A bill that does not receive a calendar assignment is probably out of the running.

★ The senate calendar is an artificial device. The first item on the calendar is a "blocking bill," which is never brought to the floor. Actually bringing a bill other than the "blocking bill" to the floor requires a vote by two-thirds of the senators to "suspend the rule" and vote on the bill out of its calendar order. Given that two-thirds of the senate must vote in the affirmative even to bring a measure to the floor, most bills that reach the floor are approved.

★ To become an act of the legislature, a bill must pass both chambers with identical language. To iron out any differences, bills are sent to a conference committee, a special

joint committee with members from both chambers. The presiding officers appoint these committees. Once a conference committee report is accepted by both chambers, the bill is sent to the governor.

★ The governor can sign or refuse to sign a bill (in which circumstance it eventually becomes law without the governor's signature). The governor can also veto a bill. If the bill contains an appropriations clause, the governor can strike it out with an item veto. In theory, the legislature could override a veto, but by the time the veto is issued, the legislature is usually no longer in session.

★ The institutional powers of the presiding officers include control over legislative boards and commissions that manage the budgeting function of state government (the Legislative Budget Board), the auditing function (the Legislative Audit Committee), and policy research (the Legislative Council).

HOW TEXAS COMPARES

★ As the Texas legislature has balanced the state budget, it has asked state employees to share the sacrifice by contributing a larger share of their family health insurance premiums than 44 other states.

★ In the 2011 effort to balance the state budget, the state legislature cut funding to women's health clinics. Critics of this new policy pointed to Texas's rank as the third-highest for

teen pregnancy rates. The state also ranks among the highest for rates of sexually transmitted diseases like chlamydia and HIV. Texas also ranks toward the top in rates of diabetes and cardiovascular disease among women.

KEY TERMS

blocking bill, *p. 205*
bureaucratic oversight, *p. 204*
calendar, *p. 204*
chubbing, *p. 206*
cloture, *p. 208*
committee of the whole, *p. 210*
conference committee, *p. 208*
conference committee report, *p. 208*

discharge process, *p. 204*
filibuster, *p. 207*
floor action, *p. 205*
floor leaders, *p. 206*
Legislative Audit Committee, *p. 213*
Legislative Budget Board (LBB), *p. 211*
Legislative Council, *p. 213*

little legislatures, *p. 203*
mark up, *p. 203*
pigeonhole, *p. 203*
point of order, *p. 206*
quorum, *p. 205*
recorded votes, *p. 207*
Sunset Advisory Commission, *p. 214*

suspension of the rule, *p. 205*
tagging, *p. 204*
voice vote, *p. 207*

REVIEW QUESTIONS

1. Describe the procedural tools of leadership. Explain why each increases the powers of the presiding officers.

2. Describe the institutional tools of leadership. Explain why each increases the powers of the presiding officers.

3. Describe the process for a bill to become a law.

4. List the restraints on the powers of the presiding officers.

LOGGING ON

A complete summary of the legislative process in Texas is available at **www.tlc.state.tx.us/gtli/legproc/process.html**.

You can research legislation pending before the legislature. Go to the legislature online at **www.capitol.state.tx.us/**. Enter what you are searching for in "Search Legislation."

More information about the Legislative Budget Board can be found at **www.lbb.state.tx.us/**, on the Legislative Council at www.tlc.state.tx.us/, on the State Auditor's Office at **www.sao.state.tx.us**, and on the Sunset Advisory Commission at **www.sunset.state.tx.us/**.

The Texas State Library is a source for legislative, administrative, and judicial research as well as general information about many political, economic, and social aspects of Texas. The library can be accessed at **www.tsl.state.tx.us/**.

The Legislative Reference Library is another source of information about the Texas legislature. The address is **www.lrl.state.tx.us/**.

Sources of political information, issues, and information about campaign contributions that student researchers may find interesting include **www.followthemoney.org/**, **www.opensecrets.org/**, and **www.speakout.com/**.

The Texas Public Policy Foundation is a prominent and influential conservative think tank that plays an important part in issue initiative and policy formulation, especially now that Republicans control all branches of state government. Go to **www.texaspolicy.com/**.

Texans for Public Justice is a nonpartisan, nonprofit policy and research organization that tracks the influence of money in politics: **www.tpj.org/**.

Tree huggers is a cornucopia of websites for liberal, environmental, consumer, and other issues: **www.afn.org/~afn49740/**.

The Texas Hispanic Research Council at www.tshrc.org/ is a good source for several links on state and national government as well as for legislative information. This site also has other resource and organizational links relating to civil rights and civil liberties.

News information from any state newspaper can be found through **www.refdesk.com/paper.html**. The *Dallas Morning News* at **www.dallasnews.com/** and the *Houston Chronicle* at **www.chron.com/** are two excellent sources for state political news.

Chapter 9

The Governor

LEARNING OBJECTIVES

★ Discuss the reasons for decentralization in Texas's administration.

★ List and describe the informal requirements for the Texas governor.

★ Describe the process, other than election, for removing a Texas governor from office, including the order of succession.

★ List the governor's formal and informal legislative tools of persuasion.

★ Describe the item veto and its purpose.

★ Describe the importance of bargaining to the governor and the powers the governor brings to the bargaining table as well as some of his limitations.

★ Explain why appointments are one of the most important administrative powers of the governor.

★ Describe the governor's administrative tools for persuasion, and explain how they are weaker than other governors' and the president's.

★ Explain the chief of state function and how it is important for the governor's political influence.

GET *Active*

★ Follow the conservative view of Governor Perry at the *Texas Insider* at **www .texasinsider.org/** and compare it with the liberal view of him at the *Burnt Orange Report* at **www.burntorangereport.com/**. See the governor's official views at **www .governor.state.tx.us/**.

★ Trace the links among Governor Perry, lobbyists, campaign contributors, and the governor's appointments to office with Texans for Public Justice at **www.tpj.org/**.

★ Investigate who contributed to Rick Perry's campaigns for governor and what special interests they represent at the National Institute on Money in State Politics at **www.followthemoney.org/**.

★ Probe the influence of the Texas Public Policy Foundation on the governor's policies on higher education at **www .texaspolicy.com**, and search for other links between this think tank and the governor's policies.

★ Learn about the governor's major public policy initiatives. Choose the initiatives that interest you, research them, and express your opinion to the governor concerning your support or opposition. Suggest policy issues for future gubernatorial consideration, explaining why you think they deserve to be public policy. Contact the governor's office at **www.governor .state.tx.us** or Governor Rick Perry, P.O. Box 12428, Austin, TX 78711; phone: (512) 463-2000; fax: (512) 463-1849. The governor's website is located at **www.governor.state .tx.us.**

*A*lthough the Texas Constitution designates the governor as chief executive, the executive branch is splintered into various offices and agencies that are often beyond the governor's effective control. The division of Texas executive power is largely based on the Jacksonian democratic theory that most major officeholders should be elected. The current Texas Constitution further weakened the power of the Texas governor because it was written in the wake of an experiment in centralized administrative power during the Reconstruction administration of Governor E. J. Davis.

The legislature has recently strengthened the governor's administrative influence over several agencies, but the continued preference for decentralized government by powerful special interest groups, bureaucrats, the legislative leadership, and the general public ensures the continuation of the weak governor administrative structure for Texas. As a result, Texas government has evolved into a hodge-podge of administratively independent entities, with no single official formally responsible for either policy initiation or implementation.

The lack of administrative authority does not mean the governor's office lacks the potential for meaningful political power. The governor's legislative powers, media access, party influence, and appointive powers to boards,

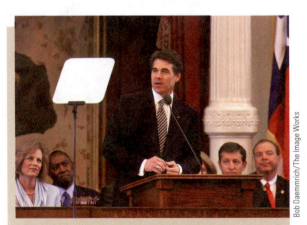

Bob Daemmrich/The Image Works

Governor Perry delivers the State of the State address to the Texas Legislature.

What purposes do such high-profile official duties serve for the governor?

commissions, and the judiciary provide enough political muscle for an astute, savvy officeholder to exert significant influence on both legislative and administrative policy.

Long tenure, solid interest group support, and the willingness to penalize opponents are also important factors in a governor's influence. A long-serving governor with the support of powerful interest groups can wield a dominant influence over the enactment and implementation of public policy. Such a governor will have appointed most members of administrative boards and commissions, convinced legislators that he or she will punish errant behavior, and have his or her authority backed by the political and financial muscle of special interests.

QUALIFICATIONS, TENURE, AND STAFF

To become governor, a candidate must meet formal or legal qualifications as well as informal qualifications that are imposed by the state's political culture.

Formal Qualifications

As is usual with elective offices, the legal requirements for becoming governor are minimal: One must be 30 years of age, an American citizen, and a citizen of Texas for five years before running for election.

Informal Criteria

Whereas the formal qualifications for governor are easily met, the informal criteria are more restrictive.

WASP Since the Texas Revolution, governors have all been WASPs (i.e., white Anglo-Saxon Protestants). They have been white Protestants, usually Methodist or Baptist, and also Anglo American, with family names originating in the British Isles.

Gender The governor is historically male. The only female governor of Texas before Ann Richards (1991–1995) was Miriam A. Ferguson, who served for two nonconsecutive terms (1925–1927 and 1933–1935). She ran on the slogan "Two Governors for the Price of One" and did not really represent a deviation from male dominance in Texas politics, for it was clear that her husband, former governor James E. Ferguson, exercised the power of the office. In reality, Governor Richards was the first woman to serve as the governing Texas chief executive.

Elected state treasurer in 1982, Ann Richards was the first woman to win a statewide election in Texas since Governor Miriam "Ma" Ferguson. Richards won the governor's office in 1990 after hard-fought and bitter primaries and general election contests, disproving the assumption that Texans will not support an assertive politician who also happens to be a woman. Richards was also an exception to several other informal criteria for becoming Texas's governor. She was moderate-to-liberal politically, a single divorcee, and a recovering alcoholic.

Middle-Aged Businessperson or Attorney The typical governor will usually be successful in business or law; in fact, more than one-half of the governors who have served since 1900 have been lawyers. The governor will probably be between 40 and 60 years of age, have a record of elective public service in state government or some other source of name recognition, and be a participant in service, social, and occupational organizations.

Conservative Republican Texas was a two-party state for top-of-the-ticket elections for president, U.S. senator, and governor for more than two decades but was basically Democratic for most other offices. It became an authentic two-party state with the 1990 election of two Republicans to the down-ticket offices of state treasurer and commissioner of agriculture.

However, Texas had effective two-party politics for only a few years before it completed its evolution into a strong Republican one-party state. Republicans first swept statewide offices in 1998, electing the governor, lieutenant governor, and all elected down-ticket administrators, including the Texas Railroad Commission. The down-ticket Republican victories have additional political significance.

Statewide elective offices provide political experience and name recognition that can serve as a springboard to higher office. In 1998, Rick Perry moved from Commissioner of Agriculture to lieutenant governor, and in 2002, he was elected governor. That same year, Attorney General John Cornyn was elected to the U.S. Senate.

The Democratic gubernatorial primary is usually a match between pro-business moderate and more liberal candidates. The Democratic nominee must forge a slippery coalition of business leaders, ethnic minorities, unions, intellectuals, teachers, conservationists, and consumer advocates, but even then, a Democratic candidate has little chance of prevailing in the general election because Texas has become reliably Republican in statewide elections.

The Republican primary is a joust between conservative-to-moderate candidates, with the more conservative candidate usually being the winner. Republican gubernatorial candidates usually have the campaign funds to outspend their Democratic opponents, thereby purchasing the all-important political image and name recognition and being able to identify and define the issues of the campaign.

Money Money is a critical factor in any serious campaign for Texas governor. Although the candidate who spends the most does not always win the office, a hefty bankroll is necessary for serious consideration. Challengers will usually spend more than incumbents to buy name recognition. Paul Taylor, executive director of the Alliance for Better Campaigns, commented that "the legacy is a political culture in which we auction off the right to free speech 30 seconds at a time to the highest political bidder."[1]

Tenure, Removal, and Succession

As in 47 other states, Texas governors serve a four-year term. Unlike most states, however, there is no limit on the number of terms that a governor may serve, and as Governor Perry has demonstrated, unlimited terms can become one of the governor's greatest sources of power to overwhelm the normal legal checks on the power of the office. If the governor can get reelected to several terms, long tenure in office gives the governor the power to appoint members to every state board, to establish working relationships with powerful lobbyists and campaign contributors, and to win powerful allies in the legislature.

Impeachment

Officially charging an office holder with improper conduct in office.

The governor may be removed from office only by **impeachment** by the house of representatives and conviction by the senate. Impeachment is the legislative equivalent of indictment and requires only a simple majority of members present. Conviction by the senate requires a two-thirds majority. If the office is vacated, the lieutenant governor becomes governor; the next in the line of succession is the president pro tempore of the senate.

---

[1]Colleen McCain Nelson, *The Dallas Morning News*, November 7, 2002.

If the governor is removed or vacates the office, the lieutenant governor becomes governor for the remainder of the elected term. The Texas Senate then elects a senator as acting lieutenant governor, who serves in both positions until the next general election.

Compensation

The governor's salary is set by the legislature. At present, it is $150,000 yearly and stands in marked contrast to the low salaries paid to legislators. Although the governor's salary is among the highest in the nation, several other Texas state officials earn more.

In addition to the governor's mansion, an expense account is necessary to keep it maintained and staffed. The governor also has a professional staff and security detail with offices in the capitol or mansion. An adequate staff is important because the modern chief executive depends heavily on staff to carry out the duties of office.

Staff

The governor's greater involvement in legislative affairs and appointments and increasing demands on government by the general public have placed intensified pressure on the time and resources of the executive. The Texas governor, like all executives in modern government, depends on others for advice, information, and assistance before making decisions and recommendations. A good staff is a key ingredient for a successful chief executive.

Among the most important concerns of the governor's staff are political appointments. Each year, the governor makes several hundred appointments to various boards, commissions, and executive agencies. The executive also fills newly created judicial offices and those vacated because of death or resignation. Staff evaluation of potential appointees is necessary because the governor may not personally know many of the individuals under consideration.

Legislative assistants provide liaison between the office of the governor and the legislature. Their job is to stay in contact with key legislators, committee chairs, and the legislative leadership. These assistants are, in practice, the governor's lobbyists. They keep legislators informed and attempt to persuade them to support the governor's position on legislation. Often the success of the governor's legislative program rests on the staff's abilities and political expertise.

Some administrative assistants head executive offices that compile and write budget recommendations and manage and coordinate activities within the governor's office. Staff members also exercise administrative control over the governor's schedule of ceremonial and official duties.

The governor is the official planning officer for the state, although coordination and participation by affected state agencies is voluntary. The planning divisions also help coordinate local and regional planning between the councils of governments in an effort to bring the work of these jurisdictions into harmony with state goals. In addition, national and state funds are available through the governor's office to local units of government for comprehensive planning (master planning).

AP Images/Harry Cabluck

The governor congratulates the president of Zachry Construction on winning the contract for a major highway privatization construction project. Federal and state highway administrators and the chairman of the Group Ferrovial also participate. Public policy formulation is often a group project including the governor, bureaucrats, and special interest groups.

How do politicians, bureaucrats, and special interests mutually benefit politically and economically from government contracts? Should public services like highways be provided by for-profit corporations?

The Texas governor's office ranks below the average of other state governors in authority to actually see that the laws are administered. In fact, the Texas governor's combined administrative and legislative power ranking is 34th among the 50 states. By comparison, Utah's governor ranks 1st and Vermont's ranks 50th.

Using a 1- to 5-point scale with 5 having the greatest power in a 2007 study, Thad Beyle ranked the various institutional powers of U.S. governors on several important categories. With a Governor's Institutional Powers (GIP) rating of 3.2, the Texas governor ranked above only 10 other state governors and slightly below the GIP average of 3.5. Beyle also ranked the governors on personal power, awarding Texas's governor a Governor Personal Power (GPP) index ranking of 3.8, above the governors in 12 other states but slightly below the GPP index average of 3.9. Both the Congressional Quarterly and Beyle ranked the powers of the Texas governorship as slightly below average but above the even lower rankings often associated with the Texas governor's office.

FOR DEBATE

1. How can Texas's governor use personal political power to overcome the formal legal and institutional limits on the office? From your reading in this chapter, identify ways that the executive branch could be restructured to give the governor more institutional power.

2. Would Texas benefit from having a stronger governor? Why? Why not?

Sources: Kendra A. Hovey and Harold A. Hovey, *CQ's State Fact Finder 2003: Rankings across America* (Washington, DC: CQ Press/Congressional Quarterly, 2003), p. 406; Thad Beyle, *The Institutional Power Ratings for the 50 Governors of the United States*, University of North Carolina at Chapel Hill, 2007, http://www.unc.edu/~beyle/gubnewpwr.html

The governor's staff, although primarily responsible for assisting with the everyday duties of the office, also attempt to persuade legislators, administrators, and the representatives of various local governments to follow the governor's leadership in solving common problems.

TOOLS OF PERSUASION

The governor's ability to influence the making and executing of government policy depends on his or her bargaining skills, persuasiveness, and ability to broker effectively between competing interests—the tools of persuasion. Thus the **informal, or extralegal, powers** of the office are as important as its formal or legal powers (those granted by the constitution or by law). The governor's ability to use informal power is largely determined by the extent of the **formal, or legal, powers**. Compared to governors of other states (especially other populous, industrialized states), the governor of Texas has weak formal administrative powers. However, some Texas governors have been able to exert substantial influence on policy formulation and even on policy execution when the formal and informal powers are enhanced by a fortunate blending of other conditions such as a strong personality, political expertise, prestige, a knack for public relations and political drama, good relations with the press, supporters with political and economic strength, a favorable political climate, and simple good luck.

Informal (extralegal) powers

Powers that are not stated in rules, a law, or a constitution but are usually derived from these legal powers.

Formal (legal) powers

Powers stated in rules, a law, or a constitution.

Legislative Tools of Persuasion

Ironically, the most influential bargaining tools that the Texas governor has are legislative. How these tools are used largely determines the governor's effectiveness.

The Veto One of the governor's most powerful formal legislative tools is the veto. After a bill has passed both houses of the legislature in identical form, it is sent to the governor. If signed, the bill becomes law; if vetoed, the bill is sent back to the legislature with a message stating the reasons for opposition. The legislature has the constitutional power to override the governor's **veto** by a two-thirds vote, but in practice vetoes are usually final.

Because legislative sessions in Texas are short, the vast majority of important bills are passed and sent to the governor in the final days of the session. The governor need take no action on the legislation for 10 days when the legislature is in session (20 days when it is not in session), so he can often wait until the legislature has adjourned and thereby ensure that a veto will not be overridden. In fact, it is so difficult to override a veto that it has happened only once since World War II. Thus the veto gives the Texas governor a strong bargaining position with legislators.

The Texas governor, however, lacks the pocket veto that is available to many other chief executives, including the president of the United States. The pocket veto provides that if the executive chooses to ignore legislation passed at the end of a session, it dies without ever taking effect. By contrast, if the Texas governor neither signs nor vetoes a bill, it becomes law. By not signing a bill and allowing it to become law, the governor may register a protest against the bill or some of its provisions.

The Item Veto The most important single piece of legislation enacted in a legislative session is the appropriations bill. If it should be vetoed in its entirety, funds for the operation of the government would be cut off, and a special session would be necessary. Thus Texas, like most other states, permits the governor an item veto, which allows the governor to veto funds for specific items or projects without killing the entire bill.

If used to its fullest potential, the item veto is a very effective negative legislative tool. Money is necessary to administer laws; therefore, by vetoing an item or a category of items, the governor can, in effect, kill programs or whole classes of programs. The governor cannot, however, reduce the appropriation for a budgetary item, as some governors may. Because the appropriations bill is usually passed at the end of the session, the item veto is virtually absolute.

Threat of Veto An informal legislative power of the governor not mentioned in the constitution or the law is the **threat of veto**. Nevertheless, it is a very real and effective tool for the governor, but like all informal power, its effectiveness depends on existing formal powers.

Both the veto and the item veto are negative tools that simply kill bills or programs; they do not let the governor shape legislation. However, by threatening to use these formal powers, the governor can often persuade the legislative supporters of a bill to change its content or face the probability of a veto. In this way, a compromise can often be negotiated. Although the veto itself is negative, the threat of veto can be used to positively affect the content of bills during the legislative process.

Veto
The executive power to reject a proposed law unless an unusual majority of the legislature (usually two-thirds) votes to override the governor's opposition. This is almost an absolute power in Texas because the legislature is seldom in session when the governor issues the veto.

Did You Know? Governor Perry has vetoed 307 bills—far more than any other single governor. He vetoed 78 bills in one day that resentful legislators dubbed the "Father's Day Massacre."

Threat of veto
An informal power of the Texas governor. Threatening in advance to veto legislation enhances the governor's bargaining power with legislators, enabling the governor to shape the content of legislation while it is still in the legislature.

Bob Daemmerich/Photo Edit

Governor Rick Perry signs a bill authorizing the creation of the Tejano Monument on the south lawn of the Texas Capitol to honor the contributions of people of Latino heritage.

What human need do monuments fulfill? What political purpose do they serve?

The governor can also use this powerful informal tool of persuasion to influence bureaucrats. Bureaucrats are very active in the legislative process, often seeking increased funding for favorite programs and projects or seeking authorization to administer new programs. Because of this, the governor may be able to influence the administration of existing programs by threatening to withhold funds or veto bills actively supported by an agency. The agency's legislative liaison personnel (its lobbyists) may also be encouraged to support the governor's legislative program in exchange for support (or neutrality) with respect to agency-supported bills.

HOW DOES TEXAS COMPARE
The Politics of the Item Veto

Forty-three governors have the item veto (or line-item veto), and some reformers have long advocated that the U.S. president should also be given this tool as a way to reduce federal budget deficits and help eliminate "earmarks" or "pork barrel"— wasteful special spending projects included in spending bills at the request of individual members of Congress to benefit a few of their constituents or campaign supporters.

However, at the state level, there is little evidence that chief executives have the political courage to use the tool to confront special interests, nor has it been an effective tool for responsible fiscal management. State legislatures have avoided the threat of the item veto by simply passing broad categories of spending that include funding for essential services that the governor is unwilling to veto. States with governors who have the item veto have about the same level of per-capita state spending as those without. In 2011, Texas Governor Rick Perry used the item veto only to kill funding for legislative proposals that had not become law during the session. In other words, Perry used the item veto as a housekeeping operation to cut spending that did not fund any existing program.

Although there is little evidence that the item veto is an effective tool for financial discipline, governors can use the item veto as a bargaining chip with legislators. For example, in 2005, when Texas Governor Perry item-vetoed the entire $35.3 billion appropriation for the Texas Education Agency (one-fourth of state spending), he put pressure on the state legislature to pass his own version of educational spending in a 30-day special session. This action forced the legislature to act because without a compromise between the governor and the legislature, Texas public schools would have closed.

FOR DEBATE

1. Should the U.S. Constitution be amended to give presidents the line item veto? Why? Why not?

The threat of veto can also be used to consolidate lobby support for the governor's legislative proposals. Lobbyists may offer to support the governor's position on legislation if the governor will agree not to veto a particular bill that is considered vital to the interests of their employers. The governor can thus bargain with both supporters and opponents of legislation in order to gain political allies.

Bargaining The governor's bargaining with legislators, lobbyists, and administrators is often intense as other political forces attempt to gain gubernatorial neutrality, support, or opposition for legislation. If the governor or political and financial supporters have not made particular legislation an explicit part of their legislative program, avenues are left open for political bartering to gain hard political support for the governor's legislative program or equally firm resistance to proposals that the governor opposes. Whoever seeks the governor's support must be willing to give something of real political value in return. All sides of the negotiation want to gain as much as possible and give as little as possible. There is, of course, a vast difference in political resources among politicians, just as among interest groups.

The flexibility and intensity that the governor brings to the bargaining table depend on several very real political factors:

1. The depth of the governor's commitment to the bill is a factor. If the governor is committed to a position, because of either a political debt or ideological belief, this support or opposition may not be open to negotiation.
2. Timing is also important. Politicians often try to be the ones to tip the scales for the winning side.
3. The political and financial support given the governor during a campaign may determine his or her flexibility. This does not mean that all campaign contributions buy political decisions, but they do increase the chances that contributors will get a favorable hearing.
4. Future campaign support is another major factor. Bargaining may involve financial or political support for the reelection or advancement of an ambitious politician.
5. Who supports and who opposes the bill? For political reasons, the governor may not want to align with a political group that is unpopular with either financial supporters or the general electorate—for example, advocates for the legalization of marijuana or a graduated state income tax.
6. The amount of firm legislative support for or opposition to the proposal is important. Even if the chief executive is inclined to a particular position, backing a losing cause could mean a loss of prestige.
7. The political benefits to be gained must be carefully considered. Some groups may be more willing or more able than others to pay a high price for the governor's support. Thus, an important consideration is the relative strength of the supporters and the opponents of a bill and their ability to pay their political and financial debts. For example, because medical patients in Texas have no organization and few political allies, their interests are not as well represented as those of the Texas Medical Association, health maintenance organizations, or insurance companies, which have strong organizations and ample political and financial resources.
8. Some governors may be hesitant to alienate interests that could provide post-gubernatorial economic opportunities or political assistance. Other governors may have extensive investments and are unlikely as governor to make political decisions that could mean personal financial loss.

Presession Bargaining If, before the legislative session begins, the governor, the legislative leadership, concerned administrators, and special interest groups can arrive at successful bargains and compromises, through **presession bargaining**, the prospect for passage of a proposal is greatly enhanced.

Presession bargaining seeks compromises, but harmonious relationships seldom develop immediately. Powerful and often competing political forces may continue bargaining throughout the legislative session. Failure to reach an amicable settlement usually means either defeat of a bill in the legislature or a veto by the governor.

Presession bargaining

Negotiations that let the governor and the legislative leaders reach the necessary compromises prior to the start of the legislative session. This usually ensures passage of the legislation.

Texas INSIDERS

Mike Toomey: The Governor's Friend and Ally or Crass Influence Peddler?

Shown here with his close friend and ally Rick Perry in 2003, Mike Toomey has become the ultimate political insider, fixer, lobbyist, campaign fundraiser, and chief of staff for two governors.

Explain how personal relationships with public officials is an invaluable resource for lobbyists.

After befriending fellow legislator Rick Perry in 1985, Mike Toomey became one of Perry's most powerful political allies and confidants, even serving briefly as the governor's chief of staff. Toomey maintained that close relationship as Perry ascended through the offices of agriculture commissioner and lieutenant governor, finally to become governor.

Meanwhile, Toomey was establishing himself as a lobbyist and a force to be reckoned with. Appointed as Bill Clements' chief of staff, Toomey exercised enough behind-the-scenes influence to be labeled "Governor Toomey" by fellow political operatives. Moving seamlessly between his lobbyist and government roles, Toomey became a key figure in "The Lobby," a group of influential fixers in Texas politics, and earned a seat in the gallery of the Texas House of Representatives known ironically as "the owners' box."

Perry and Toomey have developed a mutually beneficial relationship; Toomey has capitalized on his friendship with Perry to effectively represent his clients, and Perry has benefitted from Toomey's skillful fundraising and adept political strategies. Many of Governor Perry's greatest political successes and failures bear Toomey's fingerprint. Toomey helped hand over the House of Representatives to the Republicans in the 2002 election by raising enormous sums from the Texas Association of Business and his clients like AT&T and Aetna. As lobbyist and chief of staff, Toomey helped Perry persuade the legislature to pass the governor's signature bill to limit the damage awards that plaintiffs could receive in court. He urged his lobbying clients to contribute to the super PAC "Make Us Great Again," an independent group supporting Perry's run for the presidency.

Toomey's association with Perry has not always turned out well for the governor. Opponents used the fact that Toomey's clients had gotten $2 billion in state government contracts to tarnish Perry's presidential campaign, charging him with running a "pay to play" operation. As a lobbyist for Merck pharmaceuticals, which

Texas State Library & Archives Commission

(*continued*)

manufactures a human papillomavirus vaccine, Toomey persuaded Perry to issue an executive order requiring that sixth-grade schoolgirls be vaccinated against HPV, a cause of cervical cancer. The mandate outraged Christian fundamentalists and antigovernment conservatives, and it was reversed by the Texas legislature. Representing controversial gambling interests, Toomey also urged the governor to expand legalized gambling as a way to raise state revenue.

Thinking about elites in Texas politics What are the dangers in public officials taking the advice of friends who get paid to influence public policy? Do public officials have any sources of unbiased advice?

Sources: Jay Root, Ross Ramsey and Mr. Bacarisse, "For Perry, Lobbyist Is a Take-No-Prisoners Ally," *The New York Times,* October 15, 2011, p. A1; Jay Root, "Pro-Rick Perry PAC Raised $5.5 Million," *The Texas Tribune,* January 31, 2012, at http://www.texastribune.org/texas-politics/2012-presidential-election/pro-perry-pac-raised-55-million/.

There are several advantages if advance agreement can be reached on a given bill:

1. The advocates of the bill are assured that both the legislative leadership and the governor are friendly to the legislation.
2. The governor need not threaten a veto to influence the content of the bill. This keeps the chief executive on better terms with the legislature.
3. The legislative leaders can guide the bill through their respective houses, secure in the knowledge that the legislation will not be opposed or vetoed by the governor.

Special Sessions The constitution gives the governor exclusive power to call the legislature into special session and to determine the legislative subjects to be considered by the session. The legislature may, however, consider any nonlegislative subject, such as confirmation of appointments, resolutions, impeachment, and constitutional amendments, even if the governor does not include it in the call. Special sessions are limited to a 30-day duration, but the governor may call them as often as he or she wants.

Often when coalitions of legislators and lobbyists request a special session so that a "critical issue" can be brought before the legislature, other coalitions of legislators and interests oppose consideration of the issue and therefore oppose calling the special session. Because there is seldom any legislation that does not hurt some and help others, the governor has an opportunity to use the special session as a valuable bargaining tool. The governor may or may not call a special session on the basis of some concession or support to be delivered in the future. The supporters and opponents of legislation may also have to bargain with the governor over the inclusion or exclusion of specific policy proposals for the special session. Of course, this position may not be open to negotiation if the governor has strong feelings about the proposal and is determined to call (or not to call) a special session. If the governor does think that an issue is critical, the attention of the entire state can be focused on the proposal during the special session much more effectively than during the regular session.

Message Power As a constitutional requirement, the governor must deliver a state-of-the-state message at the beginning of each legislative session. This message includes the outline for the governor's legislative program. Throughout the session, the governor may also submit messages calling for action on individual items of legislation. The receptiveness of the legislature to the various messages is influenced by the governor's popularity, the amount of favorable public opinion generated for the proposals, and the governor's political expertise.

Message power

The influence a person gains merely by being in the public eye. For example, message power allows the governor to focus the attention of the press, legislators, and citizens on legislative proposals that he or she considers important. The visibility of high office draws instant public attention for the officeholder's proposals, a power that led Teddy Roosevelt to refer to the presidency as the "bully pulpit."

Blue-ribbon commission

A group assembled by the governor (or legislature) that may have both fact-finding and recommending authority. It often contains public personages or authorities on the subject that is being considered. Such commissions can help measure public reaction to proposals and may also let the governor delay consideration of issues that may be politically uncomfortable.

The **message power** of the governor is a formal power and is enhanced by the visibility of the office. Through the judicious use of the mass media (an informal power), the governor can focus public attention on a bill when it might otherwise be buried in the legislative maze. He or she must not overuse the mass media, however, because too many attempts to urge legislative action can result in public apathy for all gubernatorial appeals. An effective governor "goes to the people" only for the legislation considered vital to the interest of the state or to the governor's political and financial supporters.

Fact-Finding Commissions   Governors also appoint **blue-ribbon commissions** consisting of influential citizens, politicians, and members of concerned special interest groups. Commissions can serve either as trial balloons to measure public acceptance of the proposal or as a means to inform and increase public and interest-group support. Blue-ribbon commissions are also commonly used to delay the actual consideration of a political hot potato until it has cooled. Politicians know that the attention span of the public is short and that other personally important issues, such as jobs, families, and favorite soap operas or sports teams, easily distract people. Once the public becomes distracted, meaningful action may become unnecessary.

Proposals by the 1984 blue-ribbon commission appointed by former governor Mark White and headed by Ross Perot resulted in several public education reforms by the 1985 legislature. Governor George W. Bush appointed a similar commission to make proposed property tax reforms to the 1997 legislature, but his recommendations were not immediately adopted by the legislature, and property tax reform was not adopted for several years to come.

Executive Tools of Persuasion

The Texas Constitution charges the governor, as the chief executive, with broad responsibilities. However, it systematically denies the governor the power to meet these responsibilities through direct executive action. In fact, four other important elective executive offices—lieutenant governor, comptroller of public accounts, attorney general, and commissioner of the General Land Office—are established in the same section of the constitution and are legally independent of the governor, thus undermining the governor's executive authority (see Figure 9.1).

Other provisions in the constitution further fragment executive power. For example, the constitution establishes the elected Railroad Commission of Texas and creates the Board of Education, which the Texas legislature has determined shall also be elected. Moreover, the Texas legislature, by statute, has systematically continued to assume executive functions such as budgeting and auditing. It has also created the Department of Agriculture and a multitude of boards and commissions to administer state laws that are independent of direct gubernatorial control. Although these commissions are usually gubernatorial appointees, their terms are staggered, and it may be several years before one governor's appointees constitute a majority of a board or commission. Boards and commissions hire and fire top executives and establish general agency rules and policies.

Appointive Powers   An effective governor will use the power of appointment to the maximum. Probably the most important appointments that the governor makes are to the independent boards and commissions. The members of these boards establish general administrative and regulatory policy for state agencies or institutions and choose the top administrators to carry out these policies (see Figure 9.2).

The governor's ability to affect board policy through appointments is not immediate, however, because the boards are usually appointed for fixed, six-year staggered terms. Because only one-third of these positions become vacant every two years, the governor will only have appointed a majority of most boards in the second half of his or her first term.

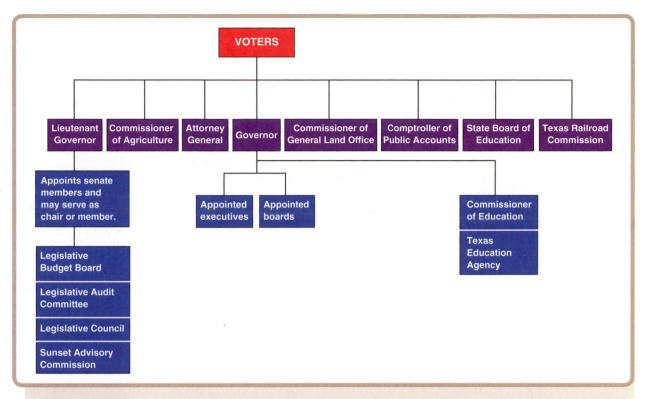

Figure 9.1

Texas's Elected Officials

A combination of political culture and Texas's Constitution have created one of the most structurally fragmented state governments in the nation and limited the governor's formal administrative bargaining powers.

How could the state executive branch be streamlined? Why would there be resistance to centralizing power in a unified executive branch responsible to the governor? What are the arguments for and against electing so many state administrators?

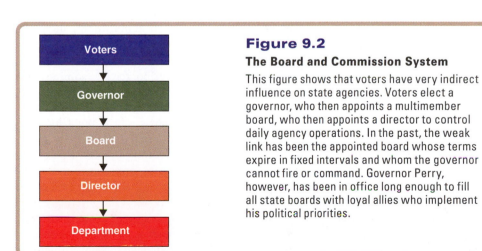

Figure 9.2

The Board and Commission System

This figure shows that voters have very indirect influence on state agencies. Voters elect a governor, who then appoints a multimember board, who then appoints a director to control daily agency operations. In the past, the weak link has been the appointed board whose terms expire in fixed intervals and whom the governor cannot fire or command. Governor Perry, however, has been in office long enough to fill all state boards with loyal allies who implement his political priorities.

How does the board and commission system reflect Texans' traditional fear of executive power?

Interest groups in Texas are vitally concerned with seeing that the "right kinds" of appointees are selected to serve on these boards and commissions. In the present age of consumerism, industry interest groups are particularly anxious to have an industry advocate (often an ex-lobbyist or industry executive) appointed to the board that oversees and sets policy for their industry. Such a close relationship develops between industries and the state agencies that industries often regard agencies that regulate them as "their" agencies. Appointment of a consumer advocate could disorient the close relationship that usually exists between an industry and its agency (see Chapter 10, "The Bureaucracy"). There may also be competing interest groups within one industry that may bargain individually with the governor for an appointee who is favorable to their particular viewpoint. Thus, an appointment to important boards often results in intense lobbying by special interest groups, which conversely gives the governor opportunities to develop support for policies and to help secure funds for future political campaigns.

Senatorial courtesy

The tradition of allowing a senator to reject the governor's appointment of a political enemy from the senator's district. The senator declares the appointee "personally obnoxious," and the other senators vote to reject the appointee.

Senators may also influence appointments from their districts as the result of **senatorial courtesy**. Senators will usually refuse to vote for confirmation if a senator announces that an appointee from his or her district is "personally obnoxious." Other senators show courtesy to the disgruntled senator by refusing to confirm a political enemy.

Administrators want sympathetic commissioners appointed to govern their agency who share their goals. Appointments that are friendly to administrator interests can strengthen a governor's influence with these administrators.

The governor can also use appointive powers to exert a great deal of influence on the state's judiciary. Because judges are elected (except for municipal judges, who are appointed by city officials), many underestimate the governor's real influence on the judiciary. Yet, the governor has a major role in the selection of judges because the governor fills vacancies on state courts. Many judges die or resign from their office before the end of their terms, and the governor has the power to fill their positions with appointees until the next election. The governor's temporary appointees then capitalize on the advantages of incumbency and usually win the next election. They become long-term fixtures in the Texas court system and the governor's judicial philosophy gradually comes to dominate the state courts.

Removal Powers   Although the governor possesses broad appointive power to boards and commissions, the powers of removal are limited. He or she may remove members of the executive office and a few minor administrators. The governor may also remove, for cause and with the consent of two-thirds of the senate, his or her own appointments to boards and commissions. If the governor decides that an elected official is administering a law so as to violate its spirit, there is no official way to force a revision of such administrative interpretation or procedures. In general, the governor cannot issue directives or orders to state agencies or remove executive officials who do not abide by his or her wishes. Only by focusing public attention on the agency and garnering public support can the governor force an administrator to change positions or resign.

Planning Powers   The office of the governor has become a focal point for planning activities at all levels of government in the state of Texas. This increase in the governor's planning authority is a first step toward comprehensive coordination of the planning, policy formulation, and administrative activities of local units of government and of the various independent agencies in the state government. But again, the governor's office has been granted responsibility without the necessary enforcement powers. The governor has no power to enforce compliance from the various local governments and state agencies involved.

The power that does exist in the governor's office to encourage compliance is derived from a requirement of the federal government that the state undertake some planning prior to the issuance of federal grants. This requirement was necessary because previously there had been little comprehensive planning to coordinate the goals of the various local governments with those of the state government. In fact, very little coordination of any kind existed for city, county, or even special district governments between these local governments and state government or between different departments in the state government. The federal government attempted to help (that is, to force) Texas to develop some kind of overall plan for program development. Thus encouraged, the state government designed rudimentary coordination and cooperation between the various government units and subunits in the state. The natural center for such statewide planning is the governor's office, which has the scope to determine whether grant requests are in accord with state wide plans. The result is a centralization of planning in the office of the Texas governor.

Chief of State The governor, as the first citizen of Texas, serves as a symbol of Texas as surely as the bluebonnet or the pecan tree. A significant part of the governor's job is related to the pomp and ceremony of the office. These ceremonial duties include throwing out the first baseball of the season, greeting Boy Scout troops at the state capitol, visiting disaster areas, and riding in parades for peanut festivals, county fairs, or cow-chip–throwing contests.

This ceremonial role is important because it can contribute indirectly to the governor's leadership effectiveness through increased popularity and prestige. The governor also broadens the image as first citizen to that of the first family of Texas whenever possible; voters identify with the governor's family, and so the governor's spouse is often included in the visual enactment of the office—particularly if the spouse is attractive and articulate.

Three notable facets to the role of **chief of state** that supplement the other formal and informal powers discussed here can be summarized as follows:

1. The governor serves as a member of (or appoints representatives to) numerous multistate organizations and conferences that work to coordinate relations between Texas and other state governments. These conferences deal with oil, civil defense, nuclear energy, and other important matters. It is also the governor's responsibility to ask other states to extradite fugitives from Texas law and to grant or refuse like requests from other states.

2. To facilitate the governor's job of coordinating the activities of state agencies and local governments with the national grant-in-aid programs, the Texas government has established an office in the nation's capital, the Office of State–Federal Relations (OSFR). The governor appoints (and may remove) the director of this office, who serves as a representative from Texas to the federal bureaucracy. "Our person in Washington" tries to keep current on the numerous federal aid programs and grants that might be available to either state agencies or local governments. The director also serves as spokesperson for state agencies and local governments when their ideas and points of view differ from those held by the federal government.

3. The governor may request federal aid when the state has suffered a disaster, a drought, or an economic calamity. As chief of state, the governor often flies over or visits a disaster area to make a personal assessment of the damage—and also to show the victims that the governor is concerned for their welfare. Then, as a "voice of the people," the governor may make a highly publicized request for federal aid to the area.

Budget Powers The governor is designated as the chief budget officer of the state. Every other year, the various agencies and institutions submit their appropriation requests to the governor's staff and to the staff of the Legislative Budget Board. Working from these estimates, the governor and staff prepare a budget that

Chief of state

The governor, who serves as the symbol of Texas, performs ceremonial duties and represents the state at meetings with foreign officials and other governors.

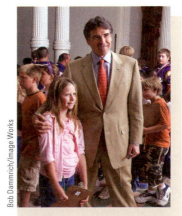

Bob Dammrich/Image Works

High School Champions Day at the state capitol; Governor Perry poses with members of championship teams.

Which role is the governor playing in this photo? How does the chief of state role enhance the governor's credibility with the public?

is determined by both the state's estimated income and the estimated cost of program proposals. When completed, the budget is submitted to the legislature. However, the governor's proposals are usually not as influential as those prepared by the Legislative Budget Board.

Law Enforcement Powers The governor has little law enforcement power. Following Texas tradition, the state's law enforcement power is decentralized at both the state and local levels.

At the state level, the Texas Rangers and the Highway Patrol are responsible for law enforcement. Both agencies are under the direction of the director of public safety, who is chosen by the Public Safety Commission. The five members of the Public Safety Commission are appointed by the governor for six-year staggered terms.

At the local level, police functions are under the jurisdiction of county sheriffs and constables (who are elected) and city chiefs of police (who are appointed by city officials). Criminal acts are prosecuted either by elected district or county attorneys or by appointed city attorneys.

The judiciary, which tries and sentences criminals, is elective (except for municipal judges, who are appointed by city officials).

Military Powers The governor is commander in chief of the state militia, which consists of the Texas National Guard and the Texas State Guard. The governor appoints (and can remove) an adjutant general who exercises administrative control over both units.

The governor may declare an area under martial law (usually after a riot or a natural disaster) and send units of the militia to keep the peace and protect public property. The governor may also employ the militia, according to Article 4, Section 7, of the Texas Constitution, "to execute the laws of the state, to suppress insurrection, and to repel invasions." The Texas National Guard has both army and air force components and is financed by the U.S. government. It is required to meet federal standards and may be called to active duty by the president. In the event the Guard is nationalized, command passes from the governor to the president.

The Texas State Guard was established during World War II and serves as a backup organization in the event that the National Guard is called to active duty by the president. It cannot be called into active duty by the federal government, and its members receive no pay unless mobilized by the governor.

Clemency powers

Executive authority to grant relief from criminal punishment; Texas's governor's clemency powers are very limited.

Clemency Powers The 1876 Texas Constitution granted the governor virtually unlimited power to pardon, parole, and grant reprieves to convicted criminals; these are known as **clemency powers**. Several governors were very generous with these powers, resulting in a 1936 constitutional amendment that established the Board of Pardons and Paroles. Many of the powers that had been held by the governor were transferred to the board, which grants, revokes, and determines the conditions for parole and makes clemency recommendations to the governor. However, the governor appoints the board's members and can grant less clemency than recommended by the board but not more. Nor can the governor any longer interfere in the parole process by blocking early releases from prison. The governor can postpone executions, but only for 30 days (see Chapter 12, "Law and Due Process").

Governor as Party Chief

Although there are varying degrees of competition from other elected officials and from political activists, the governor usually maintains the leadership of his or her party by controlling the membership of its executive committee. Although formally elected at the party's state convention, the chair and a majority of the executive committee are typically selected by the governor.

Party control is a useful channel of influence for a governor, and it permits what is often considered one of the most effective tools of persuasion of the governor's office: rewarding supporters with political patronage. Influential party members who support the governor's party choices and proposals and contribute to his or her election may influence the several hundred appointments that the governor makes each year.

The Texas governor can also be a major player in national politics if so inclined. Unless the Texas governor experiences serious public relations problems, any candidate from the governor's party who seeks the nomination for president would want the support of the governor of the nation's second-most-populous state. Texas's number of electoral votes also makes the governor an attractive candidate for president or vice president. A governor's support for a winning presidential candidate provides influence over the political patronage that flows from Washington into the state. Of course, patronage to the state can be dramatically increased if the Texas governor becomes president.

Did You Know? Governor Perry's catastrophic campaign for the Republican presidential nomination in 2011 only briefly damaged his standing with his political supporters in Texas.

National politics also affords the governor an opportunity to build a firm, clear image for the people back home. The governor can take positions on political issues that do not involve the Texas government and over which, as governor, he or she has no control but with which people can easily identify (such as foreign aid or national defense). Issues of state government are often hazy and indistinct (attributable to either the complexities of the issues or inadequate reporting by the mass media), so the electorate can more easily make political identifications through national issues.

Governor Perry: Leadership by Appointments

Richard Huckaby,
North Central Texas College

INTRODUCTION

Fear of executive power has been a prominent feature of Texas's political culture, and its constitution and statutes have been written to limit the power of the governor in almost every imaginable way. The chief executive's appointive power is limited by the fact that the governor usually does not directly appoint agency heads. Instead, the governor appoints multimember supervisory boards that serve for fixed, staggered terms and must wait for these terms to expire before filling vacancies. A further weakness is that the governor generally lacks the power to issue direct binding orders to many agencies or to fire state officers except under very limited circumstances. This article shows how Governor Perry's long tenure in office and his astute use of political skills have made his appointive powers a formidable tool of political influence.

The familiar warning "Don't Mess with Texas" seems to capture the character of Texas and Texans. The phrase had its origins in the 1980s as an anti-litter campaign slogan to encourage Texans not to toss their trash onto the landscape, but it has become much more. It may well describe the feelings of many Texans after the Civil War and Reconstruction to note their dissatisfaction with the then Republican Governor E. J. Davis.

The Texas Constitution of 1869, formulated under pressure from Washington,[2] was disputed by a large constituency of Texans. They might well have described this document as Washington, "Messing with Texas." Under this constitution, Governor Davis enjoyed substantial power as the chief executive.[3]

By 1875, Reconstruction had come to an end, and Democrats had regained power in Texas. One of their first acts was to call a constitutional convention to undo the hated 1869 Constitution.[4] The new 1876 Constitution reflected the lack of faith in government that the delegates had formed over the Reconstruction years, and slashed the power of officials, including the governor. It is this 1876 Constitution and the structurally weak executive it established that all subsequent Texas governors have had to deal with. Some have fared better than others.

The current Texas Constitution provides Texas governors precious few formal leadership tools. Nevertheless, Governor Perry has successfully spread his influence throughout the state by exercising his authority to make governmental appointments. During a four-year term, a governor will make approximately 3,000 appointments. The majority of these appointments are volunteer positions, representative of our citizen government. Most appointments include[5] the following:

★ State officials and members of state boards, commissions, and councils that carry out the laws and direct the policies of state government activities
★ Members of task forces that advise the governor or executive agencies on specific issues and policies
★ State elected and judicial offices when vacancies occur by resignation or death of the officeholder

Most boards and commissions have six-year staggered terms, with one-third of the members' terms expiring every two years.[6] Governor Perry's longevity in office has a significant impact on his influence on the makeup of Texas boards and commissions. If you do the math, since becoming governor in 2000, Governor Perry has appointed literally thousands of Texans to the various boards and commissions that operate our state agencies. Given the average length of a board or commission member's term of office, Governor Perry can be credited or blamed with having appointed or reappointed most members now serving. This relationship, with few exceptions, can provide the governor with loyalty and a support system unmatched in our history. No previous governor has been in office long enough to achieve this end. Some appointments can garner positive public recognition, while others may expose the governor to criticism by political opponents.

Some of Governor Perry's appointments have made history and generated a very positive public reaction to the governor. For example, in March 2001, Governor Perry appointed the first African American, Wallace Jefferson, to the Texas Supreme Court to fill a vacancy. As required by Texas law, Justice Jefferson had to run for the position in the next scheduled election, but he did so as the incumbent and was elected in his own right in November 2002. Governor Perry subsequently appointed Justice Wallace to Chief Justice of the Court in September 2004.[7]

Likewise, in October 2009, Governor Perry appointed the first Hispanic woman, Eva Guzman, to serve on the Texas Supreme Court, also to fill a vacancy.[8] Similar to Chief Justice Wallace, Justice Guzman successfully ran for the position in her own right in the March 2010 Republican primary as the incumbent.[9] As the Republican nominee, she faced Blake Bailey, the Democratic candidate, for Place 9 on the court in the November 2, 2010, general election. Justice Guzman's appointment was well received by the public, and she was reelected despite some criticism from the governor's political opponents.

During the contested Republican primary, in which Justice Guzman successfully defeated her Republican opponent and Governor Perry succeeded in defeating Senator Kay Bailey Hutchinson for the Republican nomination to run in the November 2010 general election, pejorative comments of "favored candidate" (Guzman) and accusations of "cronyism" (Perry) were leveled by the opposition.

Another example, with more serious political implications to Governor Perry in seeking yet another term as governor, was the controversy over appointments to the Texas Forensic Science Commission. The Texas Forensic Science Commission was created by the Texas Legislature in 2005 to investigate complaints that alleged professional negligence or misconduct by a laboratory, facility, or entity that had been accredited by the Director of the Texas Department of Public Safety would substantially affect the integrity of the results of a forensic analysis.[10]

In 2006, the *Innocence Project* (founded in 1992 to assist prisoners who could be proven innocent through DNA testing)[11] requested that the Texas Forensic Science Commission launch a full investigation into the Cameron Todd Willingham case. Willingham was executed in 2004 for the 1991 arson-related death of his three children at his home in Corsicana, Texas. In 2008, the Texas Forensic Science Commission agreed to investigate the case.[12]

The Texas Forensic Science Commission hired the noted fire scientist Craig Beyler to investigate the case and scheduled a hearing for October 2, 2009, to review his report.

---

[2]*Handbook of Texas Online*, www.tshaonline.org/handbook/online/articles/CC/mhc6.html

[3] Texas Governor Edmund J. Davis, "An Inventory of Records at the Texas State Archives," 1869–1874, *Handbook of Texas Online*, www.tshaonline.org/handbook/online/articles/CC/mhc6.html

[4] *Texas Constitution of 1876*, Texas State Library and Archives Commission, www.tsl.state.tx.us/treasures/constitution/index.html

[5]Office of the Governor, http://governor.state.tx.us/appointments/

[6]Ibid., governor.state.tx.us/appointments/process/

[7]The Supreme Court of Texas, www.supreme.courts.state.tx.us/court/justice_wjefferson.asp

[8]Ibid., http://www.supreme.courts.state.tx.us/court/justice_eguzman.asp

[9]Office of Texas Secretary of State, http://www.sos.state.tx.us/elections/forms/enrrpts/2010rp.pdf.

[10]Texas Forensic Commission, www.fsc.state.tx.us/

[11]Innocence Project, 100 Fifth Avenue, 3rd Floor New York, NY 10011, http://www.innocenceproject.org/Content/The_Texas_Forensic_Science_Commission_and_the_Willingham_Case.php.

[12]Ibid., www.innocenceproject.org/Content/2170.php

Beyler reportedly concluded that a finding of arson could not be sustained based on a "standard of care" grounded in science. If Beyler was correct, there was no arson and there was no murder for which to try or execute Willingham. Other experts and Texas officials dispute the Beyler findings. Numerous judicial, legal, criminal, and scientific experts have investigated this case and expressed contrary opinions.[13]

Two days before the scheduled hearing, Governor Perry removed three of the nine members. The three members' terms had officially expired, and Governor Perry told reporters that it would be better to replace them during the "start" of any investigation rather than after it had begun. Critics suggest that both the firings of the commission members and the now inevitable delay in the release of the commission's final report—probably until after the then upcoming Texas primary gubernatorial election in which Governor Perry was a candidate—were politically motivated. Governor Perry strongly denied both suggestions and maintained that the execution of Willingham was appropriate and that Texas did not execute an innocent man. He called the controversy "nothing more than propaganda from the anti-death-penalty people across the country."

An editorial in the *Austin American-Statesman* on October 25, 2009, put the controversy into perspective and demonstrates the contentiousness of almost any decision made in a political environment. Supporters and critics lined up to have their say. "There's no doubt that Gov. Rick Perry has the authority to appoint Texas Forensic Science Commission members. And there's no doubt that some members' terms ended recently. . . . When Perry recently shuffled the board and—two days before a crucial meeting about a controversial execution—put a tough-on-crime prosecutor in charge of the panel, we supported his right to do so. And in the face of cries of protest, we counseled patience and expressed confidence the commission would do the right thing."[14]

The *Statesman* continued to scold the Governor, "Perry, in the face of unavoidably important new input about the case, either reacted politically or, perhaps worse, evidenced an inability or unwillingness to think his way through the new material." The *Statesman* added, "Perhaps because it is campaign season, Perry doesn't seem to have it in him to do anything other than act and react as a candidate. It is unattractive and invites discredit upon Texas and its death penalty."[15]

Despite the potential for criticism for particularly visible and/or controversial appointments, most of the appointments and reappointments made by the governor go virtually unnoticed. Likewise, the work of these appointees is virtually invisible to the general public. However, their continuing presence on state boards and commissions significantly enhances the governor's influence in every aspect of state operations. For the most part, they remain loyal to the governor's agenda and programs, provide a network of supporters throughout the various state agencies, and provide a solid political base among centers of influence throughout the state.

JOIN THE DEBATE

1. How has Governor Perry's long tenure in office given him control over members of virtually every board and commission member? How can appointing loyalists to these boards give the governor control over state agencies despite his limited power to fire state officers or to issue orders to state agencies?

2. What political implications can you see in Governor Perry's appointment of Jefferson and Guzman to the Texas Supreme Court? What would have been the likely political consequences if it were determined that Texas executed an innocent man during Governor Perry's tenure?

---

[13]*The Austin Chronicle*, www.austinchronicle.com/gyrobase/Issue/story?oid=oid%3A891716
[14]*Austin American-Statesman*, www.statesman.com/opinion/content/editorial/stories/2009/10/25/1025perry_edit.html
[15]Ibid.

CHAPTER SUMMARY

★ The government of Texas was conceived in the post-Reconstruction era, after an unfortunate and unhappy experience with a centralized, alien, and unpopular state government.

★ The state government has been systematically weakened and decentralized by both the constitution and statutes as voters exhibit a basic distrust in government in general and in the executive branch in particular. This distrust is reflected in a governor's office with extensive appointive powers to boards and commissions but without meaningful removal or direct administrative powers.

★ The governor is given relatively strong legislative prerogatives with the veto and the item veto. These formal powers, together with the astute use of the informal powers inherent in the office, enable the governor to exert considerable influence on the direction and to some degree on the operation of the state's government.

★ The office of the governor in Texas is administratively weak when compared to the office in other states.

★ This denial of power to the governor (and the legislature) has created a power vacuum in government that has been willingly filled by interest groups and administrative agencies. Thus, nonelective institutions may supersede elected officials, especially in the area of policy formulation and initiation.

★ Because much of the real power in Texas government rests with these institutions, the legislature and governor are frequently placed in the position of merely ratifying, as public policy, the proposals advocated by dominant economic and other interest groups and their allies in the administrative agencies.

HOW TEXAS COMPARES

★ Like 48 governors and the U.S. President, Texas's chief executive is elected to a four-year term. However, unlike 37 states and the national government, there are no limits on the number of terms the chief executive may serve.

★ The Texas governor's institutional powers are somewhat weaker than the typical state governor. The Texas governor has especially weak administrative powers because he or she shares power with numerous other elected executives in a plural executive system, and unlike most governors, the Texas governor does not have a cabinet. The Texas governor appoints supervisory boards and commissions, but directly appoints only some agency directors. The Texas governor has relatively limited powers to remove state officers. Unique to Texas is a budget system in which the governor's budget proposals are largely ignored in favor of the recommendations of the Legislative Budget Board.

★ As in most states, the Texas governor has the power to call special sessions and line-item veto spending bills. Of course, the governor also wields considerable influence within his or her political power and commands greater access to publicity than any other state politician. Still, more than most chief executives, the Texas governor must develop leadership power through informal personal relationships, manipulation of publicity, and vigorous bargaining among special interests.

KEY TERMS

blue-ribbon commissions, *p. 234*
chief of state, *p. 237*
clemency powers, *p. 238*
formal (legal) powers, *p. 228*

impeachment, *p. 226*
informal (extralegal) powers,
  p. 228
message power, *p. 234*

presession bargaining, *p. 231*
senatorial courtesy, *p. 236*

threat of veto, *p. 229*
veto, *p. 229*

REVIEW QUESTIONS

1. Contrast the formal qualifications for governor with the informal criteria for being elected to the office. What are the informal criteria? Do you foresee a change in the kinds of candidates Texans will elect in the future? Why or why not?

2. Discuss the various functions of the governor's staff. Why is a competent staff important for a successful administration?

3. Describe the governor's legislative tools of persuasion. What are informal powers, and how can they be more important than formal powers?

4. Describe the executive tools of persuasion. Why are they weaker powers than the governor's legislative powers?

5. How did Jacksonian Democracy and the Reconstruction period following the Civil War affect the creation of the Texas governor's office?

LOGGING ON

★ To check out the how the governor's office staff is organized, go to **governor.state.tx.us/organization/.**

★ Learn about the governor's appointments and the process he uses to select candidates at **governor.state.tx.us/appointments//.**

★ To learn about the governor's powers as commander in chief of the militia, check out the Texas Adjutant General at **www.txmf.us//.**

★ To send an email to Governor Rick Perry about an issue of concern to you, go to the governor's page at **governor.state.tx.us/initiatives/.**

★ Find the legislation passed and vetoed during each governor's time in office at **www.lrl.state.tx.us/.**

★ To follow the money in state politics and look at contributions to the governor, go to the Texas Public Interest Research Group site at www.texpirg.org and to the Campaign Finance Information Center at **www.campaignfinance.org/.**

Chapter 10

The Bureaucracy

LEARNING OBJECTIVES

★ Demonstrate knowledge of the administrative structure and functions within the Texas executive branch.

★ Understand the civil law and criminal law functions of the Texas Attorney General. Explain how the attorney general's opinion is an important function in both the formulation and the administration of Texas's public policy.

★ Understand the comptroller's function in the formulation of public policy.

★ Explain the concept of bureaucratic neutrality and the various ways that Texas governments have been organized to try to accomplish it.

★ Describe the principal of hierarchy and explain how the principle is evident in the Texas bureaucracy as well as how it is not evident.

★ Describe the interconnecting web of support and interests that comprise the Iron Texas Star. Explain how each political player could benefit both personally and professionally from a system like this. Explain how economic interests benefit.

★ Understand how the powers inherent in the bureaucracy, such as expertise, information, and administrative review, are also a source of power within the political system.

GET Active

Use state and federal agencies to protect your rights as a consumer. Contact the Consumer Protection Division of the Office of the Attorney General to learn about your rights and how to exercise them. Copies of the Deceptive Practices Act and consumer brochures are available. The office also provides instructions on how to file a complaint and a copy of a consumer complaint form.

This office is for your protection—use it! The Web contact is **www.oag.state.tx.us/consumer/,** or write to Consumer Protection Division, Office of the Attorney General, P.O. Box 12548, Austin, TX 78711. The Texas consumer protection hotline is 800-621-0508.

Also check the Federal Trade Commission's Bureau of Consumer Protection at **www.ftc.gov/bcp/consumer.shtm**. Numbers to call for specific questions can be found at **www.ftc.gov/ftc/contact.shtm**.

Work with private organizations that advocate for consumer rights. Get tips on homeowner insurance from Texas Watch at **www.texaswatch.org/consumer-tips/insurance-tips/**.

Check Public Employees for Environmental Responsibility at **www.TXPEER.org** to support a cleaner environment for Texas. Write letters to elected officials and organize study groups to become more aware of environmental concerns.

You can also contact the U.S. Environmental Protection Agency at **www.epa.gov/** for more information about specific environmental topics and concerns.

The executive branch is the part of government that administers the law and implements public policy. When a highway is built, when a police officer writes a ticket, when taxes are collected, or when a public school teacher conducts a class, an executive (or administrative) function is being performed. Executive branch employees check gas pumps and meat scales for accuracy; they license morticians, insurance agents, and doctors; they check food for purity; and they arrest poachers for illegal hunting. The executive branch of government enforces public policies and is responsible for the day-to-day management of the government. It is the operational branch of the government and basically does what government does. Almost all of a citizen's contacts with the government are with the executive branch.

THE TEXAS ADMINISTRATION

The most distinctive characteristic of the Texas administration is that no one is officially in charge of the administrative apparatus.[1] As in many other states, the administration of laws in Texas is fragmented into several elective and numerous appointive positions. Although an agency director heads each executive department, no single official in Texas government bears ultimate responsibility for the actions of the Texas **bureaucracy**. And no single official can coordinate either planning or program implementation among the many agencies,

Bureaucracy
The system of officials and their employees administering or managing government policies and programs.

---

[1] Information in this section is drawn from the *Guide to Texas State Agencies,* 11th ed. (Austin: Office of Publications, Lyndon B. Johnson School of Public Affairs, The University of Texas at Austin, 2001); Legislative Budget Board, *Texas Fact Book* 2012 (Austin: Legislative Budget Board, 2012), www.lbb.state.tx.us/Fact_Book/FactBook2012.pdf; and Texas Online, www.state.tx.us.

Texas Attorney General Gregg Abbott with Luis Carlos Trevinio Berchelmann, the Attorney General of Nuevo León, Mexico, after signing a memorandum of understanding commemorating the two border states' commitment to combat transnational crime. Abbott has also made national headlines for lawsuits against the national government challenging health care reform, enforcement of voting rights laws, and environmental regulations.

Explain why the Texas Attorney General is considered one of the state's most powerful elected officials.

commissions, and departments. The Texas bureaucracy can be visualized as more than 200 separate entities, each following its own path of endeavor, often oblivious to the goals and ambitions of other (often companion) agencies.

Various divisions of the executive branch of government can be grouped according to whether their top policy maker is a single-elected administrator, a single-appointed executive, or a multimember board or commission, which may be elected, ex officio, or appointed.

Elected Executives

The constitutional and statutory requirement that several administrators (in addition to the governor) be elected was a deliberate effort to decentralize administrative power and prevent any one official from gaining control of the government. Thus, Texas has a plural executive, meaning that the governor shares executive power with several other independently elected executives and boards. These elected officials are directly accountable to the people rather than to the governor. The fact that few Texans can name the individuals in these offices, much less judge their competence or honesty, tends to contradict the democratic theory of the popular election of administrators.

Attorney General The attorney general is elected for a four-year term, with no limit on the number of terms that may be served. Holding one of the four most powerful offices in Texas government, the attorney general is the lawyer for all officials, boards, and agencies in state government. The office is authorized to employ more than 4,000 persons, many of them lawyers. The legal functions of the office range from assisting in child support enforcement, antitrust actions, Medicaid fraud investigation, crime victim compensation, consumer protection, and other civil actions concerning insurance, banking, and securities. A broad spectrum of the state's business—oil and gas, law enforcement, environmental protection, highways, transportation, and charitable trusts, to name only a few—is included under the overall jurisdiction of the attorney general.

Attorney general's opinion

Interpretation of the constitution, statutory laws, or administrative laws by Texas's attorney general. Government officials may request opinions, and although they are not legally binding, government officials usually follow them.

The attorney general performs two major functions for the state. One is to give an **attorney general's opinion**. As the state's chief lawyer, the attorney general advises his or her client. In the absence of a prior judicial interpretation, the attorney general has the power to interpret law or to give an opinion that a law or practice does or does not violate other laws or the Texas or U.S. constitutions. Although these advisory opinions are technically not legally binding, they carry great weight in the Texas government. If an official ignores the opinions, the attorney general will not defend the action in court.

The attorney general's opinion is usually requested only after the legal staff of another agency or official has been unable to reach a decision. The requests usually concern difficult questions, and several staff attorneys general consider each question. Only agencies and officials may request these opinions, and then only for official business. Occasionally a legislator will request an attorney general's opinion during the legislative session (sometimes merely to delay and thus help kill the legislation). The vagueness of laws and, particularly, the ambiguity of the Texas Constitution require the attorney general to give numerous opinions.

The second major function of the attorney general is to represent the state and its government in both civil and criminal litigation. This includes conflicts with the national government, such as the defense of Texas's poll tax, abortion, segregation, and obscenity laws and federal challenges to state legislative and congressional redistricting, voter identification requirements, and the interpretation of environmental protection laws. The attorney general also represents Texas in legal conflicts with the governments of other states, as with Louisiana and Oklahoma over the exact boundary between the two states and Texas. The attorney general initiates suits against corporations for antitrust violations or consumer protection. However, the attorney general's criminal power is relatively narrow because the primary responsibility for criminal prosecution in Texas lies with the locally elected district and county attorneys.

Part of the importance of the office is that it is viewed as a stepping-stone to the governor's chair, even though only four of the twenty-one governors since 1900 have served as attorney general. Political as well as legal considerations must therefore be taken into account. When opinions are handed down and litigation is conducted, the ambitious attorney general must not sever connections to campaign funds and political support if he or she hopes for higher office.

HARRY CABLUCK/Landov

Comptroller Susan Combs is the state's chief accountant and tax collector.

How do the comptroller's revenue estimates affect the appropriations process?

Comptroller of Public Accounts

The comptroller is elected for a term of four years, with no limit on the number of terms that may be served. The functions of the comptroller's office encompass either directly or indirectly almost all financial activities of state government. The comptroller is the chief tax collector and the chief pre-audit accounting officer in the Texas government. The comptroller manages state deposits and investments and pays warrants on state accounts.

The comptroller's most important constitutional duty is to certify the state's approximate biennial revenue. The constitution requires a balanced budget, and the state legislature may not appropriate more funds than are anticipated as income for any two-year period. The comptroller also certifies the financial condition of the state at the close of each fiscal year. Any surplus funds can give the governor and legislature fiscal flexibility for tax cuts or increased appropriations without increasing taxes.

Commissioner of the General Land Office

The commissioner of the General Land Office is elected for a term of four years. Principal duties of the commissioner are managing and collecting rentals and leases for state-owned lands; awarding oil, gas, sulfur, and other hard-mineral leases for exploration and production on state lands; and leasing mineral interests in the state's riverbeds and tidelands, including bays, inlets, and the marginal sea areas. (Out-of-state oil and gas leases require Railroad Commission review.)

As is the case with many officials, the land commissioner serves ex officio on several boards and chairs the important Veterans Land and the School Land boards, whose programs are administered by the General Land office. (Ex officio members hold their positions because they hold some other elective or appointed office.) The Veterans Land Board was established by a grateful state after World War II. The board loans money to veterans for land purchases and home purchases or improvements.

The School Land Board oversees approximately twenty million acres of public land and mineral rights properties, of which four million are submerged tidelands along the

Gulf Coast. The lease and mineral income from these public lands varies with the production and price of oil and gas, but revenues from the management of public lands are dedicated to the Permanent School Fund, which benefits the state's public schools.

Commissioner of Agriculture

The commissioner of agriculture is elected for four years to oversee the Texas Department of Agriculture, which is responsible for the administration of all laws as well as research, educational, and regulatory activities relating to agriculture. The duties of the department range from checking the accuracy of scales in meat markets and gas pumps at service stations to determining labeling procedures for pesticides and promoting Texas agricultural products in national and world markets. The commissioner also administers the Texas Agricultural Finance Authority, which provides grants and low-interest loans to businesses that produce, process, market, and export Texas agricultural products.

Like the U.S. Department of Agriculture, the Texas Department of Agriculture is charged with administering laws for protection of both consumers and farmworkers, as well as the other laws related to the agribusiness industry. The possibility of a conflict of interest between these potentially incompatible groups is likely, especially if the department begins to protect consumers to the perceived disadvantage of the more powerful economic interests.

Lieutenant Governor

Although technically part of the executive branch, the source of executive powers for the office of lieutenant governor comes from the legislative branch. The lieutenant governor, as president of the senate, is an ex officio chair of the Legislative Budget Board, the Legislative Council, and the Legislative Audit Board and, if he or she desires, can exercise considerable personal influence on the Sunset Advisory Commission and the Legislative Criminal Justice Board. These legislative boards and commissions are not part of the bureaucracy, but they conduct continuing studies of administrative policies and make recommendations to the legislature.

Appointed Executives

Besides the executives that voters directly elect, several executives are appointed by the governor. In most states, the governor appoints the heads of most state agencies, but in Texas, only a few agency heads answer directly to the governor. These include the secretary of state, the adjutant general, the insurance commissioner, and the health and human services commissioner.

Secretary of State

Appointed by the governor, with confirmation by the senate, the secretary of state serves at the pleasure of the governor. The secretary is keeper of the Seal of the State, serves as the chief election officer for Texas, administers Texas's election laws, maintains voter registration records, and receives election results. The secretary of state's office also serves as a repository for official, business, and commercial records filed with the office.

The secretary publishes government rules and regulations and commissions notaries public. By executive orders, Governor Rick Perry has also directed the secretary of state to serve as his liaison for Texas border and Mexican affairs, and to represent him and the state at international and diplomatic events.

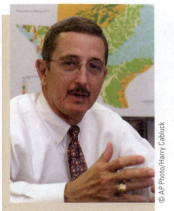

© AP Photo/Harry Cabluck

With a wind energy classification map in the background, Texas Land Commissioner Jerry Patterson announces the search for companies to lease state land, both inland and in the Gulf of Mexico, to build and operate windmills to generate energy.

Why does the land commissioner have anything to do with leasing land in the Gulf of Mexico?

© AP Photo/Harry Cabluck

Agriculture Commissioner Todd Staples discusses the accuracy of Texas gasoline pumps, a function of the Texas Agriculture Department.

What are some of the other functions of the agriculture commissioner?

Adjutant General Also appointed by the governor with the consent of the senate for a two-year term, the adjutant general is the state's top-ranking military officer and exercises administrative jurisdiction over the Texas National Guard and Texas State Guard. It is one of the few state agencies under the direct administrative control of the governor.

Health and Human Services Commissioner The executive commissioner of the Health and Human Services Commission is appointed by the governor with the advice and consent of the senate. The commissioner heads the Consolidated Texas Health and Human Services System, an umbrella or super agency that oversees and manages four major health and welfare departments (see Chapter 13).

The director of the commission is also granted extensive administrative and policy-making authority over the departments. The power within the commission clearly rests with the commissioner, who reports directly to the governor, unlike most agency directors who answer to a multimember board. The 2003 legislature significantly increased the power of the governor to act as a chief executive when it gave the governor's office direct cabinet-style control over such an important state agency.

Insurance Commissioner The commissioner of the Texas Department of Insurance is directly appointed by the governor for a two-year fixed term, subject to senate confirmation. The department monitors and regulates the Texas insurance industry. It provides consumer information; monitors corporate solvency; prosecutes violators of insurance law; licenses agents and investigates complaints against them; develops statistics for rate determination; and regulates specific insurance lines such as property, liability, and life.

Boards and Commissions

About 200 boards and commissions supervise state agencies; some of these board members are elected, many are appointed, and others serve ex officio. Some members are paid a salary or serve only for expenses. There are also considerable differences in their political power. Generally speaking, the most important boards are those concerned with chartering or regulating the business, industrial, and financial powers within the state.

A board's power is usually measured by the number of people affected by its decisions or the size of its agency's appropriations. These measures are general, however, because a relatively minor licensing board such as the Real Estate Board could be the most important agency in state government to a real estate broker whose license was about to be revoked.

Elective Boards Elective boards include the Texas Railroad Commission and the State Board of Education.

Texas Railroad Commission One of the most important state regulatory boards in the United States is the Railroad Commission, a constitutionally authorized elective board whose three members serve for overlapping six-year terms. The governor fills vacancies on the board, and these appointees serve until the first election, at which time they may win election to the board in their own right. The commission is politically partisan and its members must first win their party's nomination before being elected. The chair is elected by the commissioners from the membership.

The commission's duties almost exclusively deal with the oil and gas industry, specifically the regulation of gas utilities, pipelines, and drilling and pumping activities. It is also responsible for regulation of waste disposal and the protection of both surface and subsurface water supplies from oil- or gas-related residues.

The Railroad Commission regulated intrastate motor carriers until 1994, when the U.S. Congress deregulated Texas's trucking industry because the state's regulations were an "obstacle to free commerce among the states." The 1995 Legislature transferred the commission's remaining motor carrier responsibilities to the Departments of Transportation and Public Safety.

The state's railroad regulation function has also been largely preempted by the U.S. Government, and although the name of the commission was not changed, the remaining railroad regulatory duties were transferred by the 2005 Legislature to the Texas Department of Transportation.

The Texas State Board of Education The State Board of Education (SBOE) is elected to serve as policy-making body for the Texas Education Agency (TEA), and the commissioner of education is appointed by the governor for a two-year term to serve as its chief executive officer. The SBOE is elected in partisan elections for four-year staggered terms from fifteen single-member districts. The 2012 board consisted of eleven Republicans and four Democrats. The SBOE establishes policy, implements policy established by law, and oversees the TEA as it manages and regulates the Texas public school system below the college level as it administers national and state education law and SBOE rules and regulations.

Texas historically had a decentralized school system in which most educational and administrative policy was established by local school boards. Recently, however, the legislature, the courts, and the TEA began mandating more educational policy. The TEA writes regulations for and compels local compliance with legislative and judicial mandates and reforms; dispenses state funds; serves as a conduit for some funds from the national government to the local schools; and screens the textbooks to be purchased at state expense for use by local districts.

As the role of the TEA has grown in importance, the State Board of Education has developed from a relatively invisible state government body into one that wields considerable impact on Texans' lives, as shown in our essay feature at the end of the chapter. It attracted national attention as well as internal conflict in 2010 while establishing what Texas schoolchildren would be taught about U.S. history and other social studies for the next 10 years. Among the many issues in conflict were the "separation of church and state" and the study of the benefits versus the effects of the free enterprise system. These curriculum standards determined content and emphasis for both textbook and achievement test criteria.

The Democratic minority charged the Republican majority with interjecting its religious and political philosophies into the curriculum by minimizing the contributions of ethnic minorities and liberals, while exaggerating the political contributions of conservatives, Anglo-Americans, and Christians. Democratic board members also charged that the advice and recommendations of Texas's history teachers were largely ignored.

Ex Officio Boards Many Texas boards have memberships that are completely or partly ex officio—that is, boards whose members are automatically assigned due to their holding some other position. There are two basic reasons for creating such boards. One is that when travel to Austin was expensive and time-consuming, it seemed logical to establish a board with its members already in Austin. Another reason is that subject-matter expertise on the part of the ex officio members is assumed.

The Texas Bond Review Board is an example of an ex officio board. It has four ex officio members—the governor, lieutenant governor, speaker, and comptroller of public accounts.

It reviews and approves all bonds and other long-term debt of state agencies and universities. It also engages in various other functions pertaining to state and local long-term debt.

A number of agency boards have some ex officio members. The Texas Appraiser Licensing and Certification Board (nine members, one ex officio) and the Texas Racing Commission (nine members, two ex officio) are examples of such boards.

Appointed Boards Appointed boards vary greatly in terms of importance, administrative power, and salary. The members of these boards, who may or may not receive a salary, set the policies for their agencies and appoint their own chief administrators. The governor, with the consent of the senate, usually appoints board members, but many mixed boards have members who are appointed by the governor or by some other official or have partly ex officio membership. Because of the usual practice of appointing members to staggered terms, six years may lapse before a governor can appoint a complete board.

> **Did You Know?** Governor Perry appointed to office more than 900 people who, along with their spouses, donated more than $17 million to his election campaigns.

One example of an appointed board is The Texas Commission on Environmental Quality (TCEQ), which operates under three commissioners who are appointed by the governor for six-year staggered terms. The commissioners appoint a director who oversees its approximately 3,000 employees.

The TCEQ is the primary environmental regulator for the state. It oversees cleanups, licensing, permits, and registration and writes the rules and policies that govern all areas of the Texas environment.

In 2010, the TCEQ policy called the "flexible permit system" ran afoul of the U.S. Environmental Protection Agency (EPA). Flexible permit rules issued by the TCEQ allow one part of a plant to pollute more than the federal Clean Air Act allows so long as another part of the plant pollutes less than the maximum and as long as the total plant emissions do not violate federal air standards. The EPA argues that this policy violates the Clean Air Act and that Texas's flexible permits must be invalidated, requiring reapplication and possibly plant upgrades to be granted the more demanding EPA permits. Industry shutdowns are not expected during the process.

Whether the state or the federal view is correct, it is clear that different agencies have different views on how to implement the same law. The actual impact of a law depends on bureaucratic interpretation and rule-making.[2]

In addition to this TCEQ example, we will discuss some of the most powerful appointed boards and commissions in Chapters 12 and 13, including the Texas Juvenile Justice Board, the Board of Pardons and Paroles, the Board of Criminal Justice, the Texas Workforce Commission, the Texas Transportation Commission, the Texas Higher Education Coordinating Board, and university boards of regents.

Advisory Boards Texas also has advisory committees and boards that do not make official government decisions but instead study special issues or make recommendations to operating agencies. Texas has hundreds of advisory boards with their total membership in the thousands.

Board appointees are often representatives of groups that have an economic interest in the rules and policies of the board. Appointments may be either a reward for political support or an attempt to balance competing interest groups whose economic well-being is affected by board rules and policies.

---

[2]R. G. Ratcliffe, "Flexible Emissions Disallowed," San Antonio Express-News, July 1, 2010, p. 1B.

CHARACTERISTICS OF BUREAUCRACY

Although bureaucracy is often thought of as exclusive to government, it is also common to corporations, universities, churches, and foundations.[3] Bureaucracies develop wherever human beings organize themselves to systematically accomplish goals, but in the process, they lose some of their flexibility and efficiency. However, our focus is on Texas government bureaucracies, and we will discuss the classical model of bureaucratic organization and evaluate how well Texas's administrative agencies measure up to its ideal standards.

Size

The complexities of twenty-first-century society, together with increased demands on government at all levels, has resulted in a dramatic increase in the number of people employed by public administrations; large numbers of employees mean large bureaucracies. Much of the harshest criticism of government bureaucracy comes either from those who have simply lost confidence in our federal system or from propagandist demagogues in economic, political, and religious special interest groups who, for their own reasons, attack public employees as a means of discrediting specific government programs.

Public officials occasionally attempt to streamline both national and state bureaucracies and to make them more efficient and receptive to the wishes of policy makers. These attempts may or may not have positive results, but their level of success varies widely and is based largely on the expectations, perceptions, and political ideology of the reviewer.

HOW DOES TEXAS COMPARE?
The Size of Government and the Public Sector Workforce

Critics have frequently charged that the national government has grown to overshadow state and local governments. They may have some valid points, but Table 10.1a shows that state and local government bureaucracies are actually much larger than those of the national government. In fact, the 50 states employ more than twice as many civilian workers as the federal government, and local governments employ over six times as many. State and local governments are responsible for providing far more direct public services and functions than the federal government.

TABLE 10.1a Civilian Government Employees for the United States and Texas (In Thousands)				
	All Governments	**United States**	**State**	**Local**
United States	18,799	1,992	4,399	12,408
Texas	1, 570	140	300	1,130

Source: U.S. Census Bureau, "Federal Government Finances and Employment," *Statistical Abstract 2012*, Table 498, p. 326; "Paid Civilian Employment in the Federal Government by State: 2009," *Statistical Abstract 2012*, Table 466, p. 304; "State and Local Government by State: 2009," *Statistical Abstract 2012*, Table 466, p. 304.

---

[3]The characteristics of bureaucracy are described in detail in Max Weber, *Theory of Social and Economic Organization*, ed. Talcott Parsons (New York: Oxford University Press, 1974). Weber's book was originally published in 1920.

Despite Texas's reputation for favoring small, lean governments, Table 10.1b shows that, accounting for population, states like California and Illinois have fewer state employees than Texas. Even when local employees are included, California still has leaner public employment than Texas. Comparing total state and local employees per 10,000 residents, Texas ranks slightly *above* the average state in the number of public employees per 10,000 residents with a total of 577, compared to the 547 national average.

The patterns of public employment also tell us something about relative decentralization of state government and how important local governments are in the various states. At one extreme is Hawaii—the most centralized state government—with a rate of 463 per 10,000 residents but only 116 local government employees. In sharp contrast is New York with only 133 state workers but 507 local government employees per 10,000 residents.

TABLE 10.1b Civilian Federal, State, and Local Employees by Selected States, Per 10,000 Population

Federal		State	Local	State and Local
U.S.	65	143	404	547
CA	46	111	388	499
GA	80	125	419	544
HI	193	463	116	579
IL	40	106	407	513
LA	49	205	414	619
MA	44	147	375	522
MO	65	150	399	549
MT	113	215	369	584
NE	56	179	486	665
NH	30	151	408	559
NM	134	244	408	652
NY	37	133	509	642
OH	45	124	413	537
PA	56	130	351	481
TX	56	121	456	577
UT	104	187	323	510

Source: U.S. Census Bureau, "Federal Government Finances and Employment," *Statistical Abstract 2012,* Table 498, p. 326; "Paid Civilian Employment in the Federal Government by State: 2009," *Statistical Abstract 2012,* Table 466, p. 304; "State and Local Government by State: 2009," *Statistical Abstract 2012,* Table 466, p. 304.

FOR DEBATE

1. From your reading, identify and evaluate the criticisms of bureaucracy. Explain why arguments against "big government" agencies resonate especially well with Texas conservatives.

2. Describe the positive contributions public employees make to society. Which reforms would make bureaucratic agencies more responsive to people's needs? How can bureaucrats be made accountable for their decisions?

Attacking *the bureaucracy* remains an effective political strategy. It is unfair, however, to compare only the bureaucracies of the state governments. Each state has its own organizational system, and great variations may relate to whether a specific service is provided by the state or by one of its political subdivisions. A reduction in public bureaucracy almost invariably results in either reducing services, government contracting with private firms, or requiring the administration of specific services or programs by lower governments.

One way governments have attempted to shrink their size has been to shift responsibilities to lower levels of government. The national government has increasingly mandated policies and regulations but has left the burden for funding and implementation to state and local governments, often forcing them to increase taxes or decrease services (or both). The state of Texas has also shifted responsibility for public services to local governments through unfunded mandates.

Yet another approach to trimming bureaucracy has been through **privatization**. Since the 1980s, privatization has increased as governments have turned to the private sector for services ranging from police protection, prison management, and garbage collection. Texas has privatized some of its prisons and state jails and has experimented with privatizing determining eligibility for social service programs. The state still has some more modest plans for privately operated for-profit highways even though it has now dropped sweeping plans for the massive Trans-Texas Corridor (TTC). The TTC scheme caused a public uproar because the state proposed using powers of eminent domain to take private property away from its owners to make way for investors to profit from building and operating a huge private system of highways, railways, and pipelines.

Conservative, pro-business interests often vocally support privatization of public programs and argue that contracting with private businesses to provide traditional public services both increases efficiency and reduces the size and power of government. They contend that government agencies lack the powerful forces of the profit motive and competition that energize the private marketplace. In short, they have faith that that private enterprise is inherently more effective than the public sector.

Privatization's skeptics argue that private businesses are profiteering at public expense because they are likely to cut corners on services to improve their bottom line. Opponents also contend that private businesses are not as accountable to the public because the internal operations of private businesses are not as well publicized as government activities.

Skeptics also suspect that political contacts and campaign contributions grease the wheels for contractors. In addition, critics see a new kind of spoils system developing. Unlike the historic spoils system in which elected officials hired campaign workers as public employees, they believe that today's new **spoils system** is based on a network of **contract spoils**, or contract patronage, in which politicians now award contracts to their political supporters in the business community. Although the contract patronage system is not new, critics believe that it has become a major political reason for support of the privatization movement.

Privatization
The hiring of private contractors to perform government services and functions..

Spoils system
A system that gives elected officials considerable discretion in employment and promotion decisions.

Contract spoils
The practice by which public officials award government contracts to benefit their campaign contributors, supporters, and allies. Also referred to as *contract patronage.*

Hierarchy
A pyramid-shaped administrative organization in which several employees report to a single higher administrator until only one person with ultimate authority remains at the top.

Hierarchy

All bureaucracies are formally characterized as **hierarchical** structures, with formal authority and control exercised at successive levels from the top to the bottom. Theoretically, formal authority and directives flow down through the chain of command to lower levels, and information filters up through channels to the top from lower-level employees in the field. A framework of rigid rules and regulations formally assigns

authority to various levels and defines the relationship between those individual bureaucrats who are of near-equal rank.

An ideal hierarchy looks like the military chain of command for the U.S. Army, where the president as commander in chief outranks the secretary of defense, who outranks the secretary of the army, who outranks all the generals, who in turn outrank all the colonels, and so on, down to the new private E-1, who is outranked by everybody. Actually, a hierarchy seldom functions according to its organizational chart. Usually, it can be influenced at all levels by legislators, the chief executive, interest groups, and other bureaucrats, regardless of the formal lines of authority.

Department of Transportation

Although the formal theory of hierarchy is evident in each administrative unit, the Texas government as a whole is not arranged hierarchically because authority is not centralized in a single executive. For example, Figure 10.1 shows that the Texas Department of Transportation is not under the direct administrative control of the governor, and the direct lines of authority and communication stop abruptly when they reach the Texas Transportation Commission. The governor appoints the five-member commission for six-year staggered terms with the advice and consent of the senate, and in turn, it selects the executive director of the department, who serves as the actual chief executive officer for the department.

The authority to appoint members of most boards and commissions, together with close personal and political ties to powerful special interest groups, makes the governor an important player in shaping the direction of Texas administrative policy. However, the governor has little direct legal authority over most agency administrators.

Expertise

To function smoothly, individual bureaucrats should have an understanding of their jobs and the effects of their decisions on others. Students of administration have concluded that this can be accomplished by clearly defining the duties of the job and the limit of its authority. Thus individual bureaucrats, through training and experience in specific job classifications, become experts in specialized areas of administration. In principle, bureaucrats' expertise and experience should result in better, more efficient administration, but it is not clear that the agencies' management is always competent. It *is* clear that specialized knowledge and access to internal agency information gives bureaucrats a great deal of power.

Neutrality

Administration of the laws in a neutral fashion—the separation of politics and administration—has long been an aim of reformists in American government. Ideally, elected public officials should establish and define a program's priorities, goals, or services. Administrators should then administer the law the best way and equally to all, rich or poor, black or white, powerful or weak, male or female.

The national government took the lead in bureaucratic reform when it established a strong **civil service (merit) system** with competitive examinations or objective measures of qualifications for hiring and promoting employees. The employee spoils system—government employment and promotion based on political support—was replaced by a merit system.

Many other states also adopted a merit system of public employment. However, Texas never implemented systematic statewide civil service reform; it still depends on a spoils or patronage system of public employment. Elected officials in Texas appoint major campaign supporters to top-level positions. Some of Texas's local governments use a merit system.

Civil service (merit) system

An employment system used by governments that takes merit into account in hiring and promotions.

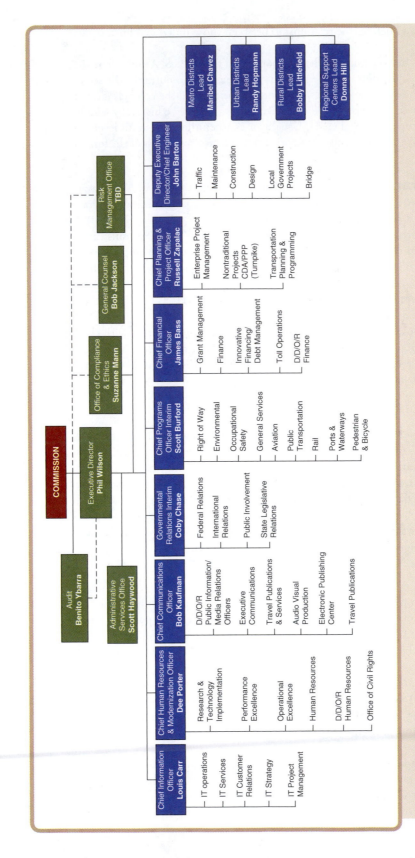

Figure 10.1
Texas Department of Transportation Organizational Structure

Source: Texas Department of Transportation.

How would you describe this organizational structure?

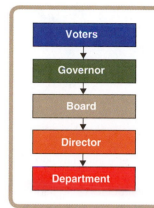

Figure 10.2

The Board and Commission System

Voters elect the governor as the chief executive, but the governor does not directly appoint most agency administrators. Multimember boards add another layer of bureaucracy between voters and agency decision-making.

Why is the structural organization of the board and commission system widely used in the Texas executive branch? Has it effectively limited the power of the governor to serve as the chief executive?

Figure 10.2 shows how Texans have historically attempted to depoliticize the state bureaucracy through the board and commission system. They tried to insulate the bureaucracy from the legislature and the governor, both of whom are elected and hence political by definition. Both agency policy and administrative oversight are the responsibility of the boards. Their terms are usually fixed at six years and staggered to delay the governor's control over the board for four years.

Board members cannot be removed until the expiration of their terms unless they have been appointed by the sitting governor, and then only with the concurrence of two-thirds of the senate. However, the governor may *encourage* board members to resign by publicly criticizing the board members or the board's policies. The board appoints a chief executive officer to manage the department and see to the administration of public policy. Administrative power is thus removed from politics and excludes the governor from direct executive control over the state bureaucracy. This system also placates Texans' basic fear of power concentrated in the chief executive.

With these safeguards, reformers believed that administrators could and would treat everyone equally and fairly, simply carrying out the policies of the elected officials. However, the theory of executive neutrality proved to be naive because public administration cannot be separated from politics—it is politics.

THE BUREAUCRACY, POLITICS, AND PUBLIC POLICY

Each attempt to depoliticize the bureaucracy simply meant that one kind of politics was substituted for another. Most political observers today agree that the Texas bureaucracy is deeply engaged in politics, that politics strongly affects public policy, and that policy formulation cannot, in fact, be separated from policy administration.

Public administration is "in politics" because it operates in a political environment and must seek political support from somewhere if it is to accomplish goals, gain appropriations, or even survive. The result of strong political support for an agency is increased size, jurisdiction, influence, and prestige. The less successful agency may experience reduced appropriations, static or reduced employment, narrowed administrative jurisdiction, and possibly extinction.

Where then, does a unit of the bureaucracy look for the political support so necessary for its bureaucratic well-being? It may look to clientele interest groups, the legislature, the chief executive, and the public. Political power also comes from factors within the bureaucracy, such as expertise, control of information, and discretion in the interpretation and administration of laws.

Clientele Groups

Clientele interest groups

The groups most concerned with the laws and policies being administered by a government agency.

The most natural allies for an agency are its constituent or **clientele interest groups**—the groups that benefit directly from agency programs. The agency reciprocates by protecting its clients within the administration. At the national level, examples of such a close-knit alliance of an interest group and agency are defense contractors and the Department of Defense; agribusiness and the Department of Agriculture; and drug manufacturers and the Food and Drug Administration. In Texas, some of the closer bedfellows are the oil, gas, and transportation industries and the Texas Railroad Commission; the banking industry and the Department of Banking; and the Texas Medical Association and the State Department of Health. Agitation by such groups often leads to the establishment of a state agency, and its power and importance are usually directly related to the power and influence of its clientele groups and the intensity of their support.

Did You Know? Industry groups do not always resist government intervention and sometimes welcome friendly regulation. The oil industry agitated for the Texas Railroad Commission to regulate oil production, and homebuilder Bob Perry was a crucial force in creating the Texas Residential Construction Commission.

The agency and its clientele groups are usually allied from the very beginning, and this alliance continues to grow and mature as mutual convenience, power, and prosperity increase. Economic and political ties are cemented by mutual self-interest. Agencies and clients share information, have common attitudes and goals, exchange employees, and lobby the legislature together for agency appropriations and government policies that favor the interest groups. Mutual accommodation becomes so accepted that the clientele groups often speak of "our agency" and spend considerable time and money lobbying for it. The agency reciprocates by protecting its clients within the administration.

Because neither the bureaucracy nor the special interests are single entities, there is often competition among the various special interests and the agencies for appropriations, so both seek allies in the legislative branch.

As discussed in Chapter 6, the "revolving-door" practices of special interest groups help them gain influence over public policy. Corporations employ ex-administrators and ex-legislators as executives, lobbyists, or consultants. The practice of government employees resigning and accepting lucrative employment with a corporation, an organization, or an individual that has profited financially by that employee's actions casts a shadow of doubt over the whole public policy-making process. In this environment, current legislators, administrators, and regulators, expecting industry jobs in the future, may become promoters of industries that they regulate. Unfortunately, this sleaze factor negatively affects public perception of all public servants and prompts cynicism toward all government.

The revolving door between special interests and government officials is a permanent fixture in Texas. Literally hundreds of former administrators and legislators work for special interests as lobbyists, consultants, and executives.[4]

The Legislature, the Lieutenant Governor, and the Speaker

Bureaucratic power is enhanced by the support of powerful legislators, often including the chair of the committee that exercises legislative oversight over the agency. The agency is dependent on legislative allies for laws that expand its powers, increase the scope of its duties,

---

[4]Texans for Public Justice, *"Million-Dollar Clients," Austin's Oldest Profession: Texas's Top Lobby Clients and Those Who Service Them* (Austin, TX: Texans for Public Justice, 2002), www.tpj.org/reports/lobby02/page4.html.

protect it from unfriendly interests, and appropriate the funds for its operation. Therefore, administrators seek the favor of influential lawmakers.

Although committee chairs are important in the Texas legislature, the short session and the power of the presiding officers limit their influence. For this reason, an agency seeks the support of the lieutenant governor and the speaker of the house as well as members of the finance and appropriations committees, the Legislative Budget Board, and the Legislative Council.

The importance of legislative support explains the intense lobbying activity that surrounds the appointment of legislators to powerful committees and the campaign activity that precedes election to positions of legislative leadership. If the interest group and its agency are unable to get allies appointed or elected to positions of influence in the legislature, they are forced to try to win support after the influential legislators are chosen—a more difficult endeavor.

The Governor

The need of administrative agencies for the governor's support depends on the extent of the governor's formal and informal powers and how successful the agency has been in finding other powerful political allies.

Even when an executive has extensive administrative powers (as the U.S. president does), most agencies have considerable independence. In Texas, where the executive is decentralized and the governor has few direct administrative powers, administrative autonomy is enhanced. Agencies still need the support of the governor, however, because a governor can influence the legislature when it considers appropriations bills and other matters important to the agency. The governor's item veto can also seriously affect an agency's funding.

The governor's cooperation is also important because of his or her appointive power to policy-making boards and commissions. Agency employees develop shared attitudes, esprit de corps, and a sense of communality with the employees of the agency's constituency interest groups. Because an agency's interests are usually similar to those of its constituency, both want the governor to appoint board members who will advance their mutual political goals. Moreover, the governor's support gives the agency greater bargaining power with legislators and interest groups in achieving its goals. Although the Texas governor has few direct administrative powers, she or he can influence and shape agency programs and success through veto power and appointments to policy-making boards and commissions.

Public Policy and the Iron Texas Star

The explanation of how public policy is made and implemented is a complex endeavor. Teachers and writers often use models as a means of simplification to explain the process. A model is a simplification of reality in order to explain reality.

One such model, the **Iron Texas Star**, is depicted in Figure 10.3. This model attempts to explain the relationships among the political actors in Texas government that make legislative and administrative public policy happen (see also "iron triangles" in Chapter 6).

Texas has weak legislative committees when compared with their counterparts in the U.S. Congress. This is attributable to the hands-on authority of the lieutenant governor and the speaker of the Texas House of Representatives, who select most of the members and all of the chairs of the standing committees, conference committees, and legislative boards and commissions. Their exercise of this power includes them in the iron star coalitions that formulate and implement public policy in Texas. The governor is also included as a result of the item veto power, the power to appoint members of state policy-making boards and commissions, and close ties with powerful special interests. The virtual absence of a civil service for Texas government employees makes them more vulnerable to influence by the appointed

Iron Texas Star

A model depicting policy making in Texas by a coalition of interests that includes interest groups, the lieutenant governor, the speaker, standing committees, the governor, administrators, and boards and commissions.

Figure 10.3
The Iron Texas Star Model

What are the bargaining chips that each of the entities at the five points of the Iron Texas Star bring to the table when engaging in the formulation of Texas public policy?

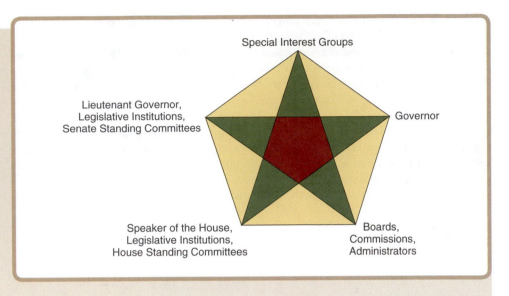

boards. Finally, economic interest groups provide the mortar that builds and holds together this five-pointed coalition of administrators, legislators, presiding officers, the governor, and clientele interests.

All economic interests want friendly government policies. Some industries, such as insurance, oil, and gas, have little need for direct appropriations and basically want only to be free of government interference. This class of interests may, however, want to use the powers of government for favorable regulations and protection from consumers and competitors. Other interests, such as the Texas State Teachers Association and the Texas Good Roads and Transportation Association, literally survive on government appropriations.

The basic goal of special interests is to accumulate friends in the policy-making and regulatory areas of government. It is equally critical for political operatives to acquire friends among economically powerful individuals and special interest groups. The members of the coalition also support the friends of their friends at the other points of the iron star and thereby develop a mutual support group from which all can benefit.

Legislators, administrators, the governor, and the presiding officers rely to varying degrees on the support of their interest group friends for campaign contributions, supplemental income, political advancement, financial advice and opportunity, and after-office employment and income. As time passes and members of the coalition become more interdependent, each looks to the other for support. Legislators bargain for the interest of the coalition in the legislature. Administrators issue favorable regulations and support their friends' viewpoints in administrative decisions. The presiding officers may shepherd the proposals of their friends through the legislative process and also place the friends of economic special interests on powerful legislative committees and legislative boards and commissions. Also, the governor appoints friends and friends of friends to various boards and commissions that make policy affecting these same friends. Other government officials may also broker with political operatives for decisions favorable to their friends and to the friends of their friends inside the iron star coalition. Our Texas Insiders feature illustrates one example of mutual accommodation and support between elected officials and special interests.

Texas INSIDERS

The Texas Enterprise Fund Insiders: Job Creators or Crony Capitalists?

The Texas Legislature created the Texas Enterprise Fund (TEF) in 2003 with a $295 million initial investment. With the approval of the Governor, Lieutenant Governor, and Speaker of the Texas House, the TEF grants taxpayer-funded subsidies to businesses that move their operations to Texas or expand their existing operations here. Since it began operations, the TEF has been at the center of ideological and political controversy.

Supporters argue that Texas must compete with the incentives being offered by other states and nations to bring jobs and economic growth to the state. Governor Perry touts the TEF as the "deal-closing" fund, and his official website claims the fund has brought more than 56,000 new jobs to the state and generated more than $14.7 billion in capital investment. What is not known is how many would have made the same move without the lure of taxpayer money.

Its detractors have described the TEF as a slush fund for the governor's supporters and dubbed it "Perry's Piggy Bank." TEF has awarded huge grants to highly profitable corporations whose executives and PACs have contributed to Governor Perry's campaign or to the Republican Governors' Association. Among them, General Electric, Hewlett-Packard, Lockheed Martin, Texas Instruments, Home Depot, and other contributors have received over $300 million from the enterprise fund.

Critics argue that giving top elected officials the opportunity to choose grant recipients creates a pay-to-play political environment in which elected officials can demand campaign contributions in exchange for government subsidies. They charge that the TEF creates "crony capitalism" in which success in business depends on close relationships with government officials, and that government officials should not have the power to use taxpayer funds to pick winners and losers in a free enterprise system.

Thinking about the role of elites in Texas politics Texas's elected politicians are trapped in a system that forces them to ask wealthy donors, special interest lobbyists, and other insiders for the funds necessary to conduct their expensive media-driven campaigns. To be successful fund-raisers, candidates must bring something of value to the table, and it usually takes the form of a general understanding that the candidate, once elected, will be sensitive to donors' interests during the policy-making process.

Such a general unspoken understanding between donors and candidates does not constitute legal bribery. Actual bribery is difficult to prove because it requires a quid pro quo—that is, a specific verbal agreement to make a particular policy decision in exchange for an agreed sum of money. Hence, actual bribery is probably rare even though no one can be certain. Still, public policy decisions are surely shaped by the influence of large campaign contributions.

What sort of campaign finance reforms would mitigate insider influence in bureaucratic decisions?

Sources: Office of the Governor, *Economic Development and Tourism—Texas Enterprise Fund,* www.governor.state.tx.us/ecodev/financial_resources/texas_enterprise_fund/; Texans for Public Justice, "Perry's Piggybank,," October, 2011, www.tpt.org; Mark Maremont, "Behind Perry's Jobs Success, Numbers Draw New Scrutiny," *The Wall Street Journal,* October 11, 2011, http://online.wsj.com/; David Mann, "Report: Nearly Half of Enterprise Fund Companies Gave to Perry," *The Texas Observer,* October 13, 2011, www.texasobserver.org/.

Public Support

Good public relations with the electorate are usually beneficial for any agency, both in its appropriations requests and in its battles with other agencies over areas of jurisdiction. Favorable propaganda combined with myth, literature, and the entertainment media have created broadly based public support for such agencies as the Texas Department of Criminal Justice, the Texas Rangers, and to some extent the Texas Highway Patrol.

Information

A kind of power inherent in any professional bureaucracy stems from administrators' ability to shape public policy because of their knowledge of a given subject. Policy-making officials such as the legislature and governor can seldom be as well-versed in all policy-making areas as the administrative personnel, who have often made a lifetime career of administration in a single area of government activity. Policy-making officials, whether appointed or elected, frequently find themselves forced to rely on longtime government employees for advice concerning both content and procedural matters. Persons whom the public may see as only the administrators of the law are often important players in its conception, promotion, and enactment.

Because the bureaucracy is the branch of government that works most directly with constituent interest groups and the general public, administrative agencies gather the information used by these groups or the general public to determine what laws are needed or wanted. Information of this nature is valuable to legislators as well as to elected or appointed administrators but may be available only at the discretion of top government administrators. In other words, these administrators may dispense or interpret information in a way that benefits their agency or constituency interests, thus affecting the formation of public policy.

Administration of the Law

Administrative review

Administrators' study and interpretation of a law and writing the rules and regulations to implement the law's enforcement. All laws undergo administrative review, whereas relatively few undergo judicial review, which is the courts' interpretation of the law.

Administrative law

The rules and regulations written by administrators to administer a law. The effectiveness of a law is often determined by how administrative law is written.

Just as judges use judicial review to interpret the meaning of the law and to write case law for its implementation, bureaucrats use what might be termed **administrative review** in the process of administering the law. When administrators interpret the law and write the rules and regulations for its enforcement, they are making law that is known as **administrative law**. Administrative law defines the meaning of the law and determines its effect on both special interests and the public.

Whether written or unwritten, decisions by administrators to enforce a dog leash, speed limit, pure food, or underage smoking law either leniently or not at all alter the spirit of the law and dilute its impact. Although the law may remain on the books indefinitely, its effect is diminished with lax or selective enforcement. In this way, administrators establish public policies that not only affect the lives of the general public but can also, to an extent, modify the decisions of the state's elected policy makers. Although administrative decisions can be overturned by the courts and statutory law can be rewritten by legislatures, administrative review is the first and usually the last determination of the meaning of a law and how rigidly it will be enforced.

Bureaucratic Accountability

Throughout the history of the United States, people have tried to hold government responsible for its policies. The rise of the bureaucratic state is the most recent challenge to responsible government. The size and political power of modern bureaucracy make the problem of administrative accountability ever more acute. Various organizational arrangements and legal restrictions have been used in attempts to make the bureaucracy accountable to the citizenry, or at least to someone whom the citizens can hold responsible.

Elective Accountability The simplest approach has been to make the bureaucracy directly accountable to the people through the democratic process—the theory of **elective accountability**. In Texas, this goal was to be accomplished through the election of the governor, lieutenant governor, attorney general, comptroller of public accounts, commissioner of the General Land office, commissioner of agriculture, Railroad Commission, and State Board of Education. The reasoning was that the public, if given an opportunity, would keep a close watch on elected administrators and refuse to reelect those who were incompetent or dishonest. Administrators would therefore be sensitive to the wishes of the voters and would administer the laws only in the interest of the general public.

Several problems have developed with the application of this theory. The most obvious is the difficulty of determining the will of the people or even of determining the public interest. Texas is a mixture of many divergent groups with several often-incompatible public interests—to please one group frequently means displeasing another.

A further problem is the relative invisibility of elected executives. As shown in Figure 10.4, the list of elected executives is so long that few voters are even aware of the names of many officeholders, much less their administrative competence. Common everyday ineptitude, inefficiency, corruption, or incompetence goes unnoticed by the public and an apathetic press. Administrators, once elected, are usually returned to office until they die, retire, anger powerful client special interests, or commit an act so flagrant that the voters finally "throw

Elective accountability

The obligation of officials to be directly answerable to the voters for their actions. This allows elected administrators to ignore the wishes of the chief executive.

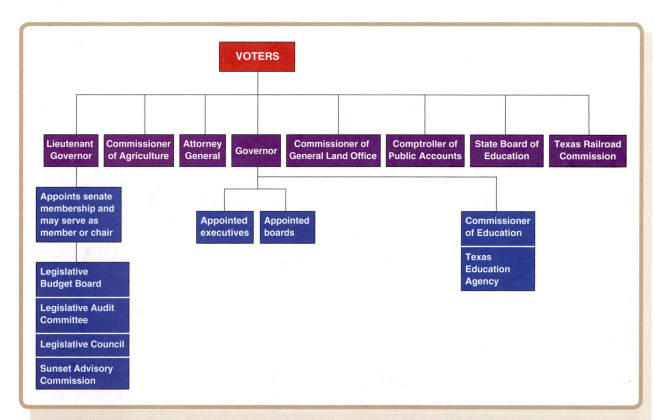

Figure 10.4
Texas's Elected Executives and Boards

Why do you think Texas elects so many people? Would a simpler process be better or worse for Texas?

the rascals out." Although elective accountability for local offices may be more practical in rural areas, in an increasingly urban society, accountability to the general public seems an ineffective method of either influencing administrative behavior or enforcing accountability.

Legislative Accountability Some advocates of administrative reform argue that the bureaucracy should be accountable to the legislature because many view the legislature as the branch of government closest to the people. Because it is elected to protect constituent interests and because legislators establish policies, many argue that these elected representatives should determine whether those policies are being administered according to legislative intent. This principle has been implemented in Texas by establishing various auditing, budgeting, and oversight boards as well as legislative committees to try to hold administrators accountable. For example, the Texas legislature established the Sunset Advisory Commission to make recommendations as to the alteration, termination, or continuation of about 130 state boards, commissions, and agencies. Agencies and their operations are reviewed periodically, usually in 12-year cycles, and cease to exist without specific legislative action to renew them. Functions may be expanded, diminished, or reassigned to other agencies by legislative action. If renewed, the Sunset Commission evaluates agency compliance with legislative directives. The state auditor also evaluates any management changes recommended by the commission. It is reasoned that periodic legislative evaluation, together with agency self-evaluation, should result in better, more efficient administration.

The principle of accountability to the legislature is questionable, however. Not only is the ability of any government to separate policy formulation from policy administration in doubt, but the assumption that the legislative branch best represents the people is also debatable. Legislators' independent judgments may be compromised by financial conflicts of interest, campaign contributions from special interest groups, and political ambition. Another problem with legislative accountability is the invisibility of the committee hearings and the decision-making processes in the legislature; the public is just not aware of many policy decisions made in its name by the legislature. Although interests of the individual legislators and special interests might well be served, the general public may or may not.

Finally, because the Texas legislature is seldom in session, permanent legislative institutions such as the Legislative Budget Board and the Legislative Council are given the task of overseeing the administration. These institutions are incapable of enforcing accountability by the autonomous agencies in Texas government; they also lack the visibility necessary for effective operation in the public interest. Accordingly, a major problem of responsible government is identifying who is watching the watchers.

Accountability to the Chief Executive Some reformers advocate a Texas administration patterned after the **cabinet system** of the federal government. As shown in Figure 10.5, this would entail a reorganization and consolidation of the executive branch into larger subject-matter departments, with the governor being given power to appoint and remove top administrators and to control the budget. Administrative authority would be concentrated at the top. (Advocates argue that this is only proper because the governor usually receives the blame for administrative blunders anyway.) Furthermore, a governor who had these powers could hold the appointed bureaucrats accountable for their actions.

Theoretically, several benefits could result from accountability to the governor. The office is visible to the general public, so the problem of who watches the watchers would be solved. There would be no question regarding final responsibility for any corruption or incompetence in the administration. Administrative control could be simplified, resulting in coordinated planning and policy implementation. Waste and duplication could be reduced.

Consolidation and reorganization of the Texas administration is, without a doubt, necessary for an orderly, modern executive branch. Analysis of the national government

Cabinet system

A system that allows the chief executive to appoint and remove top-level administrators, thereby giving the chief executive more control over the administration.

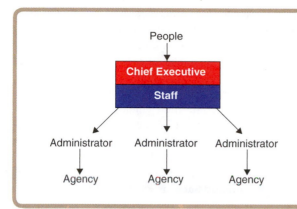

Figure 10.5
Structure of the Cabinet System

In a cabinet system used in some states and the national government, the chief executive directly appoints agency administrators and is ultimately responsible for their performance.

What are the advantages and disadvantages of a cabinet system headed by a strong chief executive?

demonstrates that no individual person can control the dozens of agencies, their chiefs, and the thousands of government employees who work in these agencies. One means by which the president can hold this bureaucracy accountable is through the executive office. If public administration in Texas could be reorganized according to the federal model, the governor would need a similar executive office. This executive staff, although relatively invisible to the public, would nevertheless be accountable to the governor.

This chain of accountability—administrative agency to appointed executive to staff to governor to the people—is weakened by the close ties usually found among administrators, constituent interest groups, and legislators. Interest groups would continue to influence administrative appointments and removals in "their agencies" just as they now influence appointments to the boards and commissions under the present system. Even under a cabinet system, the governor would have problems enforcing the accountability of agencies that have allies among powerful interest groups and legislators.

Other Forms of Bureaucratic Accountability

To whom is the Texas administrator really accountable? The answer is, in all probability, to the interest groups that benefit from the service programs the administrator provides (clientele groups). Politics works on the basic principles of mutual accommodation among allies and conflict among opponents, coalition building, and compromise. Agency officials are often obligated to administer the law and make policy decisions in ways that are favorable to the goals and aspirations of their political allies among private economic interests. Appointees to boards and administrative positions are usually chosen from the industry concerned, and the policy decisions they make tend to benefit the most influential operatives in the industry. In turn, when government employees leave government service, many find jobs in the industry where their expertise lies. Thus, because the success of their agency, their government career, and possible after-government employment often depend on their actions while in the bureaucracy, it is understandable that many administrators feel more directly accountable to the economic powers they affect than to the public at large.

How then, can the Texas administration be made more accountable to the public? There is no single answer. One possibility could be more openness. A basic concept of democratic government is that policy made in the name of the public should be made in full view of the public. Texas has made great strides in this area. **Open-meetings laws** require that meetings of government bodies at all levels of government be open to the general public except when personnel, land acquisition, or litigation matters are being discussed. The laws further prohibit unannounced sessions and splitting up to avoid a quorum, and they require that public

Open-meetings laws

With some exceptions, laws that require meetings of government bodies that make decisions concerning the public interest to be open to public scrutiny.

Open-records laws

Laws that require most records kept by government to be open for the examination of the parties involved.

Whistle-blowers

Government employees who expose corruption, incompetence, and criminal acts by other government employees.

Ombudsman

An official who hears complaints of employees and citizens concerning government administrators or policy administration. Ombudsmen usually lack authority to force administrative compliance, but they can bring the complaints to the proper authorities and represent the interests of the complaining individual within the administration.

notice be posted for both open and closed sessions. However, these laws are continuously being tested by policy makers, who feel more comfortable operating in secret.

Openness is further encouraged by the state's **open-records law**, which requires that the records of all government proceedings be available to the public for only the expense involved in assembling and reproducing them.

Another source of openness is **whistle-blowers**—government employees who expose bureaucratic excesses, blunders, corruption, or favoritism. These employees should be commended and protected from retribution, but too often they are instead exiled to the bureaucratic equivalent of Siberia or fired for their efforts. To its credit, Texas's whistle-blowers law prohibits governments from acting against employees who report law violations. But enforcement is difficult and time-consuming, and whistle-blowers often suffer.

Reformers argue that the appointment of **ombudsmen** at every level of government would give each individual increased access to the bureaucracy regarding real or imagined administrative injustices. In this way, administrative error, injustice, or oversight could be rectified, allowing individual citizens to have a more positive attitude toward government. Any lack of public accountability by Texas administrators cannot wholly be blamed on poor structural organization or the lack of consumer- or citizen-oriented agencies. No amount of reorganization and no number of consumer agencies can overcome the willingness of an apathetic or indifferent public to accept bureaucratic errors, inefficiency, excesses, favoritism, or corruption.

God, Man, and the Texas State Board of Education

Malcolm L. Cross
Tarleton State University

issue of teaching evolution in the public schools. These decisions have a major impact on the thinking of future generations of Texans and, as this article makes clear, have a significant influence in much of the rest of the nation as well.

INTRODUCTION

State agencies make some of the most important and politically sensitive policy decisions in Texas. The following article shows how the Texas State Board of Education, elected by voters and dominated by conservatives, has dealt with the

What should we teach our children in Texas's public schools about God and man? Did humans evolve from lower life forms, or were they specially created by God himself?

Perhaps no issue in public education is more contentious. Political and religious activists, regardless of party, ideology, or faith, see the classroom as a battleground in the war to shape children's minds. "I would rather have a thousand school board members," said Ralph Reed, former head of televangelist Pat Robertson's Christian Coalition, "than one president and no school board members."[5]

[5]Russell Shorto, "How Christian Were the Founders?" *New York Times Magazine*, February 14, 2010. The Ralph Reed quote is on p. 2 of the article as posted on www.nytimes.com/2010/02/14/magazine/14texbooks-t.html?em=&pagewanted=print. The article is a fascinating and invaluable analysis of the politics and processes by which the Texas State Board of Education develops curriculum standards, although its focus is on the development of social science standards.

No school board in America has more power over curriculum issues than the Texas State Board of Education. Its 15 members, elected by party to 4-year terms, approve the curricula for Texas's public schools, and each year, they buy or distribute 48 million textbooks to its children.

And the influence of the SBOE extends well beyond Texas. Texas is the largest state with centralized adoption and purchase of textbooks. Therefore the nation's textbook publishers, eager to do business in Texas's vast market, produce books to conform to the SBOE's curriculum standards. Other state and local school boards, knowing the reluctance of publishers to produce alternative versions of their texts, accept Texas's guidelines and purchase books initially written for the Texas market. It is estimated that currently as many as 47 states use books written for Texas's schoolchildren.[6]

Of particular interest to SBOE observers are its guidelines for teaching biology, which it has had to develop within the context of the long history of legal and political conflict over how—or even whether—Charles Darwin's theory of evolution should be taught in America's public schools. Since Darwin first published *The Origin of Species* in 1859, Christian creationists and social conservatives have continuously challenged the validity of Darwin's ideas.

Creationism is the doctrine that life, humanity, and the universe itself were created by a supernatural being. Whether creationism and evolution are in conflict is debatable. Darwin wrote that all life forms today share a common ancestry—all, including humans, are descended from primordial microscopic organisms, from which they gradually evolved during the course of billions of years through natural selection. Many theologically liberal Christians who consider the Bible allegorical accept evolution, considering God the creator and evolution the humanly discernable means by which He creates. But more conservative Christian creationists interpret the Book of Genesis to say that God created each species of animal suddenly and independently of all others, and created man to exercise dominion over all other life. They further note that Darwin, an agnostic, made almost no mention of God in *The Origin of Species* other than a perfunctory reference, in the last sentence of the book, to "life, with its several powers, having been originally breathed by the Creator into a few forms or into one …" The apparent conflict between Darwin's views and Genesis, and Darwin's failure to attribute to God any meaningful role in evolution, lead creationists to see evolution as an argument for atheism. Many atheists, in fact, do cite Darwin's work as contributing to their lack of religious faith.[7]

Some social conservatives charge Darwin with undermining values on which Western civilization is based. For example, the Seattle-based Discovery Institute, a leading social conservative think tank, says, "The proposition that human beings are created in the image of God is one of the bedrock principles on which Western civilization was built," and influenced the development of "representative democracy, human rights, free enterprise, and progress in the arts and sciences." But by "debunking the traditional conceptions of both God and man," Darwin helped call into question the idea that humans were "moral and spiritual beings," subject to inflexible laws governing human behavior. The Discovery Institute blames Darwin, along with Karl Marx and Sigmund Freud, for the rise of moral relativism and the decline in a sense of personal responsibility.[8] Other critics have charged Darwin with contributing to the rise of racism, Nazism, and communism.[9]

One of the earliest attempts to fight evolution was the passage of laws such as Tennessee's Butler Act, in 1925, which made it illegal, in the Tennessee public schools, "to teach any theory that denies the Story of the Divine Creation of man as taught in the Bible and to teach instead that man has descended from a lower order of animals."[10] In the only trial based on the Butler Act, the 1925 Scopes Monkey Trial, three-time Democratic presidential nominee William Jennings Bryan prosecuted teacher John T. Scopes for teaching evolution in a high school biology class. Scopes, defended by legendary defense attorney Clarence Darrow, was convicted, but his conviction was overturned on a technicality. The Bryan–Darrow clash, featuring Darrow's cross-examination of Bryan on the witness stand, was immortalized in *Inherit the Wind*, a Broadway play that has been made into a theatrical film and three made-for-TV movies.[11]

The Butler Act itself was repealed in 1967. In 1968, the United States Supreme Court declared the teaching of creationism in public schools an unconstitutional violation of the First Amendment's Establishment Clause, which prohibits government promotion of religion. In 1987, the Supreme Court, again citing the Establishment Clause, likewise banned the teaching in the public schools of creation science, a branch of creationism that says the creation story and other events in Genesis are supported by science.[12]

---

[6]Ibid.

[7]Darwin's quote can be found in any edition of *The Origin of Species.* Of the numerous books discussing the relationship between religion and evolution, a representative sample would include Lee Strobel, *The Case for a Creator: A Journalist Investigates Scientific Evidence That Points toward God* (Grand Rapids, MI: Zondervan, 2004); Kenneth R. Miller, *Finding Darwin's God: A Scientist's Search for Common Ground between God and Evolution* (New York: HarperCollins Books, 2000). Strobel and Miller are both devout Christians. Strobel rejects evolution in favor of Intelligent Design, while Miller is one of America's leading defenders of evolution.

[8]The quotations and summary of the Discovery Institute's views can be found in "The Wedge," a statement published by the Discovery Institute's Center for the Renewal of Science and Culture and accessible at www.antievolution.org/features/wedge.pdf.

[9] A fascinating summary of the political uses to which evolutionary theory has been put can be found in James Burke, *The Day the Universe Changed* (Boston and Toronto: Little, Brown and Company, 1985), pp. 260–273.

[10]The complete text of both the Butler Act (Section 49, 1922, *Tennessee Code Annotated*) and the 1967 law that repealed it can be found at www.law.umkc.edu/faculty/projects/ftrials/scopes/tennstat.htm.

[11]The trial is formally known as *Scopes* v. *The State of Tennessee.* Also see Jerome Lawrence and Robert E. Lee, *Inherit the Wind* (New York: Ballantine Books, 2003). The play was first produced in 1955.

[12]The relevant cases are *Epperson* v. *Arkansas* (1968) 393 U.S. 97 (1968); *Edwards* v. *Aguillard*, 482 U.S. 578 (1987).

These rulings stimulated the development of the newest prospective rival to evolution, Intelligent Design (ID). The Discovery Institute defines ID as the doctrine that "certain features of the universe and of living things are best explained by an intelligent cause, not an undirected process such as natural selection," on which evolution is based. In other words, some aspects of life are so complex they could not have merely evolved without guidance. Therefore, they must have been designed. Left open is the question of who the Designer really is, but the rational inference is that the Designer is God.[13]

But in a 2005 trial over whether ID could be presented as an alternative theory to evolution in biology classes taught in the public schools of Dover, Pennsylvania, federal Judge John E. Jones, III, ruled that ID was simply a restatement of creationism, and teaching it was therefore unconstitutional. Indeed, trial testimony established that the leading ID textbook that the Dover students were urged (but not required) to read was simply an updated edition of a text based on creation science.[14]

The response of evolution's opponents on the SBOE reflects the latest strategy to challenge evolution with creationism. Of the 15 members currently on the SBOE, 4 are Democrats and 11 Republicans. Seven Republicans have formed a Christian conservative voting bloc attempting to promote creationism by questioning the strength of the evidence for evolution. For example, evolution stresses the gradual modification of species over time as they develop from their ancient ancestors. But evolution's critics say that the fossil record shows gaps. While evolution's supporters argue that with each passing year paleontologists are discovering more fossils of intermediate species, the critics say gaps exist because evolution is wrong—the Designer created the species suddenly, as Genesis says.

So far, the Christian conservatives on the SBOE have had mixed results. In 2009, when the SBOE reviewed and revised its standards for science textbooks, it voted eight to seven to remove language requiring students to study the "strengths and weaknesses" of evolution and other scientific theories, and also rejected a requirement that students study the "sufficiency or insufficiency" of evolution. Supporters of evolution, believing that questioning it might permit the reintroduction of ID, hailed these votes as a triumph. But the SBOE did vote to require students to "analyze, evaluate and critique" evolution and other theories, and examine "all sides" of issues in science—decisions that the Discovery Institute hailed as victories for evolution's critics.[15]

So the battle over evolution continues, with the SBOE's 2009 decisions giving support to both sides in the conflict. Moreover, the issues raised are increasingly reflected in other fights before the SBOE. In 2010, the SBOE reviewed and revised standards for social science textbooks, and a major question was whether America is a Christian nation. In one sense, the answer is undeniably yes—after all, about 75 percent of Americans say they are Christians. But some religious conservatives argue that America was actually created by God to spread Christianity to the rest of the world, and that the Declaration of Independence and the Constitution of the United States are divinely inspired and based on biblical principles. This cultural dispute will be not be completely resolved now or in the near future, and the impact of the SBOE decisions in the rest of the country remains to be seen. SBOE membership is changing, and textbook publishers are developing new digital publishing technologies to facilitate publishing and distributing different versions of the same book for different states. But the overall issue of man's relationship to God will no doubt continue to be debated as long as God and man exist.

JOIN THE DEBATE

1. How do SBOE decisions reflect Texas's conservative political culture? How should public schools deal with culturally sensitive issues in a democracy?

2. Do you agree or disagree with court rulings that the teaching of creationism, creation science, and intelligent design are unconstitutional because they are based on religion?

3. In what ways should bureaucratic agencies be held politically accountable for their decisions when they may have such a sweeping impact on society?

---

[13]See www.discovery.org/csc/topQuestions.php for the Discovery Institute's discussion of Intelligent Design. The Discovery Institute denies that ID is either based on the Bible or the same as creationism and claims to be "agnostic regarding the source of design …".

[14]The relevant case is *Tammy Kitzmiller et al.* v. *Dover Area School District et al.* (400 F. Supp. 2d 707, Docket no. 4cv2688). The text in question was Percival Davis and Dean H. Kenyon, *Of Pandas and People: The Central Question of Biological Origins* (Richardson, TX: Foundation for Thought and Ethics 1989, 2nd ed. 1993). Copies of the text had been donated to Dover's schools.

[15]A sample of articles on the debate before the SBOE includes Stephanie Simon, "Texas Opens Classroom Door for Evolution Doubts," *The Wall Street Journal*, March 28, 2009, http://online.wsj.com/article/SB123819751472561761.html; Gordy Slack, "Texas on Evolution: Needs Further Study, *Salon.com,* March 28, 2009, www.salon.com/environment/-feature/2009/03/28/texas-evolution-case/index.html; Terrence Stutz, "Conservatives Lose Another Battle over Evolution, *The Dallas Morning News*, March 29, 2009, www.dallasnews.com/sharedcontent/dws/texassouthwest/stories/DN-evolution; "Texas Board Comes Down on Two Sides of Creationism Debate," CNN.com, www.cnn.com/2009/US/03/27/texas.education.evolution/. The Discovery Institute hailed the outcome of the SBOE's deliberations at www.evolutionnews.org/2009/03/dallas_news_ofers_alt.html. Also visit www.tea.state.tx.us/index3.aspx?id=1156 for the Texas State Board of Education official records.

CHAPTER SUMMARY

★ Public administration can be seen as a government activity that applies the power of government to enforce its policies. Size, hierarchy, expertise, and neutrality characterize all bureaucracies. The size of the bureaucracy has increased dramatically in the past century as demands for government action, assistance, and regulation have increased. Government bureaucracies in the United States are large and may seem overwhelming to individuals or small businesses that must deal with them. This leads many people to conclude that we live in an "administrative state" ruled by bureaucrats who are largely independent and lack real accountability to any politically responsible official. Thus, big government, which is really big bureaucracy, is increasingly criticized by people on both sides of the political spectrum.

★ Bureaucracies are legally organized into hierarchies with centralized control and accountability at the top. The lines of authority and communication are clearly established, although in practice they may not be followed. In contrast, the most notable characteristic of the Texas administration

is that no single official is responsible for the execution of policy. Numerous elected and appointed officials sit atop a multitude of little hierarchies and are normally accountable to no one in particular except their clientele interest groups.

★ Bureaucrats develop extensive specialization and experience in particular job classifications. Ideally, this results in increased job efficiency, but it is also a major source of bureaucratic power.

★ Although administrative neutrality is a goal long pursued by reformists, it remains a myth because politics cannot be separated from administration. All attempts to develop neutrality, such as the civil service and independent boards and commissions, have simply substituted one kind of politics for another.

★ Elected officials and public interest groups have devised various techniques to hold Texas administrations accountable, but real administrative accountability will ultimately rest with the agency's clientele interest group.

HOW TEXAS COMPARES

★ Texas's bureaucracy is less controlled by its chief executive than in most states. Texas's governor is part of a plural executive system in which more independently elected officers share executive power than is typical. Texas is among the few states that lack a cabinet system to coordinate programs, to supervise agencies, and to advise the governor. The governor's power to appoint, remove, and direct agency heads is more limited than in most states. In no state is the chief executive's influence over agency budgets limited by the dominant influence of the competing Legislative Budget Board.

★ State and local employees in Texas outnumber federal government employees by a substantial number. The largest total of Texas's government employees by far are those of cities, counties, and special districts. Most public services are provided by state and local governments rather than by federal agencies.

KEY TERMS

administrative law, *p. 262*
administrative review, *p. 262*
attorney general's opinion, *p. 246*
bureaucracy, *p. 245*
cabinet system, *p. 264*

civil service (merit) system, *p. 255*
clientele interest groups, *p. 258*
contract spoils or patronage, *p. 254*

elective accountability, *p. 263*
hierarchy, *p. 254*
Iron Texas Star, *p. 259*
ombudsman, *p. 266*
open-meetings laws, *p. 265*

open-records law, *p. 266*
privatization, *p. 254*
spoils system, *p. 254*
whistle-blowers, *p. 266*

REVIEW QUESTIONS

1. Define and explain the characteristics of a bureaucracy. What are the characteristics of the Texas bureaucracy? How does the Texas bureaucracy differ from the hierarchy model of Max Weber?

2. Discuss the importance of the Texas bureaucracy in policy formation, development, and implementation.

3. Describe the interaction of political players illustrated by the Iron Texas Star model. Discuss the various methods used to hold the bureaucracy accountable to the people. Which methods are used in Texas government? Which method do you believe is most effective?

4. How do the open-records and open-meetings laws affect bureaucratic behavior? Why are these laws important?

5. Become familiar with Texas's elected executives and elected boards. To whom are they responsible? How do they affect the governor's ability to serve as the chief executive of Texas?

6. What is the structural organization of Texas's appointed and ex officio boards and commissions? What role do they play in Texas government? To whom are they responsible?

LOGGING ON

Each member of the statewide elected executives has a separate Web site:

★ Governor: **www.governor.state.tx.us**

★ Attorney general: **www.oag.state.tx.us**

★ Comptroller of public accounts: **www.cpa.state.tx.us**

★ Commissioner of the General Land Office: **www.glo.state.tx.us**

★ Commissioner of agriculture: **www.agr.state.tx.us**

★ Lieutenant governor: **www.ltgov.state.tx.us/**

The key appointed executives also have Web sites:

★ Secretary of state: **www.sos.state.tx.us**

★ Adjutant general: **www.agd.state.tx.us**

The key elected boards in Texas have the following sites:

★ Railroad Commission: **www.rrc.state.tx.us**

★ Texas Education Agency: **www.tea.state.tx.us**

★ State Board of Education: **http://www.tea.state.tx.us/index3.aspx?id=1156.**

To follow money in politics, try OpenSecrets.org at **www.opensecrets.org**, Public Citizen of Texas at **www.citizen.org/texas**, and Texans for Public Justice at **www.tpj.org.**

Chapter 11

Texas Judiciary

LEARNING OBJECTIVES

★ Demonstrate knowledge of the judicial branch of Texas government.

★ Distinguish the differences between criminal and civil cases.

★ Understand the differences between original and appellate jurisdiction.

★ Explain how the courts are organized in Texas and identify the jurisdiction of each major court.

★ Distinguish the types of cases handled by the Texas Supreme Court from those decided by the Texas Court of Criminal Appeals.

★ Understand the role of grand juries and trial juries and analyze the responsibilities of citizens in the legal system in Texas.

★ Compare the most common methods of judicial selection in the United States to the methods Texas uses to select judges.

★ Understand the major criticisms of the Texas judicial system and predict whether reformers will be successful in their efforts to revise the system.

★ Support independent courts at **www .justiceatstake.org/**. On the state drop-down menu, click on "Your State's National Map."

★ Fight for the independence, ethics, and unbiased selection of judges with the American Judicature Society at **www.ajs .org/**.

★ Track money and corporate influence in Texas politics at Texans for Public Justice at **www.tpj.org/**.

★ Team up with groups that advocate using the courts to protect consumers, workers, and patients, such as the American Association for Justice at **www.atla.org/** and its associated state organization, the Texas Trial Lawyers Association at **www .ttla.com/tx**.

★ Be an intelligent juror. Check out the jury selection system in your county at **www .juryduty.org/JuryDuty.htm**.

An attorney addresses the jury in a civil trial.

Why have civil suits become so common in Texas? Explain the differences between civil and criminal law.

© 2012 Stockbyte/Jupiterimages Corporation

American society has increasingly turned to the judiciary to find answers to personal, economic, social, and political problems. Courts are often asked to determine our rights, and important legal questions touch almost every aspect of our lives. For example, what level of privacy should we expect in our cars, offices, and homes? What treatment should people of different racial, gender, or age groups expect? In a divorce proceeding, with which parent should the children live? Should an accused person go to jail, and if so, for how long? Should a woman be allowed to terminate her pregnancy? Should a patient be allowed to refuse potential lifesaving treatment? These are among the thousands of questions asked and answered daily by courts in the United States.

In fact, we are considered the most litigious society in the world. We have approximately one-quarter of the world's lawyers.[1] There are more than 1 million attorneys in the United States today.[2] Whereas 1 out of approximately every 700 people was a lawyer in 1951, that figure is now 1 out of approximately 260 people.[3] As a comparison, Japan has almost 29,000 lawyers, or 1 for every 4,700 people.[4]

---

[1]G. Alan Tarr, *Judicial Process and Judicial Policymaking*, 5th ed. (Belmont, CA: Wadsworth, 2009), p. 97.
[2]American Bar Association, *National Lawyer Population by State, 2011*, www.americanbar.org/content/dam/aba/ migrated/marketresearch/PublicDocuments/lawyer_count_by_state_20012011_1.pdf.
[3]G. Alan Tarr, *Judicial Process and Judicial Policymaking*, 5th ed. (Belmont, CA: Wadsworth, 2009), p. 98.
[4]Robert Carp, Ronald Stidham, and Kenneth L. Manning, *Judicial Process in America*, 8th ed. (Washington, DC: CQ Press, 2009), p. 111; Japan Federation of Bar Association, 2010 Fiscal Year Country Report, http://www .nichibenren.or.jp/library/en/document/data/2010CountryReport_JFBA.pdf.

Texas clearly fits into this general pattern of using the courts often. Texas has been found to rank 18th among the states in terms of litigation.[5] In recent years, it was found to have 292 people per attorney.[6] Texas also has more than 2,700 courts and approximately 3,400 justices or judges.[7] These courts dealt with more than 9 million cases in 2011, or on average, almost one case for every three residents of the state.[8] In recent years, Texas courts have heard important or controversial cases involving topics such as flag burning, the death penalty, school desegregation, school finance, sexual orientation, the welfare of children in a polygamist sect, and one of the largest civil cases in history in which Texaco was found liable to Pennzoil for more than $8.5 billion.

In this chapter, our focus will be the Texas judicial system and general attributes of American legal procedure and process. What will quickly become clear is the sheer size and complexity of the Texas court system. Furthermore, courts are undeniably important because they affect our lives. This is due to the subject matter they consider, which determines our legal rights and often shapes public policy. What should also become clear is that various controversies surround the selection of Texas judges and the politics connected to these courts.

CIVIL AND CRIMINAL CASES

In the American legal system, cases are generally classified as either civil or criminal; Table 11.1 shows the most important differences between these two types of cases. A **civil case** concerns private rights and remedies and usually involves private parties or organizations (*Smith* v. *Jones*), although the government may occasionally be a party to a civil case. A personal injury suit, a divorce case, a child custody dispute, a breach-of-contract case, a challenge to utility rates, and a dispute over water rights are all examples of civil suits.

A **criminal case** involves a violation of penal law. If convicted, the lawbreaker may be punished by a fine, imprisonment, or both. The action is by the state against the accused (*State of Texas* v. *Smith*). Typical examples of criminal actions range from arson, rape, murder, armed robbery, and embezzlement to speeding and jaywalking.

One of the most important differences between civil and criminal cases, such as these, is the **burden of proof** (the duty and degree to which a party must prove its position). In civil cases, the standard used is a **preponderance of the evidence**. This means that whichever party has more evidence or proof on its side should win the case, no matter how slight the differential is. However, in a criminal case, the burden of proof falls heavily on the government or prosecution. The prosecution must prove that the defendant is guilty **beyond a reasonable doubt**. The evidence must overwhelmingly, without serious question or doubt, point to the defendant's guilt; otherwise, the defendant should be found "not guilty."

Civil case
Nonpenal case dealing with private rights and responsibilities.

Criminal case
Case prosecuted by the state, seeking punishment for a violation of the penal code.

Burden of proof
The duty of a party in a court case to prove its position.

Preponderance of the evidence
The amount of evidence necessary for a party to win in a civil case; proof that outweighs the evidence offered in opposition to it.

Beyond a reasonable doubt
The standard used to determine the guilt or innocence of a person criminally charged. To prove a defendant guilty, the state must provide sufficient evidence of guilt such that jurors have no doubt that might cause a reasonable person to question whether the accused was guilty.

---

[5]*NACD Magazine*, June 11, 2010, www.directorship.com/the-annual-litigation-guide.
[6]*U.S. Census Bureau, State and County Quickfacts*, January 17, 2012, quickfacts.census.gov/qfd/states/48000.html; *State Bar of Texas Membership, Attorney Statistical Profile*, December 31, 2010, www.texasbar.com/AM/Template .cfm?Section=Demographic_and_Economic_Trends&Template=/CM/ContentDisplay.cfm&ContentID=13344.
[7]*Annual Statistical Report for the Texas Judiciary, Fiscal Year 2011* (Austin: Office of Court Administration, Texas Judicial Council, 2012), www.txcourts.gov/pubs/AR2011/toc.htm; "Texas Court System Study," unpublished manuscript, 2012, Adrianna Brosovic, Jesse Calderon, Olivia Llanes, Neal Parekh, and Phariborze Shavandy.
[8]Ibid.

TABLE 11.1 Major Differences between Civil and Criminal Cases

Civil Cases	Criminal Cases
Deal primarily with individual or property rights and involve the concept of responsibility but not guilt.	Deal with public concepts of proper behavior and morality as defined in penal law. A plea of guilty or not guilty is entered.
Plaintiff, or petitioner, who brings suit is often a private party, as is the defendant or respondent.	Case is initiated by a government prosecutor on behalf of the public.
Dispute is usually set out in a petition.	Specific charges of wrongdoing are spelled out in a grand jury indictment or a writ of information.
A somewhat more relaxed procedure is used to balance or weigh the evidence; the side with the preponderance of the evidence wins the suit.	Strict rules of procedure are used to evaluate evidence. The standard of proof is guilt beyond a reasonable doubt.
Final court remedy is relief from or compensation for the violation of legal rights.	Determination of guilt results in punishment.

Civil and criminal cases involve very different concepts of law based on different court procedures, who brings the case, and the consequences that result from court decisions in each type of case.

▲ **Why should criminal cases require a higher standard of proof than civil cases?**

ORIGINAL AND APPELLATE JURISDICTION

Original jurisdiction

The authority of a court to consider a case in the first instance; the power to try a case, as contrasted with appellate jurisdiction.

Appellate jurisdiction

The power vested in an appellate court to review and revise the judicial action of an inferior court.

Brief

A written argument prepared by the counsel arguing a case in court that summarizes the facts of the case, the pertinent laws, and the application of those laws to the facts supporting the counsel's position.

Double jeopardy

A second prosecution for the same offense after acquittal in the first trial.

Original jurisdiction is the power to try a case being heard for the first time. It involves following legal rules of procedure in hearing witnesses, viewing material evidence, and examining other evidence (such as documentary evidence) to determine guilt in criminal cases or responsibility in civil cases. The judge oversees procedure, but evaluating evidence is the jury's job (unless the right to a jury trial has been waived, in which case the judge weighs the evidence). The verdict or judgment is determined and the remedy set. A trial involves the determination of fact and the application of law.

Appellate jurisdiction refers to the power of an appellate court to review the decisions of a lower court. Such appeals do not involve a new trial but rather a review of the law as it was applied in the original trial. Many appeals are decided by review of the record (transcript) of the case and the lawyers' **briefs** (written arguments); sometimes lawyers may appear and present oral arguments. Appellate proceedings are based on law (legal process), not fact (no witnesses or material or documentary evidence). A reversal does not necessarily mean that the individual who was convicted is innocent, only that the legal process was improper. Consequently, that person may be tried again, and questions of **double jeopardy** (being prosecuted twice for the same offense) are not involved because the individual waives the right against double jeopardy by appealing the case.

Sometimes an action may have both civil and criminal overtones. Suppose that in the course of an armed robbery, the thief shoots a clerk at a convenience store. The state could prosecute for the robbery (criminal action), and the clerk could sue for compensation for medical expenses, lost earning power, and other damages (civil action). This dual nature is not unusual.

Did you know? Former Texas Supreme Court Chief Justice Tom Phillips summarized the problem of Texas court organization when he said "We simply have too many courts."

COURT ORGANIZATION

Figure 11.1 shows the organizational structure of the Texas court system and the various types and levels of courts in the system. It is important to note that some courts within this rather large and complicated system have overlapping jurisdiction.

Municipal Courts

The state authorizes incorporated cities and towns to establish municipal courts, and city charters or municipal ordinances provide for their status and organization.

Legally, the municipal courts have exclusive jurisdiction to try violations of city ordinances. They also handle minor violations of state law—class C misdemeanors for which punishment is a fine of $500 or less and does not include a jail sentence. (Justice of the peace courts have overlapping jurisdiction to handle such minor violations.) Most municipal court cases in Texas involve traffic and parking violations (see Figure 11.2).[9]

The legislature has authorized the city governments to determine whether their municipal courts are *courts of record*. Normally they are not. However, when they are so designated, records from such courts are the basis of appeal to the appropriate county court. (Only slightly more than one percent of all cases are appealed from municipal courts.) Otherwise, where records are not kept, defendants may demand a completely new trial (trial *de novo*) in overworked county courts, where most such cases are simply dismissed. Where it is available, drivers frequently use this procedure to avoid traffic convictions and higher auto insurance rates. Latin for "anew," a *de novo* trial is a new trial conducted in a higher court (as opposed to an appeal). In *de novo* cases, higher courts completely retry cases. On appeal, higher courts simply review the law as decided by the lower courts.

People who favor the court-of-record concept point to the large amount of revenue lost because trials *de novo* usually result in dismissal. Opponents of the concept argue that municipal courts are too often operated as a means of raising revenue rather than for achieving justice. The fact that municipal courts collected $751 million in 2011 lends some support to the latter argument.[10]

Judges of the municipal courts meet whatever qualifications are set by the city charter or ordinances. Some cities require specific legal training or experience. Other charters say very little about qualifications. Judges may serve for one year or indefinitely. Most are appointed for two-year terms but serve at the pleasure of the governing bodies that have selected them. Furthermore, these judges' salaries are paid entirely by their respective cities and vary widely. Where statutes authorize them, some cities have established more than one municipal court or more than one judge for each court. In view of the volume of cases pending before these courts, the need for a number of judges is obvious.

As will be discussed in the next section, public confidence in municipal courts is low. Out-of-town, out-of-county, or out-of-state residents often expect to be found guilty regardless of the evidence presented. Interestingly, 41.6 percent of all cases filed in municipal courts in 2011 were settled before trial.[11] Such large percentages of settlement could indicate guilt or that many people fear that the legal process will not be fair. It could also indicate people's desire to avoid the inconvenience or expense of going through a trial.

Justices of the Peace

The *justice of the peace* courts in Texas are authorized by the Texas Constitution, which requires that county commissioners establish at least one and not more than eight justice precincts per county (the area from which the justice of the peace is elected for each four-year term). County commissioners determine how many justices of the peace shall be elected (determined by the population) and where their courts shall sit. Changes are made continuously, making it difficult to determine the number of justices of the peace at any given time. The Texas Judicial Council determined that there were 817 justices of the peace in 2011.[12]

De novo

Latin for "anew"; a *de novo* trial is a new trial conducted in a higher court (as opposed to an appeal). In *de novo* cases, higher courts completely retry cases. On appeal, higher courts simply review the law as decided by the lower courts.

---

[9]Ibid.
[10]Ibid.
[11]Ibid.
[12]Ibid.

Figure 11.1

Court Structure of Texas

This court organizational chart arranges Texas courts from those that handle the least serious cases (bottom) to the highest appeals courts (top). As you read the text, look for ways to simplify and professionalize the state's court structure.

Source: Office of Court Administration, Texas Judicial Council, *Texas Judicial System Annual Report 2011,* (March 2012), p.2 at www.courts.state .tx.us/pubs/AR2011/jud_ branch/1-court-structure-chart.pdf.

How can Texas voters intelligently choose between candidates for so many judicial positions? How could the court structure be simplified?

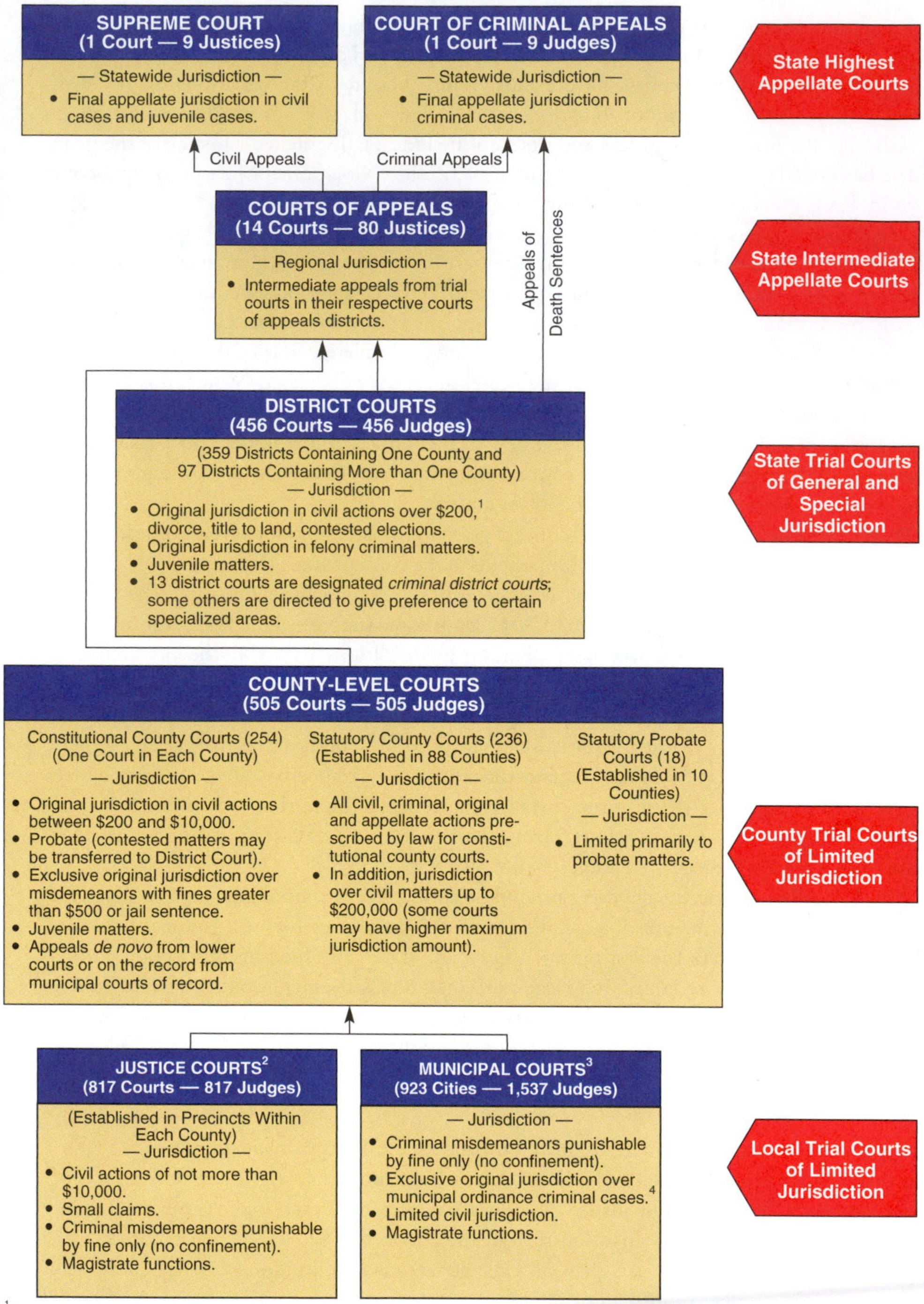

SUPREME COURT
(1 Court — 9 Justices)

— Statewide Jurisdiction —
- Final appellate jurisdiction in civil cases and juvenile cases.

COURT OF CRIMINAL APPEALS
(1 Court — 9 Judges)

— Statewide Jurisdiction —
- Final appellate jurisdiction in criminal cases.

State Highest Appellate Courts

Civil Appeals → | Criminal Appeals → | Appeals of Death Sentences

COURTS OF APPEALS
(14 Courts — 80 Justices)

— Regional Jurisdiction —
- Intermediate appeals from trial courts in their respective courts of appeals districts.

State Intermediate Appellate Courts

DISTRICT COURTS
(456 Courts — 456 Judges)

(359 Districts Containing One County and 97 Districts Containing More than One County)
— Jurisdiction —
- Original jurisdiction in civil actions over $200,[1] divorce, title to land, contested elections.
- Original jurisdiction in felony criminal matters.
- Juvenile matters.
- 13 district courts are designated *criminal district courts*; some others are directed to give preference to certain specialized areas.

State Trial Courts of General and Special Jurisdiction

COUNTY-LEVEL COURTS
(505 Courts — 505 Judges)

Constitutional County Courts (254)
(One Court in Each County)
— Jurisdiction —
- Original jurisdiction in civil actions between $200 and $10,000.
- Probate (contested matters may be transferred to District Court).
- Exclusive original jurisdiction over misdemeanors with fines greater than $500 or jail sentence.
- Juvenile matters.
- Appeals *de novo* from lower courts or on the record from municipal courts of record.

Statutory County Courts (236)
(Established in 88 Counties)
— Jurisdiction —
- All civil, criminal, original and appellate actions prescribed by law for constitutional county courts.
- In addition, jurisdiction over civil matters up to $200,000 (some courts may have higher maximum jurisdiction amount).

Statutory Probate Courts (18)
(Established in 10 Counties)
— Jurisdiction —
- Limited primarily to probate matters.

County Trial Courts of Limited Jurisdiction

JUSTICE COURTS[2]
(817 Courts — 817 Judges)

(Established in Precincts Within Each County)
— Jurisdiction —
- Civil actions of not more than $10,000.
- Small claims.
- Criminal misdemeanors punishable by fine only (no confinement).
- Magistrate functions.

MUNICIPAL COURTS[3]
(923 Cities — 1,537 Judges)

— Jurisdiction —
- Criminal misdemeanors punishable by fine only (no confinement).
- Exclusive original jurisdiction over municipal ordinance criminal cases.[4]
- Limited civil jurisdiction.
- Magistrate functions.

Local Trial Courts of Limited Jurisdiction

[1] The Texas Judicial Council reports that the dollar amount is currently unclear under Texas law.
[2] All justice courts and most municipal courts are not courts of record. Appeals from these courts are by trial *de novo* in the county-level courts, and in some instances in the district courts.
[3] Some municipal courts are courts of record—appeals from those courts are taken on the record to the county-level courts.
[4] An offense that arises under a municipal ordinance is punishable by a fine not to exceed: (1) $2,000 for ordinances that govern fire safety, zoning, and public health or (2) $500 for all others.

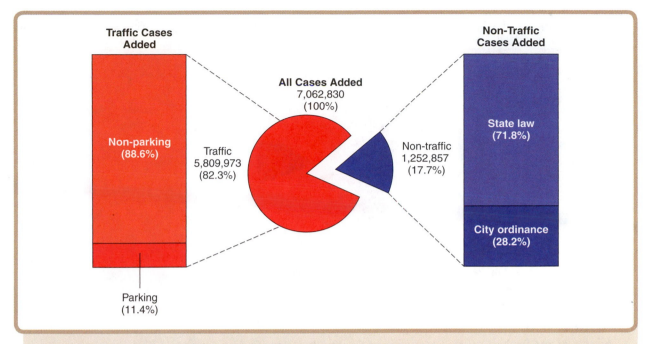

Figure 11.2

Cases Filed in Municipal Courts, Year Ending August 31, 2011

Notice that the largest slice of the pie chart is for traffic cases.

Texas Judicial System Annual Report, 2011. Activity Report for Municipal Courts (Austin: Office of Court Administration, Texas Judicial Council, 2011), www.courts.state.tx.us/pubs/AR2011/mn/2-mn-courts-overall-activity.pdf.

Should municipal courts serve as a major source of city revenue? What is the argument for making these courts of record?

The functions of the justice of the peace courts are varied. They have jurisdiction over criminal cases where the fine is less than $500. Original jurisdiction in civil matters extends to cases where the dispute involves less than $10,000. They may issue warrants for search and arrest, serve ex officio as notaries public, conduct preliminary hearings, perform marriages, serve as coroners in counties having no medical examiner, and serve as small claims courts. Figure 11.3 shows that most cases filed in justice courts were criminal and involved traffic violations.[13]

Qualifications and Objectivity

All these functions are performed by an official whose only qualification is to be a registered voter. No specific statutory or constitutional provisions require that a justice of the peace must be a lawyer. A justice of the peace who is not a licensed attorney is required by statute to take a 40-hour course in the performance of the duties of the office, plus a 20-hour course each year thereafter at an accredited state-supported institution of higher education. Serious questions have arisen as to the constitutionality of this provision because it adds a qualification for the office not specified in the constitution. Also, justice of the peace salaries vary a great deal from county to county and possibly from justice to justice within the same county.

The public's perception of justices of the peace is often not flattering; many justices are regarded as biased individuals, untrained in the law, and incompetent to hold the office.

[13]Ibid.

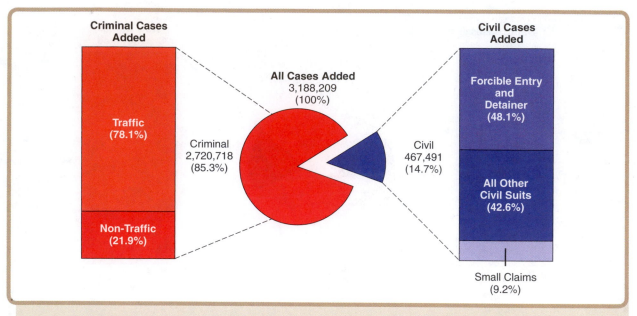

Criminal Cases Added

Traffic (78.1%)

Non-Traffic (21.9%)

All Cases Added
3,188,209 (100%)

Criminal 2,720,718 (85.3%)

Civil 467,491 (14.7%)

Civil Cases Added

Forcible Entry and Detainer (48.1%)

All Other Civil Suits (42.6%)

Small Claims (9.2%)

Figure 11.3

Justice of the Peace Courts: Categories of Cases Filed, Year Ending August 31, 2011

The pie chart for All Cases Added shows that most cases in justice of the peace courts are criminal, and the breakdown chart shows that most of these are traffic cases.

Source: Office of Court Administration, Texas Judicial Council, *Texas Judicial System Annual Report, 2011*: Justice Courts, Overall Activity.

What problems might drivers experience as they seek justice in justice of the peace courts?

Skepticism about receiving a fair trial may be a major factor in the settlement of a high percentage of cases before trial. If a person appears before a justice of the peace in a county other than that of his or her home, the general assumption is that fairness and decency are the exception rather than the rule.

Justices of the peace who are conscientious, objective, and fair find it difficult to overcome the stereotype, and this negative image is reinforced by the activities of justices of the peace who act as coroners. Though the function of the coroner is to determine the cause of death in specified cases, for decades, stories have been told about such verdicts that left more questions than answers.

Thus, despite changes affecting the qualifications, salaries, and responsibilities of justices of the peace, they still do not inspire confidence in many people. Defenders traditionally refer to the justice courts as the "people's courts" and maintain that elimination of the justice courts would remove the close contact many treasure. To eliminate them, it is argued, would put judicial power in the hands of professionals and would ignore the amateur status of these courts, which depend to a considerable extent on common-sense law. This is consistent with the widely held view that government is best when it is closest to the people. Critics counter that incompetence, bias, or stupidity is not justified simply because these courts are close to the people.

County Courts

Each of the 254 counties in Texas has a *county court* presided over by the county judge (sometimes referred to, respectively, as the *constitutional county court* and the *constitutional county judge*). The Texas Constitution requires that the county judge be elected by voters for a four-year term and be "well informed in the law of the state"—a rather ambiguous stipulation. Thus, the constitution does not require that a county judge possess a law degree. Salaries are paid by the county and vary greatly. County courts handle probate and other civil matters in which the dispute is between $200 and $10,000, and their criminal jurisdiction is confined to serious misdemeanors for which punishment is a fine greater than $500 or a jail sentence not to exceed one year.

Because the constitutional county judge also has administrative responsibilities as presiding officer of the commissioners' court (the governing body for Texas counties and not a judicial entity at all), he or she may have little time to handle judicial matters. The legislature has responded to this by establishing county courts-at-law in certain counties to act as auxiliary or supplemental courts, in some, but not all of Texas's counties. The qualifications of the judges of the statutory county courts-at-law vary according to the statute that established the particular court. In addition to residence in the county, a court-at-law judge usually must have four years of experience as a practicing attorney or judge.

Various state laws determine whether these courts have either civil or criminal jurisdiction or a combination of both. Their civil jurisdiction involves cases less than $100,000. Their criminal jurisdiction includes misdemeanors that are more serious than those tried by the justice of the peace and municipal courts or misdemeanors that include a jail sentence or a fine in excess of $500. More than two-thirds of cases disposed in county-level courts are criminal (see Figure 11.4), with cases involving theft and driving while intoxicated or under the influence of drugs being the most common. Civil cases include probate matters and suits to collect debt.

Administration of justice is very uneven in Texas county courts. Although many of the judges are competent and run their courts in an orderly manner, others regard their courts and

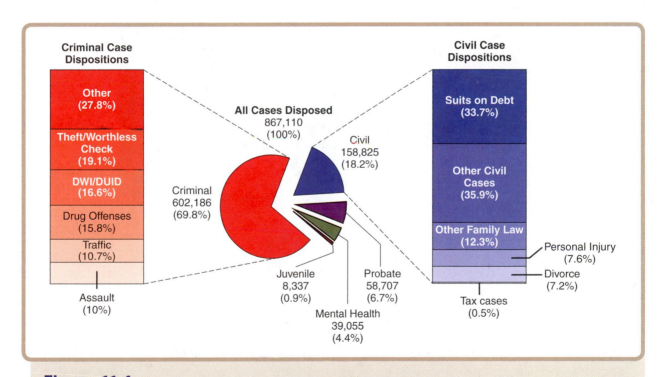

Figure 11.4

County Level Courts: Categories of Cases Disposed, Year Ending August 31, 2010

The pie chart shows that county-level courts mostly handle criminal cases, and the bar graphs show that a wide range of cases are decided by these courts.

Source: Office of Court Administration, Texas Judicial Council, *Texas Judicial System Annual Report, 2010*: County-Level Courts, Summary of Activity by Case Type; updated stats and labels for graph: www.txcourts.gov/pubs/AR2010/AR10.pdf.

What are the differences between constitutional county courts and statutory county courts-at-law?

official jurisdictions as personal fiefdoms, paying little attention to the finer points of law or accepted procedures. Opportunities for arbitrary action are compounded if the county judge is performing as a judicial officer as well as the chief administrative officer of the county.

District Courts

District courts are often described as the *chief trial courts* of the state, and as a group, these courts are called the *general trial courts.* The names of these courts and their jurisdictions vary (e.g., constitutional district courts, civil district courts, criminal district courts, and so on, through more than 40 jurisdictions). Currently, there are 456 district courts, all of which function as single-judge courts. Each judge, elected for four-year terms by voters in their districts, must be at least twenty-five years of age, a resident of the district for two years, a citizen of the United States, and a licensed practicing lawyer or judge for a combined four years. Texas pays $125,000 of the salary of each district judge, and although each county may supplement the salary, the total must be at least $1,000 less than that received by justices of the courts of appeals.

District courts possess jurisdiction in felony cases, which comprise approximately one-third of their caseload.[14] Civil cases in which the matter of controversy exceeds $200 may also be tried in district courts, and such cases constitute the greatest share of their workload (see Figure 11.5).

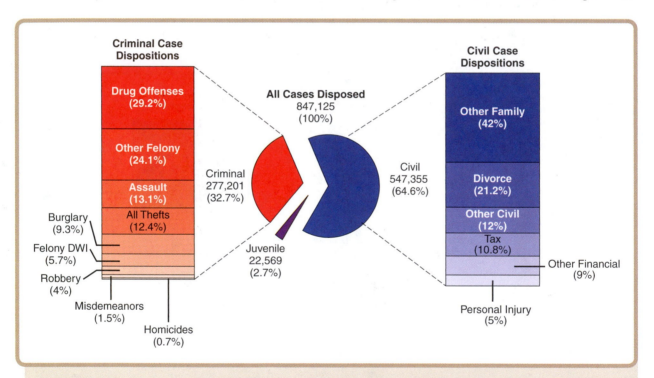

Figure 11.5

District Courts: Categories of Cases Disposed, Year Ending August 31, 2010

The pie chart and bar graphs show the kind of serious legal matters that district courts decide. Explain how many of these district court cases are settled by negotiated agreements between the parties.

Source:Office of Court Administration, Texas Judicial Council, *Texas Judicial System Annual Report, 2010*: District Courts, Summary of Activity by Case Type. www.courts.state.tx.us/pubs/AR2010/dc/4-summary-of-activity-by-case-type.pdf.

What are the benefits and problems resulting from legal negotiations such as plea bargaining?

[14]Ibid.

In addition, juvenile cases are usually tried in district courts. Although most district courts exercise both criminal and civil jurisdiction, there is a tendency in metropolitan areas to specialize in criminal, civil, or family law matters.

The caseload for these courts is so heavy that **plea bargaining** is often used to dispose of criminal cases. Plea bargaining refers to a situation in which the prosecutor and defense attorney negotiate an agreement whereby the accused pleads guilty to a less serious crime than originally charged or in return for a reduction in the sentence to be served. This process saves the state a tremendous amount of time and cost. For example, it is often estimated that approximately 90 percent of criminal cases are disposed of in this way. If plea bargaining were not used in many urban areas, court delays would be increased by months if not years. Although efficient, this practice raises many issues concerning equity and justice because it often encourages innocent people to plead guilty and allows guilty people to escape with less punishment than provided for by the law.

Likewise, many civil lawsuits are resolved by negotiated settlements between the parties. At times this may be an appropriate and just recourse, yet in many urban areas, there is such a backlog of cases before the courts that it can take years for a matter to be heard and settled. As a result, litigants often choose to settle their case out of court for reasons other than justice.

Plea bargaining
Negotiations between the prosecution and the defense to obtain a lighter sentence or other benefits in exchange for a guilty plea by the accused.

Courts of Appeals

Fourteen *courts of appeals* hear immediate appeals in both civil and criminal cases from district and county courts in their area. Actually, only a small percentage of trial court cases are appealed; for example, in 2011, the courts of appeals disposed of 11,936 cases, and the appeals courts reversed the decision of the trial court in only 700 of those cases.[15]

The state pays each chief justice $140,000 and each associate justice $137,500, and counties may pay a supplement to appeals judges. Appeals judges are elected from their districts for six-year terms (see Figure 11.6) and must be at least thirty-five years of age, with a minimum of ten years of experience as a lawyer or judge.

Court of Criminal Appeals

Texas has a dual system of courts of last resort. The Texas Supreme Court is the highest state appellate court in civil matters, and the Texas Court of Criminal Appeals is the highest state appellate court in criminal matters. Only Oklahoma has a similar system.

Although most criminal cases decided by the fourteen courts of appeals do not advance further, some are heard by the court of criminal appeals, which consists of a presiding judge and eight other judges. Criminal court judges are elected statewide in partisan elections for six-year overlapping terms. They must be at least thirty-five years of age and be lawyers or judges with ten years of experience. The presiding judge of the court of criminal appeals receives a salary of $150,000; other judges receive $137,000.

The court of criminal appeals has exclusive jurisdiction over automatic appeals in death penalty cases. Since the U.S. Supreme Court restored the use of capital punishment in 1976, Texas has executed far more citizens than any other state.

As of January 2012, the state had executed 478 people since 1976.[16] Since 1990, the average has been approximately 13 a year.[17] Death penalty cases have led to a number of headline stories, including controversies regarding the use of lethal injection, persons who

---

[15]Ibid.
[16]State by State Database," *Death Penalty Information Center*, February 2012.
[17]Ibid.

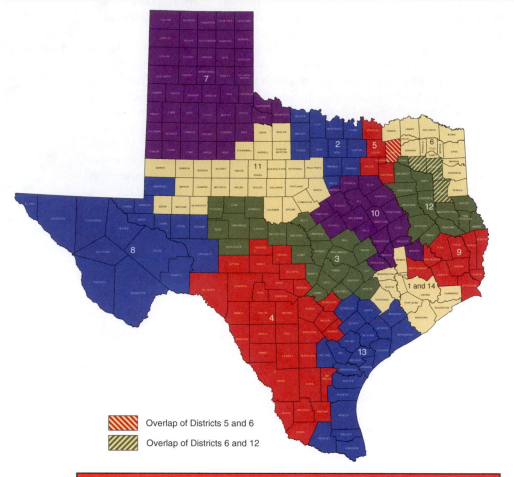

Overlap of Districts 5 and 6		
Overlap of Districts 6 and 12		

Court No.	Location	Number of Judges
1	Houston	9
2	Fort Worth	7
3	Austin	6
4	San Antonio	7
5	Dallas	13
6	Texarkana	3
7	Amarillo	4
8	El Paso	4
9	Beaumont	4
10	Waco	3
11	Eastland	3
12	Tyler	3
13	Corpus Christi	6
14	Houston	9

Figure 11.6

Appeals Court Districts (Map with Table)

Fourteen courts of appeals serve the geographical areas shown on this map. These courts handle both criminal and civil appeals from district courts in their area.

Texas Legislative Council, Courts of Appeals Districts, www.tlc.state.tx.us/redist/pdf/COA05_map.pdf; Office of Court Administration, Annual Report for the Texas Judiciary: 2011, p. 31.

How does appellate jurisdiction differ from original jurisdiction?

were juveniles at the time of their crime, those who receive poor legal counsel, or persons who might actually be innocent of the crime.[18]

Supreme Court

The Texas Supreme Court is the final court of appeals in civil and juvenile cases. Original jurisdiction of the court extends to the issuance of writs and the conduct of proceedings for involuntary retirement or removal of judges. All other cases are in appellate jurisdiction. The court also has the power to establish rules for the administration of justice—rules of civil practice and procedure for courts having civil jurisdiction. In addition, it makes rules governing licensing of members of the state bar.

The supreme court consists of one chief justice and eight associate justices—all elected statewide after their nominations in party primaries. Three of the nine justices are elected every two years for six-year terms. Texas Supreme Court justices must be at least thirty-five years of age, a citizen of the United States, a resident of Texas, and a lawyer or judge of a court of record for at least ten years. The salary of the chief justice is $152,500, and the salary of associate justices is $150,000.

The Texas Supreme Court spends much of its time deciding which petitions for review will be granted because not all appeals are heard. Generally, it only takes cases it views as presenting the most significant legal issues. It should also be noted that the supreme court at times plays a policy-making role in the state. For example, in 1989, the court unanimously declared, in *Edgewood* v. *Kirby* (777 S.W.2d 391), that the huge disparities between rich and poor school districts were unacceptable and ordered changes in the financing of Texas's public schools. The supreme court has also made important decisions in terms of oil, gas, and water rights.[20]

Courtesy of the Texas Court of Criminal Appeals

The Texas Court of Criminal Appeals is the final court for criminal appeals in Texas and automatically reviews death penalty cases. In the text, find what percentage of trial court verdicts result in appeal.

How likely is it that a conviction will be reversed on appeal?

JURIES

Juries are an important and controversial aspect of the American judicial system. Some people argue that juries are beneficial because they allow for community input and the use of common sense in the legal system. Others claim that they often do not fairly represent the

[18]"Ruling Reopens Door to Injection," *The Dallas Morning News*, April 17, 2008; "Man Executed for 1988 Revenge Killing," *Fort Worth Star-Telegram*, November 21, 2002; "Death Penalty Debate Reopens," *Fort Worth Star-Telegram*, November 8, 2002; "At Last Name Is Cleared," *The Dallas Morning News*, October 6, 2004; "Old Enough to Kill, Too Young to Die," *The Dallas Morning News*, October 10, 2004; "Trial by Fire: Did Texas Execute an Innocent Man?" *The New Yorker*, September 7, 2009.

[19]"Sharon Keller is Texas' Judge Dread," *Dallas Observer*, January 17, 2008.

[20]"Groundwater Owned by Property Owners, Texas Supreme Court Rules," *The Dallas Morning News*, February 25, 2012.

Courtesy of the Supreme Court of Texas

The Texas Supreme Court is the final court of appeals only in civil cases. Such civil cases can have a broad impact on society, and they generate much attention from interest groups when they affect business regulation or corporate liability.

Why would corporations and plaintiffs' attorneys have an interest in making contributions to the campaigns of candidates for the Texas Supreme Court?

Grand jury

In Texas, 12 persons who sit in pretrial proceedings to determine whether sufficient evidence exists to try an individual and therefore return an indictment.

Information

A written accusation filed by the prosecutor against a party charged with a minor crime; it is an alternative to an indictment and does not involve a grand jury.

Indictment

A formal written accusation issued by a grand jury against a party charged with a crime when it has determined that there is sufficient evidence to bring the accused to trial.

True bill

An indictment returned by a grand jury.

No bill

A grand jury's refusal to return an indictment filed by the prosecutor.

community and that their reasons for their decisions are often inappropriate or suspect. What is certain is that while millions of Americans serve on juries every year, the frequency of their use is declining, and the overwhelming number of cases in our legal system are not decided by them.[21]

Grand Jury

In Texas, when a person is accused of a crime, the matter is likely to be taken to a twelve-member **grand jury**. (Some states do not have grand juries, but in those that do, the size ranges from five to twenty-three members.) An alternative to a grand jury indictment is the **information**, which is used for minor offenses not punishable in the state penitentiary. Filed by the prosecutor with the appropriate court, an information must be based on an investigation by the prosecutor after receiving a complaint and a sworn affidavit that a crime has been committed.

The grand jury does not determine the guilt or innocence of the accused but rather whether there is sufficient evidence to bring the accused to trial. If the evidence is determined to be sufficient, the accused is indicted. An **indictment** is sometimes referred to as a **true bill** by the grand jury, and the vote of at least nine of the twelve grand jurors is needed to indict. If an indictment is not returned, the conclusion of the grand jury is a **no bill**.

At times, a grand jury may return indictments simply because the district attorney asks for them. In fact, grand juries return true bills in approximately 95 percent of the cases brought before them.[22] This high indictment rate is attributable at least in part to the fact that the accused cannot have an attorney in the room during questioning. Some grand juries, known as *runaway* grand juries, may consider matters independently of the district attorney's recommendation. In general, prosecutors do not like a grand jury to be so assertive and are likely to refer only routine matters to it. To bypass it, the prosecutor may refer cases to a second grand jury meeting simultaneously or postpone action for another, more favorable grand jury.

The process of selecting the grand jury has also come under criticism in recent years. Because it can be chosen by a grand jury commission (of three to five members) appointed by the district judge, the grand jury panel might not be truly representative of the county's citizenry. A total of 15 to 20 people are nominated by the commission, and 12 are selected to become the grand jury for the term of the court. In some counties, grand juries are chosen through random selection by computer.

The district attorney may determine whether or not a person indicted for a crime will be prosecuted. Some district attorneys will prosecute only if the odds are high that a conviction can be secured. This improves their statistical record, which can be taken to the voters when reelection time comes. Other prosecutors may take most indicted persons to trial, even if the

[21]G. Alan Tarr, *Judicial Process & Judicial Policymaking*, 5th ed. (Boston: Wadsworth Publishing, 2009), p. 139.
[22]Henry J. Abraham, *The Judicial Process*, 7th ed. (NY: Oxford University Press, 1998), p. 119.

chances for conviction are low, but this may prove politically costly and can make the prosecutor appear ineffective.

Petit (Trial) Jury

A jury in a criminal or civil trial is known as a **petit jury**. Trial by jury in criminal cases is a right guaranteed by the Texas Constitution and the Sixth Amendment of the U.S. Constitution. Even if the accused waives the right to trial by jury, expecting to be tried by the judge, the state may demand a jury trial in felony cases. Although not required by the U.S. Constitution, in Texas, the parties to a civil case generally decide whether a jury trial will be held. If a jury is to be used in a civil case in district court, the party requesting it pays a nominal fee to see that a jury panel is called. After the panel is summoned, the per diem for each juror is paid from public funds, which can entail considerable expense to the public if a trial becomes lengthy. County courts have six-person juries, whereas twelve people are on juries at the district court level.

Petit jury

Trial jury for a civil or criminal case.

> **Did You Know?** Only about 1 percent of the cases handled in the county and district courts of Texas involve jury trials.

A *venire*, or jury panel, is randomly selected from among those individuals who have registered to vote, hold a Texas driver's license, or hold a Texas identification card. Jurors must be literate citizens at least 18 years of age, qualified to vote, and not indicted or convicted for a theft or felony. Exemptions for jury service are now severely restricted. Persons older than 70 years of age, actively attending students, and women with custody of a child younger than the age of 10 are automatically exempt from jury service but may serve if they desire. Fathers have sought to claim the same exemption when they are legally responsible for children. Other excuses from jury service are at the discretion of the judge.

> **Did You Know?** Some counties used to select potential jurors by drawing names from a lottery drum. Today potential jurors are usually selected randomly by a sophisticated computer program called a "jury wheel."

In cases that receive a great deal of publicity, a special venire may consist of several hundred persons. Jury selection (voir dire) may last days or weeks, sometimes even longer than the trial itself. If either side believes that a prospective juror has a preconceived opinion about guilt or innocence, the prosecutor or defense attorneys may bring a **challenge for cause**. Challenges for cause extend to any factor that might convince a judge that the juror could not render a fair and impartial decision. No limits are placed on the number of challenges for cause, but the judge decides whether to grant each specific challenge.

Challenge for cause

A request to a judge that a certain prospective juror not be allowed to serve on the jury for a specific reason, such as bias or knowledge of the case.

Statutes also allow challenges of jurors without cause. Known as a **peremptory challenge**, no reason needs to be provided to remove a juror. The possibility exists, therefore, that nothing other than intuition can cause an attorney in a case to ask that a juror be dismissed. The only limitations of this type of challenge occur when the judge believes that prospective jurors are being eliminated solely because of their race or sex. Although peremptory challenges provide lawyers with a great deal of freedom in deciding to remove jurors, each side is given only a limited number of these challenges in each case.

Peremptory challenge

A challenge made to a prospective juror without being required to give a reason for removal; the number of such challenges allotted to the prosecution and defense is limited.

Many lawyers maintain that jury selection is more significant than the actual argument of a case. Some firms hire jury and trial consulting firms to assist in the selection process. Psychological profiles of ideal jurors may be used to try to avoid jurors who might be unfavorable to a client and to identify those who might be supportive. For example, the prosecution would quite possibly want a grandparent or parent of young children on a jury dealing with child molestation, while the defense would wish to avoid such a juror. Many trial law firms and prosecutors also maintain a file on jurors from completed cases to help them select or avoid prospective jurors based on past behavior.

Whereas some states allow non-unanimous jury verdicts in both criminal and civil matters, juries in criminal cases in Texas must agree unanimously (this is not required in civil

Hung jury

A jury that is unable to agree on a verdict after a suitable period of deliberation; the result is a mistrial.

cases). Even if only one juror disagrees, the result is a **hung jury**. In this event, the prosecutor must decide whether to try the case again with a different jury or drop the matter. (Because no verdict was reached with a hung jury, the accused person is not put in double jeopardy by a second trial.) Usually, in the event of a second hung jury, the prosecution drops the case.

SELECTION OF JUDGES

Merit plan or **Missouri plan**

A method of selecting judges on the basis of the merit or quality of the candidates and not on political considerations. Under this system, the governor fills court vacancies from a list of nominees submitted by a judicial commission, and these appointees later face retention elections.

States use several methods to select judges. In fact, some states use different methods for different types of courts. One principal variant is often called the **merit plan** or **Missouri plan**. This plan has been adopted by a number of states and will be described in more detail. A relatively large number of states elect judges; in some states, the elections are partisan (candidates are officially affiliated with a political party), and in the others they are nonpartisan. Some states also provide for the appointment of judges by governors and a few allow the legislature to make the selections. Table 11.2 compares Texas's Supreme Court selection method with other states' selection methods.

Reformers developed the merit plan in an attempt to make the selection of judges less political. This style of selection supposedly bases its choices on the merit or quality of the candidates as opposed to political considerations. Under this system, the governor fills court vacancies from a list of three nominees submitted by a judicial commission chaired by a judge and composed of both lawyers and laypersons. Individuals who are selected hold their posts for at least one year, until the next election. Their names are then put on a retention ballot, which simply asks whether a judge should be retained. It is a "yes" or "no" vote for the candidate with no other competition. Historically, more than 90 percent of such votes result in the candidate's election (or reelection). It is important to note that researchers have overwhelmingly found that this process is no less political than other selection methods and that there is no clear evidence that this process produces different or more meritorious judges.[23]

Officially, Texas elects its judges (except municipal court judges) in partisan elections. However, such a statement oversimplifies the process and is somewhat misleading. Actually, the system operates as an appointive–elective one because it is quite common for judges to first assume office through appointment to fill vacancies to complete unexpired terms. These appointments between elections are made by the governor with the advice and consent of the senate. Except in the largest metropolitan counties, the vast majority of all Texas judges are reelected unopposed, and open competition for judicial posts between nonincumbents is uncommon.[24]

The Politics of Judicial Selection in Texas

The system of judicial selection in Texas and practices related to it have been under attack. Some critics have alleged that Texas has the best justice that money can buy. We shall examine why the courts and judges of Texas are criticized and in doing so gain a clearer understanding of the political nature of the court system.

---

[23]For example, see Bradley Canon, "The Impact of Formal Selection Process on the Characteristics of Judges, Reconsidered," *Law and Society Review* 6 (1972), pp. 579–593; Victor Flango and Craig Ducat, "What Difference Does the Method of Judicial Selection Make?" *Justice System Journal* 5 (1979), pp. 25–44; Henry Glick and Craig Emmert, "Selection Systems and Judicial Characteristics: The Recruitment of State Supreme Court Judges," *Judicature* 70 (1986), pp. 228–235; Roy Schotland, "New Challenges to States' Judicial Selection," *Georgetown Law Journal* 95 (2007), pp. 1077–1105.

[24]Melinda Gann Hall, "Voting in State Supreme Court Elections: Competition and Context as Democratic Incentives," *Journal of Politics* 69 Issue 4 (2007), pp. 1147–1159.

Voter Apathy Because Texas elects judges, a natural question arises: How knowledgeable are voters in these judicial elections? In other words, are voters cognizant of the candidates and their records in office? Research on the U.S. Supreme Court has repeatedly shown that the vast majority of the public knows little about its rulings and actions.[25] Therefore, if most Americans know very little about the U.S. Supreme Court—the court that receives the most media attention in this country—how much do voters know about state and local courts? A voter in Texas could be asked to vote for candidates running for the Texas Supreme Court, the court of criminal appeals, the courts of appeal, district courts, county courts, and for justices of the peace.

In addition to the more systematic research conducted, an abundance of anecdotal evidence indicates that most voters in Texas are unaware of candidates' qualifications or experience. As a result, many do not vote in judicial elections at all, and those who do often select candidates based on any sort of name recognition—candidates with names similar to those of movie stars, historical figures, or public personages are often candidates for judicial positions.[26]

Partisanship Because voters know so little about individual candidates, they may use party identification as a cue to determine how to vote. In other words, a voter who has no knowledge of the views or backgrounds of the candidates on the ballot may make a choice based on the candidates' political party affiliation. In Texas, this appears to be a common approach for making selections in judicial elections.

HOW DOES TEXAS COMPARE?
Selecting Judges

States use different methods to choose judges. A few states allow their governor or legislature to make the choices. More commonly, states use elections to select their judges. There are three general types of judicial elections. Texas (along with seven other states) holds partisan elections, whereas fourteen other states do not include partisan designations on the ballot. The most popular method of selection is the merit, or Missouri, plan that claims to be less political and combines an initial appointment with retention elections (also see Figure 3.2).

TABLE 11.2 Number of State Supreme Courts Selected by Various Methods	
Merit plan	16
Nonpartisan election	14
Partisan election	7
Gubernatorial or legislative appointment	5
Combined merit selection and other methods	9

Source: American Judicature Society, *Judicial Selection in the States* (Des Moines, IA: American Judicature Society, 2009), www.ajs.org/selection/docs/Judicial%20Selection%20Charts.pdf; includes the District of Columbia.

[25]For example, see Gibson Caldeira and Spence, "Measuring Attitudes Toward the United States Supreme Court," *American Journal of Political Science* 47 Issue 2 (2003), pp. 354–367; Benesh, "Understanding Public Confidence in American Courts," *Journal of Politics* 68 Issue 3 (2006), pp. 697–707; Ramirez, "Procedural Perceptions and Support for the U.S. Supreme Court," *Political Psychology* 29 Issue 5 (2008), pp. 675–698; Gibson and Caldeira, "Knowing the Supreme Court? A Reconsideration of Public Ignorance of the High Court," *Journal of Politics* 71 Issue 2 (2009), pp. 429–441.

[26]"Kelly's Swan Song?" *The Dallas Morning News*, March 2, 2008.

FOR DEBATE

What are the advantages and disadvantages of selecting judges through partisan election? Evaluate the alternative methods for choosing judges used in many other states.

Where judicial campaigns are competitive, the Republican judicial candidates usually have a distinct political advantage. However, Democrats have had some success at the local level in some counties, and in large politically competitive metropolitan counties, either of the two parties has been able to sweep to power when they have a good year. Democrats took all judicial positions in Dallas County in 2006, and surged in Harris County in 2008.[27] In 2010, Democrats again swept all the races in which they competed in Dallas County, but Republicans won nearly as many judicial positions in Harris County as they had lost there in the previous election.[28]

It has been argued that because judges, especially at the appellate level, make significant policy decisions, it is reasonable for voters to select judges on the basis of political party affiliation.[29] Party affiliation may provide accurate information concerning the general ideology and thus the decision-making pattern of judges. However, even if this is true, voting based solely on a candidate's political party can lead to controversial results.

Campaign Contributions Because voters often look for simple voting cues (such as name familiarity or party identification), candidates often want to spend as much money as possible to make their name or candidacy well known. In recent years, spending in judicial races has increased dramatically. Candidates need to win two elections—their party's nomination and the general election. In modern politics, this can be an expensive endeavor, and for more than a decade, Republican candidates have dominated the race for campaign contributions. For example, in 2006, a Democratic challenger was outfunded 387 to 1 ($937,000 to $2,549) by the Republican justice;[30] and in 2008, the three Republican incumbents raised more than $2.8 million, whereas their Democratic challengers raised just more than $1 million.[31] Not surprisingly, the Republican candidates were successful.

In addition to questions concerning fairness or the advantages of incumbency surrounding campaign finances, many critics have also asked whether justice is for sale in Texas. More directly, individuals or organizations often appear before judges to whose election campaigns they have contributed. Do such contributions affect a judge's impartiality in deciding a case? In 1998, research indicated that 40 percent of campaign contributions to supreme court justices came from sources with cases before the court.[32] In 2008, Texas Supreme Court incumbents running for reelection received half their support from lawyers, law firms, and lobbyists.[33] More recently, a public advocacy group sued Texas over this system, claiming that it violates due process and the right to a fair trial. The group cited surveys indicating

---

[27]"Dallas County Judges Lose Seats in Democratic Deluge," *The Dallas Morning News*, November 8, 2006; "Sweep Revives. Debate on Election of Judges," *Houston Chronicle*, November 8, 2008.

[28]"Democrats Maintain Their Dominance in Dallas County," *The Dallas Morning News*, November 3, 2010; "Here's What We Can Say About The Near-Final Results Of Today's Elections in Harris County," *The Houston Chronicle*, November 3, 2010.

[29]Du Bois, *Judicial Elections and the Quest for Accountability* (Austin: University of Texas Press, 1980).

[30]"Judge Aims to Boot a Justice," *The Dallas Morning News*, August 4, 2006.

[31]"Interested Parties: Who Bankrolled Texas' High Court Justices in 2008?" *Texans for Public Justice*, October 2009.

[32]"Lawyers Give Most to High Court Hopefuls," *The Dallas Morning News*, February 28, 1998, p. A26.

[33]Texans for Public Justice, *Interested Parties: Who Bankrolled Texas' High-Court Justices in 2008?* October. 2009, http://info.tpj.org/reports/supremes08/InterestedParties.oct09.pdf.

that 83 percent of the Texas public, 79 percent of Texas lawyers, and 48 percent of Texas judges believe that campaign contributions significantly affect judicial decisions.[34] The Texas Insiders feature puts a face on major contributors to Texas Supreme Court candidates.

In 2009, the United States Supreme Court weighed in on the question of judicial bias where litigants significantly influenced the election of judges hearing their cases. In *Caperton v. A. T. Massey Coal Co., Inc.,* the U.S. Supreme Court held that the chairman of A. T. Massey Coal had created such a question by donating $3 million to help finance the successful election of a new justice to the Supreme Court of Appeals of West Virginia. The possible conflict of interest arose because A. T. Massey Coal Company had a $50 million civil suit appeal pending before the court at the time; it was later decided in their favor by a 3-to-2 vote with the new justice voting with the majority. A 5-to-4 U.S. Supreme Court majority reversed and remanded the case holding "there is a serious risk of actual bias …

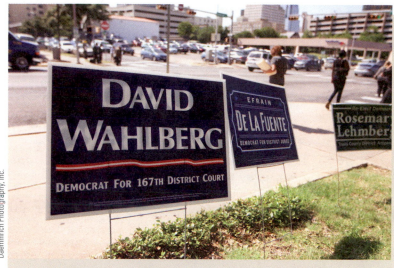

Daemmrich Photography, Inc.

Judicial campaigns in Texas are partisan and expensive affairs.

How much does justice depend on party affiliation and the influence of large campaign contributors?

Texas INSIDERS

Following the Money: Campaign Contributors in Supreme Court Elections

Table 11.3a shows the total contributions raised by the Republican and Democratic nominees for the Texas Supreme Court in 2010.

Republicans won all three positions and outraised the Democrats more than five to one. No Democrat has been elected to the Texas Supreme Court since 1994.

As usual, the list of top contributors to Texas Supreme Court candidates includes the preeminent corporate defense law firms

TABLE 11.3A Campaign Contributions to Candidates for the Texas Supreme Court		
Candidates	**Winners' Total Contributions**	**Losers' Total Contributions**
Places 3, 5, and 9*	$2,231,298	$401,025

*Serving six-year overlapping terms, only three of the nine Supreme Court justices are usually elected in each general election held every two years. The *place* simply refers to the particular seat for which a candidate is running, but all of the state's voters may cast one vote for each of the three seats being contested.

(continued)

---

[34]"State Sued over Judicial Elections," *Fort Worth Star-Telegram*, April 4, 2000.

in the state, along with health care providers and those representing businesses that are often sued. Among the top contributors is Texans for Lawsuit Reform, a group that seeks to limit the right to bring suits against individuals and businesses. These interests are closely allied with the Republican Party.

Table 11.3b shows the largest contributors to Texas Supreme Court campaigns in 2010. Lawyers are, by far, the single largest group of contributors in all judicial campaigns for both trial and appellate courts.

Notably missing from this list of top contributors are important plaintiffs' attorneys and their umbrella organization, the once-powerful Texas Trial Lawyers Association. Plaintiffs' lawyers primarily represent injured workers, patients, consumers, and the insured in liability suits against corporations, insurance companies, and medical providers. These attorneys are mostly aligned with the Democratic Party.

Thinking about the role of political elites in Texas politics Is there a conflict of interest when a law firm represents a client before a judge whom their contributions helped elect? Do the pro-business rulings of the Texas Supreme reflect the corporate philosophy of their campaign contributors?

TABLE 11.3B Top 10 Contributors in Texas Supreme Court Races

Contributor	Total	% of Total	Sector
Vinson & Elkins	$117,000	3.64%	Lawyers and lobbyists
Texans for Lawsuit Reform	$70,172	2.19%	General business
Hillco Partners	$65,000	2.02%	Lawyers and lobbyists
Fulbright & Jaworski	$55,000	1.71%	Lawyers and lobbyists
Haynes & Boone	$42,500	1.32%	Lawyers and lobbyists
Judge Debra Lehrmann for Texas Supreme Court	$41,159	1.28%	Candidate contributions
Texas Medical Association	$40,173	1.25%	Health
Andrews & Kurth	$33,500	1.04%	Lawyers and lobbyists
K & L Gates	$32,333	1.01%	Lawyers and lobbyists
USAA	$30,000	0.93%	Finance, insurance, and real estate

Source: National Institute on Money in State Politics at www.followthemoney.org/database/. The institute's searchable database relies on Texas Ethics Commission reports. The Judicial Campaign Fairness Act limits individual contributions and forbids corporate contributions. These totals represent contributions from affiliated individuals and political action committees.

when a person with a personal stake in a particular case had a significant and disproportionate influence in placing the judge on the case.[35]

Recently, the issue of corporate campaign financing became politically salient again. In 2010, the United States Supreme Court decided the case of *Citizens United* v. *Federal Election Commission*. A divided court, in a 5-to-4 decision, ruled in favor of Citizens United, a nonprofit organization accused of violating the Bipartisan Campaign Reform Act of 2002. The ruling upheld disclosure requirements for corporate campaign contributions, but removed all financial restrictions on those contributions, allowing for individuals and corporate entities to donate unlimited funds to political action committees. The decision

---

[35]*Caperton* v. *A. T. Massey Coal Co., Inc.*, 556 U.S.__(2009).

impacted campaign finance laws at the state level and began a debate about whether corporations will have increased influence on elected officials.[36] In 1995, Texas passed the Judicial Campaign Fairness Act, which set limits on contributions to judicial candidates from law firms, individuals, and PACs.[37] That law continues to be enforced but is facing numerous legal challenges under *Citizens United*.[38] For a more detailed discussion on the issue of campaign financing, refer to the section "Money In Political Campaigns" in Chapter 4 of this text.

Part of this debate of possible impropriety involves the battle between plaintiffs' attorneys and defense attorneys in civil cases. Texas has traditionally been a conservative, pro-business state. This perspective was usually reflected in the decisions of the judiciary, which often favored big business and professional groups (such as the medical profession). Plaintiffs' lawyers and their related interest group, the Texas Trial Lawyers Association, have made a concerted effort in the past few decades to make the judiciary more open to consumer suits, often filed against businesses, doctors, and their insurance companies. The plaintiffs' lawyers poured millions of dollars into the political funds of candidates they believed would align more favorably with their perspective. Defense and business attorneys responded with millions of dollars of their own contributions. These lawyers, from both vantage points, then often appear before the very judges to whom they have given these large sums of money.

Minority Representation

A final major criticism of the current partisan elective system involves questions concerning diversity and minority representation. In 2011, of the state's 98 appellate judges, only 10 were Latino and 3 were African American.[39] Within the district courts, only 81 of 456 judges were Latino or African American.[40] Out of the total of 4,294 statewide judges, 1,097 are female.[41] Minorities are still underrepresented when compared to their white male counterparts. The system thus continues to be harshly criticized by representatives of minority groups.

Clearly, the current system is quite political, and many people oppose it for a number of distinct reasons. This has led to repeated attempts to reform the current selection style or change what is permissible in campaign fund-raising. Proposals for change have come from many sources, including chief justices of the state supreme court and a committee formed by the lieutenant governor. However, with such divergent interests involved and no clear alternative acceptable to all groups, very little judicial reform has occurred.

---

[36]*Citizens United* v. *Federal Election Commission*, 558 U.S. 50 (2010).

[37]"Judicial Campaigns and Elections: Texas," American Judicature Society, http://www.judicialselection.us/ judicial_selection/campaigns_and_elections/campaign_financing.cfm?state=TX.

[38]"Three Campaign Finance Lawsuits on The Heels of 'Citizens'," *The National Law Journal*, January 3, 2012.

[39]Texas Courts Online, *Profile of Appellate and Trial Judges (As of September 1, 2011)* (Austin, TX: State of Texas Office of Court Administration, 2011).

[40]Ibid.

[41]Ibid.

New-Style Judicial Elections in Texas: Examining the Costs and Effects of Electing Judges

Brent Boyea
University of Texas-Arlington

INTRODUCTION

This article examines how the election of judges has evolved in recent years. It raises issues about how increasing campaign contributions and party politics might bias court decisions, especially in tort litigation cases. Students should consider whether or how Texas could change its judicial selection methods to reduce the impression and the reality of conflict of interest in its courts.

Following the decision of the U.S. Supreme Court in *Republican Party of Minnesota* v. *White* (2002)[42] and the Court's subsequent decision in *Caperton* v. *A. T. Massey Co.* (2009),[43] attention to the practice of electing judges has increased as a salient concern affecting state courts. The recent decision of the U.S. Supreme Court in *Caperton* featured a question relating to bias when elected judges, like those in Texas, receive contributions and subsequently make decisions involving parties that have made contributions. The U.S. Supreme Court reasoned that elected judges are obligated to recuse themselves when "a risk of actual bias" presents itself, whether or not bias would actually occur.[44] The linkage between contributions and the decisions of judges and fear about the appearance of impropriety featured prominently in the opinion of the Court.

The question of whether judges should be accountable to their constituents or independent from political pressures makes elective state court systems subject to controversy.[45] Twenty-two states, including Texas, use elective methods of judicial selection for their highest appellate court, meaning voters are charged with selecting the jurists of their state courts.[46] Further, among states using elective court systems, Texas and six additional states use judicial election formats that designate the political party affiliation of judicial candidates.

EVOLVING JUDICIAL ELECTIONS IN TEXAS

One prominent yet understated reason for concern about judicial elections relates to the changing nature of judicial campaigns during the last quarter century. Although judicial elections were traditionally low-information and staid campaigns, the new style of judicial election resembles elections for alternative offices, including those for more political offices like the U.S. House of Representatives or a state's legislature.[47] A consequence of this new-style transformation has been the development of more expensive and controversial judicial campaigns. For states that assign political parties a formal role in the selection and retention of judges, contemporary judicial elections cause apprehension about the correctness of having judges seek money to conduct their campaigns. Further, contemporary judicial elections are often qualified as mean-spirited affairs that are expensive to wage.[48] The result has caused increased criticism from a variety of opponents from former U.S. Supreme Court Justice Sandra Day O'Connor to advocacy groups such as the American Judicature Society and the American Bar Association.

Twenty-five years ago, opposition to judicial elections and descriptions of judicial elections as noisy, nasty, and costly affairs were unusual.[49] Today in Texas, these descriptions are increasingly accurate. Fitting neatly within the

[42]*Republican Party of Minnesota* v. *White*, 536 U.S. 765 (2002).

[43]*Caperton* v. *A. T. Massey Co.*, 556 U.S. ___ (2009).

[44]Ibid., Justice O'Conner concurring.

[45]*Republican Party of Minnesota*, 536 U.S. 765 (2002).

[46]Melinda Gann Hall, "State Courts: Politics and the Judicial Process," in Virginia Gray and Russell L. Hanson (eds.), *Politics in the American States: A Comparative Analysis,* 9th ed. (Washington, DC: CQ Press, 2008).

[47]Anthony Champagne, "Tort Reform and Judicial Selection," *Loyola of Los Angeles Law Review* 38 (2005), pp. 1483–1515.

[48]Chris W. Bonneau, "What Price Justice(s)? Understanding Campaign Spending in State Supreme Court Elections," *State Politics and Policy Quarterly* 5 (2005), pp. 107–125.

[49]Champagne, "Tort Reform and Judicial Selection," pp. 1483–1515.

constraints imposed by partisan elections and competition between the two major parties (i.e., the Republican Party and the Democratic Party), plaintiffs' attorneys are often linked with the Democratic Party, whereas defense attorneys in civil cases are conventionally tied to the Republican Party.[50] For the Democratic Party, this development has been challenging with the ascendency of the Republican Party in the modern two-party era in Texas. From 1999 through the 2008 judicial elections, judges serving in the Texas Supreme Court, the highest Texas court assigned to civil appeals, were universally affiliated with the Republican Party.

EXPENDITURES AND CONTRIBUTIONS TO JUDICIAL CAMPAIGNS

As for the role of money, judicial races in Texas are now expensive affairs. Compared with spending in other states with judicial elections, Texas ranked ninth nationally from 1990 to 2004.[51] A judicial contest in 2006 and 2008 for seats on the Texas Supreme Court cost an average of $515,463, considering the amount spent by all major party candidates.[52] In 2008, when three elections were featured for seats on the Texas Supreme Court, including a race for the position of chief justice, an average election cost $723,426. Relating to the cost of running a campaign, candidates for judicial office from 2006 to 2008 collected an average of $619,659, and winning candidates collected an average of $755,251.[53] Without exception, the candidate who collected more money than his opponent was the victor. Republicans universally collected more contributions and spent more in their campaigns than their Democratic opposition, leading to Republican success in both 2006 and 2008. Although the costs of judicial races in Texas are milder than contests in states like Alabama or Pennsylvania, access to contributions and larger expenditures equates to success in these new-style judicial elections.

CONSEQUENCES OF CAMPAIGN SPENDING

Despite the costs of judicial elections, the public in states with elective courts remain strongly in favor of their elective system.[54] Obscured by broad support for judicial elections is the impact of spending in judicial races on participation by

voters and political competition. One method for exploring participation by voters is the roll-off vote, which reflects the percentage of voters who do not participate in the judicial office section of a state's election ballot. Spending appears related to decreased roll-off. From 1990 to 2004, roll-off in judicial races for the Texas Supreme Court and Texas Court of Criminal Appeals averaged 13.0 percent, or 9.9 percent less than the average among all state high court elections.[55] Questions about judicial elections also relate to the competitiveness of judicial races. Incumbent campaigns that spend more than their challengers are generally more successful, whereas contests between candidates with similar resources are more closely contested. In Texas, incumbent candidates received an average of 59.9 percent of the vote, compared to the cross-state average of 70.2 percent.[56] In addition to narrow elections where incumbents seek reelection, judicial races in Texas are nearly always contested (97.6 percent of races), and defeats among incumbent candidates are commonplace (26.9 percent of incumbent reelection bids).[57]

PARTY POLITICS, CONTRIBUTORS, AND TORT LITIGATION

With partisan elections as the device for selecting judges, different groups in the Texas legal environment use judicial elections to promote their causes. With the success of Republican candidates in judicial elections since 1996, voters have placed their support with pro-business candidates aligned with the Republican moniker. In both 2006 and 2008, when Republican candidates for the Texas Supreme Court swept aside their Democratic Party opposition, 13 of the top 20 contributors to high court candidates were law firms engaged largely in defense litigation in civil cases.[58] For civil-case defense law firms and interest groups in Texas, a financial relationship between candidates and contributors is strengthened by the necessities of judicial elections. Of the remaining contributors in both 2006 and 2008, several were anti-lawsuit groups seeking tort reform.[59] In reviewing the civil docket of the Texas Supreme Court from 1995 to 1998, 50.8 percent of the docket applied to tort litigation.[60] Of those cases, only 46.2 percent were decided in favor of the original plaintiff.

The environment of the Texas court system is well-suited for concerns about judicial elections. With expensive

[50]Deborah Goldberg, "Interest Group Participation in Judicial Elections," in Matthew J. Streb (ed.), *Running for Judge: The Rising Political, Financial, and Legal Stakes of Judicial Elections* (New York: New York University Press, 2007).

[51]Chris W. Bonneau and Melinda Gann Hall, *In Defense of Judicial Elections* (New York: Routledge, 2009).

[52]Judicial expenditures data was obtained and is available through the Texas Ethics Commission, http://www.ethics.state.tx.us/.

[53]Judicial contribution data was obtained and is available through the National Institute on Money in State Politics, http://www.followthemoney.org/.

[54]Bonneau and Hall, *In Defense of Judicial Elections.*

[55]Texas Ethics Commission, http://www.ethics.state.tx.us/.

[56]Ibid.

[57]Ibid.

[58]National Institute on Money in State Politics, http://www.followthemoney.org/.

[59]Torts represent a civil rather than criminal wrong, where "damages" are claimed by a plaintiff (or plaintiffs) seeking an award.

[60]Data obtained from the State Supreme Court Data Archive, http://www.ruf.rice.edu/~pbrace/statecourt/index.html.

elections that favor Republican candidates and pro-business interests, the Texas Supreme Court reflects a prominent display of the new style of judicial elections. To succeed, candidates for the Texas Supreme Court are required to raise and spend considerable sums of money. With the transformation of the Texas courts largely structured around the battle over tort reform, the influx of money could suggest the appearance of impropriety.[61] Although evidence exists of linkage between contributions and behavior,[62] an equally significant revelation is the utility of judicial elections in Texas for structuring electoral conflict. Judicial elections in Texas encourage a strong association between interests within the law and their representation on the courts; this association thereby affects the costs of elections, democratic participation within the public, and judicial representation by pro-business and Republican judges.

JOIN THE DEBATE

1. Should Texas judges be elected? Why or why not?

2. Can elected judges set aside the interests of their largest campaign contributors when those contributors appear before them in court? Are there ways to hold judges accountable to the electorate without forcing judicial candidates to solicit campaign contributions?

3. How would justice in Texas be affected if Texas used alternative methods of judicial selection such as nonpartisan elections or appointment?

4. How would the Texas Supreme Court's inclination to rule for business in tort litigation be changed if Democrats controlled the court? Can litigants expect fair rulings when either party controls all seats on the court?

[61]Donald W. Jackson and James W. Riddlesperger, Jr., "Money and Politics in Judicial Elections: The 1988 Election of the Chief Justice of the Texas Supreme Court," Judicature 74 (1991), pp. 184–189.
[62]Madhavi M. McCall and Michael A. McCall, "Campaign Contributions, Judicial Decisions, and the Texas Supreme Court: Assessing the Appearance of Impropriety," *Judicature* 90 (2007), pp. 214–225.

CHAPTER SUMMARY

★ Cases in the legal system can be classified in two ways: (1) *Civil cases* deal primarily with individual or property rights, and (2) *criminal cases* deal with violations of penal law.

★ There are two types of jurisdiction: (1) *Original jurisdiction* is the basic power to try a case for the first time. Courts with original jurisdiction determine guilt in criminal cases or responsibility in civil cases. (2) *Appellate jurisdiction* is the ability to review the decisions of a lower court.

★ The Texas judiciary has many critics and perceived flaws. The Texas court system is often viewed as too big and complicated. Lines of jurisdiction sometimes overlap. Legislation dealing with court personnel, organization, and procedures is often a maze of confusion. Crowded court dockets usually result in new courts, not court realignment. Reorganization of the courts along more simplified lines has been urged for decades.

★ Juries are an important aspect of the American judicial system. The judicial system has two primary types of juries: (1) A *grand jury* issues indictments that indicate whether sufficient evidence exists to bring the accused to trial. (2) A *petit jury* is a jury in a criminal or civil trial. Potential jury members can be excluded from service through either a challenge for cause or a peremptory challenge.

★ The judiciary performs a vital role in our society. Courts make life-altering decisions and often shape public policy. In Texas, where judges are chosen in partisan elections, the selection of judges is very politicized. The politics of the Texas court system have led to numerous controversies and suggested reforms. Judicial reform in Texas is difficult to achieve and continues to be unlikely to occur.

HOW TEXAS COMPARES

★ Many states use a *merit plan* for the selection of judges. Variations of this plan, sometimes called the Missouri plan, include the nomination of judges by a judicial qualifying commission. After a short-term appointment by the governor, voters are allowed to decide whether to retain the judge. In some states with the merit plan, candidates are allowed to run against the incumbent judge, whereas in others, voters simply vote on the issue of whether to retain or remove the judge. Supporters argue that this judicial selection plan emphasizes qualifications and reduces the effects of campaigning and politics.

★ Some states use a system of *nonpartisan election* in which judges do not run as a party's nominee and their party affiliation does not appear on the ballot. Supporters of this judicial selection method argue that justice is not a partisan matter and that voters should not elect candidates simply because of their party membership.

★ Including Texas, fewer than 10 states use *partisan elections* to select judges. Supporters of partisan elections argue that judges are public officials and that voters should not be denied the right to elect them in the same way that they elect other public officials. Defenders argue that party labels are relevant because they give voters cues about a judicial candidate's political philosophy. Critics reason that campaigning for judicial positions introduces conflicts of interest due to campaign contributions from special interest groups with a stake in court decisions. They argue that party labels, ethnicity, personality, and organization overshadow judicial competence in political campaigns.

KEY TERMS

appellate jurisdiction, *p. 274*
beyond a reasonable doubt, *p. 273*
brief, *p. 274*
burden of proof, *p. 273*
civil case, *p. 273*

challenge for cause, *p. 285*
criminal case, *p. 273*
de novo, *p. 275*
double jeopardy, *p. 274*
grand jury, *p. 284*
hung jury, *p. 286*

indictment, *p. 284*
information, *p. 284*
merit plan or Missouri plan, *p. 286*
no bill, *p. 284*
original jurisdiction, *p. 274*

peremptory challenge, *p. 285*
petit jury, *p. 285*
plea bargaining, *p. 281*
preponderance of the evidence, *p. 273*
true bill, *p. 284*

REVIEW QUESTIONS

1. How do Americans rank in terms of lawyers and litigation? How do court decisions affect society?

2. Describe the characteristics that distinguish criminal and civil cases. What is the nature of the parties involved in both types of cases? What are the requisite standards of proof regarding evidence?

3. What is the difference between original and appellate jurisdiction? What types of issues and evidence are considered in each?

4. What types of jurisdiction do the various courts have? What basic elements of a case determine where the case is heard?

How do the qualifications of judges vary from court to court?

5. Compare and contrast grand juries and petit juries. How are jurors selected to serve on panels? How many are chosen? In what instances are exemptions from jury duty granted? What is the function of each type of jury?

6. What are some of the methods employed for selecting judges? How are judges chosen in Texas? Is the process of judicial selection a political one? How knowledgeable is the public in terms of making judicial selections? What are some criticisms of the manner in which judges are chosen?

LOGGING ON

★ The courts of the state of Texas can be accessed at the Texas Judicial Server located at **www.courts.state.tx.us/**.

★ The 14 courts of appeals can be accessed at **www.courts.state.tx.us/courts/coa.asp**.

★ You can access the court of criminal appeals at **www.cca.courts.state.tx.us**.

★ The Texas Supreme Court is at **www.supreme.courts.state.tx.us/**.

★ Find out who the municipal court judges are in your community. These are judges who hear cases involving traffic tickets or violations of municipal ordinances. Go to **www.courts.state.tx.us/courts/mn.asp** and click on the link to the Texas Judicial System Directory.

★ The Texans for Public Justice Web site, located at **www.tpj.org/**, has a section devoted to the judiciary branch.

Chapter 12

Law and Due Process

LEARNING OBJECTIVES

★ Identify citizens' basic rights in the courts, and evaluate how well they are protected in practice.

★ Give examples of major types of civil cases.

★ Describe the important controversies in civil law.

★ Identify the major types of crimes and the major factors contributing to them.

★ Describe the groups most often victimized by crime.

★ Define the due process of law.

★ Explain the rights of the accused, step-by-step, between arrest and the final verdict.

★ Define and evaluate the functions of correctional institutions.

© Glowimages / Getty Images, Inc.

GET Active

Deal intelligently with your personal legal matters:

★ For tips on civil legal matters, browse **texaslawhelp.org** to get free legal advice, do-it-yourself, and low-cost legal strategies relating to bankruptcy, consumer complaints, divorce, identity theft, tenant rights, utility bills, and a wide range of other topics.

★ Take control of legal issues in your life—learn about family law, tenants' rights, and how to sue in small claims court at **texasbar.com**. Click on "News and Publications" and then on "Free Legal Information."

★ Learn how to deal with identity theft and how to identify registered sex offenders in your neighborhood from the Texas Department of Public Safety at **www .txdps.state.tx.us/**.

Link up with the group that reflects your position on civil lawsuits.

★ Fight frivolous lawsuits that drive up the costs of doing business and support limits on civil judgments with Texans for Lawsuit Reform at **www.tortreform.com/**.

★ Support workers', patients', and consumers' rights to compensation for negligence from businesses, medical providers, and insurance companies with Texas Watch at **www.texaswatch.org/**.

Join with those who share your views on crime and punishment.

★ Fight the death penalty by joining Texas Students Against the Death Penalty at **www.texasabolition.org/** or the Texas Coalition to Abolish the Death Penalty at **www.tcadp.org/**. Help The Innocence Project free the innocent at **ipoftexas.org/**.

★ Support capital punishment with Pro-Death Penalty.com, at **www .prodeathpenalty.com/**. Fight for a vigorous criminal justice system and victims' rights with Justice for All at **www.jfa.net/**.

Civil law

Nonpenal law dealing with private rights and responsibilities.

Criminal law

Law prosecuted by the state, seeking punishment for violations of public concepts of morality.

Plaintiff

The party bringing a civil suit; often a private person or institution.

Remedy

The means to redress an injury, including relief from ongoing injury or compensation for past damages.

A s we mentioned in Chapter 11, there are substantial differences between criminal and civil law. **Civil law** deals largely with private rights and individual relationships, obligations, and responsibilities. **Criminal law** is concerned with public morality—concepts of right and wrong as defined by government.

Hence, criminal cases are prosecuted by public officials (usually county or district attorneys) in the name of the public. Civil suits are brought by **plaintiffs**, who are usually private citizens or corporations, although agents of government occasionally initiate civil suits when seeking to enforce antitrust laws, abate public nuisances, or pursue other noncriminal matters.

Perhaps the most important distinction between civil and criminal law is the way each deals with court findings. In criminal law, the aim is punishment, but in civil law, the **remedy** (the means used to redress an injury) is relief or compensation. For example, criminal law might punish a thief, but the civil law remedy for the unlawful seizure of property might be the return of the property to its rightful owner. Juvenile proceedings, which are regarded as civil rather than criminal, are an interesting illustration of the difference between civil and criminal law. Assigning juveniles to the custody of reform schools is not intended as punishment but as an effort to correct their delinquency. Assigning an adult to the penitentiary, however, is considered punishment.

CIVIL LAW

The primary focus of civil law is defining and civilizing interpersonal relationships; it also enforces legitimate contracts between parties and assigns responsibilities for personal injuries. We will provide a sample of some civil laws, but you should remember that Texas civil law fills volumes of printed matter. Texas's civil statutes are organized into 28 codes ranging from the Agriculture Code to *Vernon's Annotated Civil Statutes*. It is impossible to discuss the state's civil laws in detail—even the most competent attorneys tend to specialize in specific fields of law.

Types of Civil Law

Precedent

A previously decided legal case used as a guiding principle for a current or future case.

Stare decisis

The principle of following precedents in deciding legal cases.

Civil law in the states today is based in large part on centuries-old English *common law*. (We first discussed common law and statutory law in Chapter 3.) Common law is judge-made law; whether written or unwritten, it is based on **precedents**, or previous cases. If the essential elements of a current case are like those of a case already decided, the judge makes the same decision as was made in the earlier case. The principle of following these precedents is called *stare decisis*, and over the years, these cumulative decisions have fallen into patterns that form the basis of common law. In contrast, *statutory law* is law that has been passed by legislative bodies and is written in codebooks. Legislatures have incorporated many common-law principles into civil statutes and thereby reduced the need to rely directly on common law.

The family is protected by civil law in Texas. For example, even if a man and a woman have not participated in a formal ceremony of marriage in the presence of authorized officers of religious organizations or judges, the law may nevertheless recognize the existence of a marriage. A man and a woman who live together, agree they are married, and publicly present themselves as husband and wife will have a common-law marriage, their children will be legitimate, and the marriage can be terminated through a legal divorce. However, divorce action must be taken within one year of separation, or the marriage will be treated as if it never existed.

Texas courts may require alimony between the filing and granting of a divorce or when one spouse is incapable of self-support and the marriage has existed at least 10 years. As a *community property* state, Texas requires that a couple divide property acquired during marriage, and one spouse is not usually responsible for the other's support after divorce. Children, however, have the right to be supported by their parents even if the parents are divorced. Either parent might be given legal custody of the children, but the other parent may be responsible for part of their support. State licenses, including drivers' licenses, can now be revoked from parents who are delinquent in child support.

Titles to real property, like land and buildings, are registered in the office of the county clerk, and the legitimate use of any property by its owner is enforceable in the courts.

Did You Know? An individual may gain ownership of another's property through "adverse possession" by fencing it and using it for 10 years without objection by the owner of record.

A person cannot lose title to a *homestead* in a civil suit except to satisfy tax liens, home-improvement loans, mortgage loans for initial purchase of the property, or home equity loans. The protected family homestead includes the home and 200 acres of land in rural areas or 10 acres in the city.

Probate

The procedure for proving the validity of a will.

Even in death, property rights are protected because a person may control transfer of his or her estate through a will. If a will exists at the time of death, the function of the courts (usually the county courts) is to **probate** the will, which means to determine that it is the last and valid will of the deceased. If the deceased departed intestate (without leaving a will), civil law defines the right to inherit among various relatives; if there are no living relatives, the property passes to the state.

The right to inherit, bequeath, sell, lease, or transfer property is protected by law, but the rights of ownership do not include the privilege of misuse. The right to own a gun does not convey the right to use it as a weapon in murder; the privilege of opening an industrial plant does not include the right to pollute. The regulation of private property for public purposes is one of the oldest functions of law.

Texas law includes thousands of provisions regulating private property, and it establishes hundreds of courts and administrative agencies to elaborate, interpret, and enforce those regulations. State regulatory agencies include the Texas Railroad Commission, the Commissioner of Insurance, the Texas Finance Commission, the Public Utilities Commission, and occupational licensing boards. Their administrative regulations (administrative law) have the same binding effect as civil law and are usually enforced by civil courts.

Corporations secure permission from the state to conduct business; the secretary of state issues them a **charter**, which defines their structure, purposes, and activities. For corporations chartered in other states ("foreign" corporations), the secretary of state also issues permits to operate in Texas. Civil law holds that when a new corporation is chartered, a new legal person is created—one who can sue, be sued, or be fined for criminal activity. The attorney general is responsible for bringing civil suits to seek **writs of injunction** (court orders compelling or prohibiting specific actions) to end violations of the Texas antitrust and consumer protection laws.

When two parties enter into a valid contract, the courts will enforce the terms of the contract. However, certain kinds of contracts are not enforceable in the courts—for example, contracts with minors. Texas's **right-to-work laws** also forbid contracts between labor and management that establish a **closed shop** (in which management agrees to hire only labor union members) or a **union shop** (management agrees to require all new employees to join the union as a condition for their continued employment). Because of these restrictions, Texas is considered inhospitable to unions.

Civil law is also designed to protect a person's reputation against false and malicious statements. **Slander** (spoken defamation) or **libel** (published defamation) may result in a lawsuit to recover monetary compensation for damage to one's reputation and earning potential. The law effectively extends the protection against libel to vegetables, and farmers may sue people who make unfounded allegations against their products.

Negligence—failure to act with the prudence or care that an ordinary person would exercise—may result in someone's bodily harm or other injury, and negligent persons are liable for damages. If a personal injury suit results, it is a **tort** action (a case involving a private or civil wrong or injury other than a breach of contract).

Issues in Civil Law

These are only a few selected illustrations of civil law. More valuable to the average Texas citizen is an understanding of the major political issues surrounding civil suits. In fact, efforts to change civil law have been a major issue in Texas election campaigns and have occupied much of the legislature's time and energy.

Tort Reform Insurance companies, corporations, medical practitioners, and others have argued that society has become too litigious (inclined to go to court to settle differences). They asserted that "frivolous" lawsuits have overcrowded court dockets, and excessive damage awards have unnecessarily driven up insurance premiums and other business costs. As a result, Governor Rick Perry and most Republican leaders joined with groups representing defendants in civil actions, the Texas Civil Justice League, Texans for Lawsuit Reform, insurance companies, and a wide range of business and medical interest groups to urge **tort reform**.

Charter
The organizing document for a corporation or a municipality.

Writ of injunction
A court order to compel or restrain a particular action.

Right-to-work laws
Laws that prohibit union shop agreements requiring new employees to join a union.

Closed shop
A workplace in which management hires only labor union employees (illegal in Texas).

Union shop
A workplace in which management requires all new employees to join a union or pay dues as a condition for employment (illegal in Texas).

Slander
Spoken falsehood defaming a person's character.

Libel
Published falsehood defaming a person's character.

Negligence
Failure to act with the prudence or care that an ordinary person would exercise.

Tort
A private or civil injury or wrong other than a breach of contract.

Tort reform
Efforts to limit liability in civil cases.

Because of the power of this political alliance (see the *Texas Insiders* feature), Texas has restricted lawsuits by prison inmates, has given judges the power to dismiss frivolous lawsuits, has limited liability in civil cases involving multiple defendants, and has capped jury awards for **punitive damages** (judgments in excess of actual damages that are intended to punish the defendant). Texans narrowly approved a constitutional amendment to allow the legislature to limit claims for pain and suffering and punitive damages.

Punitive damages

Judgments in excess of actual damages intended to punish a defendant in a civil suit.

Consumer and environmentalist groups, Public Citizen, Texas Watch, Texans for Public Justice, the Texas Trial Lawyers Association, and most Democratic Party leaders generally oppose sweeping tort reform of the type Texas enacted. They argue that isolated anecdotal instances of lawsuit abuse should not be used as a justification to restrict the fundamental right to trial by jury. They contend that only a jury hearing all evidence presented by both sides can make an appropriate judgment in cases of extreme negligence and abuse of an individual's rights.

Plaintiffs' attorneys view tort reform as a big business attack on the laws protecting consumers against defective products and deceptive trade practices and argue that the threat of meaningful civil action is the only way to hold manufacturers and professionals responsible for their actions and force companies to improve safety procedures. Tort reform makes lawyers reluctant to take the risk of bringing costly and time-consuming lawsuits against well-funded corporations. Under Texas's new "loser pays" system, if either party refuses an out-of-court settlement and if the jury awards damages significantly different from the settlement offer, the loser must pay all of the "winner's" legal expenses in the case.

Tort reform issues are becoming the primary driving force in judicial campaigns. Corporations, insurance companies, health professionals, and frequently sued business groups generally contribute money to Republican judicial candidates who are inclined to interpret the law to limit damages in civil lawsuits. Consumer groups, environmentalists, plaintiffs' lawyers, patient-rights groups, and workers' organizations usually rally around Democratic judicial candidates, who tend to be friendlier to their causes.

Texas INSIDERS

Texans for Lawsuit Reform: Interest-Group Style Justice

Whether one agrees with the goals of Texans for Lawsuit Reform, there is no doubt that the group has used political means to change Texas's concept of justice. Organized by Dick Trabulsi, Texans for Lawsuit Reform (TRL) became a fund-raising juggernaut and a major force in Texas politics with the election of Governor George W. Bush. Mostly funded by only two dozen megadonors, TRL has become the largest and most prominent interest group to bankroll Republican candidates for the legislature, the governorship, and the Texas Supreme Court.

Presenting itself as a simple opponent of frivolous lawsuits and excessive damage awards, TRL has succeeded in fundamentally altering Texas's civil justice system, dramatically limiting the rights of injured parties to sue businesses, medical providers, and insurance companies. TRL persuaded the legislature and voters to amend the Texas Constitution to restrict the right to trial by jury, limiting jury awards of punitive damages and recently adopting a "loser pays" system for legal fees to discourage civil suits.

TRL's opponents, like plaintiffs' lawyers, who represent consumers, injured workers, patients, and the insured, believe that tort reform "went far beyond limiting excessive

(continued)

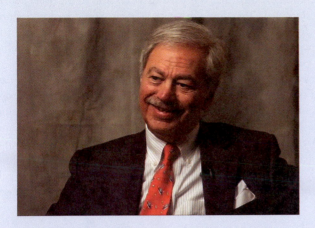

A wealthy owner of a chain of upscale liquor stores, Dick Trabulsi founded Texans for Lawsuit Reform and parlayed the single issue of tort reform to become a real player in Texas's political establishment.

Explain why tort reform catapulted Trabulsi into Texas's inner circle of political influence.

jury awards and effectively barred the courtroom door to injured Texans with legitimate claims." Mark Kincaid of the Texas Trial Lawyers Association asked, "What else is left for them to do?"

Thinking about the role of elites in Texas politics Texas's political system tends to over-represent concentrated interests at the expense of diffused interests. Insurance companies, health care providers, manufacturers, and retailers are often sued and have a strong interest in organizing to limit legal actions that raise their cost of doing business.

Meanwhile, workers, patients, and consumers have little motivation to organize to protect their right to recover damages on the off chance that they will be injured by lax workplace safety standards, medical malpractice, or defective products. How do unorganized interests protect themselves in the political system?

Sources: Ross Ramsay, "What Comes With Tort Reform?" *Texas Tribune,* August 29, 2011, www.texastribune.org/texas-special-interest-groups/texans-for-lawsuit-reform/collateral-politics-what-comes-tort-reform/ and www.texastribune.org/texas-special-interest-groups/texans-for-lawsuit-reform/about/; Nate Blakeslee, Paul Burka, and Patricia Kilday Hart, "Power Company: Who Are the Most Influential People Determining the Fate of Texas—and What Do They Want?" *Texas Monthly,* Volume 32, number 2, February, 2011, pp. 92–3.

Liability Insurance

Automobile insurance is one area for tort reform that the Texas legislature has not seriously considered. A **no-fault insurance** plan would allow an insured person to collect damages from the individual's own insurance company regardless of who is at fault in an accident. Under Texas's **liability insurance** plan, an expensive and time-consuming legal effort is often required to determine which of the individuals involved in an accident is to blame and thus legally responsible for damages. With no-fault insurance, insurance company costs for court trials could be substantially reduced, and the resulting savings could presumably be passed on to policyholders. Although there have been some instances of insurance fraud, at least a dozen states have successfully used limited no-fault insurance programs.

Eminent domain

Since the time of the Republic, Texas constitutions, like the U.S. Constitution, have required that owners must be given "adequate" or "just" compensation when government takes their private property for public "use." Just compensation has long been interpreted to mean fair market value. Recently, however, the meaning of public use has become controversial. In *Kelo* v. *City of New London Connecticut,* 545 U.S. 469 (2005), the U.S. Supreme Court interpreted public use to include private commercial development so long as it benefits the community as a whole. In its ruling, the Court approved seizing private residences to make way for a resort hotel, office buildings, and posh apartments.

No-fault insurance
An insurance plan allowing the insured person to collect from the individual's own insurance company regardless of who is at fault in a vehicular accident.

Liability insurance
Insurance against negligence claims such as those arising from auto accidents.

Although this is the interpretation of "use" that was used in Texas and many other states, property rights advocates were outraged. They hoped that the Court would ban taking, or condemning, private property for the benefit of other investors. Property rights activists argued that wealthy, politically well-connected buyers have the power to profit by influencing government to displace homeowners from property to use it for their own purposes.

Eminent domain

Government taking private property for public purposes with compensation.

In response, Texas joined several other states in limiting government's power of eminent domain. The legislature banned state and local governments from condemning private property for economic development projects except roads, parks, libraries, auditoriums, ports, and utilities. Voters confirmed these property rights with a state constitutional amendment and allowed property owners to sue state and local governments to invalidate certain policies that devalue their property by 25 percent or more.

However, some property rights advocates are disappointed that local governments are still allowed to transfer property from one owner to another for flood control and urban renewal projects.

THE ELEMENTS OF CRIME

Crime is a national issue, but despite the popularity of "law and order" as a campaign slogan in national elections, only 5 percent of crimes are prosecuted under federal law. The activities of the criminal justice system are primarily state, not federal, functions.

An act of Congress provides that federal offenses include crimes (1) committed on the high seas; (2) committed on federal property, territories, and reservations; (3) involving the crossing of state or national boundaries; (4) interfering with interstate commerce; or (5) committed against the national government or its employees while they are engaged in official duties. Otherwise, the vast majority of crimes are violations of state rather than federal law.

The Crime

As commonly used, the word *crime* refers to an act that violates whatever an authorized body (usually a state legislature) defines as the law. Many obey the law simply because it is law; others obey out of fear of punishment. Nevertheless, it is people's basic attitudes and values that are most important in determining whether they will respect or disobey a law. If a law reflects the values of most of society, as the law against murder does, it is usually obeyed. However, if a large element of society does not accept the values protected by law, as was the case with Prohibition in the 1920s, violation becomes widespread.

Felony

In Texas, a serious crime punishable by state institutions.

Felonies (see Table 12.1) are serious crimes. Murder is the illegal, willful killing of another human being. Robbery is attempting to take something from a person by force or threat of force. It is inaccurate to say that "a house was robbed"—this implies that a masked bandit stood at the front door with a pistol drawn on the doorbell and demanded that the building deliver up all its valuables. Buildings are burglarized—unlawfully entered to commit a felony or theft.

Did You Know? Texas makes it illegal to wear a bulletproof vest while committing murder.

Theft (larceny) is simply taking property from the rightful possession of another. Grand larceny—taking something valued more than $1,500—is a felony. Regardless of value, livestock rustling is a felony. It is also a felony for an adult to have sexual relations with a child less than 17 years of age. In Texas, it is a crime to disturb game hunters or for a commercial fisherman to possess a flounder less than 12 inches in length. Possession of tobacco by minors is outlawed. Most traffic violations are crimes, and the resulting fine is a form of punishment. Such minor crimes are called **misdemeanors** and are punishable by a sentence in county jail or a fine (or both).

Misdemeanor

A minor crime punishable by a county jail sentence or fine.

TABLE 12.1 Crime and Punishment under the Texas Penal Code

Offense	Terms*	Maximum Fine
Capital murder: including murder of a police officer, firefighter, prison guard, or child younger than the age of 6; murder for hire; murder committed with certain other felonies; mass murder	Execution or life sentence without parole	N\a
First-degree felony: including aggravated sexual assault, theft of money or property greater than $200,000, robbery, murder, sale of more than 4 grams of "hard" drugs such as heroin	5 to 99 years	$10,000
Second-degree felony: including theft of money or property greater than $100,000, burglary of a habitation	2 to 20 years	$10,000
Third-degree felony: including theft of money or property greater than $20,000, drive-by shootings, involuntary manslaughter	2 to 10 years	$10,000
State jail felony: including theft of money or property greater than $1,500, burglary of a building other than a habitation, sale of less than 1 gram of narcotics, auto theft, forgery	180 days to 2 years	$10,000
Class A misdemeanor: including theft of money or property greater than $500, driving while intoxicated, resisting arrest, stalking	Up to 1 year	$4,000
Class B misdemeanor: including theft of money or property greater than $50, possession of small amounts of marijuana, reckless conduct (such as pointing a gun at someone)	Up to 180 days	$2,000
Class C misdemeanor: including theft of money or property less than $50, smoking on a public elevator, disorderly conduct (such as indecent exposure)	—	$500

*Punishments may be reduced for murder committed in "sudden passion" or enhanced to the next level for crimes involving gang activity (three or more persons), the use of deadly weapons, previous convictions, or hate crimes (motivated by bias on the basis of ethnicity, religion, or sexual orientation).

Whether felonies or misdemeanors, some criminologists consider such crimes as prostitution, gambling, and illegal drug possession as being **victimless crimes** because their primary victims are the criminals themselves. However, the families of these criminals and society also pay a price for these activities, and they are often linked to more serious crimes. Now we will look at what causes people to commit crimes and what leads them to adopt values different from those reflected by the laws of society.

The Criminal

Persons who become criminals vary across the broad spectrum of human personality and come from virtually any of the multitudes of social and economic classes. Yet persons who *typically* commit serious crimes are astonishingly similar. For one reason or another, they are unwilling to accept the **mores** (the beliefs about "right" and "wrong") of the people who write the law. Lawbreakers are disproportionately young, poor, and members of racial or ethnic minority groups; many have acute emotional and social problems. They have little stake in the values that lawmakers hold dear.

With the decline of traditional family life and the rise of single-parent households, many young people are inadequately socialized by adults and generally lack a useful and rewarding role in society. They lack the sense of responsibility that usually goes with a job or a

© Yellow Dog Productions/Getty Images

First-offense driving while intoxicated is a misdemeanor punishable in the county jail. Here a city police officer conducts a field sobriety test. Students can access alcohol-related regulations at www.tabc.state.tx.us/.

How much should the law regulate individual conduct when it has an impact on society at large?

Victimless crime

A crime such as prostitution, gambling, or drug possession that primarily victimizes oneself rather than society at large.

Mores

Society's strong beliefs about right and wrong.

family. The young person who has dropped out of school or who is unemployed has difficulty functioning in legitimate society.

In some neighborhoods, street gangs provide the sole opportunity for social life and capitalistic endeavor. Membership in a gang is a powerful source of approval and a sense of belonging—often a member's only source—and thus gangs become training grounds in crime for successive generations. Lessons not learned on the streets may be picked up from the thousands of demonstrations of crime seen in movies and on television.

Whether as gangs or individuals, persons younger than the age of 25 commit a disproportionate share of crime. In Texas in 2010, those young people made up just 38 percent of the population but accounted for 55 percent of all arrests for theft, 63 percent for burglary, and 56 percent for arson.[1] Americans younger than age 25 accounted for 43 percent of all arrests nationwide for violent crimes (murder, non-negligent manslaughter, forcible rape, aggravated assault, and robbery) and 51 percent of property crimes (burglary, theft, motor vehicle theft, and arson).[2] Most of these make up **FBI index crimes**, which are used as a barometer of the crime rate.

FBI index crimes

Crimes used as a national barometer of the crime rate (murder and non-negligent manslaughter, forcible rape, robbery, aggravated assault, burglary, grand theft, and motor vehicle theft).

Many people refuse to recognize that the young are major perpetrators of crime, and others are convinced that they will "grow out of it." The truth is that disproportionate numbers of young people commit crimes and, rather than growing out of it, graduate into more serious crime; yet little is done to rehabilitate juveniles early in their criminal careers. Juvenile courts in Texas provide only limited social services for delinquents, and many have no access to vocational training, employment placement, emergency shelter, foster homes, or halfway houses. Severely limited in resources and facilities, Texas juvenile facilities not only fail to correct but also serve as breeding grounds for adult crime.

Far more men than women are arrested for crimes. In 2010, men accounted for 89 percent of Texans arrested for burglary, 87 percent for robbery, and 78 percent for aggravated assault.[3] Perhaps traditional masculine roles, social positions, and psychological attitudes make it difficult for some of them to accept certain mores of society. Aggression, violent sports, assertiveness, protectiveness, and earning money are often regarded as essentials of a boy's training for manhood. Apparently, many young men fail to learn the distinction between the kind of assertiveness that society approves and the kind it condemns.

Certain members of minority groups are arrested disproportionately for crime. Although African Americans consisted of only 12 percent of Texas's population in 2010, they accounted for 44 percent of Texans arrested for robbery, 35 percent of murder arrests, and 24 percent of arrests for rape. Meanwhile, 38 percent of Texans were Latinos and accounted for a fairly proportionate share of arrests—41 percent of arrests for murder, 42 percent for rape, and 37 percent for robbery.[4] Prejudice among law enforcement agencies may account for some of the disproportionate number of African Americans arrested, but it is likely that they actually commit a larger share of crime.

Poverty is among the social injustices experienced disproportionately by ethnic minorities, but it is by no means unique to them. Poor education and substantial psychological problems are also a result of poverty. The poor, regardless of racial or ethnic background, are more likely to commit violent crimes than members of the middle and upper classes.

[1]Calculated from data provided in Texas Department of Public Safety, *Texas Crime Report for 2010* (Austin: Department of Public Safety, 2011), pp. 75–80 and Census 2010 Summary File 1 (machine-readable data file), prepared by the U.S. Census Bureau, 2011 11AUG11 for *Texas Profile* prepared by the Texas State Data Center, (http://txsdc.utsa.edu), p. 2.

[2]Calculated using data from the Federal Bureau of Investigation, *Crime in the United States, 2010* (Washington, DC: Uniform Crime Reports, 2011), Table 38.

[3]*Texas Crime Report for 2010,* pp. 21–25.

[4]*Texas Crime Report for 2010*, pp. 16–21; *Texas Profile*, p. 2.

Crime is more likely in large metropolitan areas. More than three-fourths of all Texans live in densely populated metropolitan areas of more than 50,000 people (called *metropolitan statistical areas*). The character of urban life may contribute to crime in that cities are more anonymous, and social sanctions seem less effective there than in rural areas and small towns. Not only is there greater freedom in the city to act criminally, but there are also gangs and other organizations that openly encourage criminal activity. A majority of inmates in Texas prisons are from the San Antonio, Dallas, and Houston areas.

Addiction contributes to crime in a variety of ways. In 2010, some 144,602 Texans were arrested for narcotics violations,[5] and it is impossible to estimate what percentage of robberies, burglaries, and thefts are committed to finance illegal habits. Narcotics and alcohol also reduce inhibitions, and at least one-third of all crimes are committed under their influence.

Most violent crimes are committed by citizens who in one way or another are on the fringes of society. In many instances, these perpetrators simply live in an environment that promotes despair, low self-esteem, and weak emotional ties to the "legitimate" society. Some criminals consciously identify themselves as victims and rationalize their conduct based on their victim psychology.

In contrast to street criminals, few people think of a successful businessperson or a college professor as being a criminal; yet these people may stretch the meaning and intent of federal income tax laws, keep fraudulent business accounts, and pollute the environment. But because they seldom rob, rape, murder, or commit other violent acts, they are often punished less severely. Crimes such as bribery, tax fraud, business fraud, price-fixing, and embezzlement are **white-collar crimes**, committed by people who have often benefited from the very best advantages that society has to offer.

The American people have paid the costs of white-collar crime for centuries, but the recent near collapse of the economy has focused the public's attention, as never before, on white-collar crime. High-profile cases of fraud such as that committed by Bernie Madoff, R. Allen Sanford, and officials at Enron, and the resulting loss in confidence in the economy and stock values cost victims many times more than all robberies, burglaries, and thefts in recent years.

Contrary to the impression created by violence-centered local news coverage, Figure 12.1 shows that the crime rate has actually declined considerably since 1990.[6])

White-collar crime
Bribery, tax fraud, business fraud, embezzlement, and other nonviolent crimes usually committed by more prosperous individuals than those who commit street crimes.

The Victim

Although more affluent areas of the state and nation are sometimes victimized by perpetuators of street crime, police reports continue to demonstrate that the greatest rates of victimization remain in the poor sections of our cities. Crime is largely a neighborhood affair and is often committed against friends and families of the criminal. Acquaintance rape, or date rape, has been well publicized, and at least 45 percent of Texas killers were acquainted with their victims. In fact, 19 percent of all murder victims were killed by members of their own family. Young people and African Americans were most likely to become murder victims—35 percent were African American.[7]

Victims have the right to be informed of investigations and court proceedings against the accused and to have their victim impact statements taken into account during sentencing and parole action. The Texas Crime Victims' Compensation Fund is administered by the attorney general and financed by small fees collected from criminals when they are convicted. These meager funds are available to victims with extreme personal hardships resulting from physical injury during a crime. However, most victims are not eligible, nor is there compensation for the billions of dollars of property stolen each year.

---

[5]*Texas Crime Report for 2010*, p. 33.
[6]*Texas Crime Report for 2010*, p. 8.
[7]*Texas Crime Report for 2010*, p. 16.

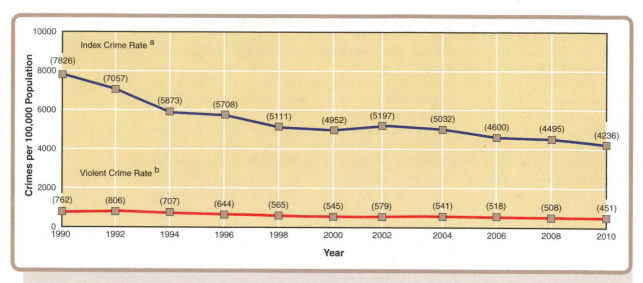

Figure 12.1

Texas Crime Rates Since 1990

This figure shows that the violent crime rate and total index crime rate per 100,000 citizens in Texas have decreased over most of the past two decades.

[a]Total of violent and property crimes (burglary, theft, and motor vehicle theft) per 100,000 population.
[b]Murder, rape, robbery, and aggravated assault.

Source: Department of Public Safety, *Crime in Texas, 2010* (Austin: Department of Public Safety 2011), p. 8.

Why do news media continue to focus on crime at a time when crime rates are declining?

THE DUE PROCESS OF LAW

It is in the courts that the most general concept of justice and the broadest norms of society are enforced against specific individuals. The courts must blend two conflicting goals of society: (1) to protect society according to the state's legal concepts of right and wrong and (2) to protect the rights of the individual charged with wrongdoing. As a result, elaborate traditions of court process and procedure have developed over the centuries; many of these traditional procedures came from the English experience, while others were developed more recently in the American states. Some court procedures have been written into state and national constitutions and statutes; others are included in written and unwritten traditional codes of court process. Such procedures are designed to promote justice and protect the individual from the government, and together they constitute what is called **due process**.

The rights guaranteed to the accused are very nearly meaningless unless courts, prosecutors, and law enforcement agents are careful to protect them—in practice, due process depends on the values of those who administer and interpret the law.

Due process

The following of proper legal procedures. Due process is essential to guaranteeing fairness before the government may deprive a person of life, liberty, or property.

Searches

At certain crucial points in the investigation and apprehension of suspected criminals, society has for centuries demanded various external checks and limits on law enforcement agencies to protect the innocent and the presumption of innocence. For example, the Texas Constitution and the Fourth Amendment to the U.S. Constitution prohibit "unreasonable" searches.

However, warrants are not always required; warrantless searches of prisoners (to protect law enforcement personnel) and pedestrians (to protect the public safety) are permitted. Motor vehicles may be searched without warrants because it is simply impractical to require a warrant when evidence may be driven away.

For the most part, the reasonableness of a search is determined by supposedly neutral and independent courts, which supervise the law enforcement agencies that propose to intrude on private premises in search of evidence. In Texas, justices of the peace, municipal court judges, or other magistrates appointed by district courts usually determine **probable cause**— whether the facts and circumstances are sufficient to lead a "reasonable person" to believe that evidence is probably contained on the premises and thus a warrant for the invasion of privacy is justified.

To make the Fourth Amendment effective, the U.S. Supreme Court, in the 1914 case of *Weeks* v. *United States* (232 U.S. 383), established the **exclusionary rule**, under which evidence acquired in violation of the Fourth Amendment could not be admitted in federal courts. The decision discouraged law enforcement agents in federal cases from engaging in illegal invasions of privacy because the evidence obtained could not be used against the accused. In the 1961 case of *Mapp* v. *Ohio* (367 U.S. 643), the U.S. Supreme Court held the exclusionary rule also to be essential to the "due process of law" that the Fourteenth Amendment requires states to respect.

The U.S. Supreme Court has begun to modify the exclusionary rule. For example, under the "good faith" rule, evidence may be admitted when law enforcement agents acted on a search warrant they believed valid even though it was not (*United States* v. *Leon*, 468 U.S. 897, 1984); improperly obtained evidence may also be admitted under the "inevitable discovery" rule if agents otherwise would have discovered the evidence during their routine legal investigation (*Nix* v. *Williams*, 467 U.S. 431, 1984).

Arrests

Like privacy, an individual's liberty is a particularly valued right. The mere fact that a person has been arrested may damage his or her reputation in the community. In short, arrest is in itself a form of punishment. To prevent arrests for frivolous causes, the courts may authorize police to arrest suspects. In Texas, magistrates issue a warrant to take a person into custody when they are presented with probable cause that the person has committed a crime, when a prosecutor files for a *writ of information* (usually charging a person for a misdemeanor) or when a *grand jury* issues an *indictment* (usually for a felony).

Police officers may make arrests without a warrant when they have probable cause and when circumstances do not permit their obtaining one. They may make arrests for crimes they witness or those that are reported directly to them by a witness. Although an arrest resulting from investigation is technically illegal without a warrant, police have considerable flexibility. By contrast, *citizens' arrests* are legal only for felonies or other offenses against the public peace committed in the citizens' presence.

Detention

The time between a person's arrest and appearance before a magistrate is critical. Historically, this period was a time of much police abuse, during which law enforcement officers sometimes used physical violence or *third-degree* psychological tactics. Police would also delay taking a suspect before a magistrate, where probable cause for arrest would have to be shown and the suspect informed of certain constitutional rights. As a result, law enforcement agents were able to extract confessions or other evidence from the frightened and sometimes abused suspects. Confessions obtained in this manner are unreliable and violate the Fifth and Fourteenth Amendments of the U.S. Constitution.

Probable cause

Sufficient information to convince a reasonably cautious person that a search or arrest is justified.

Exclusionary rule

The requirement that illegally obtained evidence may not be used against the accused.

In Arizona, the Phoenix police unknowingly set the stage for a far-reaching U.S. Supreme Court decision when they extracted a confession from Ernesto Miranda, a young Latino. Having only an eighth-grade education, the suspect could not possibly have been expected to know his constitutional right to remain silent, and his interrogators did not inform him of his rights. The Court declared that confessions such as Miranda's could not be admitted as evidence. Its ruling established guidelines for informing a person of the following rights before a confession could be admitted as evidence:

1. The suspect has the right to remain silent.
2. Any statement made may be used against the suspect.
3. The suspect has the right to an attorney, whether or not he or she can afford one.

A suspect may knowingly waive these rights and agree to talk to police. The decision of the U.S. Supreme Court in *Miranda* v. *Arizona* (384 U.S. 436, 1966) was one of its most controversial, and many people claimed that the Court was "coddling criminals." Others argued that no system worth preserving should have to fear an accused person's being aware of basic constitutional rights.

Despite the outcry and controversy, there is little evidence that conviction rates have declined as a result of the *Miranda* decision. It is less sweeping than has been assumed—its purpose is to ensure that confessions are voluntary when they result *from interrogation*. An interrogation occurs when police focus questioning on a primary suspect, expecting to extract a confession. Information resulting from unsolicited confessions or general questioning is admissible. There are many exceptions to the Miranda rule, including a public safety exception[8] and that admitting an improper confession at trial does not automatically result in reversal of conviction—if other evidence is sufficient to convict.[9]

Pretrial Court Activities

After arrest, the suspect is jailed while reports are completed and the district attorney's office decides whether or not to file charges and what bail to recommend. As soon as is practical, the accused is presented before a justice of the peace or other magistrate. This initial **arraignment** has four major purposes:

Arraignment
A prisoner's initial appearance before a magistrate in which the charges and basic rights (to an attorney and bail) are explained.

1. Explain the charges against the accused.
2. Remind the suspect of the rights to remain silent and to be represented by counsel and to request a written acknowledgment that the Miranda warning was given and understood.
3. Set bail.
4. Inform the accused of the right to an examining trial.

The suspect is usually told the charges multiple times—upon arrest, in the arraignment, and again in subsequent proceedings. Being told the nature of charges is one of the most fundamental aspects of due process. Because the states have governments of "laws and not men," a person should never be held in custody on whim but only for *legal* cause. In other words, there must be sufficient justification—probable cause—for being held. If the law no longer justifies imprisonment, counsel may secure release through a *writ of habeas corpus* (see Chapter 3), a court order requiring that the prisoner be presented in person and legal cause shown for imprisonment. The right to counsel is vital to the accused—an attorney should clearly understand the constitutional rights of the accused and be familiar with the intricacies of the law and the courts. So important is the assistance of counsel that many suspects will contact an attorney even before they first appear in front of a magistrate.

[8]*New York* v. *Quarles,* 467 U. S. 649 (1984).
[9]*Arizona* v. *Fulminante,* 499 U.S. 279 (1991).

Yet this right to counsel has never been absolute. Guaranteed in both the U.S. and Texas Constitutions, the right to counsel had traditionally been interpreted to mean that the accused has a right to counsel if he or she could afford one. In 1932, the U.S. Supreme Court ruled that the Sixth Amendment requires state courts to appoint counsel for the poor, but only in capital cases.[10] Later, the Court extended an indigent's right to counsel in other felony cases and in serious misdemeanor cases in which imprisonment might be involved, but it does not extend to petty offenses such as traffic violations.[11] However, the right to court-appointed counsel does not necessarily guarantee equal justice for the poor.

Some Texas counties still rely on an assigned counsel system in which private lawyers are selected and paid on a case-by-case basis or in which they work by contract to defend a group of indigent cases assigned to them. Paid by the county, some attorneys find that time spent defending poor people does not significantly advance either their practice or their income. Other attorneys have developed highly successful practices based on indigent defense, and some judges have been charged with cronyism for assigning cases to lawyers who have contributed to their political campaigns.

A number of Texas counties have established a system of salaried full-time public defenders to serve as advocates for indigents in serious criminal cases. Supporters of a public defender system have argued that it is more professional and less costly than the assigned counsel system. Despite the reforms adopted in some counties, the quality of indigent representation varies tremendously from county to county and from defendant to defendant.

> **Did You Know?** The federal Fifth Circuit Court of Appeals reversed one conviction because the defendant's attorney repeatedly fell asleep during the trial.

Bail is the security deposit required for the release of a suspect awaiting trial. Some persons released on bail fail to appear in court, and their security deposit is forfeited. Others commit still more crimes while out on bail. However, the legal system presumes that an individual is innocent unless convicted, and bail supports this assumption by permitting the accused to resume a normal professional and social life while preparing a defense.

Bail
The security required for release of a suspect awaiting trial.

Although bail may be reset or denied following indictment, the Texas Constitution guarantees the right to bail immediately after arrest, except where proof is "evident" in capital cases or when the defendant is being charged with a third felony after two previous felony convictions. The state constitution allows bail to be denied if the defendant is charged with committing a felony while released on bail or under indictment for another felony.

In practice, the right to bail exists only for those who can afford it. Private, licensed bonding companies may be willing to post bond for a fee (usually 10 to 50 percent of the bail as set by the court), which, unlike bail, is not refunded. Many defendants cannot afford even this fee, and unless released on **personal recognizance** (the defendant's personal promise to appear), the prisoner will await trial in jail. Bail was designed to free a person not yet found guilty of a crime, but some innocent people await trial in jail, unable to work, carry on their family life, or gather evidence for their own defense. In our criminal justice system, bail procedures, more than any other single practice, punish the poor for their poverty. Professional criminals released on bail often return to work. They may even commit more crimes to pay their attorneys' retainers and bonding fees.

Personal recognizance
A defendant's personal promise to appear; sometimes allowed instead of cash bail or bond.

Although few defendants request one, the accused has the right to an **examining trial** in felony cases. A magistrate reviews the facts and decides whether the case should be bound over to a grand jury. Or, if the facts warrant, the charges may be dismissed or bail adjusted.

Examining trial
An initial court hearing to determine if there is sufficient evidence to send a case to a grand jury.

> **Did You Know?** A majority of Texas's jail inmates are simply awaiting trial and have not yet been convicted.

---

[10]*Powell* v. *Alabama*, 287 U.S. 45 (1932).
[11]*Gideon* v. *Wainwright*, 372 U.S. 335 (1963); *Argersinger* v. *Hamlin*, 407 U.S. 25 (1972).

Formal Charges

Although indictment sometimes precedes arrests, a felony case is usually bound over to a grand jury for indictment following arraignment. A grand jury should not be confused with a petit, or trial, jury. Grand juries do not determine a person's guilt or innocence as trial juries do; the accused may not even be asked to appear before the grand jury. Instead of hearing the defense, the grand jury primarily weighs the evidence in the hands of the prosecutor to determine whether there is a ***prima facie* case** (sufficient evidence to convict when the case is taken to trial). If it determines the existence of such evidence, the grand jury issues an indictment (a *true bill*), which constitutes formal charges that enable the case to go to trial (a *no-bill* is a refusal to indict).

A *prima facie* case is necessary to bring formal charges because if the prosecutor does not have enough evidence to convict, there is no point in bringing the case to trial. Trying a case on flimsy evidence not only costs the taxpayers money but also causes the accused to suffer needless expense, lost time, and a damaged reputation. The right to a grand jury indictment is guaranteed in both the Texas and federal courts to protect the rights of innocent citizens against harassment on unjustified charges.

In practice, grand juries are usually made up of ordinary citizens who have never been trained to critically evaluate cases and so usually act as a rubber stamp for the prosecutors. Some states have abolished the grand jury in favor of writs of information in which a judge evaluates the evidence to determine if there is sufficient evidence to go to trial. Texas guarantees the right to indictment in all felony cases but uses the writ of information to charge people with misdemeanors.

Pretrial Hearings

After the indictment, the defendant has the right to yet another hearing, sometimes called the *second arraignment*. A district judge (rather than a justice of the peace) presides as the formal indictment is read, and the defendant enters a plea. If the plea is guilty, a later hearing is scheduled to set punishment. Most often the defendant pleads not guilty at this point, and the case is placed on the docket (schedule of court activity) for subsequent trial. A variety of motions may be presented, including a motion for delay (continuance) or for the suppression of certain evidence. Other subjects of pretrial hearings concern possible insanity or **change of venue** (change in the site of a trial).

A person cannot be held morally and criminally responsible for a crime if at the time of the offense, mental illness made it impossible for the person to recognize that it was wrong. There is considerable controversy as to the effects of mental disorder, so professional testimony may be necessary to establish legal insanity, and psychiatric opinion is frequently divided. It is rare that the courts find a defendant not guilty by reason of insanity.

A change of venue may be necessary when the news media have so publicized a case that it becomes impossible to select an unbiased jury locally or when inflamed public opinion may prevent a fair trial. A real tension exists between the rights of the free press and the rights of the accused, and in a modern society, the rights of the accused can be protected only with great vigilance by our courts.

Plea Bargaining

Ideally, the trial is the final step in society's elaborate guarantees of due process. Only through the deliberations in the courtroom can our system's genuine concern for justice emerge. Yet for most people who are accused of a crime, their final day in court never comes. In fact, the system is designed to discourage and even punish those who choose to exercise their right to trial. Most cases end in *plea bargaining*—a secret bargaining session with the prosecutor.

Prima facie case
Sufficient evidence to convict if unchallenged at trial; the amount of evidence necessary to indict a defendant.

Change of venue
A change in the location of a trial.

Facing overcrowded dockets and limited staff, prosecuting attorneys usually meet with the accused and offer a deal in exchange for a plea of guilty, which eliminates the need for a trial. The usual deal is to offer to drop some of the charges, to recommend probation or a lighter sentence, or to charge the accused with a lesser crime. The prosecutor may agree to delay prosecution (this is known as *deferred adjudication*) and later drop charges if the defendant agrees to meet conditions like those required under probation. Such plea agreements save tax money and court time and may be useful to law enforcement, such as when certain defendants are given a lighter sentence in exchange for testifying against fellow criminals who have committed more serious crimes.

On the other hand, the guilty obviously benefit from plea bargaining because they are not punished for the full measure of their crimes. Justice is thus exchanged for a cheaper system that benefits the guilty. Defense attorneys frequently encourage their clients to accept the bargain to save them the effort of a courtroom trial, and some become as much agents for the prosecution as advocates for the defense. The innocent and those who are unwilling to trade their rights for a secret backroom bargain take the chance of being punished more severely for demanding a trial.

The Trial

Unless the defense waives the right to a trial by jury, the first major step is the selection of a jury. The right to a trial by jury is often regarded as one of the most valuable rights available in the criminal justice system. In fact, every state provides for trial by jury in all but the most minor cases, and Texas goes even further, providing for the right to trial by jury in every criminal case.[12]

Nevertheless, the right to trial by jury in a criminal case is one of the most frequently waived rights, especially in cases where the defendant is an object of community prejudice (a member of an unpopular political group or ethnic minority) or if the alleged crime is particularly outrageous. If the right to a jury trial is waived, the presiding judge determines the verdict. Regardless of whether or not a person chooses to exercise it, the right to trial by jury remains a valuable alternative to decisions by possibly arbitrary judges.

During initial questioning of prospective jurors (***voir dire* questioning**), they may be asked about possible biases, their previous knowledge of the case, or any opinions they may have formed. Either the prosecution or the defense may challenge a prospective juror for reason of prejudice, and the presiding judge will evaluate that challenge. Furthermore, both the prosecution and the defense may dismiss a number of jurors by peremptory challenges (without cause), also called *strikes*, depending on the kind of case involved. Considering occupations, social status, and attitudes of possible jurors, experienced attorneys and prosecutors use peremptory challenges to select a friendly jury; some have been known to use psychologists to assist in the selection process, and lucrative consulting businesses have developed to assist attorneys in jury selection.

All English-speaking countries have developed an **adversary system** in which two parties to the case (the prosecution and the defense in criminal cases) arm themselves with whatever evidence they can muster and battle in court, under the rules of law, to final judgment. An adversary system cannot operate fairly unless both the defense and the prosecution have an equal opportunity to influence the decision of the court. Hence procedural guarantees are designed to ensure that both sides have equal access to an understanding of the laws and the evidence. So that equal knowledge of the laws is guaranteed, the legal knowledge of

Voir dire questioning

The initial questioning of jurors to determine possible biases.

Adversary system

The legal system used in English-speaking countries in which two contesting parties present opposing views and evidence in a court of law.

[12]The U.S. Supreme Court held in the case of *Duncan* v. Louisiana, 391 U.S. 145 (1968) that trial by jury is an essential part of due process when state criminal proceedings involve more than petty offenses.

Compulsory process

A procedure to subpoena witnesses in court.

the prosecution is balanced by the right of the defendant to have legal counsel. Because the government (in the person of the prosecutor) has the power to seize evidence and to force witnesses to testify under oath, the defense must be given that same power (called **compulsory process**).

In the adversary system, each side can challenge the material evidence and cross-examine witnesses who have been presented by the opposition. Only evidence that is presented in court can be evaluated. The fact that both parties to a case have opposite biases and intentions means that they have an interest in concealing evidence that could benefit the opposition.

Because it is the legal responsibility of the prosecutor to prove guilt beyond a reasonable doubt (the burden of proof lies with the state), the counsel for the defense has no responsibility to present evidence of the defendant's guilt, nor can the defendant be forced to take the stand to testify. On the other hand, because the responsibility of the prosecutor is to convict the guilty rather than the innocent, it is a violation of due process for the government to withhold evidence that could benefit the accused—but it happens. There is no way of knowing how many unjust verdicts have been decided because all the evidence was not presented.

In jury trials, once the evidence has been presented, the judge reads the charge to the jury—the judge's instructions about how the law applies in the case. The judge will instruct the jurors to ignore such things as hearsay testimony and other illegal evidence to which they may have been exposed during the course of the trial. (Realistically, however, it is difficult for jurors to erase from their minds the impact of illegal testimony.) The judge is supposedly neutral and cannot comment on the weight of the evidence that has been presented.

After the judge's charge to the jury, the prosecution and defense are each allowed to summarize the case. During their summary remarks, the prosecutor will comment that the evidence points toward guilt, and the defense will conclude that the evidence is insufficient to prove guilt beyond a reasonable doubt. The jury then retires to decide the verdict—guilty or not guilty. Texas law requires that all the jurors agree on the verdict in criminal cases. If the jury cannot agree, a *hung jury* exists, and the judge will declare a **mistrial**, but the defendant may be tried again.

Mistrial

A trial not completed for legal reasons, such as a hung jury; a new trial may be possible.

Regardless of whether the judge or the jury determines guilt, the judge may prescribe the sentence, unless the defendant requests that the jury do so. In considering the character of the defendant, any past criminal record, and the circumstances surrounding the crime, the judge may assess a penalty between the minimum and maximum provided by law. An offender may be sentenced to **probation**, which allows the person to serve the sentence in free society according to specific terms and restrictions and under the supervision of a probation officer. Similarly, deferred adjudication allows judges to postpone final sentencing in criminal cases, and after a satisfactory probationary period, the charges are dismissed.

Probation

A judge's sentence of an offender to serve outside a correctional institution but under specific restrictions and official supervision.

Judges have a great deal of latitude in assessing penalties, so the fate of a defendant will depend in large part on the attitudes of the presiding judge. Different judges sometimes assess vastly different penalties for the same crime committed under similar circumstances.

Upon sentencing, the prisoner will be sent to one of the state's penal institutions. Time served in jail before and during trial is usually deducted from the sentence of the guilty. For the innocent, however, the time served awaiting trial is a casualty of an imperfect system of justice that underlines the necessity for care in accusing and trying our citizens.

Post-Trial Proceedings

To protect the accused from double jeopardy, a person who is acquitted (found not guilty) cannot be tried again for the same offense. However, protection from double jeopardy is much more limited than many citizens believe. In the event of a mistrial or an error in procedure in which a person is not acquitted, another trial may be held for the same offense on the theory that the defendant was never put in jeopardy by the first trial. A person found not guilty of one crime may be tried for other related offenses. For example, a person who is accused of driving 75 miles per hour through a school zone, going the wrong way on a one-way street, striking down a child in the crosswalk, and then leaving the scene of the accident has committed four crimes. Being acquitted of one of them does not free the defendant of possible charges for each of the other offenses. Likewise, such acts as bank robbery and kidnapping may violate both federal and state law, and the accused may be tried by both jurisdictions.

Although the state cannot appeal a not-guilty verdict, because doing so would constitute double jeopardy, prosecutors may appeal the *reversal* of a guilty verdict by a higher court, and the defendant may appeal a guilty verdict. Misdemeanor cases from justices of the peace and municipal courts may be either tried *de novo* (anew) or appealed in county courts. Appeals from county and district courts go to one of 14 courts of appeals and finally to the Texas Court of Criminal Appeals.

Appellate procedure is designed to review the law as applied by lower courts, not to evaluate evidence to determine guilt or innocence. Its major concern is procedure. Even if overruled, the antics of defense attorneys in raising frequent objections to court procedure may build a case for appeal. If serious procedural errors are found, the appellate courts may return the case to a lower court for retrial. Such a retrial does not constitute double jeopardy.

Having exhausted the rights of appeal in the Texas courts, a very few cases are appealed to the federal courts, which have jurisdiction in federal law. Thus, the grounds for appeal to federal courts would be the assertion that the state courts have violated the U.S. Constitution or other federal law.

The Special Case of Juvenile Courts

As the result of a reform effort in the nineteenth century, most states began to provide special treatment for children. In 1943, Texas followed the lead of other states in replacing all adult criminal procedures in juvenile cases with special civil procedures. Under the legal fiction that juveniles were not being punished for crimes, lax procedures were used that would never have been permitted in adult criminal courts. Court proceedings were secret, the rights to counsel and to trial by jury were ignored, standards of evidence were relaxed, and frequently charges were not specific.

As a result of federal court rulings, much of due process has since been restored to juvenile proceedings—except the rights to bail, a grand jury indictment, and a public trial. Juvenile proceedings remain civil, and juvenile records may be sealed from the public with the approval of the juvenile judge, who is usually appointed by the county's judges or juvenile board to have exclusive jurisdiction in such cases. The law allows juvenile felony arrest warrants to be entered into statewide computers, and police can gather information such as juvenile fingerprints and photographs. Children as young as 14 years of age arrested for serious crimes may be certified to stand trial as adults, but a majority of those arrested for lesser crimes are counseled and released without further proceedings.

© COMPULSORY CREDIT: UPPA/Photoshot

Children tried as adults seem to be more likely to commit future crimes than those who are dealt with in the juvenile system, according to the U.S. Centers for Disease Control and Prevention. (See www.cdc.gov/mmwr/PDF/rr/rr5609 .pdf.) Texas allows children to be tried as adults at age 14.

How should the legal rights and responsibilities of children differ from those of adults?

REHABILITATION AND PUNISHMENT

Texas jails and penitentiaries are intended to have several functions:

1. Punishment (or social vengeance) is society's way of settling accounts with those who have violated its norms. By providing public institutions that extract justice, society offers an alternative to private revenge and the resulting feuds that plagued the early stages of Western civilization. Until the eighteenth century, punishment meant imposing physical or financial pain. But ideas of human dignity led to the development of prisons to deny a person liberty as a more humane way of punishing. Today, although some prisoners brutalize each other, the death penalty is the only remnant of formal physical punishment left in the law.

2. **Deterrence** of criminals is a major rationalization for the development of prison systems. Society uses punishment of convicted criminals as an example to discourage would-be lawbreakers.

3. Isolation of criminal elements from the law-abiding population is designed to protect society from future crimes. Yet for most crimes, society is unwilling to prescribe the permanent imprisonment of convicted criminals.

4. **Rehabilitation** of convicted criminals is supposed to allow those who are ultimately released to take useful and noncriminal roles in society.

In practice, prisons and jails have performed none of these functions. Punishment and isolation are cut short because prisons are overcrowded, and criminals are released after having served only a fraction of the time assessed by judges and juries. Punishment is neither swift nor certain and cannot effectively deter crime. Texas has put a larger percentage of its population in prison than almost any other state, yet it still has one of the nation's highest crime rates. Texas has executed more people than any other state, yet it still has a murder rate greater than most other states in the nation. Rehabilitation of convicts is often unsuccessful—a majority of crimes are committed by **recidivists** (repeat offenders).

Deterrence
Discouraging criminal behavior by threat of punishment.

Rehabilitation
The effort to correct criminals' antisocial attitudes and behavior.

Recidivist
A criminal who commits another crime after having been incarcerated.

Felony Punishment

The Texas Department of Criminal Justice (DCJ) supervises the state's adult correctional functions for convicted felons—probation, prison, and parole.

Probation Probation allows convicts to serve their sentences outside prisons but under varying degrees of supervision—probationers may be required to report to probation officers, submit to electronic monitoring, undergo treatment for chemical dependency, or live in community residence facilities or restitution centers. Although probation functions are largely the responsibilities of local community supervision and corrections departments, DCJ sets standards and provides funding, training, information, and technical assistance to local officers.

Prison The criminal justice department also operates the prison units for those offenders not granted probation. Texas's prison population has tripled since the mid-1980s, and 51 prison facilities, 15 state jails, 14 transfer facilities, and other confinement units now accommodate more than 150,000 inmates.

Parole
Early release from prison under official supervision.

Parole After an initial stay in prison, **parole** allows many inmates to serve the remainder of their sentences under supervision in the community. Whereas DCJ is responsible for their supervision after release, the Board of Pardons and Paroles decides which inmates will be granted parole.

HOW DOES TEXAS COMPARE?
Crime and Punishment

Texas's crime rate is greater than that of 48 other states—it is nearly twice as high as those of New York and New Hampshire. The state's high crime rate is related to the high proportion of young, low-income, ethnic minority, poorly educated, urban residents among the population. Lack of family unity, high rates of addiction, and numerous other social factors also contribute to high crime rates. Figure 12.2 shows that the highest crime rates are generally in the southern and western states.

Texas's conservative political culture has been receptive to a "get-tough" approach to dealing with its high crime rates. Texas has officially imprisoned a far larger percentage of its population than authoritarian nations such as China, Cuba, Iran, and Russia. Among the 50 states, only 3 states have a larger number of prison inmates per 100,000 population than Texas. Table 12.2 shows that Texas also has a greater proportion of its population on parole and probation than most states.

Unfortunately, these facts do not answer the larger question of whether high rates of imprisonment serve as a deterrent to crime. One might expect states, like Texas, with high

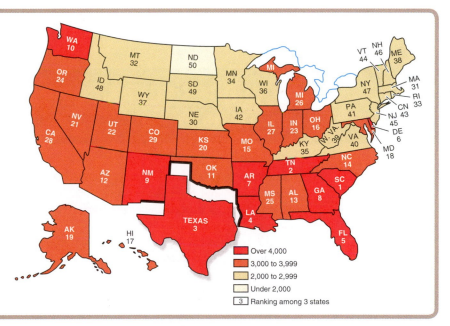

Figure 12.2

FBI Index Crime Rates per 100,000 Population, 2010

Source: Federal Bureau of Investigation, Uniform Crime Reports: Crime in the United States, 2010, Table 5 at http://www.fbi.gov/about-us/cjis/ucr/crime-in-the-u.s/2010/crime-in-the-u.s.-2010/tables/10tbl05.xls

Why do crime rates vary so dramatically from one state to another? Name the factors that affect crime rates.

Over 4,000
3,000 to 3,999
2,000 to 2,999
Under 2,000
3 | Ranking among 3 states

TABLE 12.2 Persons in Prison, on Probation, and on Parole Per 100,000 Population*

	Federal	50 States	Texas	Texas Ranking among 50 States
Prisoners	61	437	648	4
On probation	10	1,711	2,280	9
On parole	45	312	570	5

*Prisoners reported per 100,000 residents; probationers and parolees reported per 100,000 adults on December 31, 2010.

Source: Bureau of Justice Statistics, *Prisoners in 2010*, December 2011, Appendix Table 9, p. 22 (bjs.ojp.usdoj.gov/index.cfm?ty=pbdetail&iid=2230; *Probation and Parole in the United States, 2010*, November 2011, Appendix Tables 2 and 12, pp. 30 and 40 (bjs.ojp.usdoj.gov/index.cfm?ty=pbdetail&iid=2239).

rates of imprisonment would have a lower crime rate; yet ironically, Texas continues to have one of the highest crime rates in the United States.

Criminologists usually argue that *severity* of punishment is less important than the *certainty* of punishment. Many crimes are never reported, and police clear only a small share of known crimes with arrests. In fact, most criminals are never punished for the crimes they commit in Texas or in any other state.

Prisons are failures as institutions of rehabilitation. Far from being humane alternatives to corporal punishment, they are often brutal dens of violence, vice, and homosexual rape. Personal development is subordinated to personal degradation. Instead of rehabilitating prisoners, prisons have become publicly supported institutions of higher criminal learning. A large majority of those released from these human warehouses will again commit a serious crime; as many as 80 percent of all felonies may be committed by repeaters (recidivists) who have had previous contact with the criminal justice system. A major factor in crime is thus the failure of our correctional systems to correct.

FOR DEBATE

1. Does Texas have a high rate of imprisonment because it has a high crime rate, or does the state's political culture explain the high rate of imprisonment?

2. Does the threat of punishment deter crime? Why or why not?

HOW DOES TEXAS COMPARE?
The Death Penalty

States with the Death Penalty
Four states (Illinois, New York, New Jersey, Connecticut, and New Mexico) have abolished the death penalty within the past few years, leaving 33 states with death penalty laws on the books. However, many of them rarely, if ever, carry out executions.

The South is the region in which most executions take place. Between 1976 and 2011, southern states performed more than 80 percent of all executions in the United States. Texas led the nation (477), and Virginia ranked second (109). By 2011, Texas accounted for 37 percent of all executions nationwide.

Explaining Texas's Reputation as a Death Penalty State
Texas has a large population, but its population alone does not explain the state's large number of executions. Between 1976 and 2011, only Oklahoma had a greater execution rate (2.6 per 100,000 of the population) than Texas (1.9 per 100,000).

Surprisingly, Texas juries are no more likely to impose the death penalty in murder cases than juries in other states, but Texas does follow through to execute a larger share of its death row prisoners. In Texas, about 2 percent of murder cases result in a death sentence (about average in death penalty states), but Texas authorities executed 49.8 percent of those sentenced to death between 1977 and 2010—only Virginia executed a greater portion (72.5 percent) of its death row inmates.

Capital Punishment as a Deterrent

Ironically, states with capital punishment have consistently had a *greater* murder rate than the states without it. For example, in 2010, the average murder rate was 4.6 per 100,000 in states with the death penalty, while the murder rate in states without it was only 2.9. A historic pattern of such statistics has been interpreted to mean that death penalty laws do not act as a deterrent to murder. Perhaps states with a higher murder rate have been the most receptive to politicians willing to vigorously enforce the death penalty.

Alternatives to the Death Penalty

Texas was the last state to allow life without parole as an alternative to the death penalty, and initial evidence shows that prosecutors are less likely to seek the death sentence and juries are less likely to impose it when a secure and sufficiently punitive alternative is available.

Trends in Death Sentences

Across the nation, death sentences have become less frequent for four reasons: (1) the murder rate has declined; (2) the number of exonerations of death row inmates (12 in Texas) has shown that innocent persons can be convicted of crimes they did not commit; (3) actual lifetime sentences without parole are now available as an alternative to capital punishment in every state with the death penalty; and (4) the cost of carrying out the death sentence far exceeds that of lifetime imprisonment.

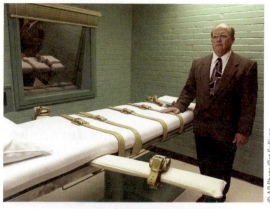

© AP Photo/Pat Sullivan

Lethal-injection gurney. Texas was the first state to use lethal injection in executions. Today, it is an option for execution in all 33 states with the death penalty. Critics argue that the lethal drug cocktail can cause excruciating pain in still-conscious subjects who show few signs of discomfort because of drug-induced paralysis. Despite these arguments, the U.S. Supreme Court ruled in 2008 that lethal injection does not violate the Eighth Amendment ban on cruel and unusual punishment.*

Can you think of ethical reasons to keep the death penalty or to abolish it?

FOR DEBATE

What is the best argument in favor of capital punishment? As an alternative, can life imprisonment serve justice as well as capital punishment? Why? Why not?

GO ONLINE

Find a wealth of information about the death penalty at the Bureau of Justice Statistics and at the Death Penalty Information Center at **www.deathpenaltyinfo.org/**. Search for studies that show capital punishment as a deterrent to murder.

**Baze et al. v. Rees et al.*, 553 U.S. 35 (2008).

Inmates serving life sentences for capital crimes are not eligible for parole, and those convicted of other violent offenses must serve at least one-half of their sentences before being considered for parole. Those convicted of other offenses must serve only one-fourth of their sentences or 15 years, whichever is less. However, additional time against the sentence is allowed for making a positive effort toward rehabilitation, good behavior, and providing various services such as serving as a prison trusty (an inmate assigned to assist prison staff). As a result, an inmate may become eligible for parole in fewer calendar years than the original sentence indicated.

The Board of Pardons and Paroles does not grant parole to prisoners automatically when they become eligible. Instead, the board examines each inmate's record for positive evidence of rehabilitation. When granted parole, the freed prisoner must abide by strict codes of conduct under the general supervision of parole officers. Parole, as the concept has developed, should not be forgiveness but a continuation of the process of correction. Parole rehabilitation is based on the idea that the elimination of antisocial attitudes can be more effectively accomplished when the individual is not severed from society. Parole is far less expensive than incarceration. Supervision of a prison inmate costs as much as 20 times that of a parolee, but parole revocations are frequent because parolees often run afoul of the law.

Misdemeanor Punishment

State government assumes the responsibility for convicted felons, but those convicted of the misdemeanors for which confinement is prescribed will serve their terms in jails operated by local governments, usually counties. Jails fail to rehabilitate for three major reasons:

1. Jail staffs and physical facilities are designed to maintain custody rather than to rehabilitate. Many prisoners in county jails are either awaiting trial or being held for other agencies (federal or state)—our jails are designed as human warehouses.
2. Those who are actually serving their sentences in the county jail will be there for only a short period of time, usually less than one year. This is insufficient time to correct criminal attitudes that the prisoner may have been forming for a lifetime.
3. Many of the people who serve their sentence in local jails have been convicted of habitual vices such as gambling, prostitution, and drunkenness, which are not amenable to rehabilitation in a jail setting.

Clemency

Although it rarely does so, the Board of Pardons and Paroles may take the initiative to recommend executive clemency (leniency) to the governor. Three types of clemency are available: pardon, commutation of sentence, and reprieve. Because conviction for crime carries a legal condemnation as well as a possible sentence, a *full pardon* is designed to absolve a citizen from the legal consequences of his or her crime. A *commutation of sentence* is a reduction in punishment. A *reprieve* is temporary interruption of punishment. The governor may grant less, but not more, clemency than the board recommends. Without board approval, the governor may grant only one 30-day reprieve to delay execution in a capital case.

Juvenile Rehabilitation

Most juvenile offenders are handled by county authorities. They are usually detained in county facilities before a disposition of the case, and minor offenders are then released (on probation) to the custody of parents or placed in county facilities.

The thirteen-member Texas Juvenile Justice Board manages state juvenile probation policies and operates training schools, boot camps, and halfway houses for more serious offenders. The Texas Youth Commission once performed many of these functions until it was abolished after becoming notorious for child neglect and abuse, including widespread sexual assault by guards against children in their custody.

Capital Punishment in Texas: Holding Steadfast in a Changing Era

David Branham, Sr.
University of Houston-Downtown

INTRODUCTION

The use of execution as a punishment for crime has been a very controversial policy issue in the United States in recent decades. As a result, society has placed the policy under a microscope, and many states have changed the way things are done when it comes to sentencing those found guilty of capital crimes. Texas's practices stand out because of the state's political culture and the structure of its death-penalty system.

During the 1930s, it was not unusual to see 150 to 200 government-sanctioned executions a year in the United States. However, the Supreme Court began focusing on the constitutional implications of the use of capital punishment in the 1940s and 50s. By 1971, with the case of *Furman* v. *Georgia*, the court questioned whether or not the death penalty was constitutional at all, and if it was constitutional, under what circumstances? The case produced nine separate opinions from the nine justices on the court. While Associate Justices Thurgood Marshall and William Brennan argued that the death penalty was a violation of the Eighth Amendment restriction against cruel and unusual punishment, the other seven justices appeared to support its use under certain conditions, primarily if the arbitrary nature of its use was eliminated and racial bias was not a factor. Four years later, the court confirmed the constitutionality of capital punishment when these precautions

were taken care of in the case of *Gregg* v. *Georgia*. By the 1980s, the number of executions in the country began to rise steadily and the increase continued for the next two decades.[13]

While it has been established that states are constitutionally able to use the death penalty, many question its value in cutting crime. These critics say that a sentence as extreme as capital punishment can be justified only if it serves to prevent more crime than would be the case if the criminal were sentenced to life in prison. In truth, constitutional protections make it difficult to make the death penalty a deterrent to crime. It takes a long time to execute a prisoner. The appeals process for capital punishment recipients is long and tedious. Over the last five years, the average conviction-to-execution process has been over 150 months.[14] The death penalty in such cases could serve as a deterrent only if a potential murderer would have to decide not to commit the crime to avoid being executed 12 years in the future.

Many studies have concluded that the death penalty is not a deterrent to murder. These studies usually compare murder rates in death penalty states to murder rates in states without capital punishment. Because murder rates are lower in non-death-penalty states, critics conclude that the death penalty is not a deterrent to committing murder. However, more sophisticated statistical research in recent studies has shown that the death penalty is a deterrent. One study found that each execution saved up to 18 lives.[15] Despite this new information, most experts are not convinced, and they still conclude that the use of the death penalty does not prevent crime. A 2008 poll showed that 88 percent of criminologists do not believe capital punishment is a deterrent, an increase of 4 percent over a similar 1996 survey, which suggests that further more sophisticated research has not changed opinions.

Lastly, many people are against the death penalty because they do not trust the criminal justice system. A nationwide poll by RT Strategies in March 2007 showed that only 10 percent of American adults were completely confident that the death penalty was administered only to those who were guilty. Specifically, DNA testing has provided numerous examples of individuals convicted of crimes they did not commit. The state of Texas alone has had over 40 exonerations from DNA testing over the last decade,[16] some of them involving death-row inmates.

The trends have some experts believing that the end of capital punishment in the United States is near.[17] Support for the death penalty is lower now than at any time since 1972,[18] the execution rate in the United States has been cut in half since 2000, and while 33 states have the death penalty as part of their criminal justice system, only 13 states had executions in 2011 and only eight states had multiple executions.

Despite the national controversy over the death penalty and its decline in popularity, Texas has seldom hesitated to use it. Since *Gregg* v. *Georgia* in 1976, Texas has executed more convicted criminals than any other state. In fact, 38 percent

[13]Snell, Tracy L. 2011. Capital Punishment, 2010-Statistical Tables. U.S. Department of Justice, Bureau of Justice Statistics. http://bjs.ojp.usdoj.gov/content/pub/pdf/cp10st.pdf, December.

[14]Ibid.

[15]Dezhbakhsh, Hashem and Joanna M. Shepherd. 2003. The Deterrent Effect of Capital Punishment: Evidence from a "Judicial Experiment." http://deathpenalty.procon.org/sourcefiles/The%20Deterrent%20Effect%20of%20Capital%20Punishment.pdf.

[16]Horton, Scott. 2011. "In Texas, 41 Exonerations from DNA Evidence in 9 Years." http://harpers.org/archive/2011/01/hbc-90007895. January 5.

[17]Baumgartner, Frank R., Suzanna De Boef, and Amber Boydstun. 2008. The Decline of the Death Penalty and the Discovery of Innocence. Cambridge University Press.

[18]Newport, Frank. 2011. In U.S., Support for Death Penalty Falls to 39-Year Low. Gallop Politics. www.gallup.com/poll/150089/Support-Death-Penalty-Falls-Year-Low.aspx. October 13.

of all executions in the United States between 1977 and 2010 were in the state of Texas. During that time period, Virginia, the state with the second-most executions, put 108 people to death compared to 464 for Texas.[19] Like other states with capital punishment, Texas uses the death penalty for only a narrow range of crimes. Texas Penal Code 19.03 defines capital crimes as murder with extended circumstances. Examples of such circumstances include the murder of a child under six years of age, murder of a police officer or firefighter in the line of duty, multiple murders, murder for hire, or murder during the commission of another crime like kidnapping or robbery.[20] This Texas definition of capital offense is not much different from other states. However, Texas is far more likely to use capital punishment for those found guilty than other states.

Texas is quite efficient in carrying out capital punishment for several reasons. At the core of Texas's political system is a traditional political culture that is hesitant to discard things of the past. So while much of the country has sought to reform its death-penalty system, Texas resisted change to its time-honored way of doing things. Capital punishment is most prevalent in states, like Texas, that allowed slavery before the Civil War ended the practice. Of the 43 executions carried out in 2011, 37 were in states where slavery was legal before the Civil War. Some experts, like David Garland, see the death penalty as an extension of slave-owning mentality.[21] If Garland is indeed correct, Texas's proficient use of capital punishment can further be explained by the death-qualified jury. In death penalty cases, all prospective jurors who do not believe that they will be able to sentence a person to death are not allowed to serve on the jury. The result is that death-penalty juries include a larger share of white men than in the population as a whole because women and minorities are significantly less likely to approve of the death penalty, and many of them are excluded from capital juries.[22] The effect in Texas is much stronger than in other former slave-holding states because Texas is far more diverse than the rest of those states. Non-Hispanic whites no longer make up the majority of the population in Texas. That said, there is evidence that Texas's use of the death penalty is not racist in nature. For instance, one Cornell study showed that African Americans who committed murder were actually less likely to be on death row in Texas than whites who committed murder.[23]

Ned Walpin of the Public Broadcasting System points out four factors in the Texas criminal justice system that are also responsible for the high execution rate in the state.[24] First, the Texas system of direct election of judges may make it more difficult for judges to disregard public opinion. Texas citizens tend to strongly favor the death penalty, especially those who vote. Incumbent judges who get the reputation of being lenient are far more vulnerable to electoral defeat than judges who are seen as tough on crime. Such circumstances may lead judges to make

rulings that increase the use of capital punishment. Second, unlike many other states, Texas does not have a statewide public defender system for indigent criminals. While some Texas counties have adopted an optional public defender system, many Texas counties still use court-appointed attorneys who are often overwhelmed with too many other cases to defend properly a person on trial for his or her life. Third, Texas does not allow juries to consider mitigating circumstances in the sentencing of capital offenders. As a result, a person who faced unfortunate circumstances before committing a crime will not get lenience. Last, Texas seems to have perfected the procedure for carrying out executions. The appeals process has been accelerated by sending all death penalty cases directly to the Texas Criminal Court of Appeals, the highest criminal court in the state. The state also gives clemency power directly to the Board of Pardons and Paroles. As a result, unlike many other states, the governor cannot grant a stay of execution without first getting permission from the board, which deliberates in secret.

The low-key but efficient nature of the Board of Pardons and Paroles is indicative of how the state goes about its business when it comes to criminal justice. While Texas has certainly earned its reputation as king of capital punishment, Texas does not flaunt its use of the death penalty. Death-row inmates are housed in the Polunsky Unit in Livingston, and state executions take place in Huntsville, a small college town between Dallas and Houston. The nearest major airport is over 60 miles away, making it difficult for the media to cover high-profile executions and tough for protesting crowds to create much fanfare.

Therefore, while the efficacy of capital punishment is in question and executions are trending down across the country, Texas continues to capably use its constitutional prerogative to carry out the death penalty for capital criminals. The state has strategically structured its criminal justice system to expedite the death-penalty process, and it has implemented its policies in a low-key manner that has avoided strong public opposition when possible. It will be interesting to see how long this trend continues. For now, Texas steadfastly continues its use of capital punishment despite the country's changing attitudes, and it doesn't look like Texas will be modifying its policy anytime soon.

JOIN THE DEBATE

1. How does Texas's political culture explain its high rates of execution at a time that the use of the death penalty is declining in other states? Explain how the state has structured its death penalty system efficiently to expedite implementation of the death penalty.

2. Evaluate the death penalty as a deterrent to crime. What are the arguments for and against the death penalty?

[19]Snell, Tracy L. 2011. Capital Punishment, 2010-Statistical Tables. U.S. Department of Justice, Bureau of Justice Statistics. http://bjs.ojp.usdoj.gov/content/pub/pdf/cp10st.pdf. December.

[20]Texas Penal Code - Section 19.03. Capital Murder. Available at http://law.onecle.com/texas/penal/19.03.00.html.

[21]Garland, David. 2010. America's Death Penalty in an Age of Abolition. Harvard University Press.

[22]Conrad, Clay. "Death-Qualification" Leads to Biased Juries - capital punishment views impact jury selection - Statistical Data Included. *USA Today* (Society for the Advancement of Education. http://findarticles.com/p/articles/mi_m1272/is_2670_129/ai_72272563/?tag=content;col.

[23]Blume, John, Theodore Eisenberg, and Martin T. Wells. 2004. Explaining Death Row's Population and Racial Composition. Journal of Empirical Legal Studies.1:1 p165–207.

[24]Walpin, Ned. Why is Texas #1 in Executions? Public Broadcasting System. www.pbs.org/wgbh/pages/frontline/shows/execution/readings/texas.html.

CHAPTER SUMMARY

★ In an attempt to impose their values on others, the dominant elements of society have turned to government with its power to define crime and punish it. Law reflects the values of the people who make and enforce it.

★ Within the American legal system, cases are classified as either civil or criminal. Civil cases primarily involve the rights of private parties or organizations. Resolution is based on the concept of responsibility rather than guilt.

★ Tort actions are common in civil law. The Texas legislature, in an effort to lighten overcrowded court dockets and limit allegedly frivolous suits, has undertaken tort reform. At the urging of business, insurance companies, and medical professionals, it has restricted lawsuits and limited awards for damages.

★ Criminal cases deal with public concepts of proper behavior and morality as defined by law. Punishment for a conviction ranges from a fine to imprisonment to a combination of both. More-serious crimes are called felonies, and minor crimes are called misdemeanors. Although younger, less-educated members of ethnic minorities living in cities are still more likely to be arrested for crime than other demographic groups, overall crime rates have declined in recent years.

★ The court procedures that constitute due process aim to promote justice and protect individuals from the government. These procedures are generally either written into state and national constitutions and statutes or included in traditional codes of court process.

★ It is largely through due process that the courts aim to blend two conflicting goals of society: (1) to protect society according to the state's legal concepts of right and wrong, and (2) to protect the rights of the individual charged with wrongdoing. Unfortunately, the goal of due process is often an ideal rather than a reality. These careful guarantees of due process are often circumvented by the practice of plea bargaining.

★ Correctional institutions such as prisons and jails are intended to punish, deter, isolate, and rehabilitate. Unfortunately, they perform these functions poorly, and a majority of inmates return to crime after their release.

HOW TEXAS COMPARES

★ Texas has a higher crime rate than most states, even though Texas has imprisoned a larger percentage of its population than China, Russia, and Iran. Texas has also incarcerated a larger percentage of its population than all but three other states and has a larger proportion of its population on probation or parole than most states.

★ On the basis of comparison with other states, no conclusive evidence shows that incarcerating a large portion of the population effectively deters crime because punishment is neither swift nor certain in Texas or any other state.

★ Texas executes more death row inmates than any other state but still has a higher murder rate than most states.

★ The most likely explanation for why Texas has a higher crime rate than most states is that it has a high proportion of young, minority, urban, poorly educated, low-income residents among its population.

KEY TERMS

adversary system, *p. 311*
arraignment, *p. 308*
bail, *p. 309*
change of venue, *p. 310*
charter, *p. 299*
civil law, *p. 297*
closed shop, *p. 299*
compulsory process, *p. 312*
criminal law, *p. 297*
deterrence, *p. 314*
due process, *p. 306*

eminent domain, *p. 302*
examining trial, *p. 309*
exclusionary rule, *p. 307*
FBI index crimes, *p. 304*
felony, *p. 302*
liability insurance, *p. 301*
libel, *p. 299*
misdemeanor, *p. 302*
mistrial, *p. 312*
mores, *p. 304*
negligence, *p. 299*
no-fault insurance, *p. 301*

parole, *p. 314*
personal recognizance, *p. 309*
plaintiff, *p. 297*
precedent, *p. 298*
prima facie case, *p. 310*
probable cause, *p. 307*
probate, *p. 298*
probation, *p. 312*
punitive damages, *p. 300*
recidivist, *p. 314*
rehabilitation, *p. 314*

remedy, *p. 297*
right-to-work laws, *p. 299*
slander, *p. 299*
stare decisis, *p. 298*
tort, *p. 299*
tort reform, *p. 299*
union shop, *p. 299*
victimless crime, *p. 303*
voir dire questioning, *p. 311*
white-collar crime, *p. 305*
writ of injunction, *p. 299*

REVIEW QUESTIONS

1. What distinguishes criminal cases from civil cases? Give examples of each type.

2. Describe the political interests underlying the controversies in civil law.

3. Discuss the root causes of crime. What are the social characteristics of the typical criminal?

4. Define the due process of law. What basic rights do the Texas and U.S. constitutions protect during the criminal justice process?

5. What are the major functions of jails and penitentiaries? Evaluate their effectiveness at preventing recidivism and deterring crime.

LOGGING ON

Use the data from the Texas Ethics Commission available at **www.texastribune.org/library/data/campaign-finance/** to compare the contributions made by tort reform groups like Texans for Lawsuit Reform with those made by their major opponents like the Texas Trial Lawyers Association. Evaluate the arguments for tort reform at the Texans for Lawsuit Reform website at **tortreform.com/**, and then click on "civil justice issues" for the case against it at the Texas Trial Lawyers Association at **www.ttla.com/**.

Evaluate Texas Supreme Court rulings to protect consumers at **www.texastribune.org/texas-courts/texas-supreme-court/supreme-court-elected-bears-perrys-stamp/**.

Always check sources and data when you read or hear assertions about crime trends. Develop a comparative analysis between

Texas and the national crime trends using Texas Department of Public Safety statistics at **www.txdps.state.tx.us/administration/crime_records/pages/crimestatistics.htm** and FBI data at **www.fbi.gov/about-us/cjis/ucr/ucr**.

Analyze trends in the rates of prosecution, prison, probation, and capital punishment using the data-rich Bureau of Justice Statistics website at **bjs.ojp.usdoj.gov/**.

See criminal punishments in the Texas Penal Code at **www.statutes.legis.state.tx.us/**. Click on "Penal Codes" and then on "Punishments." For specifics about how the criminal justice process works, check out the Texas Code of Criminal Procedure at the same site.

Chapter 13

Public Policy in Texas

LEARNING OBJECTIVES

★ Compare major state expenditures with those of other states and explain how Texas's taxing and spending decisions reflect its conservative political culture.

★ Explain why public policy decisions are political and why they create controversy.

★ Evaluate the political arguments for the various types of taxation, including progressive and regressive taxes.

★ Describe major state services and evaluate the merits of the political arguments surrounding each of these state functions.

★ Identify the decision makers who make important public choices for each major public policy focus in Texas.

★ Define the vocabulary of political controversy about Texas's public services.

GET Active

Browse progressive and conservative policy websites, and then plug into the groups that best represent your views on public policy.

Conservative Groups

★ Check out the conservative view on taxes and other policies at the Texas Public Policy Foundation at **www.texaspolicy.com**.

★ Connect with the Texas Taxpayers and Research Association representing the conservative and business perspective on taxation at **www.ttara.org**.

★ Monitor pro-business, anti-tax arguments at the Tax Foundation website at **www .taxfoundation.org**. Click on Research Areas and select State Tax and Spending Policy.

★ Probe the Lone Star Foundation and its positions on health care and poverty at **www.lonestarfoundation.org/**.

★ Check out the conservative position on taxes and business regulation at the Institute for Policy Innovation at **www.ipi.org/**.

★ Investigate the Private Enterprise Research Center at **www.tamu.edu/perc/** and learn about their research on health care, welfare, and taxes.

Liberal/Progressive Groups

★ Tune into the liberal and labor position on taxes by browsing the Citizens for Tax Justice site at **www.ctj.org**. Select State Tax Publications and News and go to Texas.

★ Engage Texas funding challenges with Texas's Center for Public Policy Priorities at **www.cppp.org**. Click on Research and sift through the latest studies on Texas's public policies.

★ Probe budget and fiscal policies in the 50 states with the Center on Budget and Policy Priorities at **www.cbpp.org**.

★ Be part of the solution for energy and environmental problems by acquainting yourself with Public Citizen—Texas at **www.citizen.org/texas/**.

The Texas legislature finally passed and sent to the governor a $173.5 billion budget for fiscal years 2012 and 2013. Counting one dollar every second without resting for weekends, holidays, and coffee breaks, it would take about 5,501 years to count these appropriations! Texas has the third-largest state budget, exceeded only by those of California and New York.

Until recently, state spending steadily rose as each successive budget was larger than the preceding one, resulting in a long succession of record expenditures. Figure 13.1 shows that inflation and population increases explained much of the historical growth in state spending.

Inflation alone explained some of the past increases in government spending; just as it drove up the costs of what citizens and families bought, it also drove up the costs of what government bought. However, inflation also drove up salaries and profits with which residents paid their taxes.

Texas's population grew more rapidly than that of most other states. Each new person had to be served, protected, and educated. Of course, the demands of a larger population for increased state services were offset by the fact that more people were

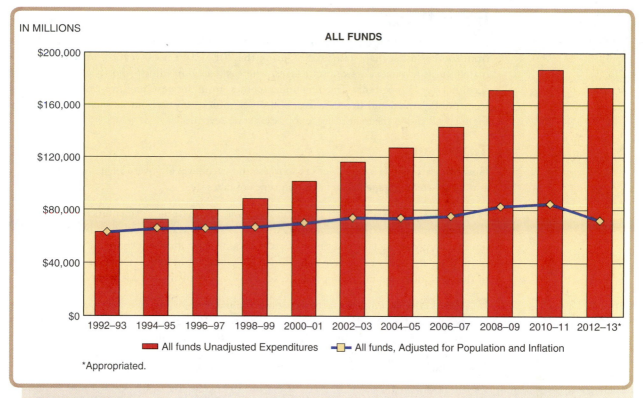

IN MILLIONS

ALL FUNDS

■ All funds Unadjusted Expenditures   ▫ All funds, Adjusted for Population and Inflation

*Appropriated.

Figure 13.1

Trends in Texas State Expenditures—All Funds, by Biennial Budget Periods 1992–2013 (in millions of dollars).

The columns show that state expenditures have grown considerably, but the line shows only modest spending growth, controlling for inflation and population growth. And contrary to past trends, the latest budget actually represents a significant reduction in state spending.

Source: Legislative Budget Board, *Fiscal Size-Up, 2012–2013* (Austin: Legislative Budget Board, 2012), p.16.

Why should measures of state spending be adjusted for inflation and population growth?

also paying taxes to support them. Adjusted for population and inflation, state spending grew at an average annual rate of 0.8 percent over the last 20 years.

However, the 2012–13 budget abruptly reverses that historical trend and represents the first real decline in state spending in generations. Texas's budget cuts were largely the result of the Great Recession of 2007–09 and the slow economic recovery in its aftermath. Rather than raise taxes to make up for revenue shortfalls, Texas's conservative state legislature took the unprecedented action of cutting already-lean state spending by a dramatic 14.6 percent after adjusting for inflation and population growth. Whether Texas continues to cut state services will be answered in the future through the continuing dynamic interplay of political elites, public opinion, and the state's political culture.

REVENUES

So, from where do the funds for this spending come? Surprisingly, much state revenue comes from sources other than state taxes. During the 2012–2013 fiscal years, 44 percent of estimated Texas revenues are from state taxes, whereas federal funding—mostly grants-in-aid—accounts for 39 percent. The remainder comes from interest on investments, revenues from public lands, and licenses, fees, and other minor non-tax sources such as the lottery. Figure 13.2 shows the major sources of Texas state revenues.

Taxation

Governments rely on a variety of tax sources, and each level of government—national, state, and local—tends to specialize in certain types of taxes.

National Taxes With the ratification of the Sixteenth Amendment to the U.S. Constitution in 1913, the income tax became available to the national government. Individual and corporate income taxes immediately became the national government's major source of funding and today constitute approximately 56 percent of federal tax revenues, with most of the remainder coming from payroll taxes for Social Security and Medicare.

State Taxes Property taxes were once the major source of state revenue, but property values collapsed during the Great Depression of the 1930s, and with them went the property tax revenues. At the same time, demands for economic assistance and other public services skyrocketed. Forced to seek other revenue sources, states came to rely on various sales taxes. Texas adopted a tax on cigarettes in 1931, on beer in 1933, and on distilled spirits in 1935. Additional selective sales taxes were adopted in the 1940s and 1950s, but it became apparent that a more general and more broadly based tax would be necessary to meet revenue needs. In 1961, Texas adopted a general sales tax on most items sold. At the same time, Texas, like most states, first drastically reduced its property taxes and then abandoned them for exclusive use by local governments. States have adopted several types of sales taxes:

1. **General sales taxes** are broadly based taxes collected on the retail price of most items.
2. **Selective sales taxes**, also known as *excise taxes*, are levied on the sale, manufacture, or use of particular items, such as liquor, cigarettes, and gasoline. Because these taxes are usually included in the item's purchase price, they are often **hidden taxes**.

General sales tax

A broad-based tax collected on the retail price of most items.

Selective sales (excise) taxes

Taxes levied on specific items only; also known as *excise taxes.*

Hidden taxes

Taxes included in the retail prices of goods and services.

Figure 13.2

Sources of Estimated State Revenues, 2012–2013 Budget Period

This figure shows that Texas's largest single revenue source is federal funding, and the largest state tax is the general sales tax.

Source: Legislative Budget Board, *Fiscal Size-Up, 2012–2013* (Austin: Legislative Budget Board, 2012), p. 29.

Besides the general sales tax, which of Texas's other taxes should be considered sales taxes? What are the arguments for and against consumer taxes?

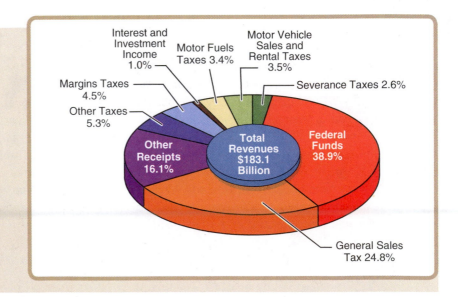

Interest and Investment Income 1.0%
Motor Fuels Taxes 3.4%
Motor Vehicle Sales and Rental Taxes 3.5%
Severance Taxes 2.6%
Margins Taxes 4.5%
Other Taxes 5.3%
Other Receipts 16.1%
Total Revenues $183.1 Billion
Federal Funds 38.9%
General Sales Tax 24.8%

3. Gross-receipts taxes are taxes on the total gross revenue (sales) of certain enterprises. A broad-based margins tax (also known as the *franchise tax*) applies to the gross sales of most corporations and limited partnerships after taking a deduction for cost of goods or personnel. Small companies, sole proprietorships, and general partnerships are exempt.

Gross-receipts tax
A tax on the gross revenues of certain enterprises.

Most state tax revenue in 2012–2013 came from various sales tax collections. The general sales tax (6.25 percent on retail sales of most items) yielded 24.8 percent of the state's revenues; the margins tax, 4.5 percent; motor fuels taxes, 3.4 percent; and motor vehicle sales and rental taxes, 3.5 percent. Once a major source of state revenue, **severance taxes** (production taxes on oil and natural gas) now account for only 2.6 percent. Texas also collects special taxes on a range of items and activities, such as tobacco, alcohol, registration of motor vehicles, hotel and motel occupancy, and insurance company operations.

Severance tax
A tax on raw materials (such as oil and natural gas) when they are extracted from their natural state.

Local Taxes Many services financed by state governments in other states are left to local governments in Texas. State government has also imposed many mandates (required services) on local governments, especially school districts, without funding them. As a result, state taxes have remained low, but local taxes are greater than in many states.

Property taxes are the major source of revenue for virtually all local governments—cities, counties, and special districts. **Ad valorem** (according to value) **taxes** may be applied to two major types of property, including **real property** (land and buildings) and **personal property** (possessions such as furniture and automobiles). Most Texas local governments primarily tax real property. A central appraisal authority in each county determines property values for all taxing units in the county according to uniform state standards and procedures. The tax rate is set by local policy-making bodies—city councils, county commissioners' courts, and boards of trustees for special districts.

Ad valorem tax
A tax assessed according to value, such as the tax on *real property* and *personal property*.

Real property
Land and buildings.

Personal property
Tangible possessions other than real estate.

Local governments also impose other taxes. For operating expenses, most Texas cities have adopted a 1 percent city sales tax applied to items taxable under the state general sales tax. Cities in counties with populations of more than 500,000 may also collect an additional sales tax up to 1 percent for economic development projects. Mass transit authorities and other special districts also collect sales taxes, but total local sales taxes are capped at 2 percent. Other local revenue sources include miscellaneous taxes, user fees, and federal grants-in-aid.

The Politics of Taxation

Taxes cannot be evaluated objectively. As with all public policy, the state's tax policy is designed by elected politicians who make tax decisions on the basis of which groups will be most affected by different types of taxes. People tend to evaluate taxes according to their social and economic position. Although their arguments are usually about the "public interest," one must recognize that the millions of dollars in campaign funds, the millions of hours devoted to campaigning, the thousands of lobbyists who fill our state and national capitols—all the resources of persuasion our political system can muster—are called into play not simply to settle some abstract academic argument. Politics, especially the politics of taxation, affects the way people live in real and concrete ways. Any evaluation of taxes must be based on the way particular taxes affect various groups in society.

The Tax Base: Who Should Pay? Not all taxes are equally effective in raising funds for the public till. **Tax rates** (the amount per unit on a given item or activity) may be raised or lowered, but simply raising the tax rate may not guarantee increased revenues because people may cut back on purchases of the taxed item.

Tax rates affect the **tax base** (the object taxed). Excessive property taxes discourage construction and repair of buildings. High income taxes can discourage general economic activity and individual initiative, undermining the tax base. To raise necessary revenue, a tax must not discourage too much of the activity that produces the revenue.

Tax rate
The amount per unit of taxable item or activity.

Tax base
The object or activity taxed.

Broad-based tax

A tax designed to be paid by a large number of taxpayers.

Most governments tax a wide variety of items and activities because they have found that **broad-based taxes** (those paid by a large number of taxpayers), such as property taxes, general sales taxes, and income taxes, are most effective at raising revenue. High tax rates on a narrow base tend to destroy the base and thus make the tax ineffective as a source of revenue.

In the battle over taxation, one of the most intense issues is what should be taxed. The decision about *what* to tax is really a decision about *whom* to tax and how heavily. Those with influence on decision makers try to get special tax treatment for themselves and other taxpayers in their group. What seems to motivate almost every group is the principle that the best tax is the one somebody else pays. The three most common political rationalizations for taxing various social groups differently are (1) to regulate their behavior, (2) to tax them according to the benefits they receive, and (3) to tax them according to their ability to pay.

Regulatory Taxes Taxes do more than simply pay for the services of government; they often serve as a tool for social or economic control. Rewarding approved behavior with lower taxation or punishing socially undesirable action with a higher tax can have a definite effect on conduct.

Regulatory tax

A tax imposed with the intent of exerting social or economic control by reducing taxes on approved behaviors or imposing higher taxes on undesirable activities.

Most state **regulatory taxes** are designed to control isolated individual choices, especially those with moral overtones, and are sometimes called *sin taxes*. The most prominent example of such state regulatory taxation is the use tax to discourage the consumption of items such as alcohol or tobacco. Texas has an excise tax (selective sales tax) on alcoholic beverages, and its cigarette tax of $1.41 per pack is among the greatest in the nation.

Did You Know? Texas charges a tax on the admission to sexually oriented businesses that is sometimes called the *pole tax* in reference to a prominent stage prop in strip clubs.

Texans continue to drink, smoke, and frequent strip clubs, so such state use taxes do not entirely prevent sin, but they place a substantial share of the tax burden on the sinner. The regulatory intent of use taxes may be a rationalization to place the tax burden on others; the most vocal advocates of alcohol and tobacco taxes are those who abstain. Proponents argue that regulatory taxes have some effect on behavior without extensive enforcement. The small annual decline in cigarette sales in Texas may be partially attributed to cost, and young people may be deterred from smoking by the high price of cigarettes.

Benefits Received On the surface, nothing would seem fairer than taxation according to benefits received—let those who benefit from a public service pay for it. Americans have become accustomed to believing that this principle operates in the private sector of the economy and should be applied in the public sector as well.

Benefits-received tax

A tax assessed according to the services received by the payers.

An example of a **benefits-received tax** in Texas is a 20-cent-per-gallon tax on gasoline. Three-fourths of the income from gasoline and diesel fuel taxes is directed into the Texas highway trust fund, which also includes the state's share of license plate fees (much of which is retained by the counties). The amount of fuel used should represent the benefits from highway building and maintenance.

Although not strictly a tax, tuition paid by students in state colleges and universities is determined on the basis of the benefits-received principle. Although much of the cost of public college education in Texas is paid out of state and local tax revenues, an increasing share of the cost of higher education is paid by student tuitions on the presumption that students should pay a larger share of the cost of the service from which they so greatly benefit. Likewise, revenues from hunting and fishing permits are used for wildlife management.

The benefits-received principle seems reasonable, but few government services are truly special services that are provided only for special groups. Although the student is a major beneficiary of state-supported higher education, society also benefits from the skills that are added to the bank of human resources. Even the elderly widow who has never owned or driven a car benefits from highways when she buys fresh tomatoes from the supermarket or goes to the hospital in the event of illness. Most services of government, like highways, schools, or law enforcement, take on the character of a public or collective good whose beneficiaries cannot be accurately determined.

The benefits-received principle cannot be applied too extensively. Although private businesses efficiently provide services on a benefits-received basis, a major reason for government to provide a *public* service is to make that service available to all. Many could not afford to pay the full cost of vital public services. For example, few people could afford to attend Texas's public colleges and universities if they had to pay the full cost of higher education.

Ability to Pay Most taxes are rationalized according to some measure of taxpayers' ability to pay them. The most common **ability-to-pay taxes** are levied on property, sales, and income. Property taxes are rationalized on the premise that the more valuable people's property, the wealthier they are and hence the greater is their ability to pay taxes. Sales taxes are based on the premise that the more a person buys, the greater is the individual's purchasing power. Income taxes are based on the assumption that the more a person earns, the greater is that person's ability to pay.

No base is completely adequate as a measure of a person's ability to pay. During Europe's feudal era, property reflected a person's wealth. With the coming of the commercial revolution, real wealth came to be measured in terms of money rather than land. Nevertheless, the taxes on real estate remained, while more modern forms of ownership, such as stocks, bonds, and other securities, are seldom taxed.

Taxes based on money (income or expenditure) also are an inadequate measure of true wealth. Income taxes reflect current taxable income and do not account for wealth accumulated in past years. Furthermore, exemptions allow the taxpayer to legally avoid taxes, even on current income. Taxes on consumption and spending (sales taxes) are an even less equitable measure of the ability to pay. Sales taxes measure wealth only as it is spent. Money saved or invested is not spent and not taxed. Because it is a general rule of economic behavior that the wealthier a person is, the more the person saves or invests, sales taxes weigh disproportionately on the have-nots and have-littles, who must spend the largest portion of their income on the necessities of life.

Tax Rates: Progressive or Regressive Taxes?
Most people would like to pay as little in taxes as possible, but it turns out that they pay quite a bit. The average working American works almost one-third of the year (from the first day of January until about mid-April) to pay taxes to all levels of government—federal, state, and local.

However, these averages obscure the real effect of taxes on the individual taxpayer. The so-called loopholes in the federal income tax structure have been well publicized, but every tax—federal, state, and local—treats various taxpayers differently. What in the political world is used to justify the unequal burden of taxation?

Progressive Tax Rates Federal income taxes illustrate **progressive tax rates** because the tax rates increase as income increases. Citizens at the very bottom of the financial totem pole have no taxable income and pay nothing, but as incomes increase, the rate increases stepwise from 10 percent to 35 percent. However, the greater rates apply only to *marginal* increments in income. For example, a single person with $400,000 in taxable income pays 10 percent on the first $8,700, just as lower-income taxpayers do; a rate of 15 percent applies only to taxable income above $8,700 and less than $35,350; and so forth, as shown in Figure 13.3. The highest rate, 35 percent, applies *only* to the amount greater than $388,350 and not to an individual's entire income.

Liberals and other supporters of progressive taxation argue that persons with greater incomes can better afford to pay greater tax rates and that lower-income persons should be left with

Ability-to-pay taxes
Taxes apportioned according to taxpayers' financial capacity.

Progressive tax rates
Tax rates that increase as income increases; for example, the federal income tax is assessed using progressive rates.

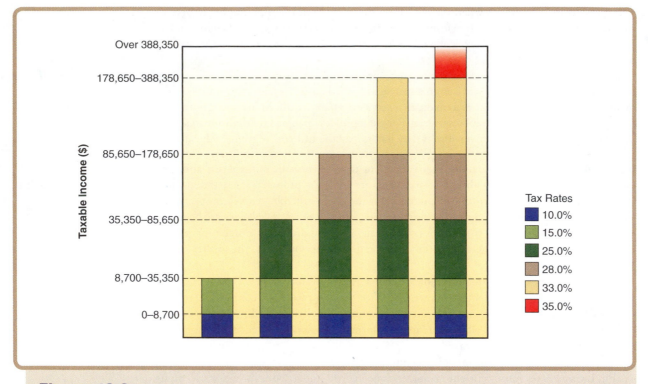

Figure 13.3

Federal Income Tax Rates for Single Individuals, 2012.

Compare the five columns representing various levels of individual taxable income and the rates that apply. Notice that, regardless of total taxable income, the tax rate on the first $8,700 is 10 percent (blue), the 15 percent rate (green) applies only to the income between $8,700 and $35,350, and so on. Note that these rates apply only to taxable income after deductions, exemptions, and exclusions; over 40 percent of Americans pay no income taxes at all. Also, capital gains tax rates are capped at a lower 15 percent rate.

Source: Internal Revenue Service, Individual.

What are the arguments for and against taxing individuals with higher income at higher rates?

enough of their incomes to maintain the necessities of life. Lower-income persons also spend a larger share of their incomes on consumption, which is the largest driving force in the economy.

Such arguments have not convinced Texans, who adopted a state constitutional amendment that forbids a state income tax unless voters approve. Even then, it can be used only for education and property tax relief.

Regressive Tax Rates By contrast, Texas has **regressive tax rates**, whereby the rate declines as income increases. For example, the state general sales tax (6.25 percent, among the highest in the nation) is proportional to the value of sales, but because of patterns of consumption, the effective rate actually declines as a person's income increases. Table 13.1 shows that if a family's income increases, so does its general sales tax payment. That fact seems reasonable—one would expect the purchases of taxable items to increase as income increases. But note that as income increases, an ever-smaller *percentage* of that income is used for taxable purchases. Presumably, more money is saved, invested, or spent on tax-exempt items. Thus, despite exemptions for certain essential items, the effective rate of the Texas general sales tax

Regressive tax rates

Tax rates that place more of a burden on low- and middle-income taxpayers than on wealthier ones; for example, sales taxes and most other consumption taxes are regressive.

TABLE 13.1 Texas General Sales Tax Paid in Dollars and as a Percentage of Taxable Income, 2011*

Taxable Income	Texas General Sales Tax	% of Taxable Income
$ 10,000	$ 269	2.69%
25,000	439	1.76
35,000	526	1.50
45,000	602	1.34
55,000	699	1.22
65,000	731	1.12
75,000	789	1.05
85,000	844	0.99
95,000	895	0.94
110,000	963	0.88
130,000	1,055	0.81
150,000	1,137	0.76
170,000	1,217	0.72
190,000	1,291	0.68
1,000,000	1,655	0.17

*For single individuals.

Source: Internal Revenue Service, *Form 1040, 2011*, p. A-12.

Follow the income column down and notice that, as income increases, sales tax payments in dollars increase, but the rate declines as a percentage of income.

▲ **What are the arguments for this kind of regressive taxation?**

declines as income increases; a working-class individual with an income of $25,000 pays an effective sales tax *rate* more than twice as high as an individual with an income of $190,000 annually. Similarly, taxpayers pay a smaller percentage of their incomes in property and excise taxes as their incomes increase.

There is a simple explanation for the regressive quality of most consumer taxes—the **declining marginal propensity to consume**. As income increases, a person saves and invests more, thus spending a smaller percentage of that income on consumer items. Compare two smokers. One earns $20,000 per year and the other $200,000 per year. Does the typical smoker who earns $200,000 per year smoke 10 times as much as the one who earns $20,000? Of course not! Let's assume that each smoker consumes one pack of cigarettes a day; each therefore pays $514.65 a year in Texas tobacco taxes. For the low-income individual, tobacco taxes represent almost 7 days of earnings, but the other smoker earned the money to pay tobacco taxes in only 5 hours and 21 minutes.

Consumption of most items follows a similar pattern. The mansion represents a smaller share of income for the millionaire than a shack does for a poor person. Proportionately, the Rolls Royce is less of a burden to its owner than the old Chevrolet to its less-affluent owner. Obviously, there are exceptions, but appetites do not increase proportionately with income. Consequently, almost any tax on consumption will not reflect ability to pay. Yet Texas's state and local taxes are based on some form of consumption—property taxes, general sales taxes, gross-receipts taxes, or selective sales taxes.

Even business taxes may be regressive for individuals because of **tax shifting**. Businesses regard their tax burden as part of their operating cost, and much of that cost is shifted to customers in the form of higher prices. When property taxes increase, landlords raise rents.

Declining marginal propensity to consume

The tendency, as income increases, for persons to devote a smaller proportion of their income to consumer spending and a larger proportion to savings or investments.

Tax shifting

Businesses passing taxes to consumers in the form of higher prices.

TABLE 13.2 Texas Major State and Local Taxes as a Percentage of House-hold Income, Fiscal 2013*					
	Lower Income	Lower Middle	Middle Income	Upper Middle	Upper Income
General sales tax	6.0%	3.4%	2.9%	2.5%	1.3%
Franchise (margins) tax	1.0	0.6	0.5	0.4	0.3
Gasoline tax	0.8	0.5	0.4	0.3	0.1
Motor vehicle sales tax	0.6	0.4	0.4	0.3	0.2
School property tax	5.3	2.9	2.4	2.2	1.6

*Estimates based on an economic model that takes into account the effect of tax shifting. Household incomes are categorized by quintiles from the lowest one-fifth to the highest one-fifth, each representing 1,919,580 households.

Source: Texas Comptroller of Public Accounts, *Exemptions and Tax Incidence*, February, 2011, pp. 44–63.

Look across each row in the table to see how major state and local taxes burden low- and middle-income taxpayers more.

▲ **Why do such consumer taxes burden high-income families least? How can a business tax like the margins tax weigh most heavily on low-income families?**

When business taxes are imposed, prices of consumer items usually increase as those taxes are passed on to customers as hidden taxes. Thus many business taxes become, in effect, *consumer* taxes and, like other consumer taxes, regressive relative to income.

Taking into account all state and local taxes and tax shifting, Texas has one of the most regressive tax structures among the 50 states. Table 13.2 shows the final incidence of major state and local taxes on Texas families. Those with the lowest fifth of household incomes paid 6.0 percent of their income in general sales taxes—more than four times the percentage that upper-income households pay. Lower-income households paid an effective school property tax rate more than three times as high as upper-income households. And, for low-income households, the gasoline tax represents more than eight times the burden that it does for the upper-income households. Lower-income families even bear a disproportionate share of the state's franchise tax on business.

> **Did You Know?** Texans in the lowest-income households pay an effective sales tax more than four times higher than upper-income households.

HOW DOES TEXAS COMPARE?
Taxes—Who Pays? And How Much?

Consistent with Texas's conservative political culture, state taxes are lower and more regressive than in most other states.

★ Only New Hampshire, Colorado, and South Dakota collect a smaller percentage of their residents' incomes than Texas, which collects approximately 4.1 percent; the average state collects 5.7 percent. Alaska has the highest tax rate in the United States because of its huge severance tax revenue, but most of this tax burden is *exported* to other states that use Alaskan oil.

★ One way Texas has kept state taxes low is by using unfunded mandates that require local governments to provide services that are usually funded at the state level in other states. As a result, local property taxes represent 3.5 percent of Texans' personal income, the 13th highest among the 50 states. Nevertheless, including local taxes and even the taxes that

Texans pay in other states, Figure 13.4 shows that Texans paid only 7.9 percent of personal income in all state and local taxes; residents of only five states paid less.

★ Most states rely heavily on sales and gross-receipts taxes, but few states are as dependent on them as Texas. Only Nevada depends more on various sales taxes (especially its gambling taxes) than Texas. Because Texas relies so much on consumer taxes, it has one of the 10 most regressive tax systems in the nation.

★ Texas is one of eight states without a progressive personal income tax and one of only five states without a corporate income tax. By contrast, progressive personal and corporate income taxes generate more revenues than regressive general sales taxes in 37 states.

FOR DEBATE

1. Do Texas's low tax rates attract business and promote economic growth? What is the effect of low state tax rates on the quality of state services?

2. Should Texas follow the lead of many other states by adopting more progressive tax policies that are less dependent on consumer taxes? Why? Why not?

Sources: Council of State Governments, *Book of the States, 2011*, pp. 267–268; Legislative Budget Board, *Fiscal Size-Up, 2012–2013*, pp. 52–55; Institute on Taxation and Economic Policy, *Who Pays? A Distributional Analysis of All 50 States* (3rd ed.), 2009, http://www.itepnet.org/whopays3.htm; and Tax Foundation, *Special Report: State and Local Tax Burdens*, February 23, 2011, www.taxfoundation.org/research/show/22320.html.

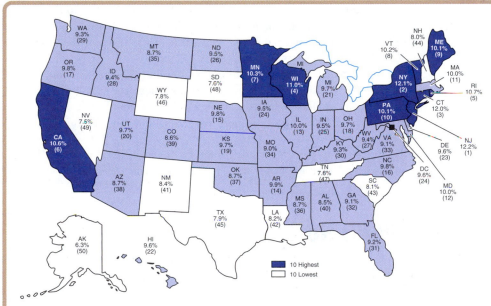

Figure 13.4

How State and Local Tax Burdens Rank among the 50 States

This figure shows the percentage of income residents paid to state and local governments in all 50 states and is based on a model that takes into account tax shifting. Note that Texans paid less than most other states.

Source: National Tax Foundation, *Special Report: State and Local Tax Burdens and Ranks, Fiscal Year 2009,* February 23, 2011, *www.taxfoundation.org/research/show/22320.html.*

Explain how lower tax rates reflect Texas's conservative political culture. How do a state's tax rates affect its economic growth potential? How do low rates of taxation impact the quality of public services that Texans receive?

© AP Photo/Harry Cabluck

Texas Comptroller of Public Accounts Susan Combs is the state's chief tax collector and financial officer. Her financial estimates are binding on the legislature during the appropriation process.

How effective are Texas's balanced budget requirements? Should the national government also be required to balance its budget? Why? Why not?

Although they usually oppose business taxes, conservatives and high-income groups who support other regressive taxes argue that taxes on higher-income individuals should be kept low to allow them to save and invest to stimulate the economy—this is known as **supply-side economics**. They argue that applying higher rates to higher incomes is unfair and that sales and property taxes are easier to collect, harder to evade or avoid, and generally less burdensome than progressive income taxes. Some advocate a national sales tax, also known as the *fair tax*, to replace the progressive federal income tax.

Other Revenues

Much of the state's revenue comes from federal grants-in-aid, and a smaller amount is generated from non-tax revenues such as licenses, fees, and borrowing.

Federal Grants-in-aid

Much federal money is provided for Texas state and local government programs. For the 2012–2013 biennium, Texas will receive approximately $71 billion in federal funds, which represents 39 percent of state revenues. Much of what Texas spends for health and human services and for transportation originates as federal grants, which we discussed in depth in Chapter 2.

Borrowing and other Revenues

At the beginning of each legislative session, the comptroller of public accounts reports to the legislature the total amount of revenues expected from current taxes and other sources, and the legislature can, in turn, appropriate no more than this amount unless it enacts new tax laws. The few exceptions to this general limit are (1) the legislature, by a nearly impossible four-fifths vote, may borrow in emergency situations, and (2) voters may amend the Texas Constitution to provide for the issuance of bonds for specific programs.

State bonds are classified as (1) **general-obligation bonds** (to be repaid from general revenues), which have been used to finance prison construction, the veterans' real estate programs, water development, and higher education; and (2) **revenue bonds**, which are to be repaid with the revenues from the service they finance, such as higher education bonds financed by tuition revenue.

Other non-tax revenues account for a small share of Texas's income from the lottery; various licenses, fines, and fees; dividends from investments; and the sale and leasing of public lands.

STATE SPENDING

Having examined the revenue side of state policy, we now turn to the appropriations process and the politics of state spending.

The Appropriations Process

It is through the **appropriations** process that the legislature legally authorizes the state to spend money to provide its various programs and services. Appropriations bills follow the same steps (described in Chapter 8) as other legislation, through standing committee consideration, floor action, conference committee compromise, final voting, and then approval by the governor. During most of the legislative process, the recommendations of the LBB (because they tend to reflect the wishes of the legislature's powerful presiding officers) carry greater weight than those of the governor. The governor may use the line-item veto to strike particular parts of the appropriations bill, but the governor rarely vetoes a significant share of state spending.

The Politics of State Spending

A wide variety of factors affects the level of state spending and complicates efforts toward rational public spending. Nowhere is the dynamic nature of politics so evident as in public finance; nowhere is the conflict between competing economic interests more visible than in the budgetary process. Behind the large figures that represent the state's final budget are vigorous conflict, compromise, and coalition building. Most of society's programs are evaluated not only according to their merit but also in light of the competing demands of other programs and other economic interests. Government programs and problems compete for a share of the public treasury—highways, education, urban decay, poverty, crime, the environment—in short, all the problems and challenges of a modern society.

Powerful political constituencies, interest groups, and their lobbyists join forces with state agencies to defend the programs that benefit them. This alliance between administrative agencies and interest groups brings great pressure to bear on the legislative process, especially targeting the powerful House Appropriations Committee, the Senate Finance Committee, and presiding officers. Individual legislators trade votes among themselves, a process called **logrolling**, to realize increased funding to benefit their districts or their supporters.

Logrolling
Trading votes among legislators, especially to fund local projects to benefit their constituents.

HOW DOES TEXAS COMPARE?
The Appropriations Process And State Spending

★ Congress and most state legislatures work with a budget plan submitted by the chief executive as they begin the appropriations process. In Texas, however, the chief executive's budget proposals have less influence than the recommendations submitted by the Legislative Budget Board; Texas's governor is not truly the state's chief budget officer.

★ Unlike the national government, most states require that either their governor must submit a balanced budget or that the legislature pass one. Texas's restrictions against borrowing are more effective than most—the average per capita state debt is almost three times higher than in Texas.

★ Texas ranked 47th among the 50 states in overall per capita spending (25 percent below the national average). Texas's per capita expenditures for education ranked 33rd among the 50 states and for hospitals it ranked 25th. The state ranked toward the bottom in per capita spending for highways (44th) and for public welfare (44th).

FOR DEBATE

1. Should the national government adopt a balanced-budget requirement like Texas has? Why? Why not?

2. Why would supporters argue that many state spending items, like education and health, are *investments* in the state's future? If they are truly investments, how will the state realize economic gains from them?

3. Would higher rates of state spending in Texas drive up taxes and discourage economic growth in the state? What arguments can you make that the state should increase its financial commitment to education, health care, and transportation programs?

Source: Legislative Budget Board, *Fiscal Size-Up, 2012–2013* (Austin: Legislative Budget Board, 2012), p. 58.

No single decision better typifies the political character of a state than the decisions made during the appropriations process. The whole pattern of spending is, in a sense, a shorthand description of which problems the state has decided to face and which challenges it has chosen to meet. The budget shows how much of which services the state will offer and to whom. Figure 13.5 shows how Texas spent its state revenues in the 2012–2013 biennium. The most costly service in Texas is education. Education accounted for 42 percent of the state budget; health and human services (including Medicaid and social services) were the second-most expensive, accounting for 31.9 percent; and transportation, primarily highways, consumed 11.4 percent. These three services consume more than four-fifths of the state's budget, with a wide variety of miscellaneous services using up the remainder.

Both individuals and groups benefit from government services, and seeking these benefits, while denying them to others, is what motivates most political activity in the state. Political controversy develops because state services affect various groups differently and these groups evaluate state programs according to their competing self-interests and their conflicting views of the public interest (see the Texas Insiders feature). It is important to outline the state's most significant services and then explore some of the major political issues surrounding them.

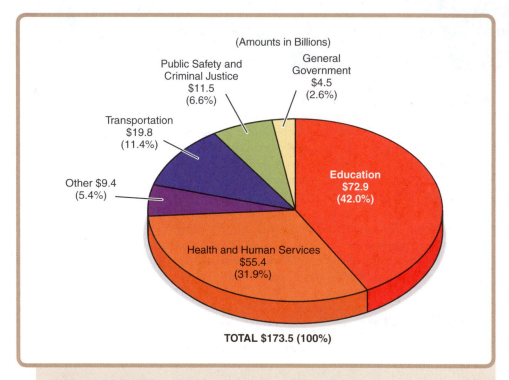

Figure 13.5

State Appropriations by Function, 2012–2013

The largest slice of Texas's budget pie goes to education, but the portion spent for health care is rapidly increasing.

Source: Legislative Budget Board, *Fiscal Size-Up, 2012–2013* (Austin: Legislative Budget Board, 2012), p. 6 and p. 433.

Explain why state spending decisions generate political controversy.

Texas INSIDERS

Information as Power: Tapping into Texas Think Tanks and Their Influence on Public Policy

Policy makers, including legislators, elected executives, and appointed administrators, are usually generalists who depend on specialists for specific information to make decisions about the details of public policy. They have historically depended on industry lobbyists, state agency bureaucrats, and their staffs to provide expert knowledge and advice in the policy-making process.

Although lobbyists and bureaucrats are usually careful to protect their reputations in Austin by providing accurate data, their information is not objective—they selectively provide state officials with the facts that support their own policy biases. Nevertheless, lobbyists and bureaucrats provide a useful public service because it is important for policy makers to know how their decisions will affect various industries and state agencies. Decision makers probably understand the biases of their information sources anyway.

Lobbyists and bureaucrats have long recognized that state officials' dependency on their data is perhaps their greatest source of power; political power is the ability to persuade, and little is more persuasive than the facts. More recently, privately funded research organizations, known as *think tanks*, have been established to harness the power of information by conducting broad-based policy research and presenting decision makers with integrated policy proposals reflecting the ideological leanings of their founders and funders. Although think tanks often bill themselves as nonprofit and nonpartisan, their work represents viewpoint-driven research.

James R. Leininger (see the Texas Insiders feature in Chapter 3) founded the conservative Texas Public Policy Foundation (TPPF), modeled after the nationally famous Heritage Foundation. TPPF continues to be funded by important conservative power-brokers like Charles G. Koch. Under Brooke Rollins's leadership, the foundation has had enormous influence on Texas's taxing, spending, criminal justice, and higher education policies.

In contrast, the liberal Center for Public Policy Priorities (CPPP) focuses its research on poverty and the needs of children. While its director F. Scott McCown has been a vocal advocate for the needy and the organization's studies have generated a great deal of press, CPPP has had only marginal success in advancing Texas's social service and health care programs.

Thinking about the role of elites in Texas politics How are political elites able to use their insiders' information to manipulate policy outcomes? Explain how information can be both accurate and biased at the same time. How important is objective information to policy makers?

Sources: Texas Public Policy Foundation at www.texaspolicy.com/; Center for Public Policy Priorities at http://cppp.org/; Nate Blakeslee, Paul Burka, and Patricia Kilday Hart, "Power Company: Who Are the Most Influential People Determining the Fate of Texas—and What Do They Want?" *Texas Monthly*, Volume 32, number 2, February, 2011, p. 92.

EDUCATION

The educational system in Texas includes elementary and secondary schools (the public schools) and the college and university system (higher education).

Elementary and Secondary Schools

History Public schools were accepted institutions in the North by the early nineteenth century, but they did not take root in the South (including Texas) until after the Civil War. Not until the Constitution of 1876 provided that alternate sections of public land grants would be set aside to finance schools did the state begin to commit itself to locally administered, optional public schools.

Meaningful state support for public education started with a compulsory attendance law, enacted in 1915, and a constitutional amendment that provided for free textbooks in 1918. In 1949, the Gilmer-Aikin law increased state funding and established the Texas Education Agency (TEA), which carries out the state's educational program.

Recent Trends Sweeping changes in education resulted when the 1984 legislature established statewide **accountability** standards for student performance and teacher competence. Former President George W. Bush later took the use of high-stakes testing nationwide with his No Child Left Behind Act.

Although the standards used to measure public school performance are sometimes controversial, there has been a recent trend toward their use to bring market forces to the public school system. Some teachers and administrators receive merit pay—bonuses for improved student achievement. To introduce the element of competition among schools, the state legislature authorized the State Board of Education to establish schools with innovative special program charters that can recruit students from across existing school district boundaries. Many conservative state legislators now also favor adding even more school competition through *privatization* by providing vouchers to help students buy their education from private businesses and organizations.

Today, public elementary and secondary education has grown from a fledgling underfinanced local function into a major state–local partnership. The TEA administers approximately 27 percent of all state expenditures, helping local school districts educate the approximately 90 percent of Texas students who enroll in public elementary and secondary schools. Public policy decisions affect the knowledge, attitudes, and earning potential of these 5 million students and the approximately 330,000 teachers who teach them.

Public School Administration As in other states, the Texas public school administration has three basic aspects:

1. Substantial local control in a joint state–local partnership.
2. Emphasis on *professional* administration supervised by laypersons.
3. Independence from the general structure of government.

State Administration The Texas Constitution, the legislature, and the State Board of Education (SBOE) have established the basic decision-making organizations and financial arrangements for public education in the state. The legislature approves the budget for the state's share of the cost of public education and sets statutory standards for public schools, but many policy decisions are left to the State Board of Education, the Texas Education Agency, and local school districts.

Members of the State Board of Education are elected to four-year overlapping terms in 15 single-member districts, and together they establish general rules and guidelines for the TEA. The SBOE approves organizational plans, recommends a budget to the governor and the Legislative Budget Board, and implements funding formulas established by the legislature. It sets curriculum standards, establishes guidelines for operating public schools, and requires management, cost accounting, and financial reports from local districts. The SBOE leaves most routine managerial decisions to the Commissioner of Education.

Accountability

Responsibility for a program's results—for example, using measurable standards to hold public schools responsible for their students' performance.

The commissioner is appointed by the governor with consent of the senate to serve as the state's principal executive officer for education. With a number of assistant and associate commissioners and professional staff, the commissioner carries out the regulations and policies established by the legislature and the SBOE concerning public school programs.

Local Administration Texas's 1,029 regular independent school districts (more than any other state) are the basic structure for local control. Voters in independent school districts elect seven or nine members (depending on the district's population) at large or from single-member electoral districts for either three- or four-year terms. These trustees set the district's tax rate and determine school policies within the guidelines established by the TEA. They approve the budget, contract for instructional supplies and construction, and hire and fire personnel. Their most important decision is the hiring of a professional superintendent, who is responsible for the executive or administrative functions of the school district.

Elected state and local school boards usually follow the recommendations of professional administrators (the commissioner and the superintendents). Most educational decisions are made independently of general government. Nevertheless, one should not conclude that independence from general government, localization, or *professionalism* keeps education free of politics. On the contrary, elected boards, especially the State Board of Education, have become quite politically assertive in recent years. Whenever important public decisions are made, political controversy and conflict arise.

The Politics of Public Education

One of the most important decisions concerning public education is what education should be. Should it promote traditional views of society, reinforce the dominant political culture, and teach *acceptable* attitudes? Or, should it teach students to be independent thinkers, capable of evaluating ideas for themselves? Because the Texas state educational system determines the curriculum, selects textbooks, and hires and fires teachers, it must answer these fundamental questions.

Curriculum Most of the basic curriculum is determined by the SBOE. Some school districts supplement this basic curriculum with a variety of elective and specialized courses, but it is in the basic courses—history, civics, biology, and English—that students are most likely to be exposed to issues that may fundamentally affect their attitudes. How should a student be exposed to the theory of evolution? Should sex education courses offer discussion of artificial birth control or present abstinence as the only reliable method of birth control? In the social sciences, should the political system be pictured in terms of its ideals or as it actually operates, with all its mistakes and weaknesses? How should the roles of women and minorities be presented? How should elective Bible courses be taught and by whom? Should students who do not speak standard English be gradually taught English through bilingual education, or should they immediately be immersed in the core curriculum taught in English?

Aside from social and political content, the substance of education in Texas has other important practical consequences as well. Although a large proportion of public school students in Texas will never enroll in an institution of higher learning, much educational effort and testing have been directed toward college preparatory courses that provide graduates with few, if any, usable job skills.

Historically, vocational, agricultural, and home economics programs were viewed as *burial grounds* for pupils who had failed in the traditional academic programs. Today, almost one-half of high school students are enrolled in career and technology programs, and one in five are in family and consumer sciences. Although program titles have changed, much remains to be done to meet the need for highly skilled technical workers who possess other practical life skills.

The Curriculum and the Culture Wars

After adopting controversial science and literature curriculum revisions in recent years, Texas's State Board of Education caused an even louder uproar in 2010 when it largely ignored the advice of professional educators and voted along party lines to establish social studies curriculum standards for the upcoming decade. Critics charged that the SBOE had hijacked the state's educational apparatus to impose a conservative, Christian fundamentalist political agenda on public school students.[1]

Critics focused on standards that require teaching the political beliefs of conservative icons like Phyllis Schlafly, Newt Gingrich, the now-disbanded Moral Majority, and the National Rifle Association. Meanwhile, students will be taught that Senator Joseph McCarthy's anti-communist crusade may have been justified. Confederate President Jefferson Davis's inaugural address will be taught alongside Abraham Lincoln's speeches, and the role of slavery as a cause of the Civil War is downplayed.

Requirements that students learn the concept of "responsibility for the common good" (which one board member described as "communistic") have been removed from the curriculum. Students will learn that the United States is a "constitutional republic" rather than a "democratic society" and that the "separation of church and state" is not in the Constitution. Students will evaluate how the United Nations undermines U.S. sovereignty and learn about the devaluation of the dollar, including the abandonment of the gold standard. The curriculum standards emphasize the biblical and Judeo-Christian influences on the Founding Fathers and the benefits of free enterprise, which is mentioned more than 80 times in the curriculum requirements.

Textbooks

The SBOE selects a list of approved textbooks that the state may buy for public school courses, and like the curriculum, the textbook selection process generates intense political battles between conservative groups (such as the Texas Public Policy Foundation and Texas Freedom Works) and liberal groups such as the Texas Freedom Network. The conservatives have dominated the battle, and some publishers have withdrawn their text offerings or changed the content of their texts to satisfy the SBOE.

Legally, the SBOE can only determine the accuracy of textbooks, but it has used this power to pressure publishers to submit texts that reflect the political and religious values of its members. One publisher eliminated references to "fossil fuels formed millions of years ago" from a science text because it conflicts with some interpretations of the timeline in the Bible. Another eliminated sections that were too kind to Muslims by asserting that Osama bin Laden's actions were inconsistent with commonly accepted Islamic teachings (even though this is the official policy view of the U.S. government). An environmental science text was rejected because it favorably mentioned the Endangered Species Act and warned of the threat of global warming—one group argued that it was unpatriotic to refer to the fact that the United States represents 5 percent of the world's population but produces 25 percent of greenhouse gases. Under pressure from religious conservatives, publishers submitted health textbooks that presented an abstinence-only approach to sex education, excluding essential information about how to prevent unwanted pregnancies and sexually transmitted diseases.

Because Texas controls the second-largest textbook market in the nation, the state's textbook decisions have historically determined the content of texts used in public schools in much of the nation. In the future, however, school systems in other states may have more alternatives to Texas-preferred texts. Electronic books, specialty publishing, and custom options are replacing market-dominant, fixed-content texts, and the national textbook market is becoming much more competitive.

---

[1] The Texas Essential Knowledge and Skills (TEKS) curriculum standards are available on the TEA website at www.tea.state.tx.us/.

Faculties Although the state board for educator certification establishes standards for qualification, conduct, and certification of public school teachers, actual hiring of teachers is a local matter. Most districts do not follow a publicly announced policy of hiring or dismissing teachers because of their political viewpoints, but in many districts, teachers are carefully screened for their attitudes.

Salary and working conditions are perpetual issues of dissatisfaction among teachers because they affect morale and recruitment. Increasing public demands for accountability have added reporting and other paperwork to teachers' workloads beyond the standard expectations for lesson planning, grading, and communicating with parents.

Expected income is certainly a factor when people choose their careers, and education simply does not compare favorably among the professions. Texas teachers earn even less than public school teachers in other states. The National Education Association reported that Texas teachers' average salary of $49,017 in 2011–2012 was 13 percent less than the national average. The TEA reported that one-third of beginning teachers leave the profession by their fifth year.

> **Did You Know?** The average annual earnings for Texas physicians is $184,300; lawyers, $131,320; pharmacists, $113,570; and elementary school teachers, $51,850.[2]

Another issue for teachers has been the use of high-stakes testing such as the Texas Assessment of Knowledge and Skills (TAKS), the new State of Texas Assessments of Academic Readiness (STAAR), and the National Assessment of Education Progress ("The Nation's Report Card"). Teachers' groups have objected to the use of these test results in retention, promotion, and salary decisions on the grounds that they do not accurately measure the full range of teachers' contributions to student knowledge and that their use causes faculty to teach the test while ignoring other valuable skills and knowledge that are not included in standardized tests.

Students Public schools have changed considerably in recent years. The number of students attending Texas public schools has been increasing at a rate of approximately 2 percent per year, and that increase is expected to continue for the next decade. Texas's students are also becoming more ethnically diverse and are increasingly from low-income backgrounds—50 percent of public school students are Latino and 13 percent are African American.

This changing student population seems to present a challenge to public schools because a significant achievement gap remains between the performance of Anglo students and that of African Americans and Latinos. Scores on the standard state performance tests like STAAR and TAKS indicate that the achievement gap is closing, but in 2011, Anglos' passing rate was still 21 percent higher than African Americans' and 15 percent higher than Latinos'.

Public School Finance In 2011–2012, expenditures for current public school operations in Texas were $8,908 per student (22 percent less than the national average). The actual distribution of these funds is governed according to extremely complex rules and mathematical formulas that occupy six chapters totaling more than 75,000 words in the Texas Education Code. Although public school accountants and financial officers must understand the nuances of these rules to maximize funding for their respective districts, you need to understand only the system's most basic features to engage intelligently in the public debate that surrounds public school finance. The following discussion is organized around the three basic sources of public school funding—federal, state, and local.

> **Did You Know?** In 2011, Texas's legislature adjusted school funding formulas to cut $4 billion from school district entitlements.

---

[2]U.S. Department of Labor, Bureau of Labor Statistics, *May 2011 State Occupational and Wage Estimates*, Texas table.

Federal grants make up a fairly small share of the cost of public education in Texas. Temporary federal stimulus funds (from the American Recovery and Reinvestment Act of 2009) have mostly been spent, and total funding for Texas public schools has declined significantly as a result. Most of the remaining federal funding pays for ongoing aid programs for child nutrition and special-needs, military, and low-income students.

State funding comes from a variety of sources. The Permanent School Fund was established in 1854 and invests receipts of rentals, sales, and mineral royalties from Texas's public lands. Only the interest and dividends from this permanent endowment may be spent. Earnings from the Permanent School Fund and one-fourth of the motor fuels tax make up the Available School Fund, some of which is used for textbooks; the remainder is distributed to local school districts based on average daily student attendance. Basing distribution of state funds on attendance focuses a school district's attention on truancy.

The Foundation School Program (FSP) accounts for the largest portion of state and local funding by far. State funds from general revenues, a margins tax on business (the franchise tax), and a portion of tobacco taxes are distributed to districts according to formulas based on district and student characteristics. The FSP is structured as a state–local partnership to bring some financial equality to local districts despite vast differences in local tax resources.

Local funding comes primarily from ad valorem property taxes. The county appraisal authority determines the market value of property for all local governments within the county, and local district boards then set the property tax rate stated as an amount per $100 of property value. Local school district trustees may set the property tax rate for maintenance and operations up to $1.17 per $100 valuation.

HOW DOES TEXAS COMPARE?
Ranking Texas Public Schools Among The 50 States

Several indicators are frequently used to measure states' educational efforts and their outcomes, but you should be extremely careful in interpreting the meaning of state rankings among the 50 states.

One measure of resources available to educate students is total state and local expenditure per student; Texas ranks 44th. However, this statistic fails to take into account the growth rate in student enrollment. Because Texas has one of the fastest-growing school systems in the nation (three times the national average), it must devote a considerable amount of resources to new construction of physical facilities and developing new school programs.

In addition, the rankings of average teacher salaries are not always fair indicators of educational inputs because they do not take into account that the cost of living varies a great deal from state to state, nor do state rankings by percentage of adults that have graduated from high school adequately measure public school performance because many Texas residents migrated to the state after their education was completed. Even comparison of high school graduation rates is suspect because states currently use different methods of reporting graduation and dropout rates. Likewise, comparison of SAT scores among the 50 states is problematic because not all students take the test. States in which a large portion of students are encouraged to take the test might be expected to have lower average scores than in those states where only a select few high-achieving students are tested.

Although no single statistic alone adequately describes the resources and performance of Texas public schools, their consistently low ranking on a variety of measures indicates that they do not compare favorably to public schools in much of the rest of the nation.

Measure	Texas's Rank
Population and Resources	
State and local expenditures per pupil in public schools	44th
Percentage of population under 18	2nd
Current expenditures per student	38th
Average teacher salary	33rd
Results	
Percentage of population older than 25 with high school diploma	50th
High school graduation rate	43rd
Scholastic Aptitude Test (SAT) scores	45th

Source: *Texas on the Brink, 2011: How Texas Ranks among the 50 States.* This publication can be accessed at the Texas Legislative Study Group website at http://texaslsg.org/.

FOR DEBATE

How can Texans evaluate the performance of their public school system? Is there any way to determine objectively how much spending on education is enough? Is this simply a political decision?

These property taxes are used to pay approximately 53 percent of the FSP basic operating expenses, with the state paying for the remainder. The state supplements local funds to ensure that each district has a basic allotment per student of $4,765 and guarantees that each additional cent in local tax above the minimum must yield at least $31.95 per student.

The system of basic allotments and guaranteed yields is designed to provide some financial equity among local school districts. However, local revenues from property taxes vary so much among school districts that the state has also been forced to establish certain *recapture* requirements. Richer districts such as those with taxable property of more than $319,000 per student may, under certain circumstances, be required to share their local revenue with poorer districts. They may choose one of several mechanisms to provide aid directly to poorer districts, but most send money to the state for redistribution to other districts.

Some local tax revenues are not subject to these recapture requirements. Without aiding poorer districts, wealthier districts may tax up to an additional 50¢ per $100 for construction, capital improvements, and debt service, and they may also collect a small amount (6¢ per $100) for educational enrichment.

School Finance Reform   The current finance system resulted from four decades of struggle, litigation, and failed reform efforts. Because the old state funding system failed to overcome significant inequalities resulting from heavy dependence on local property taxes, a lawsuit attacking the Texas system of educational finance was filed in federal court. Parents of several students in the Edgewood Independent School District in San Antonio charged that funding inequalities violated the Fourteenth Amendment to the U.S. Constitution, which guarantees that no state shall deny any person the equal protection of the laws. Ultimately, the U.S. Supreme Court declined to strike down Texas's system of school finance because it failed to find a fundamental U.S. constitutional right to equally funded public education.[3]

Later, the battle over inequality shifted to the state level. In 1987, a state district court decided a different challenge to the funding system, *Edgewood* v. *Kirby*, under a variety of provisions in the Texas Constitution guaranteeing a suitable and efficient school system.

---

[3]*San Antonio Independent School District* v. *Rodriguez*, 411 U.S. 1 (1973).

The wealthiest school district had property wealth per student 700 times greater than the poorest, and the court cited numerous other disparities resulting from heavy reliance on local property taxes.

In 1989, the Texas Supreme Court unanimously upheld the lower court decision in *Edgewood* v. *Kirby* (777 S.W.2d 391) that the funding system was unconstitutional. After a series of aborted attempts and adverse court rulings, the legislature enacted the current system as its best effort at **school finance reform**. Revenues per student now depend primarily on the tax rate (tax effort) because the state guarantees that a particular local property tax rate will produce a specific amount of revenue or the state will make up the difference. The recapture requirement that wealthier districts share their revenues with poorer districts outraged some parents and school officials, who described the system as "socialistic" or a "Robin Hood" plan that interfered with local control and the right to educate their children.

Despite the changes, some disparity still exists in revenues per student among school districts. For example, the Dallas Independent School District still has $20,700 more revenue for a class of 20 students than does the Huntsville Independent School District. Yet ironically, the poorer school district's students perform better on standard tests. And despite more equalized revenues, suburban school districts like Plano and Alamo Heights continue to have far more students passing TAKS than urban school districts like Dallas and Houston, which include the largest share of minority students and those from economically disadvantaged families. Table 13.3 shows that student TAKS test scores—and the factors sometimes thought to affect them—vary dramatically from district to district in Texas. Besides per-student revenues, ethnicity and family incomes are major variables that seem to determine public school outcomes.

School finance reform

Changes in public school financial system resulting from a Texas Supreme Court ruling that significant inequality in school financial resources violated the state constitution; note that changes in any public policy are considered *reform* by their advocates.

TABLE 13.3 Selected Texas School District Profiles

School District (1)	Enrollment (2)	Percent Minority (3)	Percent Economically Disadvantaged (4)	Percent Meeting 2011 TAKS Standard (5)	Revenue per Student (6)
Houston I.S.D.	203,294	92.2%	80.6%	73%	$ 7,701
Dallas I.S.D.	156,784	95.4	87.1	67	8,101
Plano I.S.D.	55,294	55.8	24.6	88	7,670
Edgewood I.S.D.	11,904	99.5	92.6	59	8,293
Huntsville I.S.D.	6,243	57.1	62.1	71	7,066
Alamo Heights I.S.D.	4,744	40.6	22.4	87	8,206
West Orange-Cove I.S.D.	2,529	74.7	84.9	53	7,609
Wink-Loving I.S.D.	356	41.0	34.3	77	15,728
Statewide	4,912,385	68.8	59.2	76	10,328

Source: Texas Education Agency, *2010–2011 Academic Excellence Indicator System*, District Reports available at http://ritter.tea.state.tx.us/perfreport/aeis/.

This sample of school district profiles is arranged by size of enrollment. The column on the far right shows that some financial inequity remains among school districts. Follow the Percent Meeting 2011 TAKS Standard column (column 5) down and notice that there is little relationship with district revenues per student. Now look at ethnicity (Percent Minority, column 3) and Percent Economically Disadvantaged students (column 4) to see if these factors relate to the TAKS scores (column 5).

▲ **Which factors most affect student achievement? What public policy changes would best improve student performance?**

School Privatization Adjustments to the school funding system will continue indefinitely. Among recent proposals for school finance changes are various voucher plans to use public funds to enable students to attend private and parochial schools. Supporters, often including conservatives and particular religious groups, argue that voucher plans offer poorer parents the choice to transfer their children out of underperforming public schools, an alternative now available only to wealthier families. They believe that increasing competition between public and private schools should stimulate improvements in public education.

Opponents, including teachers' organizations, charge that vouchers would damage public schools by draining their financial resources and some of their best students, leaving public schools to educate students with special problems and learning disabilities. They argue that public funds should not subsidize special private privileges; therefore, any fair voucher plan must include requirements that private schools adopt open-admissions, open-meetings, and open-records policies.

Texas public opinion surveys indicate that Texans are divided about programs to divert money from public schools to private and parochial schools.

What are the arguments for and against school vouchers?

Although the U.S. Supreme Court has upheld publicly funded voucher programs that subsidize students attending religious and private schools, opponents still contend that such programs invite state controls over parochial schools and compromise the separation of church and state. Short of vouchers for students to attend private schools, several programs offer school choice and foster competitiveness within the public school system. Local school districts have established magnet schools; charter schools and district home rule are also available options. Opponents can point to research indicating that similar students perform as well in public schools as they do in similar private schools.

Higher Education

Like public schools, higher education is a major state service, accounting for 12 percent of state expenditure during the 2012–2013 budget period. Figure 13.6 shows that public institutions enroll 90 percent of all students in Texas higher education. Texas public institutions of higher education include 38 general academic institutions and universities, nine health-related institutions, and one technical college with four campuses. Fifty public community college districts operate more than 80 campuses.

Administration of Colleges and Universities The Texas Higher Education Coordinating Board (THECB) was established to coordinate the complex system of higher education. Its 18 members are appointed by the governor with the consent of the senate, and they serve for six-year terms. The Coordinating Board appoints the commissioner of higher education to supervise its staff. Together the board and staff outline the role of each public college and university and plan future needs for programs, curricula, and physical plants. Because Texas's colleges and universities were not established systematically, the Coordinating Board has difficulty imposing a rational, coherent system on their existing operations. Politically powerful boards of regents complicate the Coordinating Board's efforts as they compete to impose their views on higher education, as do other groups.

Boards of regents or trustees set basic policies for their institutions, within the limits of state law and the rules and guidelines established by the Coordinating Board. Governing

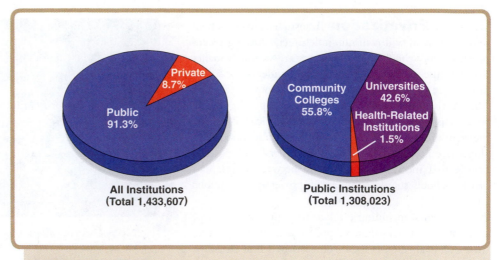

Figure 13.6

Texas Higher Education–Enrollments, Fall 2010

Higher education is overwhelmingly a responsibility of the state (left pie chart), and a majority of public college students enroll in community colleges (right pie chart).

Source: Texas Higher Education Coordinating Board and Legislative Budget Board, *Fiscal Size-Up 2012–2013*, p. 255.

What challenges do growing enrollments present to Texas's institutions of higher learning? How successful are these institutions at retaining and graduating students who have enrolled in them?

boards provide for the selection of public university administrators, including system-wide administrators (chancellors), campus presidents, deans, and other officers. Certain boards govern institutions located on several campuses:

★ The University of Texas System includes The University of Texas at Austin (with the nation's largest student population on a single campus) and other campuses located at Arlington, Brownsville, Dallas, El Paso, Permian Basin, San Antonio, and Tyler as well as University of Texas–Pan American and several medical and health units.

★ The Texas A&M System has its main campus at College Station with additional campuses at Corpus Christi, Commerce, Texarkana, Galveston, Kingsville, Prairie View A&M, Tarleton State, West Texas A&M, Texas A&M International, and several smaller campuses.

★ The Texas State University System includes Sam Houston State, Texas State University at San Marcos, Sul Ross State, and Lamar University.

★ The University of Houston has its main campus in Houston as well as a downtown campus and campuses at Clear Lake and Victoria.

★ The Texas Tech System includes the main campus at Lubbock, several other western Texas campuses, health science centers, and Angelo State University.

★ The remaining boards each govern mainly single-campus institutions.

Authorized and financed largely by the state, community colleges are also generally supervised by the Coordinating Board. However, unlike four-year institutions (which are usually designed to attract students from larger regions of the state and nation as well as international students), voters establish community colleges in one or more school districts primarily to serve area residents. They are usually governed by independently elected boards.

The traditional role of the junior college has been to serve freshmen and sophomores by offering academic courses for credits transferable to senior colleges. Although most of their students are enrolled in these transferable academic courses, two-year colleges have responded to the demands resulting from economic diversification by adopting a **community college approach**, adding adult, continuing, and special-education courses as well as technical specialties. The curriculum, low cost, and geographic and financial accessibility of community colleges have resulted in increasing enrollments, especially in academic programs. Figure 13.6 shows that a majority of Texas students enroll in two-year institutions.

Community college approach
Higher education policy based on open admissions, maximizing accessibility, and incorporating technical, compensatory, and continuing education among the traditional academic course offerings.

The Politics of Higher Education

It is difficult to measure objectively many of the benefits of higher education, such as personal satisfaction and contribution to society. Individual financial benefits, however, are very clear, contrary to critics' allegations that higher education is not worth increasing tuition costs. In 2011, high school graduates had a median annual income of $33,176 and an unemployment rate of 9.4 percent; those with an associate's degree earned $39,946 and had an unemployment rate of 6.8 percent; and those with a bachelor's degree had a median income of $54,756 and an unemployment rate of only 4.9 percent.[4] Those with college degrees earn substantially more and have a much lower risk of unemployment.

The economic benefits from investments in higher education seem quite impressive as well. According to a study funded by the Bill and Melinda Gates Foundation, every $1.00 invested in higher education yields $8.00 in enhanced productivity, greater ongoing capacity, reduced social costs, and stimulus to research and development.[5]

Despite its benefits, legislative bodies and boards of regents and trustees have often been critical in their evaluations of higher education and its results. Calls for faculty and student accountability have been frequent. Yet there are no generally agreed-upon answers to the questions raised about higher education: What should its goals be? How should it measure success in achieving those goals? To whom should it be accountable? We examine some issues concerning higher education in the remainder of this section.

© Bob Daemmrich/Alamy

Students at The University of Texas–Austin protest proposed cuts in state funding for higher education.

Explain how tuition deregulation has allowed Texas colleges and universities to raise tuition and other fees. How much of the costs of higher education should be borne by students and how much by taxpayers?

Faculty Issues   Salaries are a perpetual issue when Texas institutions of higher education recruit new faculty. Average full-time public college and university faculty salaries, for example, are still significantly below the national average.

Rationalizing their attempts as an effort to promote faculty accountability, college and university administrators have long sought to dilute job-protection guarantees for professors. State law requires governing boards to adopt procedures for periodic reevaluation of all tenured faculty. Faculties generally fear that such policies can be a threat to academic freedom and a tool for political repression by administrators.

---

[4]U.S. Census Bureau, *Current Population Survey* and Bureau of Labor Statistics *Education Pays*, March 23, 2012.
[5]The Perryman Group, *A Tale of Two States—And One Million Jobs,* March 2007, published by the Texas Higher Education Coordinating Board at www.thecb.state.tx.us/reports/PDF/1345.PDF?CFID=8408072&CFTOKEN=72550084.

Financial Issues Financing higher education is a continuing issue. Like elementary and secondary schools, most colleges and universities in Texas must struggle with relatively small budgets. Meanwhile, increasing college enrollments and demands for specialized, high-cost programs are increasing at a time when unemployment compensation, social services, health care, and other services are also placing more demands on depressed state revenues. Reluctant to raise revenues to cover the increasing cost of higher education, Texas's legislature has shifted much of the cost burden to students. (See our end-of-chapter essay.)

Student Accessibility Proposals to cope with financial pressures include closing institutions with smaller enrollments, reducing duplication, restricting student services, increasing tuition, and delaying construction plans or implementing new degree programs. Most of these policies have the effect of limiting student access to higher education, and increasing costs represent the greatest obstacle to a college education for most students.

Because the Texas legislature deregulated tuition, college and university boards have dealt with increasing costs by raising tuition, mandatory student fees, and residence costs. Between Fall 2003 and 2011, average tuition and fees for full-time in-state students at Texas public universities increased 90 percent, to $3,671 per semester. At community colleges, in-district tuition and fees increased to $868 for 12 credit hours.[6] Financial accessibility of higher education is a growing concern, especially because the size of Pell grants and other forms of financial aid are not keeping pace with increasing costs, and students are financing more of the increased cost of higher education by borrowing. Figure 13.7 shows the recent trends in costs of higher education for Texas students.

> **Did You Know?** Despite increases in tuition and fees, average tuition at Texas public community colleges is less expensive than in 44 other states and tuition at public four-year institutions is less than in 27 other states.

Student Diversity In addition to affordability, other cultural, structural, and historical factors have limited access to certain populations that have traditionally been underserved by Texas institutions of higher learning. Economically disadvantaged people, those who live in rural areas, and ethnic minorities are notably underrepresented in colleges and universities.

Institutions of higher education have struggled with minority student recruitment in an effort to increase ethnic diversity and offer more access to underserved populations. Supporters of **affirmative action** argue that ethnic, racial, and economic diversity encourages lively classroom discussions from multiple perspectives, fosters cross-racial harmony, and cultivates leaders among groups that have traditionally been at a disadvantage in society. Opponents argue that race-conscious selection of student applicants can lead to discrimination against white Anglos as they are passed over in favor of less-qualified minority applicants.

Courts have made a series of ambiguous or conflicting decisions about the constitutionality of affirmative action efforts in higher education. When the federal Fifth Circuit Court of Appeals ruled that race could not be considered in affirmative action admissions policies,[7] many states attempted to achieve diversity by considering low family income and other special nonracial obstacles that make it difficult to meet standard admission criteria. The Texas legislature responded by requiring that general academic institutions (except now for The

Affirmative action
Positive efforts to recruit ethnic minorities, women, and the economically disadvantaged. Sometimes these efforts are limited to publicity drives among target groups, but such programs have sometimes included ethnicity or gender as part of the qualification criteria.

---

[6]Texas Higher Education Coordinating Board, *College Costs, Fall 2003–Fall 2011,* March 26, 2012 at www.thecb.state.tx.us//Reports/PDF/2460.PDF?CFID=27708507&CFTOKEN=84333436; Susan Combs, *Texas in Focus: A Statewide View of Opportunities* (Austin: Office of the Comptroller of Public Accounts, January 2008); and Texas Association of Community Colleges, *Fall 2011 Tuition and Fees, Texas Public Community Colleges,* November 28, 2011 at www.tacc.org/documents/Fa11tuition_005.pdf.
[7]*Hopwood* v. *Texas,* 85 F.3d 720 (5th Cir., 1996).

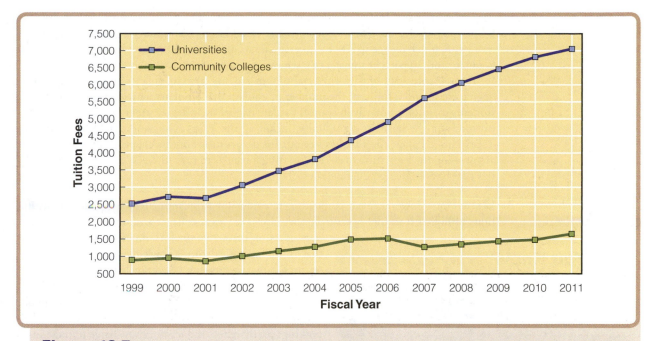

Figure 13.7

Full-Time Texas Resident Tuition and Fees per Year

This table shows the dramatic rise of tuition resulting from state budget cuts and tuition deregulation.

Sources: Texas Higher Education Coordinating Board, *College Costs, Fall 2003–Fall 2011,* March 26, 2012 at www.thecb.state.tx.us//Reports/PDF/2460. PDF?CFID=27708507&CFTOKEN=84333436; Susan Combs, *Texas in Focus: A Statewide View of Opportunities* (Austin: Office of the Comptroller of Public Accounts, January 2008); Texas Association of Community Colleges, *Fall 2011 Tuition and Fees, Texas Public Community Colleges,* November 28, 2011, at www.tacc.org/documents/Fa11tuition_005.pdf.

Evaluate the alternatives to raising tuition in Texas's institutions of higher learning. Is higher education worth the cost?

University of Texas at Austin) must automatically admit students from the top 10 percent of their high school graduating class regardless of test scores. More female, African-American, Latino, low-income, and rural students have been admitted to state universities under the "10 percent" rule than under traditional admission criteria.

When more recent U.S. Supreme Court decisions allowed race to be considered directly in college admissions policies under limited circumstances,[8] administrators at The University of Texas at Austin scrambled to find constitutionally acceptable affirmative action policies. In 2012, the U.S. Supreme Court ruled on the constitutionality of the university's use of race or ethnicity among college admission criteria.[9]

Student Retention

Of course, admission to institutions of higher learning is hardly the only measure of success. Although students may benefit from even a short experience in college and employers credit applicants for it, graduation or completion of occupational curriculum programs is society's respected measure of success.

Unfortunately, high costs, lack of course availability, inadequate academic preparation, and personal factors all contribute to the problem of student retention. Among full-time

[8]*Grutter* v. *Bollinger,* 539 U.S. 306 (2003); *Gratz* v. *Bollinger,* 539 U.S. 234 (2003).
[9]*Fisher* v. *University of Texas at Austin,* No. 11-345.

degree-seeking students at public universities, 24 percent graduate within four years, and 57 percent receive degrees within six years. In addition, community colleges have a much more difficult challenge to retain and graduate students—within three years, only 11 percent graduate and 20 percent transfer to a senior institution.[10]

Texas institutions of higher education are moving toward policies incentivizing timely degree completion, limiting the number of courses that students may drop, and counseling students to enroll primarily in courses that are part of their degree programs. Powerful political forces in the business community, including the Texas Association of Business and the Texas Public Policy Foundations (see our Insiders features in this chapter and in Chapter 5), are pressing the legislature to change funding formulas to reward Texas colleges and universities that have higher graduation rates.

Quality However, even graduation rates do not fully measure the success of institutions of higher learning. Measuring the success of Texas colleges and universities must take into account their two major functions: (1) teaching—that is, imparting existing knowledge to students, and (2) research—that is, creating new knowledge.

> **Did You Know?** By one measure, Texas has four of the top 100 national public universities in the nation—The University of Texas at Austin ranks 13th, Texas A& M University ranks 19th, University of Texas at Dallas 73rd, and Texas Tech 85th.[11]

Various rankings show that the UT and Texas A&M flagship campuses are the two most recognized public institutions of higher learning in the state. Perhaps their rankings partly reflect the resources available to these institutions. General legislative appropriations have been relatively more generous for The University of Texas (UT) at Austin and Texas A&M University, and the state Constitution earmarks revenues from more than two million acres of public land to the Permanent University Fund for the benefit of UT and Texas A&M.

A new National Research University Fund is designed to enable emerging research universities in Texas to achieve national prominence. Proposed Tier One research universities include the University of Houston, North Texas University, Texas Tech University, and University of Texas campuses at San Antonio, Dallas, Arlington, and El Paso. Of course, the results of these ambitious efforts cannot yet be fully foreseen or evaluated.

HEALTH AND HUMAN SERVICES

The second-most costly category of state spending can be broadly classified as health and human services, which encompass public assistance, Medicaid for the poor, and a variety of other programs. In the 2012–2013 budget period, these programs cost $55.4 billion (31.9 percent of the state's total budget). However, approximately 60 percent of this funding originates as grants-in-aid from the federal government.

Figure 13.8 shows that the Texas Health and Human Services Commission provides a variety of social services, including Temporary Assistance to Needy Families, Medicaid, and the Children's Health Insurance Program. The commission also coordinates planning, rule making, and budgeting among its four subsidiary social service agencies, the Department of Aging and Disability Services, the Department of Assistive and Rehabilitative Services, the Department of Family and Protective Services, and the Department of State Health Services.

---

[10]Susan Combs, *Texas in Focus: A Statewide View of Opportunities* (Austin: Comptroller of Public Accounts, 2008).

[11]"2012 Best Colleges: Top Public Schools: National Universities," *U.S. News and World Report*, http://colleges.usnews.rankingsandreviews.com/best-colleges/rankings/national-universities/top-public. These imperfect rankings are based on reputation, exclusiveness in admissions, and financial resources.

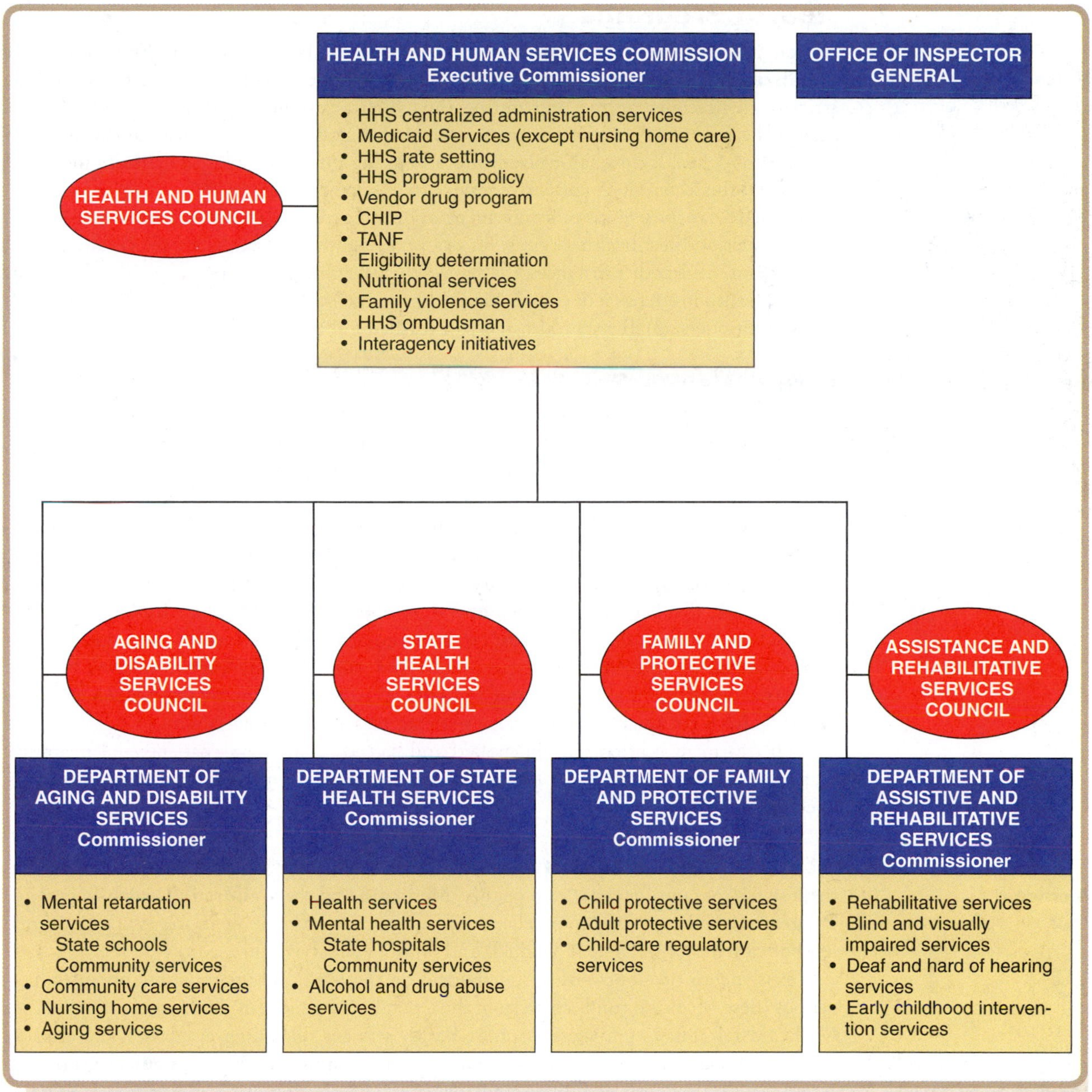

HEALTH AND HUMAN SERVICES COMMISSION
Executive Commissioner

OFFICE OF INSPECTOR GENERAL

- HHS centralized administration services
- Medicaid Services (except nursing home care)
- HHS rate setting
- HHS program policy
- Vendor drug program
- CHIP
- TANF
- Eligibility determination
- Nutritional services
- Family violence services
- HHS ombudsman
- Interagency initiatives

HEALTH AND HUMAN SERVICES COUNCIL

AGING AND DISABILITY SERVICES COUNCIL

STATE HEALTH SERVICES COUNCIL

FAMILY AND PROTECTIVE SERVICES COUNCIL

ASSISTANCE AND REHABILITATIVE SERVICES COUNCIL

DEPARTMENT OF AGING AND DISABILITY SERVICES
Commissioner

- Mental retardation services
    State schools
    Community services
- Community care services
- Nursing home services
- Aging services

DEPARTMENT OF STATE HEALTH SERVICES
Commissioner

- Health services
- Mental health services
    State hospitals
    Community services
- Alcohol and drug abuse services

DEPARTMENT OF FAMILY AND PROTECTIVE SERVICES
Commissioner

- Child protective services
- Adult protective services
- Child-care regulatory services

DEPARTMENT OF ASSISTIVE AND REHABILITATIVE SERVICES
Commissioner

- Rehabilitative services
- Blind and visually impaired services
- Deaf and hard of hearing services
- Early childhood intervention services

Figure 13.8

Texas Health and Human Service Agencies

This organizational chart illustrates the wide range of services provided by the Health and Human Services Commission.

Source: Health and Human Services Commission.

Why is it important for a single commission to coordinate so many of the state's human services?

Health Programs

Although opponents of government's assuming responsibility for public health describe it as **socialized medicine**, health has been a concern of public authorities since Moses imposed strict hygienic codes on the Jews during their biblical exodus from Egypt. In the United States, the federal government began to provide hospital care to the Merchant Marines in 1798. Today, health care has evolved into a growing public–private partnership and, after education, the second-most expensive service that Texas provides.

The state has three levels of involvement in health care: (1) In some instances, the state is the provider of direct health services, for example, it provides health care for certain special populations. (2) In other instances, the state is the payer but not the provider. When it acts as a public health insurer as it does with Medicaid, it pays for the medical services offered by private practitioners. (3) The state also acts as a regulator and buyer of private health insurance.

Direct Health Services

Texas's Department of Health Services provides personal health services for special populations. For example, the health department operates a lung and tuberculosis hospital in San Antonio and a general services hospital in Harlingen. The Department of Health Services operates general psychiatric hospitals and funds local mental health community centers and chemical dependency programs as well.

County hospitals and clinics are legally responsible for providing medical care for uninsured indigents, and therefore, they have become the health providers of last resort. County hospitals are usually operated by county hospital districts that have the authority to collect property taxes that partially fund their operations. Several government institutions also manage teaching hospitals that provide care to both indigent and non-indigent patients.

Instead of using county-funded hospitals and clinics, many uninsured and indigent patients access medical services through hospital emergency rooms because federal and state laws require them to accept emergency patients regardless of their ability to pay. The cost of such treatment is often uncompensated and passed on to paying patients and insurance companies—a practice partially responsible for the recent dramatic increase in health insurance premiums.

State Health-Insurance Programs

Texas operates two major health-insurance programs for those who qualify. **Medicaid** and the **Children's Health Insurance Program (CHIP)** are fairly comprehensive insurance programs designed to provide a minimal level of care for low-income individuals and families who have enrolled.

Texas spends one-fourth of its state budget on the Medicaid program, but about 60 percent of these Medicaid funds come from the federal government in the form of grants-in-aid. Medicaid reimburses providers for most health services, including eyeglasses, prescription drugs, physicians' fees, laboratory and X-ray services, family planning, ambulance transportation, Medicare Part B premiums, and a wide variety of other medical expenses. Generally, these providers are in managed care (HMO-type) systems.

Medicaid should not be confused with **Medicare**, which is available to most persons older than 65 years of age regardless of income, and is administered by the U.S. Department of Health and Human Services. In contrast, the Medicaid program is administered by the state and is available only to those who meet certain age and income requirements. These groups include (1) impoverished persons eligible for Temporary Assistance for Needy Families (TANF) or Supplemental Security Income (SSI), (2) individuals receiving medical assistance only (low-income persons residing in institutions who qualify for SSI except for certain income requirements), (3) children up to 19 years of age whose families would qualify for TANF, (4) children ages 6 through 18 who reside in families with income below the federal poverty level, (5) children younger than 6 whose family's income is at or less than

Sidebar

Socialized medicine

Strictly defined, socialized medicine is a health care system in which the government hires medical practitioners who work at government-owned facilities to directly provide health care, as in Great Britain and in U.S. veterans' and military hospitals. However, the term is often applied to health care systems in which the government provides health care insurance (such as Medicare) but benefit payments are made to private health care providers.

Medicaid

A program to provide medical care for qualified low-income persons; although funded largely by federal grants-in-aid, it is a state-administered program.

Children's Health Insurance Program (CHIP)

Program that provides health insurance for low-income children. It is administered by the state but funded largely by federal grants-in-aid.

Medicare

A federal program to provide medical insurance for most persons older than 65 years of age.

133 percent of the federal poverty level, and (6) pregnant women and infants younger than 1 year of age who reside in families with income less than 185 percent of the federal poverty level.[12] Of Texas's 3 million Medicaid recipients, 90 percent are elderly, disabled, or children.

CHIP helps insure children of parents with incomes less than 200 percent of the poverty level and who do not qualify for Medicaid. Even though almost 600,000 children are insured by CHIP and 2.5 million are enrolled in Medicaid, one in six Texas children remains uninsured.

Private Health Insurance Although approximately 19 percent of nonelderly Texans have some sort of public insurance coverage such as Medicaid or CHIP, most others rely on private insurance companies to pay for their medical expenses. Employer-sponsored plans cover 49 percent of Texans and private individual policies cover 4 percent. The state itself pays private insurance companies for part of the premiums for its employees and teachers. As a result, businesses, government, and individuals have been seriously impacted by health insurance premiums that have skyrocketed, more than doubling since 2001 and now costing about $14,000 for the average family premium.[13] High premium costs have caused some businesses to drop coverage for their employees, and many individuals have chosen not to buy private coverage, leaving Texas as the state with the largest share of uninsured persons in the nation.

HOW DOES TEXAS COMPARE?
How People Get Health Insurance

One of every six Americans and one in four Texans has no health insurance coverage. Texas has the nation's highest percentage of uninsured residents. In 2010, approximately 6.1 million Texans, or 25 percent of the state's nonelderly population, were uninsured, including more than one in six Texas children.

Nationally, about 56 percent of the nonelderly were covered by employment-based insurance, whereas only 49 percent had employment-based health insurance in Texas. Texas ranked 43rd among states, including the District of Columbia, in the percentage of people with employer-sponsored insurance.

Only about 5 percent of businesses with 50 or more employees did not offer health insurance, but small businesses lagged far behind. Nationwide, only 39.2 percent of businesses with fewer than 50 employees offered health care benefits, whereas an even smaller portion, 31.4 percent, of those companies in Texas offered such benefits.

Increasing health insurance costs partly explain the large number of uninsured. Between 2001 and 2010, health insurance premiums across the nation rose by an average of 104 percent. By 2010, the average premium cost for employer-sponsored family coverage in Texas was $14,526, somewhat above the national average.

The fact that many Texans are uninsured poses problems for individuals, businesses, and state and local governments, who bear extra costs to pay for uncompensated care. Medical providers of all types are forced to raise paying patients' fees to cover losses resulting from unpaid medical services to the uninsured. Costs that are not reimbursed are passed on to Texans in the form of higher taxes and insurance premiums. In 2005, Texas's insured families

---

[12]Health and Human Services Commission, "Texas Medicaid Program," www.hhsc.state.tx.us/medicaid/index.html.

[13]The Kaiser Family Foundation. See how Texas compares at www.statehealthfacts.org.

spent an extra $1,551 in premiums to cover the unpaid health care bills of the uninsured. Meanwhile, rising premiums cause private employers to drop employee insurance coverage altogether, thus compounding the problem.

FOR DEBATE

1. To what extent should health care insurance be a public policy concern?

2. The main drivers of rising health care costs include the use of more expensive technology, expensive new drugs, increasing demand for health care services due to a surging elderly population, and an epidemic of chronic diseases like diabetes. What public policy measures could be adopted to contain health care costs?

Sources: Kaiser Family Foundation, *State Health Facts* at www.statehealthfacts.org; U.S. Bureau of Census, *Current Population Survey* (Annual Social and Economic Supplements), 2010 and 2011; Susan Combs, *Texas in Focus: A Statewide View of Opportunities* (Austin: Comptroller of Public Accounts, 2008). This publication can be accessed online at www.window.state.tx.us/specialrpt/tif/index.html.

Health Care Reform (HCR)

A comprehensive federal program expanding health insurance coverage with broader Medicaid coverage, individual mandates, guaranteed-issue requirements, health insurance subsidies, and exchanges.

Guaranteed-issue requirements

Requirement that insurance companies will sell health insurance to applicants despite preexisting conditions.

The Future of Texas Health Insurance

In an effort to cope with the increasing cost of private health insurance, the large number of uninsured Americans, and objectionable insurance company practices, Congress passed the controversial Patient Protection and Affordable Care Act of 2010, also known as **Health Care Reform (HCR)**. The U.S. Supreme Court later upheld the law in the landmark case *National Federation of Independent Business* v. *Sebelius, Secretary of Health and Human Services,* 567 U.S.__(2012).

Because Texas has the largest percentage of uninsured persons of any state in the nation, HCR will have a more dramatic effect in Texas than in most states. It will expand Medicaid and CHIP eligibility by 2.1 million persons. Individual mandates, small business subsidies, affordability subsidies for middle-income families, and large business incentives will reduce the number of uninsured by as many as 4.3 million, depending on how many choose to ignore the individual mandate. The remaining uninsured will be mostly illegal immigrants who are ineligible and eligible persons who choose to pay a tax rather than buy health insurance.

Health-care reform impacts Texans in stages because its provisions are being implemented over time. The act has already ended some of the most unpopular insurance company practices as its first priority. *Rescissions* are no longer allowed, meaning health insurance companies can no longer arbitrarily drop beneficiaries when they get sick or because they have reached lifetime limits. Insurance companies may not deny insurance to children because of preexisting conditions, and adults with preexisting conditions such as diabetes or high blood pressure are now allowed to buy subsidized insurance through a new high-risk pool. Insurance companies must also allow parents to keep their children covered under their family policies until age 26.

Small businesses will have tax credits to help them buy insurance for their employees during the first phase of health reform, but the most significant and controversial elements of the reform package will take effect in 2014. At that time, insurance companies will be subject to a **guaranteed-issue** requirement that they must insure all applicants even if they are sick—a requirement that

Texas Tea Party protesters attacked Health Care Reform as being too much big government.

How does HCR expand the role of the state and federal governments? Evaluate the need for the individual mandate and government regulation of the health care industry.

AP Images/Deborah Cannon/Austin American-Statesman

insurance companies will be able to meet only because they will be able to spread risk over a larger pool of customers. Most people will be required to have health insurance or pay a tax penalty to the federal government—the **individual mandate**.

Uninsured individuals and small businesses will be allowed to buy health insurance through state insurance exchanges in which insurance companies compete by offering qualified plans with clear and comparable information on coverage options. States may agree to allow their residents to buy health insurance in their exchanges across state lines. Individuals purchasing health insurance on these exchanges will be eligible for subsidies on a sliding scale based on their incomes up to four times the federal poverty level ($92,200 in 2012). Some low-income individuals will also qualify for subsidies for a portion of out-of-pocket expenses.

Although some very low-income individuals are exempted from the mandate, most states will expand Medicaid eligibility to all persons with incomes less than 133 percent of the federal poverty level because the federal government will pay for 100 percent of the cost of this expansion during the first few years and for 90 percent of its cost thereafter. If Texas opts to accept this federal funding, the state would be able to cover an additional two million individuals under its Medicaid program.

The health-care reform law gives the Texas Department of Insurance substantial powers to enforce new federal health insurance regulations and to monitor hikes in insurance premiums. In addition, the state may assume the responsibility for operating an insurance exchange and for qualifying new Medicaid and CHIP clients. Texas's Health and Human Services Executive Commissioner Tom Suehs estimates the expansion of Medicaid and the Children's Health Insurance Program could cost the state $27 billion between 2014 and 2023.

Individual mandate

Requirement that individuals get health insurance or pay a tax penalty to the federal government.

Income Support Programs

Although health care services are by far the most expensive of the social services the state provides, income-support programs are probably more controversial because they provide cash directly to beneficiaries. While the amounts are relatively small, taxpayer funds are directly transferred or redistributed to recipients based on their need or lack of employment.

Temporary Assistance to Needy Families
Among social service programs, Temporary Assistance to Needy Families (TANF) is designed for children whose parents are incapable of providing for their children's basic needs. More than two-thirds of TANF recipients are children. Unless they are disabled or needed at home to care for very young children, adult TANF and food stamp recipients are referred for employment counseling, assessment, and job placement.

The TANF-Basic program serves those who are deprived of support because of the absence or disability of one or both parents and whose income is less than 12 percent of the poverty level. TANF grants are available for two-parent families in which the principal wage earner is unemployed and the family income does not exceed the criteria established for the basic program.

Federal and state regulations now require recipients to cooperate in identifying an absent parent and, with few exceptions, limit TANF benefits to citizens; adult eligibility is usually limited to two years at a time, with a maximum five-year lifetime benefit. By making welfare less of an entitlement, these welfare reforms were intended to force able-bodied individuals out of dependency and into productive work. Some federal funds are now distributed as block grants to the states to allow them flexibility to develop support services, child care, job training and placement, and rehabilitation programs to help welfare recipients in finding work. These reforms have substantially reduced the number of TANF recipients in Texas.

In 2012–2013, the maximum monthly TANF grant for a family of three was $263, considerably below the national average. The Texas median TANF grant is about one-half the national median. Adjusting for inflation, TANF benefits have declined considerably over the years. Today, Texas spends about 0.1 percent of its budget for this income-assistance program for the poor.

Unemployment Insurance

Unemployment insurance
Benefit program for certain workers losing their employment; a joint federal–state program financed with a tax on employers.

Whereas TANF is designed as an income supplement for the poor and is administered by the Health and Human Service Commission, unemployment compensation is designed as partial income replacement for those who have lost their jobs. Unlike TANF, which is a welfare program determined by need, unemployment compensation is a social insurance program financed by employer-paid premiums, and eligibility is based on previous earnings rather than on need or family size.

The U.S. Congress established the system of **unemployment insurance** under the Social Security Act of 1935 as a partnership between the states and the federal government. This act imposed a tax on covered employers to establish a nationwide system of unemployment insurance administered by the federal government. However, the act provided that most of this tax would be set aside in all of the states that adopted an acceptable state program. Thus every state was pressured to adopt state systems of unemployment insurance. Benefits are financed from state taxes on employers, but some administrative costs are paid with federal funds. These programs are actually administered by the states.

In Texas, unemployment insurance is administered by the Texas Workforce Commission (TWC), a three-member board appointed by the governor, with the consent of the senate, for six-year overlapping terms. Outside the authority of the Health and Human Services Commission, the TWC administers benefit payments. Usually, the maximum is 26 weekly benefit payments, but Congress usually extends the period of eligibility and pays for much of the cost of the extension during periods of severe recessions when jobs are scarce.

Under Texas's rather restrictive laws, a worker must register for job placement with the TWC and is usually ineligible to receive benefits (at least for a time) if he or she voluntarily quits or was fired for cause. Because the rate at which employers are taxed is based on claims made by former employees, employers have an interest in contesting employee claims. For these reasons and others, only one-third of unemployed Texans receive benefits.

Until recently, handling unemployment insurance claims has not been a major priority among TWC's activities; its major functions have been providing a workforce for employers, gathering employment statistics, enforcing child-labor laws, and providing various special job-training and rehabilitation services. Able-bodied welfare recipients are referred to the TWC for training and child-care services. Regional workforce development boards plan one-stop career-development centers in 28 areas across the state.

The Politics of Welfare and Income Redistribution

Income redistribution
A public policy goal intended to shift income from one class of recipients to another, regardless of whether these programs are designed to benefit lower-, middle-, or upper-income groups.

Social service programs are among a wide range of public policies that employ mechanisms for **income redistribution**; these are public taxation, spending, and regulatory policies intended to shift income from one class of recipients to another. Some redistributive programs, like regressive taxation, business subsidies, and certain government contracting policies, shift income upward from lower- and middle-income families to high-income earners; others, like unemployment compensation, TANF, Medicaid, and food stamps, primarily benefit lower-income persons. Different views about these kinds of programs drive much of the ideological conflict between liberals and conservatives in Texas. (See Chapter 1 for a more complete discussion of these competing ideologies.)

So many public policies redistribute income among various groups that the very concept of *welfare* has no uniformly recognized definition. The broadest view is that welfare is any unearned, government-provided benefit. Governments provide direct subsidies to businesses and corporations that far exceed TANF and food stamp costs combined.

Such corporate welfare includes financial bailouts, most subsidies to agribusiness, and grants to weapons manufacturers to sell weapons to foreigners.

Programs that primarily benefit the middle class, such as federal income tax deductions for mortgage interest, are also more costly than poverty programs. Because Social Security recipients now receive more benefits in the first three years of retirement than they paid in Social Security taxes during their working lifetimes, even Social Security is largely an unearned benefit and may be seen as a form of middle-class welfare. Because these programs are supported by powerful special interests or large numbers of middle-class voters, they are relatively secure from serious political threat.

More often, the term *welfare* narrowly refers to controversial programs explicitly designed to assist the poor. Accordingly, old-age, survivors', and disability insurance (commonly referred to as Social Security) as well as unemployment insurance, are **social-insurance** programs, not public welfare programs. Eligibility for social insurance programs is based not on poverty alone—that is, eligibility is not based on a **means test** but on the tax paid by beneficiaries and their employers. In this respect, they are like private insurance programs, differing primarily in that they are operated by the government and are compulsory for most employers and employees. Such programs are not aimed directly at the poor. In fact, many persons now receive public assistance for the very reason that they were ineligible to participate in adequate social insurance programs.

More myths and misunderstandings have developed about antipoverty programs than probably any other public service.

Welfare Myths There is a mistaken impression that any poor person may be eligible for state public assistance benefits. Although more than 4.6 million Texans live in poverty, fewer than 3 percent of them receive monthly TANF aid, and the only significant group of able-bodied adults now receiving income assistance is parents with sole custody of young dependent children.

There is no general program of cash assistance for able-bodied adults without children, even though they may be unemployed or in need. However, the Supplemental Nutritional Assistance Program (popularly known as food stamps) and Medicaid are available to most who fall below the federally defined poverty level, and federal Supplemental Security Income (SSI) may be available to the aged, blind, and disabled.

Resentment can be expected when shoppers waiting in grocery checkout lines to part with hard-earned cash see the customer ahead paying with federally funded food stamps. Nevertheless, contrary to popular myth, few new Cadillac drivers are legally on Texas welfare rolls because benefits furnish less than the bare essentials of life.

Nor does it seem likely, as some critics suggest, that welfare mothers have more children just to increase their monthly TANF checks. The maximum monthly TANF grant is $263 per three-person family; even when these payments are combined with food stamps and Medicaid, the average TANF child still lives in a home with resources considerably below the poverty level. Children intensify the problems of the poor. Large family size probably results from carelessness, cultural attitudes, or lack of access to birth control rather than a deliberate effort to increase welfare payments.

Several reasons explain the myths that have grown around public welfare. Because welfare benefits people according to their needs rather than according to their efforts, it seems to violate the widespread American attitude that everyone ought to be paid according to the

Did You Know? The top 20 percent of Texas households earned 51 percent of the income and the bottom 40 percent of households received only 12 percent of the income in the state. Only four states have more income inequality.[14]

Social insurance
Public insurance programs with benefits based on tax premiums paid by the beneficiary or his or her employer; for example, Social Security and unemployment compensation are social insurance programs that are not based on need alone.

Means test
A standard of benefit eligibility based on need.

[14]*Austin American-Statesman,* "Politifact Texas," January 18, 2010, www.politifact.com/texas/statements/2010/jan/28/ronnie-earle/ronnie-earle-says-income-gap-steadily-widening-tex/

work one does. Consequently, even the lowest wage earner often feels superior to the welfare recipient. Most Texans prefer to identify themselves with the economically secure rather than with the poor. There is also prejudice against some groups that benefit from welfare because a disproportionate number of welfare recipients are mothers of children born out of wedlock or members of ethnic minority groups. Whatever the cause, these myths and prejudices remain major elements in the debate over public assistance.

Welfare Realities Public welfare faces serious substantive questions. Cheating and overpayment cost taxpayers money and dilute the limited resources that would otherwise be available for those in genuine need. It is difficult to estimate the amount of cheating. Although Texas's Lone Star Card was developed as a form of positive identification to reduce fraud, it is difficult to determine the amount of cheating that occurs during the application and qualification processes.

Probably the most serious problem for the welfare system today is that it alleviates rather than cures. Most public assistance programs are designed only to relieve the most severe pains of poverty, not to cure the disease. Welfare or other assistance programs may prevent starvation, but they offer little hope that recipients will someday escape poverty and dependence. The vast majority of Texas welfare recipients are children who are too young to do much about their problems. But for the able-bodied, chronic poverty is sometimes a symptom of a disease that affects both the individual and society at large. Typically, the long-term poor dropped out of school at an early age and lack the education and skills necessary to earn a living wage. They also exhibit varying degrees of despair, alienation, hopelessness, emotional insecurity, or lethargy. Many lack a feeling that they can do much about their problem; others lack a sense of responsibility for their own fate.

TRANSPORTATION

Road-building has been has been a government function since ancient times and, representing 11.4 percent of the state budget, it remains one of the three most expensive state functions in Texas today. A relatively small share of state funding is directed to mass public transportation and the lion's share of Texas's transportation spending is for highway construction and maintenance.

Highway Programs

In Texas's early days, road construction was primarily the responsibility of the county. Most Texas counties still maintain a property tax dedicated to the construction and maintenance of roads, and in rural areas, road building remains a major function of county government. But the efforts are too small and too poorly financed to provide the expensive, coordinated statewide network of roads needed by highly mobile Texans in the modern world.

In 1916, the national government encouraged state governments to assume the major responsibility for highway construction and maintenance. The 1916 Federal Aid Road Act made available federal funds to cover one-half of the construction costs for state highways. To become eligible for those funds, a state was required to establish an agency to develop a coordinated plan for the state highway system and to administer construction and maintenance programs. Texas responded by establishing the Texas Highway Department, now known as the Texas Department of Transportation (TxDOT). The department is supervised by a five-member commission appointed by the governor, with the consent of the senate, for six-year overlapping terms. The commission appoints an executive director who oversees the department and supervises the work of regional district offices.

Newer federal aid programs and increased funding for existing ones have expanded TxDOT's responsibilities. The earliest highway-building program was designed to provide only major highways along primary routes. Federal funding later became available for secondary roads, and Texas established the farm-to-market program to assume state maintenance of many county roads as the rural road network was paved, extended, and improved. Finally, beginning in 1956, Congress made funds available for 90 percent of the cost of construction of express, limited-access highways to connect major cities in the United States. Today, the 80,000-mile state highway system carries about three-fourths of Texas's motor vehicle traffic (see Table 13.4).

The Politics of Transportation

The Good Roads and Transportation Association, a private organization supported by highway contractors and other groups, lobbied for the establishment of the state highway fund and for increases in motor fuel taxes and still attempts to guard the fund against those who would spend any part of it for other purposes. Despite the organization's efforts, per capita state highway funding is far below the national average.

Funding for the highway program is a joint federal–state responsibility. In 2012–2013, the federal government, mostly from the federal gasoline tax, provided 31 percent of the transportation department's revenues. This large federal contribution has allowed the national government to demand such restrictions as meeting clean air standards and setting a minimum drinking age of 18 as conditions for receiving federal aid.

State monies account for about 70 percent of TxDOT funding. The state highway fund is mostly supported by motor vehicle registration (license plate) fees and three-fourths of the 20-cent-per-gallon motor fuels tax, which has not been raised since 1991. Although the motor fuels tax is about average for the 50 states, Texas spends almost as much maintaining the second-most extensive highway network in the nation as it does constructing new highways.

As a result, the state has been forced to look to alternative revenue sources to pay for new highway construction to accommodate the population's transportation needs in one of the fastest-growing states in the nation. In a conservative state reluctant to raise motor fuels taxes or general revenue sources, such as the state general sales taxes, Governor Perry and other state leaders turned to the idea of privatizing new highways.

TABLE 13.4 **The Texas Highway System**

Type of Roadway	Total Miles	Percentage of Traffic Accommodated
Interstate highways and frontage roads	10,272	28
Farm-to-market roads	40,939	11
Federal and state highways	28,441	35

Note: Figures do not include almost a quarter-million miles of city streets and county roads, which accommodate approximately one-fourth of traffic.

Maintaining this extensive aging highway system is becoming so costly that the state has diminishing funds available to finance new highway construction.

Source: Legislative Budget Board, *Fiscal Size-Up, 2012–2013,* p. 456.

▲ **Does Texas have alternatives to the public highway system that would accommodate the transportation needs of its growing population? How would the state pay for these alternatives?**

Highway Privatization   TxDOT planned to use comprehensive development agreements with private entities to develop a highly ambitious and controversial 50-year program to supplement existing highways. The $200 billion, 4,000-mile Trans-Texas Corridor would have included superhighways (with separate freight and commuter lanes), railways (with high-speed, commuter, and freight lines), and utility corridors (for water, electricity, natural gas, petroleum, fiber-optic telecommunications, and broadband lines). Funded by both state taxes and private investment, the project was to be operated largely by private enterprises such as toll companies.

Facing stiff opposition from property rights groups that objected to the use of eminent domain (see Chapter 12) to enable such a massive state takeover of private land to benefit private investors, TxDOT abandoned the expansive Trans-Texas Corridor plan in favor of smaller more localized projects, but it has not yet given up on the concept of highway privatization or the use of tolls to fund new highway construction. The future of highway funding remains a tough political problem for the Texas legislature and the state's political leadership.

Mass transit

Transport systems that carry multiple passengers such as train and bus systems; whether publicly or privately owned, mass transit systems are available to the general public and usually charge a fare.

Mass Transit   Texans, like most Americans, remain unreceptive to **mass transit** as an alternative to individual motor vehicles. Only 4 to 6 percent of Texas residents regularly commute by urban mass transit. By contrast, mass transportation is a popular, viable alternative to personal vehicles in northeastern areas where one-third of all users of urban mass transit live in the New York City metropolitan area.

Automotive transportation is close to the hearts of Texans, and no other mode of transportation seems as convenient because no other is as individualized. Buses and trains cannot take individuals exactly where they want to go exactly when they want to go there. Automobiles have become a way of life, and their manufacture, maintenance, and fueling have become dominant elements of the economy.

Proponents of mass transit point to the enormous social and personal costs of automotive transportation. Texas's annual highway death toll is close to 3,700, and thousands more are injured. The motor vehicle is also the single most important contributor to atmospheric pollution, a major factor in climate change, a cause of thousands of highway deaths and injuries, and a significant source of refuse that finds its way into junkyards and landfills. As the least efficient mode of transportation presently available, dependence on the individual motor vehicle is in direct conflict with the need to conserve energy and reduce our "addiction to foreign oil."

Urban mass transit was widely used before the end of World War II, and supporters of mass transit argue that adequate public funding could once again make railroads and buses rapid and comfortable alternatives to automotive transportation. When gasoline prices increase, more Texans seem to be receptive to the use of mass transit where it is available.

Critics argue that making mass transportation a viable alternative to motor vehicle transportation would require a massive investment of public funds. And, given Texans' love affair with the automobile and their strong cultural individualism, they are skeptical that the public will respond to a costly investment in mass transit with increased ridership without a catastrophic energy or environmental crisis. In Texas's conservative political environment, it is doubtful that Texas will readily increase public funding for local mass transit authorities, but high energy prices might drive the market for other fuel-efficient alternatives.

Tuition Deregulation and the Future of Texas's Higher Education

Kevin T. Davis
North Central Texas College

Texas government had a big problem in 2003. The Texas budget had to be balanced, but the state was going to start with a $10 billion deficit! Where was the state going to find new money? There were only two answers: raise taxes or find ways to cut the budget. The Texas Legislature agreed to save $260 million by cutting Texas's higher education budget and allowing colleges and universities to increase student tuition and fees. This deregulation of tuition initiated a long, steep increase in tuition costs for colleges and universities across the state. These increases have made it more and more difficult for Texas students to afford a college education, and it looks like it will only get worse.

Although the state has saved money by reducing state funding for higher education, students' tuition has risen substantially to cover the difference, and both students and parents are complaining. This situation got worse in 2011 with a $24 billion budget deficit, and 2013 looks to be no better, so students should expect higher tuition costs.

The rising tuition costs at Texas' public colleges and universities were a natural consequence of the State of Texas cutting its education budget. Back in 2003, deregulation saved the state $260 million, which the schools had to recoup through higher tuition. In the words of State Senator Florence Shapiro of Plano, "We had a $10 billion shortfall. We didn't have the money to fund them appropriately."[15] Governor Perry agreed to this deregulation because he felt it would be better than a tax increase.

The Texas Legislature has continued to cut back on education funding, so all Texas schools have had to increase local taxes, increase tuition, or make severe cuts in their budgets.

With the state cutbacks, Texas universities have had only one option—raising student tuition. Community college districts had the option of increasing their property taxes, but many opted not to do so. Without increased revenue, these schools would have no choice but to cut back budgets by closing programs, offering fewer courses, and/or laying off employees. Although politicians try to downplay the tuition increases, the records (see Tables 13.5a and b) speak for themselves. One pattern of note: while urban areas seemed to fare better, colleges and universities in rural areas increased their tuition substantially. With large increases statewide, many parents and students are questioning the value of a college education at these prices. Obviously, these kinds of increases are making it tougher and tougher for poor and middle-class Texans to pay for a college education.

Many other states are going through a similar experience, for example, California (see Table 13.5c). Rates for California colleges and universities have risen sharply in the last couple of years due to the economic recession. Obviously, they will have many of the same problems as Texas colleges and universities, and the burden will fall on the students. With tuition increasing nationwide, going out of state for a college education will not be an option for many families.

Back in 2009, Texas accepted over $10 billion of Federal Stimulus money to balance the budget, but there was no such help in 2011. Although Texas had $9 billion in a Rainy Day Fund, the legislature opted to spend only $4 billion to pay for Medicaid overruns. Some legislators wanted to spend all of it because that is what they saved it for. Others argued that we should hold some back, in case the economy does not come back over the next two years. Because it took a supermajority, or four-fifths vote, to spend this money, the legislature decided to pay only the Medicaid cost overruns and save the rest for the 2013 session. Consequently, the 2011 state budget ended up $4 billion less than the session before it. These cuts will affect the funding for our education programs, and Texas colleges and universities will have to make do with less.

Our colleges and universities are facing an enrollment challenge. As with most economic downturns, colleges and universities are seeing an increase in student enrollment, but none of that growth was accounted for in the 2011 budget. Texas colleges and universities are accommodating the extra students without extra funding from the state. Because the number of students has grown faster than the funding, the funding per student in Texas has slowly been decreasing. This slow decrease of support from the state has led many colleges and universities to rely more on part-time faculty, increase class sizes, and offer fewer courses. These changes have brought into question the quality of the education our students are getting and what the money is being used for.

Colleges and universities have been conscious of the fact that their tuition is getting very expensive for the average Texan. As such, they have been trying to save money as best they can. Many colleges and universities have put off building projects, delayed maintenance, and hired fewer faculty and administrators. Others have experimented with discounted

[15]Patricia Kilday Hart, "(Much) Higher Education: Does Tuition Deregulation Mean That UT and A&M Cost Too Much? It's All a Matter of Degrees," *Texas Monthly*, February 2005, www.texasmonthly.com/2005-02-01/hart.php.

TABLE 13.5a Undergraduate Tuition and Fee Increases at Selected Texas Universities

Institution In-State Tuition and Fees for 12 Credit Hours

	2003	2009	2011	Percent Increase 2003–2011
University of Texas–El Paso	$1104*	$1,922	$2,809	155 %
University of Texas–Austin	1967*	4,525	4,832	146
University of North Texas	1803	3,501	3,994	122
Texas A & M University	1979	3,517	4,209	113
Texas Tech University	1104	3,339	3,689	235

*For 2002/3 academic year.

TABLE 13.5b Tuition and Fee Increases at Selected Texas Community Colleges

Institution In-District Tuition and Fees for 12 Credit Hours

	2003	2009	2011	Percent Increase 2003–2011
Brookhaven College (Dallas Community College District	$312*	$493**	$540	73 %
Odessa College	492	696	912	86
Houston Community College System	564	690	806	43
Tyler Junior College	492	768	1,088	122

*For 2002/3 academic year.
**For 2008/9 academic year.

TABLE 13.5c Undergraduate Tuition and Fee Increases at Selected California Institutions

Institution Resident Tuition and Fees for 12 Credit Hours

	2003	2009	2011	Percent Increase 2003–2011
University of California–Los Angeles	$1,938	$2,770	$4,637	140 %
California State University–Sacramento	1,256	2,450	3,286	162
Modesto Junior College	146	277	330	126
Chaffey College	150	339	459	206

Sources: Registrars and offices of records and admissions at listed institutions.

tuition in off-peak times, fixed pricing, and tapping endowments. At the same time, they are trying to accommodate more students while keeping their academic standards high. However, many colleges and universities were forced to raise tuition again with the latest budget.

It is highly unlikely that Texas will ever reregulate tuition costs. Reregulation would be extremely expensive for the state and would necessitate increased, or new, taxes. With Texas being a very conservative state, taxpayers especially dislike tax increases, which means that tuition costs will continue to rise. The Texas Legislature will determine how fast tuition costs rise based on the state's economic conditions, the needs of its colleges and universities, and the outcome of its political struggles.

JOIN THE DEBATE

1. Can you explain your personal stake in Texas's policy-making process? What arguments can be made for placing the burden of higher education on students, who benefit most directly from higher education? For some ideas, review the benefits-received concept of financing public services earlier in this chapter.

2. To what extent is higher education a collective good from which all of society benefits? Give examples of costs to society if high tuitions reduce the number of college graduates.

CHAPTER SUMMARY

★ State spending as a percentage of personal income remains fairly constant, and state tax rates remain low compared with other states. About half of state revenues are raised through taxes. A substantial portion (more than one-third) comes from federal grants-in-aid, and miscellaneous sources account for the rest. State borrowing is limited.

★ Although political self-interest actually determines which kinds of taxes are used, taxing decisions may be rationalized as serving some regulatory purpose or reflecting benefits received or ability to pay. Both narrow- and broad-based taxes are used in Texas.

★ The largest single state tax is the general sales tax, which is regressive relative to income because it falls most heavily on middle- and lower-income people. Most state taxes, including selective sales taxes and gross-receipts taxes, are also consumer taxes and regressive relative to income. Even business taxes are shifted onto consumers. Local ad valorem and sales taxes also burden those least able to pay. Among taxes that Texans pay, only the federal income tax is somewhat progressive.

★ The LBB dominates the process of proposing Texas's state budget because the state legislature frequently follows its recommendations during the appropriations process. The governor's most effective tool in spending decisions is the item veto. The spending process is political. Perhaps no other type of decision evokes more consistent and passionate political efforts from interest groups, think tanks, and administrative agencies.

★ Education, health and human services, and transportation are the major services that state government offers, together constituting more than four-fifths of the total cost of Texas's state government. These services have a significant effect on the way Texans live and even on the way they think. It is nearly impossible to evaluate them objectively because they affect different groups so differently.

★ The educational system of Texas is generally decentralized and independent of the normal course of partisan politics. Its administrators and curricula are conservative, as is much of Texas politics.

★ Health care services are both publicly and privately financed in Texas, as in the rest of the nation, and they are plagued by a similar problem: the rising costs of providing better services to more people. A smaller proportion of residents are insured to cover these costs in Texas than in any other state, but national health care reform is set to dramatically expand private health insurance in Texas.

★ Income support for the poor (such as Temporary Aid to Needy Families) is not a major state priority and it is not designed to eliminate the root causes of poverty.

★ Financed largely by motor fuels taxes and federal funds, the cost of maintaining the extensive highway system is growing faster than revenues. Construction of new highways to relieve traffic congestion has become problematic as the state seeks alternative funding sources such as use tolls. Facing budget limits, it is unlikely that TxDOT will substantially increase funding for local mass transportation authorities.

★ Individual and group positions on these and virtually all public policies differ according to who benefits and who pays the cost for which public services. The process of allocating costs and benefits is the very essence of politics.

HOW TEXAS COMPARES

★ Texans pay a smaller percentage of their incomes in state and local taxes than in most states.

★ Only Nevada relies more heavily on sales taxes than Texas. Because Texas local governments also rely on regressive taxes, Texas state and local taxes weigh more heavily on poor and middle-income families than most states. As one of only five states with neither progressive personal nor corporate income taxes, Texas has no progressive tax resources.

★ Although the governor has the line-item veto on appropriations, like 42 other governors, that power generally shows little effect in reducing wasteful state spending or earmarks for special legislative projects.

★ Fewer employers provide health insurance than in most other states, and as a result, a smaller proportion of Texans are insured to cover increasing health care costs than the residents of any other state. More Texans are likely to benefit from health care reform, but because of their individualistic culture, they are more likely to resent federal mandates than residents of most states.

★ Compared with other states, per capita expenditures for education are below average. Per student expenditures, like teacher salaries, are also considerably below average. College faculty salaries, income support for the poor, health care, investment in mass transit, and spending for virtually every public service lag behind much of the rest of the nation.

★ Although it would be tempting to attribute the Texas low-tax, limited public service environment to a basic distrust of government, some of its other public policies indicate a considerable willingness to use the power of government to control the population. More than most states, Texas limits same-sex relationships, implements the death penalty, restricts abortion, controls illegal drug use, and incarcerates a larger percentage of its population. Texas's unwillingness to use the power of government is primarily a reluctance to tax, spend, and regulate business. Texas's political culture is supportive of government power to enforce traditional values but skeptical of government intervention in the economy. In short, Texas's public policies support economic individualism and social conservatism more than most states.

KEY TERMS

ability-to-pay taxes, *p. 329*
accountability, *p. 338*
ad valorem tax, *p. 327*
affirmative action, *p. 348*
appropriations, *p. 334*
benefits-received tax, *p. 328*
broad-based tax, *p. 328*
Children's Health Insurance
   Program (CHIP),
   p. 352
community college approach,
   p. 347

declining marginal propensity
   to consume, *p. 331*
general-obligation bonds,
   p. 334
general sales tax, *p. 326*
gross-receipts tax, *p. 327*
guaranteed-issue requirement,
   p. 354
Health Care Reform (HCR),
   p. 354
hidden taxes, *p. 326*
income redistribution, *p. 356*

individual mandate, *p. 355*
logrolling, *p. 335*
mass transit, *p. 360*
means test, *p. 357*
Medicaid, *p. 352*
Medicare, *p. 352*
personal property, *p. 327*
progressive tax rates, *p. 329*
real property, *p. 327*
regressive tax rates, *p. 330*
regulatory tax, *p. 328*
revenue bonds, *p. 334*

school finance reform, *p. 344*
selective sales (excise) tax,
   p. 326
severance tax, *p. 327*
social insurance, *p. 357*
socialized medicine, *p. 352*
supply-side economics, *p. 334*
tax base, *p. 327*
tax rate, *p. 327*
tax shifting, *p. 331*
unemployment insurance,
   p. 356

REVIEW QUESTIONS

1. Describe the major types of taxes imposed by state and local governments. How does Texas compare with other states?

2. What are the advantages and disadvantages of regulatory taxes? Of taxes based on the benefits-received principle? Of taxes based on the ability-to-pay principle?

3. Define *progressive* and *regressive* tax rates. What are the arguments for and against each type? Which social groups benefit from each type?

4. Describe the functions of state and local institutions in governing Texas public elementary and secondary schools. What are the major issues that these institutions face?

5. Explain why health care is the state's second-largest expenditure. How will national health care reform affect Texas? Why are social service programs controversial?

6. Describe the state's role in providing transportation. What major political controversies have developed in planning for future transportation development?

LOGGING ON

Check out your family's tax burden compared with other Texas families in *Exemptions and Tax Incidence, 2011*, available at the Texas Comptroller of Public Accounts website, **www.window .state.tx.us**.

The Texas Education Agency is the key site for public education at **www.tea.state.tx.us**. Go to **www.capitol.state .tx.us**. Click on Statutes and then on Education Code. Scroll to Chapters 41, 42, and 43 to examine the complex funding of Texas public schools. The best national source of information about educational achievement is the National Center for Education Statistics at **http://nces.ed.gov/**.

Investigate the conservative argument that an excess of demand for higher education in America is driving its costs higher than its actual value and a bubble similar to the housing bubble is developing in higher education. See *The Economist* **www.economist.com/blogs/schumpeter/2011/04/ higher_education** and **http://techcrunch.com/2011/04/10/ peter-thiel-were-in-a-bubble-and-its-not-the-internet-its-higher-education/** and compare these arguments with those at *The Stanford Daily* at **www.stanforddaily.com/2011/05/16/ editorial-higher-education-is-not-a-bubble/**.

Get the facts on health care in Texas and the rest of the nation at the Kaiser Family Foundation website at **www .statehealthfacts.org/**. See how Texas compares in access to health professionals and how its people finance their health insurance.

Compare public policy developments in the 50 states at the Pew Center on the States website at **www.pewstates.org/ projects/stateline**. Special interest groups have very different views of public services—sample the conservative views of the American Legislative Council (ALEC) at **www.alec.org/** and the liberal views at the Texas Freedom Network site, **www .tfn.org**, or the Texas Public Interest Research group at **www .texpirg.org/**.

Use the Legislative Budget Board website at **www.lbb.state .tx.us** to learn about the financing of state services. At the Legislative Budget Board site, read the full text of the state appropriations bill (H.B. 1) and *Fiscal Size-Up for 2012–2013 Biennium*.

Find services and assistance at the Health and Human Services Commission website, **www.hhsc.state.tx.us**. Go to the Texas Workforce Commission site at **www.twc.state.tx.us/** for information on unemployment benefits or to apply for a job.

Chapter 14

Local Government

LEARNING OBJECTIVES

★ Demonstrate an understanding of the structure and functions of local political systems and their relationship with the state and federal governments.

★ Contrast the types of services provided by general-purpose governments and special districts.

★ Explain the structural and organizational differences between general-law and home-rule cities.

★ Assess the advantages and disadvantages of different forms of local government.

★ Assess the advantages and disadvantages of different local election systems.

★ Compare the different revenue sources used by local governments.

GET Active

Apply for membership on a city advisory board or commission. Go to your city's official website and check out the many boards and commissions that offer you the chance to advise the city council and city officials on matters of critical importance to your community, such as health, education, transportation, housing, and ethics.

Participate in a local campaign. Candidates often need volunteers to help organize campaign rallies and get-out-the-vote drives, stuff envelopes with campaign literature for mail-outs, work phone banks, and pass out campaign literature. You will find the names of city council candidates listed on the election ballot at the official websites of Texas cities. For county elections, you will find the candidates listed on the ballot by going to the official websites of county governments.

Attend a city council meeting or a county commissioners court meeting. Sign up to speak during the time of the meeting set aside for public comments. Let city or county officials know what improvements you think could be made in your community.

You can find a list of Texas cities and counties at Texas.gov, which is the official website of the State of Texas, **www.texas.gov/**.

General-purpose government

A municipal or county government that provides a wide range of public services. Compare *special district*.

Special district

A limited-purpose local government that provides a narrow range of services not provided by general-purpose local governments such as cities or counties. Examples of special districts include municipal utility districts, hospital authorities, and transit authorities.

Should a city place red-light cameras at high-traffic intersections? Or pass anti-loitering laws to curb the presence of the homeless? Or make it a crime for landlords to rent to undocumented immigrants? How should counties provide for mentally ill prisoners or fund the burial of indigents with no known next of kin? These issues are just a few that have been placed on the agendas of local governments throughout the nation, including Texas.

These are only some of the challenges to local officials that can generate controversies in their communities. Many issues that are nationwide in scope, such as reducing traffic fatalities, homelessness, immigration, mental health, and poverty, also have an important local dimension. Local governments, themselves, are primarily responsible for law enforcement, mass transit, sewage treatment, flood control, and emergency services.

The sheer number of local governments across Texas and the rest of the nation can challenge even the most interested members of a community who want to contact local officials occasionally or on a routine basis about pressing concerns ranging from potholes to the need for better street lighting and more police to the increase in the number of homeless families. (See Table 14.1 for a comparison of local governments in Texas and in the United States as a whole.) Anyone who lives in a metropolitan area is likely to be governed by two **general-purpose governments**, municipal and county governments, in addition to numerous **special districts** such as school districts, hospital districts, metropolitan transit authorities, and municipal utility districts.

According to the Pew Research Center, the American public has a more positive view of local governments than of the national and state governments.[1] Also, over

---

[1]"61% - Americans' View of Local Government More Favorably than Washington," Pew Research Center, April 2012, http://pewresearch.org/databank/dailynumber/?NumberID=1492.

TABLE 14.1 Local Governments and Public School Systems, United States and Texas, 2012

	Total	County	Municipal	Town or Township	Special Districts	School Districts
United States	89,004	3,031	19,522	16,364	37,203	13,884
Texas	4,856	254	1,214	0	2,309	1,079

Source: U.S. Census Bureau, 2012 Census of Governments, http://www2.census.gov/govs/cog/2012/formatted_prelim_counts_23jul2012_2.pdf.

70 percent of the public "… follow local news closely."[2] However, while information about local governments is available in a variety of print and electronic media, adequately covering thousands of local governments is no small challenge. Political scientist Doris A. Graber has observed that when it comes to local media, "Reporting, of necessity, becomes highly selective and superficial."[3]

Nor can the public depend on local political parties to provide information and generate interest about all local governments. In Texas, political parties do not nominate candidates below the county level. Municipal and special-district elections are nonpartisan—that is, no mention of party affiliation is on the ballot. It is not surprising that in the absence of party labels, voter turnout tends to be low in municipal and special-district elections.

In an effort to shed more light on the inner workings of local government, we examine in the following sections the various institutional features of cities, counties, and special districts. We also look at issues and trends facing local government. Finally, given the growing interest in finding regional solutions to local problems, we discuss the role of councils of government (COGs) at the local level.

MUNICIPALITIES

How are municipalities relevant to our lives? Cities hire police and firefighters to protect the community. Cities enforce building and safety codes, pass anti-litter ordinances, issue garage sale permits, maintain recycling programs, launch anti-graffiti programs, impound stray animals for the safety of the community, and enforce curfews. These are just a few examples of how cities routinely affect our day-to-day lives.

Did You Know? Texas has more than 4,800 local governments, most of them governed by officials who are elected by voters.

AP Photo/Rex C. Curry

The city of Farmers Branch passed a ban on the rental of apartments to illegal immigrants in 2007, but the Fifth Circuit Court of Appeals later overturned the ban on grounds the regulation of immigration is an exclusive function of the national government.[4]

Should local governments take actions to crack down on illegal immigration? Or is immigration enforcement a responsibility of the federal government?

[2]"72% of Americans Follow Local News Closely," The Pew Research Center's Internet and American Life Project Local News Survey, January 2011, http://pewresearch.org/pubs/2238/local-news-enthusiasts-newspaper-television-internet-communities.

[3]Doris A. Graber, *Mass Media and American Politics*, 8th ed. (Washington, DC: CQ Press, 2010), p. 267.

[4]*Villas at Parkside Partners, et al.* v. *City of Farmers Branch, Texas* (2012).

Cities also become involved in high-profile, controversial issues. For example, in 2012, the Fifth Circuit Court of Appeals struck down an ordinance passed in a Dallas suburb, Farmers Branch, that banned the rental of apartments to illegal immigrants. In 2010, a controversial state law was passed in Arizona requiring police officers who stop individuals for lawful reasons to check their immigration status if they suspect they are in the country illegally; the law was amended to ban racial profiling in its enforcement. In reaction to the Arizona law, the Austin City Council passed a resolution banning (with some exceptions) city employee trips to Arizona and official business dealings with the state.

All local governments are bound by federal and state laws as well as the United States and Texas Constitutions. The relationship between states and local governments follows from the fact that states, including Texas, have a *unitary system of government* (see Chapter 2). Municipalities—like counties, special districts, and school districts—are creatures of the state and have only as much power as the Texas Constitution and Texas legislature grant them. Texas has seen a marked increase in the number of municipalities in the state since the 1950s (see Table 14.2).

General-Law and Home-Rule Cities

General-law city
A city with a population of 5,000 or fewer whose structure and organization are prescribed and limited by state law.

Home-rule city
A city with a population greater than 5,000 that has exercised its legal option to write its own charter using any organizational structure that complies with state law.

Charter
The organizing document for a corporation or a municipality.

Texas cities are classified as either general-law or home-rule cities. A **general-law city** is an incorporated community with a population of 5,000 or fewer and is limited in the subject matter upon which it may legislate. A city with a population of more than 5,000 may, by majority vote, become a **home-rule city**. This means that it can adopt its own **charter** and structure its local government as it sees fit as long as charter provisions and local laws (also called ordinances) do not violate national and state constitutions and laws.

The Texas Constitution allows a home-rule city whose population has dropped to 5,000 or fewer to retain its home-rule designation. According to the Texas Municipal League, the vast majority of Texas cities—about 75 percent—are general-law cities.

Direct Democracy at the Municipal Level
Home rule permits local voters to impose their will directly on government through initiative, referendum, and recall, and most home-rule cities have all three provisions. With the initiative power, after the people obtain a designated percentage of signatures of registered voters, they can force a sometimes-reluctant city council to place a proposed ordinance on the ballot. If the proposal passes by a majority vote, it becomes law. Texas cities have used initiatives to resolve the following issues by popular vote:

★ Should a city allow stores within the city limits to sell beer and wine?
★ Should a city freeze the property tax exemption for senior citizens and people with disabilities?
★ Should a city increase the minimum wage?
★ Should a city impose a cap on the property tax rate?

TABLE 14.2 Municipal Governments in Texas, 1952–2012

1952	1962	1972	1982	1992	2002	2007	2012
738	866	981	1,121	1,171	1,196	1,209	1,214

Sources: U.S. Census Bureau, *2002 Census of Governments, Volume 1, Number 1, Government Organization*, GC02(1)-1 (Washington, DC: U.S. Government Printing Office, 2002), http://www.census.gov/prod/2003pubs/gc021x1.pdf; 2007 Census of Governments, www.census.gov/govs/cog/GovOrgTab03ss.html; 2012 Census of Governments, http://www2.census.gov/govs/cog/2012/formatted_prelim_counts_23jul2012_2.pdf.

As general-purpose governments, municipal governments provide a variety of services that are critically important to the well-being of communities.

▲ **As mayors and city councils attempt to prioritize the needs of their communities, what factors should they take into consideration?**

HOW DOES TEXAS COMPARE?
Cities and Red-Light Cameras

States have approached the use of red-light cameras in a variety of ways. The National Conference of State Legislatures reports that while some states, including Texas, permit the local adoption of red-light cameras throughout the state, others allow adoption in only select communities. Also, some states have banned the use of red-light cameras or have no policy at all on their use. According to the Insurance Institute for Highway Safety, by May 2012, red-light cameras were used in approximately 552 U.S. communities in 24 states (including Texas) and the District of Columbia.

FOR DEBATE

1. What measures should be taken to ensure that red-light cameras are used effectively?

2. How does the use of red-light cameras compare to other measures used to deter traffic accidents such as banning the use of cell phones in school zones?

Source: Insurance Institute for Highway Safety, Automated Enforcement Laws, June 2012, www.iihs.org/laws/automated_ enforcement.aspx.

Voters who want to repeal an existing ordinance can also petition the council to hold a referendum election to determine whether the law should remain in effect. For example, College Station and Houston voters approved referenda to remove red-light cameras. Smoking bans were put to a referendum vote in Lubbock and Baytown. In both cases, voters decided to retain the ban. A referendum election called by a city council can also permit voters to determine whether a law will go into effect. Finally, voters can, by petition, force the council to hold a **recall election** that would permit voters to remove the mayor or a member of the council.

The Limits of Home Rule Although home-rule cities have wider latitude than general-law cities in their day-to-day operations, they must still contend with state limitations on their authority. For example, state law determines the specific dates on which municipal elections can be held. Voters are free to amend city charters, but the Texas Constitution permits cities to hold charter elections only every two years. An election establishing a metropolitan transit authority can be held only in cities that meet a population requirement determined by the Texas legislature. Local governments in Texas are subject to "sunshine" laws such as the Public Information Act and the Open Meetings Act. Because Texas is covered under the "preclearance" requirement of the federal Voting Rights Act, all state and local election law changes must first be approved by the U.S. Justice Department or a federal district court in Washington, DC.

Forms of Government

The three common forms of municipal governments are council-manager, mayor-council, and commission.

Council-Manager System In a **council-manager form of government** (see Figure 14.1), an elected city council makes laws and hires a professional administrator who

Recall election

An election, called by citizen petition, that permits voters to remove an elected official before the official's term expires.

Council-manager form of government

A form of government that features an elected city council and a city manager who is hired by the council. The council makes policy decisions, and the city manager is responsible for the day-to-day operations of the city government.

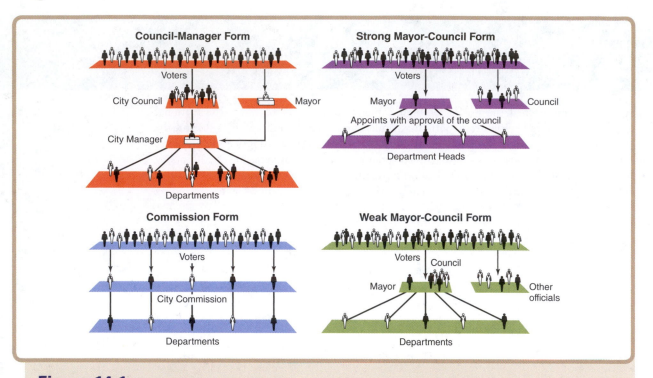

Figure 14-1

Common Forms of Municipal Government

This figure shows the four major forms of city government. Although voters are the ultimate authority in each type, scholars argue that some types are more efficient and responsive to residents' needs.

What measures can the public take to make their views known to city officials in a way that makes city hall more accountable to the people?

is responsible for both executing council policies and managing the day-to-day operations of city government and who serves at the pleasure of the council.

The powers of the city manager come from the city charter and from the delegation of authority by the council through direct assignment and passage of ordinances. For example, the city manager is responsible for selecting key personnel and for submitting a proposed budget to the council for its approval. The city council will likely seek the manager's opinion on a wide variety of matters, including what tax rate the city should adopt, whether or not the city should call a bond election, and the feasibility of recommendations made by interest groups. But these issues are ultimately up to the council, and the city manager is expected to implement whatever decisions the council makes.

In a council-manager form of government, the mayor may be either selected by the council from among its members or independently elected by the voters. The mayor presides over council meetings, has limited or no veto power, and has for the most part only the same legislative authority as members of the council. The mayor also has important ceremonial powers, such as signing proclamations and issuing keys to the city to important dignitaries. Although the office is institutionally weak, a high-profile mayor can wield considerable political influence. Mayors of the two largest Texas cities using the council-manager system, former San Antonio mayor Henry Cisneros and former Dallas mayor Ron Kirk, went on to be appointed as major federal officials.

Council-manager government was initiated as part of a reform movement during the Progressive Era (1900–1917). Reformers were attempting to substitute "efficient and businesslike management" for the then-prevalent system of boss rule, in which politics was the key consideration in city hall decisions. Although the council-manager system is seen as a means of separating politics from the administration of city government, critics charge that its principal shortcoming is that the voters do not directly elect the chief executive officer of the city.

Mayor-Council System

Although most Texas cities now use a council-manager system, a few, including Houston and Pasadena, still use a **mayor-council system** to govern their cities. The mayor-council system has many variations from one city to the next, but they are generally classified according to the relative power of their mayors.

The Strong-Mayor Form In the **strong-mayor form of government** (see Figure 14.1), the mayor, who is chosen in a citywide election, is both the chief executive and the leader of the city council. The mayor makes appointments, prepares the budget, and is responsible for the management of city government. The mayor also sets the council agenda, proposes policy, and in many cities may veto council actions.

Critics of the strong-mayor system fear that the office is too powerful and may become too politicized to distribute services fairly or efficiently. This system conjures up the image of nineteenth-century urban political party machines led by mayors who appointed political cronies as department heads, hired campaign workers as city employees, and awarded contracts to supporters.

Although the target of criticism of early twentieth-century reformers, the strong-mayor form of government did not die out but was often restructured to include an elected city comptroller (or controller) to separate the mayor from the city treasurer. (Houston, for example, elects a city controller who serves as the chief financial officer for the city.) Rules were also adopted to require that contracts be awarded to the lowest and best bidder. Other restrictions in place today that political bosses did not have to contend with include nonpartisan elections, ethics, and campaign finance laws.

The Weak-Mayor Form The **weak-mayor form of government** (see Figure 14.1) lacks unified lines of authority because the mayor and council share administrative authority. Power is, in effect, decentralized. However, it is difficult for voters to know which officials to hold accountable when problems and mismanagement occur. This type of government is usually found in small cities and is not common in Texas.

Commission System

The **commission form of government** (see Figure 14.1) is another approach to municipal government. Here, voters elect one set of officials who act as both executives and legislators. The commissioners, sitting together, are the municipal legislature, but individually each administers a city department. A manager or administrative assistant may be employed to assist the commissioners, but ultimate administrative authority still remains with the elected commissioners.

Commissioners may possess technical knowledge about city government because they supervise city departments. However, because power in the city bureaucracy is fragmented among separately elected commissioners, coordination is difficult, and the check-and-balance system is impaired because commissioners serve both legislative and executive functions—commissioners adopt the budget for the departments that they administer.

Mayor-council system

A form of municipal government consisting of a mayor and a city council; this form includes both *strong-mayor* and *weak-mayor* variations.

Strong-mayor form of government

A form of municipal government in which substantial authority over appointments and budgets is lodged in the mayor's office. The mayor is elected by voters in a citywide election.

Weak-mayor form of government

A form of municipal government in which an elected mayor and city council share administrative responsibilities, often with other elected officers.

Commission form of government

A municipal government in which individual members of the commission head city departments and collectively act as a city council to pass ordinances.

AP Photo/David J. Phillip

Houston has a strong mayor-council form of government, which gives the mayor substantial authority when it comes to setting the council agenda and proposing the budget.

How do the priorities of big-city mayors differ from those set by mayors of smaller communities? What challenges do all mayors face regardless of the size of their cities? What are key leadership traits that every mayor should have?

According to the International City/County Management Association, over 90 percent of U.S. cities with a population of 2,500 or more use either the mayor-council or city-manager form of government. Also, between 1984 and 2012, the adoption of the city-manager system steadily increased, while use of the mayor-council form declined.

Municipal Election Systems

Mayors and city council members are usually elected for terms according to their city charter, usually two years. Scheduled at a different time from the state general election, municipal elections usually require that candidates receive a majority of the vote, and a runoff election may be required if no candidate receives more than 50 percent of the vote.

Nonpartisan Elections
In Texas, all city elections are *nonpartisan,* meaning that parties do not nominate candidates or officially campaign for them. Advocates of nonpartisan elections contend that municipal issues transcend traditional party divisions and that party labels are irrelevant. They argue that the two parties are overly polarized and that qualified candidates should not be excluded simply because they belong to the minority party.

Several other states use partisan elections to select city officials. Supporters of partisan elections argue that party labels provide voters with useful cues as to how a candidate will govern; in nonpartisan elections, voters often take their cues from well-financed campaigns. Parties are useful because they help winnow the field of potential candidates; dozens of candidates sometimes clutter Texas municipal election ballots. Parties mobilize more voters and generate greater public interest than do nonpartisan campaigns. Critics of nonpartisan elections argue that they are dominated by low-visibility special interests with much to gain from city contracts and with enough money to hire campaign workers and to flood the airwaves with campaign ads.

While all municipal elections are nonpartisan in Texas, cities have the choice to use at-large and single-member district systems—a choice that has generated considerable legal and political controversy.

At-Large Systems versus Single-Member District Systems
At-large elections, which are citywide elections, usually take two forms. In the **pure at-large system**, all of the voters elect all the members of the city council. The voters simply choose from a common pool of all the candidates to fill the available council seats, with the winning candidates being those who receive the most votes. For example, if 20 candidates run for six seats, the six candidates getting the most votes are elected.

In the **at-large place system**, each candidate runs for a specific seat on the council and voters cast one vote for each seat or place. For example, on a seven-member city council, the ballot would show perhaps several candidates running for place 1, different candidates running for place 2, and still others running for each place down through place 7. Voters would be able to cast one vote for each of the seven seats, and the candidate winning the majority of votes cast citywide would win each particular seat. Variations of either system may require a specific candidate to live in a particular district of the city, but the candidates are still elected by all the voters in the city. In contrast, in a system with **single-member districts**, each council member is elected from a particular geographical district by only the voters who live in that district.

Supporters of at-large elections say that they promote the public interest because council members must take a citywide view of problems. They charge that council members elected from districts are focused on the needs of their district rather than the interests of the community as a whole. Opponents of single-member districts also claim that the election of individuals who have an outlook limited to their district makes it difficult for the council to build a consensus about the future of the city.

At-large city elections

Citywide elections. In many cities, some or all of the city council members are elected by voters of the entire municipality rather than from neighborhood districts.

Pure at-large system

An electoral system in which candidates for city council run citywide and the top vote getters are elected to fill the number of open seats. Contrast this system with an *at-large place system.*

At-large place system

An electoral system in which candidates run citywide for a *particular* seat on the city council.

Single-member districts

Election districts in which one candidate is elected to a legislative body. In city council elections, single-member districts are contrasted with at-large citywide elections. Members from single-member districts tend to feel greater loyalty to the residents of their own neighborhoods because they are not elected citywide.

Critics of at-large elections maintain that the system allows a simple majority of voters to elect all council members and that, consequently, the interests of racial, ethnic, and ideological minorities in the community are not represented at city hall. Supporters of single-member districts argue that effective neighborhood representation reflects the diverse interests of the city; neighborhoods where political, cultural, and ethnic minorities live have a chance to elect at least some members to the city council when a district system is used.

Although major Texas cities usually resisted single-member districts, civil rights organizations such as the Mexican American Legal Defense and Educational Fund, the League of United Latin American Citizens, the American GI Forum, the National Association for the Advancement of Colored People, Texas Rural Legal Aid, and the Southwest Voter Registration Education Project brought successful legal action, and the federal courts forced several of them to abandon at-large elections. Several cities have instituted a mixed system in which a majority of the council members are elected from single-member districts, although the mayor and some of the council members are elected at large.

Cumulative Voting Although the single-member district election system has served as the primary means of increasing minority representation on city councils, attention has also been drawn to other ways of achieving this goal. One alternative system is **cumulative voting**. Under this plan, members of city councils are elected in at-large elections, and the number of votes a voter can cast corresponds to the number of seats on the council. If, for example, the city council has five seats, a voter can cast all five votes for a single candidate. Or a voter can cast three votes for one candidate and the remaining two votes for another candidate. In other words, voters can distribute their votes among the candidates in whatever way they choose.

Cumulative voting
An at-large election system that permits voters to cast one or more votes for a single candidate. For example, if a voter can cast up to five votes in a city council election, all five votes could be cast for one candidate or spread among several candidates.

HOW DOES TEXAS COMPARE?
Public Financing and Municipal Elections

According to the Center for Governmental Studies, local jurisdictions that provide public financing for candidates running for public office are found in nine states, including Texas. Supporters of public financing maintain that it will reduce the overall campaign spending and level the playing field among candidates so that campaign contributions are less important in deciding the election outcome. Opponents maintain that public funding requirements overly restrict individual and group contributions, hinder a candidate's ability to campaign effectively, and limit freedom of expression.

The following jurisdictions have publicly financed campaigns:

Albuquerque, NM	Austin, TX	Miami-Dade County, FL
Long Beach, CA	Los Angeles, CA	Oakland, CA
New Haven, CT	New York, NY	Sacramento, CA
Portland, OR	Richmond, CA	Tucson, AZ
San Francisco, CA	Boulder, CO	

Although most of the jurisdictions use public financing for city council and mayoral elections, some also allow it for other city and county elective offices. Eligibility requirements vary. In Austin, funding is disbursed only in runoff elections.

Source: "Mapping Public Financing in American Elections," Jessica A. Levinson, Center for Governmental Studies, November 2009, http://policyarchive.org/handle/10207/bitstreams/95926.pdf.

According to the organization FairVote, more than 50 local jurisdictions in Texas have adopted cumulative voting since the 1990s, most of them school districts. In approximately 20 percent of the communities in which cumulative voting is used, the method has been adopted by both the school board and the city council. Civil rights organizations such as the National Association for the Advancement of Colored People and the Mexican American Legal Defense and Educational Fund have backed cumulative voting in litigation, and the adoption of this election system is credited with leading to the election of minorities in two Texas independent school districts—Atlanta ISD and Amarillo ISD. The Amarillo Independent School District is the largest jurisdiction in the country to use this election system.

Term limits

Restrictions on the number of times that a politician can be reelected to an office or the number of years that a person may hold a particular office.

Term Limits About 60 Texas cities joined the movement to limit the number of times a municipal official can be reelected. Proponents of **term limits** believe that city hall is best governed by new blood and fresh ideas and that limiting the number of terms for council members is the best way to achieve that goal. Opponents, though, worry that cities stand to lose experienced, effective council members.

These term-limit laws are not uniform. Corpus Christi, for example, allows a person who has held a seat for four consecutive two-year terms to run again for the seat after sitting out one term. In Austin, a council member is limited to two consecutive three-year terms, but that limit can be waived upon petition by 5 percent of the registered voters the council member represents. In Dallas, city council members are subject to term limits, but the mayor is not.

Attempts to weaken city term-limit laws by state law or by litigation have had mixed success. In 2000, voters in Austin rejected a proposition that would have repealed the city's term-limit law. However, in 2008, a proposal to extend the term limit to four two-year terms passed in San Antonio.

Revenue Sources and Limitations

The local political culture determines expectations about appropriate standards of services and tolerable levels of taxation. External forces—such as a downturn in the national economy, the closing of a military base, the downsizing of industries, federal and state mandates, and natural disasters—also influence the economic climate of a community.

The sources and amount of revenue used to meet a city's budgetary obligations vary greatly among Texas municipalities according to various factors, including the following:

★ The size of the city's population
★ The amount and type of taxes a city is allowed and willing to levy
★ The total assessed value of taxable property within the city limits
★ The needs of the residents

City revenues can also depend on how much aid money is available from the state and national governments. Our Insiders feature shows that some cities, as well as some counties, use aggressive lobbying efforts to protect this intergovernmental revenue.

Texas INSIDERS

Texas Cities and Counties Hire Lobbyists to Promote Local Interests

City councils and county commissioners courts are routinely lobbied by business groups, taxpayers associations, minority groups, and environmental organizations that want to influence local policies. Local officials, themselves, also lobby by making personal appeals to their state legislatures and Congress for local-friendly laws and more revenue for their communities.

Organizations such as the National Conference of Mayors and the National Association of Counties, along with state municipal and county associations, make their case to national and state lawmakers about the challenges facing local governments. Individual cities and counties send local delegations consisting of elected officials and community leaders to state capitals and Washington, DC. to meet directly with their representatives.

Another type of local government lobbying has raised some eyebrows. In an attempt to gain an inside track with state legislatures and Congress, some cities and counties hire lobbyists to promote their interests in funding for airports, roads, fire and police departments, or other special projects funded by earmarks. Texas cities and counties paid lobbyists $17 million to speak on their behalf in the nation's capital between 2006 and 2010. Harris County, along with the cities of Houston, Dallas, San Antonio, and Carrollton spent the most

lobbying Congress, according to reports required by the U.S. Senate Lobbying Disclosure Act.

Critics charge that local government advocacy is a responsibility best met by local elected officials and their staffs rather than lobbyists-for-hire. They also contend that taxpayers should not have to foot the bill for lobbyists. Instead, this money would be better spent on services and projects, *especially* when local governments face financial shortfalls. On the other hand, defenders of this practice argue that local governments need additional leverage when it comes to combating unfunded mandates and that lobbyists are needed to help secure funds from state lawmakers and Congress *especially* when a community is in economic distress.

Thinking about the role of elites in Texas politics Not all local governments have the revenue to hire lobbyists. Do local governments' lobbying efforts make state legislatures and Congress more aware of the general needs of all local governments? Or do cities with big lobbying budgets get a disproportionate share of state and federal funding?

Sources: "Let's stop cities from using tax money to seek more tax money," Chuck DeVore, *Houston Chronicle*, May 25, 2012, www .chron.com/default/article/Let-s-stop-cities-from-using-tax-money-to-seek-3586514.php; "Cities, Counties Spend Millions to Lobby in D.C.," Tristan Hallman, *The Texas Tribune*, November 11, 2010, www.texastribune.org/texas-lobbying/lobby-and-lobbyists/cities-counties-spend-millions-to-lobby-in-dc/; "Mandate fears," Gary Halter, *Houston Chronicle*, May 31, 2012, www.chron.com/opinion/letters/article/Letters-A-case-for-city-lobbyists-3600555.php; "States and Municipalities Aggressively Lobby Federal Government for Scarce Aid, Dave Levinthal, The Center for Responsive Government," September 3, 2009, www.opensecrets.org/news/2009/09/state-and-municipal-politicos.html.

Sales Taxes Texas cities are heavily dependent on the sales tax. Although all taxes are affected by economic conditions, sales tax revenue is more sensitive to economic fluctuations than property taxes. And because budgetary problems make state and national government assistance unreliable, cities need to build into their budgets a reserve fund to compensate for these somewhat-inconsistent sources of revenue.

Property Taxes Municipalities (as well as school districts and counties) are heavily dependent on ad valorem property taxes, in which the tax rate is a percentage of the assessed value of real estate (see Table 14.3). In a community with a low tax base, or total assessed value, the local government has a limited capacity to raise taxes from this source. Thus a "poor" city must set a very high tax rate to provide adequate services. Furthermore, any loss in property values causes a decline in the city's tax base.

Texas has established a countywide appraisal authority for property taxes, and all local governments must accept its property appraisals. However, Texas state law does not require full disclosure of the sales price of residential and commercial property, making it difficult to accurately appraise property values.

The property tax rate of general-law cities depends on the size of the city, but the maximum property tax rate of a general-law city is $1.50 per $100 of the assessed value of a city's property. Home-rule municipalities can set property tax rates as high as $2.50 per $100 of assessed value.

Limits on Property Taxes Some Texas cities have taken measures to limit increases in property taxes. For example, Corpus Christi's city charter sets a property tax cap of $0.68 per $100 valuation except for taxes to finance voter-approved bonds. Texas cities, towns, counties, and junior college districts may freeze property taxes for the disabled and the elderly. Once the freeze is in place, the governing body cannot repeal it. Texas cities, as well as counties and hospital districts, may also call an election to lower property taxes by raising sales and use taxes.

Rollback Elections Voters in nonschool district jurisdictions (cities, counties, and special districts) may petition for a **rollback election** to limit an increase in the property tax rate to no more than 8 percent above that required for increased debt service. For school districts, an automatic rollback election is triggered if a school board raises taxes more than 6¢ per $100 valuation.

Rollback election

An election that permits the voters to decide if a property tax increase (of more than 8 percent) approved by a local government will remain in effect or be reduced to 8 percent.

TABLE 14.3 Property Taxes Levied by Texas Local Governments in 2009

Type of Local Government	Maximum Tax Rate (in Dollars $100 Valuation)	Amount Levied* (In Billions of Dollars)
Counties	0.80	$6.5
General-law cities	1.50 ⎫	6.6
Home-rule cities	2.50 ⎭	
Special districts	Varies according to law	5.1
School districts	**	21.8
Total		40.0

*The amounts levied are not necessarily the same as the amounts collected.
**The maximum school district property tax for construction and debt service is $0.50. The maximum rate for maintenance and operations is $1.00 and for enrichment is $0.17.

Source: Texas Comptroller of Public Accounts, Property Tax Assistance Division, *Annual Property Tax Report – Tax Year 2009*, January 2011, p. 2, www.window.state.tx.us/taxinfo/proptax/annual09/96-318-09.pdf.

The property tax is the principal source of revenue for local governments in Texas.

▲ **What are the advantages and disadvantages of the property tax as a major source of funding for local services? What other funding mechanisms can be used instead of the property tax?**

User Fees When residents are charged for the services they receive, the charges are called **user fees**. Such charges are increasingly popular because voters often oppose higher taxes and generally believe that people should pay for what they actually use. Cities may charge fees for city-provided electricity, water, sewage, and garbage collection as well as swimming pools, golf courses, and ambulance services. The Texas Municipal League has found that user fees bring in approximately 20 percent of municipal revenue. Permits, business licenses, and inspection fees round out the usual sources of city revenue.

Public Debt Local governments use **public debt** (normally bond issues that must be approved by the voters in a referendum) to fund infrastructure projects such as roads, buildings, and public facilities. Texas law explicitly limits the amount of long-term debt to a percentage of assessed valuation of property within the boundaries of the government. This restriction is intended to keep local governments from going bankrupt, as many did during the Great Depression of the 1930s.

Issues and Trends

Several trends and issues dominate city politics; understanding the dynamics of municipal policy making requires us to focus on population changes, economic development issues, federal and state mandates, and annexation issues.

Population Growth and Demographic Change A community's size as well as its growth rate impact local officials' public policy choices. Growing cities must expand services ranging from sewage treatment, street building, and law enforcement to urban planning, parks and recreation, and building convention centers. Even a city with limited growth may see an internal shift in population, with one area of the city facing dramatic growth, while other areas contend with a loss of population and businesses, vacant buildings, and urban decay. Communities with stagnant or declining populations also face the challenge of funding services from a declining economic base. Cities with increasingly diverse, elderly, or youthful populations may face competing demands from the public, which will necessitate hard choices, especially if local revenue is limited.

User fees
Fees paid by the individuals who receive a particular government service, such as sewage disposal or garbage collection.

Public debt
Money owed by government, ordinarily through the issuance of bonds. Local governments issue bonds to finance major projects with voter approval.

HOW DOES TEXAS COMPARE?
Population Changes in Large U.S. Cities

Texas population grew by 20.6 percent between the 2000 and 2010 censuses, adding over four million persons. While Texas added more people than any other state, most of this growth has been outside the city limits of the largest cities. Much of Texas's growth has been in suburban and exurban communities. Nevertheless, Texas has still has three of the ten largest cities in the United States.

The city centers continue to serve as the economic and cultural hub of most metropolitan communities across the nation. Central city governments must therefore provide several services on which the smaller surrounding communities depend. In metropolitan areas, central city governments finance most economic development activities such as building sports stadiums and convention centers, financing airports, funding tourism bureaus, and providing incentives to lure business into the area.

The Ten Largest U.S. Cities: The 2000 and 2010 Census

Rank	Place	State	2000 Census	2010 Census
1.	New York	New York	8,008,278	8,175,173
2.	Los Angeles	California	3,694,820	3,792,621
3.	Chicago	Illinois	2,896,016	2,695,598
4.	Houston	Texas	1,953,631	2,099,451
5.	Philadelphia	Pennsylvania	1,517,550	1,526,006
6.	Phoenix	Arizona	1,321,045	1,445,623
7.	San Antonio	Texas	1,144,646	1,327,407
8.	San Diego	California	1,223,400	1,307,402
9.	Dallas	Texas	1,188,580	1,197,816
10.	San Jose	California	894,943	945,942

Source: United States Census Bureau, *Cities with 100,000 or More Population in 2000 ranked by Population*, www.census.gov/statab/ccdb/cit1020r.txt, and *2010 Interactive Population Map*, http://2010.census.gov/2010census/popmap/.

FOR DEBATE

1. How can slower-growing central cities finance the costs of economic development projects that benefit the faster-growing areas that surround them?

2. What challenges do changing demographics present to large urban areas?

Economic Development

The Development Corporation Act allows many Texas cities, with voter approval, to adopt additional sales taxes for economic development projects. Voters have approved such development sales taxes in more than 500 cities for property tax relief and to finance a wide range of projects, including professional and amateur sports facilities, public park improvements, and affordable housing.

Government Mandates

Texas cities—like most cities in the nation—have seen both federal and state governments cut funding even as they have increased the number of mandates imposed on local governments. A **mandate** is a federal or state requirement that a lower level of government, like a city or county, provide a service or meet certain standards. The federal government has imposed many such mandates as a condition for state or local governments to receive grants-in-aid. Some notable examples of federal mandates are the Americans with Disabilities Act, the National Voter Registration Act (Motor Voter Act), the Help America Vote Act, and the No Child Left Behind Act (see Chapter 2). Likewise, the state has imposed innumerable mandates on school districts, counties, and cities.

Supporters of mandates argue that they permit the federal and state governments to meet important needs in a uniform fashion. Critics charge that mandates—particularly those that are unfunded—impose a heavy financial burden on the governments that are required to fulfill the obligations they impose.

The Unfunded Mandates Interagency Work Group, including the state auditor, comptroller, director of the Legislative Budget Board, a senator (selected by the lieutenant governor), and a representative (selected by the speaker), keep a record of unfunded mandates the legislature passes. Mandates exempt from the list include those passed by voters and those adopted to comply with the Texas Constitution, federal law, or a court order.

Mandate

A federal or state requirement that a lower level of government, like a city or county, provide a service or meet standards, often as a condition for receiving financial aid.

Annexation According to the Texas Municipal League, "The inherent power to unilaterally annex adjoining areas is one of the most important home-rule prerogatives."[5] Big cities in Texas have suffered less than many other U.S. cities from white flight, urban decay, the evacuation of industry, and declining tax bases; one reason they have escaped some of the worst of these problems is the state's broad **annexation** laws. The Municipal Annexation Act establishes a buffer area known as **extraterritorial jurisdiction (ETJ)** that extends one-half mile to five miles beyond the city's limits, depending on the city's population. The city may enforce zoning and building codes in the ETJ, and new cities may not be incorporated within the ETJ. The law also gives home-rule cities the power to annex as much as 10 percent of their existing area each year without the consent of the inhabitants of the area to be annexed.

With this protection and long-range planning, Texas cities can keep from being boxed in by suburban "bedroom" cities. Cities often use a strategy of spoke annexation to expand their ETJ into nearby areas and to prevent smaller communities from incorporating in those areas. They annex narrow "fingers" of land along highway right-of-ways outward from the existing city limits, thereby placing the area between the fingers into the ETJ. The unincorporated areas within the ETJ may then be annexed as they become sufficiently populated to warrant such action. Cities that plan ahead are therefore free to extend their boundaries and recapture both the tax base and the population that earlier fled the city center.

In recent years, some outlying areas have raised strong objections to the state's municipal annexation laws. Critics resent that their jurisdictions can be annexed without their permission. They fear higher taxes without comparable levels of services. In response to these criticisms, Texas's legislature passed a bill to require cities to give notice of annexation plans three years in advance, participate in arbitration with areas to be annexed, and deliver most city services within two and one-half years.

Usually cities have a powerful motivation to annex outlying areas to add to their tax base. However, they have resisted annexing **colonias**, impoverished unincorporated areas along the Texas–Mexico border with a multitude of problems, including substandard housing, unsanitary drinking water, and lack of proper sewage disposal, for which they may receive state assistance. The Texas Attorney General's Office has identified more than 1,800 colonias in 29 Texas counties, most of them along the U.S.–Mexico border. To encourage cities to assume responsibility for these areas, the state has given nearby cities incentives to annex them by allowing them to remain eligible for state aid for five years after they have been annexed.

Annexation
A policy that permits a city to bring unincorporated areas into the city's jurisdiction.

Extraterritorial jurisdiction (ETJ)
A buffer area that may extend beyond a city's limits. Cities can enforce some laws such as zoning and building codes in their ETJs.

Colonias
Severely impoverished unincorporated areas facing a variety of problems, including substandard housing, unsanitary drinking water, and lack of proper sewage disposal.

COUNTIES

County government provides a variety of services and makes public policies having widespread and direct impact on the public. The county commissioners court draws voting precinct boundaries and voting locations in each county. In most counties, the county clerk administers state elections, issues marriage licenses, and records birth and death certificates. The County Tax Office collects property taxes, issues license plates and stickers, and processes vehicle transfers. County Dispute Resolution Services help mediate conflicts between landlords and tenants. Sheriffs enforce state laws, and district or county attorneys prosecute most criminal violations. County and district courts try most civil and criminal cases.

The state constitution and the legislature established Texas counties to serve as a general-purpose government *and* as an administrative arm of the state, carrying out the state's laws and collecting certain state taxes. Although the county is an arm of the state, state supervision is minimal.

---

[5]Texas Municipal League, *Handbook for Mayors and Councilmembers* (Austin: Texas Municipal League, 2011), p. 12.

With 254 counties, Texas has more counties than any other state. County government is far less flexible than municipal government in its organization and functions. Texas counties do not have home rule and cannot pass ordinances unless the state legislature specifically authorizes them to do so. New statutes or constitutional amendments are often necessary to allow the county to deal with contemporary problems; many state laws apply to only one specific county's unique circumstances and do not grant flexibility to counties throughout the state. The needs of Harris County, for example, with a population of 4,092,459 in 2010, are significantly different from those of Loving County, which had only 82 inhabitants. Yet Texas law allows only modest variations to accommodate these differences.

For example, county property taxes are limited to a rate of 80 cents per $100 of assessed valuation unless voters approve additional taxes to cover long-term debt for infrastructure such as courthouses, criminal justice buildings, flood control, and county road or bridge maintenance.

Functions of Counties

County government
A general-purpose local government that also serves as an administrative arm of the state. Texas has 254 counties—more than any other state.

County government administers county, state, and national elections but not those for municipalities, school, and other special districts. County government acts for the state in securing right-of-ways for highways; law enforcement; registering births, deaths, and marriages; housing state district courts; registering motor vehicles; recording land titles and deeds; and collecting some state taxes and fees.

County government also has optional powers specifically authorized by state law. For example, the Local Government Code authorizes counties to establish and maintain libraries, operate and maintain parks, establish recreational or cultural facilities such as auditoriums or convention centers, appoint a county historical commission, and regulate sexually oriented businesses. County governments may also enter into agreements with another local government to provide a service or program such as purchasing and maintaining parks, museums, and historical sites. Counties may contract with other local governments to carry out administrative functions such as assessing and collecting taxes or managing records or to provide public services such as police and fire protection, streets and roads, public health and welfare, and waste disposal. The Health and Safety Code gives county governments the authority to maintain a county hospital.

Structure and Organization of Counties

Commissioners court
The policy-making body of a county, consisting of a county judge (the presiding officer of the court), who is elected in a countywide election to a four-year term, and four commissioners, who are elected from individual precincts to four-year terms.

County government consists of several independent officials, elected for four-year terms in the partisan general election at the same time state officials are elected (see Figure 14.2). The county governing body, the **commissioners court**, consists of the county judge and four county commissioners. It is not a judicial body; it is a legislature with limited authority to approve the budget for all county operations, set the tax rate, and pass ordinances on a narrow range of policies. The commissioners court does not have direct control over the many elected department heads in county government, but it wields considerable influence through its budgetary power. The sheriff, for example, is responsible to county voters for enforcing the law and maintaining order and security in the county jail, but the quality of law enforcement depends a great deal on county commissioners' decisions. The commissioners court must provide the funds to build the jail and approve its staff, authorize expenditures for each vehicle and its gas and repairs, and authorize deputies, clerks, and their salaries.

County judge
An official elected countywide to preside over the county commissioners court and to try certain minor cases.

The **county judge** is elected for a four-year term from the county at large to preside over the commissioners court. In addition, the county judge has administrative functions that include preparing a budget proposal (a responsibility the county judge shares with the county clerk or auditor in counties with fewer than 225,000 population); supervising election-related activities (such as calling elections, posting election notices, and receiving and canvassing

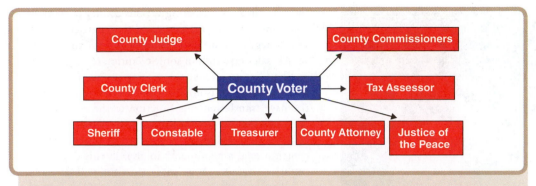

Figure 14.2
Texas County Officials Elected by Voters

Each of the 254 Texas counties has several officials, each of whom is independently elected in partisan elections.

Should counties have fewer elected offices and nonpartisan elections, as is the case with Texas municipalities? Or are the voters better served in terms of government accountability by the current county organizational structure?

of election results); conducting hearings for beer and wine permits; performing marriage ceremonies; conducting hearings on state hospital admittance for people with mental illness; and serving as the head of civil defense and disaster relief for the county. In addition, a county judge may have judicial authority in many of the smaller counties.

Four county commissioners comprise the remaining membership of the court and are elected to four-year terms. Commissioners are elected in single-member districts (or precincts, as they are called in Texas). In 1968, the U.S. Supreme Court ruled that commissioner districts must be roughly equal in population based on the one-person, one-vote principle.[6]

Commissioners are sometimes called "road commissioners" because they are responsible for the county roads and bridges within their precincts (unless a county engineer has been hired to do that job). Each is given a certain amount of money and has almost total authority to determine how it will be spent on roads and bridges. Residents of rural areas often consider building and maintaining roads to be the commissioners' primary responsibility.

Law enforcement officers are the county sheriff and constables. **Sheriffs**, next to the county judge, are usually the most powerful county officers because they have a relatively large budget and staff of deputies to assist them in enforcing state law throughout the county. In the corporate limits of cities, they usually refrain from patrolling to better use scarce resources and avoid jurisdictional disputes with the city police. The sheriff's department also operates the county jail and delivers and executes court papers (such as court orders).

Constables are elected from the same precincts as justices of the peace and serve as process officers of that court—they deliver summons and execute court orders. They are also general law enforcement officers. In some metropolitan counties, constables have added many deputies and have become important law enforcement agencies, but in others, the office is so unimportant that it has remained unfilled and some county commissioners have abolished the office altogether.

Financial officers of the county include the tax assessor-collector, the treasurer, and the auditor. The **tax assessor-collector** is probably the most important of these. The responsibilities of

Sheriff

The chief county law enforcement officer. Although the sheriff is an elected official in Texas, his or her budget must be approved by the commissioners court.

Constable

A county law enforcement official who is elected to serve as the process officer of justice of the peace courts and also has general law enforcement powers.

Tax assessor-collector

A county financial officer whose responsibilities include collecting various county taxes and fees and registering voters.

---

[6]*Avery* v. *Midland County*, 390 U.S. 474 (1968).

Courtesy of Sheriff Greg Hamilton, Travis County Sheriff's Office

The sheriff is usually the most powerful county officer, next to the county judge, because he or she has a relatively large budget and a staff of deputies to assist in enforcing state law throughout the county. But the sheriff's department budget must be approved by the commissioners court.

What should the commissioners court and the public study to determine if a sheriff's office is effectively meeting the county's law enforcement needs? How can voters hold county officials accountable when so many of them are elected to offices with divided and overlapping responsibilities?

County treasurer

In many counties, the official who is responsible for receiving, depositing, and disbursing funds.

County auditor

A financial officer whose duties may include reviewing county financial records and, in large counties, serving as chief budget officer.

County clerk

The chief record keeper and election officer of a county.

the office include collecting various county taxes and fees; collecting certain state taxes and fees, particularly motor vehicle registration fees (license plate fees) and the motor vehicle sales tax; and, in some counties, registering voters.

The **county treasurer** is responsible for receiving, depositing, and disbursing funds, although some counties have transferred this function to the county auditor. Although the treasurer holds a constitutional office, several counties have asked the legislature to propose statewide constitutional amendments to abolish this office in their counties. Because a general constitutional amendment to allow county voters to abolish the office is unlikely, elimination of this office is likely to proceed on a county-by-county basis.

The **county auditor** reviews all county financial records and ensures that expenditures are made in accordance with the law. Whereas other key county officials are elected, the county auditor is appointed to a two-year term by district judges.

Clerical officers in the county are the county and district clerks. The **county clerk** serves as the county's chief record keeper and election officer. In some ways, the office parallels that of the Texas secretary of state. The county clerk's duties include serving as clerk for the commissioners court; maintaining records for justices of the peace, county courts, and district courts in counties with a population of fewer than 8,000; recording deeds, mortgages, wills, and contracts; issuing marriage licenses and maintaining certain records of births and deaths; and serving on the county election board, certifying candidates running for county office, and carrying out other housekeeping functions related to, such as preserving the results of state, county, and special-district elections.

The **district clerk** in counties with a population of more than 8,000 assumes the county clerk's role as record keeper for the district courts, even as the county clerk continues to maintain records for the constitutional county court and any county courts-at-law.

Legal officers, known either as **county attorneys** or **district attorneys**, perform a variety of functions such as prosecuting all criminal cases, giving advisory opinions to county officials that explain their authority, and representing the county in civil proceedings. Some counties have both a county attorney and a district attorney; in these counties, the county attorney deals primarily with civil matters and the district attorney prosecutes criminal matters. District attorneys are not subordinate to county government in Texas, nor are they considered county officials, but their office space and salaries are partly paid by the counties. County attorneys are wholly county officials.

Some counties have other executive officers, such as five or more members of the county board of school trustees, a county superintendent of schools, a county surveyor, and a county weigher. Counties may authorize such appointive officers as the county election administrator, county health officer, county medical examiner, county agricultural agent, and home demonstration agent.

Issues and Trends

The institutional features of Texas county government are largely a product of the nineteenth century, yet the demands of modern society are placing an increasingly heavy burden on this level of government. The following discussion focuses on some frequently cited criticisms of county government and the measures counties can take to deal with contemporary problems.

Constitutional Rigidity
The great mass of detailed and restrictive material in the Texas Constitution creates problems of rigidity and inflexibility. Controls that are not embedded in the constitution are scattered throughout the Local Government Code and various other statutes. The result is a collection of legal requirements, many of which apply equally to the four largest counties in the state—Harris, Dallas, Tarrant, and Bexar—as well as the more than 100 counties that have populations of fewer than 20,000. The standardization of county structure and functions often fails to account for the great variation among the counties in their individual needs and problems. At present, deviations from the uniform structure and functions must be specifically authorized by the state legislature. Some reformers would entrust voters to restructure their own county governments using home-rule provisions similar to those now available to many Texas cities.

Long Ballot
So many county officials are independently elected and the operations of county government are so decentralized that the voters may find it difficult to monitor the many positions involved. Reformers recommend a **short ballot** with fewer elected (and more appointed) county officials in conjunction with the establishment of the county manager system or the elected county executive. They argue that a simplified structure with a single county executive would allow voters to hold one high-profile officer accountable for administration of county programs. They contend that a chief county executive could coordinate county programs, engage in long-range planning, and eliminate duplication among various county offices.

Defenders of the *long ballot* (see Chapter 3) counter that the current system provides for the direct election of public officials to ensure that government remains responsive to the needs and demands of the voters. They fear that concentrating too much power in a single chief executive invites abuse and threatens personal liberty.

Unit Road System
The **unit road system** takes the day-to-day responsibility for roads away from individual county commissioners and concentrates it in the hands of a professional engineer. The engineer is responsible to the commissioners court for efficient and economical construction and maintenance of county roads. The voters may petition for an election to establish the unit road system, or commissioners may initiate the change themselves.

Supporters of this system maintain that it brings greater coordination and professionalism to road building and maintenance in rural areas. Commissioners, however, are reluctant to give up the political influence that their individual control over road building brings; some voters like the idea of directly electing the officers who build their roads.

Spoils System versus Merit System
Elected county officials hire county employees using a **spoils system**, which makes their job security dependent on the continued election of and allegiance to their employer. Political loyalty rather than competence is often the main factor in the recruitment and retention of employees, and when a new official is elected, a large turnover of county employees may result.

The spoils system's defenders point out that the elected official is responsible for the employee's performance and therefore should have the authority to bring in more employees

---

District clerk
The record keeper for the district court in counties with a population exceeding 8,000.

County attorney
A county legal officer whose responsibilities may include giving legal advice to the commissioner's court, representing the county in litigation, and prosecuting crimes. In counties that also elect a district attorney, the county attorney specializes in civil matters.

District attorney
A county officer who prosecutes criminal cases and also handles civil matters in many counties.

Short ballot
The listing of only a few independently elected offices on an election ballot.

Unit road system
A system that concentrates the day-to-day responsibilities for roads in the hands of a professional engineer rather than individual county commissioners. The engineer is ultimately responsible to the commissioners court.

Spoils system
A system that gives elected officials considerable discretion in employment and promotion decisions.

Courthouses are the nerve center of county government, where courts conduct trials, the commissioners meet, taxes are collected, and vital records are kept. In Texas, county officials are elected in partisan elections on a long ballot.

What are the advantages and disadvantages of commissioners, judges, and other major officials such as the sheriff running for office on party labels? Evaluate the use of a long ballot in terms of local government efficiency and responsiveness to public needs.

than just the personnel at the top echelon. They also argue that an elected official would be foolish to release competent employees simply because they had gained their experience under a predecessor. Finally, they argue that alternatives like the merit system provide so much job security that employees become complacent and indifferent to the public.

The spoils system's opponents propose a *merit system* that bases employment and promotion on specific qualifications and performance (see Chapter 10). Because it would also prohibit termination of employment except for proven cause, the merit system offers job security, which should attract qualified personnel. Supporters of the merit system maintain that it encourages professionalism, increases efficiency, and allows uniform application of equal-opportunity requirements.

Texas counties with a population of 200,000 or more may establish a *civil service* program for some county employees, and counties with populations of more than 500,000 may establish a civil service system for the sheriff's office. According to the Texas Association of Counties, half of the 20 counties that may establish a civil service system have done so, and all seven counties eligible to establish a civil service program in the sheriffs' department have one.

Consolidation Students of county government reform point to city–county consolidation as a means to reduce the number of local governments, to eliminate duplication of government services, and to increase greater government efficiency. With **consolidation**, the county and other local governments within it are merged into a single government.

The consolidation of governments faces many challenges. Consolidation requires legislative action, followed by local voter approval. Independently elected officials at the local level are likely to resist a move that would eliminate their offices and the power that goes with them. Although many cities and counties enter into partnership agreements to provide joint services, city–county consolidation bills have failed to win passage in the Texas legislature.

HOW DOES TEXAS COMPARE?
Counties, Their Populations, and Consolidation

Texas has two of the nation's ten most populated counties. In fact, Harris County—in which Houston is located—has a population larger than that of Oregon and 23 other states. In contrast, the least populated county in the United States is Loving County, Texas, with a total population of just 82. It is easy to understand that counties have vastly different problems and needs throughout the nation.

The nation's largest counties must manage huge operations and spend enormous sums of money to finance services to their many residents. And, while the size of their operations presents numerous challenges, it also presents the opportunity to streamline services by consolidating with the cities, as Miami and Dade County, Florida, have done. Others have contracted with other units of local government to provide a single set of services and to avoid duplication of effort. For example, some offer joint city-county library systems or countywide health districts.

The Ten Largest U.S. Counties: The 2000 and 2010 Census

Rank	Geographic Area	2000 Census	2010 Census
1.	Los Angeles County, CA	9,519,338	9,818,605
2.	Cook County, IL	5,376,741	5,194,675
3.	Harris County, TX	3,400,578	4,092,459
4.	Maricopa County, AZ	3,072,149	3,817,117
5.	San Diego County, CA	2,813,833	3,095,313
6.	Orange County, CA	2,846,289	3,010,232
7.	Kings County, NY	2,465,326	2,504,700
8.	Miami-Dade County, FL	2,253,362	2,496,435
9.	Dallas County, TX	2,218,899	2,386,139
10.	Queens County, NY	2,229,379	2,230,722

Source: United States Census Bureau, *Table: Population Change for Counties*, http://www.census.gov/prod/cen2010/briefs/c2010br-01.pdf, Table 4.

FOR DEBATE

1. What are the advantages of city-county consolidation? Why might city residents resist paying for countywide services?

2. Would county government be more efficient if several small counties merged into larger regional governments? Would such a merger result in loss of local control and geographical accessibility to county services?

SPECIAL-DISTRICT GOVERNMENTS

Special districts are local governments that provide single or closely related services that are not provided by general-purpose county or municipal governments. In Chapter 13, we discussed special-purpose governments related to education—independent school districts and community college districts. Here, we focus on the non-school special districts.

These special districts do not always receive attention comparable with cities and counties, but they are no less important when it comes to serving the needs of the public. In a suburban area outside the city limits, for example, a special district may be established to provide water and sewer facilities for a housing development; such a special district has the authority to borrow to build the system and may assess taxes and user fees on property owners and residents.

Table 14.4 shows that the number of special districts has grown considerably. In fact, special districts are the most numerous of all local governments in Texas (see Table 14.1).

Consolidation

The merging of county government with other local governments to form a single local government.

TABLE 14.4 Special Districts In Texas, 1952–2012

1952	1962	1972	1982	1992	2002	2007	2012
491	733	1,215	1,681	2,266	2,245	2,291	2,309

Sources: U.S. Census Bureau, *2002 Census of Governments, Volume 1, Number 1, Government Organization*, GC02(1)-1 (Washington, DC: U.S. Government Printing Office, 2002), www.census.gov/prod/2003pubs/gc021x1.pdf.; 2007 Census of Governments, www.census.gov/govs/cog/GovOrgTab03ss.html; 2012 Census of Governments, http://www2.census.gov/govs/cog/2012/formatted_prelim_counts_23jul2012_2.pdf.

Special districts have been on the rise since the mid-twentieth century. Some special districts have their own elected governing boards that have the authority to impose a property tax.

▲ **What are the benefits of having a specialized approach to providing government services? What are the drawbacks? What issues might encourage special districts to collaborate with cities and counties, and what challenges might make collaboration difficult?**

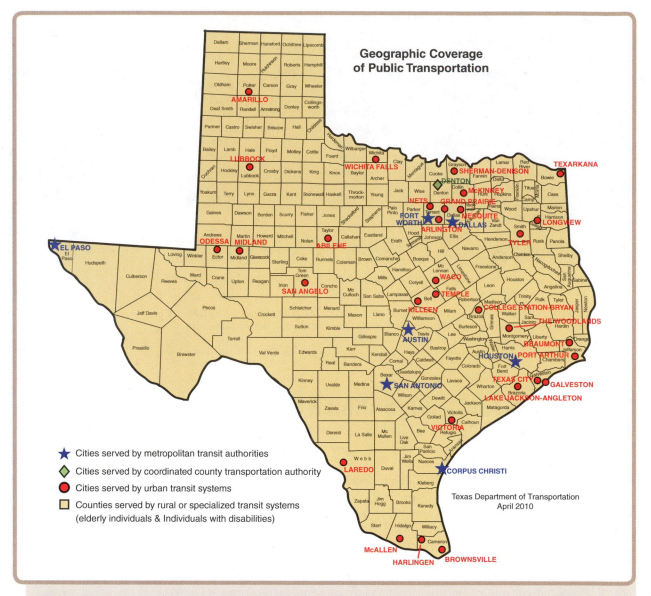

Geographic Coverage of Public Transportation

Texas Department of Transportation
April 2010

★ Cities served by metropolitan transit authorities

◆ Cities served by coordinated county transportation authority

● Cities served by urban transit systems

▢ Counties served by rural or specialized transit systems
(elderly individuals & Individuals with disabilities)

Figure 14.3
Cities and Counties Served by Public Transportation Systems

Source: Texas Department of Transportation, http://ftp.dot.state.tx.us/pub/txdot-info/ptn/small_urban_map.pdf.

Should Texas cities invest more in public transportation? What factors are likely to encourage the public to use mass transit?

Some examples are airport authorities, drainage districts, hospital authorities, municipal utility districts, library districts, navigation districts, metropolitan transit authorities (see Figure 14.3), river authorities, rural fire prevention districts, and noxious weed control districts. According to the U.S. Census Bureau, two-thirds of the special districts in Texas provide a single service. The rest are classified as "multiple-function districts," and most of those provide closely related functions like sewerage and water supply.

Multimember boards usually govern special districts. Voters elect members of some special district boards in either in partisan or nonpartisan elections; city councils and county commissioners appoint others; in some cases, city council members or county commissioners themselves serve ex officio as board members.

Special districts should not be confused with dependent agencies. The Census Bureau recognizes some government entities as "dependent agencies" rather than special districts because they are more closely tied to general-purpose governments and do not have as much independence as special districts in budgeting and administration. An example of a **dependent agency** is a crime control and prevention district, a temporary agency created with voter approval. Crime control districts have become increasingly popular since the 1990s, particularly in cities located in Tarrant County. Voters have authorized more than 60 crime control districts, and most of them collect either a one-half cent or one-fourth cent sales tax. In some communities, the establishment of crime control and prevention districts has substantially increased funding for law enforcement.

Dependent agency

A classification created by the U.S. Census Bureau for governmental entities that are closely tied to general-purpose governments but do not have as much independence as special-district governments.

Reasons for Creating Special District Governments

Having a service provided by a special district rather than a general-purpose government is appealing to many residents for a variety of reasons. A city or county may have limited revenue because of a downturn in the economy, the loss of a major industry, new unfunded mandates, or fewer federal dollars. The general-purpose government may have reached its state-mandated sales tax ceiling of 2 percent. Popular or political sentiment may be that city and county property taxes are already too high, and a strong anti-tax organization in the community may be eager to make that point. Little or no support may exist for increasing taxes or cutting other services to accommodate another service responsibility.

Furthermore, only a small area within a city or county may need the service. Why tax the entire jurisdiction? A district may be created for the benefit of "underserved areas," as is the case with library districts in Texas that serve rural and suburban areas. The demand for a service may extend beyond a single jurisdiction, calling for a special district that is multicity or multicounty in scope. For example, a river authority with the power to govern the use of water throughout the river's watershed must transcend existing political boundaries; flood control districts similarly deal with a problem that crosses political boundaries. Municipal Utilities Districts (MUDs) are often created at the insistence of developers who want to provide water and sewerage for the subdivisions they establish outside city service areas. For a host of reasons, special districts serve as alternatives to general-purpose governments and they are an attractive option as an alternative revenue source.

Issues and Trends

Although special districts provide valuable public services not provided by general-purpose governments, reformers charge that they are often too small to be efficient, too low-profile to be visible to the public, and too numerous to be readily held accountable to voters.

Multiple Governments
Although special districts can be dissolved when a municipality annexes the area and provides it with services, the trend in Texas as across the rest of the nation has been toward the proliferation of special district governments (see Table 14.4). The sheer number of special-district governments and their small size create serious challenges for special district governments.

Hidden Governments   Special districts are sometimes called *hidden* governments because the actions of district officials and employees are less visible than if a county or city provided the services. When special-district elections are held at times or places other than those for general elections, voter turnout is quite low.

Cost   Because special districts are often small, they may purchase in limited quantities at higher prices than larger governments. In addition, if special districts have little or no authority to tax, they are forced to borrow money by issuing revenue bonds, which are paid from fees collected for the service provided, rather than *general-obligation bonds*, which are paid from tax revenue. Because revenue bonds are less secure than general-obligation bonds, special-district residents are forced to pay higher interest rates just to service the bonded indebtedness. Special districts may also have a lower bond rating than larger, general-function governments, which also increases their borrowing costs.

Inefficiency   A study of special-purpose governments in more than 300 U.S. metropolitan areas concluded that the special-district approach to governing is more costly than the general-purpose approach. Moreover, social welfare functions (such as hospitals, housing, and welfare) tend to receive more revenue in metropolitan areas with fewer special districts. Housekeeping functions (including fire protection, natural resources, and police protection) and development functions (including airports, water, and highways) tend to receive more revenue in areas in which districts are more prevalent.[7]

As an alternative to inefficient special districts, reformers advocate consolidation of small special districts. To deal with problems and fiscal challenges that transcend city and county boundaries, they urge general-purpose governments to negotiate interlocal agreements to meet the needs of their respective communities. They argue that the need for special districts can be reduced by transferring their functions to general-purpose governments.

COUNCILS OF GOVERNMENT

Councils of government (COGs)

Advisory bodies consisting of representatives of various local governments brought together for the purposes of regional planning and cooperation.

Councils of government (COGs) are not governments; instead they are voluntary regional groupings of local governments that attempt to coordinate government activities and share information. Encompassing all regions of the state, 24 Texas COGs focus on such major issues as homeland security, economic development, aging, emergency communications and preparedness, and environmental quality.

By bringing local officials together, COGs provide a base for the exchange of ideas and knowledge. Although COGs do not solve the problems that local governments face, they do encourage local officials to recognize the magnitude of these problems and cooperate to manage some of them.

---

[7]Kathryn A. Foster, *The Political Economy of Special-Purpose Government* (Washington, DC: Georgetown University Press, 1997), pp. 221–224.

From the Mayor's Desk: Lessons in Governing a City

INTRODUCTION

The author of this article was a mayor of a small town in South Texas. His very personal insight into a mayor's day-to-day activities shows the difficulties of satisfying competing political demands generated in a close-knit community. Most of the lessons in decision making that this article teaches apply to larger cities, states, and the national government as well.

When you are the mayor of a small town, your phone rings a lot. Usually, the call is about the condition of the streets, an interruption in water service, or another stray dog. This call was about neither of those things—it had to do with something happening at our new city park.

"I want to make a complaint," the unidentified caller said, "I've got small kids that go down to play at the park and the older kids that are always there pick on them. Why aren't the police down there more often to keep this from happening? The police are never there."

Alone, this conversation was not unusual; what made it a lasting impression is the next call that came 20 minutes later.

"Are you the mayor?" caller number two demanded.

After assuring her I was, I asked the nature of her concern.

"I have some teenage boys that like to go over to the park with their friends after school, but they don't want to go anymore because they say the police are always down there giving them a hard time."

Every time I hear someone say that an elected official's job is to do just what the voters want—I think of those two calls. Each caller was seeking relief within the same context, but each had two totally different perspectives and two divergent requests for the action they wanted to see taken. Of course, I recognized that I had no way of knowing how many others were unhappy about the police presence in the city park, and of those who were concerned, I had no way of knowing which caller's perspective they shared. All I could do is raise the topic with the city manager and the police chief and have the department be both present and judicious at the site.

People who hope to study politics would be well advised to live in a small town for just a short time. In the national media, they talk about "retail politics" taking place when Iowa holds their presidential caucus and New Hampshire hosts the same candidates in the very personal campaigning leading to their primaries. That is a quadrennial event. If you want retail politics every day, move to a rural community. In rural Texas, most mayors and city council members serve without pay. They are, in fact, generally driven by a sense of civic purpose. They serve with no pay and have no staff to assist them. They are as responsible for the governance of a municipal corporation as their big-city counterparts but have fewer resources. Of course, they do have specific motivations like holding down the tax rate or promoting singular projects, like the city park I mentioned. People know each other in small towns, and their personalities and motivations are known by the voters on a personal level.

If the two contradictory phone calls demonstrated the elected official's role of providing constituent services to me, the following vignette clarified another political phenomenon to me:

In the 1980s, the United States economy took a dive amidst the failure of financial institutions known as savings and loan (S&L) associations. At the macro level, the whole affair, like most economic downturns, is best left to the economists to explain. I live in a small town and my experiences allow me to offer a micro-level explanation of how the S&L failure impacted government. The S&L located in our town failed and was closed by federal regulators on a Friday. At the city council meeting the next week, we were approached by a leader in the local business community. He appeared before us as the president of the local Little League. It seems the boys and girls had been playing ball on fields that sat on property owned by the S&L. They had no contract to use the fields; it was allowed on "a handshake-kind of arrangement." The federal program closing down the S&Ls planned to sell the land the fields had been built on at auction if the Little League could not buy them at a price set by the regulators. The Little League did not have the money, and the citizen was before the council asking if the city could save this recreational venue for the town's children. He conceded that it was deep within our budget year and he was requesting a sizeable expenditure that we had not planned for or foreseen. His plea was a logical and well-reasoned presentation. However, it was not over.

"One more thing," he said, "As vice-president of the Chamber of Commerce (in a small town, the civic-minded wear many hats), I would like to formally ask the city to provide a vehicle and trailer when we represent the city at out-of-town events like parades and other activities."

However, he was not done yet.

"And the street in front of my business needs repaved."

He still was not done.

"Finally, I just want to say that I don't understand why the council keeps raising taxes. You're killing us. It's time to cut back a bit."

Now let me say, I have the utmost respect for this citizen. He was concerned, he was articulate, and he was involved. He saw problems and he saw answers. What he never saw were the inherent contradictions in his requests. He wanted three ball fields purchased, use of city-owned equipment, and street improvements. Along with the wish list came a demand for lower taxes.

Plato said to understand the actions of men you had to understand society because society was just human nature writ large. I will never be accused of belonging in Plato's intellectual company, but I think to understand big government in America, you can watch small-town politics in Texas. The big picture comes with financing wars, maintaining Social Security and Medicaid, containing the damage when financial institutions collapse, and altering the tax code through the complexity of congressional operations. The small picture is Little League parks and city taxes. Either way, we see citizens making additional demands on a government while resisting the taxes it takes to meet those demands. This thinking leads candidates to pledge, "I will tax you less and give you more—Vote for me." Do I even have to ask if that sounds familiar?

Rural government stories can be examined as allegories to urban, state, and national policy making. That is what I hope my first two stories tell. The last tale I wish to tell is about how rural governance is different.

I was presiding over a council meeting in which bids were being opened for a municipal project. One of the losing bidders unleashed his rather vocal displeasure at the outcome in an unexpected breach of decorum. I let the citizen have his say as he vented his disappointment. After the meeting, our financial consultant (a resident of one of Texas's larger cities) confided that he was surprised that I had allowed such an outburst and that it was not my typical way of handling a meeting. I had to remind the consultant that I lived in a small town. Our wives could easily meet in the grocery store, and, I would certainly see his son in my classroom the next day. I knew this citizen and was well aware of the many contributions he had made to the community. Tomorrow I may well go to the citizen's business and buy something.

In rural governance, you cannot avoid the personal impact of every decision you make. That is the real nature of rural city governance, the reminder that every policy is personal. All sizes of government at all levels would be well served to remember that.

JOIN THE DEBATE

1. Is it ever possible to reconcile citizen demands to provide improved city services while trimming the budget? How does cynicism about government develop when citizens present self-contradictory demands?

2. How do personal relationships affect government decision making? Should public officials be sensitive to the effects of their decisions on individuals, or should they try to be professional by making policies that benefit the community at large without regard to their effects on particular individuals?

CHAPTER SUMMARY

★ Although local governments are responsible for providing services that are unique to the communities they serve—that is, reducing traffic violations, fixing potholes, maintaining parks—they must also contend with issues of national importance, such as immigration, homelessness, and homeland security. Municipalities, counties, and special districts provide numerous services that have a direct impact on our daily lives.

★ The examination of local governments is challenging because they number in the thousands, and they do not receive the media attention of the national and state governments. Municipal and school district elections in Texas are nonpartisan; they generate low levels of public interest and low voter turnout.

★ Municipalities with a population greater than 5,000 may adopt home rule, which allows them considerable latitude when it comes to governing. These cities can write their own charters (organic law comparable to a constitution) and ordinances, as long as they do not conflict with state or federal laws or constitutions. Cities that do not meet that population requirement must operate within the structure of a general-law charter established by the state.

★ The municipal reform movement of the twentieth century had a major effect on Texas cities. Key features of the reform era—nonpartisan elections, the council-manager form of government, and at-large elections—are characteristics of many Texas cities. Some cities with large Latino and African-American populations have, under court order, replaced at-large elections with single-member districts, modified election systems, or instituted cumulative voting. In addition to participating in city council, county, and some special-district elections, local voters may also influence their communities through initiative, referendum, and recall elections; rollback elections; term-limit elections; and economic development sales tax elections.

★ Local governments must frequently meet mandates imposed by Congress or the state legislature. Although unfunded mandates are of particular concern to local governments, supporters of mandates contend that they allow governments to address pressing needs in a uniform fashion.

★ Texas maintains broad annexation laws that facilitate the jurisdictional expansion of home-rule cities. This policy is subject to criticism by unincorporated areas that are annexed against their will, but recent reforms have facilitated greater planning and quicker service delivery after annexation.

★ Texas county government does not have home rule. Its structure and organization are determined by the Texas Constitution and the state legislature. Texas counties range considerably in terms of population, yet they are quite similar when it comes to structural features, sources of funding, and functions. County law enforcement, financial officers, and clerical officers are independently elected. The spoils system remains a feature of county government, though counties meeting certain population requirements may establish civil service systems.

★ Although city–county consolidation of governments is non-existent in Texas, local governments can establish interlocal agreements that promote regional cooperation.

★ Local governments rely on a variety of revenue sources—property and sales taxes, user fees, public debt, and state and federal dollars—to provide services.

★ Government is largely fragmented at the local level. Although friction between governments is common over policies like annexation, cooperation may also result when local governments agree to share responsibility for certain services. Nevertheless, any significant changes in the structural relationship between cities, counties, and special districts will likely continue to be more incremental than sweeping.

HOW TEXAS COMPARES

★ Like state governments, local governments are often subject to comparison on the basis of their structural features. Municipal home rule is a common feature in most states—including Texas, which allows its adoption in cities with a population of more than 5,000, contingent on voter approval.

★ The council manager form of government, nonpartisan elections, and at-large elections have been widely adopted by municipalities throughout the nation, including Texas home-rule cities.

★ Combinations of distinct features, such as election systems that include at-large and single-member district seats, may also be found. Term limits have not been widely adopted by municipalities nationwide or in Texas.

★ Texas has more counties than any other state. Whereas most states permit some variation of home rule, Texas counties are not authorized by the state to adopt home rule.

KEY TERMS

annexation, *p. 379*
at-large city elections, *p. 372*
at-large place system, *p. 372*
charter, *p. 368*
colonias, *p. 379*
commission form of
    government, *p. 371*
commissioners court, *p. 380*
consolidation, *p. 385*
constable, *p. 381*
council-manager form of
    government, *p. 369*
councils of government
    (COGs), *p. 388*
county attorney, *p. 383*

county auditor, *p. 382*
county clerk, *p. 382*
county government, *p. 380*
county judge, *p. 380*
county treasurer, *p. 382*
cumulative voting, *p. 373*
dependent agencies, *p. 387*
district attorney, *p. 382*
district clerk, *p. 382*
extraterritorial jurisdiction
    (ETJ), *p. 379*
general-law city, *p. 368*
general-purpose government,
    p. 366
home-rule city, *p. 368*

mandate, *p. 378*
mayor-council system, *p. 371*
public debt, *p. 377*
pure at-large system, *p. 372*
recall election, *p. 369*
rollback election, *p. 376*
sheriff, *p. 381*
short ballot, *p. 383*
single-member district,
    p. 372
special district, *p. 366*
spoils system, *p. 383*
strong-mayor form of
    government, *p. 371*
tax assessor-collector, *p. 381*

term limits, *p. 374*
unit road system, *p. 383*
user fees, *p. 377*
weak-mayor form of
    government, *p. 371*

REVIEW QUESTIONS

1. Why do cities adopt home rule? What are some examples of limitations that are imposed on home-rule cities?

2. Compare and contrast at-large and single-member district election systems. Describe the cumulative-voting election system alternative.

3. Explain the mayor's role and authority in the council-manager, weak-mayor, and strong-mayor forms of government.

4. Discuss the various revenue sources used by local governments, including property taxes, sales taxes, and user fees.

5. Explain how initiative, referendum, recall, and rollback elections allow voters to influence local governments.

6. Why do proponents of economic development support tax abatements? What reasons are given to oppose them?

7. Explain how county government is organized. What are the responsibilities of the county commissioners court?

8. What are the advantages and disadvantages associated with special-district governments? Is the trend toward special districts a positive feature of local government? Why or why not?

9. What services do councils of government provide local governments?

LOGGING ON

Use your Internet skills to search out which Texas cities use council-manager and mayor-council forms. Develop a table showing whether larger or smaller cities prefer one form over the other.

Use Title 2, Chapters 5 through 9 of the Texas Local Government Code at **www.statutes.legis.state.tx.us/?link=LG** to describe the structures of Texas general-law cities.

Visit the websites of the following organizations to stay informed about local government issues:

★ National Association of Counties: **www.naco.org**

★ Texas Association of Counties: **www.county.org**

★ National League of Cities: **www.nlc.org**

★ Texas Municipal League: **www.tml.org**

A useful source is the U.S. Census Bureau's "State and County QuickFacts," which provides an abundance of data on Texas counties and Texas cities and towns with a population of more than 25,000. Go to **www.census.gov**, click on QuickFacts, and then select Texas.

Go to the FairVote website (**www.fairvote.org**) to learn more about various local election methods, including cumulative voting.

Ability-to-pay taxes Taxes apportioned according to taxpayers' financial capacity.

Access The ability to contact an official either in person or by phone. Campaign contributions are often used to gain access.

Accountability Responsibility for a program's results—for example, using measurable standards to hold public schools responsible for their students' performance.

Ad valorem tax A tax assessed according to value, such as the tax on *real property* and *personal property*.

Ad-hoc committee A temporary committee.

Administrative law The rules and regulations written by administrators to administer a law. The effectiveness of a law is often determined by how administrative law is written.

Administrative review Administrators' study and interpretation of a law and writing the rules and regulations to implement the law's enforcement. All laws undergo administrative review, whereas relatively few undergo *judicial review*, which is the courts' interpretation of the law.

Adversary system The legal system used in English-speaking countries in which two contesting parties present opposing views and evidence in a court of law.

Advocacy Promotion of a particular public policy position.

Affirmative action Positive efforts to recruit ethnic minorities, women, and the economically disadvantaged. Sometimes these efforts are limited to publicity drives among target groups, but such programs have sometimes included ethnicity or gender as part of the qualification criteria.

Annexation A policy that permits a city to bring unincorporated areas into the city's jurisdiction.

Appellate jurisdiction The power vested in an appellate court to review and revise the judicial action of an inferior court.

Appropriations The process by which a legislative body legally authorizes a government to spend specific sums of money to provide various programs and services.

Arraignment A prisoner's initial appearance before a magistrate in which the charges and basic rights (to an attorney and bail) are explained.

Astroturf lobbying The fabrication of public support for issues supported by industry and special interest groups but which give the impression of widespread public support.

At-large city elections Citywide elections. In many cities, some or all of the city council members are elected by voters of the entire municipality rather than from neighborhood districts.

At-large place system An electoral system in which candidates run for a *particular* seat on the city council.

Attorney general's opinion Interpretation of the constitution, statutory laws, or administrative laws by Texas's attorney general. Government officials may request opinions, and although they are not legally binding, government officials usually follow them.

Australian ballot A ballot printed by the government (as opposed to the political parties) that allows people to vote in secret.

Bail The security required for release of a suspect awaiting trial.

Benefits-received tax A tax assessed according to the services received by the payers.

Beyond a reasonable doubt The standard used to determine the guilt or innocence of a person criminally charged. To prove a defendant guilty, the state must provide sufficient evidence of guilt such that jurors will have no doubt that might cause a reasonable person to question whether the accused was guilty.

Bicameral Consisting of two houses or chambers; applied to a legislative body with two parts, such as a senate and a house of representatives (or state assembly). Congress and 49 state legislatures are bicameral. Only Nebraska has a one-house (unicameral) legislature.

Bicultural Encompassing two cultures.

Biennial regular session Regular legislative sessions are scheduled by the constitution. In Texas, they are held once every two years; hence they are biennial.

Binational Belonging to two nations.

Block grants Federal grants to state or local governments for more general purposes and with fewer restrictions than categorical grants.

Blocking bill A bill placed early on the senate calendar that will never be considered by the full senate. Its purpose is to require two-thirds of the senators to vote to suspend the senate rule that requires bills to be considered in the order they are reported out of committee. The effect is that any bill appearing later on the calendar must have the support of two-thirds of the senate if it is to be allowed to come up for debate and passage.

Blue-ribbon commission A group assembled by the governor (or legislature) that may have both fact-finding and recommending authority. It often contains public personages or authorities on the subject that is being considered. Such commissions can help measure public reaction to proposals and may also let the governor delay consideration of issues that may be politically uncomfortable.

Brief A written argument prepared by the counsel arguing a case in court that summarizes the facts of the case, the pertinent laws, and the application of those laws to the facts supporting the counsel's position.

Broad-based tax A tax designed to be paid by a large number of taxpayers.

Budgetary power The power to propose a spending plan to the legislative body; a power limited for Texas's governor because of the competing influences of the Legislative Budget Board.

Burden of proof The duty of a party in a court case to prove its position.

Bureaucracy The system of officials and their employees administering or managing government policies and programs.

Bureaucratic oversight The legislative function of monitoring administrators to make sure they are administering the laws according to legislative intent.

Cabinet system A system that allows the chief executive to appoint and remove top-level administrators, thereby giving the chief executive more control over the administration.

Calendar The list of bills reported out of committee and ready for consideration by the house or the senate.

Categorical grants Federal aid to state or local governments for specific purposes, granted under restrictive conditions and often requiring matching funds from the receiving government.

Chad The small pieces of paper produced in punching data cards, such as punch-card ballots.

Challenge for cause A request to a judge that a certain prospective juror not be allowed to serve on the jury for a specific reason, such as bias or knowledge of the case.

Change of venue A change in the location of a trial.

Charter The organizing document for a corporation or a municipality.

Checks and balances The concept that each branch of government is assigned power to limit abuses in the others, for example, the executive veto could be used to prevent legislative excesses.

Chief of state The governor, who serves as the symbol of Texas and who performs ceremonial duties and represents the state at meetings with foreign officials and other governors.

Children's Health Insurance Program (CHIP) Program that provides health insurance for low-income children. It is administered by the state but funded largely by federal grants-in-aid.

Chubbing Slowing the legislative process by maximizing debate, amendments, and points of order on minor bills to prevent ultimate consideration of a more controversial bill further down on the calendar.

Civil case Nonpenal case dealing with private rights and responsibilities.

Civil law Nonpenal law dealing with private rights and responsibilities.

Civil service (merit) system An employment system used by governments that takes merit into account in hiring and promotions.

Clemency powers Executive authority to grant relief from criminal punishment; Texas's governor's clemency powers are very limited.

Clientele interest groups The groups most concerned with the laws and policies being administered by a government agency.

Closed primary A type of primary where a voter can participate in the primary for the party of which they are a member.

Closed shop A workplace in which management hires only labor union employees (illegal in Texas).

Cloture A parliamentary move to stop legislative debate and force a floor vote; also known as *closure*.

Coercive Federalism A relationship between the national government and states in which the former directs the states on policies they must take.

Colonias Severely impoverished unincorporated areas facing a variety of problems, including substandard housing, unsanitary drinking water, and lack of proper sewage disposal.

Commerce clause An enumerated power in Article I, Section 8 of the U.S. Constitution that gives Congress the power to regulate commerce.

Commission form of government A municipal government in which individual members of the commission head city departments and collectively act as a city council to pass ordinances.

Commissioners court The policy-making body of a county, consisting of a county judge (the presiding officer of the court), who is elected in a countywide election to a four-year term, and four commissioners, who are elected from individual precincts to four-year terms.

Committee of the whole The entire senate acting as a committee. Its purpose is to allow the senate to relax its rules and thereby expedite legislation.

Common law Customs upheld by courts and deriving from British tradition.

Community college approach Higher education policy based on open admissions, maximizing accessibility, and incorporating technical, compensatory, and continuing education among the traditional academic course offerings.

Community property Property acquired during marriage and owned equally by both spouses.

Compulsory process A procedure to subpoena witnesses in court.

Concurrent powers Those powers that are shared by both the national government and the states.

Confederal system A system of government in which member state or regional governments have all authority and any central institutions have only the power that regional governments choose to give them; also known as confederacies.

Conference committee An ad-hoc committee that meets to resolve differences between senate and house versions of the same legislation.

Conference committee report A compromise between the house and senate versions of a bill reached by a conference committee. It may not be amended by either house but must either be rejected, accepted, or sent back to the committee for more work.

Conflict of interest The situation that exists when a legislator, bureaucrat, executive, official, or judge is in a position to make a decision that might result in personal economic benefit or advantage.

Conservative A political ideology marked by the belief in a limited role for government in taxation, economic regulation, and providing social services; conservatives support traditional values and lifestyles, and are cautious in response to social change.

Consolidation The merging of county government with other local governments to form a single local government.

Constable A county law enforcement official who is elected to serve as the process officer of justice of the peace courts and also has general law enforcement powers.

Contract spoils The practice by which public officials award government contracts to benefit their campaign contributors, supporters, and allies. Also referred to as *contract patronage.*

Cooperative Federalism A relationship where "the National Government and the States are mutually complementary parts of a *single* government mechanism all of whose powers are intended to realize the current purposes of government according to their applicability to the problem in hand."

Co-optation The capturing of an institution by members of an interest group. In effect, in such a situation, state power comes to be exercised by the members of the private interest.

Council-manager form of government A form of government that features an elected city council and a city manager who is hired by the council. The council makes policy decisions, and the city manager is responsible for the day-to-day operations of the city government.

Councils of government (COGs) Advisory bodies consisting of representatives of various local governments brought together for the purposes of regional planning and cooperation.

County attorney A county legal officer whose responsibilities may include giving legal advice to the commissioner's court, representing the county in litigation, and prosecuting crimes. In counties that also elect a district attorney, the county attorney specializes in civil matters.

County auditor A financial officer whose duties may include reviewing county financial records and, in large counties, serving as chief budget officer.

County clerk The chief record keeper and election officer of a county.

County government A general-purpose local government that also serves as an administrative arm of the state. Texas has 254 counties—more than any other state.

County judge An official elected countywide to preside over the county commissioners court and to try certain minor cases.

County treasurer In many counties, the official who is responsible for receiving, depositing, and disbursing funds.

Cracking A gerrymandering technique in which concentrated political or ethnic minority groups are split into several districts so that their votes in any one district are negligible.

Creole A descendant of European–Spanish (or in some regions, French) immigrants to the Americas.

Criminal case Case prosecuted by the state, seeking punishment for a violation of the penal code.

Criminal law Law prosecuted by the state, seeking punishment for violations of public concepts of morality.

Crossover voting When members of one political party vote in the other party's primary to influence the nominee that is selected.

Cumulative voting An at-large election system that permits voters to cast one or more votes for a single candidate. For example, if a voter can cast up to five votes in a city council election, all five votes could be cast for one candidate or spread among several candidates.

De novo Latin for "anew"; a *de novo* trial is a new trial conducted in a higher court (as opposed to an appeal). In *de novo* cases, higher courts completely retry cases. On appeal, higher courts simply review the law as decided by the lower courts.

Deadwood State constitutional provisions voided by a conflicting U.S. constitutional or statutory law; also provisions made irrelevant by changing circumstances.

Dealignment The situation that arises when large numbers of voters refuse to identify with either of the two parties and become increasingly independent of party affiliation.

Decentralization Exercise of power in political parties by state and local party organizations rather than by national party institutions.

Declining marginal propensity to consume The tendency, as income increases, for persons to devote a smaller proportion of their income to consumer spending and a larger proportion to savings or investments.

Delegate To legally transfer authority from one official or institution to another.

Delegated powers Those powers that the constitution gives to the national government. These include those enumerated powers found in Article I, Section 8 of the U.S. Constitution as well as a few other powers that have evolved over time.

Demographics Population characteristics, such as age, gender, ethnicity, employment, and income, that social scientists use to describe groups in society.

Dependent agency A classification created by the U.S. Census Bureau for governmental entities that are closely tied to general-purpose governments but do not have as much independence as special-district governments.

Descriptive representation The idea that legislative bodies should represent not only voters' political views but also the demographic and geographic characteristics that affect their political perspectives.

Deterrence Discouraging of criminal behavior by threat of punishment.

Devolution The attempt to enhance the power of state or local governments, especially by substituting more flexible block grants instead of restrictive categorical grants-in-aid.

Direct primary A method of selecting the nominees from a political party where party members elect the candidates who represent them in the general election.

Directive authority The power to issue binding orders to state agencies; the directive authority of Texas's governor is severely limited.

Discharge process A rarely used legislative process for rescuing a bill pigeonholed in standing committee.

Discretion The power to make decisions on the basis of personal judgment rather than specific legal requirements.

District attorney A county officer who prosecutes criminal cases and also handles civil matters in many counties.

District clerk The record keeper for the district court in counties with a population exceeding 8,000.

Double jeopardy A second prosecution for the same offense after acquittal in the first trial.

Dual federalism The understanding that the federal government and state governments are both sovereign within their sphere of influence.

Due process The following of proper legal procedures. Due process is essential to guaranteeing fairness before the government may deprive a person of life, liberty, or property.

Early voting The practice of voting before election day at more traditional voting locations, such as schools, and other locations, such as grocery and convenience stores.

Elective accountability The obligation of officials to be directly answerable to the voters for their actions. This allows elected administrators to ignore the wishes of the chief executive.

Electronic voting Voting using video screens similar to e-ticket check-ins at most airports.

Eminent domain Government taking private property for public purposes with compensation.

Evangelical (fundamentalist) Christians A number of Christians, often conservative supporters of the Republican Party, who are concerned with such issues as family, religion, abortion, gay rights, and community morals.

Ex officio Holding a position automatically because one also holds some other office.

Examining trial An initial court hearing to determine if there is sufficient evidence to send a case to a grand jury.

Exclusionary rule The requirement that illegally obtained evidence may not be used against the accused.

Expressed powers Those delegated powers that are found in Article I, Section 8 and are clearly listed in the U.S. Constitution; also known as *enumerated powers.*

Extraterritorial jurisdiction (ETJ) A buffer area that may extend beyond a city's limits. Cities can enforce some laws such as zoning and building codes in ETJs.

FBI index crimes Crimes used as a national barometer of the crime rate (murder and nonnegligent manslaughter, forcible rape, robbery, aggravated assault, burglary, grand theft, and motor vehicle theft).

Federal system A system of government in which governmental power is divided and shared between a national or central government and state or regional governments.

Felony In Texas, a serious crime punishable by state institutions.

Filibuster An attempt by a senator to delay a bill by unlimited debate.

Floor action The entire senate or house acting as a whole to debate, amend, vote on, enact, pass, or defeat proposed legislation.

Floor leaders The legislators who are responsible for getting legislation passed or defeated. Their job is to negotiate, bargain, and compromise because they are in the center of political communication.

Formal (legal) powers Powers stated in rules, a law, or a constitution.

Fragmentation Division of power among separately elected executive officers. A plural executive is a fragmented executive.

General-law city A city with a population of 5,000 or fewer whose structure and organization are prescribed and limited by state law.

General-obligation bonds Bonds to be repaid from general taxes and other revenues; such bond issues usually must be approved by voters.

General-purpose government A municipal or county government that provides a wide range of services. Compare *special district*.

General sales tax A broad-based tax collected on the retail price of most items.

Gerrymander A district or precinct that is drawn specifically to favor some political party, candidate, or ethnic group.

Grand jury In Texas, 12 persons who sit in pretrial proceedings to determine whether sufficient evidence exists to try an individual and therefore return an indictment.

Grassroots The lowest level of party organization. In Texas, the grassroots level is the precinct level of organization.

Gross-receipts tax A tax on the gross revenues of certain enterprises.

Guaranteed-issue requirements Requirements that insurance companies will sell health insurance to applicants despite preexisting conditions.

Health Care Reform (HCR) A comprehensive federal program expanding health insurance coverage with broader Medicare coverage, individual mandates, guaranteed-issue requirements, health insurance subsidies, and exchanges.

Hidden taxes Taxes included in the retail prices of goods and services.

Hierarchy A pyramid-shaped administrative organization in which several employees report to a single higher administrator until there remains only one person with ultimate authority at the top.

Home-rule charter A document organizing a municipality with a population greater than 5,000 and allowing it to use any organizational structure or institute any program that complies with state law.

Homestead An owner-occupied property protected from forced sale under most circumstances.

Hung jury A jury that is unable to agree on a verdict after a suitable period of deliberation; the result is a mistrial.

Ideology A pattern of political beliefs about how society and the economy operate, including policy orientations consistent with that pattern; a set of beliefs consistent with a particular political perspective.

Impeachment Officially charging an officeholder with improper conduct in office.

Implementation Carrying out by members of the executive branch any policy made by the legislature and judiciary.

Implied powers Those delegated powers that are assumed to exist in order for the government to perform the functions that are expressly delegated. These powers are granted by the necessary and proper clause in Article I, Section 8.

Income redistribution A public policy goal intended to shift income from one class of recipients to another, regardless of whether these programs are designed to benefit lower-, middle-, or upper-income groups.

Incorporation doctrine Certain rights found in the Bill of Rights are rights that cannot be encroached upon by the states.

Incumbent The current holder of an office.

Independent expenditures Money that individuals and organizations spend to promote a candidate without working or communicating directly with the candidate's campaign organization.

Indictment A formal written accusation issued by a grand jury against a party charged with a crime when it has determined that there is sufficient evidence to bring the accused to trial.

Indirect appointive powers Texas governor's authority to appoint supervisory boards but not operational directors for most state agencies.

Individual mandate Requirement that individuals get health insurance or pay a tax penalty to the federal government.

Individualistic culture A political subculture that views government as a practical institution that should further private enterprise but intervene minimally in people's lives.

Informal (extralegal) powers Powers that are not stated in rules, a law, or a constitution but are usually derived from these legal powers.

Information A written accusation filed by the prosecutor against a party charged with a minor crime; it is an alternative to an indictment and does not involve a grand jury.

Inherent powers Those delegated powers that come with an office or position—generally the executive branch. While the U.S. Constitution does not clearly specify powers granted to the executive branch, over time, inherent powers have evolved as part of the powers needed to perform the functions of the executive branch.

Initiative An election method that allows citizens to place a proposal on the ballot for voter approval. If the measure passes, it becomes law (permitted in some Texas cities but not in state government).

Interest group An organization that expresses the policy desires of its members to officers and institutions of government; also known as a *pressure group*.

Interim committees Committees that meet between legislative sessions.

Internationality Having family and/or business interests in two or more nations.

Iron Texas Star A model depicting policy making in Texas by a coalition of interests that includes interest groups, the lieutenant governor, the speaker, standing committees, the governor, administrators, and boards and commissions.

Iron triangle A working coalition among administrative agencies, clientele interest groups, and legislative committees that share a common interest in seeing either the implementation or the defeat of certain policies and proposals.

Issue network Fluid alliances of individuals and organizations who are interested in a particular policy area and join together when policy-making topics affect their interests.

Item veto Executive authority to veto sections of a bill and allow the remainder to become law.

Jim Crow laws State and local laws that promulgated racial segregation.

Joint committees Committees that include members of both houses.

Ku Klux Klan (KKK) A white supremacist organization. The first Klan was founded during the Reconstruction era following the Civil War.

Late-train contributions Campaign funds given to the winning candidate after the election up to 30 days before the legislature comes into session. Such contributions are designed to curry favor with individuals whom the donors may not have supported originally.

Legislative Audit Committee The body that performs audits of state agencies and departments for the legislature.

Legislative Budget Board (LBB) The body responsible for proposing the legislature's version of the proposed biennial budget. The governor also proposes a budget to the legislature.

Legislative Council The body that provides research support, information, and bill-drafting assistance to legislators.

Legitimacy General public acceptance of government's right to govern; also, the legality of a government's existence conferred by a constitution.

Liability insurance Insurance against negligence claims such as those arising from auto accidents.

Libel Published falsehood defaming a person's character.

Liberal A political ideology marked by the advocacy of positive government action to improve the welfare of individuals, government regulation of the economy, support for civil rights, and tolerance for political and social change.

Little legislatures Another name for standing committees because most of the work of legislation occurs in committees.

Lobbying Direct contact between an interest group representative and an officer of government.

Lobbyist In state law, a person who directly contacts public officials to influence their decisions. Registered lobbyists are paid to represent the interests of their employers.

Logrolling Trading votes among legislators, especially to fund local projects to benefit their constituents.

Long ballot A ballot that results from the election of a large number of independent executive and judicial officers; giving the chief executive the power to appoint most executive and judicial officers results in a *short ballot*.

Mandate A federal or state requirement that a lower level of government, like a city or county, provide a service or meet standards, often as a condition for receiving financial aid.

Maquiladora A factory in the Mexican border region that assembles goods imported duty-free into Mexico for export. In Spanish, it literally means "twin plant."

Mark up Rewrite of a bill in standing committee, usually substantially altering it by adding or deleting major provisions.

Mass transit Transport systems that carry multiple passengers such as train and bus systems; whether publicly or privately owned, mass transit systems are available to the general public and usually charge a fare.

Mayor-council system A form of municipal government consisting of a mayor and a city council; this form includes both *strong-mayor* and *weak-mayor* variations.

Means test A standard of benefit eligibility based on need.

Medicaid A program to provide medical care for qualified low-income persons; although funded largely by federal grants-in-aid, it is a state-administered program.

Medicare A federal program to provide medical insurance for most persons older than 65 years of age.

Merit plan or **Missouri Plan** A method of selecting judges on the basis of the merit or quality of the candidates and not on political considerations. Under this system, the governor fills court vacancies from a list of nominees submitted by a judicial commission, and these appointees later face retention elections.

Merit system An employment and promotion system based on specific qualifications and performance rather than party affiliation or political support.

Message power The influence a person gains merely by being in the public eye. For example, message power allows the governor to focus the attention of the press, legislators, and citizens on legislative proposals that he or she considers important. The visibility of high office draws instant public attention for the officeholder's proposals, a power that led Teddy Roosevelt to refer to the presidency as the "bully pulpit."

Mestizo A person of both Spanish and Native-American lineage.

Metroplex The greater Dallas–Fort Worth metropolitan area.

Misdemeanor A minor crime punishable by a county jail sentence or fine.

Missouri plan See *merit plan*.

Mistrial A trial not completed for legal reasons, such as a hung jury; a new trial may be possible.

Moralistic culture A political subculture that views government as a positive force, one that values the individual but functions to benefit the general public.

Mores Society's strong beliefs about right and wrong.

Necessary and proper clause The last clause in Article I, Section 8 of the U.S. Constitution that gives Congress implied powers.

Negative campaigning A strategy used in political campaigns in which candidates attack opponents' issue positions or character.

Negligence Failure to act with the prudence or care that an ordinary person would exercise.

No bill A grand jury's refusal to return an indictment filed by the prosecutor.

No-fault insurance An insurance plan allowing the insured person to collect from the individual's own insurance company regardless of who is at fault in a vehicular accident.

North American Free Trade Agreement (NAFTA) A treaty between Canada, Mexico, and the United States that calls for the gradual removal of tariffs and other trade restrictions. NAFTA came into effect in 1994.

Office-block ballot A type of ballot used in a general election where the offices are listed across the top, in separate blocks.

Ombudsman An official who hears complaints of employees and citizens concerning government administrators or policy administration. Ombudsmen usually lack authority to force administrative compliance, but they can bring the complaints to the proper authorities and represent the interests of the complaining individual within the administration.

Open primary A type of party primary where a voter can choose on election day in which primary they will participate.

Open-meetings laws With some exceptions, laws that require meetings of government bodies that make decisions concerning the public interest to be open to public scrutiny.

Open-records laws Laws that require most records kept by government to be open for the examination of the parties involved.

Original jurisdiction The authority of a court to consider a case in the first instance; the power to try a case as contrasted with appellate jurisdiction.

Packing Gerrymandering technique in which members of partisan or minority groups are concentrated into one district, thereby ensuring that the group will influence only one election rather than several.

Pairing Placing two incumbent officeholders in the same elective district through redistricting. This is usually done to eliminate political enemies.

Parole Early release from prison under official supervision.

Participation paradox The fact that citizens vote even though a single vote rarely determines an election.

Partisan elections General elections in which candidates are nominated by political parties, and their party labels appear on the ballot.

Partisan identification A person's attachment to one political party or the other.

Party platform The formal issue positions of a political party; specifics are often referred to as planks in the party's platform.

Party realignment The transition from one dominant-party system to another. In Texas politics, it refers to the rise and possible dominance of the Republican Party in recent years.

Party–column ballot A type of ballot used in a general election where all of the candidates from each party are listed in parallel columns.

Peremptory challenge A challenge made to a prospective juror without being required to give a reason for removal; the number of such challenges allotted to the prosecution and defense are limited. Also called a *peremptory strike*.

Personal property Tangible possessions other than real estate.

Personal recognizance A defendant's personal promise to appear; sometimes allowed instead of cash bail or bond.

Petit jury The jury for a civil or criminal trial.

Pigeonhole To kill a bill in standing committee usually by setting it aside without taking any action at all.

Plaintiff The party bringing a civil suit; often a private person or institution.

Plea bargaining Negotiations between the prosecution and the defense to obtain a lighter sentence or other benefits in exchange for a guilty plea by the accused.

Plural executive An executive branch with power divided among several independent officers and a weak chief executive.

Plurality vote An election rule in which the candidate with the most votes wins regardless of whether it is a majority.

Pocket veto Chief executive's power to kill legislation by simply ignoring it at the end of the legislative session; this power is not available to Texas's governor.

Point of order A formal objection that rules of procedure are not being followed on the house floor. Successfully raising a point of order can result in the postponement or defeat of a bill.

Political action committees (PACs) Organizations that raise and then contribute money to political candidates.

Political culture The political values and beliefs that are dominant in a nation or state.

Political movement A mass alliance of like-minded groups and individuals seeking broad changes in the direction of government policies.

Popular recall A special election to remove an official before the end of his or her term, initiated by citizen petition (permitted in some Texas cities but not in state government).

Pragmatism The philosophy that ideas should be judged on the basis of their practical results rather than on an ideological basis. American political parties are pragmatic because they are more concerned with winning elections than with taking clear uncompromising stands on issues.

Precedent A previously decided legal case used as a guiding principle for a current or future case.

Precinct convention A gathering of party members who voted in the party's primary for the purpose of electing delegates to the county or district convention.

Preponderance of the evidence The amount of evidence necessary for a party to win in a civil case; proof that outweighs the evidence offered in opposition to it.

Presession bargaining Negotiations that let the governor and the legislative leaders reach the necessary compromises prior to the start of the legislative session. This usually ensures passage of the legislation.

Presidential preference primary A primary election that allows voters in the party to vote directly for candidates seeking their party's presidential nomination.

Pressure group See *interest group*.

***Prima facie* case** Sufficient evidence to convict if unchallenged at trial; the amount of evidence necessary to indict a defendant.

Primary An election held by a political party to nominate its candidates. Texas party primary elections are usually held in the spring.

Privatization The hiring of private contractors to perform government services and functions.

Probable cause Sufficient information to convince a reasonably cautious person that a search or arrest is justified.

Probate The procedure for proving the validity of a will.

Probation A judge's sentence of an offender to serve outside a correctional institution but under specific restrictions and official supervision.

Progressive tax rates Tax rates that increase as income increases; for example, the federal income tax is assessed using progressive rates.

Proposal of constitutional amendments In Texas, the proposal of a constitutional amendment must be approved by two-thirds of the total membership of each house of the Texas legislature.

Public debt Money owed by government, ordinarily through the issuance of bonds. Local governments issue bonds to finance major projects with voter approval.

Public interest The good of the whole society, without bias for or against any particular segment of the society.

Punitive damages Judgments in excess of actual damages intended to punish a defendant in a civil suit.

Pure at-large system An electoral system in which candidates for city council run citywide and the top vote getters are elected to fill the number of open seats. Compare this system with an *at-large place system*.

Quorum The number of members that the rules require to be present to conduct official business. In the Texas Senate and House, two-thirds of the total membership is necessary to take most floor actions.

Ranchero culture A quasi-feudal system whereby a property's owner, or patrón, gives workers protection and employment in return for their loyalty and service. The rancher and workers all live on the *ranchero*, or ranch.

Ratification Approval of a constitutional amendment by a majority of voters.

Real property Land and buildings.

Reapportionment The redrawing of district and precinct lines following the national census to reflect population changes.

Recall election An election, called by citizen petition, that permits voters to remove an elected official before the official's term expires.

Recidivist A criminal who commits another crime after having been incarcerated.

Recorded vote Votes in which the names of those who cast the vote are recorded in the house journal.

Reduction veto The power of some governors to reduce amounts in an appropriations bill without striking them out. Texas's governor does not have this power.

Referendum An election that permits voters to determine if an ordinance or statute will go into effect.

Regressive tax rates Tax rates that place more of a burden on low- and middle-income taxpayers than on wealthier ones; for example, sales taxes and most other consumption taxes are regressive.

Regulatory tax A tax imposed with the intent of exerting social or economic control by reducing taxes on approved behaviors or imposing higher taxes on undesirable activities.

Rehabilitation The effort to correct criminals' antisocial attitudes and behavior.

Remedy The means to redress an injury, including relief from ongoing injury or compensation for past damages.

Removal powers The authority to fire appointed officials. The Texas governor has limited removal powers; they extend only to officials he or she has appointed and are subject to the consent of two-thirds of the state senators.

Reserved powers Those powers that belong to the states. The legitimacy of these powers comes from the Tenth Amendment.

Retainers Fees charged by lawyers. Some special-interest groups place lawyer-legislators on retainer with the intent of legally compromising their objectivity on important matters of public policy.

Revenue bonds Bonds to be repaid with revenues from the projects that they finance, such as utilities or sports stadiums.

Revolving door The interchange of employees between government agencies and the private businesses with which they have dealings.

Right-to-work laws Laws that prohibit union shop agreements requiring new employees to join a union.

Rollback election An election that permits the voters to decide if a property tax increase (of more than 8 percent) approved by a local government will remain in effect or be reduced to 8 percent.

Runoff primary A second primary election that pits the two top vote-getters from the first primary, where the winner in that primary did not receive a majority. The runoff primary is used in states such as Texas that have a majority election rule in party primaries.

School finance reform Changes in public school financial system resulting from a Texas Supreme Court ruling that significant inequality in school financial resources violated the state constitution; changes in any public policy are considered *reform* by their advocates.

Selective sales (excise) taxes Taxes levied on specific items only; also known as *excise taxes*.

Senatorial courtesy The tradition of allowing a senator to reject the governor's appointment of a political enemy from the senator's district. The senator declares the appointee "personally obnoxious," and the other senators vote to reject the appointee.

Separate-but-equal doctrine Doctrine that resulted from Supreme Court ruling in *Plessey* v. *Ferguson* that legalized segregation.

Separation of powers The principle behind the concept of a government with three branches—the legislative, executive, and judicial.

Severance tax A tax on raw materials (such as oil and natural gas) when they are extracted from their natural state.

Sheriff The chief county law enforcement officer. Although the sheriff is an elected official in Texas, his or her budget must be approved by the commissioners court.

Short ballot The listing of only a few independently elected offices on an election ballot.

Single-member district system A system in which one candidate is elected to a legislative body in each election district.

Single-member districts Election districts in which one candidate is elected to a legislative body. In city council elections, single-member districts are contrasted with at-large citywide elections. Members from single-member districts tend to feel greater loyalty to the residents of their own neighborhoods because they are not elected citywide.

Slander Spoken falsehood defaming a person's character.

Social insurance Public insurance programs with benefits based on tax premiums paid by the beneficiary or his or her employer; for example, Social Security and unemployment compensation are social insurance programs that are not based on need alone.

Socialized medicine Strictly defined, socialized medicine is a health-care system in which the government hires medical practitioners who work at government-owned facilities to directly provide health care, as in Great Britain and in U.S. veterans' and military hospitals. However, the term is often applied to health-care systems in which the government provides health care insurance (such as Medicare) but benefit payments are made to private health care providers.

Soft money Money spent by political parties on behalf of political candidates, especially for the purposes of increasing voter registration and turnout.

Special district A limited-purpose local government that provides a narrow range of services not provided by general-purpose local governments such as cities or counties. Examples of special districts include municipal utility districts, hospital authorities, and transit authorities.

Special session A legislative session called by the Texas governor, who also sets its agenda.

Spoils system A system that gives elected officials considerable discretion in employment and promotion decisions.

Standing committees Permanent committees that function throughout the legislative session.

Stare decisis The principle of following precedents in deciding legal cases.

Statute-like detail Detailed state constitutional policies of narrow scope, usually handled by statutes passed by legislative bodies.

Statutory law Law passed by legislatures and written into code books.

Strong-mayor form of government A form of municipal government in which substantial authority over appointments and budgets is lodged in the mayor's office. The mayor is elected by voters in a citywide election.

Subcommittees Divisions of a committee that consider specific subtopics of a committee's primary jurisdiction.

Suffrage The legal right to vote.

Sunset Advisory Commission A body that systematically evaluates most government agencies and departments and may recommend restructuring, abolishing, or altering the jurisdiction of an agency.

Supply-side economics The theory that higher-income taxpayers should be taxed less because their savings and investments stimulate the economy.

Supremacy clause Article VI, Section 2 of the U.S. Constitution, which states that the U.S. Constitution, as well as laws and treaties created in accordance with the U.S. Constitution, supersede state and local laws.

Suspension of the rule The setting aside of the rules of the legislative body so that another set of rules can be used.

Swing voters People who cast their ballots on the basis of personality and other factors rather than strictly on the basis of party affiliation; swing voters are often those "independents" who are persuadable by either party's campaign.

Tagging A senate rule that allows a senator to demand a 48-hour advance notification before a standing committee holds hearings on a particular bill.

Tax assessor-collector A county financial officer whose responsibilities include collecting various county taxes and fees and registering voters.

Tax base The object or activity taxed.

Tax rate The amount per unit of taxable item or activity.

Tax shifting Businesses passing taxes to consumers in the form of higher prices.

Tenant farmer A farmer who does not own the land that he or she farms but rents it from a landowner.

Tenth Amendment Section of the U.S. Constitution that reserves powers to the states. It reads as follows: "The powers not delegated to the United States by the Constitution, nor prohibited by it to the States, are reserved to the States respectively, or to the people."

Term limits Restrictions on the number of times that a politician can be reelected to an office or the number of years that a person may hold a particular office.

Texas Register The official publication of the state that gives the public notice of proposed actions and adopted policies of executive branch agencies.

The Lobby The collective characterization of the most politically and economically powerful special interest groups in the state.

The Valley An area along the Texas side of the Rio Grande River known for its production of citrus fruits.

Threat of veto An informal power of the Texas governor. Threatening in advance to veto legislation enhances the governor's bargaining power with legislators, enabling the governor to shape the content of legislation while it is still in the legislature.

Ticket splitters People who vote for candidates of more than one party in a given election.

Tipping A phenomenon that occurs when a group that is becoming more numerous over time grows large enough to change the political balance in a district, state, or county.

Tort A private or civil injury or wrong other than a breach of contract.

Tort reform Efforts to limit liability in civil cases.

Traditionalistic culture A political subculture that views government as an institution to maintain the dominant social and religious values.

True bill An indictment returned by a grand jury.

Two-party system A political system characterized by two dominant parties competing for political offices. In such systems, minor or third parties have little chance of winning.

Umbrella organization An organization created by interest groups to promote common goals. Several interest groups may choose to coordinate their efforts to influence government when they share the same policy goal. The organization may be temporary or permanent.

Unemployment insurance Benefit program for certain workers losing their employment; a joint federal–state program financed with a tax on employers.

Unfunded mandates Obligations that the federal government imposes on state governments with little or no funding to help support the program.

Union shop A workplace in which management requires all new employees to join a union or pay dues as a condition for employment (illegal in Texas).

Unit road system A system that concentrates the day-to-day responsibilities for roads in the hands of a professional engineer rather than individual county commissioners. The engineer is ultimately responsible to the commissioners court.

Unitary system A system of government in which one central government has ultimate authority; any regional or local governments are subordinate to the central government.

User fees Fees paid by the individuals who receive a particular service, such as sewage disposal or garbage collection.

Veto The executive power to reject a proposed law unless an unusual majority of the legislature (usually two-thirds) votes to override the governor's opposition. This is almost an absolute power in Texas because the legislature is seldom in session when the governor issues the veto.

Victimless crime A crime such as prostitution, gambling, or drug possession that primarily victimizes oneself rather than society at large.

Voice vote An oral vote cast by lawmakers that is not recorded in the official record.

Voir dire **questioning** The initial questioning of jurors to determine possible biases.

Voter turnout The percentage of people who are eligible to vote who actually vote.

Voting-age population The total number of persons in the United States who are 18 years of age or older regardless of citizenship, military status, felony conviction, or mental state.

Weak-mayor form of government A form of municipal government in which an elected mayor and city council share administrative responsibilities, often with other elected officers.

Whistle-blowers Government employees who expose corruption, incompetence, and criminal acts by other government employees.

White primary The practice of excluding African Americans from Democratic Party primary elections in Texas. First enforced by law and later by party rules, this practice was found unconstitutional in *Smith* v. *Allwright*, 321 U.S. 649 (1944).

White-collar crime Bribery, tax fraud, business fraud, embezzlement, and other nonviolent crimes usually committed by more prosperous individuals than those who commit street crime.

Writ of habeas corpus A court order requiring that an individual be presented in person and that legal cause be shown for confinement; it may result in release from unlawful detention.

Writ of injunction A court order to compel or restrain a particular action.

Index